A HISTORY OF
THE ENGLISH-SPEAKING
PEOPLES

WINSTON CHURCHILL

A HISTORY OF
THE ENGLISH-SPEAKING
PEOPLES

A New One-volume Abridgement by
Christopher Lee

CASSELL&CO

Cassell & Co.
Wellington House
125 Strand
London
WC2R OBB

This edition first published in 2000
This one-volume abridgement first published in 1998
First published as four volumes *The Birth of Britain* (1956), *The New World* (1956),
The Age of Revolution (1957), *The Great Democracies* (1958)

British Library Cataloguing-in-Publication Data
A catalogue entry for this book is available from the British Library

ISBN 0-304-35741-3

Printed and bound in Great Britain by Mackays of Chatham PLC, Kent

⤛ CONTENTS ⤜

CONTENTS

⊷ EDITOR'S NOTE ⊷

Shortly before the Second World War, Winston Churchill started to write *A History of the English-speaking Peoples*. When the conflict with Germany began, some half a million words had been written. On September 3, 1939, Churchill went to the Admiralty, and *HESP*, as it became known, went to the filing tray marked 'Pending'. The war done, Churchill set about his version of those five years between 1939 and 1945, and it was not until 1956 that the first of the four volumes of this history appeared.[1]

This is the fortieth anniversary of the publication of the complete work, and during those four decades it has not been out of print. There are those, perhaps preferring other versions of great events (including their own), who may wonder if that says more for the name Churchill than for his powers as a historian. Yet as he wrote in the preface to his first manuscript, Churchill did not set out to write something that would "rival the works of professional historians". His history was his own account of the events which appeared significant to him and which in some way showed how English-speaking peoples had "achieved their distinctive position and character". Although his history was a personal view, Churchill called on some of the best historians of the day to help. Dr Maurice Ashley notes that Churchill "hired a whole team of qualified historians to help him, some of whom he had never met; and he employed a kind of editorial staff which checked and re-checked his facts and his fancies".[2]

Churchill's team was as distinguished a gathering of dons as ever worked on one manuscript. F.W. Deakin, G.M Young, Keith Feiling, Alan Hodge, A.R. Myers, Joel Hurstfield, D.H. Pennington, A.L. Rowse, Steven Watson, Asa Briggs, Maurice Shock, Frank Freidal and M.A. Jones.

The huge task was well received. Alan Taylor, then Fellow in Modern History at Oxford, described the volume as "one of the wisest, most exciting works of history ever written".[3] Sir Arthur Bryant thought the second book better than the first. "The most comprehensive and discerning ever written of the English-speaking Nations"[4] he wrote. Flattery for the master? Geoffrey Baraclough thought it "a major piece of historical writing in an age when

---

1   *The Birth of Britain* (1956), *The New World* (1956), *The Age of Revolution* (1957), *The Great Democracies* (1958).
2   *Churchill as Historian*, Maurice Ashley, Secker & Warburg, 1968.
3   *Daily Herald*, 1956.
4   *Sunday Times*, 1956.

historians are more inclined to take a microscopic than a telescopic view".[5] And Michael Howard, then Professor of Military History at the University of London, wrote, "This work will be, for generations of common readers, *the* history of England. From it millions throughout the world may learn the only history they will ever know. That it should be balanced, accurate and reliable is thus a matter of the profoundest importance; it is by no means the least of the debts which the world owes to this amazing man...."[6]

It is possible that J.H. Plumb, the eminent Cambridge historian, best judged the four volumes. "This history will endure; not only because Sir Winston has written it, but because of its own inherent virtues – its narrative power, its fine judgement of war and politics, of soldiers and statesmen, and even more of what Englishmen in the hey-day of their empire thought and felt about their country's past."[7] Of course, Churchill felt a strong link with that past. From the seventeenth century onwards, there was usually a Churchill to be found making The Headlines, as it would be called today. Certainly, from the days of his ancestor and hero Marlborough, Churchill regarded British history as his (WSC's) history.

And so to the immediate question: why edit the original into a single volume? For a short period during the 1980s, I was left alone at Emmanuel College, Cambridge, to research the historical factors that influenced post-World War II political and diplomatic decision making. I started to write my own history of Britain. It must be said, immediately, that this was not an attempt to produce a definitive academic work. Rather, it was a chronological history from the Romans – a sort of history handbook, albeit one of some 250,000 words. It was during this writing that I started to think of *A History of the English-speaking Peoples* as something which could easily satisfy an even larger readership than Michael Howard had anticipated. But, or so I felt, the way of doing that would be to edit the original to produce a one-volume *History of the English-speaking Peoples*. Five years later, Sean Magee of Cassell came to me with the same thought. And so this single volume was born.

But discarding some forty per cent of the text has been a two-year task, and an agonizing one. This was not a simple abridgement. It was not good enough to remove sections simply because of questions raised by new research, or because the readership might now be more historically aware than, say, forty years ago. I had to remember why Churchill wrote this work and I was ever mindful that *A History of the English-speaking Peoples* was a reflection of what Englishmen in the hey-day of their empire thought and felt about their country's past. Thus, it could not simply be treated as a history which needed updating. Nevertheless, I have inserted considerable numbers of footnotes, expanding and explaining Churchill's text, whereas he felt little need for such appendage. There were moments when I imagined the ghost of the man himself in the corner of my study. As I pondered, rewrote, deleted, expanded,

5   *Manchester Guardian*, 1958.
6   *New Statesman*, 1956.
7   *Daily Telegraph*, 1957.

I could hear that unmistakable voice upbraiding, questioning, admonishing as yet another pencil line or note was made. Why would he not? After all, *HESP* went through as many as twelve draft versions until Churchill thought it perfect. So, I hope that most of the changes are difficult to spot, even for those with reasonable knowledge of the original. However, there are two great chunks removed. They cover the War of American Independence and the American Civil War. I fear Churchill would have argued against their removal. In the full sense of the title, Churchill felt that *A History of the English-speaking Peoples* was part of his contribution to the link between the Old World and the New World. Therefore I have tried to retain that sense, by emphasizing the importance of what was happening in America, without giving the details of battles and campaigns that Churchill found so attractive.

The overall task has been harder than I imagined. I am grateful to Nigel Wilcockson at Cassell who has performed the unusual task of an editor controlling another editor with aplomb. I am also indebted to Lydia Darbyshire, whom I have never met, nor spoken to, but who fixed my work with an uncompromising eye when I strayed from the path of her strict copy-editing. My one hope is that I have retained the idea of *A History of the English-speaking Peoples* as Churchill's own 1956 perspective on the world and some of its history, and that this comes across when the volume is being read.

Christopher Lee, Cambridge, 1998

CHAPTER ONE

BRITANNIA

*Julius Caesar – Cassivellaunus – Claudius orders invasion of
Britain – the resistance of Caractacus – the revenge of Boadicea and
the vengeance of Suetonius – the Battle of Mons Graupius – the building
of London – the villa system – Hadrian's Wall*

IN THE summer of the Roman year 699, now described as the year 55
before the birth of Christ, the Proconsul of Gaul, Gaius Julius Caesar,
turned his gaze upon Britain. In the midst of his wars in Germany and
in Gaul he became conscious of this heavy Island which stirred his
ambitions and already obstructed his designs. He knew that it was inhabited by
the same tribesmen who confronted the Roman arms in Germany, Gaul, and
Spain. The Islanders had helped the local tribes in the late campaigns along
the northern coast of Gaul. They were the same Celtic stock, somewhat intensified by insular life. British volunteers had shared the defeat of the
Veneti on the coasts of Brittany in the previous year. Refugees from momentarily conquered Gaul were welcomed and sheltered in Britannia. To Caesar,
the Island now presented itself as an integral part of his task of subjugating
the Northern barbarians to the rule and system of Rome. The land not covered
by forest or marsh was verdant and fertile. The climate, though far from
genial, was equable and healthy. The natives, though uncouth, had a certain
value as slaves for rougher work on the land, in mines, and even about the
house. There was talk of a pearl fishery, and also of gold. Even if there was
not time for a campaign that season, Caesar thought it would be of great
advantage to him merely to visit the Island, to see what its inhabitants were
like, and to make himself acquainted with the lie of the land, the harbours, and
the landing-places. Other reasons added their weight. Caesar's colleague in the
Triumvirate, Crassus, had excited the imagination of the Roman Senate and
people by his spirited march towards Mesopotamia. Here, at the other end of
the known world, was an enterprise equally audacious. The Romans hated and
feared the sea. By a supreme effort of survival they had two hundred years
before surpassed Carthage upon its own element in the Mediterranean, but the
idea of Roman legions landing in the remote, unknown, fabulous Island of the
vast ocean of the North would create a novel thrill and topic in all ranks of
Roman society.

Thus, in this summer fifty-five years before the birth of Christ he withdrew his army from Germany, broke down his massive and ingenious timber bridge across the Rhine above Coblenz, and throughout July marched westward by long strides towards the Gallic shore somewhere about the modern Calais and Boulogne.

Late in August 55 B.C. Caesar sailed with eighty transports and two legions at midnight, and with the morning light saw the white cliffs of Dover crowned with armed men. He judged the place "quite unsuitable for landing", since it was possible to throw missiles from the cliffs on to the shore. He therefore anchored till the turn of the tide, sailed seven miles farther, and descended upon Albion on the low, shelving beach between Deal and Walmer. But the Britons, observing these movements, kept pace along the coast and were found ready to meet him. There followed a scene upon which the eye of history has rested. The Islanders, with their chariots and horsemen, advanced into the surf to meet the invader. Caesar's transports and warships grounded in deeper water. The legionaries, uncertain of the depth, hesitated in face of the shower of javelins and stones, but the eagle-bearer of the Tenth Legion plunged into the waves with the sacred emblem, and Caesar brought his warships with their catapults and arrow-fire upon the British flank. The Romans, thus encouraged and sustained, leaped from their ships, and, forming as best they could, waded towards the enemy. There was a short, ferocious fight amid the waves, but the Romans reached the shore, and, once arrayed, forced the Britons to flight.

Caesar's landing however was only the first of his troubles. His cavalry, in eighteen transports, which had started three days later, arrived in sight of the camp, but, caught by a sudden gale, drifted far down the Channel, and were thankful to regain the Continent. The high tide of the full moon which Caesar had not understood wrought grievous damage to his fleet at anchor. "A number of ships", he says, "were shattered, and the rest, having lost their cables, anchors, and the remainder of their tackle, were unusable, which naturally threw the whole army into great consternation. For they had no other vessels in which they could return, nor any materials for repairing the fleet; and, since it had been generally understood that they were to return to Gaul for the winter, they had not provided themselves with a stock of grain for wintering in Britain."

The Britons had sued for peace after the battle on the beach, but now that they saw the plight of their assailants their hopes revived and they broke off negotiations. In great numbers they attacked the Roman foragers. But the legion concerned had not neglected precautions, and discipline and armour once again told their tale. It shows how much food there was in the Island that two legions could live for a fortnight off the cornfields close to their camp. The British submitted. Their conqueror imposed only nominal terms. Breaking up many of his ships to repair the rest, he was glad to return with some hostages and captives to the mainland. He never even pretended that his expedition had been a success. To supersede the record of it he came again the next year, this time with five legions and some cavalry conveyed in eight hundred ships. The Islanders were overawed by the size of the armada. The landing was unimpeded, but again the sea assailed him. Caesar had marched twelve miles into the interior when he was recalled by the news that a great storm had shattered or damaged a large portion of his fleet. He was forced to spend ten days in hauling all his ships on to the shore, and in fortifying the camp of which they then formed part. This done he renewed his invasion, and, after easily destroying the forest stockades in which the British sheltered, crossed the Thames near Brentford. But the British had found a leader in the chief Cassivellaunus, who was a master of war under the prevailing conditions. Dismissing to their homes the mass of untrained foot-soldiers and peasantry, he kept pace with the invaders march by march with his chariots and horsemen. Caesar gives a detailed description of the chariot-fighting:

> In chariot-fighting the Britons begin by driving all over the field hurling javelins, and generally the terror inspired by the horses and the noise of the wheels are sufficient to throw their opponents' ranks into disorder. Then, after making their way between the squadrons of their own cavalry, they jump down from the chariots and engage on foot. In the meantime their charioteers retire a short distance from the battle and place the chariots in such a position that their masters, if hard pressed by numbers, have an easy means of retreat to their own power of infantry; and by daily training and practice they attain such proficiency that even on a steep incline they're able to control the horses at full gallop, and to check and turn them in a moment. They can run along the chariot pole, stand on the yoke, and get back into the chariot as quick as lightning.[1]

Cassivellaunus, using these mobile forces and avoiding a pitched battle with the Roman legions, escorted them on their inroad and cut off their foraging parties. None the less Caesar captured his first stronghold; the tribes began to make terms for themselves; a well-conceived plan for destroying Caesar's base on the Kentish shore was defeated. At this juncture Cassivellaunus, by a prudence of policy equal to that of his tactics, negotiated a further surrender of hostages and a promise of tribute and submission, in return for which Caesar was again content to quit the Island. In a dead calm "he set sail late in the evening and brought all the fleet safely to land at dawn". This time he proclaimed a conquest. Caesar had his triumph, and British captives trod their dreary path at his tail through the streets of Rome; but for nearly a hundred years no invading army landed upon the Island Coasts.[2]

During the hundred years which followed Julius Caesar's invasion the British Islanders remained unmolested. The Belgic cities developed a life of their own, and the warrior tribes enjoyed amid their internecine feuds the comforting illusion that no one was likely to attack them again. However, their contacts with the mainland and with the civilisation of the Roman

---

1   Caesar, *The Conquest of Gaul*, translated by S.A. Handford, Penguin Classics, 1951.
2   The importance of the Roman period is sometimes forgotten because, to many, Roman Britain was simply 55 B.C., villas, and Hadrian's Wall. Yet it is well to remember that the Romans were in Britain for nearly four hundred years; that is, roughly the same length of time as from the end of Henry VIII's reign to the present.

Empire grew, and trade flourished in a wide range of commodities. Roman traders established themselves in many parts, and carried back to Rome tales of the wealth and possibilities of Britannia, if only a stable government were set up.

In the year A.D. 41 the murder of the Emperor Caligula, and a chapter of accidents, brought his uncle, the clownish scholar Claudius, to the throne of the world. No one can suppose that any coherent will to conquest resided in the new ruler, but the policy of Rome was shaped by the officials of highly competent departments. It proceeded upon broad lines, and in its various aspects attracted a strong and growing measure of support from many sections of public opinion. Eminent senators aired their views, important commercial and financial interests were conciliated, and elegant society had a new topic for gossip. Thus, in this triumphant period there were always available for a new emperor a number of desirable projects, well thought out beforehand and in harmony with the generally understood Roman system, any one of which might catch the fancy of the latest wielder of supreme power. Hence we find emperors elevated by chance, whose unbridled and capricious passions were their only distinction, whose courts were debauched with lust and cruelty, who were themselves vicious or feeble-minded, who were pawns in the hands of the counsellors or favourites, decreeing great campaigns and setting their seal upon long-lasting acts of salutary legislation.

The advantages of conquering the recalcitrant Island Britannia were paraded before the new monarch, and his interest was excited. He was attracted by the idea of gaining a military reputation. He gave orders that this dramatic and possibly lucrative enterprise should proceed. In the year 43, almost one hundred years after Julius Caesar's evacuation, a powerful, well-organised Roman army of some twenty thousand men was prepared for the subjugation of Britain.

The internal situation favoured the invaders. Cunobelinus (Shakespeare's Cymbeline) had established an overlordship over the south-east of the Island, with his capital at Colchester. But in his old age dissensions had begun to impair his authority, and on his death the kingdom was ruled jointly by his sons Caractacus[1] and Togodumnus. They were not everywhere recognised, and they had no time to form a union of the tribal kingdom before the Roman commander, Plautius, and his legions arrived. The people of Kent fell back on the tactics of Cassivellaunus, and Plautius had much trouble in searching them out; but when he did find them he first defeated Caractacus, and then his brother somewhere in East Kent. Then, advancing along Caesar's old line of march, he came on a river he had not heard of, the Medway. "The barbarians thought that the Romans would not be able to cross without a bridge, and consequently bivouacked in rather careless fashion on the opposite bank"; but the Roman general sent across "a detachment of Germans, who were accustomed to swim easily in full armour across the most turbulent streams.

---

[1] Caratacus or Caradoc, who led the Silures in the west. Churchill prefers the popular spelling, Caractacus.

These fell unexpectedly upon the enemy, but instead of shooting at the men they disabled the horses that drew the chariots, and in the ensuing confusion not even the enemy's mounted men could save themselves." Nevertheless the Britons faced them on the second day, and were only broken by a flank attack, Vespasian — some day to be Emperor himself — having discovered a ford higher up. This victory marred the stage-management of the campaign. Plautius had won his battle too soon, and in the wrong place. Something had to be done to show that the Emperor's presence was necessary to victory. So Claudius, who had been waiting on events in France, crossed the seas, bringing substantial reinforcements, including a number of elephants. A battle was procured, and the Romans won. Claudius returned to Rome to receive from the Senate the title of "Britannicus" and permission to celebrate a triumph.

But the British war continued. The Britons would not come to close quarters with the Romans, but took refuge in the swamps and the forests, hoping to wear out the invaders, so that, as in the days of Julius Caesar, they should sail back with nothing accomplished. Caractacus escaped to the Welsh border, and, rousing its tribes, maintained an indomitable resistance for more than six years. It was not till A.D. 50 that he was finally defeated by a new general, Ostorius, the successor of Plautius, who reduced to submission the whole of the more settled regions from the Wash to the Severn.

The conquest was not achieved without one frightful convulsion of revolt. "In this year A.D. 61", according to Tacitus, "a severe disaster was sustained in Britain." Suetonius, the new governor, had engaged himself deeply in the West. He transferred the operational base of the Roman army to Chester. Because it was the centre of Druid resistance he prepared to attack "the populous island of Mona (Anglesey), which had become a refuge for fugitives, and he built a fleet of flat-bottomed vessels suitable for those shallow and shifting seas. The infantry crossed in the boats, the cavalry went over by fords: where the water was too deep the men swam alongside of their horses. The enemy lined the shore, a dense host of armed men, interspersed with women clad in black like the Furies, with their hair hanging down and holding torches in their hands. Round this were Druids uttering dire curses and stretching their hands towards heaven. These strange sights terrified the soldiers. They stayed motionless, as if paralysed, offering their bodies to the blows. At last, encouraged by the general, and exhorting each other not to quail before the rabble of female fanatics, they advanced their standards, bore down all resistance, and enveloped the enemy in their own flames.

"Suetonius imposed a garrison upon the conquered and cut down the groves devoted to their cruel superstitions; for it was part of their religion to spill the blood of captives on their altars, and to inquire of the gods by means of human entrails."

This dramatic scene on the frontiers of modern Wales was the prelude to a tragedy. The king of the East Anglian Iceni had died. Hoping to save his kingdom and family from molestation, he had appointed Nero, who had succeeded Claudius as Emperor, as heir jointly with his two daughters. "But", says Tacitus, "things turned out differently. His kingdom was plundered by centurions, and his private property by slaves, as if they had been captured in war; his widow Boadicea (relished by the learned as Boudicca) was flogged, and his daughters outraged; the chiefs of the Iceni were robbed of their ancestral properties as if the Romans had received the whole country as a gift, and the king's own relatives were reduced to slavery." Thus the Roman historian.[1]

Boadicea's tribe, at once the most powerful and hitherto the most sub-missive, was moved to frenzy against the Roman invaders. They flew to arms. Boadicea found herself at the head of a numerous army, and nearly all the Britons within reach rallied to her standard. There followed an up-rush of hatred from the abyss, which is a measure of the cruelty of the conquest. It was a scream of rage against invincible oppression and the superior culture which seemed to lend it power.

In all Britain there were only four legions, at most twenty thousand men. The Fourteenth and Twentieth were with Suetonius on his Welsh campaign. The Ninth was at Lincoln, and the Second at Gloucester. The first target of the revolt was Camulodunum[2] (Colchester), the centre of Roman authority and Roman religion, where the recently settled veterans, supported by the soldiery, who hoped for similar licence for themselves, had been ejecting the inhabitants from their houses and driving them away from their lands. The Britons were encouraged by omens. The Statue of Victory fell face foremost, as if flying from the enemy. The sea turned red. Strange cries were heard in the council chamber and the theatre. The Roman officials, business men, bankers, usurers, and the Britons who had participated in their authority and profits, found themselves with a handful of old soldiers in the midst of a "multitude of barbarians". Suetonius was a month distant. The Ninth Legion was a hundred and twenty miles away. There was neither mercy nor hope. The town was burned to ashes. The temple, whose strong walls resisted the conflagration, held out for two days. Everyone, Roman or Romanised, was massacred and everything destroyed. Meanwhile the Ninth Legion was marching to the rescue. The victorious Britons advanced from the sack of Colchester to meet it. By sheer force of numbers they overcame the Roman infantry and slaughtered them to a man, and the commander, Petilius Cerialis, was content to escape with his cavalry. Such were the tidings which reached Suetonius in Anglesey. He realised at once that his army could not make the distance in time to prevent even greater disaster, but, says Tacitus, he, "undaunted, made his way through a hostile country to Londinium, a town which, though not dignified by the title of colony, was a busy emporium for traders". This is the first mention of London in literature. Though fragments

1   Extracts from Tacitus' *Annals* are from G.G. Ramsay's translation; passages from the *Agricola* come from the translation of Church and Brodribb. [Churchill]

2   The early tenth-century name was Colneceastre. In Domesday Book it is given as Colecestra – or Roman town on the Colne river – but the full Romano-British name would have been Colonia Camulodunum – that is, colony for retired legionnaires.

of Gallic or Italian pottery which may or may not antedate the Roman conquest have been found there, it is certain that the place attained no prominence until the Claudian invaders brought a mass of army contractors and officials to the most convenient bridgehead on the Thames.

Suetonius reached London with only a small mounted escort. He had sent orders to the Second Legion to meet him there from Gloucester, but the commander, appalled by the defeat of the Ninth, had not complied. London was a large, undefended town, full of Roman traders and their British associates, dependants, and slaves. It contained a fortified military depot, with valuable stores and a handful of legionaries. The citizens of London implored Suetonius to protect them, but when he heard that Boadicea, having chased Cerialis towards Lincoln, had turned and was marching south he took the hard but right decision to leave them to their fate. The commander of the Second Legion had disobeyed him, and he had no force to withstand the enormous masses hastening towards him. His only course was to rejoin the Fourteenth and Twentieth Legions, who were marching with might and main from Wales to London along the line of the Roman road now known as Watling Street, and, unmoved by the entreaties of the inhabitants, he gave the signal to march, receiving within his lines all who wished to go with him.

The slaughter which fell upon London was universal. No one was spared, neither man, woman, nor child. The wrath of the revolt concentrated itself upon all of those of British blood who had lent themselves to the wiles and seduction of the invader. In recent times, with London buildings growing taller and needing deeper foundations, the power-driven excavating machines have encountered at many points the layer of ashes which marks the effacement of London at the hands of the natives of Britain.

Boadicea then turned upon Verulamium (St Albans). Here was another trading centre, to which high civic rank had been accorded. A like total slaughter and obliteration was inflicted. "No less", according to Tacitus, "than seventy thousand citizens and allies were slain" in these three cities. "For the barbarians would have no capturing, no selling, nor any kind of traffic usual in war; they would have nothing but killing, by sword, cross, gibbet, or fire." Some high modern authorities think these numbers are exaggerated; but there is no reason why London should not have contained thirty or forty thousand inhabitants, and Colchester and St Albans between them about an equal number. If the butcheries in the countryside are added the estimate of Tacitus may well stand. This is probably the most horrible episode which our Island has known. We see the crude and corrupt beginnings of a higher civilisation blotted out by the ferocious uprising of the native tribes. Still, it is the primary right of men to die and kill for the land they live in, and to punish with exceptional severity all members of their own race who have warmed their hands at the invaders' hearth.

"And now Suetonius, having with him the Fourteenth Legion, with the veterans of the Twentieth, and the auxiliaries nearest at hand, making up a force of about ten thousand fully armed men, resolved ... for battle." The day was bloody and decisive. The barbarian army, eighty thousand strong, attended, like the Germans and the Gauls, by their women and children in an unwieldy wagon-train, drew out their array, resolved to conquer or perish. Here was no thought of subsequent accommodation. On both sides it was all for all. At heavy adverse odds Roman discipline and tactical skill triumphed. No quarter was given, even to the women. Boadicea poisoned herself. The camp commander of the Second Legion, who had both disobeyed his general and deprived his men of their share in the victory, on hearing of the success of the Fourteenth and Twentieth fell upon his sword.

Suetonius now thought only of vengeance, and indeed there was much to repay. Reinforcements of four or five thousand men were sent by Nero from Germany, and all hostile or suspect tribes were harried with fire and sword. Worst of all was the want of food; for in their confident expectation of capturing the supplies of the Romans the Britons had brought every available man into the field and left their land unsown. Yet even so their spirit was unbroken, and the extermination of the entire ancient British race might have followed but for the remonstrances of a new Procurator, supported by his Treasury seniors at Rome, who saw themselves about to be possessed of a desert instead of a province. As a man of action Suetonius ranks high, and his military decisions were sound. But there was a critical faculty alive in the Roman state which cannot be discounted as arising merely through the jealousies of important people. It was held that Suetonius had been rashly ambitious of military glory and had been caught unaware by the widespread uprising of the province, that "his reverses were due to his own folly, his successes to good fortune", and that a Governor must be sent, "free from feeling of hostility or triumph, who would deal gently with our conquered enemies". The Procurator, Julius Classicianus, whose tombstone is now in the British Museum, kept writing in this sense to Rome, and pleaded vehemently for the pacification of the warrior bands, who still fought on without seeking truce or mercy, starving and perishing in the forests and the fens. In the end it was resolved to make the best of the Britons. German unrest and dangers from across the Rhine made even military circles in Rome disinclined to squander forces in remoter regions. The loss in a storm of some of Suetonius's warships was made the pretext and occasion of his supersession. The Emperor Nero sent a new Governor, who made a peace with the desperate tribesmen which enabled their blood to be perpetuated in the Island race.

In A.D. 78 Agricola, a Governor of talent and energy, was sent to Britannia. Instead of spending his first year of office in the customary tour of ceremony, he took field against all who still disputed the Roman authority. One large tribe which had massacred a squadron of auxiliary cavalry was exterminated. The island of Mona, from which Suetonius had been recalled by the rising of Boadicea, was subjugated. With military ability Agricola united a states-manlike humanity. According to Tacitus (who had married his daughter), he proclaimed that "little is gained by conquest if followed by oppression". He mitigated the severity of the corn tribute. He encouraged and aided the building of temples, courts of justice, and dwelling-houses. He provided a liberal education for the sons of the chiefs, and showed "such a preference for the natural powers of the Britons over the more laboured style of the Gauls" that the well-to-do classes were conciliated and became willing to adopt the toga and other Roman fashions. "Step by step they were led to practices which disposed to vice – the lounge, the bath, the elegant banquet. All this in their ignorance they called civilisation, when it was but part of their servitude."

Although in the Senate and governing circles in Rome it was constantly explained that the Imperial policy adhered to the principle of the great Augustus, that the frontiers should be maintained but not extended, Agricola was permitted to conduct six campaigns of expansion in Britannia. In the third he reached the Tyne, the advances of his legions being supported at every stage by a fleet of sea-borne supplies. In the fifth campaign he reached the line of the Forth and Clyde, and here on this wasp-waist of Britain he might well have dug himself in. But there was no safety or permanent peace for the British province unless he could subdue the powerful tribes and large bands of desperate warriors who had been driven northwards by his advance. Indeed, it is evident that he would never of his own will have stopped in any direction short of the ocean shore. Therefore in his sixth campaign he marched northwards again with all his forces. The position had now become formidable. Past misfortunes had taught the Britons the penalties of disunion.

The decisive battle was fought in A.D. 83 at Mons Graupius, a place unidentified, though some suggest the Pass of Killiecrankie. Tacitus describes in unconvincing detail the course of this famous struggle. The whole of Caledonia, all that was left of Britannia, a vast host of broken, hunted men, resolved on death or freedom, confronted in their superiority of four or five to one the skilfully handled Roman legions and auxiliaries, among whom no doubt many British renegades were serving. It is certain that Tacitus greatly exaggerated the dimensions of the native army in these wilds, where they could have no prepared magazines. The number, though still considerable, must have been severely limited. Apparently, as in so many ancient battles, the beaten side were the victims of misunderstanding and the fate of the day was decided against them before the bulk of the forces realised that a serious engagement had begun. Reserves descended from the hills too late to achieve victory, but in good time to be massacred in the rout. The last organised resistance of Britain to the Roman power ended at Mons Graupius. Here, according to the Roman account, "ten thousand of the enemy were slain, and on our side there were about three hundred and sixty men".

The way to entire subjugation of the Island was now open, and had Agricola been encouraged or at least supported by the Imperial Government the course of history might have been altered. But Caledonia was to Rome only a sensation: the real strain was between the Rhine and the Danube. Counsels of prudence prevailed, and the remnants of the British fighting men were left to moulder in the Northern mist.

In the wild North and West freedom found refuge among the mountains, but elsewhere the conquest and pacification were at length complete and Britannia became one of the forty-five provinces of the Roman Empire. The great Augustus had proclaimed as the Imperial ideal the creation of a commonwealth of self-governing cantons. Each province was organised as a separate unit, and within it municipalities received their charters and rights. The provinces were divided between those exposed to barbarian invasion or uprising, for which an Imperial garrison must be provided, and those which required no such protection. The military provinces were under the direct supervision of the Emperor. The more sheltered were controlled, at least in form, through the medium of the Senate, but in all provinces the principle was followed of adapting the form of government to local conditions. No prejudice of race, language, or religion obstructed the universal character of the Roman system. The only divisions were those of class, and these ran unchallenged throughout the ordered world. There were Roman citizens, there was an enormous mass of non-Roman citizens, and there were slaves, but movement to full Roman citizenship was possible to fortunate members of the servile class. On this basis therefore the life of Britain now developed.

For nearly three hundred years Britain, reconciled to the Roman system, enjoyed in many respects the happiest, most comfortable, and most enlightened times its inhabitants have had. Confronted with the dangers of the frontiers, the military force was moderate. The Wall was held by the auxiliaries, with a legion in support at York. Wales was pinned down by a legion at Chester and another at Caerleon-on-Usk. In all, the army of occupation numbered less than forty thousand men, and after a few generations was locally recruited and almost of purely British birth. In this period, almost equal to that which separates us from the reign of Queen Elizabeth I, well-to-do persons in Britain lived better that they ever did until late Victorian times. From the year 400 till the year 1900 no one had central heating and very few had hot baths. A wealthy British-Roman citizen building a country house regarded the hypocaust which warmed it as indispensable. For fifteen hundred years his descendants lived in the cold of unheated dwellings, mitigated by occasional roasting at gigantic wasteful fires. As for baths, they were completely lost till the middle of the nineteenth century. In all this long, bleak intervening gap cold and dirt clung to the most fortunate and highest in the land.

In culture and learning Britain was a pale reflection of the Roman scene, not so lively as the Gallic. But there was law; there was order; there was peace; there was warmth; there was food, and a long-established custom of life. The population was free from barbarism without being sunk in sloth or luxury. Some culture spread even to the villages. Roman habits percolated; the use of Roman utensils and even of Roman speech steadily grew. The British thought themselves as good Romans as any. Indeed, it may be said that of all the provinces few assimilated the Roman system with more aptitude that the Islanders. The British legionaries and auxiliaries were rated equal or second only to the Illyrians as the finest troops in the Empire. There was a sense of pride in sharing in so noble and widespread a system. To be a citizen of Rome was to be a citizen of the world, raised upon a pedestal of unquestioned superiority above barbarians or slaves. Movement across the great Empire was as rapid as when Queen Victoria came to the throne, and no obstruction of frontiers, laws, currency, or nationalism hindered it.

The experts dispute the population of Roman Britain, and rival estimates vary between half a million and a million and a half. It seems certain that the army, the civil services, the townsfolk, the well-to-do, and their dependants amounted to three or four hundred thousand. To grow food for these, under the agricultural methods of the age, would have required on the land perhaps double their number. We may therefore assume a population of at least a million in the Romanised area. There may well have been more. But there are no signs that any large increase of population accompanied the Roman system. In more than two centuries of peace and order the inhabitants remained at about the same numbers as in the days of Cassivellaunus. This failure to foster and support a more numerous life spread disappointment and contraction throughout Roman Britain. The conquerors who so easily subdued and rallied the Britons to their method of social life brought with them no means, apart from stopping tribal war, of increasing the annual income derived from the productivity of the soil. The new society, with all its grace of structure, with its spice of elegance and luxury – baths, banquets, togas, schools, literature, and oratory – stood on no more sumptuous foundation than the agriculture of prehistoric times. The rude plenty in which the ancient Britons had dwelt was capable of supporting only to a moderate extent the imposing façade of Roman life. The cultivated ground was still for the most part confined to the lighter and more easily cultivated upland soils, which had for thousands of years been worked in a primitive fashion. The powerful Gallic plough on wheels was known in Britain, but it did not supplant the native implement, which could only nose along in shallow furrows. With a few exceptions, there was no large-scale attempt to clear the forests, drain the marshes, and cultivate the heavy clay soil of the valleys, in which so much fertility had been deposited. Such mining of lead and tin, such smelting, as had existed from times immemorial may have gained something from orderly administration; but there was no new science, no new thrust of power and knowledge in the material sphere. Thus the economic basis remained constant, and Britain became more genteel rather than more wealthy. Urban life in Britannia was a failure, not of existence, but of expansion. It ran on like the life of some cathedral city, some fading provincial town, sedate, restricted, even contracting, but not without grace and dignity.

We owe London to Rome. The military engineers of Claudius, the bureaucracy which directed the supply of the armies, the merchants who followed in their wake, brought it into a life not yet stilled. Trade followed the development of their road system. An extensive and well-planned city with mighty walls took the place of the wooden trading settlement of A.D. 61, and soon achieved a leading place in the life of the Roman province of Britain, superseding the old Belgic capital, Colchester, as the commercial centre. At the end of the third century money was coined in the London mint, and the city was the headquarters of the financial administration. In the later days of the province London seems to have been the centre of civil government, as York was of the military, although it never received the status of a *municipium*.

The efflorescence of Rome in Britain was found in its villa population all over the settled area. The villas of country gentlemen of modest station were built in the most delightful spots of a virgin countryside, amid primeval forests and the gushing of untamed streams. A very large number of comfortable dwellings, each with its lands around it rose and thrived. At least five hundred have been explored in the southern counties. None is found farther north than Yorkshire or farther west than the Glamorgan sea-plain. The comparative unsuccess of urban life led the better-class Roman Britain to establish themselves in the country, and thus the villa system was the dominant feature of Roman Britain in its heyday. The villas retained their prosperity after the towns had already decayed. The towns were shrunken after the third century. The villas still flourished in the fourth, and in some cases lingered on into the darkening days of the fifth.

The need for strong defences at the time when the expansion of the Empire had practically reached its limits was met by the frontier policy of the Flavian emperors. Domitian was the first to build a continuous line of fortifications. About A.D. 89 the great earth rampart was constructed on the Black Sea, and another connecting the Rhine with the Danube. By the end of the first century a standard type of frontier barrier had been evolved. The work of Agricola in Northern Britain had been left unfinished at his hasty recall. No satisfactory line of defence had been erected, and the position which he had won in Scotland had to be gradually abandoned. The legions fell back on the line of the Stanegate, a road running eastwards from Carlisle. The years which followed revealed the weakness of the British frontier. The accession of Hadrian was marked by a serious disaster. The Ninth Legion disappears from history in combating an obscure rising of the tribes in Northern Britain. The defences were disorganised and the province was in danger. Hadrian came to Britain in 122, and the reorganisation of the frontier began.

During the next five years a military barrier was built between the Tyne and the Solway seventy-three miles long. It consisted of a stone rampart eight to ten feet thick, sustained by seventeen forts, each garrisoned by an auxiliary cohort, about eighty castles, and double that number of signal towers. In front of the wall was a 30-foot ditch and behind it another ditch which seems to have been designed as a customs frontier and was probably controlled and staffed by the financial administration. The works needed a supporting garrison of about fourteen thousand men, not including some five thousand who, independent of the fighting units in the forts, were engaged in patrol work along the wall. The troops were provisioned by the local population, whose taxes were paid in wheat, and each fort contained granaries capable of holding a year's supply of food.

Twenty years later, in the reign of the Emperor Antoninus Pius, the Roman troops pushed northwards again over the ground of Agricola's conquests, and a new wall was built across the Forth-Clyde isthmus thirty-seven miles in length. The object was to control the tribes of the eastern and central Lowlands; but the Roman forces in Britain were not able to man the new defences without weakening their position on Hadrian's Wall and in the West. The middle years of the second century were troubled in the military area. Somewhere about the year 186 the Antonine Wall was abandoned and the troops were concentrated on the original line of defence. Tribal revolts and Scottish raids assailed the northern frontier system, and in places the Wall and its supporting camps were utterly wrecked.

It was not until the Emperor Severus came to Britain in 208 and flung his energies into the task of reorganisation that stability was achieved. So great had been the destruction, so massive were his repairs, that in later times he was thought to have built the Wall, which in fact he only reconstructed. He died at York in 211; but for a hundred years there was peace along the Roman Wall.

The first half-century after the Claudian invasion was very active in road-building. In the second century we find most of the work concentrated upon the frontiers of the military districts. By the third century the road system was complete and needed only to be kept in repair. It is true that for the period of Constantine the Great no fewer than four milestones have been unearthed, which point to some fresh extension, but by 340 all new work was ended, and though repairs were carried out as long as possible no later milestones proclaim a forward movement. The same symptoms reproduced themselves in Gaul after the year 350. The pedestrian facts are one measure of the rise and decline of the Roman power.

The Roman Empire was an old system. Its sinews and arteries had borne the strain of all that the ancient world had endured. Every generation after the middle of the second century saw an increasing weakening of the system and a gathering movement towards a uniform religion. Christianity asked again all the questions which the Roman world deemed answered for ever, and some that it had never thought of. Although the varieties of status, with all their grievous consequences, were accepted during these centuries, even by those who suffered from them most, as part of the law of nature, the institution of slavery, by which a third of Roman society was bound, could not withstand indefinitely the new dynamic thoughts which Christianity brought with it. The alternations between fanatic profligacy and avenging puritanism which marked the succession of the emperors, the contrast between the morals at the centre of power and those practised by wide communities in many subject lands, presented problems of ever-growing unrest. At the moment when mankind seemed to have solved a very large proportion of its secular difficulties and when a supreme Government offered unlimited freedom to spiritual experiment, inexorable forces both within and without drove on the forward march. Before the Roman system lay troubles immeasurable – squalor, slaughter, chaos itself, and the long night which was to fall upon the world. From outside the uncouth barbarians smote upon the barriers.

CHAPTER TWO

THE LOST ISLAND

*Picts and Scots — Hadrian's Wall breached — legions recalled to defend
Rome — the end of Roman Britain — the Pelagian heresy — the great
migration from Germany — the Saxon invasion — Anglo-Saxon
Chronicle — Hengist and Horsa — the legend of King Arthur*

ROM THE end of the third century, when Roman civilisation in Britain
and the challenge to the supreme structure were equally at their
height, inroads of barbarian peoples began, both from Europe and
from the forlorn Island to the westward. The Scots, whom nowadays
we should call the Irish, and the Picts from Scotland began to press on
Hadrian's Wall, to turn both flanks of it by sea raids on a growing scale. At the
same time the Saxons rowed in long-boats across the North Sea and lay heavy
all along the east coast from Newcastle to Dover. From this time forth the
British countryside dwelt under the same kind of menace of cruel, bloody, and
sudden inroad from the sea as do modern nations from the air. Many proofs
have been drawn from the soil in recent years. All point to the same conclusion. The villa life of Britain, upon which the edifice of Roman occupation
was now built, was in jeopardy. We see the signs of fear spreading through the
whole country. Besides the forts along the east and south coasts, and the
system of galleys based upon them, a host of new precautions become evident.
The walls of London were furnished with bastion towers, the stones for which
were taken from dwelling-houses, now no longer required by a dwindling
town-population. Here and there the broad Roman gateways of townships
were narrowed to half their size with masonry, a lasting proof of the
increasing insecurity of the times. All over the country hoards of coins have
been found, hardly any of which are later than the year A.D. 400. Over this
fertile, peaceful, ordered world lay the apprehension of constant peril.

For nearly a hundred years our Island was one of the scenes of conflict
between a dying civilisation and lusty, famishing barbarism. Continuous
efforts were made by the Roman-British community to repel the inroads, and
for two or three generations there were counter-strokes by flotillas of galleys,
and hurried marchings of cohorts and of British auxiliaries towards the
various thrusts of raid or invasion. But although the process of wearing down

was spread over many years, and misery deepened by inches, we must recognise in the year 367 circumstances of supreme and murderous horror.

In that fatal year the Picts, the Scots, and the Saxons seemed to work in combination. All fell together upon Britannia. The Imperial troops resisted manfully. The Duke of the Northern Marches and the Count of the Saxon Shore were killed in the battles. A wide-open breach was made in the defences, and murderous hordes poured in upon the fine world of country houses and homesteads. Everywhere they were blotted out. The ruins tell the tale. The splendid Mildenhall silver dinner service, now in the British Museum, is thought to have been buried at this time by its owners, when their villa was surprised by raiders. Evidently they did not live to dig it up again. The villa life of Britain only feebly recovered from the disaster. The towns were already declining. Now people took refuge in them. At least they had walls.

After the disasters of 367 the Emperor Valentinian sent a general, Theodosius, with a considerable force to relieve the province. Theodosius achieved his task, and once again we find on the coastal fortifications the traces of a further strong reconstruction. Untaught however by continuing danger, the garrison and inhabitants of Britain in 383 yielded themselves willingly to a Spaniard, Magnus Maximus, who held the command in Britain and now declared himself Emperor. Scraping together all the troops he could find, and stripping the Wall and the fortresses of their already scanty defenders, Maximus hastened to Gaul, and defeated the Emperor Gratian near Paris. Gratian was murdered at Lyons by his troops and Maximus became master of Gaul and Spain as well as Britain. For five years he struggled to defend his claim to these great dominions, but Theodosius, who had succeeded Gratian, at length defeated and slew him.

Meanwhile the Wall was pierced again, and Britain lay open to the raiders both from the North and from the sea. Seven years more were to pass before Theodosius could send his general, Stilicho, who was a Romanised barbarian, to the Island. This great soldier drove out the intruders and repaired the defences. The writings of Claudian, the court poet, described in triumphant terms the liberation of Britain from its Saxon, Pictish, and Scottish assailants in the year 400. In celebrating the first consulship of Stilicho he tells how Britain has expressed her gratitude for her deliverance from the fear of these foes. This sentiment soon fades.

Stilicho had returned to Rome, and was in chief command when in the same year Alaric and the Visigoths invaded Italy. He was forced to recall a further part of the British garrison to defend the heart of the Empire. In 402 he defeated Alaric in the great Battle of Pollentia, and drove him out of Italy. No sooner was this accomplished than a new barbarian invasion swept down upon him under Radagaisus. By 405 Stilicho had completely destroyed this second vast host. Italy was scarcely clear when a confederacy of Suevi, Vandals, Avars, and Burgundians broke through the Rhine frontiers and overran Northern Gaul. The indomitable Stilicho was preparing to meet this onslaught when the British army, complaining that the province was being neglected, mutinied. They set up a rival Emperor named Marcus, and on his speedy murder elected a Briton, Gratianus, in his stead. After his assassination four months later the soldiers chose another Briton, who bore the famous name of Constantine. Constantine, instead of protecting the Island, found himself compelled to defend upon the Continent the titles he had usurped. He drained Britain of troops, and, as Magnus Maximus had done, set forth for Boulogne to try his fortune. In the supreme theatre for three years, with varying success, he contended with Stilicho, and was finally captured and executed, as Maximus had been before him. None of the troops who had accompanied him ever returned to Britain. Thus in these fatal years the civilised parts of the Island were stripped of their defenders, both in order to aid the Empire and to strike against it.

By the beginning of the fifth century all the legions had gone on one errand or another, and to frantic appeals for aid the helpless Emperor Honorius could only send his valedictory message in 410, that "the cantons should take steps to defend themselves".

The first glimpse of the British after the Roman Government had withdrawn its protection is afforded by the visit of St Germanus in 429. The Bishop came from Auxerre in order to uproot the Pelagian heresy, which in spite of other preoccupations our Christian Island had been able to evolve. This doctrine consisted in assigning an undue importance to free will, and cast a consequential slur upon the doctrine of original sin. It thus threatened to deprive mankind, from its very birth, of an essential part of our inheritance. The Bishop of Auxerre and another Episcopal colleague arrived at St Albans, and we are assured that they soon convinced the doubters and eradicated the evil opinions to which they had incautiously hearkened. What kind of Britain did he find? He speaks of it as a land of wealth. There is treasure; there are flocks and herds; food is abundant; institutions, civil and religious, function; the country is prosperous, but at war. An invading army from the North or the East is approaching. It was an army said to be composed of Saxons, Picts, and Scots in ill-assorted and unholy alliance.

The Bishop had been a distinguished general in his prime. He organised the local forces. He reconnoitred the surrounding districts. He noticed in the line of the enemy's advance a valley surrounded by high hills. He took command, and lay in ambush for the ferocious heathen hordes. When the enemy were entangled in the defile, suddenly "The priests shouted a triple Alleluia at their foes. ... The cry was taken up with one mighty shout and echoed from side to side of the enclosed valley; the enemy were smitten with terror, thinking that the rocks and the very sky were falling upon them; such was their fear that they could hardly run quickly enough. They threw away their arms in their disorderly flight, glad to escape naked; a river devoured many in their headlong fear, though in their advance they had crossed it in good order. The innocent army saw itself avenged, a spectator of a victory gained without exertion. The abandoned spoils were collected ... and the Britons triumphed over an enemy routed without loss of blood; the victory was won by faith and not by might. ... So the Bishop returned to Auxerre, having settled the affairs of that most wealthy Island, and overcome their foes both spiritual and carnal, that is to say, both the Pelagians and Saxons."[1]

Another twelve years passed and a Gaulish chronicler records this sombre note in A.D. 441 or 442: "The Britons in these days by all kinds of calamities and disasters are falling into the power of the Saxons." What happened? Something more than the forays of the fourth century: the mass migration from North Germany had begun. Thereafter the darkness closes in.

Upon this darkness we have four windows, each obstructed by dim or coloured glass. First we have the tract of Gilda, upon whom the gratitude of the Middle Ages bestowed the title of "the wise". The tract was written in approximately A.D. 545, and therefore a hundred years after the curtain fell between Britannia and the continent. Nearly two hundred years later the Venerable Bede, whose main theme was the history of the English Church, lets fall some precious scraps of information, outside his subject, about the settlement itself. A compilation known as the *Historia Britonum* contains some documents earlier than Bede. Finally, in the ninth century, and very likely at the direction of King Arthur, various annals preserved in different monasteries were put together as the *Anglo-Saxon Chronicle*.[2] Checking these by each other, and by such certainties as archaeology allows us to entertain, we have the following picture.

Imitating a common Roman practice, the dominant British chief about A.D. 450 sought to strengthen himself by bringing in a band of mercenaries from over the seas. They proved a trap. Once the road was open fresh fleet-loads made their way across and up the rivers, from the Humber perhaps as far round as Portsmouth. But the British resistance stiffened as the invaders got away from the coast, and their advance was brought to a standstill for nearly fifty years by a great battle won at Mount Badon.

So far this tale is confirmed, historically and geographically. Gildas could have heard the story of the mercenaries from old men whom he had known in his youth, and there is no real ground for doubting the statements of Nennius,

1   Constantine of Lyons, a near contemporary biographer of St Germanus. [Churchill]

2   Churchill uses references from the Eyre & Spottiswoode edition of *The Anglo-Saxon Chronicle*. Arguments over exact translations and interpretation should be approached with caution. The Chronicle was not the work of one writer; it was set down by monks working at different times and at different monasteries – Winchester, Peterborough, Abingdon, Worcester, and Canterbury. In defence of Churchill's selection, it is certainly true that the substantial "fact" of the record does not much alter, whoever the writer and whatever the date of the translation. In the preface of the translation by James Ingram, Professor of Anglo-Saxon in the University of Oxford in the nineteenth century, there is the memorable claim that "philosophically considered, this ancient record is the second great phenomenon in the history of mankind". For the present readers' (and Churchill's) purpose, it has to be remembered that the importance of the Chronicle – and of the other references used in this text – is that they survived. Equally, the Chronicle and other references followed by Churchill – Dio's *Roman History*, Tacitus's *Annals*, and Caesar's *Conquests*, for example – have one thing in common: just as the early part of the Chronicle may have been inspired by King Alfred, each reference work is a version of history encouraged by understandable prejudice. Few, even Churchill, escaped that charge.

a compiler probably of the ninth century, and Bede, who agree that the name of the deceived chief who invited these deadly foes was Vortigern. Hengist, a name frequently mentioned in northern story, like a medieval mercenary was ready to sell his sword and his ships to anyone who would give him land on which to support his men; and what he took was the future kingdom of Kent. Gildas has a tale to tell of this tragedy.

> No sooner have they [the Britons] gone back to their land than the foul hosts of the Picts and Scots land promptly from their coracles. ... These two races differ in part in their manners, but they agree in their lust for blood, and in their habit of covering their hang-dog faces with hair, instead of covering with clothing those parts of their bodies which demand it. They seize all the northern and outlying part of the country as far as to the Wall. Upon this Wall stands a timorous and unwarlike garrison. The wretched citizens are pulled down from the Wall and dashed to the ground by the hooked weapons of their naked foes. What shall I add? The citizens desert the high Wall and their towns, and take to a flight more desperate than any before. Again the enemy pursue them, and there is slaughter more cruel than ever. As lambs by butchers, so are our piteous citizens rent by their foes, till their manner of sojourning might be compared to that of wild beasts. For they maintained themselves by robbery for the sake of a little food. Thus calamities from outside were increased by native feuds; so frequent were these disasters that the country was stripped of food, save what could be procured in the chase.
>
> Therefore again did the wretched remnants send a letter to Ætius, a powerful Roman – "To Ætius, three times, Consul, the groans of the Britons": "The barbarians drive us to the sea, the sea drives us to the barbarians: between these two methods of death we are either massacred or drowned." But they got no help. Meantime dire famine compelled many to surrender to their spoilers. ... But others would in no wise surrender, but kept on sallying from the mountains, caves, passes, and thick coppices. And then, for the first time, trusting not in man but in God, they slaughtered the foes who for so many years had been plundering their country. ... For a time the boldness of our enemies was checked, but not for our own countrymen: the enemy left our citizens, but our citizens did not leave their sins.

Nennius tells us, what Gildas omits, the name of the British soldier who won the crowning mercy of Mount Badon, and that name takes us out of the mist of dimly remembered history into the daylight of romance. There looms, large, uncertain, dim but glittering, the legend of King Arthur and the Knights of the Round Table. Somewhere in the Island a great captain gathered the forces of Roman Britain and fought the barbarian invaders to the death. Around him, around his name and his deeds, shine all that romance and poetry can bestow. Twelve battles, all located in scenes untraceable, with foes unknown, except that they were heathen, are punctiliously set forth in the Latin of Nennius. Other authorities say, "No Arthur; at least, no proof of any Arthur." It was only when Geoffrey of Monmouth six hundred years later was praising the splendours of feudalism and martial aristocracy that chivalry, honour, the Christian faith, knights in steel and ladies bewitching, are enshrined in a glorious circle lit by victory. Later these tales would be retold and embellished by the genius of Mallory, Spenser, and Tennyson. True or false, they have gained an immortal hold upon the thoughts of men. It is difficult to believe it was all an invention of a Welsh writer. If it was he must have been a marvellous inventor.

A broader question is keenly disputed. Did the invaders exterminate the native population, or did they superimpose themselves upon them and become to some extent blended with them? Here it is necessary to distinguish between the age of fierce forays in search of plunder and the age of settlement. Gildas is speaking of the former, and the scenes he described were repeated in the Danish invasions three centuries later. But to the settler such raids are only occasional incidents in a life mainly occupied in subduing the soil, and in that engrossing task, labour is as important as land. The evidence of place-names suggests that in Sussex extermination was the rule. Farther west there are grounds for thinking that a substantial British population survived, and the oldest West Saxon code of A.D. 694 makes careful provision for the rights of "Welshmen" of various degrees – substantial landowners, and "the King's Welshmen who ride his errands", his native gallopers in fact, who knew the ancient track-ways. Even where self-interest did not preserve the native villagers as labourers on Saxon farms, we may cherish the hope that somewhere a maiden's cry for pity, the appeal of beauty in distress, the lustful needs of an invading force, would create some bond between victor and vanquished. Thus the blood would be preserved, thus the rigours of subjugation would fade as generations passed away. The complete obliteration of an entire race over large areas is repulsive to the human mind. There should at least have been, in default of pity, a hearing for practical advantage or the natural temptations of sex. Thus serious writers contend that the Anglo-Saxon conquest was for the bulk of the British community mainly a change of masters. The rich were slaughtered; the brave and proud fell back in large numbers upon the Western mountains. Other numerous bands escaped betimes to Brittany, whence their remote posterity were one day to return.

The Saxon was moreover a valley-settler. His notion of an economic hold-ing was a meadow for hay near the stream, the lower slopes under the plough, the upper slopes kept for pasture. But in many places a long time must have passed before these lower grounds could be cleaned and drained, and while this work was in progress what did he live on but the produce of the upland British farms? It is more natural to suppose that he would keep his natives working as serfs on the land with which they were familiar until the valley was ready for sowing. Then the old British farms would go down to grass, and the whole population would cluster in the village by the stream or the spring. But the language of the valley-settlers, living in compact groups, would be dominant over that of the hill-cultivators, scattered in small and isolated hold-ings. The study of modern English place-names has shown that hill, wood, and stream names are often Celtic in origin, even in regions where the village names are Anglo-Saxon. In this way, without assuming any wholesale extermination, the disappearance of the British language can be explained even in areas where we know a British population to have survived. They had to learn the language of their masters: there was no need for their master to learn theirs. Thus it came about that both Latin and British yielded to the speech of the newcomers so completely that hardly a trace of either is to be found in our earliest records.

No uniformity of practice prevailed in the Island. There is good reason to think that the newcomers in Kent settled down beside the old inhabitants, whose name, Cantiaci, they adopted. In Northumbria there are strong traces of Celtic laws. In Hants and Wilts a broad belt of British names, from Liss to Deverill, seems to show the natives still cultivating their old fields on the downs, while the Saxon was clearing the valleys. There was no colour bar. In physical type the two races resembled each other; and the probabilities are that in many districts a substantial British element was incorporated in the Saxon stock.

The invaders themselves were not without their yearnings for settled security. Their hard laws, the rigours they endured, were but the results of the immense pressures behind them as the hordes of avid humanity spread westward from Central Asia. The warriors returning from a six months' foray liked to sprawl in lazy repose. Evidently they were not insensible to progressive promptings; but where, asked the chiefs and elders, could safety be found? In the fifth century, as the pressure from the East grew harder and as the annual raiding parties returned from Britain with plunder and tales of wealth, there was created in the ruling minds a sense of the difficulty of getting to the Island, and consequently of the security which would attend its occupation by a hardy and valiant race. Here, perhaps, in this wave-lapped Island men might settle down and enjoy the good things of life without the haunting fear of subjugation by a stronger hand, and without the immense daily sacrifices inseparable from military and tribal discipline on the mainland. To these savage swords Britain seemed a refuge. In the wake of the raiders, there grew steadily the plan and system of settlement. Thus, with despair behind and hope before, the migration to Britain and its occupation grew from year to year.

Of all the tribes of the Germanic race none was more cruel that the Saxons. Their very name, which spread to the whole confederacy of Northern tribes, was supposed to be derived from the use of a weapon, the seax, a short one-handed sword. Although tradition and the Venerable Bede assign the conquest of Britain to the Angles, Jutes, and Saxons together, and although the various settlements have tribal peculiarities, it is probable that before their general exodus from Schleswig-Holstein the Saxons had virtually incorporated the other two strains.

The history books of our childhood attempted courageously to prescribe exact dates for all the main events. In 449 Hengist and Horsa, invited by

Vortigern, founded the Jutish kingdom of Kent upon the corpses of its former inhabitants. In 477 Ella and his three sons arrived to continue the inroad. In 495 Cerdic and Cynric appeared. In 501 Port, the pirate, founded Portsmouth. In 514 the West Saxons Stuf and Wihtgar descended in their turn and put the Britons to flight. In 544 Wihtgar was killed. In 547 came Ida, founder of the kingdom of Northumberland. All that can be said about these dates is that they correspond broadly to the facts, and that these successive waves of invaders, bringing behind them settlers, descended on our unhappy shores.

Other authorities draw an alternative picture. "The bulk of the homesteads within the village", J. R. Green tells us,

> were those of its freemen or ceorls; but amongst these were the larger homes of eorls, or men distinguished among their fellows by noble blood, who were held in an hereditary reverence, and from whom the leaders of the village were chosen in war-time, or rulers in time of peace. But the choice was a purely voluntary one, and the man of noble blood enjoyed no legal privilege among his fellows.[1]

If this was so we might thus early have realised the democratic ideal of "the association of us all through the leadership of the best". In the tribal conceptions of the Germanic nation lie, no doubt, many of those principles which are now admired, and which have formed a recognisable part of the message which the English-speaking peoples have given to the world. But the conquerors of Roman Britain, far from practising these ideals, introduced a whole scheme of society which was fundamentally sordid and vicious. The invaders brought into Britain a principle common to all Germanic tribes, namely, the use of money power to regulate all the legal relations of men. If there was any equality it was liberty for the rich. If there were rights they were primarily the rights of property. There was no crime committed which could not be compounded by a money payment. Except failure to answer a call to join an expedition, there was no offence more heinous than that of theft.

An elaborate tariff prescribed in shillings the "wergild" or exact value or worth of every man. An atheling, or prince, was worth 1500 shillings, a shilling being the value of a cow in Kent, or of a sheep elsewhere; an eorl, or nobleman, 300 shillings. A ceorl, now degraded to the word "churl", who was a yeoman farmer, was worth 100 shillings, a laet, or agricultural serf, 40–80 shillings, and a slave nothing. All these laws were logically and mathematically pushed to their extremes. If a ceorl killed an eorl he had to pay three times as much in compensation as if the eorl were the murderer. And these laws were applied to the families of all. The life of a slaughtered man could be compounded for cash. With money all was possible; without it only retribution or loss of liberty. However, the atheling, valued at 1500 shillings, suffered in certain respects. The penalty for slander was the tearing out of the tongue. If an atheling were guilty of this offence his tongue was worth five times that of

1 *Short History of the English People.* [Churchill]

an eorl and fifteen times as much as that of a common laet, and he could ransom it only on these terms. Thus the abuse of a humble tongue was cheap. Wergild, at least, as Alfred[1] said long afterwards, was better than the blood feud.

The foundation of the Germanic system was blood and kin. The family was the unit, the tribe was the whole. The great transition which we witness among the emigrants is the abandonment of blood and kin as the theme of their society and its replacement by local societies and lordship based on the ownership of land. This change arose, like so many of the lessons learned by men, from the grim needs of war. Fighting for life and foothold against men as hard pressed as themselves, each pioneering band fell inevitably into the hands of the bravest, most commanding, most fortunate war-leader. This was no longer a foray of a few months, or at the outside a year. Here were settlements to be founded, new lands to be reclaimed and cultivated, lands which moreover offered to the deeper plough a virgin fertility. These must be guarded, and who could guard them except the bold chieftains who had gained them over the corpses of their former owners?

Thus the settlement in England was to modify the imported structure of Germanic life. The armed farmer-colonists found themselves forced to accept a stronger state authority owing to the stresses of continued military action. In Germany they had no kings. They developed them in Britain from leaders who claimed descent from the ancient gods. The position of the king continually increased in importance, and his supporters or companions gradually formed a new class in society, which carried with it the germ of feudalism, and was in the end to dominate all other conventions. But the lord was master; he must also be protector. He must stand by his people, must back them in the courts, feed them in time of famine, and they in return must work his land and follow him in war.

The king was at first only the war-leader made permanent; but, once set up, he had his own interests, his own needs, and his own mortal dangers. To make himself secure became his paramount desire. "To be thus is nothing, but to be safely thus ...". But how was this to be achieved? Only by the king gathering round him a band of the most successful warriors and interesting them directly in the conquest and in the settlement. He had nothing to give them except land. There must be a hierarchy. The king must be surrounded by those who had shared his deeds and his bounty. The spoils of war were soon consumed, but the land remained for ever. Land there was in plenty, of varying quality and condition, but to give individual warriors a title to any particular tract was contrary to the whole tradition of the Germanic tribes. Now under the hard pressures of war and pioneering, land increasingly became private property. Insensibly, at first, but with growing speed from the seventh century onwards, a landed aristocracy was created owing all it had to the king. While the resistance of the Britons was vigorously maintained, and the fortunes of the struggle swung this way and that way for nearly two hundred years, this new

1 Alfred the Great (A.D. 849–899).

institution of personal leadership established in the divinely descended war-chief sank deeply into the fibre of the Anglo-Saxon invaders.

But with this movement towards a more coherent policy or structure of society there came also a welter or conflicting minor powers. Distances were usually prohibitive, and writing virtually unknown. Districts were separated from each other like islands in rough seas, and thus a host of kings and kinglets sprang into existence behind the fighting frontier of the intruding tribes. In marking the many root faults and vices which they possessed a high place be assigned to their inability to combine. For a long time the Island presented only the spectacle of a chaos arising from the strife of small fiercely organised entities. Although from the time of the immigration the people south of the Humber were generally subject to a common overlord, they were never able to carry the evolution of kingship forward to a national throne. They remained marauders; but they had taken more pains to be sure of their booty.

Much has been written about the enervating character of Roman rule in Britain, and how people were rendered lax and ineffectual by the modest comforts which it supplied. There is no doubt that Gildas, by his writings, imparted an impression, perhaps in this case well founded, of gross incompetent and fatuity in the society and administration which followed Roman power. But justice to this vanished epoch demands recognition of the fact that the Britons fought those who are now called the English for nearly two hundred and fifty years. For a hundred years they fought them under the aegis of Rome, with its world organisation; but for a hundred and fifty years they fought them alone. The conflict ebbed and flowed. British victories were gained, which once for a whole generation brought the conquest to a halt; and in the end the mountains which even the Romans had been unable to subdue proved an invincible citadel of the British race.

CHAPTER THREE

ANGLO-SAXON ENGLAND

Spreading Christianity – St Patrick, St David, St Columba – Augustine
sent from Rome – he re-founds the Church at Canterbury – Ethelbert and
Edwin – Paulinus and the conversion of York – the final battle between
Britons and Saxons – the destruction of Cadwallon and Penda – the
Synod of Whitby – the Venerable Bede – Offa, rex Anglorum

A RED SUNSET; a long night; a pale, misty dawn! But as the light grows it becomes apparent to remote posterity that everything has changed. Night had fallen on Britannia. Dawn rose on England, humble, poor, degraded and divided, but alive. Britannia had been an active part of a world state; England was once again a barbarian island. It had been Christian, it was now heathen. Its inhabitants had rejoiced in well-planned cities, with temples, markets, academies. They had nourished craftsmen and merchants, professors of literature and rhetoric. For four hundred years there had been order and law, respect for property, and a widening culture. All had vanished. The buildings, such as they were, were of wood, not stone. The people had lost entirely the art of writing. Some miserable runic scribblings were the only means by which they could convey their thoughts or wishes to one another at a distance. Barbarism reigned in its rage, without even the stern military principles which had animated and preserved the Germanic tribes. The confusion and conflict of petty ruffians sometimes called kings racked the land. There was nothing worthy of the name of nationhood, or even of tribalism; yet this is a transition which the learned men of the nineteenth century banded themselves together to proclaim as an onward step in the march of mankind. We wake from an awful and, it might well have seemed, endless nightmare to a scene of utter prostration. Nor did the seeds of recovery spring from the savage hordes who had wrecked the Roman culture. They would certainly have continued to welter indefinitely in squalor, but for the fact that a new force was stirring beyond the seas which, moving slowly, fitfully, painfully, among the ruins of civilisation, reached at length by various paths the unhappy Island, to which, according to Procopius, the souls of the dead upon the mainland were ferried over by some uncouth Charon.

Christianity had not been established as the religion of the empire during the first two centuries of the Roman occupation of Britain. It grew with many other cults in the large and easy tolerance of the Imperial system. There arose however a British Christian Church which sent its bishops to the early councils, and had sufficient vitality to develop the Pelagian heresy from its own unaided heart-searchings. When the evil days overtook the land and the long struggle with the Saxons was fought out, the British Church fell back with other survivors upon the western parts of the Island. Such was the gulf between the warring races that no attempt was made at any time by the British bishops to Christianise the invaders. Perhaps they were not given any chance of converting them. After an interval one of their leading luminaries, afterwards known as St David, accomplished the general conversion of what is now Wales. Apart from this, British Christianity languished in its refuges, and might well have become moribund but for the appearance of a remarkable and charming personality.

St Patrick was a Roman Briton of good family dwelling probably in the Severn valley. His father was a Christian deacon, a Roman citizen, and a member of the municipal council. One day in the early fifth century there descended upon the district a band of Irish raiders, burning and slaying. The young Patrick was carried off and sold into slavery in Ireland. Whether he dwelt in Connaught or in Ulster is disputed, and the evidence is contradictory. It may well be that both versions are true and that both provinces may claim the honour. For six years, wherever it was, he tended swine, and loneliness led him to seek comfort in religion. He was led by miraculous promptings to attempt escape. Although many miles separated him from the sea he made his way to a port, found a ship, and persuaded the captain to take him on board. After many wanderings we find him in one of the small islands off Marseilles, then a centre of the new monastic movement spreading westward from the Eastern Mediterranean. Later he consorted with Bishop Germanus of Auxerre. He conceived an earnest desire to return good for evil and spread the tidings he had learned among his former captors in Ireland. After fourteen years of careful training by the Bishop and self-preparation for what must have seemed a forlorn adventure Patrick sailed back in 432 to the wild regions which he had quitted. His success was speedy and undying. He organised the Christianity already in existence, he converted kingdoms which were still pagan, and he brought Ireland into touch with the Church of Western Europe and made it indissolubly part of universal Christendom. On a somewhat lower plane, although also held in perpetual memory, was the banishing of snakes and reptiles of all kinds from the Irish soil, for which from age to age his fame has been celebrated.

It was therefore in Ireland and not in Wales or England that the light of Christianity now burned and gleamed through the darkness. And it was from Ireland that the Gospel was carried to the North of Britain and for the first time cast its redeeming spell upon the Pictish invaders. Columba, born half a century after St Patrick's death, but an offspring of his church, and imbued with his grace and fire, proved a new champion of the faith. From the monastery which he established in the island of Iona his disciples went forth to the

British kingdom of Strathclyde, to the Pictish tribes of the North, and to the Anglian kingdom of Northumbria. He is the founder of the Scottish Christian Church. Thus the message which St Patrick had carried to Ireland came back across the stormy waters and spread through wide regions. There was however a distinction in the form of Christianity which reached England through the mission of St Columba and that which was more generally accepted throughout the Christianised countries of Europe. It was monastic in its form, and it travelled from the East through Northern Ireland to its new home without touching at any moment the Roman centre. The Celtic churches therefore received a form of ecclesiastical government which was supported by the loosely knit communities of monks and preachers, and was not in these early decisive periods associated with the universal organisation of the Papacy.

In spite of the slow means of travel and scanty news, the Papacy had from an early stage followed with deep attention the results of St Columba's labours. Its interest was excited not only by the spread of the Gospel, but also by any straying from the true path into which new Christians might be betrayed. It saw with thankfulness an ardent Christian movement afoot in these remote Northern islands, and with concern that it was from the outset independent of the Papal throne. These were the days when it was the first care of the Bishop of Rome that all Christ's sheep should be gathered into one fold. Here in the North, where so much zeal and fervour were evident, the faith seemed to be awkwardly and above all separately planted.

For various reasons, including the spreading of the Gospel, it was decided in the closing decade of the sixth century that a guide and teacher should be sent to England to diffuse and stimulate the Faith, to convert the heathen, and also to bring about an effective working union between British Christians and the main body of the Church. For this high task Pope Gregory, afterwards called "the Great", and the ecclesiastical statesmen gathered in Rome selected a trusty and cultured monk named Augustine.[1] St Augustine, as he is known to history, began his mission in 596 under hopeful auspices. Kent has always been the part of the British Island most closely in contact with Europe, and in all its various phases the most advanced in culture. The King of Kent had married Bertha, a daughter of the Frankish king, the descendant of Clovis, now

[1] Churchill gives only a hint of Augustine's character when he writes of his "tactless arrogance". This is, according to wider opinion, an understatement. Augustine did not feel an awesome calling to convert the people of these islands. In fact, he did not wish to make the journey, which at the time (the sixth century) was considered an awesome trek and a dangerous destination. There was even a point at which he and his fellow monks stopped in southern Gaul and refused to go any nearer to the barbarians of Britannia. Augustine returned to Rome to explain their ecclesiastic reservations, and only the diplomatic patience and determination of Pope Gregory (who did feel inspired) saved the day and the crusade. Letters written by the pope encouraging Augustine, and the others and dated A.D. 596 have survived. If nothing else, these documents show that Pope Gregory and not Augustine (who was the prior of Gregory's monastery) was the mastermind of the crusade. The journey to conversion was not on the byways of England but in the royal courts, which is why this text refers to the conversions of princes and kings. The people followed the crown – or mattered not.

enthroned in Paris. Although her husband still worshipped Thor and Woden Queen Bertha had already begun to spread the truth through courtly circles. Her chaplain, an earnest and energetic Frank, was given full rein, and thus a powerful impulse came to the people of Kent, who were already in a receptive mood towards the dominant creed of Western Europe. St Augustine, when he landed in Kent, was therefore aware that much had been prepared beforehand. His arrival infused a mood of action. With the aid of the Frankish princess he converted King Ethelbert, who had for reasons of policy long mediated this step.[1] Upon the ruins of the ancient British church of St Martin he refounded the Christian life of Canterbury, which was destined to become the centre and summit of religious England.

Ethelbert, as overlord of England, exercised an effective authority over the kingdom of the South and West. His policy was at once skilful and ambitious; his conversion to Christianity, however sincere, was also in consonance with his secular aims. He was himself, as the only English Christian ruler, in a position where he might hold out the hand to the British princes, and, by using the Christian faith as a bone of union, establish his supremacy over the whole country. This, no doubt, was also in accordance with the ideas which Augustine had carried from Rome. Thus at the opening of the seventh century Ethelbert and Augustine summoned a conference of the British Christian bishops. The place chosen in the Severn valley was on the frontier between the English and British domains, and far outside the bound of the Kentish kingdom. Here, then, would be a chance of a general and lasting peace for both races, reconciled in the name of Christ; and this settlement Ethelbert and his descendants could securely expect to be the heirs. We must regret that this hope, sustained by sagacious and benevolent politics, was not realised. It failed for two separate reasons: first, the sullen and jealous temper of the British bishops, and, secondly, the tactless arrogance of St Augustine.

There were two conferences, with an interval. The discussions were ostensibly confined to interesting but uncontroversial questions. There was the date of Easter, which is still debated, and also the form of the tonsure. Augustine urged the Roman custom of shaving only the top of the head. The British bishops had perhaps imitated the Druidical method of shaving from the centre to the ears, leaving a fringe on the forehead. It was a choice of the grotesque. These were matters well capable of adjustment, but they conveniently offered ample pasture upon which the conferences could browse in public, while the vital issues were settling themselves in an atmosphere of goodwill, or being definitely compacted behind the scenes.

But the British bishops were found in no mood to throw themselves into the strong embraces of Rome. Why should they, who had so long defended the Faith against horrible cruelties and oppression, now receive their guidance

---

1   Christian baptism is to play a significant part in the rest of the story. Almost immediately, we will find that after a bloody and dreadful battle, the successful English king will baptise his defeated foe and stand godparent to the other's sons. It was more than zealousness: this Christian act was also a form of protection.

from a Saxon Kentish king whose conversion was brand-new, and whose political designs however inspiring, were none the less obvious? The second conference ended in a complete rupture. When Augustine found himself in the presence of what he deemed to be unreasonable prejudice and deep-seated hostility, when he saw the few bishops who had been won over reproached by their brethren as backsliders and traitors, he fell back quite quickly upon threats. If British Christianity would not accept the fair offers now made the whole influence and prestige of Rome would be thrown against them upon the English side. The Saxon armies would be blessed and upheld by Rome and by the unbroken traditions of the main Christian Church, and no sympathy would be felt for these long-faithful British Christians when they had their throats cut by the new English convert states. "If", the Saint exclaimed, "you will not have peace from your friends, you shall have war from your foes." But this was no more than the British had faced for two hundred years. It was language they understood. The conference separated in enmity; the breach was irreparable. All further efforts by Rome through Ethelbert and the Kentish kingdom to establish even the slightest contact with Christian Britain were inexorably repulsed.

Augustine's mission therefore drew to a dignified but curtailed end. Except for the consecration of Mellitus as Bishop of the East Saxons in a church on the site of St Paul's, he had made little attempt to proselytise outside Kent. From the title loosely accorded him of "Apostle of the English" he enjoyed for many centuries the credit of having re-converted the once-famous Roman province of Britannia to the Christian faith; and this halo has shone about him until comparatively recent times.

Almost a generation passed before envoys from Rome began to penetrate into Northern England and rally its peoples to Christianity, and then it came about in the wake of political and dynastic developments. By a series of victories Redwald, King of the East Angles, had established a wide dominion over the lands of Central England from the Dee to the Humber. With Redwald's aid the crown of Northumbria was gained by an exiled prince, Edwin, who by his abilities won his way, step by step, to the foremost position in England. Even before the death of his ally Redwald, Edwin was recognised as overlord of all the English kingdoms except Kent, and the isles of Anglesey and Man were also reduced by his ships. He not only established his personal primacy, but the confederation founded by him foreshadowed the kingdom of all England that was later to take shape under the kings of Mercia and Wessex. Edwin married a Christian princess of Kent, whose religion he had promised to respect. Consequently, in her train from Canterbury to Edwin's capital at York there rode in 625 the first Roman missionary to Northern England, Paulinus, an envoy who had first come to Britain in the days of St Augustine, twenty-four years before.

We have a picture agreeable and instructive of Edwin: "There was then a perfect peace in Britain wheresoever the dominion of King Edwin extended, and, as it is still proverbially said, a woman with her new-born babe might walk throughout the island from sea to sea without receiving any harm. That King took such care for the good of his nation that in several places where he had seen clear springs near the highways he caused stakes to be fixed with proper drinking vessels hanging on them for the refreshment of travellers, nor durst any man touch them for any other purpose than that for which they were designed, either for the great fear that they had of the King or for the affection which they bore him." He revived the Roman style: "Not only were his banners borne before him in battle, but even in peace when he rode about his cities, townships, or provinces with his thanes. A standard-bearer was always wont to go before him when he walked anywhere in the streets in the Roman fashion."

Such in his heyday was the prince to whom Paulinus resorted. Paulinus converted Edwin, and the ample kingdom of Northumbria, shaped like England itself in miniature, became Christian. But this blessed event brought with it swift and dire consequences. The overlordship of Northumbria was fiercely resented by King Penda of Mercia, or, as we should now say, of the Midlands. The drama unfolded with staggering changes of fortune. In 633 Penda, the heathen, made an unnatural alliance with Cadwallon, the Christian British King of North Wales, with the object of overthrowing the suzerainty of Edwin and breaking the Northumbrian power. Here for the first time noticed in history British and English fought side by side. Politics for once proved stronger than religion or race. In a savage battle near Doncaster Edwin was defeated and slain, and his head – not the last – was exhibited on the ramparts of captured York. It may be that York, long the home of a legion, still preserved Roman-British traditions which led them to welcome the British victors. This sudden destruction of the greatest king who had hitherto ruled in the Island brought in recoil an equally speedy vengeance. British Cadwallon had triumphed over Northumbria. Here at last was the chance, so long expected, of British vengeance upon their Saxon foes. Here was the faithful paying off of very old but very heavy debts. We might almost be seeing again the spirit of Boadicea.

But the inherent power of Northumbria was great. The name and fame of the slaughtered Edwin rang through the land. His successor, Oswald, of the house of Bernicia, which was one of the two provinces of the kingdom, had but to appear to find himself at the head of the newly Christianised and also infuriated Saxon warriors. Within a year of the death of Edwin Oswald destroyed Cadwallon and his British forces in a hard battle which fell out along the line of the Roman Wall. This was the last pitched battle between the Britons and the Saxons; and it must be admitted that the Britons fared as badly in conduct as in fortune. They had joined with the heathen Saxon Midlands to avenge their wrongs and had exploited an English movement towards the disunity of the land. They had shattered this bright hope of the Christianity they professed, and now they were themselves overthrown and cast aside. The long story of their struggle with the invaders ended thus in no fine way; but what is important to our tale is that it had ended at last.

The destruction of Cadwallon and the clearance from Northumbria of the wild Western Britons, whose atrocities had united all the Saxon forces in the North, was the prelude to the struggle with King Penda. He was regarded by the Saxon tribes as one who had brought boundless suffering and slaughter upon them through a shameful pact with the hereditary foe. Nevertheless he prospered for a while. He upheld the claims of Thor and Woden with all the strength of Mercia for seven years. He defeated, decapitated, and dismembered King Oswald, as he had destroyed his predecessor before him. But a younger brother of Oswald, Oswy by name, after a few years, settled the family account, and Penda fell by the sword he had drawn too often. Thus the power of Northumbria rose the stronger from the ordeal and eclipse through which its people had passed.

The failure of Ethelbert's attempt to make a Christian reunion of England and Britain left the direction of the immediate future with the Northumbrian Court. It was to York and not to Canterbury that Rome looked, and upon English, not British, armies that the hopes of organised Christendom were placed. When the disasters had overtaken Northumbria Paulinus had hastened back by sea to Canterbury. Neither he nor Augustine was the kind of man to face the brutal warfare of those times. Carefully trained as they were in the doctrines, interests, and policy of the Papacy, they were not the stuff of which martyrs or evangelists are made. This British incursion was too rough. But the lieutenant of Paulinus, one James the Deacon, stuck to his post through the whole struggle, and preached and baptised continually in the midst of rapine and carnage. Still more important than his work was that of the Celtic mission to Northumbria under St Aidan. Much of Mercia and East Anglia, as well as Northumbria, was recovered to Christianity by the Celtic missionaries. Thus two streams of the Christian faith once more met in England, and the immediate future was to witness a struggle for supremacy between them.

With the defeat and death of Penda, and upon the surge of all the passions which had been loosed, Anglo-Saxon England was definitely rallied to the Christian faith. There was now no kingdom in which heathen practices prevailed. Indeed, apart from individuals, whose private adherence to Woden was overlooked, the whole Island was Christian. But this marvellous event, which might have brought in its train so many blessings, was marred by the new causes of division which now opened between the English and British people. To the ferocious British-English racial feud there was added a different view of Church government, which sundered the race almost as much as the difference between Christianity and heathenism. Henceforward the issue is no longer whether the Island shall be Christian or pagan, but whether the Roman or the Celtic view of Christianity shall prevail. These differences persisted across the centuries, much debated by all the parties concerned.

The celebrated and largely successful attempt to solve them took place at the Synod of Whitby in 663. There the hinging issue was whether British Christianity should conform to the general life-plan of Christendom or whether it should be expressed by the monastic orders which had founded the Celtic Churches of the North. The issues hung in the balance, but in the end after much pious dissertation the decision was taken that the Church of Northumbria should be a definite part of the Church of Rome and of the Catholic system. Mercia soon afterwards conformed. Though the Celtic leader and his following retired in disgust to Iona, and the Irish clergy refused to submit, the importance of this event cannot be overrated. Instead of a religion controlled by the narrow views of abbots pursuing their strict rule of life in their various towns or remote resorts there was opened to every member of the English Church the broad vista of a world-state and universal communion. These events brought Northumbria to her zenith. In Britain for the first time there was achieved a unity of faith, morals, and Church government covering five-sixths of the Island. The decisive step had been taken in the spiritual sphere. The Island was now entirely Christian, and by far the greater and more powerful part was to be directly associated with the Papacy.

Rome had had little reason to be satisfied with the mission of either Augustine or Paulinus. The Papacy realised that its efforts to guide and govern British Christianity through the kingdom of Kent had been misplaced. It now made a new plan, which illustrates the universal character of the Catholic Church. Two fresh emissaries were chosen in 668 to carry the light into the northern mists, the first a native of Asia Minor, Theodore of Tarsus, the second an African named Hadrian from Carthage. These missionaries were of a strong type than their precursors, and character and integrity shone before all. When they arrived at Canterbury there were but three bishops from all England to greet them. When their work was finished the Anglican Church raised its mitred front in a majesty which has not yet been dimmed. Before he died in 690 Theodore had increased the number of bishoprics from seven to fourteen, and by his administrative skill he gave the Church a new cohesion. This remarkable Asiatic was the earliest of the statesmen of England, and guided her steps with fruitful wisdom.

There followed a long and intricate rivalry for leadership between the various Anglo-Saxon kings which occupied the seventh and eighth centuries. It was highly important to those whose span of life was cast in that period, but it left small marks on the subsequent course of history. Let a few words suffice. The primacy of Northumbria was menaced and finally ended by the inherent geographical and physical weakness of its position. It was liable to be beset from every quarter, from the north by the Picts, on the west by the British kingdom of Strathclyde, in the south by Mercia, those jealous Midlands still smarting from the suppression of Penda and the punishments inflicted upon his adherents. These antagonisms were too much for Northumbria to bear, and although great efforts were made and amid the exhausting feuds of rival kings some wise chieftains occasionally prevailed, its collapse as the leading community in the Island was inevitable.

Northumbria was fortunate however in having in this twilight scene a chronicler, to whom we have already referred, whose words have descended to us out of the long silence of the past. Bede, a monk of high ability, working unknown in the recesses of the Church, now comes forward as the most effective and almost the only audible voice from the British islands in these dim times. Unlike Gildas, Bede wrote history, and the name of "the Venerable Bede" still carries with it a proud renown. He alone attempts to paint for us, and, so far as he can, explain the spectacle of Anglo-Saxon England in its first phase: a Christian England, divided by tribal, territorial, dynastic, and personal feuds into what an Elizabethan antiquary called the Heptarchy, seven kingdoms of varying strength, all professing the Gospel of Christ, and striving over each other for mastery by force and fraud. For almost exactly a hundred years, from 731 to 829, there was a period of ceaseless warfare, conducted with cruelty and rapine under a single creed.

The leadership of Saxon England passed to Mercia. For nearly eighty years two Mercian kings asserted or maintained their ascendancy over all England south of the Humber. Ethelbald and Offa reigned each for forty years. Ethelbald had been an exile before he became an autocrat. As a fugitive he consorted with monks, hermits, and holy men. On attaining power he did not discard his Christian piety, but he found himself much oppressed by the temptations of the flesh. St Guthlac had comforted him in misfortune and poverty, but St Boniface was constrained to rebuke him for his immorality.

The moral sense had grown so strong in matters of sex that Churchmen could now brand a king as licentious. Boniface from Germany censured Ethelbald for the "twofold sin" which he committed in nunneries by using the advantages of his royal position to gain himself favours otherwise beyond his reach. The chronicles of this sovereign are scanty. He showed charity to the poor; he preserved law and order; in the South in 733 he raided Wessex; and in 740 he laid parts of Northumbria waste while its harassed chief was struggling with the Picts. After this last victory he took to styling himself "King of the Southern English" and "King of Britain". South of the Humber these claims were made good.

Ethelbald, having been at length murdered by his guards, was succeeded by a greater man. Little is know of Offa, who reigned for the second forty years, but the imprint of his power is visible not only throughout England but upon the Continent. Offa was the contemporary of Charlemagne.[1] His policy interlaced with that of Europe; he was reputed to be the first "King of the English", and he had the first quarrel since Roman times with the mainland.

---

1   Charlemagne's importance should not be underrated, although in some respected English history reference books, Charlemagne does not appear. A term used at this time is Carolingian – the dynasty of Charles. The name Charles meant brave warrior and it was the first Charles, Charles Martel (the hammer), who conquered the Saracens and ruled Austrasia. He died in 741. His son, Pepin the Short, expanded the Carolingian empire, and in 754 it was he who gave the pope the city of Rome. One of Pepin's sons was also named Charles. Such were Charles's powers that he was given the title Charles the Great, "Carolus Magna", this translated into eighth-century French and English as Charlemagne. He was crowned emperor in Rome by Pope Leo III in A.D. 800. Charlemagne should be seen in Churchill's story as the most powerful ruler in the whole of Europe.

Charlemagne wished one of his sons to marry one of Offa's daughters. Here we have an important proof of the esteem in which the Englishman was held. Offa stipulated that his son must simultaneously marry a daughter of Charlemagne. The founder of the Holy Roman Empire appeared at first incensed at this assumption of equality, but after a while he found it expedient to renew his friendship with Offa. It seems that "the King of the English" had placed an embargo upon Continental merchandise, and the inconvenience of this retaliation speedily overcame all points of pride and sentiment. Very soon Offa was again the Emperor's "dearest brother", and Charlemagne is seen agreeing to arrange that there should be reciprocity of royal protection in both countries for merchants, "according to the ancient custom of trading". Apparently the commodities in question were "black stones", presumably coal, from France, in return for English cloaks. There were also questions of refugees and extradition. Charlemagne was interested in repatriating a Scot who ate meat in Lent. He sent presents of an ancient sword and silken mantles. Thus we see Offa admitted to equal rank with the greatest figure in Europe. It is evident that the Island Power must have counted for a great deal in these days. Monarchs of mighty empires do not make marriage contracts for their children and beat out the details of commercial treaties with persons of no consequence.

The advantage given by these two long reigns when everything was in flux had reinstated the Island again as a recognisable factor in the world. We know that Offa styled himself not only *rex Anglorum*, but also "King of the whole land of the English" (*rex totius Anglorum patriae*). This expression *rex Anglorum* is rightly signalised by historians as a milestone in our history. Here was an English king who ruled over the greatest part of the Island, whose trade was important, and whose daughters were fit consorts for the sons of Charles the Great. We learn about Offa almost entirely through this impact on his neighbours. It is clear from their record that he suppressed the under-kings of the Severn valley, that he defeated the West Saxons in Oxfordshire and subjugated Berkshire, that he decapitated the King of East Anglia, that he was master of London, that he extirpated the monarchy which Hengist had founded in Kent, and put down a Kentish rising with extreme severity. Henceforth he gave his own orders in Kent. He captured its mint and inscribed his name upon the coins issued by the Archbishop of Canterbury.

In studying Offa we are like geologists who instead of finding a fossil find only the hollow shape in which a creature of unusual strength and size undoubtedly resided. Alcuin, one of the few recorders of this period at the Court of Charlemagne, addresses Offa in these terms: "You are a glory to Britain and a sword against its enemies." We have a tangible monument of Offa in the immense dyke which he caused to be built between converted Saxon England and the still unconquered British. The tables were now turned, and those who had never faltered in the old faith and had always maintained their independence had sunk in the estimation of men from the mere fact that they lived in barren mountainous lands, while their successful ravishers strode on in pomp and even dignity. This dyke, which runs over the hills and dales, leaving gaps for the impenetrable forests, from the mouth of the Severn to the neighbourhood of the Mersey, attests to our day the immense authority of the state over which Offa presided. When we reflect how grim was the struggle for life, and how the getting of enough food to keep body and soul together was the prime concern not only of families but of whole peoples, the fact that this extensive rampart could have been mainly the work of the lifetime and the will of a single man is startling. It conveys to us an idea of the magnitude and force of Offa's kingdom. Such works are not constructed except upon a foundation of effective political power. But "Offa's Dyke" shows policy as well as man-power. In many sections it follows lines favourable to the British, and historians have concluded that it was a boundary rather than a fortification and resulted from an agreement reached for common advantage. It was not a Roman wall, like those of Antoninus or Hadrian, between savagery and civilisation, but rather the expression of a solemn treaty which for a long spell removed from Offa's problem the menace of a British incursion, and thus set him free with his back secure to parley and dispute with Europe.

CHAPTER FOUR

THE VIKINGS

The Vikings – the sacking of Lindisfarne and Iona – the founding of
Dublin – the fyrd – Ragnar Lodbrok – Ivar the Boneless – the Treaty of
Nottingham

A FTER THE fall of Imperial Rome the victorious barbarians were in
their turn captivated and enthralled by the Gospel of Christ.
Though no more successful in laying aside their sinful promptings than religious men and women are today, they had a common
theme and inspiration. There was a bond which linked all the races of Europe.
There was an international organisation which, standing erect in every
country, was by far the most powerful, and indeed the only coherent surviving
structure, and at the head of which the Bishop of Rome revived in a spiritual,
or at least in an ecclesiastical form, the vanished authority of the Caesars. The
Christian Church became the sole sanctuary of learning and knowledge. It
sheltered in its aisles and cloisters all the salvage of ancient days. It offered to
men in their strife and error "the last solace of human woe, the last restraint of
earthly power". Thus, while the light of pagan civilisation was by no means
wholly extinguished, a new effulgence held, dazzled, and dominated the barbaric hordes, not only in our Island but throughout Europe. They were
tamed and uplifted by the Christian revelation. Everywhere, from the
Euphrates to the Boyne, old gods were forsworn, and a priest of Christ could
travel far and wide, finding in every town an understanding of brotherhood
and a universal if sometimes austere hospitality.

Amid the turbulence and ignorance of the age of Roman decay all the
intellectual elements at first found refuge in the Church, and afterwards
exercised mastery from it. Here was the school of politicians. The virtual
monopoly of learning and the art of writing made the Churchmen indispensable to the proud and violent chieftains of the day. The clerics became the
civil servants, and often the statesmen, of every Court. They fell naturally,
inevitably, into the place of the Roman magistrate whose garb they wore, and
wear today. Triumphant barbarism yielded itself insensibly to a structure,
reliance upon which was proved on numberless occasions to give success in the
unending struggle for power. After the convulsions and disorders of the Dark
Ages, when at last daylight fell again on the British Island, she awoke to a
world also profoundly changed, but devoid neither of form nor majesty.
There was even a gentler breeze in the air.

The fervour of the converted heathen brought however in its train mischiefs which opened new calamities. The Church was bound by its spirit to inculcate mildness and mercy. It was led by zeal and by its interests to fortify in every way the structure of its own power. The humility and faith of the descendants of the invaders soon exposed them in their human frailty, to an organised exploitation which during the sixth and seventh centuries led in many countries to an engrossment by the Church of treasure and lands out of all proportion to its capacity to control events. We are presented with Christendom pious but forward; spiritually united, but a prey to worldly feuds; in a state of grace, but by no means free from ambition.

Upon this revived, convalescent, loosely knit society there now fell two blasting external assaults. The first came from the East. In Arabia Mahomet had unfurled the martial and sacred standards of Islam. At the beginning of the next century Islam crossed the Straits of Gibraltar and prevailed in Spain, whence it was not finally to be dislodged for nearly eight hundred years. At one moment France too seemed about to succumb, but the Arabs were beaten back by Charles Martel, grandfather of Charlemagne, in 732 at Poitiers. Thus, all the way from Mecca the power of Islam came almost within striking distance of these islands.

For Britain however was reserved the second invading wave. It came from the North. In Scandinavia the Vikings fitted out their long-boats for sea. This double assault by Arab infidels and Nordic pirates distracted the weakened life of Europe for ten generations. It was not until the eleventh century that the steel-clad feudalism of medieval Christendom, itself consisting largely of the converted descendants of the Vikings, assigned limits to the Arab conquests, and established at the side of the Christian church ample and effective military power.

Measure for measure, what the Saxon pirates had given to the Britons was meted out to the English after the lapse of four hundred years. In the eighth century a vehement manifestation of conquering energy appeared in Scandinavia. Norway, Sweden, and Denmark threw up bands of formidable fighting men, who, in addition to all their other martial qualities, were the hardy rovers of the sea. The causes which led to this racial ebullition were the spontaneous growth of their strength and population, the thirst for adventure, and the complications of dynastic quarrels. There was here no question of the Danes or Norsemen being driven westward by new pressures from the steppes of Asia. They moved of their own accord. Their prowess was amazing. One current of marauding vigour struck southwards from Sweden, and not only reached Constantinople, but left behind it potent germs which across the centuries made their mark upon European Russia. Another contingent sailed in their long-boats from Norway to the Mediterranean, harried all the shores of the inland sea, and were with difficulty repulsed by the Arab kingdom of Spain and the north coast of Africa. The third far-ranging impulse carried the Scandinavian buccaneers to the British Isles, to Normandy, to Iceland, and presently across the Atlantic Ocean to the American continent.

The soul of the Vikings lay in the long-ship. They had evolved, and now, in the eighth and ninth centuries, carried to perfection a vessel which by its shallow draught could sail far up rivers, or anchor in innumerable creeks and bays, and which by its beautiful lines and suppleness of construction could ride out the fiercest storms of the Atlantic Ocean.

Such was the vessel which, in many different sizes, bore the Vikings to the plunder of the civilised world – to the assault of Constantinople, the siege of Paris, to the foundation of Dublin, and the discovery of America. Its picture rises before us vivid and bright: the finely carved, dragon-shaped prow; the high, curving stern; the long row of shields, black and yellow alternately, ranged along the sides; the gleam of steel, the scent of murder.

One summer day, probably in 789, while "the innocent English people, spread through their plains, were enjoying themselves in tranquillity and yoking their oxen to the plough", news was carried to the King's officer, the Reeve of Dorchester, that three ships had arrived on the coast. The Reeve "leapt on his horse and rode with a few men to the harbour [probably Portland], thinking that they were merchants and not enemies. Giving his commands as one who had authority, he ordered them to be sent to the King's town; but they slew him on the spot and all who were with him." This was a foretaste of the murderous struggle which, with many changes of fortune, was to harry and devastate England for two hundred and fifty years. It was the beginning of the Viking Age.[1]

In 793, on a January morning , the wealthy monastic settlement of Lindisfarne (or Holy Island), off the Northumbrian coast was suddenly attacked by a powerful fleet from Denmark. They sacked the place, devoured the cattle, killed many of the monks, and sailed away with a rich booty in gold, jewels, and sacred emblems, and all the monks who were likely to fetch a good price in the European slave-market. This raid had been planned with care and knowledge. It was executed by complete surprise in the dead of winter before any aid from the shore could reach the island. The news of the atrocity travelled far and wide, not only in England but throughout Europe, and the loud cry of the Church sounded a general alarm. Alcuin, the Northumbrian, wrote home for the Court of Charlemagne to condole with his countrymen:

> Lo, it is almost three hundred and fifty years that we and our fore-fathers have dwelt in this fair land, and never has such a horror before appeared in Britain, such as we have just suffered from the heathen. It was not thought possible that they could have made such a voyage. Behold the church of St Cuthbert sprinkled with the blood of the priests of Christ, robbed of all its ornaments. ...
> In that place where, after the departure of Paulinus from York, the Christian

1   Some recent research suggests that the Vikings weren't nearly so cruel as claimed. But beware the temptation to dismiss all early assessments as deliberately ghoulish or of doubtful scholarship. Right through to the later Danes, there is, in many accounts, a constant claim of harrying, burning and slaying. See also *England Before The Conquest* (Cambridge University Press) edited by the late Professor Peter Clemoes.

faith had its beginning among us, there is the beginning of woe and calamity. ... Portents of this woe came before it. ... What signifies that rain of blood during Lent in the town of York?

When the next year the raiders returned and landed near Jarrow they were stoutly attacked while harassed by bad weather. Many were killed. Their "king" was captured and put to a cruel death, and the fugitives carried so grim a tale back to Denmark that for forty years the English coasts were unravaged. In this period the Vikings were little inclined for massed invasion or conquest, but, using their sea-power, made minor descents upon the east coast of Scotland and the Scottish islands. The monastic colonies which had hitherto found a safe retreat in these islands now became a particularly vulnerable prey. Their riches and their isolation left them the most attractive quarry of the sea-rovers. Iona was pillaged and destroyed in 802. The Irish religious establishments also presented attractive prizes to marauding greed, and from now onward their sufferings were unceasing. The vitality of the Church repaired the ruin with devoted zeal. The Vikings, having a large choice of action, allowed an interval of recovery before paying another visit. Iona was sacked thrice, and the monastery of Kildare no fewer than fourteen times.

Buccaneering had become a steady profession, and the Church was their perpetually replenished treasure-house. Charlemagne's historian, Eginhard, records that the ravages were continuous, and a new shadow of fear spread over Christendom. No effective measures were however taken, and the raiding business was so profitable that the taste for it spread throughout Scandinavia. "These merry, clean-limbed, stout-hearted gentlemen of the Northlands", as one of their Scottish eulogists describes them, sailed every year in greatly increasing numbers upon their forays, and returned triumphant and enriched; and their example inspired all audacious spirits and younger sons.

It was not until 835 that the storm broke in fury, and fleets, sometimes of three or four hundred vessels, rowed up the rivers of England, France, and Russia in predatory enterprises on the greatest scale. For thirty years Southern England was constantly attacked. Paris was more than once besieged. Constantinople was assaulted. The harbour towns in Ireland were captured and held. Dublin was founded by the Viking under Olaf.[1] In many cases now the raider settled upon the conquered territory. The Swedish element penetrated into the heart of Russia, ruling the river towns and holding the trade to ransom. The Norwegian Vikings, coming from a still more severe climate, found the Scottish islands good for settlement. They colonised the Shetlands, the Faroes, and Ireland. They reached Greenland and Stoneland (Labrador). They sailed up the St Lawrence. They discovered America, but they set little store by the achievement.

---

1 Dublin was one of the three important Viking towns (with Rouen and York). It was settled by at least A.D. 841. Churchill's Olaf might not have been the founder, but he (Olaf the White) certainly ruled there as did Olaf Guthricsson (d.942) and Olaf Sihtricsson (d.981). From 995 Viking kings minted coins to show their command of the Irish city.

For a long time no permanent foothold was gained in Britain or France. It was not until 865, when resistance on the Continent had temporarily stiffened, that the great Danish invasion of Northumbria and Eastern England began.

Saxon England was at this time ripe for the sickle. The invaders broke in upon the whole eastern seaboard, once guarded by the "Count of the Saxon Shore", with its Imperial fortresses in ruins, buried already under the soil of centuries. No Roman galleys plied their oars upon the patrol courses. There was no Imperial Government to send a great commander or legion to the rescue. But on all sides were abbeys and monasteries, churches, and even cathedrals, possessed in that starveling age of treasures of gold and silver, of jewels, and also large stores of food, wine, and such luxuries as were known. The pious English had accepted far too literally the idea of the absolution of sins as the consequence of monetary payment to the church. Their sins were many, their repentances frequent, and the Church had thrived. Here were easy prizes for sharp swords to win.

To an undue subservience to the Church the English at this time added military mismanagement. Their system of defence was adapted to keeping the survivors of the ancient Britons in their barren mountain-lands or guarding the frontier against an incursion by a Saxon neighbour. The local noble, upon the summons of his chief or king, could call upon the able-bodied cultivators of the soil to serve in their own district for about forty days. The service, in the "fyrd", was grudgingly given, and when it was over the army dispersed without paying regard to the enemies who might be afoot or the purposes for which the campaign had been undertaken. Now the English were confronted with a different type of enemy. The Danes and Norsemen had not only the advantages of surprise which sea-power so long imparted, but they showed both mobility and skill on land. They adopted the habit of fortifying their camps with almost Roman thoroughness. Their stratagems also have been highly praised. Among these "feigned flight" was foremost. Again and again we read that the English put the heathen army to rout, but at the end of the day the Danes held the field. On one occasion their leader, who was besieging a town, declared himself to be dying and begged the bishop of the place to give him Christian burial. The worthy Churchman rejoiced in the conversion and acceded to the request, but when the body of the deceased Viking was brought into the town for Christian burial it suddenly appeared that the attendants were armed warriors of proved quality, disguised in mourning, who without more ado set to work on sack and slaughter. There are many informing sidelights of this kind upon the manners and customs of the Vikings. They were, in fact, the most audacious and treacherous type of pirate and shark that had ever yet appeared, and, owing to the very defective organisation of the Saxons and the conditions of the period they achieved a fuller realisation of their desires than any of those who have emulated their proficiency – and there have been many.

In Viking legend at this period none was more famous than Ragnar

Lodbrok, or "Hairy-breeches". He was born in Norway but was connected with the ruling family of Denmark. He was a raider from his youth. "West over seas" was his motto. His prow had ranged from the Orkneys to the White Sea. In 845 he led a Viking fleet up the Seine and attacked Paris. The onslaught was repulsed, and plague took an unforeseeable revenge upon the buccaneers. He turned his mobile arms against Northumbria. Here again fate was adverse. According to Scandinavian story, he was captured by King Ella of Northumbria, and cast into a snake-pit to die. Amid the coiling mass of loathsome adders he sang to the end his death-song. Ragnar had four sons, and as he lay among the venomous reptiles he uttered a potent threat: "The little pigs would grunt now if they knew how it fares with the old boar." The skalds tell us how his sons received the news. Bjorn "Ironside" gripped his spear shaft so hard that the print of his fingers remained stamped upon it. Hvitserk was playing chess, but he clenched his fingers upon a pawn so tightly that the blood started from under his nails. Sigurd "Snake-eye" was trimming his nails with a knife, and kept on paring until he cut into the bone. But the fourth son was the one who counted. Ivar, "the Boneless", demanded the precise details of his father's execution, and his face "became red, blue, and pale by turns, and his skin was swollen with anger".[1]

A form of vengeance was prescribed by which sons should requite the killer of their fathers. It was known as the "Blood-red Eagle". The flesh and ribs of the killer must be cut and sawn out in an aquiline pattern, and then the dutiful son with his own hands would tear out the palpitating lungs. This was the doom which in legend overtook King Ella. But the actual consequences to England were serious. Ivar "the Boneless" was a warrior of command and guile. He was the master-mind behind the Scandinavian invasion of England in the last quarter of the ninth century. He it was who planned the great campaigns by which East Anglia, Deira in Northumbria, and Mercia were conquered. Hitherto he had been fighting in Ireland, but he now appeared in 865 in East Anglia. In the spring of 866 his powerful army, organised on the basis of ships' companies, but now all mounted not for fighting but for locomotion, rode north along the old Roman road and was ferried across the Humber.

He laid siege to York. And now – too late – the Northumbrians, who had been divided in their loyalties between two rival kings, forgot their feuds and united in one final effort. They attacked the Danish army before York. At first they were successful; the heathens were driven back upon the city walls. The defenders sallied out, and in the confusion the Vikings defeated them all with

1   From *The Vikings and their Voyages*, by A. MacCallum Scott. The detail of vengeance known as Blood-red Eagle has been questioned; yet saga evidence (often the only source available to acceptor and revisionist) suggests such practice was not imagined even though the translation of the rite may be wanting. The further complication is that Ivar the Boneless is sometimes thought to have been an imaginary character dreamed up in the twelfth century. The Anglo-Saxon Chronicle of Æthelweard, coming from earliest sources, gives us *Igwares*. Yet there is ample evidence of the existence of Ivar (and of his brother Halfdan or Halfdane), and we have here a reminder not to demand exact names, transliterations nor translations – especially at a distance.

grievous slaughter, killing both their kings and destroying completely their power of resistance. This was the end of Northumbria. The North of England never recovered its ascendancy.

But Ivar's object was nothing less than the conquest of Mercia which, as all men knew, had for nearly a hundred years represented the strength of England. Ivar lay before Nottingham. The King of Mercia called for help from Wessex. The old King of Wessex was dead, but his two sons, Ethelred and Alfred, answered the appeal. They marched to his aid, and offered to join him in his attack upon the besiegers' lines; but the Mercians flinched, and preferred a parley. Ivar warred with policy as well as arms. He had not harmed churches at York and Ripon. He was content to set up a vassal king, one Egbert, in Northumbria, and after ending the campaign of 868 by a treaty which left him master of Nottingham he spent the winter fortifying himself in York.

While the Danes in their formidable attempt at conquest spread out from East Anglia, subdued Mercia, and ravaged Northumbria, the King of Wessex and his brother Alfred quietly built up their strength. Their fortunes turned on balances so delicate and precarious that even the slightest addition to their burdens must have been fatal. It was therefore a deliverance when Ivar, after breaking the Treaty of Nottingham and subjecting King Edmund of East Anglia to martyrdom, suddenly quitted England for ever. The annals of Ulster explain that Olaf and Ivar, the two kings of the Northmen, came again to Dublin in 870 from Scotland, and "a very great spoil of captives, English, British, and Pictish, was carried away to Ireland". But then there is this final entry: "872. Ivar, King of the Northmen of all Ireland and Britain, ended his life." He had conquered Mercia and East Anglia. He had captured the major stronghold of the kingdom of Strathclyde, Dumbarton. Laden with loot and seemingly invincible, he settled in Dublin, and died there peacefully two years later. The pious chroniclers report that he "slept in Christ". Thus it may be that he had the best of both worlds.

The Danish raiders now stayed longer every year. In the summer the fleets came over to plunder and destroy, but each year the tendency was to dally in a more genial and more verdant land. At last the warrior's absence on the raids became long enough and the conditions of his conquest sure enough for him to bring over his wife and family. Thus again behind piracy and rapine there grew the process of settlement. But these settlements of the Danes differed from those of the Saxons; they were the encampment of armies, and their boundaries were the fighting fronts sustained by a series of fortified towns. Stamford, Nottingham, Lincoln, Derby, Leicester were the bases of the new invading force. Behind their frontier lines the soldiers of one decade were to become the colonists and landowners of the next. The Danish settlement in England was essentially military. They cut their way with their swords, and then planted themselves deeply in the soil. The warrior type of farmer asserted from the first a status different from the ordinary agriculturist. Without any coherent national organisation to repel from the land on which they had settled the ever-unknowable descents from the seas, the Saxons, now for four centuries entitled to be deemed the owners of the soil, very nearly succumbed completely to the Danish inroads. That they did not was due – as almost every critical turn of historic fortune had been due – to the sudden apparition in an era of confusion and decay of one of the great figures of history.

CHAPTER FIVE

ALFRED THE GREAT

*Alfred the Great – the Danes and the Wessex wars – the Battle
of Ashdown – Ethelred – Viking settlement of eastern England – the
building of Durham Cathedral – the Danegeld – Alfred in hiding –
the Battle of Edington – the baptism of Guthrum the Viking – Laws of
Alfred – the Lady of the Mercians*

THE STORY of Alfred is made known to us in some detail in the pages of Asser, a monk of St David's, who became Bishop of Sherborne.[1] The Bishop dwells upon the religious and moral qualities of his hero; but we must also remember that, in spite of ill-health, he was renowned as a hunter, and that his father had taken him to Rome as a boy, so that he had a lively comprehension of the great world. Alfred began as second-in-command to his elder brother, the King. There were no jealousies between them, but a marked difference of temperament. Ethelred inclined to the religious view that faith and prayer were the prime agencies by which the heathen would be overcome. Alfred, though also devout, laid the emphasis upon policy and arms.

In earlier years the overlordship of Mercia had never been popular, and her kings had made the serious mistake of quarrelling with the See of Canterbury. When, in 825, the Mercian army, invading Wessex, was overthrown by Alfred's grandfather, King Egbert, at Ellandun, near Swindon, all the South and East made haste to come to terms with the victor, and the union of Kent, the seat of the Primate, with Wessex, now the leading English kingdom, created a solid Southern *bloc*. This, which had been the aim of West Saxon policy for many generations, was achieved just in time to encounter the invasion from the North. Wessex was strategically strong, with sharp ridges facing north, and none of those long, slow rivers up which the Danes used to steer their long-ships into the heart of Mercia. Wessex had moreover

---

1   Asser's *Life of Alfred*. It has been generally accepted (and certainly was when Churchill was writing) that Asser wrote the story of Alfred in A.D. 893. Asser was a scribe and therefore, not surprisingly for the time, a monk. He seems to have observed the king shortly after 890 and the not entirely critical style may have been due to his place at court rather than his objective assessment. As important as Asser's document is, it is just possible that it was written long after the king's (and Asser's) death and is therefore bogus and intended to perpetuate a legend. On balance, *Life of Alfred* should be accepted as a not unreasonable account of one of the most important figures of the ninth century.

developed a local organisation which gave her exceptional resiliency under attack: the alderman at the head of the shire could act on his own account. The advantages of this system were later to be proved. Definite districts, each under an accepted commander, or governor, for civil and military purposes, constituted a great advance on the ancient tribal kingdoms, or the merely personal union of tribes under a single king. When the dynasties of Kent, Northumbria, and Mercia had disappeared all eyes turned to Wessex, where there was a royal house going back without a break to the first years of the Saxon settlement.

The Danes had occupied London, not then the English capital, but a town in the kingdom of Mercia, and their army had fortified itself at Reading. Moving forward, they met the forces of the West Saxons on the Berkshire downs, and here, in January 871, was fought the Battle of Ashdown. Both sides divided their forces into two commands. Ethelred tarried long at his devotions. The Vikings, with their brightly painted shields and banners, the finery and golden bracelets, made the West Saxons seem modest by contrast. As they slowly approached they clashed their shields and weapons and raised long, repeated, and defiant war-cries. Although archery was not much in use, missiles began to fly. The King was still at his prayers. God came first, he declared to those who warned him that the battle must soon be joined.

The fight was long and hard. King Ethelred, his spiritual duty done, soon joined his brother. "The heathens", said the Bishop, "had seized the higher ground, and the Christians had to advance uphill. There was in that place a single stunted thorn-tree which we have seen with our own eyes. Round about this tree, then, the opposing ranks met in conflict, with a great shouting from all men – one side bent on evil, the other side fighting for life and their loved ones and their native land." At last the Danes gave way, and, hotly pursued, fled back to Reading. They fled till nightfall; they fled through the night and the next day, and the whole breadth of Ashdown – meaning the Berkshire hills – was strewn with their corpses, among which were found the body of one of the Viking kings and five of his earls.

The results of this victory did not break the power of the Danish army; in a fortnight they were again in the field. But the Battle of Ashdown justly takes its place among historic encounters because of the greatness of the issue. If the West Saxons had been beaten all England would have sunk into heathen anarchy. Since they were victorious the hope still burned for a civilised Christian existence in this Island. This was the first time the invaders had been beaten in the field. The last of the Saxon kingdoms had withstood the assault upon it. Alfred had made the Saxons feel confidence in themselves again. They could hold their own in open fight. The story of this conflict at Ashdown was for generations a treasured memory of the Saxon writers. It was Alfred's first battle.

All through the year 871 the two armies waged deadly war. King Ethelred soon fell sick and died. Although he had young children there was no doubt who his successor must be. At twenty-four Alfred became King, and entered upon a desperate inheritance. To and fro the fighting swayed, with varying fortunes. The Danes were strongly reinforced from overseas; "the summer army", as it was called, arrived to join them. Seven or eight battles were fought, and we are told the Danes usually held the field. At Wilton, in the summer, about a month after Alfred had assumed the crown, he sustained a definite defeat in the heart of his own country. His numbers had been worn down by death and desertion, and once again in the field the Vikings' ruse of a feigned retreat was successful.

On the morrow of this misfortune Alfred thought it best to come to terms while he still had an army. We do not know the conditions, but there is no doubt that a heavy payment was among them. "The Saxons made peace with the heathen on the condition that they should depart from them, and this they did", declares the *Chronicle* laconically. But as they took three or four months before retiring upon London it seems that they waited for the Danegeld to be paid. Nevertheless Alfred and his Saxons had in all this fighting convinced the Vikings of their redoubtable force. By this inglorious treaty and stubborn campaign Alfred secured five years in which to consolidate his power.

The reasons which led the Danes to make a truce with Alfred are hard to analyse at this date. They were certainly convinced that only by prolonged and bloody fighting could they master the West Saxons. Both sides relished war, and this had been ding-dong; there was little to show but scars and corpses on either side. But Alfred had always counted upon the invaders dividing, and the stresses at work within the heathen army justified his policy.

Still maintaining their grip on London, the Danes moved back to the Midlands which were now in complete submission. "The Mercians made peace with the army." Their king, Burgred, in 874 was driven overseas, and died in piety under the Papal compassion in Rome. "After his expulsion", says Asser, "the heathen subjected the whole kingdom of the Mercians to their lordship." They set up a local puppet, in a fashion which has often been imitated since, after he had given hostages and taken an oath "that he would not obstruct their wishes, and would be obedient in everything".

But now in the last quarter of the century a subtle, profound change came over the "Great Heathen Army". Alfred and the men of Wessex had proved too stubborn a foe for easy subjugation. Some of the Danes wished to settle on the lands they already held; the rest were for continuing the war at a suitable moment till the whole country was conquered. Perhaps these two bodies acted in concert, the former providing a sure and solid base, the latter becoming an expeditionary force. Thus, after mauling the kingdom of Strathclyde and carrying off the stock and implements of agriculture nearly half of the sea-pirates settled themselves in Northumbria and East Anglia. Henceforward they began to till the ground for a livelihood. Here was a great change. We must remember their discipline and organisation. The ships' companies, acting together, had hitherto fought ashore as soldiers. All their organisation of settlements was military. The sailors had turned soldiers, and the soldiers had turned yeomen. They preserved that spirit of independence, regulated only by comradeship and discipline for vital purposes, which was the life of the long-ship.

The whole of the East of England thus received a class of cultivator who, except for purposes of common defence, owed allegiance to none; who had won his land with the sword, and was loyal only to the army organisation which enabled him to keep it. From Yorkshire to Norfolk this sturdy, upstanding stock took root. As time passed they forgot the sea; they forgot the army; they thought only of the land – their own land. They liked the life. Although they were sufficiently skilful agriculturists, there was nothing they could teach the older inhabitants; they brought no new implements or methods, but they were resolved to learn.

They were not dependent wholly upon their own labour. They must have exploited the former possessors and their serfs. The distribution of the land was made around a unit which could support a family. What eight oxen could plough in a certain time under prescribed conditions, much disputed by students, became the measure of the holding. They worked hard themselves, but obviously they used the local people too.

Thus the Danish differs in many ways from the Saxon settlement four hundred years earlier. There was no idea of exterminating the older population. The two languages were not very different; the way of life, the methods of cultivation, very much the same. The colonists – for such they had now become – brought their families from Scandinavia, but also it is certain that they established human and natural relations with the expropriated English. The reformed and placated pirate-mariners brought with them many Danish customs. They had a different notation, which they would have been alarmed to hear described as the "duodecimal system". They thought in twelves instead of tens, and in our own day in certain parts of East Anglia the expression "the long hundred" (i.e., 120) is heard on market days.

They had a different view of social justice from that entertained by the manorialised Saxons. Their customary laws as they gradually took shape were an undoubted improvement upon the Saxon theme.

Scandinavian England reared a free peasant population which the burdens of taxation and defence had made difficult in Wessex and English Mercia. And this population related itself so closely to the original invaders that students seek in the Domesday Book of the eleventh century for the means of estimating the size of the Viking armies in the ninth. We shall see presently the equitable, deferential terms which even after their final victory the Anglo-Saxon monarchs proffered to the districts settled by the Danes, known as the Danelaw. It remained only for conversion to Christianity to mingle these races inextricably in the soul and body of a nation. These considerations may aptly fill the five years' breathing-space which Alfred had gained by courageous fighting and politic Danegeld. In this interval Halfdene, the Viking leader, departed like Ivar from the scene. The tortured, plundered Church requited his atrocities by declaring that God punished him in the long run by madness and a smell which made his presence unendurable to his fellows.

At Lindisfarne, in Dane-ravaged Northumbria, a pathetic tale is told. The ruined monks quitted their devastated, polluted sanctuary and carried on their shoulders the body of St Cuthbert and the bones of St Aidan. After seven years of pilgrimage by land and sea they established themselves in a new patrimony of St Cuthbert at Chester-le-Street. The veneration felt throughout the North for St Cuthbert brought such wealth to his see that in 995 its bishops began to build a new cathedral on the rock at Durham. Thither St Cuthbert's bones were taken, and so great was his prestige that until the twentieth century the Bishops of Durham were Prince-bishops, exercising immense power in North-Eastern England.

Alfred's dear-bought truce was over. Guthrum, the new war-leader of the mobile and martial part of the heathen army, had formed a large design for the subjugation of Wessex. He operated by sea and land. The land army marched to Wareham, close to Portland Bill, where the sea army joined him in Poole harbour. In this region they fortified themselves, and proceeded to attack Alfred's kingdom by aid and storm from every quarter. The prudent King sought peace and offered an indemnity. At the same time it seems probable that he had hemmed in the land army very closely at Wareham. The Danes took the gold, and "swore upon the Holy Ring" they would depart and keep a faithful peace. With a treachery to which all adjectives are unequal they suddenly darted away and seized Exeter. Alfred, mounting his infantry, followed after, but arrived too late. "They were in the fortress, where they could not be come at." But let all heathen beware of breaking oaths! A frightful tempest smote the sea army. They sought to join their comrades by sea. They were smitten in the neighbourhood of Swanage by the elements, which in those days were believed to be personally directed by the Almighty. A hundred and twenty ships were sunk, and upwards of five thousand of these perjured marauders perished as they deserved. Thus the whole careful plan fell to pieces, and Alfred, watching and besetting Exeter, found his enemies in the summer of 877 in the mood for a new peace. They swore it with oaths of still more compliant solemnity, and they kept it for about five months.

Then in January 878 occurred the most surprising reversal of Alfred's fortunes. His headquarters and Court lay at Chippenham, in Wiltshire. It was Twelfth Night, and the Saxons, who in these days of torment refreshed and fortified themselves by celebrating the feasts of the Church, were off their guard, engaged in pious exercises, or perhaps even drunk. Down swept the ravaging foe. The whole army of Wessex, sole guarantee of England south of the Thames, was dashed into confusion. Many were killed. The most part stole away to their houses. A strong contingent fled overseas. Refugees arrived with futile appeals at the Court of France. Only a handful of officers and personal attendants hid themselves with Alfred in the marshes and forests of Somerset and the Isle of Athelney which rose from the quags. This was the darkest hour of Alfred's fortunes. It was some months before he could even start a guerrilla. He led "with thanes and vassals an unquiet life in great tribulation. ... For he had nothing wherewith to supply his wants except what in frequent sallies he could seize either stealthily or openly, both the heathen and from the Christians who had submitted to their rule." He lived as Robin Hood did in Sherwood Forest long afterwards.

This is the moment when those gleaming toys of history were fashioned for the children of every age. We see the warrior-king disguised as a minstrel harping in the Danish camps. We see him acting as kitchen-boy to a Saxon housewife. The celebrated story of Alfred and the cakes first appears in a late edition of Bishop Asser's life.

To the people of Wessex it seemed that all was over. Their forces were dispersed, the country overrun; their King, if alive, was a fugitive in hiding. It is the supreme proof of Alfred's quality that he was able in such a plight to exercise his full authority and keep contact with his subjects. Towards the end of Lent the Danes suffered an unexpected misfortune. The crews of twenty-three ships, after committing many atrocities in Wales, sailed to Devon and marched to the attack of one of Alfred's strongholds on Exmoor.

Eight hundred Danes were killed, and the spoils of the victory included an enchanted banner called the Raven, of which it was said that the three daughters of Ragnar Lodbrok had woven it in a single day, and that "in every battle in which that banner went before them the raven in the middle of the design seemed to flutter as though it were alive if they were going to have the victory". On this occasion it did not flutter, but hung listlessly in its silken folds. The event proved that it was impossible for the Danes to win under these conditions.

Alfred, cheered by this news and striving to take the field again, continued a brigand warfare against the enemy while sending his messengers to summon the "fyrd", or local militia, for the end of May. The news that he was alive and active caused widespread joy. All the fighting men came back. After all, the country was in peril of subjugation, the King was a hero, and they could always go home again. The troops of Somerset, Wiltshire, and Hampshire concentrated near Selwood. A point was chosen near where the three shires met, and we can see from this the burdens which lay upon Alfred's tactics.

Battle must be sought before they lost interest. The Danes still lay upon their plunder at Chippenham. Alfred advanced to Ethandun – now Edington – and on the bare downs was fought the largest and culminating battle of Alfred's wars. All was staked. All hung in the scales of fate. On both sides the warriors dismounted; the horses were sent to the rear. The shield-walls were formed, the masses clashed against each other, and for hours they fought with sword and axe. But the heathen had lost the favour of God through their violated oath, and eventually from this or other causes they fled from the cruel and clanging field. This time Alfred's pursuit was fruitful. Guthrum, king of the Viking army, so lately master of the one unconquered English kingdom, found himself penned in his camp. Bishop Asser says, "the heathen, terrified by hunger, cold and fear, and at the last full of despair, begged for peace". They offered to give without return as many hostages as Alfred should care to pick and to depart forthwith.

But Alfred had had longer ends in view. It is strange that he should have wished to convert these savage foes. Baptism as a penalty of defeat might lose its spiritual quality. The workings of the spirit are mysterious, but we must still wonder how the hearts of these hard-bitten swordsmen and pirates could be changed in a single day. Indeed these mass conversions had become almost a matter of form for defeated Viking armies. But Alfred meant to make a lasting peace with Guthrum. He had him and his army in his power. He could have starved them into surrender and slaughtered them to a man. He wished instead to divide the land with them, and that the two races, in spite of fearful injuries given and received, should dwell together in amity. He received Guthrum with thirty prominent buccaneers in his camp. He stood godfather to Guthrum; he raised him from the font; he entertained him for twelve days; he presented him and his warriors with costly gifts; he called him his son.

This sublime power to rise above the whole force of circumstances, to remain unbiased by the extremes of victory or defeat, to persevere in the teeth of disaster, to greet returning fortune with a cool eye, to have faith in men after repeated betrayals, raises Alfred far above the turmoil of barbaric wars to his pinnacle of deathless glory.

Fourteen years intervened between the victory of Ethandun and any serious Danish attack. In spite of much uneasiness and disturbance, by the standards of those days there was peace. Alfred worked ceaselessly to strengthen his realm. He had been content that the Danes should settle in East Anglia, but he cultivated the best relations with the harassed kingdom of Mercia, which had become tributary to the Danes, though still largely unoccupied by them. In 886 he married his eldest daughter to the regent Ethelred, who was striving to bear the burden abandoned to him by the fugitive king, Burgred. There had already been several inter-marriages in the Mercian and Wessex royal families, and this set the final seal upon the co-operation of the South and the Midlands.

The first result of this new unity was the recovery of London in 886. London had long been the emporium of Christian England. Ancient Rome had seen in this bridgehead of the Thames, at the convergence of all the roads and sea routes, the greatest commercial and military centre in the Island. Now the city was set on the road to becoming the national capital.

The King fortified the whole country by boroughs, running down the Channel and then across to the Severn estuary and so back by the Thames valley, assigning to each a contributory district to man the walls and keep the fortifications in repair. He saw too the vision of English sea-power. To be safe in an island it was necessary to command the sea. Still, the beginning of the English Navy must always be linked with King Alfred.

In spite of the disorders a definite treaty was achieved after the reconquest of London in 886. Significance attaches to the terms in which the contracting parties are described. On Alfred's side there are "the counsellors of the

English nation", on Guthrum's "the people who dwell in East Anglia". The organisation of the Danelaw, based entirely upon the army and the subjugated inhabitants, had not yet assumed the form of a State. The English, on the other hand, had already reached the position of "King and Witan"; and none did more to enforce the idea than Alfred himself.

King Alfred's Book of Laws, or Dooms, as set out in the existing laws of Kent, Wessex, and Mercia, attempted to blend the Mosaic code with Christian principles and old Germanic customs. He inverted the Golden Rule. Instead of "Do unto others as you would that they should do unto you", he adopted the less ambitious principle, "What ye will that other men should not do to you, that do ye not to other men", with the comment, "By bearing this precept in mind a judge can do justice to all men; he needs no other law-books. Let him think of himself as the plaintiff, and consider what judgement would satisfy him." The King, in his preamble, explained modestly that "I have not dared to presume to set down in writing many laws of my own, for I cannot tell what will meet with the approval of our successors."

The Laws of Alfred, continually amplified by his successors, grew into that body of customary law administered by the shire and hundred courts which, under the name of the Laws of St Edward (the Confessor), the Norman kings undertook to respect, and out of which, with much manipulation by feudal lawyers, the Common Law was founded.

The King encouraged by all his means religion and learning. Above all he sought the spread of education. He sought to reform the monastic life, which in the general confusion had grossly degenerated. He it was who set on foot the compiling of the Saxon Chronicle. The fact that the early entries are fragmentary gives confidence that the compilers did not draw on their imagination. From King Alfred's time they are exact, often abundant, and sometimes written with historic grasp and eloquence.

We discern across the centuries a commanding and versatile intelligence, wielding with equal force the sword of war and of justice; using in defence arms and policy; cherishing religion, learning, and art in the midst of adversity and danger; welding together a nation, and seeking always across the feuds and hatreds of the age a peace which would smile upon the land.

One final war awaited Alfred. It was a crisis in the Viking story. In 885 they had rowed up the Seine with hundreds of ships and an army of forty thousand men. For six years they ravaged the interior of Northern France. Famine followed in their footsteps. The fairest regions had been devoured; where could they turn?

Guthrum died in 891, and the pact which he had sworn with Alfred, and loosely kept, ended. Suddenly in this autumn of 892 a hostile armada of two hundred and fifty ships appeared off Lympne, carrying to the invasion of England "the Great Heathen Army" that had ravaged France. They disembarked and fortified themselves at Appledore, on the edge of the forest. They were followed by eighty ships conveying a second force of baffled raiders from the Continent, who sailed up the Thames and established themselves on its southern bank at Milton, near Sittingbourne. Thus Kent was to be attacked from both sides. This immense concerted assault confronted Alfred with his third struggle for life. The English, as we may call them – for the Mercians and West Saxons stood together – had secured fourteen years of unquiet peace in which to develop their defences. Many of the Southern towns were fortified; they were "burhs". The "fyrd" had been improved in organisation, though its essential weaknesses had not been removed. There had been a re-gathering of wealth and food; there was a settled administration, and the allegiance of all was given to King Alfred. Unlike Charlemagne, he had a valiant son. At twenty-two Edward could lead his father's armies to the field. The Mercians also had produced an Ethelred, who was a fit companion to the West Saxon prince. The King, in ill-health, is not often seen in this phase at the head of armies; we have glimpses of him, but the great episodes of the war were centred, as they should be, upon the young leaders.

The English beat the Vikings in this third war. Owning the command of the sea, the invaders gripped the Kentish peninsula from the north and south. Alfred had tried to buy them off, and certainly delayed their full attack. He persuaded Haesten, the Viking leader, at least to have his two young sons baptised. He gave Haesten much money, and oaths of peace were interchanged, only to be broken. Meanwhile the Danes raided mercilessly, and Alfred tried to rouse England to action. In 893 a third expedition composed of the Danish veterans who had settled in Northumbria and East Anglia sailed round the south coast, and, landing, laid siege to Exeter. But now the young leaders struck hard. Apparently they had a strong mounted force, not indeed what we should call cavalry, but possessing swiftness of movement. They fell upon a column of the raiders near the modern Aldershot, routed them, and pursued them for twenty miles till they were glad to swim the Thames and shelter behind the Colne. Unhappily, the army of the young princes was not strong enough to resume the attack, and also it had run out of provisions. The pursuit therefore had to be abandoned and the enemy escaped.

The Danes had fortified themselves at Benfleet, on the Thames below London, and it is said that their earthworks can be traced to this day. Thence, after recovering from their defeat, they sallied forth to plunder, leaving a moderate garrison in their stronghold. This the princes now assaulted. It had very rarely been possible in these wars to storm a well-fortified place; but Alfred's son and his son-in-law with a strong army from London fell upon Benfleet and "put the army to flight, stormed the fort, and took all that there was within, goods as well as women and children, and brought all to London. And all the ships they either broke in pieces or burnt or brought to London or Rochester." Such are the words of the *Saxon Chronicle*. When in the nineteenth century a railway was being made across this ground the charred fragments of the ships and numbers of skeletons were unearthed upon the site of Benfleet. In the captured stronghold the victors found Haesten's wife and his two sons. These were precious hostages, and King Alfred was much criticised at the time, and also later, because he restored them to Haesten. He sent back his wife on broad grounds of humanity. As for the two sons, they had been baptised; he was godfather to one of them, and Ethelred of Mercia to the other. They were therefore Christian brethren, and the King protected them from the consequences of their father's wrongful war. The ninth century found it very hard to understand this behaviour when the kingdom was fighting desperately against brutal marauders, but that is one of the reason why in the after-time the King is called "Alfred the Great". The war went on, but so far as the records show Haesten never fought again. It may be that mercy and chivalry were not in vain.

In 896 the war petered out, and the Vikings, whose strength seemed at this time to be in decline, dispersed, some settling in the Danelaw, some going back to France. "By God's mercy", exclaims the *Chronicle*, in summing up the war, "the [Danish] army had not too much afflicted the English people." Alfred had well defended the Island home. He had by policy and arms preserved the Christian civilisation in England. He had built up the strength of that mighty South which has ever since sustained much of the weight of Britain, and later of her Empire. He had liberated London, and happily he left behind him descendants who, for several generations, as we shall see, carried his work forward with valour and success.

Alfred died in 899, but the struggle with the Vikings had yet to pass through strangely contrasted phases. Alfred's blood gave the English a series of great rulers, and while his inspiration held victory did not quit the Christian ranks. In his son Edward, who was immediately acclaimed King, the armies had already found a redoubtable leader. A quarrel arose between Edward and his cousin, Ethelwald, who fled to the Danelaw and aroused the Vikings of Northumbria and East Anglia to a renewed inroad upon his native land. In 902 Ethelwald and the Danish king crossed the upper reaches of the Thames at Cricklade and ravaged part of Wiltshire. Edward in retaliation ordered the invasion of East Anglia, with an army formed of the men of Kent and London. They devastated Middle Anglia; but the Kentish contingent, being slow to withdraw, was overtaken and brought to battle by the infuriated Danes. The Danes were victorious, and made a great slaughter; but, as fate would have it, both Eric, the Danish king, and the renegade Ethelwald perished on the field and the new king, Guthrum II, made peace with Edward on the basis of Alfred's treaty of 886, but with additions which show that the situation had changed. It is now assumed that the Danes are Christians and will pay their tithes, while the parish priest is to be fined if he misleads his flock as to the time of a feast-day or a festival.

In 910 this treaty was broken by the Danes, and the war was renewed in Mercia. The main forces of Wessex and Kent had already been sent by Edward, who was with the fleet, to the aid of the Mercians, and in heavy fighting at Tettenhall, in Staffordshire, the Danes were decisively defeated. This English victory was a milestone in the long conflict. The Danish armies in Northumbria never recovered from the battle, and the Danish Midlands and

East Anglia thus lay open to English conquest. Up to this point Mercia and Wessex had been the defenders, often reduced to the most grievous straits. But now the tide had turned. Fear camped with the Danes.

Edward's sister had been married to Earl Ethelred of Mercia. Ethelred died in 911, and his widow, Ethelfleda, succeeded and surpassed him. In those savage times the emergence of a woman ruler was enough to betoken her possession of extraordinary qualities. Edward the Elder, as he was afterwards called, and his sister, "the Lady of the Mercians", conducted the national war in common, and carried its success to heights which Alfred never knew. The policy of the two kingdoms, thus knit by blood and need, marched in perfect harmony, and the next onslaught of the Danes was met with confident alacrity and soon broken. The victors then set themselves deliberately to the complete conquest of the Danelaw and its Five Boroughs. This task occupied the next ten years, brother and sister advancing in concert upon their respective lines, and fortifying towns they took at every stage. In 917, when Edward stormed Tempsford, near Bedford, and king Guthrum was killed, the whole resistance of East Anglia collapsed, and all the Danish leaders submitted to Edward as their protector and lord. They were granted in return their estates and the right to live according to their Danish customs. At the same time "the Lady of the Mercians" conquered Leicester, and received even from York offers of submission. In this hour of success Ethelfleda died, and Edward, hastening to Tamworth, was invited by the nobles of Mercia to occupy the vacant throne.

Alfred's son was now undisputed King of all England south of the Humber, and the British princes of North and South Wales hastened to offer their perpetual allegiance. Driving northwards in the next two years, Edward built forts at Manchester, at Thelwall in Cheshire, and at Bakewell in the Peak country. The Danes of Northumbria saw their end approaching. It seemed as if a broad and lasting unity was about to be reached. Edward the Elder reigned five years more in triumphant peace, and when he died in 924 his authority and his gifts passed to a third remarkable sovereign, capable in every way of carrying on the work of his father and grandfather.

CHAPTER SIX

THE SAXON DUSK

*The first King of England – the Battle of Brunanburh – King Edward –
the beginnings of modern English institutions – the creation of
the Hundreds – Shire courts – St Dunstan – Ethelred the Unready –
St Brice's Day massacre – Canute – Emma of Normandy – Godwin –
Archbishop Stigand – Edward the Confessor*

THELSTAN, THE third of the great West Saxon kings, sought at first, in accordance with the traditions of his house, peaceful relations with the unconquered parts of the Danelaw; but upon disputes arising he marched into Yorkshire in 926, and there established himself. Northumbria submitted; the Kings of the Scots and of Strathclyde acknowledged him as their "father and lord", and the Welsh princes agreed to pay tribute.[1] There was an uneasy interlude; then in 933 came a campaign against the Scots, and in 937 a general rebellion and renewed war, organised by all the hitherto defeated characters in the drama. The whole of North Britain – Celtic, Danish, and Norwegian, pagan and Christian – together presented a hostile front under Constantine, King of the Scots, and Olaf of Dublin, with Viking reinforcements from Norway. On this occasion neither life nor time was wasted in manoeuvres. The fight that followed is recorded for us in an Icelandic saga and an English poem. According to the saga-man, Athelstan challenged his foes to meet him in a pitched battle, and to this they blithely agreed. The English king even suggested the place where all should be put to the test.[2] The armies, very large for those impoverished times, took up their stations as if for the Olympic Games, and much parleying accompanied the process. Tempers rose high as these masses of manhood flaunted their shields and blades at one another and flung their gibes across a narrow space; and there was presently a fierce clash between the Northumbrian and the Icelandic Vikings on the one hand and a part of the English army of the other. In this, although the Northumbrian commander

---

1   We come to the moment when we can say that there is a King of England. Until this stage, no king has had control of all England. Churchill tells us that Athelstan arrived in Yorkshire in 926. The significant point is that York was the centre of the Scandinavian kingdom, which Athelstan defeated in 927.

2   The Battle of Brunanburh, perhaps in the East Midlands. The poem is the first great English epic war eulogy and, as a source of historical information, should be read with some caution.

fled, the English were worsted. But on the following day the real trial of strength was staged. The rival hosts paraded in all the pomp of war, and then in hearty goodwill fell on with spear, axe and sword. All day long the battle raged.

The original victory-song on Brunanburh opens to us a view of the Anglo-Saxon mind, with its primitive imagery and war-delight. "Here Athelstan King, of earls the lord, the giver of the bracelets of the nobles, and his brother also, Edmund the Ætheling, an age-long glory won by slaughter in battle, with the edges of swords, at Brunanburh. The wall of shields they cleaved, they hewed the battle shafts with hammered weapons, the foe flinched ... the Scottish people and the ship-fleet. ... The field was coloured with the warrior's blood! After that the sun on high, ... the greatest star, glided over the earth, God's candle bright! till the noble creature hastened to her setting there lay soldiers, many with darts struck down, Northern men over their shields shot. So were the Scotch; weary of battle, they had had their fill! They left behind them, to feast on carrion, the dusty-coated raven with horned beak, the black-coated eagle with white tail, the greedy battle-hawk, and the grey beast, the wolf in the wood."

The victory of the English was overwhelming. Constantine, "the perjured" as the victors claimed, fled back to the North, and Olaf retired with his remnants to Dublin. Thus did King Alfred's grandson, the valiant Athelstan, become one of the first sovereigns of Western Europe. He styled himself on coin and charter *Rex totius Britanniae*. These claims were accepted upon the Continent. His three sisters were wedded respectively to the Carolingian king, Charles the Simple, to the Capetian, Hugh the Great, and to Otto the Saxon, a future Holy Roman Emperor. He even installed a Norwegian prince, who swore allegiance and was baptised as his vassal at York. Here again one might hope that a decision in the long quarrel had been reached; yet it persisted; and when Athelstan died, two years after Brunanburh, and was succeeded by his half-brother, a youth of eighteen, the beaten forces welled up once more against him. Edmund, in the spirit of his race, held his own. He reigned only six years, but when he died in 946 he had not ceded an inch or an ell. Edmund was succeeded by his brother Edred, the youngest son of Alfred's son Edward the Elder. He too maintained the realm against all comers, and, beating them down by force of arms, seemed to have quenched for ever the rebellious fires of Northumbria.

Historians select the year 954 as the end of the first great episode in the Viking history of England. A hundred and twenty years had passed since the impact of the Vikings had smitten the Island. For forty years English Christian society had struggled for life. For eighty years five warrior kings – Alfred, Edward, Athelstan, Edmund, and Edred – defeated the invaders. The English rule was now restored, though in a form changed by the passage of time over the whole country. Yet underneath it there had grown up, deeply rooted in the soil, a Danish settlement covering the great Eastern plain, in which Danish blood and Danish customs survived under the authority of the English king.

In the brilliant and peaceful reign of Edgar all this long building had reached its culmination. The reconquest of England was accomplished step by step by a conscious administrative reconstruction which has governed the development of English institutions from that day to this. The shires were reorganised, each with its sheriff or reeve, a royal officer directly responsible to the Crown. The hundreds, subdivisions of the shire, were created, and the towns prepared for defence. An elaborate system of shire, hundred, and borough courts maintained law and order and pursued criminals. Taxation was reassessed. Finally, with this military and political revival marched a great re-birth of monastic life and learning and the beginning of our native English literature. The movement was slow and English in origin, but advanced with great strides from the middle of the century as it came in contact with the religious revival on the Continent. The work of Dunstan, Archbishop of Canterbury, and his younger contemporaries, Oswald, Bishop of Worcester, and Ethelwold, Bishop of Winchester, was to revive the strict observance of religion within the monasteries, and thereby indirectly to reform the Episcopate as more and more monks were elected to bishoprics. Another and happy, if incidental, result was to promote learning and the production of splendid illuminated manuscript, which were much in demand in contemporary Europe. Many of these, designed for the religious instruction of the laity, were written in English. The Catholic Homilies of Elfric, Abbot of Eynsham, mark, we are told, the first achievement of English as a literary language – the earliest vernacular to reach this eminence in the whole of Europe. From whatever point of view we regard it, the tenth century is a decisive step forward in the destinies of England. Despite the catastrophic decline of the monarchy which followed the death of Edgar, this organisation and English culture were so firmly rooted as to survive two foreign conquests in less than a century.

It must have seemed to contemporaries that with the magnificent coronation at Bath in 973, on which all coronation orders since have been based, the seal was set on the unity of the realm. Everywhere the courts are sitting regularly, in shire and borough and hundred; there is one coinage, and one system of weights and measures. The arts of building and decoration are reviving; learning begins to flourish again in the Church; there is a literary language, a King's English, which all educated men write. Civilisation had been restored to the Island. But now the political fabric which nurtured it was about to be overthrown. Hitherto strong men armed had kept the house. Now a child, a weakling, a vacillator, a faithless, feckless creature, succeeded to the warrior throne. Twenty-five years of peace lapped the land, and the English, so magnificent in stress and danger, so invincible under valiant leadership, relaxed under its softening influences. We have reached the days of Ethelred the Unready. But this expression, which conveys a truth, means literally Ethelred the Ill-counselled, or Ethelred the "Redeless".

In 980 serious raids began again. Chester was ravaged from Ireland. The people of Southampton were massacred by marauders from Scandinavia or Denmark. Thanet, Cornwall, and Devon all suffered butchery and pillage.

We have seen that Alfred in his day had never hesitated to use money as well as arms. Ethelred used money instead of arms in ever-increasing quantities, with ever-diminishing returns. He paid as a bribe in 991 twenty-two thousand pounds of gold and silver, with rations for the invaders. In 994, with sixteen thousand pounds, he gained not only a brief respite, but the baptism of the raider, Olaf, thrown in as a compliment. In 1002 he bought a further truce for twenty-four thousand pounds of silver, but on this occasion he was himself to break it. In their ruin and decay the English had taken large numbers of Danish mercenaries into their service. Ethelred suspected these dangerous helpers of a plot against his life. Panic-stricken, he planned the slaughter of all the Danes in the south of England, whether in his pay or living peaceably on the land. This atrocious design was executed in 1002 on St Brice's Day. Among the victims was Gunnhild, the wife of one of the principal Vikings, and sister of Sweyn, King of Denmark. Sweyn swore revenge, and for two years executed it upon the wretched Islanders. Exeter, Wilton, Norwich, and Thetford all record massacres, which show how widely the retaliation was applied. The fury of the avenger was not slaked by blood. It was baffled, but only for a space, by famine. The Danish army could no longer subsist in the ruined land, and departed in 1005 to Denmark. But the annals of 1006 show that Sweyn was back again, ravaging Kent, sacking Reading and Wallingford. At last Ethelred, for thirty-six thousand pounds of silver, bought another short-lived truce.

There is the record of a final payment to the Vikings in 1012. This time forty-eight thousand pounds' weight of silver was exacted, and the oppressors enforced the collection by the sack of Canterbury, holding Archbishop Alphege to ransom, and finally killing him at Greenwich because he refused to coerce his flock to raise the money.

It is vain to recount further the catalogue of miseries. In earlier ages such horrors remain unknown because unrecorded. Just enough flickering light plays upon this infernal scene to give us the sense of its utter desolation and hopeless wretchedness and cruelty. It suffices to note that in 1013 Sweyn, accompanied by his younger son, Canute,[1] came again to England, subdued the Yorkshire Danes and the Five Boroughs in the Danelaw, was accepted as overlord of Northumbria and Danish Mercia, sacked Oxford and Winchester in a punitive foray, and, though repulsed from London, was proclaimed King of England, while Ethelred fled for refuge to the Duke of Normandy, whose sister he had married. On these triumphs Sweyn died at the beginning of 1014. There was another respite. The English turned again to Ethelred, "declaring that no lord was dearer to them than their natural lord, if he would but rule them better than he had done before".

But soon the young Danish prince, Canute, set forth to claim the English

---

1   Sometimes, and perhaps more appropriately, written, Cnut.

crown. At this moment the flame of Alfred's line rose again in Ethelred's son, Edmund – Edmund Ironside, as he soon was called. At twenty he was famous. Although declared a rebel by his father, and acting in complete disobedience to him, he gathered forces, and in a brilliant campaign struck a succession of heavy blows. He gained battles, he relieved London, he contended with every form of treachery; the hearts of all men went out to him. New forces sprang from the ruined land. Ethelred died, and Edmund, last hope of the English, was acclaimed King. In spite of all odds and a heavy defeat he was strong enough to make a partition of the realm, and then set himself to rally his forces for the renewal of the struggle; but in 1016, at twenty-two years of age, Edmund Ironside died, and the whole realm abandoned itself to despair.

The ecclesiastical aristocracy which played so great a part in politics dwelt long upon the prophecies of coming woe ascribed to St Dunstan. At Southampton, even while Edmund lived, the lay and spiritual chiefs of England agreed to abandon the descendants of Ethelred for ever and recognise Canute as King. All resistance, moral and military, collapsed before the Dane.

There were three principles upon which sovereignty could be erected: conquest, which none could dispute; hereditary right, which was greatly respected; and election, which was a kind of compromise between the two. It was upon this last basis that Canute began his reign. It is possible that the early English ideal of kingship and just government in Alfred and Canute was affected by the example of Trajan. This Emperor was a favourite of Pope Gregory, who had sent the first missionaries. There is evidence that stories of Trajan's virtue were read aloud in the English church service. Canute may also have studied, and certainly he reproduced, the poise of the Emperor Augustus. Everyone knows the lesson he administered to his flatterers when he sat on the seashore and forbade the tide to come in. He made a point of submitting himself to the laws whereby he ruled. He even in his military capacity sub-jected himself to the regulations of his own household troops. At the earliest moment he disbanded his great Danish army and trusted himself broadly to the loyalty of the humbled English. He married Emma of Normandy, the widow of Ethelred, and so forestalled any action by the Duke of Normandy on behalf of her descendants by Ethelred.

Canute became the ruling sovereign of the North, and was reckoned as having five or six kingdoms under him. He was already King of Denmark when he conquered England, and he made good his claim to be King of Norway. Scotland offered him its homage. The Viking power, although already undermined, still stretched across the world, ranging from Norway to North America, and through the Baltic to the East. But of all his realms Canute chose England for his home and capital. He liked, we are told, the Anglo-Saxon way of life. He wished to be considered the "successor of Edgar", whose seventeen years of peace still shone by contrast with succeeding times. He ruled according to the laws, and he made it known that these were to be administered in austere detachment from his executive authority.

He built churches, he professed high devotion to the Christian faith and to the Papal diadem. He honoured the memory of St Edmund and St Alphege, whom his fellow-countrymen had murdered, and brought their relics with pious pomp to Canterbury. From Rome, as a pilgrim in 1027, he wrote a letter to his subjects couched in exalted and generous terms, promising to administer equal justice, and laying particular emphasis upon the payment of Church dues. His daughter was married to the Emperor Conrad's eldest son, who ultimately carried his empire across Schleswig to the banks of the Eider. These remarkable achievements, under the blessing of God and the smiles of fortune, were in large measure due to his own personal qualities. Here again we see the power of a great man to bring order out of ceaseless broils and command harmony and unity to be his servants, and how the lack of such men has to be paid for by the inestimable suffering of the many.

Meanwhile across the waters of the English channel a new military power was growing up. The Viking settlement founded in Normandy in the early years of the tenth century had become the most vigorous military state in France. In less than a hundred years the sea-rovers had transformed themselves into a feudal society.

In Normandy a class of knights and nobles arose who held their land in return for military service, and sublet to inferior tenants upon the same basis. The Normans, with their craving for legality and logic, framed a general scheme of society, from which there soon emerged an excellent army. Order was strenuously enforced. No one but the Duke might build castles or fortify himself. The Court or "Curia" of the Duke consisted of his household officials, of dignitaries of the Church, and of the more important tenants, who owed him not only military service but also personal attendance at Court. Here the administration was centred. Respect for the decisions and interests of the Duke was maintained throughout Normandy by the Vicomtes, who were not merely collectors of taxes from the ducal estates, but also, in effect, prefects, in close touch with the Curia, superintending districts like English counties. The Dukes of Normandy created relations with the Church which became a model for medieval Europe. They were the protectors and patrons of the monasteries in their domains. They welcomed the religious revival of the tenth century, and secured the favour and support of its leaders. But they made sure that bishops and abbots were ducal appointments.

It was from this virile and well-organised land that the future rulers of England were to come. Between the years 1028 and 1035 the Viking instincts of Duke Robert of Normandy turned him seriously to plans of invasion. His death and his failure to leave a legitimate heir suspended the project, but only for a while.

The figure of Emma, sister of Robert of Normandy, looms large in English history at this time. Ethelred had originally married her from a reasonable desire to supplement his failing armaments by a blood-tie with the most vigorous military state in Europe. Canute married her to give him a united England. Of her qualities and conduct little is known. Nevertheless few women have stood at the centre of such remarkable converging forces. In fact Emma had two husbands and two sons who were Kings of England.

In 1035 Canute died, and his empire with him. He left three sons, two by a former wife and one, Hardicanute, by Emma. These sons were ignorant and boorish Vikings, and many thoughts were turned to the representative of the old West Saxon line, Alfred and Edward, sons of Ethelred and Emma, then living in exile in Normandy. The elder, Alfred, "the innocent Prince" as the chronicler calls him, hastened to England in 1036, ostensibly to visit his again-widowed mother, the ex-Queen Emma. A Wessex earl, Godwin, was the leader of the Danish party in England. He possessed great abilities and exercised the highest political influence. The venturesome Alfred was arrested and his personal attendants slaughtered. The unfortunate prince himself was blinded, and in this condition soon ended his days in the monastery at Ely. The guilt of this crime was generally ascribed to Godwin. The succession being thus simplified, Canute's sons divided the paternal inheritance. Sweyn reigned in Norway for a spell, but his two brothers who ruled England were short-lived, and within seven years the throne of England was again vacant.

Godwin continued to be the leading figure in the land, and was now master of its affairs. There was still living in exile in Normandy Edward, the remaining son of Ethelred and Emma, younger brother of the ill-starred Alfred. In these days of reviving anarchy all men's minds turned to the search for some stable institution. This could only be found in monarchy, and the illustrious line of Alfred the Great possessed unequalled claims and titles. It was the Saxon monarchy which for five or six generations had provided the spearhead of resistance to the Danes. The West Saxon line was the oldest in Europe. Two generations back the house of Capet were lords of little more than Paris and the Île de France, and the Norman dukes were Viking rovers. A sense of sanctity and awe still attached to any who could claim descent from the Great King, and beyond him to Egbert and immemorial antiquity. Godwin saw that he could consolidate his power and combine both English and Danish support by making Edward King. He bargained with the exile, threatening to put a nephew of Canute on the throne unless his terms were met. Of these the first was the restriction of Norman influence on England. Edward made no difficulty; he was welcomed home and crowned; and for the next twenty-four years, with one brief interval, England was mainly governed by Godwin and his sons. "He had been to such an extent exalted", says the *Chronicle* of Florence of Worcester, "as if he had ruled the King and all England."

Edward was a quiet, pious person, without liking for war or much aptitude for administration. His Norman upbringing made him the willing though gentle agent of Norman influence, so far as Earl Godwin would allow. Norman prelates appeared in the English Church, Norman clerks in the royal household, and Norman landowners in the English shires. To make all smooth Edward was obliged to marry Godwin's young and handsome daughter, but we are assured by contemporary writers that this union was no more than formal. According to tradition the King was a kindly, weak, chubby albino. Some later writers profess to discern a latent energy in a few of his dealings with that formidable group of Anglo-Danish warriors that surrounded him. Nevertheless his main interest in life was religious, and as he grew older his outlook was increasingly that of a monk. In these harsh times he played much the same part as Henry VI, whose nature was similar, during the War of the Roses. His saintliness brought him as the years passed by a reward in the veneration of his people, who forgave him his weakness for the sake of his virtues.

Meanwhile the Godwin family maintained their dictatorship under the crown. Nepotism in those days was not merely the favouring of a man's own family; it was almost the only way in which a ruler could procure trustworthy lieutenants. The family tie, though frequently failing, gave at least the assurance of a certain identity of interest. Statistics had not been collected, but there was a general impression in these primitive times that a man could trust his brother, or his wife's brother, or his son, better than a stranger. We must not therefore hasten to condemn Earl Godwin because he parcelled out the English realm among his relations; neither must we marvel that other ambitious magnates found a deep cause of complaint in this distribution of power and favour. For some years a bitter intrigue was carried on between Norman and Anglo-Danish influences at the English Court.

A crisis came in the year 1051, when the Norman party at Court succeeded in driving Godwin into exile. During Godwin's absence William of Normandy is said to have paid an official visit to the Confessor in England in quest of the succession to the crown. Very likely King Edward promised that William should be his heir. But in the following year Godwin returned, backed by a force raised in Flanders, and with the active help of his son Harold. Together father and son obliged King Edward to take them back into power. Many of the principal Norman agents in the country were expelled, and the authority of the Godwin family was felt again throughout the land. The territories that they directly controlled stretched south of a line from the Wash to the Bristol Channel.

Seven months after his restoration Godwin died, in 1053. Since Canute first raised him to eminence he had been thirty-five years in public life. Harold, his eldest surviving son, succeeded to his father's great estates. He now filled his part to the full, and for the next thirteen adventurous years was the virtual ruler of England. In spite of the antagonism of rival Anglo-Danish earls, and the opposition of the Norman elements still attached to the Confessor's Court, the Godwins, father and son, maintained their rule under what we should now call a constitutional monarchy. A brother of Harold's became Earl of East Anglia, and a third son of Godwin, Tostig, who courted the Normans, and was high in the favour of King Edward, received the Earldom of Northumbria, dispossessing the earls of those regions. But there was now no unity within the house of Godwin. Harold and Tostig soon became bitter foes.

All Harold's competence, vigour, and shrewdness were needed to preserve the unity of the realm. Even so, as we shall see, the rift between the brothers left the land a prey to foreign ambitions.

The political condition of England at the close of the reign of Edward the Confessor was one of widespread weakness. Illuminated manuscripts, sculpture, metalwork and architecture of much artistic merit were still produced, religious life flourished, and a basis of sound law and administration remained, but the virtues and vigour of Alfred's posterity were exhausted and the Saxon monarchy itself was in decline. A strain of feeble princes, most of whom were short-lived, had died without children. Even the descendants of the prolific Ethelred the Unready died out with strange rapidity, and at this moment only a sickly boy and his sister and the aged sovereign represented the warrior dynasty which had beaten the Vikings and reconquered the Danelaw. The great earls were becoming independent in the provinces.

Though England was still the only state in Europe with a royal treasury to which sheriffs all over the country had to account, royal control over the sheriffs had grown lax. The King lived largely upon his private estates and governed as best he could through his household. The remaining powers of the monarchy were in practice severely restricted by a little group of Anglo-Danish notables. The main basis of support for the English kings had always been this select Council, never more than sixty, who in a vague manner regarded themselves as the representatives of the whole country. It was in fact a committee of courtiers, the greater thanes, and ecclesiastics. But at this time this assembly of "wise men" in no way embodied the life of the nations. It weakened the royal executive without adding any strength of its own. Its character and quality suffered in the general decay. It tended to fall into the hands of the great families. As the central power declined a host of local chieftains disputed and intrigued in every county, pursuing private family aims and knowing no interest but their own. Feuds and disturbances were rife. The people, too, were hampered not only by the many conflicting petty authorities, but by the deep division of custom between the Saxon and the Danish districts. Absurd anomalies and contradictions obstructed the administration of justice. The system of land-tenure varied from complete manorial conditions in Wessex to the free communities of the Danelaw in the North and East. There was no defined relation between Lordship and Land. A thane owed service to the King as a personal duty, and not in respect of lands he held. The Island had come to count for little on the Continent, and had lost the thread of its own progress. The defences, both of the coast and of the towns, were neglected. To the coming conquerors the whole system, social, moral, political, and military, seemed effete. The figure of Edward the Confessor comes down to us faint, misty, frail. The medieval legend, carefully fostered by the Church, whose devoted servant he was, surpassed the man. The lights of Saxon England were going out, and in the gathering darkness a gentle, grey-beard prophet foretold the end. When on his death-bed Edward spoke of a time of evil that was coming upon the land his inspired muttering struck terror into the hearers. Only Archbishop Stigand, who had been Godwin's stalwart, remained unmoved, and whispered in Harold's ear that age and sickness had robbed the monarch of his wits. Thus on January 5, 1066, ended the line of the Saxon kings. The national sentiment of the English, soon to be conquered, combined in the bitter period that lay before them with the gratitude of the Church to circle the royal memory with a halo. As the years rolled by his spirit became the object of popular worship. His shrine at Westminster was a centre of pilgrimage. Canonised in 1161, he lived for centuries in the memories of the Saxon folk. The Normans also had an interest in his fame. For them he was the King by whose wisdom the crown had been left, or so they claimed, to their Duke. Hence both sides blessed his memory, and until England appropriated St George during the Hundred Years War St Edward the Confessor was the kingdom's patron saint. St George proved undoubtedly more suitable to the Islanders' needs, mood, and character.

CHAPTER SEVEN

THE NORMAN INVASION

*William the Bastard — Norman claims to the English throne — King
Harold — Hardrada and Tostig unite against Harold — the Battle of
Stamford Bridge — the Norman Invasion — the Battle of Hastings — the
Conquest begins — the execution of Waltheof — William and his son meet
in combat — Domesday, the great account — the end of the old English
nobility — the new aristocracy — the death of William the Conqueror*

ONE MORNING Duke Robert of Normandy, the fourth descendant
of Rollo, was riding towards his capital town, Falaise, when he
saw Arlette, daughter of a tanner, washing linen in a stream. His
love was instantly fired. He carried her to his castle, and,
although already married to a lady of quality, lived with her for the rest of his
days. To this romantic but irregular union there was born in 1027 a son,
William, afterwards famous.

Duke Robert died when William was only seven, and in those harsh times a
minor's hold upon his inheritance was precarious. The great nobles who were
his guardians came one by one to violent ends, and rival ambitions stirred
throughout Normandy. Were they to be ruled by a bastard? Was the grandson
of a tanner to be the liege lord of the many warrior families? The taint
of bastardy clung, and sank deep into William's nature. It embittered and
hardened him. When, many years afterwards, he besieged the town of
Alençon the citizens imprudently hung out hides upon the walls, shouting,
"Hides for the tanner!" William repaid this taunt by devastating the town, and
mutilating or flaying alive its chief inhabitants.

William, like his father, was in close touch with the Saxon Court, and had
watched every move on the part of the supporters of the Anglo-Danish party,
headed by Godwin and his son Harold. Fate played startlingly into the hands
of the Norman Duke. On some visit of inspection, probably in 1064, Harold
was driven by the winds on to the French coast. The Count of Ponthieu, who
held sway there, looked upon all shipwrecked mariners and their gear as
treasure-trove. He held Harold to ransom for what he was worth, which was
much. The contact between the Norman and English Courts were at this time
close and friendly, and Duke William asked for the release of King Edward's
thane, acting at first by civil request, and later by armed commands. The

Count of Ponthieu reluctantly relinquished his windfall and conducted Harold to the Norman Court. A friendship sprang up between William and Harold. Politics apart, they liked each other well. We see them, falcon on wrist, in sport; Harold taking the field with William against the Bretons, or rendering skilful service in hazardous broils. He was honoured and knighted by William. But the Duke looked forward to his future succession to the English crown. Here indeed was the prize to be won. Harold had one small streak of royal blood on his mother's side; but William, through his father, had a more pointed or at least less cloudy claim to the Island throne.[1] This claim he was resolved to assert. He saw the power which Harold wielded under Edward the Confessor, and how easily he might convert it into sovereignty if he happened to be on the spot when the Confessor died. He invited Harold to make a pact with him whereby he himself should become King of England, and Harold Earl of the whole splendid province of Wessex, being assured thereof and linked to the King by marriage with William's daughter. It is probable however that Harold swore a solemn oath to William to renounce all rights or designs upon the English crown, and it is likely that if he had not done so he might never have seen either crown or England again.

At length, in January 1066, Edward the Confessor died, absolved, we trust, from such worldly sins as he had been tempted to commit. With his dying breath, in spite of his alleged promise to William, he is supposed to have commended Harold, his young, valiant counsellor and guide, as the best choice for the crown which the Witan, or Council, could make. At any rate, Harold, at the beginning of the fateful year 1066, was blithely accepted by London, the Midlands, and the South, and crowned King with all solemnity in Westminster Abbey. This event opened again the gates of war. The entire structure of the feudal world rested upon the sanctity of oaths. Against the breakers of oaths the censures both of chivalry and the Church were combined with blasting force. It was a further misfortune for Harold that Stigand, the Archbishop of Canterbury, had himself received the pallium from a schismatic Pope. Rome therefore could not recognise Harold as King.

Two rival projects of invasion were speedily prepared. The first was from Scandinavia. The successors of Canute in Norway determined to revive their traditions of English sovereignty. An expedition was already being organised when Tostig, Harold's exiled and revengeful half-brother, ousted from his Earldom of Northumbria, arrived with full accounts of the crisis in the Island and of the weak state of its defences. King Harold Hardrada set forth to conquer the English crown. He sailed at first to the Orkneys, gathering recruits from the Scottish isles and from the Isle of Man. With Tostig he wended towards the north-east coast of England with a large fleet and army in the late summer of 1066.

---

1 His father was cousin to Edward the Confessor. William of Normandy visited Edward in 1051, and there is evidence that the Saxon king promised William the English throne.

Harold of England was thus faced with a double invasion from the north-east and from the south. In September 1066 he heard that a Norwegian fleet, with Hardrada and Tostig on board, had sailed up the Humber, beaten the local levies under Earls Edwin and Morcar, and encamped near York at Stamford Bridge. He now showed the fighting qualities he possessed. The news reached him in London, where he was waiting to see which invasion would strike him first, and where. At the head of his Danish household troops he hastened northwards up the Roman road to York, calling out the local levies as he went. His rapidity of movement took the Northern invaders completely by surprise. Within five days of the defeat of Edwin and Morcar Harold reached York, and the same day marched to confront the Norwegian army ten miles from the city. The battle began. The Englishmen charged, but at first the Norsemen, though without their armour, kept their battle array. After a while, deceived by what proved to be a feint, the common ruse of those days, they opened up their shield rampart and advanced from all sides. This was the moment for which Harold had waited. The greatest crash of weapons arose. Hardrada was hit by an arrow in the throat, and Tostig, assuming the command, took his stand by the banner "Land-ravager". In this pause Harold offered his brother peace, and also quarter to all Norsemen who were still alive; but "the Norsemen called out all of them together that they would rather fall, one across the other, than accept of quarter from the Englishmen".[1] Harold's valiant house-carls, themselves of Viking blood, charged home, and with a war shout the battle began again. At this moment a force left on board ship arrived to succour the invaders. They, unlike their comrades, were clad in proof, but, breathless and exhausted from their hurried march, they cast aside their ring-mail, threw in their lot with their hard-pressed friends, and nearly all were killed. The victorious Harold buried Hardrada in the seven feet of English earth he had scornfully promised him, but he spared his son Olaf and let him go in peace with his surviving adherents. Tostig paid for his restless malice with his life. Though the Battle of Stamford Bridge has been overshadowed by Hastings it has a claim to be regarded as one of the decisive contests of English history. Never again was a Scandinavian army able seriously to threaten the power of an English king or the unity of the realm.

At the moment of victory news reached the King from the south that "William the Bastard" had landed at Pevensey. William's invasion of England was planned like a business enterprise. The resources of Normandy were obviously unequal to the task; but the Duke's name was famous throughout the feudal world, and the idea of seizing and dividing England commended itself to the martial nobility of many lands. The barons of Normandy at the Council of Lillebonne refused to countenance the enterprise officially. It was the Duke's venture, and not that of Normandy. But the bulk of them hastened to subscribe their quota of knights and ships. Brittany sent a large contingent. It must be remembered that some of the best stocks from Roman Britain had

---

1   From the *Heimskringla Saga* of Snorri Sturluson. [Churchill]

found refuge there, establishing a strong blood strain which had preserved a continuity with the Classic Age and with the British race. But all France was deeply interested. Mercenaries came from Flanders, and even from beyond the Alps; Normans from South Italy and Spain, nobles and knights, answered the advertisement. The shares in this enterprise were represented by knights or ships, and it was plainly engaged that the lands of the slaughtered English would be divided in proportion to the contributions, subject of course to a bonus for good work in the field. During the summer of 1066 this great gathering of audacious buccaneers, land-hungry, war-hungry, assembled in a merry company around St Valery, at the mouth of the Somme. Ships had been built in all the French ports from the spring onwards, and by the beginning of August a considerable fleet, carrying about seven thousand fighting men, of whom the majority were persons of rank and quality, was ready to follow the renowned Duke and share the lands and wealth of England.

But the winds were contrary. For six whole weeks there was no day when the south wind blew. The heterogeneous army, bound by no tie of feudal allegiance, patriotism, or moral theme, began to bicker and grumble. Only William's repute as a managing director and the rich pillage to be expected held them together. At length extreme measures had to be taken with the weather. The bones of St Edmund were brought from the church of St Valery and carried with military and religious pomp along the sea-shore. This proved effective, for the very next day the wind changed, not indeed to the south, but to the south-west. William thought this sufficient, and gave the signal. The whole fleet put to sea, with all their stores, weapons, coats of mail, and great numbers of horses. Special arrangements were made to keep the fleet together, the rendezvous being at the mouth of the Somme, and the Duke by night having a lamp of special brilliancy upon his masthead. The next morning all steered towards the English coast. The Duke, who had a faster vessel, soon found himself alone in mid-channel. He hove to and breakfasted with his staff "as if he had been in his own hall". Wine was not lacking, and after the meal he expressed himself in enthusiastic terms upon his great undertaking and the prizes and profit it would bring to all engaged therein.

On September 28 the fleet hove in sight, and all came safely to anchor in Pevensey Bay. There was no opposition to the landing. The local "fyrd" had been called out this year four times already to watch the coast, and having, in true English style, come to the conclusion that the danger was past because it had not yet arrived had gone back to their homes. William landed, as the tale goes, and fell flat on his face as he stepped out of the boat. "See", he said turning the omen into a favourable channel, "I have taken England with both my hands." He occupied himself with organising his army, raiding for supplies in Sussex, and building some defensive works for the protection of his fleet and base. Thus a fortnight passed.

Meanwhile Harold and his house-carls, sadly depleted by the slaughter of Stamford Bridge, jingled down Ermine Street on their ponies, marching night and day to London. They covered the two hundred miles in seven days. In

London the King gathered all the forces he could, and most of the principal persons in Wessex and Kent hastened to join his standard, bringing their retainers and local militia with them. Remaining only five days in London, Harold marched out towards Pevensey, and in the evening of October 13 took up his position upon the slope of a hill which barred the direct march upon the capital.[1]

The military opinion of those, as of these, days has criticised his staking all upon an immediate battle. The loyalty of the Northern earls, Edwin and Morcar, was doubtful. They were hastening south with a substantial reinforcement, but he could not be sure which side they would join. In the event they "withdrew themselves from the conflict". Some have suggested that he should have used the tactics which eleven hundred years before Cassivellaunus had employed against Caesar. But these critics overlooked the fact that whereas the Roman army consisted only of infantry, and the British only of charioteers and horsemen, Duke William's was essentially a cavalry force assisted by archers, while Harold had nothing but foot-soldiers who used horses only as transport. It is one thing for mounted forces to hover round and harry an infantry army, and the opposite for bands of foot-soldiers to use these tactics against cavalry. King Harold had great confidence in his redoubtable axe-men, and it was in good heart that he formed his shield-wall on the morning of October 14. There is a great dispute about the numbers engaged. Some modern authorities suppose the battle was fought by five or six thousand Norman knights and men-at-arms, with a few thousand archers, against eight to ten thousand axe- and spear-men, and the numbers on both sides may have been fewer. However it may be, at the first streak of dawn William set out from his camp at Pevensey, resolved to put all to the test; and Harold, eight miles away, awaited him in resolute array.

As the battle began Ivo Taillefer, the minstrel knight who had claimed the right to make the first attack, advanced up the hill on horseback, throwing his lance and sword into the air and catching them before the English army. He then charged deep into the English ranks, and was slain. The cavalry charges of William's mail-clad knights, cumbersome in manoeuvre, beat in vain upon the dense, ordered masses of the English. Neither the arrow hail nor the assaults of the horsemen could prevail against them. William's left wing of cavalry was thrown into disorder, and retreated rapidly down the hill. On this the troops on Harold's right, who were mainly the local "fyrd", broke their ranks in eager pursuit. William, in the centre, turned his disciplined squadrons upon them and cut them to pieces. The Normans then re-formed their ranks and began a second series of charges upon the English masses, subjecting them in the intervals to severe archery. It has often been remarked that this part of the action resembles the afternoon at Waterloo, when Ney's cavalry exhausted themselves upon the British squares, torn by artillery in the intervals. In both cases the tortured infantry stood unbroken. Never, it was said, had the

1 Probably Senlac Hill on what is now called the A2100 road north of the coast at Hastings (a Roman settlement, Haestingaceaster).

Norman knights met foot-soldiers of this stubbornness. They were utterly unable to break through the shield-walls, and they suffered serious losses from deft blows of the axe-men, or from javelins, or clubs hurled from the ranks behind. But the arrow showers took a cruel toll. So closely, it was said, were the English wedged that the wounded could not be removed, and the dead scarcely found room in which to sink upon the ground.

The autumn afternoon was far spent before any result had been achieved, and it was then that William adopted the time-honoured ruse of a feigned retreat. He had seen how readily Harold's right had quitted their positions in pursuit after the first repulse of the Normans. He now organised a sham retreat in apparent disorder, while keeping a powerful force in his own hands. The house-carls around Harold preserved their discipline and kept their ranks, but the sense of relief to the less trained forces after these hours of combat was such that seeing their enemy in flight proved irresistible. They surged forward on the impulse of victory, and when half-way down the hill were savagely slaughtered by William's horsemen. There remained, as the dusk grew, only the valiant bodyguard who fought round the King and his standard. His brothers, Gyrth and Leofwine, had already been killed. William now directed his archers to shoot high into the air, so that the arrows would fall behind the shield-wall, and one of these pierced Harold in the right eye, inflicting a mortal wound.[1] He fell at the foot of the royal standard, unconquerable except by death, which does not count in honour. The hard-fought battle was now decided. The last formed body of troops was broken, though by no means overwhelmed. They withdrew into the woods behind, and William, who had fought in the foremost ranks and had three horses killed under him, could claim the victory. Nevertheless the pursuit was heavily checked. There is a sudden deep ditch on the reverse slope of the hill of Hastings into which large numbers of Norman horsemen fell, and in which they were butchered by the infuriated English lurking in the wood.

The dead king's naked body, wrapped only in a robe of purple, was hidden among the rocks of the bay. His mother in vain offered the weight of the body in gold for permission to bury him in holy ground. The Norman Duke's answer was that Harold would be more fittingly laid upon the Saxon shore which he had given his life to defend. The body was later transferred to Waltham Abbey, which he had founded. Although here the English once again accepted conquest and bowed in a new destiny, yet ever must the name of Harold be honoured in the Island for which he and his famous house-carls fought indomitably to the end.

Duke William knew that his work was but begun. The very disunity which

[1] There remains continuing debate on the contents of the Bayeux Tapestry. For example, it does not really show that Harold died from an arrow wound in his eye. Abbot Baudin de Bourgueil, writing towards the end of the century, claimed death was from an arrow. But the Tapestry shows a second view of Harold which suggests that he was, indeed, wounded by an arrow but was then struck down and killed by Norman knights. But even when read with the texts of Abbot Baudin and William of Poitiers, no line may yet be drawn beneath the so-called real meaning of the Bayeux Tapestry.

had made assault successful made subjugation lengthy. Saxon lords in the North and in the West might carry on endless local struggles and cut communications with the Continent. Cautiously, with a compact force of Normans, French, and Bretons, he advanced through Kent upon the capital, and at first no native came to his camp to do him homage. The people of Romney had killed a band of Norman knights. Vengeance fell upon them. The news spread through the country, and the folk flocked "like flies settling on a wound" to make their submission and avoid a similar fate. The tale of these events bit deep into the hearts of the people.

When William arrived near London he marched round the city, isolating it by a belt of cruel desolation. From Southwark he moved to Wallingford, and thence through the Chilterns to Berkhamsted, where the leading Saxon notables and clergy came meekly to his tent to offer him the crown. On Christmas Day Aldred, Archbishop of York, crowned him King of England at Westminster. He rapidly established his power over all England south of the Humber. Within two years of the conquest Duchess Matilda, who ruled Normandy in William's absence, came across the sea to her coronation at Westminster on Whit Sunday 1068, and later in the year a son, Henry, symbol and portent of dynastic stability, was born on English soil.

The North still remained under its Saxon lords, Edwin and Morcar, unsubdued and defiant. The King gathered an army and marched towards them. The track of William in the North was marked for generations upon the countryside and in the memories of the survivors and their descendants. From coast to coast the whole region was laid desolate, and hunted men took refuge in the wooded valleys of Yorkshire, to die of famine and exposure, or to sell themselves into slavery for food. For long years after tales were told of the "waste" and of the rotting bodies of the famine-stricken by the roadside. At Christmas 1069 William wintered at York, and, the feasting season over, continued the man-hunt. Only one town in England had not been subjected to the Conqueror's will – Chester. Across England in the depth of the winter of 1070 he marched his army. The town surrendered at the summons, and submitted to the building of a castle.

England north of the Humber was now in Norman control. The great Earldom of Richmond was created, possessing broad estates in Yorkshire and in the adjacent counties as well. The Bishopric of Durham was reorganised, with wide powers of local government. It was now clear that Normandy had the force and spirit to absorb all Saxon England; but whether William would retain the whole of his conquests unchallenged from without was not settled till his closing years. The period of English subjugation was hazardous. For at least twenty years after the invasion the Normans were an army camped in a hostile country, holding the population down by the castles at key points. The Saxon resistance died hard. Legends and chroniclers have painted for us the last stand of Hereward the Wake in the broad wastes of the fens round Ely. Not until five years after Hastings, in 1071, was Hereward put down. In his cause had fallen many of the Saxon thanage, the only class from whose ranks new leaders could spring. The building of Ely Castle symbolised the end of their order.

Other internal oppositions arose. In 1075 a serious revolt of disaffected Norman knights broke out in the Midlands, East Anglia, and on the Welsh border, and one surviving Saxon leader, Waltheof, who had made his peace with William, joined them. The King in Normandy must hasten back to crush the rebels. The Saxon population supported the Conqueror against chaos. The "fyrd" took the field. Vengeance was reserved for Waltheof alone, and his execution upon a hill outside Winchester is told in moving scenes by the Saxon-hearted monkish chroniclers of the time. Medieval legend ascribed the fate of William in his later years to the guilt of this execution. It marked also the final submission of England. Norman castles guarded the towns, Norman lords held the land, and Norman churches protected men's souls. All England had a master, the conquest was complete, and the work of reconstruction began.

In their early days the Normans borrowed no manners and few customs from the Islanders. The only culture was French. Surviving Saxon notables sent their sons to the monasteries of France for education. The English repeated the experience of the Ancient Britons; all who could learnt French, as formerly the contemporaries of Boadicea had learnt Latin. At first the conquerors, who despised the uncouth English as louts and boors, ruled by the force of sharpened steel. But very soon in true Norman fashion they intermarried with the free population and identified themselves with their English past.

William's work in England is the more remarkable from the fact that all the time as Duke of Normandy he was involved in endless intrigues and conflicts with the King of France. Though England was a more valuable possession than Normandy, William and his sons were always more closely interested in their Continental lands. The French kings, for their part, placed in the forefront of their policy the weakening of these Dukes of Normandy, now grown so powerful, and whose frontiers were little more than twenty miles from Paris. Hence arose a struggle that was solved only when King John lost Normandy in 1203. Meanwhile years passed. Queen Matilda was a capable regent at Rouen, but plagued by the turbulence of her sons. The eldest, Robert, a Crusading knight, reckless and spendthrift, with his father's love of fighting and adventure but without his ruthless genius or solid practical aims, resented William's persistent hold on life and impatiently claimed his Norman inheritance. Many a time the father was called across the Channel to chastise rebellious towns and forestall the conspiracies of this son with the French Court. Robert, driven from his father's lands, found refuge in King Philip's castle of Gerberoi. William marched implacably upon him. Beneath the walls two men, visors down, met in single combat, father and son. Robert wounded his father in the hand and unhorsed him, and would have killed him but for a timely rescue by an Englishman, one Tokig of Wallingford, who remounted the overthrown Conqueror. Both [Robert and William] were sobered by this chance encounter, and for a time there was reconciliation.

The Normans introduced into England their system of land tenure based upon military service. A military caste was imposed from above. A revolution not only in warfare, but also in the upper reaches of society, had taken place. William aimed first at securing an effective and compact army, and the terms of knight-service and the quota of men due from each of his greater subjects interested him more than the social relationships prevailing on the lands they held. The Normans, a small minority, had destroyed the Saxon governing class and had thrust an alien domination upon England. But the mass of the inhabitants were only indirectly affected by the change, and the feudal super-structure was for many years as unsure as it was impressive. There were interminable controversies among the new masters of the country about the titles to their lands, and how these fitted the customs and laws of Anglo-Saxon England. The bishoprics and abbeys were especially loud in their complaints, and royal legates repeatedly summoned great assemblies of the shire courts to settle these disputes. Finally in 1086 a vast sworn inquiry was made into the whole wealth of the King's feudal vassals, from whom he derived a large part of his own income. The inquest or description, as it was called, was carried through with a degree of minuteness and regularity unique in that age and unequalled for centuries after. The history of many an English village begins with an entry in Domesday Book. The result of this famous survey showed that the underlying structure of England and its peasant life were little changed by the shock of the invasion.

But the holding of the great Domesday inquest marks a crisis. The Norman garrison in England was threatened from abroad by other claimants. The rulers of Scandinavia still yearned for the Island once the west of their empire. They had supported the rising in the North in 1069, and again in 1085 they threatened to intervene with greater vigour. A fleet was fitted out, and though it never sailed, because its leader was murdered, William took precautions. It became necessary that all feudal controversies arising out of the Conquest should be speedily settled, and it was under the shadow of this menace that Domesday Book was compiled. In 1086 William called together at Salisbury "all the land-holding men of any account throughout England, whosoever men they were". The King had need of an assurance of loyalty from all his feudal tenants of substance, and this substantial body bound itself together by oath and fealty to his person.

With increasing years William became fiercer in mood particularly after the death, in 1083, of his consort, Queen Matilda. Stung to fury by the forays of the French, he crossed the frontier, spreading fire and ruin till he reached the gate of Mantes. His Normans surprised the town, and amid the horrors of the sack fire broke out. As William rode through the streets his horse stumbled among the burning ashes and he was thrown against the pommel of the saddle. He was carried in agony to the priory of St Gervase at Rouen. There, high above the town, he lay, through the summer heat of 1087, fighting his grievous injury. When death drew near his sons William and Henry came to him.

William, whose one virtue had been filial fidelity, was named to succeed the Conqueror in England. The graceless Robert would rule in Normandy at last. For the youngest, Henry, there was nothing but five thousand pounds of silver, and the prophecy that he would one day reign over a united Anglo-Saxon nation. This proved no empty blessing.

Fear fell upon the Conqueror's subject when it was known that he was dying. What troubles would follow the end of a strong ruler? On Thursday, September 9, 1087, as the early bells of Rouen Cathedral echoed over the hills, William and his authority died. The caitiff attendants stripped the body and plundered the chamber where he lay. The clergy of Rouen bore him to the church of St Stephen at Caen, which he had founded. Even his final journey was disturbed. In the graveyard one Ascelin cried out that his father had been deprived by the dead Duke of this plot of ground, and before all the concourse demanded justice from the startled priests. For the price of sixty shilling the Conqueror came thus humbly to his grave.

The Norman achievement in England was not merely military in character. Although knight-service governed the holding of property and produced a new aristocracy, much was preserved of Saxon England. The Normans were administrators and lawyers rather than legislators. Their centre of government was the royal Curia, the final court of appeal and the instrument of supervision; here were preserved and developed the financial and secretarial methods of the Anglo-Saxon kingdom. The whole system of Saxon local government, also of immense usefulness for the future – the counties, the sheriffs, and the courts – survived, and through this the King maintained his widespread contact with the country. In fact the Conqueror himself by these means collected the information for Domesday. Not only the courts, but also the dues and taxes such as Danegeld, were preserved for the sake of the Norman revenues. The local militia raised by the counties survived the Conquest, and proved serviceable to William and his successors. Thus in the future government of England both Norman and Saxon institutions were unconsciously but profoundly blended.

In some respects all this was a sudden acceleration of the drift toward the manorial system, a process which had already gone a long way in Anglo-Saxon England, and certainly in Wessex. But even in Wessex the idea still persisted that the tie of lord and man was primarily personal, so that a free man could go from one lord to another and transfer his land with him. The essence of Norman feudalism, on the other hand, was that the land remained under the lord, whatever the man might do. Thus the landed pyramid rose up tier by tier to the King, until every acre in the country could be registered as held of somebody by some form of service. But besides the services which the man owed to the lord in arms there was the service of attending the courts of the hundred and the county, which were, apart from exemptions, courts of the King, administering old customary law. This survival of the hundred, the county court, and the sheriff makes the great difference between English and Continental feudalism. In England the monarch is everywhere – in

Northumberland as in Middlesex; a crime anywhere is a breach of his peace; if he wants to know anything he tells his officer, the sheriff, to impanel a jury and find out, or, in later days, to send some respectable persons to Westminster and tell him. But perhaps when they got to Westminster they told him that he was badly advised, and that they would not pay any taxes till he mended his ways. Far ahead we see the seventeenth-century constitutional issue. There were in Norman days no great mercantile towns in England, except London. If William had not preserved the counties and hundreds as living and active units there would have been no body of resistance or counter-poise to the central Government, save in the great baronial families.

In the Norman settlement lay the germ of a constitutional Opposition, with the effect if not the design of controlling the Government, not breaking it up. The seat of this potential Opposition was found in the counties, among the smaller nobility and their untitled descendants, Justices of the Peace and knights of the shire. They were naturally for the Crown and a quiet life. Hence after centuries they rallied to the Tudor sovereigns; and in another age to the Parliament against the Crown itself. Whatever else changed they were always *there*. And the reason why they were there is that William found the old West Saxon organisation, which they alone could administer, exceedingly convenient. He did not mean to be treated as he had treated the King of France. He had seen, and profited by seeing, the mischief of a country divided into great provinces. The little provinces of England, with the King's officers at the head of each, gave him exactly the balance of power he needed for all purposes of law and finance, but were at the same time incapable of rebelling as units. The old English nobility disappeared after the Battle of Hastings. But all over Domesday Book the opinion of what we should later call the gentry of the shire is quoted as decisive. This is the class – people of some considera- tion in the neighbourhood, with leisure to go to the sheriff's court and thereafter to Westminster. Out of this process in time the Pyms and Hampdens arose.

The Conquest was the supreme achievement of the Norman race. It linked the history of England anew to Europe, and prevented for ever a drift into the narrower orbit of a Scandinavian empire. Henceforward English history marched with that of races and lands south of the Channel. The effect of the Conquest on the Church was no less broad and enlivening. The bishoprics and abbeys and other high posts were now as a matter of course given to Normans, and insular customs supplanted by the newest fashions from abroad. The age of the Conquest coincided with the many-sided reforms of the Church and advances in Papal power initiated by Hildebrand, who became Pope as Gregory VII in 1073. Under its new leaders England was brought into the van on this movement. New abbeys sprang up all over the country which attested the piety of the conquerors, though few of the new houses attained to the wealth or standing of the older foundations. These monasteries and bishoprics were the chief centres of religion and learning, until after a century they were gradually eclipsed by the rise of the universities.

CHAPTER EIGHT

GROWTH AMID TURMOIL

*William Rufus – the barons' revolt – Rufus killed hunting in the
New Forest – Henry I – the Battle of Tinchebrai – the Curia Regis –
establishment of the Exchequer – Stephen of Blois – Empress
Maud – the marriage with Anjou – the death of Henry I – Robert
of Gloucester – Civil War – the Battle of the Standard – Henry
Plantagenet – Eleanor of Aquitaine*

T HE ACCESSION of the Conqueror's second surviving son[1] to the
throne of England did not pass without dispute. William I's
decision to divide his English from his Norman lands brought new
troubles in its train. The greater barons possessed property on both
sides of the Channel. They therefore now owed feudal allegiance to two
sovereign lords, and not unnaturally they sought to play one against the other.
Both Duke Robert and William II were dissatisfied with the division, and their
brotherly ties did not mitigate their covetous desires. During the thirteen years
of the reign of William Rufus the Anglo-Norman realms were vexed by
fratricidal strife, and successive baronial revolts. The Saxon inhabitants of
England, fearful of a relapse into the chaos of pre-Conquest days, stood by the
King against all rebels. The "fyrd" obeyed every summons, and supported
him in the field as it had his father in 1075. Thus he was able finally to bring
Cumberland and Westmorland into the kingdom. The feckless Robert, who
had plagued the Conqueror so long, eventually departed in a fit of gallantry
on the First Crusade,[2] leaving Normandy pawned to Rufus for the loan of
10,000 marks.

Rufus's extortions and violent methods had provoked the baronage
throughout his reign. In August 1100 he was mysteriously shot through the
head by an arrow while hunting in the New Forest, leaving a memory of
shameless exactions and infamous morals, but also a submissive realm to his

---

1   William II known as William the Red or William Rufus (1060–1100).
2   The Crusades were wars against enemies of the Christian Church and blessed by the popes. The
    three great crusades took place over a hundred years against the Muslim armies in what became
    the Middle East (crusades were not always against Muslims). The First Crusade (1095–9) led to
    the capture of Jerusalem from Islamic governors. The Second Crusade (1147–8) led to very
    little. The Third Crusade (1189–92) was led by Richard the Lionheart (see below).

successor. The main progress in his reign was financial; but the new feudal monarchy was also more firmly established, and in territory its sway was wider than at Rufus's accession. The Norman lords whom the Conqueror had settled upon the Welsh Marches had fastened a lasting grip upon Southern Wales. The Northern counties had been finally brought under Norman control, and a military frontier drawn against the Scots. While the rough hands of Rufus chafed and bruised the feudal relationship, they had also enforced the rights of a feudal king.

Prince Henry, the youngest of the royal brothers, had been a member of the fatal hunting party in the New Forest. There is no proof that he was implicated in the death of his brother, but he certainly wasted no time in mourning. He made straight for the royal treasury at Winchester, and gained possession of it after a sharp argument with its custodians. Evidently he represented a strong movement of opinion among the leading classes, and he had a policy of his own. For a layman his scholarship deserved the title of Beauclerc which the custom of his day accorded him. He set the precedent, which his successor followed, of proclaiming a charter upon his accession. By this he sought to consolidate those powerful forces in Church and State which had been alienated by the rapacity and tactlessness of his predecessor. He guaranteed that the rights of the baronage and the Church should be respected. At the same time, having seen the value of Saxon loyalty in the reigns of his father and his brother, he promised the conquered race good justice and the laws of Edward the Confessor. He knew that the friction caused by the separation of Normandy from England was by no means soothed. Duke Robert was already on his way back from his Crusade with his mortgage to redeem. The barons on both sides of the Channel would profit from fraternal strife to drive hard bargains in their own interest. Henry's desire to base himself in part at least upon the Saxon population of England led him, much to the suspicion of the Norman barons, to make a marriage with Matilda, niece of the last surviving Saxon claimant to the English throne, and descendant of the old English line of kings. The barons, mollified by the charter, accepted his decisive step. The ceaseless gigantic process of intermarriage received the highest sanction.

Henry was now ready to face Robert whenever he should return. In September 1100 this event occurred. Immediately the familiar incidents of feudal rebellion were renewed in England, and for the next six years the King had to fight to make good his title under his father's will. The great house of Montgomery formed the head of the opposition in England. By a series of persevering sieges the family's stronghold fell one by one, and Henry at length destroyed their power and annexed their estates to the Crown. But the root evil lay in Normandy, and in 1105, having consolidated his position in England, Henry crossed the Channel. In September 1106 the most important battle since Hastings was fought at Tinchebrai. King Henry's victory was complete. Duke Robert was carried to his perpetual prison in England. Normandy acknowledged Henry's authority, and the control of Anglo-

Norman policy passed from Rouen to London. The Saxons, who had fought heartily for Henry, regarded this battle as their military revenge for Hastings. By this new comradeship with the Crown, as well as by the marriage with Matilda, they felt themselves relieved from some at least of the pangs of being conquered. The shame was gone; the penalties could be endured. Through these two far-reaching factors a certain broad measure of unity was re-established in the Island.

There was now no challenged succession. The King of England's authority was established on both sides of the Channel. The Saxon people had proved their loyalty and the more powerful barons had been cowed. Foreign dangers having also been repelled, Henry was free for the time being to devote himself to internal government and to strengthening the power of the Crown throughout the land. He sought to invest the Anglo-Norman kingship with new and powerful attributes. There survived in medieval Europe a tradition of kingship more exalted than that of the feudal overlord. The king was not merely the apex of the feudal pyramid, but the anointed Vicegerent of God upon earth. The collapse of the Roman Empire had not entirely destroyed this Roman conception of sovereignty, and Henry now set himself to inject this idea of kingship into the Anglo-Norman state; and in so doing he could not help reviving, whether consciously or not, the English conception of the King as the keeper of the peace and guardian of the people.

The centre of government, the Curia Regis, was an ill-defined body consisting of those tenants-in-chief whose feudal duty it was to attend when summoned, and those personal servants of the monarch who could be used for Government service as well as for their household duties. Henry realised that royal servants who were members of the minor baronage, if formed into a permanent nucleus, would act as a brake upon the turbulence of the greater feudatories. Here were the first beginnings, tentative, modest, but insinuating, of a civil administrative machinery, which within its limits was more efficient and persistent than anything yet known. These officials soon developed a vested interest of their own. Families like the Clintons and the Bassetts, whom the King, as the chronicler put it, had "raised from the dust to do him great service", entrenched themselves in the household offices, and created what was in fact an official class.

The power of any government depends ultimately upon its finances. It was therefore in the business of gathering and administering the revenue that this novel feature first became apparent. There was no distinction in feudal society between the private and public resources of the Crown. The King in feudal theory was only the greatest of the landowners in the State. The sheriffs of counties collected not only the taxes and fines accruing to the Crown, but also the income from the royal estates, and they were responsible, when they appeared yearly at the royal treasury, for the exact payment of what was due from each of their counties. Henry's officials created a special organ to deal with the sheriffs and the business the sheriffs transacted. This was the Exchequer, still regarded simply as the Curia meeting for financial purposes, but gradually acquiring a life of its own. It took its name from the chequered boards used for greater ease of calculation in Roman numerals, and its methods included the keeping of written records, among them the important documents called the Pipe Rolls because they were kept rolled up in the shape of a pipe. Thus the King gained a surer grip over the finances of the realm and the earliest specialised department of royal administration was born. Its offspring still survives.

Henry took care that the sheriffs of the counties were brought under an increasingly strict control, and several commissions were appointed during the reign to revise their personnel. In troublous times the office of sheriff tended to fall into the hands of powerful barons and to become hereditary. The King saw to it that whenever possible his own men held these key positions. One of the most fertile sources of revenue arose from the fines imposed by the courts upon delinquents. The barons realised this as soon as the King, and their manorial courts provided them with important incomes, which could at once be turned into armed retainers. Within their domains they enjoyed a jurisdiction over nearly all laymen. But in the county courts and in the courts of the hundreds the Crown had at its disposal the old Saxon system of justice. These time-honoured institutions could well be used to rival the feudal courts of the baronage. Henry therefore revised and regularised the holding of the county courts, and made all men see that throughout the land there was a system of royal justice. King's officers – judges, as they became – in their occasional circuits administered this justice, and the very nature of their function brought them often into clash not only with humble suitors and malefactors, but with proud military magnates.

The King entered into a nation-wide competition with the baronage as to who could best deserve the rich spoils of the law. Through his control of the sheriffs he bound together the monarchy and the old Saxon system of local justice. The Conqueror had set the example when in the Domesday survey he combined the Continental system of getting information by means of bodies of men sworn to tell the truth with the English organisation by shire and hundred. His son for other purposes continued and intensified the process, sending officials constantly from his household through the kingdom, and convening the county courts to inquire into the claims of the royal revenue and to hear cases in which the Crown was interested. From these local inquiries by royal officials there were to spring far-reaching consequences in the reign of Henry II. The chroniclers spoke well of Henry I. "Good man he was", they declared, "and there was great awe of him. In his days no man dared to harm another." They bestowed upon him the title "Lion of Justice", and none has sought to rob him of it.

We must regard his reign as a period when the central Government, by adroit and sharp accountancy and clerking, established in a more precise form the structure and resources of the State. The Anglo-Norman State was now powerful. Henry was lord of England, Normandy, and Maine. In 1109 his only legitimate daughter, Matilda, was betrothed to Henry V, Holy Roman

Emperor and King of Germany. On the other hand, the reunion of England and Normandy after Tinchebrai had stirred the hostility of France. The forces of anarchy grew, and every noble in his castle balanced his chances upon who would succeed to the Crown.

There were two claimants, each of whom had a fair share or right. The King had a daughter, Matilda, or Maud as the English called her, but although there was no Salic Law in the Norman code this clanking, jangling aristocracy, mailed and spurred, did not take kindly to the idea of a woman's rule.[1] Against her stood the claim of Stephen, son of the Conqueror's daughter Adela. Stephen, Count of Blois, was leader of the Norman barons, and possessed great estates in England; after his elder brother had waived his claim, he was the rightful male heir. The feudal system lived entirely through the spirit of sworn allegiance. Throughout Christendom the accusation of violating an oath was almost mortal. Only great victories could atone and absolve. But here was a dilemma which every man could settle for himself according to his interests and ambitions. Split – utter, honest, total!

King Henry in the grey close of his life set himself to fill the void with his daughter Maud as female king. He spent his remaining years in trying to establish a family succession which would spare his widespread domains from civil war. At the age of thirteen Maud had been married to the Holy Roman Emperor. In 1125, he died, and at twenty-two she was a widow and an Empress. We have many records of this remarkable princess, of whom it was said "she had the nature of a man in the frame of a woman". Fierce, proud, hard, cynical, living for politics above all other passions, however turbulent, she was fitted to bear her part in any war and be the mother of one of the greatest English kings.

Upon this daughter, after mature consideration, Henry founded all his hopes. On two separate occasions he called his murmuring barons together and solemnly swore them to stand by Maud. Subsequently, in order to enhance her unifying authority, and to protect Normandy from the claims of Anjou after his death, he married her to the Count of Anjou, thus linking the interests of the most powerful state in Northern France with the family and natural succession in England. The English mood has never in later ages barred queens, and perhaps queens have served them best. But here at this time was a deep division, and a quarrel in which all parties and all interests could take sides. The gathered political arrays awaited the death of the King. The whole interest of the baronage, supported at this juncture by the balancing weight of the Church, was to limit the power of the Crown and regain their control of their own districts. Now in a division of the royal authority they saw their chance.

After giving the Island thirty years of peace and order and largely reconciling the Saxon population to Norman rule, Henry I expired on December 1,

1   Salic law, supposedly taken from French law, would exclude females from dynastic succession.

1135, in the confident hope that his daughter Maud would carry on his work. But she was with her husband in Anjou and Stephen was first on the spot. Swiftly returning from Blois, he made his way to London and claimed the crown. The secular forces were divided and the judgement of the Church would be decisive.

There was an additional complication. Henry I had a bastard son, Robert of Gloucester, a distinguished soldier and a powerful magnate in the West Country, who is usually regarded as one of the rare examples of a disinterested baron. Robert did not rate his chances sufficiently high to compete with either of the legitimate heirs. Almost from the beginning he loyally supported his half-sister Maud, and became one of Stephen's most determined opponents.

To the north, persuaded of the English decay, King David of Scotland, who was Maud's uncle, crossed the Border and laid claim to Northumbria. The Archbishop of York advanced against him, with the support of the mass of the Northern counties. He displayed the standards of the Yorkshire saints, and in a murderous battle at Northallerton, henceforward know as the Battle of the Standard, repulsed and slaughtered the invaders. This reverse, far from discouraging the malcontents, was the prelude to civil war. In 1139 Maud, freed from entanglements that had kept her in France, entered the kingdom to claim her rights. As Stephen had done, she found her chief support in the Church. The men who had governed England under Henry I, antagonised by Stephen's weakness towards the barons, joined his enemies. In 1141 a more or less general rebellion broke out against his rule, and he himself was taken prisoner at the Battle of Lincoln. The Bishop of Winchester, Stephen's own brother and hitherto his main supporter, now went over to Maud's side. For nearly a year Maud, uncrowned, was in control of England. The Londoners after some trial liked her even less than Stephen. Rising in fury, they drove her out of the capital. She fought on indomitably. But the strain upon the system had been too great. The Island dissolved into confused civil war. During the six years that followed there was neither law nor peace in large parts of the country.

The civil war developed into the first successful baronial reaction against the centralising policy of the kings. Stephen, faded with powerful rivals, had failed to preserve the rights of the Crown. The royal revenues decreased, royal control of administration lapsed; much of the machinery itself passed for a time out of use. Baronial jurisdiction reasserted its control; baronial castles overawed the people. It seemed that a divided succession had wrecked the work of the Norman kings. Men looked back with yearning to the efficient government of Henry I. But a greater than he was at hand.

In 1147 Robert of Gloucester died and the leadership of Maud's party devolved upon her son. Henry Plantagenet was born to empire. His grandfather, Fulk, had made of the Angevin lands, Anjou, Touraine, and Maine, a principality unsurpassed in France, and in resources more than the equal of Normandy. Fulk died in 1143, King of Jerusalem, leaving two sons to succeed him on that precarious throne, and a third, Geoffrey, as heir to his French dominions. Geoffrey's marriage with Maud had united the Norman and Angevin lands, and the child of this marriage was from his birth in 1133 recognised as the "master of many peoples". To contemporaries he was best known as Henry Fitz-Empress; but he carried into English history the emblem of his house, the broom, the *Planta Genesta*, which later generations were to make the name of this great dynasty, the Plantagenets. He embodied all their ability, all their energy, and not a little of that passionate, ruthless ferocity which, it was whispered, came to the house of Anjou from no mortal source, but from a union with Satan himself.

When scarcely fifteen, in 1147, Henry had actively championed his claim to the English throne on English soil. His small band of followers was then defeated by Stephen's forces, and he took refuge in Normandy. The Empress Maud gave up her slender hopes of success in the following year and joined her son in the duchy. Nineteen years of life remained before her, but she never set foot in England again. Work of piety, natural to the times, filled many of her days.

For a few years of comparative peace King Stephen was left in uneasy possession. In the meantime Henry was invested by his parents in 1150 as Duke of Normandy. The next year his father's death made him also Count of Anjou, Touraine, and Maine. In his high feudal capacity Henry repaired to Paris to render homage to his lord the King of France, of which country he already possessed, by the accepted law of the age, a large part.

Louis VII was a French Edward the Confessor; he practised with faithful simplicity the law of Christ. All his days were spent in devotion, and his nights in vigil or penance. When he left his own chapel he would delay the whole Court by waiting till the humblest person present had preceded him. These pious and exemplary habits did not endear him to his queen. Eleanor of Aquitaine was in her own right a reigning princess, with the warmth of the South in her veins. She had already complained that she had "married a monk and not a king" when this square-shouldered, ruddy youth, with his "countenance of fire", sprightly talk, and overflowing energy, suddenly presented himself before her husband as his most splendid vassal. Eleanor did not waste words in coming to a decision. The Papacy bowed to strong will in the high feudal chiefs, and Eleanor obtained a divorce from Louis VII in 1152 on the nominal ground of consanguinity. But what staggered the French Court and opened the eyes of its prayerful King was the sudden marriage of Eleanor to Henry two months later. Thus half of France passed out of royal control into the hands of Henry. Rarely have passion and policy flowed so buoyantly together. The marriage was one of the most brilliant political strokes of the age. Henry afterwards admitted his designs, and accepted the admiration of Europe for their audacity. He was nineteen and she was probably thirty; and, uniting their immense domains, they made common cause against all comers. To Louis VII were vouchsafed the consolations of the spirit; but even these were jarred upon by the problems of government.

War in all quarters lay before the royal pair. From all sides the potentates confronted the upstart. The King of France, who certainly had every conceivable cause of complaint; King Stephen of England, who disputed Henry's title to the Norman duchy, though without force to intervene across the Channel; the Count of Champagne; the Count of Perche; and Henry's own brother, Geoffrey – all spontaneously, and with good reason, fell upon him.

A month after the marriage these foes converged upon Normandy. But the youthful Duke Henry beat them back, ruptured and broken. The Norman army proved once again its fighting quality. Before he was twenty Henry had cleared Normandy of rebels and pacified Anjou. He turned forthwith to England. It was a valiant figure that landed in January 1153, and from all over England, distracted by civil wars, hearts and eyes turned towards him. Merlin had prophesied a deliverer; had he not in his veins blood that ran back to William the Conqueror, and beyond him, through his grandmother Matilda, wife of Henry I, to Cedric and the long-vanished Anglo-Saxon line? A wild surge of hope greeted him from the tormented Islanders, and when he knelt after his landing in the first church he found "to pray for a space, in the manner of soldiers", the priest pronounced the wish of the nation in the words, "Behold there cometh the Lord, the Ruler, and the kingdom is in his hand."

The baronage, on the other hand, saw their interest favoured by a stalemate; they wanted neither a victorious Stephen nor a triumphant Henry. The weaker the King the stronger the nobles. A treaty was concluded at Winchester in 1153 whereby Stephen made Henry his adopted son and his appointed heir. And when a year later Stephen died he was acclaimed and crowned King of England with more general hope and rejoicing than had ever uplifted any monarch in England since the days of Alfred the Great.

CHAPTER NINE

HENRY PLANTAGENET

*Henry II — royal government — assizes — war with the Church — the
Constitution of Clarendon — Becket —the invasion of Ireland — the
English pope — foundations of English Common Law — Royal Courts of
Justice — Henry's sons plot against their father — the death of Henry II*

THE ACCESSION of Henry II in 1154 began one of the most preg-
nant and decisive reigns in English history. The new sovereign
ruled an empire, and, as his subjects boasted, his warrant ran "from
the Arctic Ocean to the Pyrenees". England to him was but one —
the most solid though perhaps the least attractive — of his provinces. But he
gave to England that effectual element of external control which, as in the
days of William of Orange, was indispensable to the growth of national unity.
He was accepted by English and Norman as the ruler of both races and of the
whole country. The memories of Hastings were confounded in his person, and
after the hideous anarchy of civil war between robber barons all due attention
was paid to his commands. Thus, though a Frenchman, with foreign speech
and foreign modes, he shaped our country in a fashion of which the outline
remains to the present day.

After a hundred years of being the encampment of an invading army and
the battleground of its quarrelsome officers and their descendants England
became finally and for all time a coherent kingdom, based upon Christianity
and upon that Latin civilisation which recalled the message of ancient Rome.
Henry Plantagenet first brought England, Scotland, and Ireland into a certain
common relationship; he re-established the system of royal government which
his grandfather, Henry I, had prematurely erected. He relaid the foundations
of a central power, based upon the Exchequer and the judiciary, which was
ultimately to supersede the feudal system of William the Conqueror. The
King gathered up and cherished the Anglo-Saxon tradition of self-
government under royal command in shire and borough; he developed and
made permanent "assizes" as they survive today. By his Constitutions of
Clarendon he sought to fix the relationship of the Church and State and to
force the Church in its temporal character to submit itself to the life and law
of the nation. In this endeavour he had, after a deadly struggle, to retreat, and
it was left to Henry VIII, though centuries later, to avenge his predecessor by
destroying the shrine of St Thomas at Canterbury.

A vivid picture is painted of this gifted and, for a while, enviable man: square, thick-set, bull-necked, with powerful arms and coarse, rough hands; his legs bandy from endless riding; a large, round head and closely cropped red hair; a freckled face; a voice harsh and cracked. Intense love of the chase; other loves, which the Church deplored and Queen Eleanor resented; frugality in food and dress; days entirely concerned with public business; travel unceasing; moods various. It was said that he was always gentle and calm in times of urgent peril, but became bad-tempered and capricious when the pressure relaxed. "He was more tender to dead soldiers than to the living, and found far more sorrow in the loss of those who were slain than comfort in the love of those who remained." He journeyed hotfoot around his many dominions, arriving unexpectedly in England when he was thought to be in the South of France. He carried with him in his tours of each province wains loaded with ponderous rolls which represented the office files of his day. His Court and train gasped and panted behind him. Sometimes, when he had appointed an early start, he was sleeping till noon, with all the wagons and pack horses awaiting him fully laden. Sometimes he would be off hours before the time he had fixed, leaving everyone to catch up as best they could. Everything was stirred and moulded by him in England, as also in his other much greater estates, which he patrolled with tireless attention.

But this twelfth-century monarch, with his lusts and sports, his hates and his schemes, was no materialist; he was the Lord's Anointed, he commanded, with the Archbishop of Canterbury, the whole allegiance of his subjects. Such was the man who succeeded to the troubled and divided inheritance of Stephen. But when in one hour Henry II was King of England, Duke of Normandy, Lord of Aquitaine, Brittany, Poitou, Anjou, Maine, and Guienne, ruler from the Somme to the Pyrenees of more than half of France, all balance of power among the feudal lords was destroyed.

No episode opens to us a wider window upon the politics of the twelfth century in England than the quarrel of Henry II with his great subject and former friend, Thomas Becket, Archbishop of Canterbury. We have to realise the gravity of this conflict. The military State in feudal Christendom bowed to the Church in things spiritual; it never accepted the idea of the transference of secular power to priestly authority. But the Church, enriched continually by the bequests of hardy barons, anxious in the death agony about their life beyond the grave, became the greatest landlord and capitalist in the community. Rome used its ghostly arts upon the superstitions of almost all the actors in the drama. The power of the State was held in constant challenge by this potent interest. Questions of doctrine might well have been resolved, but how was the government of the country to be carried on under two conflicting powers, each possessed of immense claims upon limited national resources? This conflict was not confined to England. It was the root question of the European world, as it then existed.

Under William the Conqueror schism had been avoided in England by tact and compromise. Under Lanfranc the Church worked with the Crown, and each power reinforced the other against the turbulent barons or the oppressed commonalty. But now a great personality stood at the summit of the religious hierarchy, Thomas Becket, who had been the King's friend. He had been his Chancellor, or, as Ranke first remarked, "to use a somewhat equivalent expression, his most trusted cabinet minister". He had in both home and foreign affairs loyally served his master. He had reorganised the imposition of scutage, a tax that allowed money to commute personal service in arms, and thus eventually pierced the feudal system to its core. He had played his part in the acquisition of Brittany. The King felt sure that in Becket he had his own man – no mere servant, but a faithful comrade and colleague in the common endeavour. It was by the King's direct influence and personal effort that Becket was elected Archbishop.

From that moment all his gifts and impulses ran in another channel. Something like the transformation which carried Henry V from a rollicking prince to the august hero-King overnight was now witnessed in Becket. His private life had always been both pious and correct. He had of course been immersed in political affairs; nor was it as a sombre figure behind the throne. But whereas hitherto as a courtier and a prince he had rivalled all in magnificence and pomp, taking his part in the vivid pageant of the times, he now sought by extreme austerities to gather around himself the fame and honour of a saint. Becket pursued the same methods and ambitions in the ecclesiastical as previously he had done in the political sphere; and in both he excelled. He now championed the Church against the Crown in every aspect of their innumerable interleaving functions. He clothed this aggressive process with those universal ideas of the Catholic Church and the Papal authority which far transcended the bounds of our Island, covering Europe and reaching out into the mysterious and the sublime. After a tour upon the Continent and a conclave with the religious dignitaries of France and Italy he returned to England imbued with the resolve to establish the independence of the Church hierarchy of the State as represented by the King. Thus he opened the conflict which the wise Lanfranc had throughout his life striven to avoid. At this time the mood in England was ripe for strife upon this issue.

In a loose and undefined way Saxon England had foreshadowed the theory to which the Elizabethan reformers long afterwards returned. Both thought of the monarch as appointed by God, not only to rule the State, but to protect and guide the Church. In the eleventh century however the Papacy had been reinvigorated under Pope Gregory VII and his successors. Rome now began to make claims which were hardly compatible with the traditional notions of the mixed sovereignty of the King in all matters temporal and spiritual. The Gregorian movement held that the government of the Church ought to be in the hands of the clergy, under the supervision of the Pope. According to this view, the King was a mere layman whose one religious function was obedience to the hierarchy. The Church was a body apart, with its own allegiance and its own laws. By the reign of Henry II the bishop was not only a spiritual officer; he was a great landowner, the secular equal of earls; he could put forces in the field; he could excommunicate his enemies, who might be the King's friends. Who, then, was to appoint the bishop? And, when once appointed, to whom, if the Pope commanded one thing and the King another, did he owe his duty? If the King and his counsellors agreed upon a law contrary to the law of the Church, to which greater authority was obedience due? Thus there came about the great conflict between Empire and Papacy symbolised in the question of Investiture, of which the dispute between Henry II and Becket is the insular counterpart.

The struggle between Henry II is confused by the technical details over which it was fought. There was however good reason why the quarrel should have been engaged upon incidents of administration rather than upon the main principles which were at stake. The Crown resented the claim of the Church to interfere in the State; but in the Middle Ages no king dared to challenge the Church outright, or, much as he might hope to limit its influence, thought of a decisive breach. It was not till the sixteenth century that an English king in conflict with Papacy dared to repudiate the authority of Rome and nakedly declare the State supreme, even in spiritual matters. In the twelfth century the only practicable course was compromise. But the Church at this time was in no mood for a bargain. In every country the secular power took up the challenge; but it was hard to meet, and in Central Europe at least the struggle ended only in the exhaustion of both the Holy Roman Empire and the Papacy.

The Church in England, like the baronage, had gained greatly in power since the days of William the Conqueror and his faithful Archbishop Lanfranc. Stephen in his straits had made sweeping concessions to the Church, whose political influence then reached its zenith. These concessions, Henry felt, compromised his royal rights. He schemed to regain what had been lost, and as the first step in 1162 appointed his trusted servant Becket to be Archbishop of Canterbury, believing he would thus secure the acquiescence of the Episcopacy. In fact he provided the Church with a leader of unequalled vigour and obstinacy. He ignored or missed the ominous signs of the change in Becket's attitude, and proceeded to his second step, the publication in 1164 of the Constitutions of Clarendon. In these Henry claimed, not without considerable truth, to be re-stating the customs of the kingdom as they had been before the anarchy of Stephen's reign. He sought to retrace thirty years and to annul the effects of Stephen's surrender. But Becket resisted. He regarded Stephen's yieldings as irrevocable gains by the Church. He refused to let them lapse. Though he nominally accepted the Constitutions of Clarendon, he was soon at odds with the King over their application in his archdiocese. When, in October 1164, he was summoned to appear before the Great Council and explain his conduct he haughtily denied the King's authority and placed himself under the protection of the Pope and God.

Thus he ruptured that unity which had hitherto been deemed vital in the English realm, and in fact declared war with ghostly weapons upon the King. Stiff in defiance Becket took refuge on the Continent, where the same conflict was already distracting both Germany and Italy. The whole thought of the ruling classes in England was shaken by this grievous dispute. It endured for six years, during which the Archbishop of Canterbury remained in his French exile. Only in 1170 was apparent reconciliation brought about between him and the King at Fretéval, in Touraine. Each side appeared to waive its claims in principle. The King did not mention his rights and customs. The Archbishop was not called upon to give an oath. He was promised a safe return and full possession of his see. King and Primate met for the last time in the summer of 1170 at Chaumont. "My lord," said Thomas at the end, "my heart tells me that I part from you as one whom you shall see no more in this life." "Do you hold me as a traitor?" asked the King. "That be far from thee, my lord," replied the Archbishop; but he returned to Canterbury resolved to seek from the Pope unlimited power of excommunication wherewith to discipline his ecclesiastical forces. "The more potent and fierce the prince is," he wrote, "the stronger stick and harder chain is needed to bind him and keep him in order." "I go to England", he said, "whether to peace or destruction I know not; but God has decreed what fate awaits me."

Meanwhile, in Becket's absence, Henry had resolved to secure the peaceful accession of his son, the young Henry, by having him crowned in his own lifetime. The ceremony had been performed by the Archbishop of York, assisted by six other bishops. This action was bitterly resented by Becket as an infringement of a cherished right of his see. After the Fretéval agreement Henry supposed that bygones were to be bygones. But Becket had other views.

His welcome home after the years of exile was astonishing. At Canterbury the monks received him as an angel of God. "I am come to die among you," he said in his sermons, and again, "in this church there are martyrs, and God will soon increase their number." He made a triumphal progress through London, scattering alms to the beseeching and exalted people. Then hot-foot he proceeded to renew his excommunication of the clergy who had taken part in the crowning of young Henry. These unfortunate priests and prelates travelled in a bunch to the King, who was in Normandy. They told a tale not only of an ecclesiastical challenge, but of actual revolt and usurpation. They said that the Archbishop was ready "to tear the crown from the young King's head".

Henry Plantagenet, first of all his line, with all the fire of his nature, received these tidings when surrounded by his knights and nobles. He was transported with passion. "What a pack of fools and cowards," he cried, "I have nourished in my house, that not one of them will avenge me of this turbulent priest!" Another version says "of this upstart clerk". A council was immediately summoned to devise measures for reasserting the royal authority. In the main it shared the King's anger. Second thoughts prevailed. With all the stresses that existed in that fierce and ardent society, it was not possible that the realm could support a fearful conflict between the two sides of life represented by Church and State.

But meanwhile another train of action was in process. Four knights had heard the King's bitter words spoken in the full circle. They travelled fast to the coast. They crossed the Channel. They called for horses and rode to Canterbury. There on December 29, 1170, they found the Archbishop in the cathedral. The scene and the tragedy are famous. He confronted them with Cross and mitre, fearless and resolute in warlike action, a master of the histrionic arts. After haggard parley they fell upon him, cut him down with their swords, and left him bleeding like Julius Caesar, with a score of wounds to cry for vengeance.

This tragedy was fatal to the King. The murder of one of the foremost of God's servant, like the breaking of a feudal oath, struck at the heart of the age. All England was filled with terror. They acclaimed the dead Archbishop as a martyr; and immediately it appeared that his relics healed incurable diseases, and robes that he had worn by their mere touch relieved minor ailments. Here indeed was a crime, vast and inexpiable. When Henry heard the appalling news he was prostrated with grief and fear. All the elaborate process of law which he had sought to set on foot against this rival power was brushed aside by a brutal, bloody act; and though he had never dreamed that such a deed would be done there were his own hot words, spoken before so many witnesses, to fasten on him, for that age at least, the guilt of murder, and still worse, sacrilege.

The immediately following years were spent in trying to recover what he had lost by a great parade of atonement for his guilt. By the Compromise of Avranches in 1172 he made his peace with the Papacy on comparatively easy terms. Becket's sombre sacrifice had not been in vain. Until the Reformation the Church retained the system of ecclesiastical courts independent of the royal authority, and the right of appeal to Rome, two of the major points upon which Becket had defied the King.

Eighteen years of life lay before the King after Becket's death. In a sense they were years of glory. All Europe marvelled at the extent of Henry's domains, to which in 1171 he had added the lordship of Ireland.[1] Through the marriages of his daughters he was linked with the Norman King of Sicily, the King of Castile, and Henry the Lion of Saxony, who was a most powerful prince in Germany.

Yet Henry knew well that his splendour was personal in origin, tenuous and transient in quality; and he had also deep-clouding family sorrows. During these years he was confronted with no fewer than four rebellions by his sons. For the three eldest he had provided glittering titles: Henry held Normandy, Maine, and Anjou, Richard was given Aquitaine, and to Geoffrey went Brittany. These boys were typical sprigs of the Angevin stock. They wanted power as well as titles, and they bore their father no respect. Urged on by their

1   Henry's interest in Ireland was part military (the Normans had, with their Irish allies, captured Dublin in 1171) and part crusade that would relieve him from the uncompromising European disapproval that followed the murder of Becket. The papal bull issued for Henry's expedition came from Pope Adrian IV, born Nicholas Breakspear and the only Englishman to become pope. It was Henry's youngest son, John, who received the title, Lord of Ireland, in 1177.

mother, Queen Eleanor, who now lived in Poitiers apart from her husband, between 1173 and 1186 they rose in revolt in various combinations. On each occasion they could count of the active support of the watchful King of France.

John, whom he had striven to provide with an inheritance equal to that of his brothers, joined the final plot against him. In 1188 Richard, his eldest surviving son, after the death of young Henry, was making war upon him in conjunction with King Philip. Already desperately ill, Henry was defeated at Le Mans and recoiled into Touraine. When he saw in the list of conspirators against him the name of his son John, upon whom his affection had strangely rested, he abandoned the struggle with life. "Let things go as they will," he gasped. "Shame, shame on a conquered King." So saying, this hard, violent, brilliant, and lonely man expired at Chinon on July 6, 1189.

England has had greater soldier-kings and subtler diplomatists than Henry II, but no man has left a deeper mark upon our laws and institutions. The names of his battles have vanished with their dust, but his fame will live with the English Constitution and the English Common Law.[1] The disasters of Stephen's reign determined Henry not only to curb baronial independence and regain the ground lost by his predecessor, but to go much further. In place of a multitude of manorial courts where local magnates dispensed justice whose quality and character varied with the customs and temper of the neighbourhood, he planned a system of royal courts which would administer a law common to all England and all men.

The policy was not without peril. The King was wise enough to avoid a direct assault, for he knew, as the Conqueror had known, that to lay a finger upon the sanctity of customary rights would provoke disaster. His plan was to stretch old principles to take on new meaning. In an unwritten Constitution the limits of the King's traditional rights were vaguely defined. This opened a shrewd line of advance. For centuries before the Conquest Church and King had been the enemies of seigneurial anarchy, but there had been no question of swiftly extending the Crown's jurisdiction. Fastening upon the elastic Saxon concept of the King's Peace, Henry used it to draw all criminal cases into his courts. Every man had his own Peace, which it was a crime to break, and the more important the man the graver the breach. The King's Peace was the most important of all, and those who broke it could be tried in the King's

1   During the reign of Henry I (1100–35) the laws of England were written so that the ruling of the feudal system appeared quite separate from Saxon law. By the time of Henry II (1154–89) these two systems have been brought together. The great work that defined those laws was called *Treatise on the Laws and Customs of England*. For a long time it was thought that the author of the treatise was the famous justiciar (the chief officer of the Crown) Ranulf de Glanvill (sometimes *Glanvil*) – the work is still known as *Glanvill* – but now there is some doubt, although there is a good case for suggesting that if Glanvill did not write the treatise, then "by his wisdom" it was written. However, it is certainly true that this period of constitutional history gave England the basis for Common Law as it is practised today. Perhaps the irony of Glanvill's position is that Richard I got rid of him because it was said that he (Glanvill) was corrupt. He died on a Crusade in 1190.

court. But the King's Peace was limited, and often embraced only offences committed in the King's presence or on the King's highway or land. When the King died his Peace died with him and men might do as they willed. Cautiously and quietly Henry began to claim that the King's Peace extended over all England, and that no matter where it was broken offenders should be tried in the King's courts. Civil cases he attracted by straining a different principle, the old right of the King's court to hear appeals in cases where justice had been refused and to protect men in possession of their lands. He did not brandish what he was about; the changes that he made were introduced gradually and without legislation, so that at first they were hardly perceived. Rarely is it possible to state the date at which any innovation was made; yet at the King's death a clever man might have looked back and seen how much had been altered in the thirty-five years that Henry II had sat on the English throne.

But if Henry was to pose as a conservative in the legal sphere he must be consistent. Compulsion could play little part in his programme; it had to be the first principle of his policy to attract cases to his courts rather than to compel them. A bait was needed with which to draw litigants to the royal courts; the King must offer them better justice than they could have at the hands of their lords. Henry accordingly threw open to litigants in the royal courts a new procedure for them – trial by jury. *Regale quoddam beneficium* a contemporary called it – a royal boon; and the description illuminates both the origin of the jury and the part it played in the triumph of the Common Law. Henry did not invent the jury; he put it to a new purpose. The idea of the jury is the one great contribution of the Franks to the English legal system, for, unknown in this country before the Conquest, the germ of it lies far back in the practice of the Carolingian kings. In origin the jury was a royal instrument of administrative convenience: the King had the right to summon a body of men to bear witness under oath about the truth of any question concerning the royal interest. It was through this early form of jury that William the Conqueror had determined the Crown rights in the great Domesday survey. The genius of Henry II, perceiving new possibilities in such a procedure, turned to regular use in the courts as an instrument which so far had only been used for administrative purposes.

Only the King had the right to summon a jury. Henry accordingly did not grant it to private courts, but restricted it to those who sought justice before the royal judges. It was an astute move. Until this time both civil and criminal cases had been decided through the oath, the ordeal, or the duel. The court would order one of the litigants to muster a body of men who would swear to the justice of his cause and whom it was hoped God would punish if they swore falsely; or condemn him, under the supervision of a priest, to carry a red-hot iron, or eat a morsel of bread, or be plunged in a pool of water. If the iron did not burn or the bread choke or the water reject him, so that he could not sink, the Divine Providence was adjudged to have granted a visible sign that the victim was innocent.

The jury of Henry II was not the jury that we know. There were various forms of it; but in all there was this essential difference: the jury men were witnesses as well as judges of the facts. Good men and true were picked, not yet for their impartiality, but because they were the men most likely to know the truth. The modern jury, which knows nothing about the case till it is proved in court, was slow in coming. The process is obscure. A jury summoned to Westminster from distant parts might be reluctant to come. The way was long, the roads unsafe, and perhaps only three or four would arrive. The courts could not wait. An adjournment would be costly. To avoid delay and expense the parties might agree to rely on a jury *de circumstantibus*, a jury of bystanders. The few jurors who knew the truth of the matter would tell their tale to the bystanders, and then the whole body would deliver their evidence in open court to a jury entirely composed of bystanders.

Trial by jury became popular. Professional judges removed from local prejudice, whose outlook ranged above the interested or ignorant lord or his steward, armed with the King's power to summon juries, secured swifter decisions, and a strong authority to enforce them. Henry accordingly had to build up almost from nothing a complete system of royal courts, capable of absorbing a great rush of new work. The instrument to which he turned was the royal Council, the organ through which all manner of governmental business was already regularly carried out. It was to be the common parent of Chancery and Exchequer, of Parliament, of the Common Law courts, and those Courts of Prerogative on which the Tudors and Stuarts relied. At the onset of Henry II's reign it dealt almost indiscriminately with every kind of administrative business. On the judicial side the Court of the Exchequer, which tried cases affecting the royal revenue, was beginning to take shape; but in the main the Council in this aspect was scarcely more than the King's feudal court, where he did justice, like any other lord, among his vassals. Under Henry II all this was changed. The functions of the King's justices became more and more specialised. During the reigns of his sons the Council began to divide into two great courts, the King's Bench and the Common Pleas. They did not become fully separate till a century later. Thereafter, with the court of the Exchequer, they formed the backbone of the Common Law system down to the nineteenth century. In addition, travelling justices – "justices in eyre" – were from time to time appointed to hear all manner of business in the shires, whose courts were thus drawn into the orbit of royal justice.

But all this was only a first step. Henry also had to provide means whereby the litigant, eager for royal justice, could remove his case out of the court of his lord into the King's court. The device which Henry used was the royal writ. At all costs baronial rights must be formally respected; but by straining the traditional rights of the Crown it was possible to claim that particular types of case fell within the King's province. The whole course of a case might depend on the writ with which it was begun, for every writ had its special procedure, mode of trial, and eventual remedy. Thus the Saxon spirit of formalism survived. Henry II had only been able to break down the primitive methods of the early courts by fastening upon the law a procedure which became no less rigid. Yet, cumbersome though it was, the writ system gave to English law a conservative spirit which guarded and preserved its continuity from that time on in an unbroken line.

It is a maxim of English law that legal memory begins with the accession of Richard I in 1189. The date was set for a technical reason by a statute of Edward I. It could scarcely have been more appropriately chosen however, for with the close of the reign of Henry II we are on the threshold of a new epoch in the history of English law. With the establishment of a system of royal courts, giving the same justice all over the country, the old diversity of local law was rapidly broken down, and a law common to the whole land and to all men soon took its place. A modern lawyer, transported to the England of Henry's predecessor, would find himself in strange surroundings; with the system that Henry bequeathed to his son he would feel almost at home. That is the measure of the great King's achievement. He had laid the foundations of the English Common Law, upon which succeeding generations would build. Changes in the design would arise, but its main outlines were not to be altered.

It was in these fateful and formative years that the English-speaking peoples began to devise methods of determining legal disputes which survive in substance to this day. By the time Henry II's great-grandson, Edward I, had died English criminal and civil procedure had settled into a mould and a tradition which in the mass govern the English-speaking peoples today.

Most of it was then unwritten, and in England much still remains so. Lawyers could only ascertain it by studying reports and records of ancient decisions. For this they had already in this early age made their own arrangements. A century after Henry's death they began to group themselves into professional communities in London, the Inns of Court, half colleges, half law-schools, but predominantly secular, for the presence of clerics learned in the laws of Rome and the Canon Law of the Roman Church was not encouraged, and here they produced annual law reports, or "Year Books", as they were then called, whose authority was recognised by the judges, and which continued in almost unbroken succession for nearly three centuries. In all this time however only one man attempted a general and comprehensive statement of the English Common Law. About the year 1250 a Judge of Assize named Henry of Bracton produced a book of nearly nine hundred pages entitled *A Tract on the Laws and Customs of England*.[1] Nothing like it was achieved for several hundred years, but Bracton's method set an example, since followed throughout the English-speaking world, not so much of stating the Common Law as of explaining and commenting on it, and thus encouraging and helping later lawyers and judges to develop and expand it.

---

1   Written after Glanvill, and, since Churchill's manuscript was finished, there is some evidence that Bracton was not the author although he may have made distinguished amendments. Nevertheless, this Common Law "bible" remains known as "Bracton".

CHAPTER TEN

RICHARD, COEUR DE LION

Richard, Coeur de Lion — William the Marshal — the Crusades — the
capture of Cyprus — Saladin — Richard I held ransom — the legend
of Blondel — the treachery of Prince John — Archbishop Hubert
Walter — Justices of the Peace — the first mayor of London —
the death of the Lionheart

THE CHRISTIAN kingdom founded at Jerusalem after the First
Crusade had stood precariously for a century, guarded by the
military orders of the Knights Templars and Hospitallers. Its continued existence was largely due to the disunity that prevailed
among the Moslem lands surrounding it. At length the rise of the great
national leader of the Turks, or Saracens, united the Moslem power. In 1169
Saladin became Vizier of Egypt. Shortly afterwards he proclaimed himself
Sultan. By origin he was a Kurd, and by culture a Damascene. Soon his power
was stretching out into Syria, encircling the Crusaders' principalities on the
Levantine coast. He took Damascus in 1774 and Aleppo in 1183. In their
anxieties at these gathering dangers the Christian community in Jerusalem,
and Guy of Lusignan, the King, offered the threatened crown first to Philip of
France and then to Henry II, and made the West ring with cries for help. But
the quarrels of the Western princes prevented effective measures being taken
in time. In 1186 Saladin in his turn proclaimed a Holy War. He promised his
warlike hordes booty and adventure in this world and bliss eternal in the next,
and advanced upon Jerusalem. The Christian army of occupation which took
the field against him, perhaps ten thousand strong, was caught at a disadvantage in the thirsty desert and cut to pieces by greatly superior numbers
at Hattin. The King, the Grand Master of the Templars, and many of the great
nobles were taken prisoners. In October 1187 Jerusalem surrendered, and
thereafter all Palestine and Syria, except Tyre, Antioch, and Tripoli, fell again
into Moslem hands.

The shock of these events resounded throughout Europe. The Pope shared
the general horror of the Christian West. His legates traversed the Courts
enjoining peace among Christians and war against the infidel. The sovereigns
of the three greatest nations of the West responded to the call, and an intense
movement stirred the chivalry of England, France and Germany. To the
religious appeal was added the spur of the tax-gatherer. The "Saladin tithe"

was levied upon all who did not take the Cross. On the other hand, forgiveness of taxes and a stay in the payment of debts were granted to all Crusaders. The strongest armies ever yet sent to the East were raised. Germany marshalled a large array round the standard of Frederick Barbarossa. A Scandinavian fleet bore twelve thousand Norsemen through the Straits of Gibraltar. Thus did armoured Europe precipitate itself upon Asia. Meanwhile the first of the rescuers, Conrad of Montferrat, who, hastening from Constantinople, had saved Tyre, was already besieging Acre.

In the midst of these surgings Henry II died in sorrow and disaster. He made no attempt to prescribe the succession, and it passed naturally to Richard. The new King affected little grief at the death of a father against whom he was in arms. During his rebellion against his father he had pressed hard upon Henry II's rout at Le Mans in the very forefront of the cavalry without even wearing his mail. In the rearguard of the beaten army stood Henry's faithful warrior, William the Marshal. He confronted Richard and had him at his mercy. "Spare me!" cried Richard in his disadvantage; so the Marshal turned his lance against the prince's horse and killed it, saying with scorn, "I will not slay you. The Devil may slay you." This was humiliation and insult worse than death. It was not therefore without anxiety that the Marshal and his friends awaited their treatment at the hands of the sovereign to whom their loyalties must now be transferred. But King Richard rose at once above the past. He spoke with dignity and detachment of the grim incident so fresh and smarting in his mind. He confirmed his father's true servant in all his offices and honours, and sent him to England to act in his name. He gave him in marriage a Crown ward, the rich heiress of Pembroke, and at a stroke the Marshal became one of the most powerful of English barons.

Richard, with all his characteristic virtues and faults cast in a heroic mould, is one of the most fascinating medieval figures. He has been described as the creature and embodiment of the age of chivalry. In those days the lion was much admired in heraldry, and more than one king sought to link himself with its repute. When Richard's contemporaries called him "Coeur de Lion" they paid a lasting compliment to the king of beasts. Little did the English people owe him for his services, and heavily did they pay for his adventures. He was in England only twice for a few short months in his ten years' reign; yet his memory has always stirred English hearts, and seems to present throughout the centuries the pattern of the fighting man. He loved war, not so much for the sake of glory or political ends, but as other men love science or poetry, for the excitement of the struggle and the glow of victory. His life was one magnificent parade, which, when ended, left only an empty plain.

The King's heart was set upon the new Crusade. This task seemed made for him. The English would greatly have liked their King to look after their affairs, to give them peace and order, to nourish their growing prosperity, and to do justice throughout the land. But they understood that the Crusade was a high and sacred enterprise, and the Church taught them that in unseen ways it would bring a blessing upon them. Richard was crowned with peculiar state, by a ceremonial which, elaborating the most ancient forms and traditions of the Island monarchy, is still in all essentials observed today. Thereafter the King, for the sake of Christ's sepulchre, virtually put the realm up for sale. Money he must have at all costs for his campaign in far-off Palestine. He sold and re-sold every office in the State. He made new and revolutionarily heavy demands for taxation. He called for "scutage", the commutation of military service for a money payment, and later reintroduced "carucage", a levy on every hundred acres of land. Thus he filled his chests for the Holy War.

Confiding the government to two Justiciars, William Longchamp, Bishop of Ely, and Hugh de Puiset, Bishop of Durham, under the supervision of the one trustworthy member of his family, his mother, the old Queen, Eleanor of Aquitaine, he started for the wars in the winter of 1189. He had promised Philip of France to marry his sister Alice, about whom, except for her looks, the tales were none too good. Philip claimed that Richard had tried to seduce her, and there was bad feeling between the monarchs. However that may be, after Richard had marched across France and sailed to Sicily, where he rested for the winter, his mother brought out to him Berengaria, daughter of the King of Navarre, whom he had known and admired, and now resolved to marry. It was fitting that the "Lion-heart" should marry for love and not for policy, but the rejection of Alice prevented a tie between the Kings of France and England which had been deemed essential to their comradeship in the Crusade. Philip was little soothed for the affront by a compensation of ten thousand marks. The quarrels of England and France were not so lightly set aside, and jealousies and bickerings distressed the winter sojourn of the two allies in Sicily. The Anglo-French armies did not quit Sicily till the spring of 1191. Philip sailed direct to Acre. Richard paused in Cyprus. He quarrelled with the local Greek ruler, declared that an insult had been offered to his betrothed, conquered the island, and there wedded Berengaria. It was not until June 8, that he arrived with powerful forces before Acre.

The glamours of chivalry illumine the tale of the Third Crusade. All the chief princes of Europe were now in line around the doomed stronghold of Saladin, rivalling each other in prowess and jealousy. The sanctity of their cause was no bar to their quarrels and intrigues. King Richard dominated the scene. Fighting always in the most dangerous places, striking down the strongest foes, he negotiated all the time with Saladin. An agreement was in fact almost reached. To save his garrison Saladin offered to surrender his Christian captives, to pay a large indemnity, and to give up the cross, captured by him in Jerusalem, on which Christ – though this after twelve hundred years was not certain – had suffered. But the negotiations failed, and Richard in his fury massacred in cold blood the two thousand Saracen hostages who had been delivered as guarantees. Within five weeks of his arrival he brought the two years' siege to a successful conclusion.

By the time Acre fell King Richard's glory as a warrior and also his skill as a general were the talk of all nations. But the quarrels of the allies paralysed the campaign. Guy of Lusignan, the exiled King of Jerusalem, was disputing with Conrad of Montferrat for the crown. Richard took the one side and Philip the other. A compromise was arranged, but immediately the French king returned home to prosecute his designs in Flanders and to intrigue with Prince John against his absent brother. Duke Leopard of Austria, whom Richard had personally insulted, also took his departure. In these circumstances the Crusading army, ably led by Richard, in spite of the victory at Arsuf, where many thousand infidels were slain, could do no more than reach an eminence which commanded a distant view of the Holy city. The King veiled his eyes, not bearing to look upon the city he could not enter. He resolved to retreat to the coast. In the next year, 1192, he captured Jaffa. Once again the distant prospect of Jerusalem alone rewarded the achievements of the Crusaders, and once again they fell back frustrated.

By now the news from England was so alarming that the King felt it imperative to return home. Late in 1192 the King set out for home. Wrecked in the Adriatic, he sought to make his way through Germany in disguise, but his enemy the Duke of Austria was soon upon his track. He was arrested, and held prisoner in a castle. So valuable a prize was not suffered to remain in the Duke's hands. The Emperor himself demanded the famous captive. For many months his prison was a secret of the Imperial court, but, as a pretty legend tells us, Blondel, Richard's faithful minstrel, went from castle to castle striking the chords which the King loved best, and at last was rewarded by an answer from Richard's own harp.

William Longchamp, Bishop of Ely, and, with magnificent pluralism, Papal Legate, Chancellor, and Justiciar, had addressed himself with fidelity and zeal to the task of governing England, entrusted to him by Richard in 1189. Emulating the splendour of a monarch, he moved about the country with a pompous retinue, and very soon drew upon himself the envy and then the active hatred of the whole nobility. As the King's faithful servant he saw that the chief danger lay in the over-mighty position of Prince John. The indulgence of Richard had allowed his brother to form a state within a state. John held the shires of Derby, Nottingham, Somerset, Dorset, Devon, and Cornwall; the Earldom of Gloucester, with wide lands in South Wales; the honours of Lancaster, Wallingford, Eye, and Peverel. For the revenues which John drew from these lands he rendered no account to the Exchequer. Their sheriffs were responsible to him alone; their judicial business was transacted by his servants, their writs issued by his chancery and in his name. The royal officers and judges dared not enter John's shires. Bishop Longchamp determined to resist this dual system of government. His personal ostentation and arrogant airs had already multiplied his difficulties. Socially of humble origin, and by race a foreigner, he antagonised the other members of the Council, and provoked them to side with John, who knew well how to turn all this to his profit.

In the summer of 1191 there was open conflict between the two parties, and Longchamp marched against a revolt of John's adherents in the North Midlands. This was a serious crisis. Fortunately however the King, far off in the Levant, had sent home Walter de Coutances, the Archbishop of Rouen, to watch the royal interests. The Archbishop formed a third party, loyal to the King, offended by Longchamp, but unwilling to support John; and presently he succeeded to Longchamp's position when the latter fled from England in October. The return of Philip Augustus from the Crusade in this same autumn brought new opportunities to John's ambition. The French king saw in Richard's absence the chance of breaking up the Angevin power and driving the English out of France. In John he found a willing partner. It was agreed between them that Philip Augustus should attack Normandy, while John raised a revolt in England.

Early in 1193, at a moment already full of peril, the grave news reached England that the King was prisoner "somewhere in Germany". There was general and well-founded consternation among the loyal bulk of his subjects. John declared that Richard was dead, appeared in arms, and claimed the crown. That England was held for Richard in his long absence against all these powerful and subtle forces is a proof of the loyalties of the feudal age. A deep sense of his heroic character and sacred mission commanded the allegiance of a large number of resolute, independent people whose names are unknown to history. The Church never flinched; Walter de Coutances of Rouen stood firm; the Queen-Mother with septuagenarian vigour stood by her eldest son; these dominated the Council, and the Council held the country. The coasts were guarded against an impending French invasion. John's force melted. In April the strain was relieved by the arrival of authoritative news that Richard was alive. Prince John put the best face he could upon it and stole away to France.

The Holy Roman Empire demanded the prodigious ransom of a hundred and fifty thousand marks, twice the annual revenue of the English Crown. One hundred thousand was to be ready in London before the King was liberated. Richard approved and the English Council agreed. Meanwhile Philip and John were active on the other side. They offered the Emperor eighty thousand marks to keep the English king under lock and key till Michaelmas 1194, or a hundred and fifty thousand marks to deliver him into their hands. But the Emperor felt that his blackmailing honour was engaged to Richard, with whom he had, perhaps precipitately, settled the figure. Once Philip knew that the Emperor would not go back upon his bargain he sent John his notorious message: "Have a care – the Devil is unloosed."

It remained to collect the ransom. The charge staggered the kingdom. Yet nothing was more sacred than the feudal obligation to ransom the liege lord, above all when he enjoyed the sanctity of a Crusader. The Justiciar, the Archbishops, and Queen Eleanor addressed themselves to their grievous task. The Church faced its duty. It was lawful to sacrifice even the most holy ornaments of the cathedrals for the ransom of a Christian lost in the Holy War. From all the lands a new scutage was taken. All laymen had to give a quarter of their movables. The Church lands bore an equal burden; they gave their plate and treasure, and three of the monastic orders yielded unresistingly a year's wool crop. Prince John of course set an example in collecting these taxes throughout his shires. His agents dwelt upon the sacred duty of all to pay, and he kept the proceeds of their faith and loyalty for himself. Three separate attempts were made to gather the money, and although England and Normandy, taxed to the limit, could not scrape together the whole of the sum required, the Emperor, satisfied that he could get no more, resolved to set his captive at liberty.

At the end of 1193 the stipulated first instalment was paid, and at the beginning of February 1194 Richard Coeur de Lion was released from bondage. He picked his way, we may be assured, with care across Europe, avoiding his French domains, and on March 16 arrived again in London among citizens impoverished but still rejoiced to see him and proud of his fame. He found John again in open rebellion, having seized castles and raised forces with French aid. The new Justiciar and the Council were already acting against the traitor prince, and Richard lent the weight of his strong right arm as well as the majesty of his name to the repression of the revolt. John fled once more to France. The King was re-crowned in London with even more elaborate ceremony than before. As he was now plainly at war with Philip Augustus, his first, last, and only measures of government were to raise money and gather knights. These processes well started, he crossed the Channel to defend his French possessions. He never set foot in England again. But the Islanders owed him no grudge. All had been done as was right and due.

The mere arrival of the mighty warrior in France was enough to restore the frontiers and to throw King Philip and his forces upon an almost abject defensive. John sought pardon from the brother and liege lord he had so foully wronged. He did not sue in vain. With the full knowledge that if John had had his way he would still be a captive in a German castle, dethroned, or best of all dead – with all the long story of perfidy and unnatural malice in his mind, Coeur de Lion pardoned John, embraced him in fraternal love, and restored him to some of his estates, except certain fortresses which the barest prudence obliged him to reserve. This gesture was admired for its grandeur, though not perhaps for its wisdom, by the whole society, lay and spiritual, of Christendom.

The five remaining years of Richard's reign were spent in defending his French domains and raising money for that purpose from England. Once again the country was ruled by a deputy, this time Hubert Walter, a man bred in the traditions of Henry II's official Household as the right-hand man of Rannulf Glanvill; no feudal amateur, but a professional administrator by training and experience. Hubert Walter was now Archbishop of Canterbury, and Richard's Justiciar. He was to become King John's Chancellor. Thus for ten years he was the kingdom's chief Minister. He had been extremely useful to Richard on the Crusade, on which he had accompanied him, and had been prominent in the organisation of the ransom. With determination, knowledge, and deft touch he developed the system of strong centralised government devised by Henry II. Hubert Walter stands out as one of the great medieval administrators. The royal authority was reasserted in the North; commissions of inquiry dealt with unfinished judicial and financial business; other commissions, with the help of local juries, carried out exhaustive inquiries into royal rights and the administration of justice. A new machinery for keeping the peace was devised, to which the origin of the Justices of the Peace can be traced, and the office of Coroner now emerged clearly for the first time. As head of the Exchequer, Walter de Coutances, Archbishop of Rouen, attempted the revision of taxation and of the existing military system. New assessments of land were begun, weights and measures standardised, and the frauds of cloth-workers and dealers purged or curbed. New concessions, involving the precious privilege of local self-government, were granted to London[1] and the principal towns. Throughout the length and breadth of the land the machinery of government was made to work easily and quietly.

The system of administration devised by Henry II – the Civil Service as we may call it – had stood the test, and, undisturbed by royal interventions, consolidated itself to the general convenience and advantage. It was proved that the King, to whom all allegiance had been rendered, was no longer the sole guarantee for law and order. There were other sureties upon which in addition the English nation could rely.

In France the war with Philip proceeded in a curious fashion. The negotiations were unceasing. Every year there was a truce, which every year was broken as the weather and general convenience permitted. In 1199, when the difficulties of raising revenue for the endless war were at their height, good news was brought to King Richard. It was said there had been dug up near the castle of Chaluz, on the lands of one of his vassals, a treasure of wonderful quality; a group of golden images of an emperor, his wife, sons, and daughters, seated round a table, also of gold, had been unearthed. The King claimed this treasure as lord paramount. The lord of Chaluz resisted the demand, and the King laid siege to his small, weak castle. On the third day, as he rode daringly near the wall, confident in his hard-tried luck, a bolt from a crossbow struck him in the left shoulder by the neck. The wound, already deep, was aggravated by the necessary cutting out of the arrow-head. Gangrene set in, and Coeur de Lion knew that he must pay a soldier's debt. He prepared for death with fortitude and calm, and in accordance with the principles he had followed. He arranged his affairs; he divided his personal belongings among his friends or bequeathed them to charity. He sent for his mother, the redoubtable Eleanor, who was at hand. He declared John to be his heir, and made all present swear fealty to him, and died in the forty-second year of his age on April 6, 1199, worthy, by the consent of all men, to sit with King Arthur and Roland and other heroes of martial romance at some Eternal Round Table, which we trust the Creator of the Universe in His comprehension will not have forgotten to provide.

---

1   Henry Fitz Ailwin became the first mayor of London in 1191.

CHAPTER ELEVEN

⊰ MAGNA CARTA ⊱

*King John — the murder of Prince Arthur — Normandy returned
to the French — the death of Eleanor of Aquitaine — war with the
Church — the papal interdict — the King excommunicated — the barons'
revolt — Magna Carta*

THE CHARACTER of the prince who now ascended the throne of
England and became Lord of Normandy, Anjou, Touraine, and
Maine, claimant to Brittany and heir to Queen Eleanor's Aquitaine,
was already well known. Richard had embodied the virtues which
men admire in the lion, but there is no animal in nature that combines the
contradictory qualities of John. He united the ruthlessness of a hardened
warrior with the craft and subtlety of a Machiavellian. Although from time to
time he gave way to furious rages, in which "his eyes darted fire and his
countenance became livid", his cruelties were conceived and executed with a
cold, inhuman intelligence. Monkish chroniclers have emphasised his violence, greed, malice, treachery, and lust. But other records show that he was
often judicious, always extremely capable, and on occasions even generous.
Moreover, when the long tally is added it will be seen that the British nation
and the English-speaking world owe far more to the vices of John than to the
labours of virtuous sovereigns; for it was through the union of many forces
against him that the most famous milestone of our rights and freedom was in
fact set up.

Although Richard had declared John to be King there were two views upon
the succession. Geoffrey, his elder brother, had left behind him a son, Arthur,
Prince of Brittany. It was already possible to hold that this grandson of Henry
II of an elder branch had a prior right against John, and that is now the law of
primogeniture. William the Marshal put the point before the Archbishop of
Canterbury, but they both decided that John had the right. Queen Eleanor
stood by her son against the grandson, whose mother she had never liked. John
was accepted without demur in England. In the French provinces however the
opposite view prevailed. King John found himself compelled to fight at
greater odds than his predecessors for his possessions on the Continent. He
was also opposed by an increasing resistance to taxation for that purpose in
England.

From the first John feared Arthur. He had been in Brittany and at Arthur's

Court when the news of Richard's death reached him. He had made good haste out of so dangerous an area. Arthur was received at Le Mans with enthusiasm. He did homage to Philip for Anjou, Maine, and Touraine. John's strength lay only in Aquitaine and in Normandy. The war and negotiations continued in the fitful style of the preceding reign, but without the prestige of Coeur de Lion on the side of the English Crown. In 1202 Philip, as John's overlord in respect of certain territories, issued a summons in due form citing John before his Court to answer charges made against him by the barons of Poitou. John replied that he was not amenable to such a process. Philip answered that he was summoned as Count of Poitou. John declared that the King of England could not submit himself to such a ritual. Philip rejoined that the King of France could not lose his rights over a vassal because that vassal happened to acquire another dignity. All legal expedient being exhausted, John, who was not even promised safe-conduct for his return, refused to attend the Court, and was accordingly sentenced to be deprived of all the lands which he held in France because of his failure of service to his overlord. Thus armed with a legal fight recognised by the jurists of the period, Philip invaded Normandy in the summer of 1202, capturing many towns with practically no resistance. The French King knighted Arthur, invested him with all the fiefs of which John had been deprived, except Normandy and Guienne, and betrothed him to his daughter Mary. Arthur was now sixteen.

When we reflect that the French provinces counted just as much with the Plantagenet kings as the whole realm of England it is obvious that a more virtuous man than John would be incensed at such treatment, and its consequences. His pent-up feelings roused in him an energy unexpected by his foes. Arthur, hearing that his grandmother Eleanor was at the castle of Mirabeau in Poitou with a scanty escort, surrounded the castle, stormed the outworks, and was about to gain custody of this important and hostile old Queen. Eleanor contrived in the nick of time to send word to John, who was at Le Mans. Her son with ample forces covered the eighty miles between them in forty-eight hours, surprised Arthur and the besiegers at daybreak, and, as he declared, "by the favour of God" got the lot. Arthur and all who stood with him, Hugh of Lusignan and a cluster of barons who had revolted, two hundred knights or more, fell at a stroke into John's power, and his mother was delivered from her dangerous plight.

Arthur was imprisoned at Falaise and then at Rouen. No one doubted that he lay in mortal peril. All those barons of Brittany who were still loyal to John asked that the Prince should be released, and on John's refusal went into immediate rebellion. John felt that he would never be safe so long as Arthur lived. This was certainly true. The havoc of disunity that was being wrought throughout the French provinces by the French king using Arthur as a pawn might well have weighed with a better man than John. Arthur, caught in open fight besieging his own grandmother, was a prisoner of war. The horrid crime of murder has often been committed for reasons of state upon lesser temptations than now assailed this exceptionally violent king. No one knows what happened to Arthur. An impenetrable veil descends upon the tragedy of Rouen. The officer commanding the fortress, one Hubert de Burgh, of whom more and better hereafter, gave out that upon the King's order he had delivered his prisoner at Easter 1203 to the hands of agents sent by John to castrate him, and that Arthur had died of the shock. This explanation by no means allayed the ill-feeling aroused in Brittany and elsewhere. Hubert then declared that Arthur was still alive, and John stated that he was glad his orders had been disobeyed. However it may be, Arthur was never seen again. That he was murdered by John's orders was not disputed at the time nor afterwards, though the question remains unanswered.[1]

Although high nobles and common people in large numbers were in those times frequently put to death without trial and for reasons of hate or policy, the murder by a king of an equal confirmed the bad impression which all the world had formed of John. Brittany and the central provinces of the Angevin Empire revolted. Philip had come to terms with each province, and at Easter 1203 he made a voyage down the Loire to Saumur. A deep wedge had already been driven between the northern and the southern halves of John's Continental possessions. Having encircled Normandy, Philip prepared to strike at the stronghold of the Angevin power. John, awake to his danger, poured in treasure and supplies to strengthen his defences. The military position was not yet desperate, and if John had not at the end of 1203 after a series of savage but ineffectual raids precipitately quitted Normandy he might, drawing supplies from England, have held the duchy indefinitely. But, as Philip took fortress after fortress in Central Normandy, John's nerve failed, and the Normans, not unwilling to find an excuse for surrender, made English indifference their justification. In March 1204 King Richard's "fair child", the frowning Château Gaillard, fell, and the road to Rouen lay open. Three months later the capital itself was taken, and Normandy finally became French.

No English tears need have been shed over this loss. The Angevin Empire at its peak had no real unity. Time and geography lay on the side of the French. The separation proved as much in the interest of England as of France. It rid the Island of a dangerous, costly distraction and entanglement, turned its thought and energies to its own affairs, and above all left a ruling class of alien origin with no interest henceforth that was not English or at least insular. These consolations did not however dawn on John's contemporaries, who saw only a disastrous and humiliating defeat, and blamed a King already distrusted by the people and at variance with the nobility.

The very success of Henry II in re-establishing order and creating an efficient central administration had left new difficulties for those who came after him. Henry II had created an instrument so powerful that it needed

---

1 There is strong opinion that, in a fit of drunken rage, King John himself killed Arthur on April 3, 1203 and had his body thrown into the River Seine. See, for example, *Domesday Book to Magna Carta, 1087–1216*, A.L. Poole (Oxford University Press, 1955, second edition).

careful handling. He had restored order only at the cost of offending privilege. His fiscal arrangements were original, and drastic in their thoroughness. His work had infringed feudal custom at many points. All this had been accepted because of the King's tactful management and in the reaction from anarchy. Richard I, again, had left England in the hands of able administrators, and the odium of their strict government and financial ingenuity fell on them directly, and stopped short of the King, radiant in the halo of a Crusader and fortunate in his absence. John was at hand to bear the brunt in person.

John, like William Rufus, pressed to logical limits the tendencies of his father's system. There were arrears in the payment of scutage from Richard's reign, and more money was needed to fight the French king, Philip Augustus. But a division had opened in the baronage. The English barons of John's reign had become distinct from his Norman feudatories and not many families now held lands on both sides of the Channel. Even King Richard had met with refusals from his English nobles to fight abroad. Disputes about foreign service and payment of scutage lay at the root of the baronial agitation. By systematic abuse of his feudal prerogatives John drove the baronage to violent resistance. English society was steadily developing. Class interests had assumed sharper definition. Many barons regarded attendance or suit at Court as an opportunity for exerting influence rather than for rendering dutiful service. The sense of Church unity grew among the clergy, and corporate feeling in the municipalities. All these classes were needed by the new centralised Government; but John preferred to emphasise the more ruthless aspects of the royal power.

The year 1205 brought a crisis. The loss of Normandy was followed by the death of John's mother, Eleanor, to whose influence he had owed much of his position on the mainland. The death of Archbishop Hubert Walter, who for the last ten years had controlled the whole machinery of administration, deprived him of the only statesman whose advice he respected and whose authority stood between the Crown and the nation. It also re-opened the thorny question of who should elect the Primate of England.

The Papal throne at this time was occupied by Innocent III, one of the greatest of the medieval Popes, renowned for his state-craft and diplomacy, and intent on raising to its height the temporal power of the Church. The dispute between John and the monastery of Canterbury over the election to the Archbishopric offered Innocent the very chance he sought for asserting Papal authority in England. Setting aside the candidates both of the Crown and of the Canterbury clergy, he caused Stephen Langton to be selected with great pomp and solemnity at Rome in December 1206. King John, confident of his sufficient influence in the Papal Court to secure the election of his own candidate, had imprudently acknowledged the validity of the Papal decision beforehand. It was with pardonable anger that he learned how neatly Innocent had introduced a third and successful candidate, whose qualifications were unimpeachable. Stephen Langton was an English cardinal of the highest character, and one of the most famous doctors of the Paris schools. In his wrath, and without measuring the strength of his opponents, the King proceeded to levy a bloodless war upon the Church. Innocent III and Stephen Langton were not men to be browbeaten into surrender and they possessed in an age of faith more powerful weapons than any secular monarch. When John began to persecute the clergy and seize Church lands the Pope retaliated by laying all England under an interdict. For more than six years the bells were silent, the doors of the churches were closed against the devout; the dead must be buried in unconsecrated ground and without the last communion. Many of John's subjects were assured of damnation for themselves or their loved ones on this account alone.

When John hardened his heart to the interdict and redoubled the attacks upon Church property, the Pope, in 1209, took the supreme step of excommunication. The King's subjects were thereby absolved from their allegiance; his enemies received the blessing of the Church and were sanctified as Crusaders. But John was stubborn and unabashed. Interdict and excommunication brought no ghostly terrors to his soul. Indeed they aggravated the violence of his measures to a point which his contemporaries could only attribute to insanity. The royal administration, never more efficient, found little difficulty in coping with the fiscal and legal problems presented to it or in maintaining order. The interdict, if a menace, was also an opportunity for which John's plans were well matured. The ecclesiastical property of clerics who fled abroad was seized as forfeit by the Crown; and as more and more bishoprics and abbeys fell vacant their revenues were exploited by royal custodians. Thus the Exchequer overflowed with the spoils. But for the combination of the Church quarrel with stresses of mundane politics, the Crown might have established a position not reached till the days of Henry VIII.

After the loss of Normandy John had embarked upon a series of grandiose schemes for a Continental alliance against Philip Augustus. He found allies in the Emperor Otto IV and the Counts of Toulouse and Flanders; but his breach with the Church hastened a far more formidable league between the King of France and the Papacy, and in 1213 he had to choose between submission and a French invasion, backed by all the military and spiritual resources which Innocent III could set in motion. The King's insecurity at home forced him to bow to the threat, and Innocent rejoiced in victory upon his own terms.

John however was not at the end of his devices, and by a stroke of cunning choice enough to be called political genius he turned defeat into something very like triumph. If he could not prevail he would submit; if he submitted he would repent; if he repented there must be no limit to his contrition. At all costs he must break the closing circle of his foe. He spread before Innocent III the lure of temporal sovereignty which he knew that the Pontiff could never resist. He offered to make England a fief of the Papacy, and to do homage to the Pope as his feudal lord. Innocent leapt at this addition to his worldly dignities. He forgave the penitent King; he took him and the realm of England under his especial protection. He accepted the sovereignty of England from the hands of John, and returned it to him as his vassal with his blessing.

This turned the tables upon John's secular enemies. He was now the darling of the Church. Philip Augustus, who at heavy expense had gathered his armies to invade England as a Crusader for his own purposes, thought himself ill-used by the sudden tergiversation of his spiritual ally. He was indignant, and not at all inclined to relinquish the prey he had so long held in view. The barons also found meagre comfort in this transformation. Their grievances remained unredressed, their anger unappeased. Even in the English Church there was a keen division. The English Episcopate saw themselves now carried into a subjection to Rome far beyond what their piety or interest required, and utterly at variance with the tradition in which they had been reared. Obedience to the Supreme Pontiff was a sacred duty, but it could be carried into excessive interpretations. Stephen Langton himself, the Pope's elect, was as good an Englishman as he was a Churchman. He foresaw the unbridled exploitation by Rome of the patronage of the English Church and the wholesale engrossment of its benefices by Italian nominees. He became almost immediately an opposing force to the Pope. King John, who had lain at Dover, quaking but calculating, may have laughed while he pulled all these strings and threw his enemies into confusion.

Both John and Innocent persevered in their new partnership, and the disaffected barons drew together under the leadership of Stephen Langton. The war with the French king was continued, and John's demands in money and service kept the barons' anger hot. In 1214 an English expedition which John had led to Poitou failed. In Northern France the army commanded by his nephew, Otto of Saxony, and by the Earl of Salisbury, was defeated by King Philip at Bouvines. This battle destroyed in a day the whole Continental combination on which John's hopes had been based. Here again was the opportunity of the King's domestic enemies. They formed plans to restrain the rule of a despotic and defeated King, and openly threatened revolt unless their terms were accepted. Left to themselves, they might have ruined their cause by rancorous opposition and selfish demands, but Archbishop Langton, anxious for a just peace, exercised a moderating influence upon them. Nor could the King, as a Papal vassal, openly disregard Langton's advice.

But John still had one final resource. Encouraged by the Pope, he took the vows of a Crusader and invoked sentence of excommunication upon his opponents. This was not denied him. The conditions of 1213 were now entirely reversed. The barons, who had thought to be Crusaders against an excommunicated King, were now under the ban themselves. But this agile use of the Papal thunders had robbed them of some of their virtues as a deterrent. The barons, encouraged by the King's defeat abroad, persisted in their demands in spite of the Papal Bull. A great party in the Church stood with them. In vain did John manoeuvre, by the offer to grant freedom of election to the Church, to separate the clergy from the barons. Armed revolt seemed the only solution. Although in the final scene of the struggle the Archbishop showed himself unwilling to go to the extreme of civil war, it was he who persuaded the barons to base their demands upon respect for ancient custom and law, and who gave them some principle to fight for besides their own class interests. After forty years' experience of the administrative system established by Henry II the men who now confronted John had advanced beyond the magnates of King Stephen's time. They had learned to think intelligently and constructively. In place of the King's arbitrary despotism they proposed, not the withering anarchy of feudal separatism, but a system of checks and balances which would accord the monarchy its necessary strength, but would prevent its perversion by a tyrant or a fool. The leaders of the barons in 1215 groped in the dim light towards a fundamental principle. Government must henceforward mean something more than the arbitrary rule of any man, and custom and the law must stand even above the King. It was this idea, perhaps only half understood, that gave unity and force to the barons' opposition and made the Charter which they now demanded imperishable.

On a Monday morning in June, between Staines and Windsor, the barons and Churchmen began to collect on the great meadow at Runnymede. A small cavalcade appeared from the direction of Windsor. Gradually men made out the faces of the King, the Papal Legate, the Archbishop of Canterbury, and several bishops. They dismounted without ceremony. Someone, probably the Archbishop, stated briefly the terms that were suggested. The King declared at once that he agreed. He said the details should be arranged immediately in his chancery. The original "Articles of the Barons" on which Magna Carta is based exist to day in the British Museum. They were sealed in a quiet, short scene, which has become one of the most famous in our history, on June 15, 1215. Afterwards the King returned to Windsor. Four days later, probably, the Charter itself was engrossed. In future ages it was to be used as the foundation of principles and systems of government of which neither King John nor his nobles dreamed.[1]

At the beginning of the year 1216 there had seemed to be every chance that John would still defeat the baronial opposition and wipe out the humiliation of Runnymede. Yet before the summer was out the King was dead, and the Charter survived the denunciation of the Pope and the arbitrament of war. In the next hundred years it was reissued thirty-eight times, at first with a few substantial alterations, but retaining its original characteristics. Little more was heard of it until the seventeenth century. After more than two hundred years a Parliamentary Opposition struggling to check the enrichments of the Stuarts upon the liberty of the subject rediscovered it and made of it a rallying cry against oppression. Thus was created the glorious legend of the "Charter of an Englishman's liberties".

If we set aside the rhetorical praise which has been so freely lavished upon the Charter and study the document itself we may find it rather surprising reading. It is in a form resembling a legal contract, and consists of sixty-one clauses, each dealing either with the details of feudal administration and custom or with elaborate provisions for securing the enforcement of the

1   There are four surviving copies, made at the time, of Magna Carta. Two are in the British Library, one at Lincoln Cathedral and the fourth at Salisbury Cathedral.

promises which it embodies. It is entirely lacking in any spacious statement of the principles of democratic government or the rights of man. It is not a declaration of constitutional doctrine, but a practical document to remedy current abuses in the feudal system. In the forefront stand the questions of scutage, of feudal reliefs and of wardship. The word "freeman" was a technical feudal term, and it is doubtful whether it included even the richer merchants, far less the bondmen or humbler classes who make up the bulk of a nation. It implies on the king's part a promise of good government for the future, but the terms of the promise are restricted to the observance of the customary privileges and interests of the baronial class. The barons on their part were compelled to make some provision for their tenants, the limits forced on John being vaguely applied to the tenants-in-chief as well; but they did as little as they safely and decently could. The villeins, in so far as they were protected, received such solicitous attention as befitted valuable chattels attached to the manor and not as free citizens of the realm.

The thirteenth century was to be a great age of Parliamentary development and experiment, yet there is no mention in Magna Carta of Parliament or representation of any but the baronial class. The great watchwords of the future here find no place. The actual Charter is a redress of feudal grievances extorted from an unwilling king by a discontented ruling class insisting on its privileges. If the thirteenth-century magnates understood little and cared less for popular liberties or Parliamentary democracy, they had all the same laid hold of a principle which was to be of prime importance for the future development of English society and English institutions. Throughout the document it is implied that here is a law which is above the King and which even he must not break. This reaffirmation of a supreme law and its expression in a general charter is the great work of Magna Carta; and this alone justifies the respect in which men have held it. The reign of Henry II, according to the most respected authorities, initiates the rule of law. But the work as yet was incomplete: the Crown was still above the law; the legal system which Henry had created could become, as John showed, an instrument of oppression.

Now for the first time the King himself is bound by the law. The root principle was destined to survive across the generations and rise paramount long after the feudal background of 1215 had faded in the past. The Charter became in the process of time an enduring witness that the power of the Crown was not absolute.[1]

1 Magna Carta had such authority that, if the king broke his promises, the Charter gave the council of twenty-five barons the right to go to war with the monarch. The term Magna Carta, at the time, was more a reference to its size than its then constitutional significance; this Great Charter was larger than the very much shorter Forest Charter of 1217. From the mid-fourteenth century Magna Carta was a benchmark in law making. The seventeenth-century authors of the Grand Remonstrance and Petition of Right believed they were following its sound constitutional footsteps. By the twentieth century there was a school that believed the document was nothing to do with common man and all to do with baronial interests. The true meaning of Magna Carta may be what it has come to signify.

CHAPTER TWELVE

THE MOTHER OF PARLIAMENTS

The death of King John – Prince Henry becomes Henry III – the Dauphin
lands in England to claim the throne – William the Marshal rules
England – Archbishop Langton fights for English rights – Hubert de
Burgh, the last of the great Justiciars – the Fair of Lincoln – the
Dauphin leaves England – re-issue of Magna Carta – Henry III assumes
his majority – the fall of de Burgh – Peter des Roches, the scheming
bishop – the rise of the Poitevins – Robert Grosseteste opposes Rome –
the rise of Simon de Montfort – the Barons' Wars – the Provisions of
Oxford and Westminster – the emergence of Parliament – the Battle of
Lewes – Prince Edward captured – the King surrenders to de Montfort –
Llewelyn ap Gruffudd recognised as Prince of Wales – Edward escapes –
Simon de Monfort slain at the Battle of Evesham – the Statute of
Marlborough – the death of Henry III

K ING JOHN died in the toils; but he died at bay. The mis-govern-
ment of his reign had brought against him what seemed to be an
overwhelming combination. He was at war with the English
barons who had forced him to grant the Charter. They had invited
Louis, son of the implacable Philip, King of France, into the country to be
their liege lord, and with him came foreign troops and hardy adventurers. The
insurgent barons north of the Humber had the support of Alexander, King of
Scots; in the West the rebellion was sustained by Llewellyn, the powerful
Prince of North Wales. The towns were mainly against the King; London was
vehemently hostile. The Cinque Ports were in enemy hands. Winchester,
Worcester, and Carlisle, separated by the great distances of those times, were
united in opposition to the Crown.

On the other hand, the recreant King had sacrificed the status of the realm
to purchase the unswerving aid of the Papacy. A strong body of mercenaries,
the only regular troops in the kingdom, were in John's pay. Some of the
greatest warrior-nobles, the venerable William the Marshal, and the famous,
romantic Ranulf, Earl of Chester, with a strong following of the aristocracy,
adhered to his cause. The mass of the people, bewildered by this new quarrel
of their master, on the whole inclined to the King against the barons, and

certainly against the invading foreigners. Their part was only to suffer at the hands of both sides. Thus the forces were evenly balanced; everything threatened a long, stubborn civil war and a return to the anarchy of Stephen and Maud. John himself, after a lifetime of subtleties and double-dealing, of illegal devices and sharp, unexpected twists of religious policy, showed himself possessed, in the last months of his life, of a warlike energy and resource which astonished friend and foe. It was at this moment that he died of dysentery, aggravated by fatigue and too much food and drink.

The death of the King in this convulsion of strife changed the conditions of the conflict without ending it. The rival interest and factions that were afoot had many purposes beyond the better government of England. Louis was in the Island, and fighting. Many had plighted him their faith, already once forsworn. The rebel lords were deeply involved with their Scottish and Welsh allies; none was in the humour for peace. Yet the sole reason and justification for revolt died with John. Henry, a child of nine, was the undoubted heir to all the rights and loyalties of his grandfather's wide empire. He was the rightful King of England. Upon what grounds could the oppressions of the father be visited upon his innocent son? A page of history had been violently turned; the new parchment was blank and clear. All parties were profoundly sensible of these considerations. Nevertheless John for the moment was missed by those whose lives and fortunes were devoted to the national cause. William the Marshal acted with honesty and decision. Had he failed in his duty to the Crown the strong centralised monarchy which Henry II had created, and upon which the growing civilisation of the realm depended, might have degenerated into a heptarchy of feudal princes, or even worse. The Papal Legate, sure of the unchanging policy of Rome, aided William the Marshal. The boy King was crowned at Gloucester, and began his reign of fifty-six years on October 28, 1216. He was anointed by the Legate, and in default of the diadem which John had lost in crossing the Wash a plain gold circlet was placed upon his brow. This was to prove no inadequate symbol of his rule.

William the Marshall, aged seventy, reluctantly undertook what we should now call the Regency. He joined to himself the Earl of Chester, who might well have been his rival but did not press his claims, and Hubert de Burgh, John's faithful servant. The wisdom and the weakness of the new Government were alike revealed in the reissue of the charter, which had been too rashly quashed by the Pope in 1215. The religious character of the King's party had become predominant. The Royalists wore white crosses, the church preached a virtual Crusade, and the chiefs of the opposing factions were excommunicated. "At a time," said Henry in after-years to Bishop Grosseteste, "when we were orphan and minor, when our subjects were not only alienated from us, but were organised against us, it was our mother, the Roman Church, which brought this realm once more under our authority, which consecrated us King, crowned us and placed us on the throne."

The confusion and monotony of the barons' warfare, against each other, or against the King, sometimes with the Church, more often against the Church, have repelled many readers of history. But the fact is that King Henry III survived all his troubles and left England enjoying a prosperity and peace unknown when he was a child. The cruel war and anarchy lie only upon the surface; underneath, unformulated and largely unrealised by the hard-pressed actors, coursed all the tides which were to flow in Europe five hundred years later; and almost all the capital decisions which are demanded of the modern world were rife in this medieval society. From out of the conflict there rises the figures of heroes, both warriors and statesmen, from whose tribulations we are separated by long ages, but whose work and outlook unite them to us, as if we read their acts and words in the morning newspaper.

We must examine some of these figures at close quarters. Stephen Langton, the great Archbishop, was the indomitable, unwearying builder of the rights of Englishmen against royal, baronial, and even ecclesiastical pretensions. He stood against King John; he stood against the Pope. Both cast upon him at times their utmost displeasure, short of taking his life. Here is a man who worked for the unity of Christendom through the Catholic Church; but also for the interest of England against the Papacy. Here is a faithful servant of the Crown, but at the same time a champion of the charter, and all it meant, and still means. A commanding central figure, practical, resourceful, shifting from side to side as evils force him, but quite unchanging and unchangeable in his broad, wise, brave, workaday, liberal purpose. Here was, if not an architect of our Constitution, at least a punctual and unfailing Clerk of the Works.

The second personality which emerges from the restless scene is Hubert de Burgh. Here is a soldier and a politician, armed with the practical wisdom which familiarity with courts and camps, with high authorities, ecclesiastical and armoured, may infuse into a man's conduct, and even nature. John's Justiciar, identified with the crimes and the follies of the reign, was yet known to all men as their constant resolute opponent. Under the Marshal, who was himself a star of European chivalry, Hubert was an outstanding leader of resistance to the rebellion against the monarchy. At the same time, above the warring factions, he was a solid champion of the rights of England. The Island should not be ravaged by greedy nobles, nor pillaged by foreign adventurers, or mutilated unduly even for the high interests of the Papacy.

The rebellion of the barons was quelled by fights on land and sea. At Lincoln the King's party gained a fantastic but none the less decisive victory. In the streets of Lincoln, during a whole day, we are told that four hundred royal knights jostled and belaboured six hundred of the baronial party. Only three were killed in combat. Contemporary opinion declined to accord the name of battle to this brawl. It was called "the Fair of Lincoln". It is difficult to form a general picture of what was happening. One must suppose that the knights had upon the average at least eight or ten stalwart retainers each, and that the almost invulnerable, chain-mailed monsters waddled about in the throng, chasing away or cutting down the unarmoured fold, and welting each other when they met, hard, but perhaps not too hard.

After a year of fighting Louis of France was compelled to leave the country in 1217, his hopes utterly dashed. The great Charter was now reissued for the second time in order to show that the Government meant its word. In 1219 the old victorious Marshal died, and Hubert ruled the land for twelve years. He was a stern ruler. When Fawkes de Breauté, who had been the chief mercenary of John and William the Marshal during all these recent tumults, grew over-mighty and attempted to disturb the new-found peace of the land Hubert determined to expel him. On taking Fawkes's stronghold of Bedford Castle in 1224, after two months' siege, Hubert hanged in front of its walls the twenty-four surviving knights who had commanded the garrison. In the following year, as a sign of pacification, the Great Charter was again reissued in what was substantially its final form. Thus it became an unchallenged part of English law and tradition. But for the turbulent years of Henry III's minority, it might have mouldered in the archives of history as a merely partisan document.

No long administration is immune from mistakes, and every statesman must from time to time make concessions to wrongheaded superior powers. But Hubert throughout his tenure stood for the policy of doing the least possible to recover the King's French domains. This he carried out not only by counsel, but by paralysing action, and by organising ignominious flight before the enemy when battle seemed otherwise unavoidable. He hampered the preparation for fresh war; he stood firm against the incursions of foreign favourites and adventurers. He resisted the Papacy in its efforts to draw money at all costs out of England for its large European schemes. He maintained order, and as the King grew up he restrained the Court party which was forming about him from making inroads upon the Charter. His was entirely the English point of view.

At last in 1229 he had exhausted his goodwill and fortune and fate were upon him. The King, now twenty-two years of age, crowned and acting, arrived at Portsmouth with a large army raised by the utmost exercise of his feudal power to defend those estates in France which after the loss of Normandy still pertained to the English Crown. Hubert could not control this, but the transporting of the expedition lay apparently in his department. The King found no ships, or few, awaiting him; no supplies, no money, for his oversea venture. He flew into a rage. Although usually mild, affable, scholarly, and artistic, he drew his sword and rushed upon the Justiciar, reproaching him with having betrayed his trust and being bribed by France. It certainly was a very unpleasant and awkward situation, the Army wishing to fight abroad, and the Navy and the Treasury unable or unwilling to carry them thither. The quarrel was smoothed down; the King recovered his temper; the expedition sailed in the following year and Hubert retained his place. But not for long. In 1232 he was driven from power by a small palace clique. Threatened in his life, he took sanctuary at Brentwood. He was dragged from this asylum, but the common, humble blacksmith who was ordered to put the fetters on him declared he would die any death rather than do so; and he is said to have used the words which historians have deemed to the true monument of Hubert de Burgh: "Is he not that most faithful Hubert who so often saved England from the devastation of foreigners and restored England to England?"

De Burgh's conduct had been far from blameless, but his fall had been deliberately engineered by men whose object was not to reform administration but to gain power. The leader of this intrigue was his former rival Peter des Roches, the Bishop of Winchester. Des Roches himself kept in the background, but at the Christmas Council of 1232 nearly every post of consequence in the administration was conferred upon his friends, most of them, like him, men of Poitou. More was involved in the defeat of de Burgh than the triumph of des Roches and his party. De Burgh was the last of the great Justiciars who had wielded plenary and at times almost sovereign power. Henceforward the Household offices like the Wardrobe, largely dependent upon the royal will and favour, began to overshadow the great "national" offices, like the Justiciarship, filled by the baronial magnates. As they came to be occupied increasingly by foreign intruders, Poitevins, Savoyards, Provençals, the national feeling of the baronage became violently hostile. Under the leadership of Richard the Marshal, a second son of the faithful William, the barons began to growl against the foreigners. Des Roches retorted that the King had need of foreigners to protect him against the treachery of his natural subjects; and large numbers of Poitevin and Breton mercenaries were brought over to sustain this view. But the struggle was short. In alliance with Prince Llewellyn the young Marshal drove the King among the Welsh Marches, sacked Shrewsbury, and harried des Roches's lands. In the spring of 1234 Henry was forced to accept terms, and, although the Marshal was killed in April, the new Archbishop, Edmund Rich, insisted on the fulfilment of the treaty. The Poitevin officials were dismissed, des Roches found it convenient to go on a journey to Italy, and de Burgh was honourably restored to his lands and possessions.

The Poitevins were the first of the long succession of foreign favourites whom Henry III gathered round him in the middle years of his reign. Hatred of the aliens, who dominated the King, monopolised the offices, and made scandalous profits out of a country to whose national interest they were completely indifferent, became the theme of baronial opposition. The King's affection was reserved for those who flattered his vanity and ministered to his caprices. He developed a love for extravagant splendour, and naturally preferred to his morose barons the brilliant adventurers of Poitou and Provence. The culture of medieval Provence, the home of the troubadours and the creed of chivalry, fascinated Henry. In 1236 he married Eleanor, the daughter of Raymond of Provence. With Eleanor came her numerous and needy kinsmen, chief among them her four uncles. A new wave of foreigners descended upon the profitable wardships, marriages, escheats, and benefices, which the disgusted baronage regarded as their own.

An even more copious source of discontent in England was the influence of the Papacy over the grateful and pious King. Pope Gregory IX, at desperate grips with the Holy Roman Emperor Frederick II, made ever greater demands for money, and his Legate, Otto, took an interest in English Church reform. Otto's demand in 1240 for one-fifth of the clergy's rents and movables raised a storm. The rectors of Berkshire published a manifesto denying the right of Rome to tax the English Church, and urging that the Pope, like other bishops, should "live of his own". Nevertheless, early in 1241 Otto returned to Rome with a great treasure; and the Pope rewarded the loyalty of the Italian clergy by granting them the next three hundred vacant English benefices. The election of Innocent IV in 1243 led to renewed demands. In that year the Papal envoy forbade bishops in England to appoint to benefices until the long list of Papal nominees had been exhausted. Robert Grosseteste, scholar, scientist, and saint, a former Master of the Oxford Schools and since 1235 Bishop of Lincoln, led the English clergy in evasion or refusal of Papal demands. He became their champion. Although he still believed that the Pope was absolute, he heralded the attacks which Wyclif was more than a century later to make upon the exactions and corruption of the Roman Court.

The Church, writhing under Papal exaction, and the baronage, offended by Court encroachments, were united in hatred of foreigners. A crisis came in 1244, when a baronial commission was appointed to fix the terms of a money grant to the King. The barons insisted that the Justiciar, Chancellor, and Treasurer, besides certain judges, should be elected by the Great Council, on which they were strongly represented. Four of the King's Council were to be similarly elected, with power to summon the Great Council. The King turned in his distress to the already mulcted Church, but his appeal was rejected through the influence of Grosseteste.

In the last years of Grosseteste's life he had come to hope great things of his friend, Simon de Montfort.[1] Simon had married the King's sister and had inherited the Earldom of Leicester. He had been governor of the English lands in Gascony for four years. Strong and energetic, he had aroused the jealousy and opposition of the King's favourites; and as a result of their intrigues he had been brought to trial in 1252. The commission acquitted him; but in return for a sum of money from the King he unwillingly agreed to vacate his office. Friendship between him and the King was at an end; on the one side was contempt, on the other suspicion. In this way, from an unexpected quarter, appeared the leader whom the baronial and national opposition had long lacked.

There were many greater notables in England, and Simon's relationship to the King was aspersed by the charge that he had seduced his bride before he married her. None the less there he stood with five resolute sons, an alien leader, who was to become the brain and driving force of the English aristocracy. Behind him gradually ranged themselves most of the great feudal

---

1   Simon de Montfort (1208–65). Born in Normandy, de Montfort arrived in England in 1230 to claim (through his grandmother) the Earldom of Leicester. It was not until 1239 – the year after he married the princess, Eleanor – that his claim was recognised.

chiefs, the whole strength of London as a corporate entity, all the lower clergy, and the goodwill of the nation. A letter of a court official, written in July 1258, has been preserved. The King, so it says, had yielded to what he felt was overwhelming pressure. A commission for reform of government was set up; it was agreed that "public offices should only be occupied by the English", and that "the emissaries of Rome and the foreign merchants and bankers should be reduced to their proper station".

The commission for reform set about its works seriously, and in 1258 its proposals were embodied in the Provisions of Oxford, supplemented and extended in 1259 by the Provisions of Westminster.[1] This baronial movement represented something deeper than dislike of alien counsellors. The two sets of Provisions, taken together, represent a considerable shift of interest from the standpoint of Magna Carta. The Great Charter was mainly concerned to define various points of law, whereas the Provisions of Oxford deal with the overriding question of by whose advice and through what officials royal government should be carried on. Many of the clauses of the Provisions of Westminster moreover mark a limitation of baronial rather than of royal jurisdiction. The fruits of Henry II's work were now to be seen; the nation was growing stronger, more self-conscious and self-confident. The notable increase in judicial activity throughout the country, the more frequent visits of the judges and officials – all of them dependent upon local co-operation – educated the country knights in political responsibility and administration. This process, which shaped the future of English institutions, had it first effects in the thirteenth century.

The staple of the barons' demand was that the King in future should govern by a Council of Fifteen, to be elected by four persons, two from the baronial and two from the royal party. It is significant that the King's proclamation accepting the arrangement in English as well as French is the first public document to be issued in both languages since the time of William the Conqueror. For a spell the Council, animated and controlled by Simon de Montfort, governed the land. They held each other in proper check, sharing among themselves the greater executive offices and entrusting the actual administration to "lesser men", as was then widely thought to be desirable. The magnates, once their own class interests were guarded, and their rights – which up to a certain point were the rights of the nation – were secure, did not wish to put the levers of power in the hands of one or two of their number. This idea however of a Cabinet of politicians, chosen from the participate, with highly trained functionaries of no political status operating under them, had in it a long vitality and many resurrections.

It is about this time that the world "Parlement" – Parliament – began to be

---

1   A reminder that although a form of Parliament – or Parlement – existed, it was not yet an established body and it did not have a home. "Parliament" met wheresoever the king decided. So, the Provisions of Oxford were the reforms issued by the committee of twenty-four men selected by the meeting, or great council, at Oxford. The Provisions of Westminster were issued by the "parliament" that met in October 1259 at Westminster.

current. In 1086 William the Conqueror had "deep speech" with his wise men before launching the Domesday inquiry. In Latin this would have appeared as *colloquium*; and "colloquy" is the common name in the twelfth century for the consultations between the King and his magnates. The occasional colloquy "on great affairs of the Kingdom" can at this point be called a Parliament. But more often the word means the permanent Council of officials and judges which sat at Westminster to receive petitions, redress grievances, and generally regulate the course of the law. By the thirteenth century Parliament establishes itself as the name of two quite different, though united, institutions.

The King, the Court party, and the immense foreign interests associated therewith had no intention of submitting indefinitely to the thraldom of the Provisions. Every preparation was made to recover the lost ground. In 1259 the King returned with hopes of foreign aid from Paris, where he had been away to sign a treaty of peace with the French. His son, Edward was already the rising star of all who wished to see a strong monarchy. Supporters of this cause appeared among the poor and turbulent elements in London and the towns. The enthusiasm of the revolution – for it was nothing less – had not been satisfied by a baronial victory. Ideas were afoot which would not readily be put to sleep. It is the merit of Simon de Montfort that he did not rest content with a victory by the barons over the Crown. He turned at once upon the barons themselves. If the King should be curbed, so also must they in their own spheres show respect for the general interest. Upon these issues the claims of the middle classes, who had played a great part in carrying the barons to supremacy, could not be disregarded. The "apprentice" or bachelor knights, who may be taken as voicing the wishes of the country gentry, formed a virile association of their own entitled "the Community of the Bachelors of England". Simon de Montfort became their champion. Very soon he began to rebuke great lords for abuse of their privileges. He wished to extend to the baronial estates the reforms already undertaken in the royal administration. He addressed himself pointedly to Richard, Earl of Gloucester, who ruled wide estates in the South-West and in South Wales. He procured an ordinance from the Council making it plain that the great lords were under the royal authority, which was again – though this he did not stress – under the Council. Here was dictatorship in a new form. It was a dictatorship of the Commonwealth, but, as so often happens to these bold ideas, it expressed itself inevitably through a man and a leader. These developments split the baronial party from end to end; and the King and his valiant son Edward, striking in with all their own resources upon their divided opponents, felt they might put the matter to the proof.

At Easter in 1261 Henry, freed by the Pope from his oath to accept the Provisions of Oxford and Westminster, deposed the officials and Ministers appointed by the barons. There were now two Governments with conflicting titles, each interfering with the other. The barons summoned up the representatives of the shires to meet them at St Albans; the King summoned them to

Windsor. Both parties competed for popular support. The barons commanded greater sympathy in the country, and only Gloucester's opposition to de Montfort held them back from sharp action. After the death of Gloucester in July 1262 the baronial party rallied to de Montfort's drastic policy. Civil war broke out, and Simon and his sons, all of whom played vigorous parts, a moiety of barons, the middle class, so far as it had emerged, and powerful allies in Wales together faced in redoubtable array the challenge of the Crown.

Simon de Montfort was a general as well as a politician. Nothing in his upbringing or circumstances would naturally have suggested to him the course he took. It is ungratefully asserted that he had no real conception of the ultimate meaning of his actions. Certainly he builded better than he knew. By September 1263 a reaction against him had become visible: he had succeeded only too well. Edward played upon the discontent among the barons, appealed to their feudal and selfish interest, fomented their jealousy of de Montfort, and so built up a strong royalist party. At the end of the year de Montfort had to agree to arbitration by Louis IX, the French king. The decision went against him. Loyal to his monarchical rank, the King of France defended the prerogative of the King of England and declared the Provisions to be illegal. As Louis was accepted as saint in his own lifetime this was serious. Already however the rival parties had taken up arms. In the civil war that followed the feudal party more or less supported the King. The people, especially the towns, and the party of ecclesiastical reform, especially the Franciscans, rallied to de Montfort. New controls were improvised in many towns to defeat the royalist sympathies of the municipal oligarchies. In the summer of 1264 de Montfort once again came south to relieve the pressure which Henry and Edward were exerting on the Cinque Ports.

The King and Prince Edward met him in Sussex with a superior power. At Lewes a fierce battle was fought. In some way it was a forerunner of Edgehill. Edward, like Rupert four hundred years later, conquered all before him, pursued incontinently, and returned to the battlefield only to find that all was lost. Simon had, with much craft and experience of war, laid a trap to which the peculiar conditions of the ground lent themselves, whereby when his centre had been pierced his two wings of armoured cavalry fell upon the royal main body from both flanks and crushed all resistance. He was accustomed at this time owing to a fall from his horse to be carried with the army in a sumptuous and brightly decorated litter, like the coach of an eighteenth-century general. In this he placed two or three hostages for their greater security, and set it among the Welsh in the centre, together with many banners and emblems suggesting his presence. Prince Edward, in his charge, captured this trophy, and killed the unlucky hostages from his own party who were found therein. But meanwhile the King and all his Court and principal supporters were taken prisoners by de Montfort, and the energetic prince returned only to share their plight.

Simon de Montfort was now in every respect master of England, and if he had proceeded in the brutal manner of modern times in several European countries by the wholesale slaughter of those who were in his grip he might long have remained so.[1] In those days however, for all their cruelty in individual cases, nothing was pushed to the last extreme. The influences that counted with men in contest for power at the peril of their lives were by no means only brutal. Force, though potent, was not sovereign. Simon made a treaty with the captive King and the beaten party, whereby the rights of the Crown were in theory respected, though in practice the King and his son were to be subjected to strict controls. The general balance of the realm was preserved, and it is clear from Simon's action not only that he felt the power of the opposing forces, but that he aimed at their ultimate unification. He saw himself, with the King in his hands, able to use the authority of the crown to control the baronage and create the far broader and better political system which, whether he aimed at it or not, must have automatically followed from his success. Thus he ruled the land, with the feeble King and the proud Prince Edward prisoners in his hands. This opens the third and final stage in his career.

All the barons, whatever party they had chosen, saw themselves confronted with an even greater menace than from which they had used Simon to deliver them. The combination of Simon's genius and energy with the inherent powers of a Plantagenet monarchy and the support of the middle classes, already so truculent, was a menace to their class privileges far more intimate and searching than the misgovernment of John or the foreign encumbrances of Henry III. Throughout these struggles of lasting significance the English barony never deviated from their own self-interest. At Runnymede they had served national freedom when they thought they were defending their own privilege. They had now no doubt that Simon was its enemy. He was certainly a despot, with a king in his wallet and the forces of the Court not in Simon's hands schemed night and day to overthrow him.

For the moment de Montfort was content that the necessary steps should be taken by a Council of nine who controlled expenditure and appointed officials. Any long-term settlement could be left until the Parliament which he had summoned for 1265. The earl's autocratic position was not popular, yet the country was in such a state of confusion that circumstances seemed to justify it.

In January 1265 a Parliament met in London to which Simon summoned representatives both from the shires and from the town. Its purpose was to give an appearance of legality to the revolutionary settlement, and this, under the guidance of de Montfort, it proceeded to do. Its importance lay however more in its character as a representative assembly than in its work. The constitutional significance which was once attached to it as the first Parliament in our history is somewhat discounted by modern opinion. The practical reason for summoning the strong popular element was de Montfort's desire to weight

1 Churchill published the first volume in 1956, although much of the text had been written by the outbreak of World War II. Here, he is making reference to what had happened in the Soviet Union and Nazi Germany.

the Parliament with his own supporters: among the magnates only five earls and eighteen barons received writs of summons. Again he fell back upon the support on the country gentry and the burgesses against the hostility or indifference of the magnates. In this lay his message and his tactics.

The Parliament dutifully approved of de Montfort's actions and accepted his settlement embodied in the Provisions. but Clare's[1] withdrawal to the West could only mean the renewal of war. King Henry III abode docilely in Simon's control, and was treated all the time with profound personal respect. Prince Edward enjoyed a liberty which could only have been founded upon his parole not to escape. However, as the baronial storm gathered and many divisions occurred in Simon's party, and all the difficulties of government brought inevitable unpopularity in their train, he went out hunting one day with a few friends, and forgot to return as in honour bound. He galloped away through the woodland, first after the stag and then in quest of larger game. He at once became the active organising head of the most powerful elements in English life, to all of which the destruction of Simon de Montfort and his unheard-of innovations had become the supreme object. By promising to uphold the Charters, to remedy grievances and to expel the foreigners, Edward succeeded in uniting the baronial party and in cutting away the ground from under de Montfort's feet. The Earl now appeared as no more than the leader of a personal faction, and his alliance with Llewellyn, grandson of Llewellyn the Great, by which he recognised the claims of the Welsh prince to territory and independence, compromised his reputation. Out-manoeuvred politically by Edward, he had also placed himself at a serious military disadvantage. While Edward and the Marcher barons, as they were called, held the Severn valley de Montfort was penned in, his retreat to the east cut off, and his forces driven back into South Wales. At the beginning of August he made another attempt to cross the river and to join the forces which his son, Simon, was bringing up from the south-east. He succeeded in passing by a ford near Worcester, but his son's forces were trapped by Edward near Kenilworth and routed. Unaware of this disaster, the Earl was caught in turn at Evesham; and here on August 4 the final battle took place.

It was fought in the rain and half darkness of a sudden storm. The Welsh broke before Edward's heavy horse, and the small group around de Montfort were left to fight desperately until sheer weight of numbers overwhelmed them. De Montfort died a hero on the field. The Marchers massacred large numbers of fugitives and prisoners and mutilated the bodies of the dead. The old King, a pathetic figure, who had been carried by the Earl in all his wander-

[1] Gilbert de Clare, 8th Earl of Gloucester (1243–95), one of the Oxford barons and knighted by de Montfort shortly before the Battle of Lewes (May 12, 1264). By the following year he had fallen out with the younger de Montforts and had "withdrawn himself and made excuses for staying away from court". Gilbert de Clare and his brother, Thomas, became part of the conspiracy against de Montfort and Gilbert's defection should be seen as an important factor in the fall of de Montfort.

ings, was wounded by his son's followers, and only escaped death by revealing his identity with the cry, "Slay me not! I am Henry of Winchester, your King."

A reversion to feudal independence and consequent anarchy appeared imminent. In these troubles Pope Clement IV and his Legate Ottobon enjoined moderation; and after a six-months' unsuccessful siege of Kenilworth Edward realised that this was the only policy. In the last years of his life, with de Montfort dead and Edward away on Crusade, the feeble King enjoyed comparative peace. More than half a century before, at the age of nine, he had succeeded to the troubled inheritance of his father in the midst of civil war. At times it had seemed as if he would also die in the midst of civil war. At last however the storms were over: he could turn back to the things of beauty that interested him far more than political struggles. The new Abbey of Westminster, a masterpiece of Gothic architecture, was now dedicated; its consecration had long been the dearest object of King Henry III's life. And here in the last weeks of 1272 he was buried.

The quiet of these last few years should not lead us to suppose that de Montfort's struggle and the civil war had been in vain. Among the common people he was for many years worshipped as a saint, and miracles were worked at his tomb. De Montfort had lighted a fire never to be quenched in English history. Already in 1267 the Statute of Marlborough had re-enacted the chief of the Provisions of Westminster. Not less important was his influence upon his nephew, Edward, the new King, who was to draw deeply upon the ideas of the man he had slain. In the this way de Montfort's purposes survived both the field of Evesham and the reaction which succeeded it, and in Edward I the great Earl found his true heir.

CHAPTER THIRTEEN

KING EDWARD I

Edward I — Robert Burnell — local government reform — the Statutes of Westminster, Gloucester and Winchester — land reform — persecution of the Jews — the Exchequer, Chancery, the Wardrobe and the Privy Seal — the Council of Reading — war with France — the barons in revolt — the first English Prince of Wales — the Maid of Norway — John Balliol, King of Scotland — the sack of Berwick — William Wallace defeats British at Stirling Bridge — Wallace captured and executed — Bruce crowned at Scone — the death of Edward I

EW PRINCES had received so thorough an education in the art of rulership as Edward I when at the age of thirty-three his father's death brought him to the Crown. He was an experienced leader and a skilful general. He had carried his father on his shoulders; he had grappled with Simon de Montford, and, while sharing many of his views, had destroyed him. He had learned the art of war by tasting defeat. When at any time in the closing years of King Henry III he could have taken control he had preferred a filial and constitutional patience, all the more remarkable when his own love of order and reform is contrasted with his father's indolence and incapacity and the general misgovernment of the realm.

He was of elegant build and lofty stature, a head and shoulders above the height of the ordinary man. His hair, always abundant, changed from yellow in childhood to black in manhood and snow-white in age, and marked the measured progress of his life. His proud brown and regular features were marred only by the drooping left eyelid which had been characteristic of his father. If he stammered he was also eloquent. There is much talk of his limbs. His sinewy, muscular arms were those of a swordsman; his long legs gave him a grip of the saddle, and the nickname of "Longshanks". The Dominican chronicler Nicholas Trivet, by whom these traits are recorded, tells us that the King delighted in war and tournaments, and especially in hawking and hunting. When he chased the stag he did not leave his quarry to the hounds, nor even to the hunting spear; he galloped at breakneck speed to cut the unhappy beast to the ground.

All this was typical of his reign. He presents us with qualities which are a mixture of the administrative capacity of Henry II and the personal prowess and magnanimity of Coeur de Lion. He sought a national kingship, an extension of his mastery throughout the British Isles, and a preponderant influence in the councils of Europe.

His administrative reforms in England were not such as to give satisfaction to any one of the strong contending forces, but rather to do justice to the whole. Here was a time of setting in order. The reign is memorable, not for the erection of great new landmarks, but because the beneficial tendencies of the three preceding reigns were extracted from error and confusion and organised and consolidated in a permanent structure. The framework and policies of the nation, which we have seen shaping themselves with many fluctuations, now set and hardened into a form which, surviving the tragedies of the Black Death, the Hundred Years War with France, and the Wars of the Roses, endured for the remainder of the Middle Ages, and some of them for longer. In this period we see a knightly and bourgeois stage of society increasingly replacing pure feudalism. The organs of government, land tenure, the military and financial systems, the relations of Church and State, all reach definitions which last nearly till the Tudors.

The first eighteen years of the reign witnessed an outburst of legislative activity for which there was to be no parallel for centuries. Nearly every year was marked by an important statute. Few of these were original, most were conservative in tone, but their cumulative effect was revolutionary. Edward relied upon his Chancellor, Robert Burnell, Bishop of Bath and Wells, a man of humble birth, who had risen through the royal chancery and Household to his bishopric and until his death in 1292 remained the King's principal adviser. Burnell's whole life had been spent in the service of the Crown; all his policy was devoted to the increase of its power at the expense of feudal privilege and influence. He had not been Chancellor for more than three weeks, after Edward's return to England in 1274, before a searching inquiry into the local administration was begun. Armed with a list of forty questions, commissioners were sent throughout the land to ask what were the rights and possessions of the King, what encroachments had been made upon them, which officials were negligent or corrupt, which sheriffs "for prayer, price, or favour" concealed felonies, neglected their duties, were harsh or bribed. Similar inquests had been made before; none was so thorough or so fertile. "Masterful, but not tyrannical", the King's policy was to respect all rights and overthrow all usurpations.

The First Statute of Westminster in the Parliament of 1275 dealt with the administrative abuses exposed by the commissioners. The Statute of Gloucester in 1278 directed the justices to inquire by writs of *Quo Warranto* into the rights of feudal magnates to administer the law by their own courts and officials within their demesnes, and ordained that those rights should be strictly defined. The main usefulness of the inquiry was to remind the great feudatories that they had duties as well as rights. In 1279 the Statute of Mortmain, *De Religiosis*, forbade gifts of land to be made to the Church, though the practice was allowed to continue under royal licence. In 1285 the Statute of Winchester attacked local disorder, and in the same year was issued the Second Statute of Westminster, *De Donis Conditionalibus*, which strengthened the system of entailed estates. The Third Statute of Westminster, *Quia Emptores*, dealt with land held, not upon condition, but in fee simple. Land held on these terms might be freely alienated, but it was stipulated for the future that the buyer must hold his purchase not from the seller, but from the seller's lord, and by the same feudal services and customs as were attached to the land before the sale. It thus called halt to the growth of sub-infeudation, and was greatly to the advantage of the Crown, as overlord, whose direct tenants now increased in number.

The purpose of this famous series of laws was essentially conservative, and for a time their enforcement was efficient. But economic pressures were wreaking great changes in the propertied life of England, scarcely less deep-cutting than those which had taken place in the political sphere. Land gradually ceased to be the moral sanction upon which national society and defence were based. It became by successive steps a commodity, which could in principle, like wool or mutton, be bought and sold, and which under certain restrictions could be either transferred to new owners by gift or testament, or even settled under conditions of entail on future lives which were to be the foundation of a new aristocracy.

Of course only a comparatively small proportion of the land of England came into this active if rude market; but enough of a hitherto solid element was fluid to make a deep stir. In those days, when the greatest princes were pitifully starved in cash, there was already in England one spring of credit bubbling freely. The Jews had unseen and noiselessly lodged themselves in the social fabric of that fierce age. They were there and they were not there; and from time to time they could be most helpful to high personages in urgent need of money; and to none more than to a king who did not desire to sue Parliament for it. The spectacle of land which could be acquired on rare but definite occasions by anyone with money led the English Jews into a course of shocking imprudence. Land began to pass into the hand of Israel, either by direct sale or more often by mortgage. Enough land came into the market to make both processes advantageous. In a couple of decades the erstwhile feudal lords were conscious that they had parted permanently for fleeting lucre with a portion of the English soil large enough to be noticed.

For some time past there had been growing a wrathful reaction. Small landowners oppressed by mortgages, spendthrift nobles who had made bad bargains, were united in their complaints. Italian moneylenders were now coming into the country, who could be just as useful in times of need to the King as the Jews. Edward saw himself able to conciliate powerful elements and escape from awkward debts, by the simple and well-trodden path of anti-Semitism. The propaganda of ritual murder and other dark tales, the commonplaces of our enlightened age, were at one invoked with general acclaim. The Jews, held up to universal hatred, were pillaged, maltreated, and finally expelled the realm. Exception was made for certain physicians without whose skill persons of consequence might have lacked due attention. Once again the sorrowful, wandering race, stripped to the skin, must seek asylum and begin afresh. To Spain or North Africa the melancholy caravan, now so familiar, must move on. Not until four centuries had elapsed was Oliver Cromwell by contracts with a moneyed Israelite to open again the coasts of England to the enterprise of the Jewish race. It was left to a Calvinist dictator to remove the ban which a Catholic king had imposed. The bankers of Florence and Siena, who had taken the place of the Jews, were in their turn under Edward I's grandson to taste the equities of Christendom.

Edward I was remarkable among medieval kings for the seriousness with which he regarded the work of administration and good government. It was natural therefore that he should place more reliance upon expert professional help than upon what has been neatly termed "the amateurish assistance of great feudalists staggering under the weight of their own dignity". By the end of the thirteenth century three departments of specialised administration were already at work. One was the Exchequer, established at Westminster, where most of the revenue was received and the accounts kept. The second was the Chancery, a general secretariat responsible for the writing and drafting of innumerable royal charters, writs, and letters. The third was the Wardrobe, with its separate secretariat, the Privy Seal, attached to the ever-moving royal household, and combining financial and secretarial functions, which might range from financing a Continental war to buying a pennyworth of pepper for the royal cook. Burnell was a typical product of the incipient Civil Service. His place after his death was taken by an Exchequer official, Walter Langton, the Treasurer, who, like Burnell, looked upon his see of Lichfield as a reward for skilful service rather than a spiritual office.

Though the most orthodox of Churchmen, Edward I did not escape conflict with the Church. Anxious though he was to pay his dues to God, he had a far livelier sense than his father of what was due to Caesar, and circumstances more than once forced him to protest. The leader of the Church party was John Pecham, a Franciscan friar, Archbishop of Canterbury from 1279 to 1292. With great courage and skill Pecham defended what he regarded as the just rights of the Church and its independence against the Crown. At the provincial Council held at Reading in 1279 he issued a number of pronouncements which angered the King. One was a canon against plurality of the clerical offices, which stuck at the principal royal method of rewarding the growing Civil Service. Another was the order that a copy of the Charter, which Edward had sworn to uphold, should be publicly posted in every cathedral and collegiate church. All who produced royal writs to stop cases in ecclesiastical court and all who violated Magna Carta were threatened with excommunication.

Pecham bowed to Edward's anger and waited his time. In 1281, when another provincial Council was summoned to Lambeth, the King, suspecting mischief, issued writs to its members forbidding them to "hold counsel concerning matters which appertain to our crown, or touch our person, our state, or the state of our Council". Pecham was undeterred. He revived almost verbatim the principal legislation of the Reading Council, prefaced it with an explicit assertion of ecclesiastical liberty, and a month later wrote a remarkable letter to the King, defending his action. "By no human constitution," he wrote, "not even by an oath, can we be bound to ignore laws which rest undoubtedly upon divine authority." "A fine letter" was the marginal comment of an admiring clerk who copied it into the Archbishop's register.

At the beginning of the reign relations between England and France were governed by the Treaty of Paris, which the baronial party had concluded in 1259. For more than thirty years peace reigned between the two countries, though often with an undercurrent of hostility. The disputes about the execution of the terms of the treaty and the quarrels between English, Gascon, and French sailors in the Channel, culminating in a great sea-fight off Saint-Matthieu in 1293, need never have led to a renewal of war, had not the presence of the English in the South of France been a standing challenge to the pride of the French and a bar to their national integrity. Even when Philip the Fair, the French king, began to seek opportunities of provocation Edward was long-suffering and patient in his attempts to reach a compromise. Finally however the Parlement of Paris declared the Duchy of Gascony forfeit. Philip asked for the token surrender of the principal Gascon fortresses, as a recognition of his legal powers as overlord. Edward complied. But once Philip was in possession he refused to give them up again. Edward now realised that he must either fight or lose his French possessions.

By 1294 the great King had changed much from his early buoyant manhood. After the long, stormy years of sustaining his father he had reigned himself for nearly a quarter of a century. Meanwhile his world had changed about him; he had lost his beloved wife Eleanor of Castile, his mother, Eleanor of Provence, and his three eldest infant sons. Burnell was now dead. Wales and Scotland presented grave problems; opposition was beginning to make itself heard and felt. Alone, perplexed, and ageing, the King had to face an endless succession of difficulties.

In June 1294 he explained the grounds of the quarrel with the French to what is already called "a Parliament" of magnates in London. His decision to go to war was accepted with approval, as has often been the case in more regularly constituted assemblies. Any enthusiasm which had been expressed at the outset wore off speedily under the inevitable increases of taxation. All wool and leather, the staple items of the English export trade, were impounded, and could only be redeemed by the payment of a customs duty of 40s. on the sack instead of the half-mark (6s. 8d.) laid down by the Parliament of 1275. In September, the clergy, to their great indignation, were ordered to contribute one-half of their revenues. The Dean of St Paul's, who attempted to voice their protests in the King's own terrifying presence, fell down in a fit and died. In November Parliament granted a heavy tax upon all moveable property. As the collection proceeded a bitter and sullen discontent spread among all classes. In the winter of 1294 the Welsh revolted, and when the King had suppressed them he returned to find that Scotland had allied itself with France. From 1296 onward war with Scotland was either smouldering or flaring.

After October 1297 the French war degenerated into a series of truces which lasted until 1303. Such conditions involved expense little less than actual fighting. Edward proposed to the barons at Salisbury that a number of them should serve in Gascony while he conducted a campaign in Flanders. This was ill received. Humphrey de Bohun, Earl of Hereford and Constable of England, together with the Marshal, Roger Bigot, Earl of Norfolk, declared that their hereditary offices could only be exercised in the King's company. Such excuses deceived nobody. Both the Earls had personal grudges against the King, and – much more important – they voiced the resentment felt by a large number of the barons who for the past twenty years had steadily seen the authority of the Crown increased to their own detriment. The time was ripe for a revival of the baronial opposition which a generation before had defied Edward's father.

For the moment the King ignored the challenge. He pressed forward with his preparations for war, appointed deputies in place of Hereford and Norfolk, and in August sailed for Flanders. The opposition saw in his absence their long-awaited opportunity. They demanded the confirmation of those two instruments, Magna Carta and its extension, the Charter of the Forest, which were the final version of the terms extorted from John, together with six additional articles. By these no aid was to be imposed in future except with the consent of the community of the realm; corn, wool, and the like must not be impounded against the will of their owners; the clergy and laity of the realm must recover their ancient liberties; the two Earls and their supporters were not to be penalised for their refusal to serve in Gascony; the prelates were to read the Charter aloud in their cathedrals, and to excommunicate all who neglected it. In the autumn the two Earls, backed by armed forces, appeared in London and demanded the acceptance of these proposals. The Regency, unable to resist, submitted. The articles were confirmed, and in November at Ghent the King ratified them, reserving however certain financial rights of the Crown.

There were large and surprising concessions. Both King and Opposition attached great importance to them, and the King was suspected, perhaps with justice, of trying to withdraw from the promises he had given. Several times the baronial party publicly drew attention to these promises before Parliament, and finally in February 1301 the King was driven by the threats and arguments of a Parliament at Lincoln to grant a new confirmation of both charters and certain further articles in solemn form.

By this crisis and its manner of resolution two principles had been established from which important consequences flowed. One was that the King had no right to despatch the feudal host wherever he might choose. This limitation sounded the death-knell of the feudal levy, and inexorably led in the following century to the rise of indentured armies serving for pay. The second point of principle now recognised was that the King could not plead "urgent necessity" as reason for imposing taxation without consent. Other English monarchs as late as the seventeenth century were to make the attempt. But by Edward's failure a precedent had been set up, and a long stride had been taken towards the dependence of the Crown upon Parliamentary grants.

In their fatal preoccupation with their possessions in France the English kings had neglected the work of extending their rule within the Island of Great Britain. There had been fitful interference both in Wales and Scotland, but the task of keeping the frontiers safe had fallen mainly upon the shoulders of the local Marcher lords. As soon as the Treaty of Paris had brought a generation's respite from Continental adventures it was possible to turn to the urgent problems of internal security. Edward I was the first of the English kings to put the whole weight of the Crown's resources behind the effort of national expansion in the West and North, and to him is due the conquest of the independent areas of Wales and the securing of the Western frontier. He took the first great step towards the unification of the Island. By Edward's Statute of Wales the independent principality came to an end. The land of Llewellyn's Wales was transferred to the King's dominions and organised into the shires of Anglesey, Carnarvon, Merioneth, Cardigan, and Carmarthen. The King's son Edward, born in Carnarvon, was proclaimed the first English Prince of Wales.

The Welsh wars of Edward reveal to us the process by which the military system of England was transformed from the age-long Saxon and feudal basis of occasional service to that of paid regular troops. We have seen how Alfred the Great suffered repeatedly from the expiry of the period for which the "fyrd" could be called out. Four hundred years had passed and Norman feudalism still conformed to this basic principle. But how were campaigns to be conducted winter and summer for fifteen months at a time by such methods? How were Continental expeditions to be launched and pursued? Thus for several reigns the principle of scutage had been agreeable alike to barons who did not wish to serve and to sovereigns who preferred a money payment with which to hire full-time soldiers. In the Welsh wars both systems are seen simultaneously at work, but the old is fading. Instead of liege service Governments now required trustworthy mercenaries, and for this purpose money was the solvent.

At the same time a counter-revolution in the balance of warfare was afoot. The mailed cavalry which from the fifth century had eclipsed the ordered ranks of the legion were wearing out their long day. A new type of infantry raised from the common people began to prove its dominating quality. This infantry operated, not by club or sword or spear, or even by hand-flung missiles, but by an archery which, after a long development, concealed from Europe, was very soon to make an astonishing entrance upon the military scene and gain a dramatic ascendancy upon the battlefields of the Continent. Here was a prize taken by the conquerors from their victims. In South Wales the practice of drawing the long-bow had already attained an astonishing efficiency. For the first time infantry possessed a weapon which could penetrate the armour of the clanking age, and which in range and rate of fire was superior to any method ever used before, or ever used again until the coming of the modern rifle.

The great quarrel of Edward's reign was with Scotland. For long years the two kingdoms had dwelt in amity. In the year 1286 Alexander III of Scotland, riding his horse over a cliff in the darkness, left as his heir Margaret, his granddaughter, know as the Maid of Norway. The Scottish magnates had been persuaded to recognise this princess of three years old as his successor. Now the bright project arose that the Maid of Norway should at the same moment succeed to the Scottish throne and marry Edward, the King's son. Thus would be achieved a union of royal families by which the antagonism of England and Scotland might be laid to rest. We can measure the sagacity of the age by the acceptance of this plan. Practically all the ruling forces in England and Scotland were agreed upon it. It was a dream, and it passed as a dream. The Maid of Norway embarked in 1290 upon stormy seas, only to die before reaching land, and Scotland was bequeathed the problem of a disputed succession, in the decision of which the English interest must be a heavy factor. The Scottish nobility were allied at many points with the English royal family, and from a dozen claimants, some of them bastards, two men stood clearly forth, John Balliol and Robert Bruce. Bruce asserted his aged father's closeness in relationship to the common royal ancestor; Balliol, a more distant descendant, the rights of primogeniture. But partisanship was evenly balanced.

Since the days of Henry II the English monarchy had intermittently claimed an overlordship of Scotland, based on the still earlier acknowledgment of Saxon overlordship by Scottish kings. King Edward, whose legal abilities were renowned, had already arbitrated in the Scottish succession. Since the alternatives were the splitting of Scotland into rival kingships or a civil war to decide the matter, the Scots were induced to seek Edward's judgment; and he, pursuing all the time a path of strict legality, consented to the task only upon the prior condition of the reaffirmation of his overlordship, betokened by the surrender of certain Scottish castles. The English King discharged his function as arbitrator with extreme propriety. He rejected the temptation presented to him by Scottish baronial intrigues of destroying the integrity of Scotland. He pronounced in 1292 in favour of John Balliol. Later judgments have in no wise impugned the correctness of his decision. But, having regard to the deep division in Scotland, and the strong elements which adhered to the Bruce claim, John Balliol inevitably became not merely his choice, but his puppet. So thought King Edward I, and plumed himself upon a just and at the same time highly profitable decision. He had confirmed his overlordship of Scotland. He had nominated its King, who stood himself in his own land upon a narrow margin. But the national feeling of Scotland was pent up behind these barriers of legal affirmation. In their distress the Scottish baronage accepted King Edward's award, but they also furnished the new King John with an authoritative council of twelve great lords to overawe him and look after the rights of Scotland. Thus King Edward saw with disgust that all his fair-seeming success left him still confronted with the integrity of Scottish nationhood, with an independent and not a subject Government, and with a hostile rather than a submissive nation.

At this very moment the same argument of overlordship was pressed upon him by the formidable French king, Philip IV. Here Edward was the vassal, proudly defending feudal interests, and the French suzerain had the lawful advantage. Moreover, if England was stronger than Scotland, France was in armed power superior to England. This double conflict imposed a strain upon the financial and military resources of the English monarchy which it could by no means meet. The rest of Edward's reign was spent in a twofold struggle North and South, for the sake of which he had to tax his subjects beyond all endurance. He journeyed energetically to and fro between Flanders and the Scottish Lowlands. He racked the land for money. Nothing else mattered; and the embryonic Parliamentary system profited vastly by the repeated concessions he made in the hope of carrying opinion with him. He confirmed the bulk of the reforms wrung from John. With some exceptions among the great lords, the nation was with him in both of his external efforts, but though time and again it complied with his demands it was to be reconciled to the crushing burden. Thus we see the wise lawgiver, the thrifty scrutineer of English finances, the administrative reformer, forced to drive his people beyond their strength, and in this process to rouse opposition which darkened his life and clouded his fame.

To resist Edward, the Scots allied themselves with the French. Since Edward was at war with France he regarded this as an act of hostility. He summoned Balliol to meet him at Berwick. The Scottish nobles refused to allow their King to go, and from this moment war began. Edward struck with ruthless severity. He advanced on Berwick. The city, then the great emporium of Northern trade, was unprepared, after a hundred years of peace, to resist attack. Palisades were hurriedly raised, the citizens seized such weapons as were at hand. The English army, with hardly any loss, trampled down these improvised defences, and Berwick was delivered to a sack and slaughter which shocked even those barbaric times. Thousands were slain. The most determined resistance came from thirty Flemish merchants who held their depot, called the Red Hall, until it was burnt down. Berwick sank in a few hours from one of the active centres of European commerce to the minor seaport which exists today.

This act of terror quelled the resistance of the ruling classes in Scotland. Perth, Stirling, Edinburgh, yielded themselves to the King's march. Here we see how Edward I anticipated the teachings of Machiavelli; for to the frightfulness of Berwick succeeded a most gracious, forgiving spirit which welcomed and made easy submission in every form. Balliol surrendered his throne and Scotland was brought under English administration. But, as in Wales, the conqueror introduced not only an alien rule, but law and order, all of which were equally unpopular. The governing classes of Scotland had conspicuously failed, and Edward might flatter himself that all was over. It was only the beginning. It has often been said that Joan of Arc first raised the standard of nationalism in the Western world. But over a century before she appeared an outlaw knight, William Wallace, arising from the recesses of South-West Scotland which had been his refuge, embodied, commanded, and led to victory the Scottish nation. Edward, warring in France with piebald fortune, was forced to listen to tales of ceaseless inroads and forays against his royal peace in Scotland, hitherto deemed so sure. Wallace had behind him the spirit of a race as stern and as resolute as any bred among men. He added military gifts of a high order. Out of an unorganised mass of valiant fighting men he forged, in spite of cruel poverty and primitive administration, a stubborn, indomitable army, ready to fight at any odds and mock defeat. The structure of this army is curious. Every four men and a fifth man as leader; every nine men a tenth; every nineteen men a twentieth, and so on to every thousand; and it was agreed that the penalty for disobedience to the leader of any unit was death. Thus from the ground does freedom raise itself unconquerable.

Warenne, Earl of Surrey, was Edward's commander in the North. When the depredations of the Scottish rebels had become intolerable he advanced at the head of strong forces upon Stirling. At Stirling Bridge, near the Abbey of Cambuskenneth, in September 1297, he found himself in the presence of Wallace's army. Many Scotsmen were in the English service. One of these warned him of the dangers of trying to deploy beyond the long, narrow bridge which spanned the river. This knight pleaded calculations worthy of a modern staff officer. It would take eleven hours to move the army across the bridge, and what would happen, he asked, if the vanguard were attacked before the passage was completed? He spoke of a ford higher up, by which at least a flanking force could cross. But Earl Warenne would have none of these things. Wallace watched with measuring eye the accumulation of the English troops across the bridge, and at the right moment hurled his full force upon them, seized the bridgehead, and slaughtered the vanguard of five thousand men. Warenne evacuated the greater part of Scotland. His fortress garrisons were reduced one after the other. The English could barely hold the line of the Tweed.

It was beyond the compass of King Edward's resources to wage war with France and face the hideous struggle with Scotland at the same time. He sought at all costs to concentrate on the peril nearest home. He entered upon a long series of negotiations with the French king which were covered by truces repeatedly renewed, and reached a final Treaty of Paris in 1303. Though the formal peace was delayed for some years, it was in fact sealed by the arrangement of a marriage between Edward and Philip's sister, the young Princess Margaret, and also by the betrothal of Edward's son and heir, Edward of Carnarvon, to Philip's daughter Isabella. This dual alliance of blood brought the French war to an effective close in 1299, although through Papal complications neither the peace nor the King's marriage were finally and formally confirmed. By these diplomatic arrangements Edward for two years was able to concentrate his strengths against the Scots.

Wallace was now the ruler of Scotland, and the war was without truce or mercy. A hated English official, a tax-gatherer, had fallen at the bridge. His skin, cut into suitable strips, covered Wallace's sword-belt for the future. Edward, forced to quit his campaign in France, hastened to the scene of disaster, and with the whole feudal levy of England advanced against the Scots. The Battle of Falkirk in 1298, which he conducted in person, bears a sharp contrast to Stirling Bridge. Wallace, now at the head of stronger powers, accepted battle in a withdrawn defensive position. He had few cavalry and few archers; but his confidence lay in the solid "schiltrons" (or circles) of spearmen, who were invincible except by actual physical destruction. The armoured cavalry of the English vanguard were hurled back with severe losses from the spear-points. But Edward, bringing up his Welsh archers in the intervals between horsemen of the second line, concentrated a hail of arrows upon particular points in the Scottish schiltrons, so that there were more dead and wounded than living men in these places. Into the gaps and over the carcasses the knighthood of England forced their way. Once the Scottish order was broken the spearmen were quickly massacred. The slaughter ended only in the depths of the woods, and Wallace and the Scottish army were once again fugitives, hunted as rebels, starving, suffering the worst of human privations, but still in arms.

The Scots were unconquerable foes. It was not until 1305 that Wallace was captured, tried with full ceremonial in Westminster Hall, and hanged, drawn, and quartered at Tyburn. But the Scottish war was one in which, as a chronicler said, "every winter undid every summer's work". Wallace was to pass the torch to Robert Bruce.

In the closing years of Edward's life he appears as a lonely and wrathful old man. A new generation had grown up around him with whom he had slight acquaintance and less sympathy. Queen Margaret was young enough to be his daughter, and sided often with her step-children against their father. Few dared to oppose the old King, but he had little love or respect in his family circle.

With Robert Bruce, grandson of the claimant of 1290, who had won his way partly by right of birth, but also by hard measures, the war in Scotland flared again. He met the chief Scotsman who represented the English interest in the solemn sanctuary of the church in the Border town of Dumfries. The two leaders were closeted together. Presently Bruce emerged alone, and said to his followers, "I doubt me I have killed the Red Comyn." Whereat his chief supporter, muttering "I'se mak' siccar!" re-entered the sacred edifice. A new champion of this grand Northern race had thus appeared in arms. King Edward was old, but his will-power was unbroken. When the news came south to Winchester, where he held his Court, that Bruce had been crowned at Scone his fury was terrible to behold. He launched a campaign in the summer of 1306 in which Bruce was defeated and driven to take refuge on Rathlin

Island, off the coast of Antrim. Here, according to the tale, Bruce was heartened by the persistent effort of the most celebrated spider known to history. Next spring he returned to Scotland. Edward was now too ill to march or ride. Like the Emperor Severus a thousand years before, he was carried in a litter against this stern people, and like him died upon the road. His last thoughts were on Scotland and on the Holy Land. He conjured his son to carry his bones in the van of the army which should finally bring Scotland to obedience, and to send his heart to Palestine with a band of a hundred knights to help recover the sacred city. Neither wish was fulfilled by his futile and unworthy heir.

Edward I was the last great figure in the formative period of English law. His statutes, which settled questions of public order, assigned limits to the powers of the seigneurial courts, and restrained the sprawling and luxurious growth of judge-made law, laid down principles that remained fundamental to the law of property until the mid-nineteenth century.

In the constitutional sphere the work of Edward I was not less durable. He had made Parliament – that is to say, certain selected magnates and representatives of the shires and boroughs – the associate of the Crown, in place of the old Court of Tenants-in-Chief. By the end of his reign this conception had been established.

Dark constitutional problems loomed in the future. The boundary between the powers of Parliament and those of the Crown was as yet very vaguely drawn. A statute, it was quickly accepted, was a law enacted by the King in Parliament, and could only be repealed with the consent of Parliament itself. But Parliament was still in its infancy. The initiative in the work of government still rested with the King, and necessarily he retained many powers whose limits were undefined. Did royal ordinances, made in the Privy Council on the King's sole authority, have the validity of law? Could the King in particular cases override a statute on the plea of public or royal expediency? In a clash between the power of King and Parliament who was to say on which side right lay? Inevitably, as Parliament grew to a fuller stature, these questions would be asked; but for a final answer they were to wait until Stuart kings sat on the English throne. Nevertheless the foundations of a strong national monarchy for a United Kingdom and of a Parliamentary Constitution had been laid.

CHAPTER FOURTEEN

BANNOCKBURN

*Edward II – Lords Ordainers – Piers Gaveston, the King's favourite and
the barons' enemy – Gaveston's execution – war with Scotland –
Bannockburn – the growing importance of Parliament – barons fighting
the Crown – Thomas of Lancaster – the emergence of a Royalist party –
the Despensers – Queen Isabella and Mortimer lead rebellion – the
execution of the King at Berkeley Castle*

E DWARD II'S reign may fairly be regarded as a melancholy appendix
to his father's and the prelude to his son's. In default of a dominating
Parliamentary institution, the Curia Regis seemed to be the centre
from which the business of Government could be controlled. On the
death of Edward I the barons succeeded in gaining control of this mixed
body of powerful magnates and competent Household officials. They set up a
committee called the "Lords Ordainers", who represented the baronial and
ecclesiastical interests of the State.

Scotland and France remained the external problems confronting these new
masters of government, but their first anger was directed upon the favourite
of the King. Piers Gaveston, a young, handsome Gascon, enjoyed his fullest
confidence. His decisions made or marred. There was a temper which would
submit to the rule of a King, but would not tolerate the pretensions of his
personal cronies. The barons' party attacked Piers Gaveston. Edward and his
favourite tried to stave off opposition by harrying the Scots. They failed, and
in 1311 Gaveston was exiled to Flanders. Thence he was so imprudent as to
return, in defiance of the Lords Ordainers. Compelling him to take refuge in
the North, they pursued him, not so much by war as by a process of
establishing their authority, occupying castles, controlling the courts, and
giving to the armed forces orders which were obeyed. Besieged in the castle of
Scarborough, Gaveston made terms with his foes. His life was to be spared;
and on this they took him under guard. But other nobles, led by the Earl of
Warwick, one of the foremost Ordainers, who had not been present at the
agreement of Scarborough, violated these conditions. They overpowered the
escort, seized the favourite at Deddington in Oxfordshire, and hewed off his
head on Blacklow Hill, near Warwick.

In spite of these successes by the Ordainers royal power remained formidable. Edward was still in control of Government, although he was under their restraint. Troubles in France and war in Scotland confronted him. To wipe out his setbacks at home he resolved upon the conquest of the Northern kingdom. A general levy of the whole power of England was set on foot to beat the Scots. A great army crossed the Tweed in the summer of 1314. Twenty-five thousand men, hard to gather, harder still to feed in those days, with at least three thousand armoured knights and men-at-arms, under the nominal but none the less baffling command of Edward II, moved against the Scottish host. The new champion of Scotland, Robert the Bruce, now faced the vengeance of England. The Scottish army, of perhaps ten thousand men, was composed, as at Falkirk, mainly of the hard, unyielding spearmen who feared nought and, once set in position, had to be killed. But Bruce had pondered deeply upon the impotence of pikemen, however faithful, if exposed to the alternations of an arrow shower and an armoured charge. He therefore, with a foresight and skill which proves his military quality, took three precautions. First, he chose a position where his flanks were secured by impenetrable woods; secondly, he dug upon his front a large number of small round holes or "pottes", afterwards to be imitated by the archers at Crécy, and covered them with branches and turfs as a trap for charging cavalry; thirdly, he kept in his own hand his small but highly trained force of mounted knights to break up any attempt at planting archers upon his flank to derange his schiltrons. These dispositions made, he awaited the English onslaught.

The English army was so large that it took three days to close up from rear to front. The ground available for deployment was little more than two thousand yards. On the morning of June 24 the English advanced, and a dense wave of steel-clad horsemen descended the slope, splashed and scrambled through the Bannock Burn, and charged uphill upon the schiltrons. Though much disordered by the "pottes", they came to deadly grip with the Scottish spearmen. "And when the two hosts so came together and the great steeds of the knights dashed into the Scottish pikes as into a thick wood there rose a great and horrible crash from rending lances and dying horses, and there they stood locked together for a space." As neither side would withdraw the struggle was prolonged and covered the whole front. The strong corps of arches could not intervene. When they shot their arrows into the air, as William had done at Hastings, they hit more of their own men than of the Scottish infantry. At length a detachment of archers was brought round the Scottish left flank. But for this Bruce had made effective provision. His small cavalry force charged them with the utmost promptitude, and drove them back into the great mass waiting to engage, and now already showing signs of disorder. Continuous reinforcements streamed forward towards the English fighting line. Confusion steadily increased. At length the appearance on the hills to the English right of the camp-followers of Bruce's army, waving flags and raising loud cries, was sufficient to induce a general retreat, which the King himself, with his numerous personal guards, was not slow to head. The retreat speedily became a rout. The Scottish schiltrons hurled themselves forward down the slope, inflicting immense carnage upon the English even before they could recross the Bannock Burn. No more grievous slaughter of English chivalry ever took place in a single day. Even Towton in the Wars of the Roses was less destructive. The Scots claimed to have slain or captured thirty thousand men, more than the whole English army, but their feat in virtually destroying an army of cavalry and archers mainly by the agency of spearmen must nevertheless be deemed a prodigy of war.

In the long story of a nation we often see that capable rulers by their very virtues sow the seeds of future evil and weak or degenerate princes open the pathway of progress. At this time the unending struggle for power had entered upon new ground. The Lord Ordainers, as we have seen, had control of the Curia Regis; but they soon found that many of the essentials of power still eluded their grasp. In those days the King was expected to rule as well as to reign. The King's sign manual, the seal affixed to a document, a writ or warrant issued by a particular officer, were the facts upon which the courts pronounced, soldiers marched, and executioners discharged their functions. One of the main charges brought against Edward II at his deposition was that he had failed in his task of government. From early in his reign he left too much to his Household officials. To the Lords Ordainers it appeared that the high control of Government had withdrawn itself from the Curia Regis into an inner citadel described as "the King's Wardrobe". There was the King, in his Wardrobe, with his favourites and indispensable functionaries, settling a variety of matters from the purchase of the royal hose to the waging of a Continental war. Outside this select, secluded circle, the rugged, arrogant, virile barons prowled morosely.

The forces were not unequally balanced. To do violence to the sacred person of the King was an awful crime. The Church by its whole structure and tradition depended upon him. A haughty, self-interested aristocracy must remember that in most parts of the country, the common people, among whom bills and bows were plentiful, had looked since the days of the Conqueror to the Crown as their protector against baronial oppression. Above all, law and custom weighed heavily with all classes, rich and poor alike, when every district had a life of its own and very few lights burned after sundown. The barons might have a blasting case against the King at Westminster, but if he appeared in Shropshire or Westmorland with his handful of guards and the royal insignia he could tell his own tale, and men, both knight and archer, would rally to him.

In this equipoise Parliament became of serious importance to the contending interests. Here at least was the only place where the case for or against the conduct of the central executive could be tried before something that resembled, however imperfectly, the nation. Thus we see in this ill-starred reign both sides operating in and through Parliament, and in this process enhancing its power. Parliament was called together no fewer than twenty-five times under King Edward II. It had no share in the initiation or control of policy. It was of course distracted by royal and baronial intrigue. Many of its knights and burgesses were but the creatures of one faction or the other. Nevertheless it could be made to throw its weight in a decisive manner from time to time. This therefore was a period highly favourable to the growth of forces in the realm which were to become inherently different in character from either the Crown or the barons.

Thomas of Lancaster, nephew to Edward I, was the forefront of the baronial opposition. Little is known to his credit. He had long been engaged in treasonable practices with the Scots. As leader of the barons he had pursued Gaveston to his death, and, although not actually responsible for the breach of faith which led to his execution, he bore henceforward upon his shoulders the deepest hate of which Edward II's nature was capable. Into the hands of Thomas and his fellow Ordainers Edward was now thrown by the disaster of Bannockburn, and Thomas for a while became the most important man in the land. Within a few years however the moderates among the Ordainers became so disgusted with Lancaster's incompetence and with the weakness into which the process of Government had sunk that they joined with the royalists to edge him from power. The victory of this middle party, headed by the Earl of Pembroke, did not please the King. Aiming to be more efficient than Lancaster, Pembroke and his friends tried to enforce the Ordinances more effectively, and carried out a great reform of the royal Household.

Edward, for his part, began to build up a royalist party, at the head of which were the Despensers, father and son, both named Hugh. These belonged to the nobility, and their power lay on the Welsh border. By a fortunate marriage with the noble house of Clare, and by the favour of the King, they rose precariously amid the jealousies of the English baronage to the main direction of affairs. Against both of them the hatreds grew, because of their self-seeking and the King's infatuation with the younger man. They were especially unpopular among the Marcher lords, who were disturbed by their restless ambitions in South Wales. In 1321 the Welsh Marcher lords and the Lancastrian party joined hands with intent to procure the exile of the Despensers. Edward soon recalled them, and for once showed energy and resolution. By speed of movement he defeated first the Marcher lords and then in the next year the Northern barons under Lancaster at Boroughbridge in Yorkshire. Lancaster was beheaded by the King. But by some perversity of popular sentiment miracles were reported at his grave, and his execution was adjudged by many of his contemporaries to have made him a martyr to royal oppression.

The Despensers and their King now seemed to have attained a height of power. But a tragedy with every feature of classical ruthlessness was to follow. One of the chief Marcher lords, Roger Mortimer, though captured by the King, contrived to escape to France. In 1324 Charles IV of France took advantage of a dispute in Gascony to seize the duchy, except for a coastal strip. Edward's wife, Isabella, "the she-wolf of France", who was disgusted by his passion for Hugh Despenser, suggested that she should go over to France to negotiate with her brother Charles about the restoration of Gascony. There she became the lover and confederate of the exiled Mortimer. She now hit on the stroke of having her son, Prince Edward, sent over from England to do homage for Gascony. As soon as the fourteen-year-old prince, who as heir to the throne could be used to legitimatise opposition to King Edward, was in her possession she and Mortimer staged an invasion of England at the head of a large band of exiles.

So unpopular and precarious was Edward's Government that Isabella's triumph was swift and complete, and she and Mortimer were emboldened to depose him. The end was a holocaust. In the furious rage which in those days led all who swayed the Government of England to a bloody fate the Despensers were seized and hanged. For the King a more terrible death was reserved. He was imprisoned in Berkeley Castle, and there by hideous methods, which left no mark upon his skin, was slaughtered. His screams as his bowels were burnt out by red-hot irons passed into his body were heard outside the prison walls, and awoke grim echoes which were long unstilled.

CHAPTER FIFTEEN

SCOTLAND AND IRELAND

Bruce and the Treaty of Northampton – Scotland divided – the beginnings
of the Royal Stuart dynasty – the ransom of King James I – the
Douglases – medieval Ireland – the legend of Tara – the O'Neill's –
"Strongbow" – Beyond the Pale – the Anglo-Irish

THE FAILURES of the reign of Edward II had permanent effects on the unity of the British Isles. Bannockburn ended the possibility of uniting the English and Scottish Crowns by force. Across the Irish Sea the dream of a consolidated Anglo-Norman Ireland also proved vain. Centuries could scarcely break down the barrier that the ruthless Scottish wars had raised between North and South Britain. From Edward I's onslaught on Berwick, in 1296, the armed struggle had raged for twenty-seven years. It was not until 1323 that Robert the Bruce at last obliged the English to come to terms. Even then Bruce was not formally recognised as King of Scots. This title, and full independence for his country, he gained by the Treaty of Northampton, sealed in 1328 after Edward's murder. A year later the saviour of Scotland was dead.

While the Bruce had lived his great prestige and the loyalty of his lieutenants served as a substitute for the institutions and traditions that united England. His death left the throne to his son, David II, a child of five, and there ensued one of those disastrous minorities that were the curse of Scotland. The authority of the Scottish kings had often been challenged by the great magnates of the Lowlands and by the Highland chiefs. To this source of weakness were now added others. The kin of the "Red Comyn",[1] never forgiving his assassination by Bruce, were always ready to lend themselves to civil strife. And the barons who had supported the cause of Balliol, and lost their Scottish lands to the followers of Bruce, constantly dreamt of regaining them with English help. David II reigned for forty-two years, but no less than eighteen of them were spent outside his kingdom. For a long spell during the wars of his Regents with the Balliol faction he was a refugee in France. On his return he showed none of his father's talents. Loyalty to France led him to invade England. In 1346, the year of Crécy, he was defeated and captured at Neville's Cross, in County Durham.

---

1   John Comyn, Lord of Badenoch and supporter of Balliol, was murdered at Dumfries by Robert Bruce, who probably saw Comyn as a contender for the Scottish throne.

Eleven years of imprisonment followed before he was ransomed for a sum that sorely taxed Scotland.

David II was succeeded by his nephew Robert the High Steward, first king of a line destined to melancholy fame. For many generations the Stuarts, as they came euphoniously to be called, had held the hereditary office from which they took their name. Their claim to the throne was legitimate, but they failed to command the undivided loyalty of the Scots. The first two Stuarts, Robert II and Robert III, were both elderly men of no marked strength of character. The affairs of the kingdom rested largely in the hands of the magnates, whether assembled in the King's Council or dispersed about their estates. For the rest of the fourteenth century, and throughout most of the fifteenth, Scotland was too deeply divided to threaten England, or be of much help to her old ally, France. A united England, free from French wars, might have taken advantage of the situation, but by the mid-fifteenth century England was herself tormented by the Wars of the Roses.

Union of the Crowns was the obvious and natural solution. But after the English attempts, spread over several reigns, had failed to impose union by force the reinvigorated pride of Scotland offered an insurmountable obstacle. Hatred of the English was the mark of a good Scot. Though discontented nobles might accept English help and English pay, the common people were resolute in their refusal to bow to English rule in any form. The memory of Bannockburn kept a series of notable defeats at the hands of the English from breeding despair or thought of surrender.

It is convenient to pursue Scottish history further at this stage. Destiny proved adverse to the house of Stuart as the story unfolded. Dogged by calamity, they could not create enduring institutions comparable to English feudalism. King Robert III sent his son, later James I, to be schooled in France. Off Flamborough Head in 1406 he was captured by the English, and taken prisoner to London. In the following month King Robert died, and for eighteen years Scotland had no monarch. Eventually the English Government was prepared to let King James I be ransomed and return to his country.

Captivity had not daunted James. He had conceived a justifiable admiration for the English monarch's position and powers and on his arrival in Scotland he asserted his sovereignty with vigour. During his effective reign of thirteen years he ruthlessly disciplined the Scottish baronage. It was not an experience they enjoyed. James put down his cousins of the house of Albany, whose family had been regents during his absence. He quelled the pretensions to independence of the powerful Lord of the Isles, who controlled much of the Northern mainland as well as the Hebrides. All this was accompanied by executions and widespread confiscation of great estates. At length a party of infuriated lords decided on revenge; in 1437 they found the opportunity to slay James by the sword. So died, and before his task had been accomplished, one of the most forceful of Scottish kings.

The throne once more descended to a child, James II, aged seven. After the inevitable tumults of his minority the boy grew into a popular and vigorous ruler. He had need of his gifts, for the "Black" Douglases, descendant of the Bruce's faithful knight, had now become over-mighty subjects and constituted a heavy menace to the Crown. Enriched by estates confiscated from Balliol supporters, they were the masters of South-West Scotland. Large territories in the East were held by their kin, the "Red" Douglases, and they also made agile use of their alliance with the clans and confederacies of the North. Moreover, they had a claim, acceptable in the eyes of some, to the throne itself.

For more than a century the Douglases had been among the foremost champions of Scotland. One of them had been the hero of the Battle of Otterburn, celebrated in the ballad of Chevy Chase. Their continual intrigues, both at home and at the English Court, with which they were in touch, incensed the young and high-spirited King. In 1452, when he had not long turned twenty-one, James invited the "Black" Douglas to Stirling. Under a safe-conduct he came; and there the King himself in passion stabbed him with his own hand. The King's attendants finished his life.

But to cut down the chief of the Douglases was not to stamp out the family. James found himself sorely beset by the Douglas's younger brother and by his kin. Only in 1455 did he finally succeed, by burning their castles and ravaging their lands, in driving the leading Douglases over the Border. In England they survived for many years, to vex the house of Stuart with plots and conspiracies, abetted by the English Crown.

James II was now at the height of his power; but fortune seldom favoured the house of Stuart for very long. Taking advantage of the English civil wars, James in 1460 laid siege to the castle of Roxburgh, a fortress that had remained in English hands. A special interest of his was cannon and fire-power. While inspecting one of his primitive siege guns the piece exploded, and he was killed by a flying fragment. James II was then in his thirtieth year.

For the fourth time in little more than a century a minor inherited the Scottish crown. James III was a boy of nine. As he grew up he showed some amiable qualities; he enjoyed music and took an interest in architecture. But he failed to inherit the capacity for rule displayed by his two predecessors. His reign, which lasted into Tudor times, was much occupied by civil wars and disorders, and its most notable achievement was the rounding off of Scotland's territories by the acquisition, in lieu of a dowry, of Orkney and Shetland from the King of Denmark, whose daughter James married.

The disunity of the kingdom, fostered by English policy and perpetuated by the tragedies that befell the Scottish sovereigns, was not the only source of Scottish weakness. The land was divided in race, in speech, and in culture. The rift between Highlands and Lowlands was more than a geographical distinction. The Lowlands formed part of the feudal world, and, except in the South-West, in Galloway, English was spoken. The Highlands preserved a social order much older than feudalism. In the Lowlands the King of Scots was a feudal magnate; in the Highlands he was the chief of a loose federation of clans. He had, it is true, the notable advantage of blood kinship both with the new Anglo-Norman nobility and with the ancient Celtic kings. The Bruces were undoubted descendants of the family of the first King of Scots in the ninth century, Kenneth MacAlpin, as well as of Alfred the Great; the Stuarts claimed, with some plausibility, to be the descendants of Macbeth's contemporary, Banquo. The lustre of a divine antiquity illumined princes whose pedigree ran back into the Celtic twilight of Irish heroic legend. For all Scots, Lowland and Highland alike, the royal house had a sanctity which commanded reverence through periods when obedience and even loyalty were lacking, and much was excused those in whom royal blood ran.

But reverence was not an effective instrument of government. The Scottish Estates did not create the means of fusion of classes that were provided by the English Parliament. In law and fact feudal authority remained far stronger than in England. The King's justice was excluded from a great part of Scottish life, and many of his judges were ineffective competitors with the feudal system. There was no equivalent of the Justice of the Peace or of the Plantagenet Justices in eyre.

Over much of the kingdom feudal justice itself fought a doubtful battle with the more ancient clan law. The Highland chiefs might formally owe their lands and power to the Crown and be classified as feudal tenants-in-chief, but their real authority rested on the allegiance of their clansmen. Some clan chiefs, like the great house of Gordon, in the Highlands, were also feudal magnates in the neighbouring Lowlands. In the West the rising of the house of Campbell played either rôle as it suited them. They were to exercise great influence in the years to come.

Meanwhile the Scots peasant farmer and the thrifty burgess, throughout these two hundred yeas of political strife, pursued their ways and built up the country's real strength in spite of the numerous disputes among their lords and masters. The Church devoted itself to its healing mission, and many good bishops and divines adorn the annals of medieval Scotland. In the fifteenth century three Scottish universities were founded, St Andrew's, Glasgow, and Aberdeen – one more than England had until the nineteenth century.

Historians of the English-speaking peoples have been baffled by medieval Ireland. Here in the westernmost of the British Isles dwelt one of the oldest Christian communities in Europe. It was distinguished by missionary endeavours and monkish scholarship while England was still a battlefield for heathen Germanic invaders.

Until the twelfth century however, Ireland had never developed the binding feudal institutions of state that were gradually evolving elsewhere. A loose federation of Gaelic-speaking rural principalities was dominated by a small group of clan patriarchs who called themselves "kings". Over all lay the shadowy authority of the High King of Tara, which was not a capital city, but a sacred hill surmounted by earthworks of great antiquity. Until about the year 1000 the High King was generally a member of the powerful Northern family of O'Neill. The High Kings exercised no real central authority, except as the final arbiters of genealogical disputes, and there were no towns of Irish founding from which Government power could radiate.

The High Kingship had been in dispute since the great Brian Boru – much lamented in song – had broken the O'Neill succession, only himself to be killed in his victory over the Danes at Clontarf in 1014. A century and a half later one of his disputing successors, the King of Leinster, took refuge at the Court of Henry II in Aquitaine. He secured permission to raise help for his cause from among Henry's Anglo-Norman knights. It was a fateful decision for Ireland. In 1169 there arrived in the country the first progenitors of the Anglo-Norman ascendancy.

Led by Richard de Clare, Earl of Pembroke, and known as "Strongbow", the invaders were as much Welsh as Norman; and with their French-speaking leaders came the Welsh rank and file. Even today some of the commonest Irish names suggest a Welsh ancestry. Other of the leaders were of Flemish origin. But all represented the high feudal society that ruled over Western Europe, and whose conquest already ranged from Wales to Syria. Irish military methods were no match for the newcomers, and "Strongbow", marrying the daughter of the King of Leinster, might perhaps have set up a new feudal kingdom in Ireland, as had been done by William the Conqueror in England, by Roger in Sicily, and by the Crusading chiefs in the Levant. But "Strongbow" was doubtful both of his own strength and of the attitude of his vigilant superior, Henry II. So the conquests were proffered to the King, and Henry briefly visited this fresh addition to his dominions in 1171 in order to receive the submission of his new vassals.

The reviving power of the Papacy had long been offended by the traditional independence of the Irish Church. By Papal Bull in 1155 the overlordship of Ireland had been granted to the English king. The Pope at the time was Adrian IV, an Englishman, and the only Englishman ever to be Pope. Here were foundations both spiritual and practical. But the Lord of England and of the greater part of France had little time for Irish problems. He left the affairs of the island to the Norman adventurers, the "conquistadores" as they have been called. It was a pattern often to be repeated.

The century that followed Henry II's visit marked the height of Anglo-Norman expansion. More than half a century was by now directly subjected to the knightly invaders. Among them was Gerald of Windsor, ancestor of the Fitzgerald family, the branches of which, as Earls of Kildare and lords of much else, were for long to control large tracts of Southern and Central Ireland. There was also William de Burgh, brother of the great English Justiciar, and ancestor of the Earl of Ulster; and Theobald Walter, King John's butler, founder of the powerful Butler family of Ormond, which took their name from his official calling. But there was organised colonisation and settlement. English authority was accepted in the Norse towns of the southern and eastern coasts, and the King's writ ran over a varying area of country surrounding Dublin. This hinterland of the capital was significantly known as "the Pale", which might be defined as a defended enclosure. Immediately outside lay the big feudal lordships, and beyond these were the "wild" unconquered Irish of the West. Two races dwelt in uneasy balance, and the division between them was sharpened when a Parliament of Ireland evolved toward the end of the thirteenth century. From this body the native Irish were excluded; it was a Parliament in Ireland of the Anglo-Irish only.

Within a few generations of the coming of the Anglo-Normans however the Irish chieftains began to recover from the shock of new methods of warfare. They hired mercenaries to help them, originally in large part recruited from the Norse-Celtic stock of the Scottish western isles. These were the terrible "galloglasses", named from the Irish words for "foreign henchmen". Supported by these ferocious axe-bearers, the clan chiefs regained for the Gaelic-speaking peoples wide regions of Ireland, and might have won more, had they not incessantly quarrelled among themselves.

Meanwhile a change of spirit had overtaken many of the Anglo-Norman Irish barons. These great feudatories were constantly tempted by the independent rôle of the Gaelic clan chief that was theirs for the taking. They could in turn be subjects of the English king or petty kings themselves, like their new Celtic allies, with whom they were frequently united by marriage. Their stock was seldom reinforced from England, except by English lords who wedded Irish heiresses, and then became absentee landlords. Gradually a group of Anglo-Irish nobles grew up, largely assimilated to their adopted land, and as impatient as their Gaelic peasants of rule from London.

If English kings had regularly visited Ireland, or regularly appointed royal princes as resident lieutenants, the ties between the two countries might have been closely and honourably woven together. As it was, when the English king was strong English laws generally made headway; otherwise a loose Celtic anarchy prevailed. King John, in his furious fitful energy, twice went to Ireland, and twice brought the quarrelsome Norman barons and Irish chiefs under his suzerainty. Although Edward I never landed in Ireland English authority was then in the ascendant. Thereafter the Gael revived. The shining example of Scotland was not lost upon them. The brother of the victor of Bannockburn, Edward Bruce, was called in by his relations among the Irish chiefs with an army of Scottish veterans. He was crowned King of Ireland in 1316, but after a temporary triumph and in spite of the aid of his brother was defeated and slain at Dundalk.

Thus Ireland did not break loose from the English Crown and gain independence under a Scottish dynasty. But the victory of English arms did not mean a victory for English law, custom, or speech. The Gaelic reaction gathered force. In Ulster the O'Neills gradually won the mastery of Tyrone. In Ulster and Connaught the feudal trapping were openly discarded when the line of the de Burgh Earls of Ulster ended in 1333 with a girl. According to feudal law, she succeeded to the whole inheritance, and was the King's ward to be married at his choice. In fact she was married to Edward III's second son, Lionel of Clarence. But in Celtic law women could not succeed to the chieftainship. The leading male members of the cadet branches of the de Burgh family accordingly "went Irish", snatched what they could of the inheritance, and assumed the clan names of Burke, or, after their founder, MacWilliam.

They openly defied the Government in Ulster and Connaught. In the Western province both French and Irish were spoken, but not English, and English authority vanished from these outer parts.

To preserve the English character of the Pale and of its surrounding Anglo-Norman lordships a Parliament was summoned in the middle of the fourteenth century. Its purpose was to prevent the English from "going Irish" and to compel men of Irish race in the English-held parts of Ireland to conform to English ways. But its enactments had little effect. In the Pale the old Norman settlers clung to their privileged position and opposed all attempts by the representatives of the Crown to bring the "mere Irish" under the protection of English laws and institutions. Most of Ireland now lay outside the Pale, either under native chiefs who had practically no dealing with the representatives of the English kings, or controlled by Norman dynasts, such as the two branches of the Fitzgeralds, who were earls or clan chiefs as suited them best. English authority stifled the creation of either a native or a "Norman" centre of authority, and the absentee "Lord of Ireland" in London could not even provide a substitute, nor even prevent his own colonists from intermingling with the population.

By Tudor times anarchic Ireland lay open to reconquest, and to the tribulations of reimposing English royal authority was to be added after Henry VIII's Reformation the fateful divisions of religious beliefs.

CHAPTER SIXTEEN

THE LONG-BOW

Edward III – England ruled by Isabella and her lover Mortimer – the execution of the Earl of Kent – Henry of Lancaster – Mortimer hanged for Edward II's murder – Edward III supports the younger Balliol – the Battle of Halidon Hill – strength of the long-bow – the Staple – start of the Hundred Years War – the Battle of Sluys – Tournai – the Normandy landing – the invasion of France – the Battle of Crécy – the Black Prince wins his spurs

THE REIGN of King Edward III passed through several distinct phases. In the first he was a minor, and the land was ruled by his mother and her lover, Roger Mortimer. This Government, founded upon unnatural murder and representing only a faction in the nobility, was condemned to weakness at home and abroad. Its rule of nearly four years was marked by concession and surrender both in France and Scotland. For this policy many plausible arguments of peace and prudence might be advanced. The guilty couple paid their way by successive abandonments of English interests. A treaty with France in March 1327 condemned England to pay a war indemnity, and restricted the English possessions to a strip of land running from Saintes in Saintonge and Bordeaux to Bayonne, and to a defenceless enclave in the interior of Gascony. In May 1328 the "Shameful Treaty of Northampton", as it was called at the time, recognised Bruce as King north of the Tweed, and implied the abandonment of all the claims of Edward I in Scotland.

The anger which these events excited was widespread. The régime might however have maintained itself for some time but for Mortimer's quarrel with the barons. After the fall of the Despensers Mortimer had taken care to put himself in the advantageous position they had occupied on the Welsh border, where he could exercise the special powers of government appropriate to the Marches. This and his exorbitant authority drew upon him the jealousies of the barons he had so lately led. His desire to make his position permanent caused him to seek from a Parliament convened in October at Salisbury the title of Earl of March, in addition to the office he already held of Justice of Wales for life. Mortimer attended, backed by his armed retainers. But it then appeared that many of the leading nobles were absent, and among them Henry, Earl of

Lancaster, brother of the executed Thomas and uncle of the King, who held a counter-meeting in London. From Salisbury Mortimer, taking with him the young King, set forth in 1328 to ravage the lands of Lancaster, and in the disorders which followed he succeeded in checking the revolt.

It was plain that the barons themselves were too much divided to overthrow an odious but ruthless government. But Mortimer made an overweening mistake. In 1330 the King's uncle, the Earl of Kent, was deceived into thinking that Edward II was still alive. Kent made an ineffective attempt to restore him to liberty, and was executed in March of that year. This event convinced Henry of Lancaster and other magnates that it might be their turn to suffer next at Mortimer's hands. They decided to get their blow in first by joining Edward III. All eyes were therefore turned to the young King. When fifteen, in 1328, he had been married to Philippa of Hainault. In June 1330 a son was born to him; he felt himself now a grown man who must do his duty by the realm. But effective power still rested with Mortimer and the Queen-Mother. In October Parliament sat at Nottingham. Mortimer and Isabella, guarded by ample force, were lodged in the castle. It is clear that very careful thought and preparation had marked the plans by which the King should assert his rights. Were he to succeed, Parliament was at hand to acclaim him. Mortimer and Isabella did not know the secrets of the castle. An underground passage led into its heart. Through this on an October night a small band of resolute men entered, surprised Mortimer in his chamber, which as usual was next to the Queen's, and, dragging them both along the subterranean way, delivered them to the King's officers. Mortimer, conducted to London, was brought before the peers, accused of the murder in Berkeley Castle and other crimes, and, after condemnation by the lords, hanged on November 29. Isabella was consigned by her son to perpetual captivity. Three thousand pounds a year was provided for her maintenance at various country manors, and Edward made it his practice to pay her a periodic visit. She died nearly thirty years later.

Upon these grim preliminaries the long and famous reign began.

The guiding spirit of the new King was to revive the policy, assert the claims, and restore the glories of his grandfather. The quarrel with Scotland was resumed. Since Bannockburn Robert Bruce had reigned unchallenged in the North. His triumph had been followed inevitably by the ruin and expulsion of the adherents of the opposite Scottish party. Edward, the son of John Balliol, the nominee of Edward I, had become a refugee at the English Court, which extended him the same kind of patronage afterwards vouchsafed by Louis XIV to the Jacobite exiles. No schism so violent as that between Bruce and Balliol could fail to produce rankling injuries. Large elements in Scotland after Bruce's death in 1329 looked to a reversal of fortune, and the exiles, or "disinherited", as they were termed, maintained a ceaseless intrigue in their own country and a constant pressure upon the English Government. In 1332 an endeavour was made to regain Scotland. Edward Balliol rallied his adherents and, with the secret support of Edward III, sailed from Ravenspur to Kinghorn in Fife. Advancing on Perth, he met and defeated the infant David's Regent at Dupplin Moor. Balliol received the submission of many Scottish magnates, and was crowned at Scone.

Henceforward fortune failed him. Within two months he and his supporters were driven into England. Edward III was now able to make what terms he liked with the beaten Balliol. He was recognised by Balliol as his overlord and promised the town and shire of Berwick. In 1333 therefore Edward III advanced to besiege Berwick, and routed the Scots at Halidon Hill. This was a battle very different in character from Bannockburn. The power of the archers was allowed to play its part, the schiltrons were broken, and the exiled party re-established for a while their authority in their native land. There was a price to pay. Balliol had to cede to the English king not only Berwickshire but the whole of South-Eastern Scotland. In exacting this concession Edward III had overshot the mark; he had damned Balliol's cause in the eyes of all Scots. Meanwhile the descendants and followers of Robert Bruce took refuge in France. The contacts between Scotland and France and the constant aid given by the French Court to the Scottish enemies of England rouse a deep antagonism. Thus the war in Scotland pointed the path to Flanders.

Here a new set of grievances formed a substantial basis for a conflict. The loss of all the French possessions, except Gascony, and the constant bickering on the Gascon frontiers, had been endured perforce since the days of John. Successive English kings had done homage in Paris for domains of which they had in large part long since been deprived. But in 1328 the death of Charles IV without a direct heir opened a further issue. Philip of Valois assumed the royal power and demanded homage from Edward, who made difficulties. King Edward III, in his mother's right – if indeed the female line was valid – had a remote claim to the throne of France. This claim, by and with the assent and advice of the Lords Spiritual and Temporal, and of the Commons of England, he was later to advance in support of his campaigns.

The dynastic and territorial disputes were reinforced by a less sentimental but none the less powerful motive, which made its appeal to many members of the Houses of Parliament.[1] The wool trade with the Low Countries was the staple of English exports, and almost the sole form of wealth which rose above the resources of agriculture. The Flemish towns had attained a high economic development, based upon the art of weaving cloth, which they had brought to remarkable perfection. They depended for their prosperity upon the wool of England. But the aristocracy under the Counts of Flanders nursed French sympathies which recked little of the material well-being of the burghers, regarding them as dangerous and subversive folk whose growth in wealth and power conflicted with feudal ascendancy. There was therefore for many years a complete divergence, economic, social, and political, between the Flemish

---

1   By the 1350s, the Lords and the Commoners had started to sit in different Houses although it was not until the end of the 14th century that the Commons took up a permanent place at Westminster. The first Presiding Officer ('Speaker') in the Commons was Peter de Montfort (1258). The first designated Speaker was Sir Thomas Hungerford in January 1377.

towns and the nobility of the Netherlands. The former looked to England, the latter to France. Repeated obstructions were placed by the Counts of Flanders upon the wool trade, and each aroused the anger of those concerned on both sides of the Narrow Sea. The mercantile element in the English Parliament, already inflamed by running sea-fights with the French in the Channel, pleaded vehemently for action.

In 1336 Edward was moved to retaliate in a decisive manner. He decreed an embargo on all exports of English wool, thus producing a furious crisis in the Netherlands. The townspeople rose against the feudal aristocracy, and under Jacques Van Arteveldt, a warlike merchant of Ghent, gained control, after a struggle of much severity, over a large part of the country. The victorious burghers, threatened by aristocratic and French revenge, looked to England for aid, and their appeals met with a hearty and deeply interested response. Thus all streams of profit and ambition flowed into a common channel at a moment when the flood-waters of conscious military strength ran high, and in 1337, when Edward repudiated his grudging homage to Philip VI, the Hundred Years War began. It was never to be concluded; no general peace treaty was signed, and not until the Peace of Amiens in 1802, when France was a republic and the French royal heir a refugee within these isles, did the English sovereign formally renounce his claims to the throne of the Valois and the Bourbons.

Edward slowly assembled the expeditionary army of England. This was not a feudal levy, but a paid force of picked men. Its backbone consisted of indentured warriors, recruited where and how their captains pleased. In consequence far less than the legal quota of unreliable militia needed to be drawn from every shire. Both knights and archers embodied the flower of the nation, and the men who gathered in the Cinque Ports formed one of the most formidable and efficient invading armies history had yet seen. These preparations were well known in France, and the whole strength of the monarchy was bent to resist them.

Philip VI looked first to the sea. For many years there had been a warfare of privateers, and bitter hatred ruled between the maritime populations on both sides of the Channel. All the resources of the French marine were strained to produce a fleet; even hired Genoese galleys appeared in the French harbours. In Normandy plans were mooted for a counter-invasion which should repeat the exploits of William the Conqueror. But Edward had not neglected the sea-power. His interest in the Navy won him from Parliament early in this reign the title of "King of the Sea". He was able to marshal a fleet equal in vessels and superior in men. A great sea battle was necessary before the transport of the English army to France and its maintenance there was feasible. In the summer of 1340 the hostile navies met off Sluys, and a struggle of nine hours ensued. The French admirals had been ordered, under pain of death, to prevent the invasion, and both sides fought well; but the French fleet was decisively beaten and the command of the Channel passed into the hands of the invading Power. The seas being now open, the army crossed to France.

Joined with the revolted Flemings, Edward's numbers were greatly augmented, and this combined force, which may have exceeded twenty thousand, undertook the first Anglo-Flemish siege of Tournai. The city was stubbornly defended, and as the grip of famine tightened upon the garrison the horrible spectacle was presented of the "useless mouths" being driven forth into No Man's Land to perish by inches without pity or relief. But the capture of this fortress was beyond Edward's resources in money and supplies. The power of the archers did not extend to stone walls; the first campaign of what was a great European war yielded no results, and a prolonged truce supervened.

This truce was imposed upon the combatants through lack of money, and carried with it no reconciliation. On the contrary, both sides pursued their quarrel in secondary ways. The French wreaked their vengeance on the burghers of the Netherlands, whom they crushed utterly, and Van Arteveldt met his death in a popular tumult at Ghent. The English retaliated as best they could. There was a disputed succession in Brittany, which they fomented with substantial aids. The chronic warfare on the frontiers of Gascony continued. Both sides looked forward to a new trial of strength. Well-trained men, eager to fight, there were in plenty, but to maintain them in the field required funds, which to us seem pitifully small, but without which all was stopped. How could these resources be obtained? The Jews had been exploited, pillaged, and expelled in 1290. The Florentine bankers, who had found the money for the first invasion, had been ruined by royal default. The main effort, not only of the Court but of Parliament, was to secure the modest sums of ready money without which knights could not ride nor archers draw their bows. But here a fertile source was at hand. The wealthiest and best organised commercial interest in England, the wool trade, was eager to profit from war. A monopoly of wool merchants was created, bound to export only through a particular town to be prescribed by the King from time to time in accordance with his needs and judgment. This system, which was called the Staple, gave the King a convenient and flexible control. By taxing the wool exports which passed through his hands at the Staple port he was assured of an important revenue independent of Parliament. Moreover, the wool merchants who held the monopoly formed a corporation interested in the war, dependent on the King, and capable of lending him money in return for considerate treatment. This development was not welcomed by Parliament, where the smaller wool merchants were increasingly represented. They complained of the favour shown to the monopolists of the Staple, and they also pointed to the menace to Parliamentary power involved in the King's independent resources.

By the spring of 1346 Parliament had at length brought itself to the point of facing the taxation necessary to finance a new invasion. The army was reconstituted, more efficiently than before; its old elements were refreshed with carefully chosen levies. In one wave 2,400 cavalry, 12,000 archers, and other infantry sailed and landed unopposed at St Vaast in Normandy on July 12, 1346. Their object this time was no less than the capture of Paris by a sudden dash. The secret was well kept; even the English army itself believed it was going to Gascony. The French could not for some time collect forces sufficient to arrest the inroad. Caen fell, and Edward advanced, burning and laying waste the country, to the very walls of Paris. But by this time the whole power of the French monarchy had gathered against him.

The thrust had failed and retreat imposed itself upon the army. The challenger was forced to quit the lists at a pace which covered sixty miles in four days. The French army moved on a parallel line to the southward and denied the Seine valley to the retreating English. They must now make for the Somme, and hope to cross between Amiens and the sea. Edward and the English host, which had tried so audacious, even foolhardy, a spring, now seemed penned in a triangle between the Somme, the seashore, and the French mass. No means had been found to bring the fleet and its transports to any suitable harbour. To cross the Somme near the mouth was a desperate enterprise. The ford was very lengthy, and the tides, violent and treacherous, offered only a few precarious hours in any day.

By hard fighting, under conditions most deadly to men encased in mail, the passage was forced. At the landing the Genoese cross-bowmen inflicted losses and delayed the deployment until the long-bow asserted its mastery. Thus did King Edward's army escape. That night they rejoiced. The countryside was full of food; the King gathered his chiefs to supper and afterwards to prayer. But it was certain that they could not gain the coast without a battle. No other resolve was open than to fight at enormous odds. The King and the Prince of Wales, afterwards famous as the Black Prince, received all the offices of religion, and Edward prayed that the impending battle should at least leave him unstripped of honour. With the daylight he marshalled about eleven thousand men in three divisions. Mounted upon a small palfrey, with a white wand in his hand, with his splendid surcoat of crimson and gold above his armour, he rode along the ranks, "encouraging and entreating the army that they would guard his honour and defend his right". Their position on the open rolling downs enjoyed few advantages, but the forest of Crécy on their flanks afforded protection and the means of a final stand.

King Philip at sunrise on this same Saturday, August 26, 1346, heard Mass in the monastery of Abbeville, and his whole army, gigantic for those times, rolled forward in their long pursuit. Four knights were sent forth to reconnoitre. About midday the King, having arrived with large masses on the farther bank of the Somme, received their reports. The English were in battle array and meant to fight. He gave the sage counsel to halt for the day, bring up the rear, form the battle-line, and attack on the morrow. These orders were carried by famous chiefs to all parts of the army. But the thought of leaving, even for a day, this hated foe, who had for so many marches fled before overwhelming forces, and was now compelled to come to grips, was unendurable to the French army. What surety had they that the morrow might not see their enemies decamped and the field bare? It became impossible to control the forward movement. All the roads and tracks from Abbeville to Crécy were black and glittering with the marching columns. King Philip's orders were obeyed by some, rejected by most. While many great bodies halted obediently, still larger masses poured forward, forcing their way through the stationary or withdrawing troops, and at about five in the afternoon came face to face with the English army lying in full view on the broad slopes of Crécy. Here they stopped.

King Philip, arriving on the scene, was carried away by the ardour of the throng around him. The sun was already low; nevertheless all were determined to engage. There was a corps of six thousand Genoese cross-bowmen in the van of the army. These were ordered to make their way through the masses of horsemen, and with their missiles break up the hostile array in preparation for the cavalry attacks. The Genoese had marched eighteen miles in full battle order with their heavy weapons and store of bolts. Fatigued, they made it plain that they were in no condition to do much that day. But the Count of Alençon, who had covered the distance on horseback, did not accept this remonstrance kindly. "This is what one gets," he exclaimed, "by employing such scoundrels, who fall off when there is anything for them to do." Forward the Genoese! At this moment, while the cross-bowmen were threading their way to the front under many scornful glances, dark clouds swept across the sun and a short, drenching storm beat upon the hosts. A large flight of crows flew cawing the air above the French in gloomy presage. The storm, after wetting the bow-strings of the Genoese, passed as quickly as it had come, and the setting sun shone brightly in their eyes and on the backs of the English. This, like the crows, was adverse, but it was more material. The Genoese, drawing out their array, gave a loud shout, advanced a few steps, shouted again, and a third time advanced, "hooted", and discharged their bolts. Unbroken silence had wrapped the English lines, but at this the archers, six or seven thousand strong, ranged on both flanks in "portcullis" formation, who had hitherto stood motionless, advanced one step, drew their bows to the ear, and came into action. They "shot their arrows with such force and quickness", says Froissart, "that it seemed as if its snowed."

The effect upon the Genoese was annihilating; at a range which their own weapons could not attain they were in a few minutes killed by thousands. The ground was covered with feathered corpses. Reeling before this blast of missile destruction, the like of which had not been known in war, the survivors recoiled in rout upon the eager ranks of the French chivalry and men-at-arms, which stood just out of arrow-shot. "Kill me those scoundrels," cried King Philip in fury, "for they stop up our road without any reason." Whereupon the front line of the French cavalry rode among the retreating Genoese, cutting them down with their swords. In doing so they came within the deadly distance. The arrow snow-storm beat upon them, piercing their mail and smiting horse and man. Valiant squadrons from behind rode forward into the welter, and upon all fell the arrow hail, making the horses caper, and strewing the field with richly dressed warriors. A hideous disorder reigned. And now Welsh and Cornish light infantry, slipping through the chequered ranks of the archers, came forward with their long knives and, "falling upon earls, barons, knights, and squires, slew many, at which the King of England was afterwards exasperated". Many a fine ransom was cast away in those improvident movements.

In this slaughter fell King Philip's ally, the blind King of Bohemia, who bade his knights fasten their bridles to his in order that he might strike a blow with his own hand. Thus entwined, he charged forward in the press. Man and horse they fell, and the next day their bodies were found still linked. His son, Prince Charles of Luxembourg, who as Emperor-elect already signed his name as King of the Romans was more prudent, and, seeing how matters lay, departed with his following by an unnoticed route. The main attack of the French now developed. The Count d'Alençon and the Count of Flanders led heavy cavalry charges upon the English line. Evading the archers as far as possible, they sought the men-at-arms, and French, German, and Savoyard squadrons actually reached the Prince of Wales's division. The enemy's numbers were so great that those who fought about the Prince sent to the windmill, whence King Edward directed the battle, for reinforcements. But the King would not part with his reserves, saying, "Let the boy win his spurs" — which in fact he did.

Continuous cavalry charges were launched upon the English front, until utter darkness fell upon the field. And all through the night fresh troops of brave men, resolved not to quit the field without striking their blow, struggled forward, groping their way. All these were slain, for "No quarter" was the mood of the English, though by no means the wish of their King. When night had fallen Philip found himself with no more than sixty knights in hand. He was slightly wounded by one arrow, and his horse had been shot under him by another. Sir John Hainault, mounting him again, seized his bridle and forced him from the field, upon the well-known principle which, according to Froissart, he exactly expounded, of living to fight another day. The King had but five barons with him on reaching Amiens the next day.

On the Sunday morning fog enshrouded the battlefield, and the King sent a strong force of five hundred lancers and two thousand archers to learn what lay upon his front. These met the columns of the French rear, still marching up from Rouen to Beauvais in ignorance of the defeat, and fell upon them. After this engagement the bodies of 1,542 knights and esquires were counted on the field. Later this force met with the troops of the Archbishop of Rouen and the Grand Prior of France, who were similarly unaware of the event, and were routed with much slaughter. They also found very large numbers of stragglers and wandering knights, and "put to the sword all they met". "It has been assured to me for fact", says Froissart, "that of foot-soldiers, sent from the cities, towns, and municipalities, there were slain, this Sunday morning, four times as many as in the battle of the Saturday."

Edward marched through Montreuil and Etaples to Boulogne, passed through the forest of Hardelot, and opened the siege of Calais. Calais presented itself to English eyes as the hive of that swarm of privateers who were the endless curse of the Channel. Here on the nearest point of the

Continent England had long felt a festering sore. Calais was what Dunkirk was to become three centuries later. The siege lasted for nearly a year. Every new art of war was practised by land; the bombards flung cannon-balls against the ramparts with terrifying noise. By sea elaborate barriers of piles stopped the French light craft, which sought to evade the sea blockade by creeping along the coast. All reliefs by sea and land failed. But the effort of maintaining the siege strained the resources of the King to an extent we can hardly conceive. When the winter came his soldiers demanded to go home, and the fleet was on the verge of mutiny. In England everyone complained, and Parliament was morose in demeanour and reluctant in supply. The King and his army lived in their hutments, and during this time he never recrossed the Channel to his kingdom. Machiavelli has shrewdly observed that every fortress should be victualled for a year, and this precaution has covered almost every case in history.

Calais held out for eleven months, and yet this did not suffice. Famine at length left no choice to the besieged. They sued for terms. Calais, then, was the fruit, and the sole territorial fruit so far, of the exertions, prodigious in quality, of the whole power of England in the war with France. But Crécy had a longer tale to tell.

CHAPTER SEVENTEEN

SOCIAL REVOLT

The Black Death – the arrival of gunpowder and the fading of the archer – Poitiers – King John of France captured – Founding of the Order of the Garter – the Queen dies of plague – increasing power of Petition – growth of the Commons – the first Speaker of the House – Wyclif and John of Gaunt become allies – Wyclif's Bible – the death of the Black Prince followed by that of the deserted King Edward III – Richard II becomes King at age ten – deserted farmlands after plague – the Statute of Labourers – the Peasants' Revolt – Wat Tyler – the Lollards – Robert de Vere – Bolingbroke defeats de Vere at Radcot Bridge – the Nottingham Declaration – the Merciless Parliament – the death of John of Gaunt – the King submits to Bolingbroke at Flint Castle – Richard II dies at Pontefract Castle

W HILE FEATS of arms and strong endeavours held the English mind a far more deadly foe was marching across the continents to their doom. Christendom has no catastrophe equal to the Black Death. Vague tales are told of awful events in China and of multitudes of corpses spreading their curse afar. The plague entered Europe through the Crimea, and in the course of twenty years destroyed at least one-third of its entire population. The privations of the people, resulting from ceaseless baronial and dynastic wars, presented an easy conquest to disease. The records in England tell more by their silence than by the shocking figures which confront us wherever records were kept. We read of lawsuits where all parties died before the cases could be heard; of monasteries where half the inmates perished; of dioceses where the surviving clergy could scarcely perform the last offices for their flocks and for their brethren; of the Goldsmiths' Company, which had four Masters in a year. These are detailed indications. But far more convincing is the gap which opens in all the local annals of the nation. A whole generation is slashed through by a hideous severance.

The character of the pestilence was appalling. The disease itself, with its frightful symptoms, the swift onset, the blotches, the hardening of the glands under the armpit or in the groin, these swellings which no poultice could resolve, these tumours which, when lanced, gave no relief, the horde of virulent carbuncles which followed the dread harbingers of death, the delirium, the insanity which attended its triumph, the blank spaces which opened on all sides in human society, stunned and for a time destroyed the life and faith of the world. This affliction, added to all the severities of the Middle Ages, was more than the human spirit could endure. The Church, smitten like the rest in body, was wounded grievously in spiritual power. If a God of mercy ruled the world, what sort of rule was this? Such was the challenging thought which swept upon the survivors. Weird sects sprang into existence, and plague-haunted cities saw the gruesome procession of flagellants, each lashing his forerunner to a dismal dirge, and ghoulish practices glare at us from the broken annals. It seemed to be the death-rattle of the race.

But at length the plague abated its force. The tumours yielded to fomentations. Recoveries became more frequent; the resistant faculties of life revived. The will to live triumphed. The scourge passed, and a European population, too small for its clothes, heirs to much that had been prepared by more numerous hands, assuaging its grief in their universality, turned with unconquerable hope to the day and to the morrow.

Philosophers might suggest that there was no need for the use of the destructive mechanism of plague to procure the changes deemed necessary among men. A more scientific reagent was at hand. Gunpowder, which we have seen used in the puny bombards which, according to some authorities, Edward had fired at Crécy and against Calais, was soon decisively to establish itself as a practical factor in war and in human affairs based on war. If canon had not been invented the English mastery of the long-bow might have carried them even farther in their Continental domination. We know no reason why the yeoman archer should not have established a class position similar in authority to that of the armoured knights, but upon a far broader foundation.

The early fifteenth century was to see the end of the rule of the armoured men. Breastplates and backplates might long be worn as safeguards to life, but no longer as the instrument and symbol of power. If the archers faded it was not because they could not master chivalry; a more convenient agency was at hand which speedily became the common property of all nations. Amid jarring booms and billowing smoke, which frequently caused more alarm to friends than foes, but none the less arrested all attention, a system which had ruled and also guided Christendom for five hundred years, and had in its day been the instrument of an immense advance in human government and stature, fell into ruins. These were plainly carted away to make room for new building.

The calamity which fell upon mankind reduced their numbers and darkened their existence without abating their quarrels. The war between England and France continued in a broken fashion, and the Black Prince, the most renowned warrior in Europe, became a freebooter. Grave reasons of State had been adduced for Edward's invasion of France in 1338, but the character of the

Black Prince's forays in Aquitaine can vaunt no such excuses. Nevertheless they produced a brilliant military episode.

In 1355 King Edward obtained from Parliament substantial grants for the renewal of active war. An ambitious strategy was adopted. The Black Prince could advance northward from the English territories of Gascony and Aquitaine towards the Loire. His younger brother, John of Gaunt, Duke of Lancaster, struck in from Brittany. The two forces were to join for a main decision. But all this miscarried, and the Black Prince found himself, with forces shrunk to about four thousand men, of whom however nearly a half were the dreaded archers, forced to retire with growing urgency before the advance of a French royal army twenty thousand strong. So grim were his straits that he proposed, as an accommodation, that he and the army should be allowed to escape to England. These terms were rejected by the French, who once again saw their deeply hated foe in their grasp. At Poitiers the Prince was brought to bay. Even on the morning of his victory his vanguard was already marching southwards in retreat. But King John of France was resolved to avenge Crécy and finish the war at a stroke. Forced against all reason and all odds to fight, the haggard band of English marauders who had carried pillage and arson far and wide were drawn up in array and position chosen by consummate insight. The flanks were secured by forests; the archers lined a hedgerow and commanded the only practicable passage.

Ten years had passed since Crécy, and French chivalry and high command alike had brooded upon the tyranny of that event. They had been forced to accept the fact that horses could not face the arrow storm. King Edward had won with an army entirely dismounted. The confusion wrought by English archery in a charging line of horses collapsing or driven mad through pain was, they realised, fatal to the old forms of warfare. King John was certain that all must attack on foot, and he trusted to overwhelming numbers. But the great merit of the Black Prince is that he did not rest upon the lessons of the past or prepare himself to repeat the triumphs of a former battle. He understood that the masses of mail-clad footmen who now advanced upon him in such towering numbers would not be stopped as easily as the horses. Archery alone, however good the target, would not save him. He must try the battle of manoeuvre and counter-attack. He therefore did the opposite to what military convention, based upon the then known facts, would have pronounced right.

The French nobility left their horses in the rear. The Black Prince had all his knight mounted. A deadly toll was taken by the archers upon the whole front. The French chivalry, encumbered by their mail, plodded ponderously forward amid vineyards and scrub. Many fell before the arrows, but the arrows would not have been enough at the crisis. It was the English spear and axe men who charged in the old style upon ranks disordered by their fatigue of move- ment and the accidents of the ground. At the same time, in admirable concert, a strong detachment of mounted knights, riding round the French left flank, struck in upon the harassed and already disordered attack. The result was a slaughter as large and a victory as complete as Crécy, but with even greater gains. The whole French army was driven into ruin. King John and the flower of his nobility were captured or slain. The pillage of the field could not be gathered by the victors; they were already overburdened with the loot of four provinces. The Black Prince, whose record is dinted by many cruel acts of war, showed himself a paladin of the age, when, in spite of the weariness and stresses of the desperate battle, he treated the captured monarch with all the ceremony of his rank, seated him in his own chair in the camp, and served him in person with such fare as was procurable. Thus by genius, valour, and chivalry he presents himself in a posture which history has not failed to salute.

King John was carried to London. Like King David of Scotland before him, he was placed in the Tower, and upon this personal trophy, in May 1360, the Treaty of Brétigny was concluded. By this England acquired, in addition to her old possession of Gascony, the whole of Henry II's possessions in Aquitaine in full sovereignty, Edward I's inheritance of Ponthieu, and the famous port and city of Calais, which last was held for nearly two hundred years.

The years of war with France are important in the history of Parliament. The need for money drove the Crown and its officials to summoning it frequently. This led to rapid and important developments. One of the main functions of the representatives of the shires and boroughs was to petition for the redress of grievances, local and national, and to draw the attention of the King and his Council to urgent matters. The stress of war forced the Government to take notice of these petitions of the Commons of England, and during the reign of Edward III the procedure of collective petition, which had started under Edward II, made progress. The fact that the Commons now petitioned as a body in a formal way, and asked, as they did in 1327, that these petitions should be transformed into Parliamentary statutes, distinguishes the lower House from the rest of Parliament. Under Edward I the Commons were not an essential element in a Parliament, but under Edward III they assumed a position distinct, vital, and permanent. They had their own clerk, who drafted their petitions and their rejoinders to the Crown's replies. The separation of the Houses now appears. The Lords had come to regard themselves not only as the natural counsellors of the Crown, but as enjoying the right of separate consultation within the framework of Parliament itself. In 1343 the prelates and magnate met in the White Chamber at Westminster, and the knights and burgesses adjourned to the Painted Chamber to discuss the business of the day. Here, in this Parliament, for the first time, the figure of a Speaker emerged. He was not on this occasion a Member of the House, and for some time to come the Commons generally spoke through an appointed deputation. But by the end of the reign the role of the Speaker was recognised, and the Crown became anxious to secure its own nominees for this important and prominent office.

The concessions made by Edward III to the Commons mark a decisive stage. He consented that all aids should be granted only in Parliament. He accepted the formal drafts of the Commons's collective petitions as the preliminary bases for future statutes, and by the time of his death it was recognised that the commons had assumed a leading part in the granting of taxes and the presentation of petitions. Naturally the Commons stood in awe of the Crown. There was no long tradition of authority behind them. The assertions of the royal prerogative in the days of Edward I still echoed in their minds, and there was no suggestion that either they or Parliament as a whole had any right of control or interference in matters of administration and government. They were summoned to endorse political settlements reached often by violence, to vote money, and to voice grievances; but the permanent acceptance of Parliament as an essential part of the machinery of government and of the Commons as its vital foundation is the lasting work of the fourteenth century.

The renewal in 1369 of serious fighting in Aquitaine found England exhausted and disillusioned. The clergy claimed exemption from taxation, though not always successfully, and they could often flaunt their wealth in the teeth of poverty and economic dislocation. Churchmen were ousting the nobility from public office and anti-clerical feeling grew in Parliament. The King was old and failing and a resurgence of baronial power was due. John of Gaunt set himself to redress the balance in favour of the Lords by a carefully planned political campaign against the Church. Ready to his hand lay an unexpected weapon. In the University of Oxford, the national centre of theological study and learning, criticism of Papal pretensions and power raised its voice. The arguments for reform set forth by a distinguished Oxford scholar named Wyclif attracted attention.[1] Wyclif was indignant at the corruption of the Church, and saw in its profound hierarchy and absolute claims a distortion of the true principles of Christianity. He declared that dominion over men's souls had never been delegated to mortals. The King, as the Vicar of God in things temporal, was as much bound by his office to curb the material lavishness of the clergy as the clergy to direct the spiritual life of the King. Though Pope and King was each in his sphere supreme, every Christian held not "in chief" of them, but rather of God. The final appeal was to Heaven, not to Rome.

Wyclif's doctrine could not remain the speculation of a harmless schoolman. Its application to the existing facts of Church and State opened deep rifts. It involved reducing the powers of the Church temporal in order to purify the Church spiritual. John of Gaunt was interested in the first, Wyclif in the second. The Church was opposed to both. Gaunt and Wyclif in the beginning each hoped to use the other for his special aim. They entered into alliance. Gaunt busied himself in packing the new Parliament, and Wyclif lent moral support by running about from church to church preaching against abuses. But counter-forces were also aroused. Wyclif's hopes of Church reform were soon involved in class and party prejudices, and Gaunt by his alliance with the

1   John Wyclif or Wycliffe (c.1330–84) was a Yorkshireman and master of Balliol College, Oxford, from c.1360. About 1376 he wrote *De dominio divino* and *De dominio civil*, claiming the Church should stick to spiritual and not temporal affairs.

revolutionary theologian consolidated the vested interest of the Episcopate against himself. Thus both suffered from their union. The bishops, recognising in Wyclif Gaunt's most dangerous supporter, arraigned him on charges of heresy at St Paul's. Gaunt, coming to his aid, encountered the hostility of the London mob. The ill-matched partnership fell to pieces and Wyclif ceased to count in high politics.

It was at this same point that his enduring influence began. He resolved to appeal to the people. Church abuses and his own reforming doctrines had attracted many young students around him. He organised his followers into bands of poor preachers, who, like those of Wesley in a later century, spread the doctrines of poetry and holiness for the clergy throughout the countryside. He wrote English tracts, of which the most famous was *The Wicket*, which were passed from hand to hand. Finally, with his students he took the tremendous step of having the Bible translated into English. The spirit of early Christianity now revived the English countryside with a keen, refreshing breeze after the weariness of sultry days. But the new vision opened to rich and poor alike profoundly disturbed the decaying society to which it was vouchsafed. The powers of Church and State were soon to realise their danger.

The long reign had reached its dusk. The glories of Crécy and Poitiers had faded. The warlike King, whose ruling passions were power and fame, who had been willing to barter many prerogatives for which his ancestors had striven in order to obtain money for foreign adventure, was now in old age a debtor to time and fortune. Harsh were the suits they laid against him. He saw the wide conquests which his sword and his son had made in France melt like snow at Easter. A few coastal towns alone attested the splendour of victories long to be cherished in the memories of the Island race. Queen Phillipa, his loving wife, had died of plague in 1369. Even before her death the old King had fallen under the consoling thrall of Alice Perrers, a lady of indifferent extraction, but of remarkable wit and capacity, untrammelled by scruple or by prudence. The spectacle of the famous King in his sixties, infatuated by an illicit love, jarred upon the haggard yet touchy temper of the times. Here was something less romantic than the courtly love that had been symbolised in 1348 by the founding of the Order of the Garter.

The King, at length worn down by war, business and pleasure subsided into senility. In 1376 the Black Prince expired, leaving a son not ten years old as heir apparent to the throne. In 1377 King Edward died deserted by all.

John of Gaunt was now head of the Council of Regency and ruled the land. Both the impact and the shadow of the Black Death dominated the scene. A new fluidity swept English society. The pang of almost mortal injury still throbbed, but with it crept a feeling that there was for the moment more room in the land. A multitude of vacant places had just been filled, and many men in all classes had the sense of unexpected promotion and enlargement about them. The belief that the English were invincible and supreme in war, that nothing could stand before their arms, was ingrained. Few recognised the difference between winning battles and making lasting conquests. Parliament in its youth was eager for war, improvident in preparation, and resentful in paying for it. While the war continued the Crown was expected to produce dazzling results, and at the same time was censured for the burden of taxation and annoyance to the realm. A peace approached inexorably which would in no way correspond to the sensation of overwhelming victory in which the English indulged themselves. This ugly prospect came to Richard II as a prominent part of his inheritance.

In medieval England the lords of the manors had often based their prosperity on a serf peasantry, whose status and duties were enjoined by long custom and enforced by manorial courts. Around each manor a closely bound and self-sufficient community revolved. Although there had been more movement of labour and interchange of goods in the thirteenth and early fourteenth centuries than was formerly supposed, development had been relatively slow and the break-up of the village community gradual. The time had now come when the compartments of society and toil could no longer preserve their structure. The convulsion of the Black Death violently accelerated this deep and rending process. Nearly one-third of the population being suddenly dead, a large part of the land passed out of cultivation. The survivors turned their ploughs to the richest soils and quartered their flocks and herds on the fairest pastures. Small-holdings were deserted, and many manors were denuded of the peasantry who had served them from time immemorial. Ploughmen and labourers found themselves in high demand, and were competed for on all sides. They in their turn sought to better themselves, or at least to keep their living equal with the rising prices.

But their masters repulsed fiercely demands for increased wages; they revived ancient claims to forced or tied labour. The pedigrees of villagers were scrutinised with a care hitherto only bestowed upon persons of quality. The villeins who were declared serfs were at least free from new claims. Assertions of long-lapsed authority, however good in law, were violently resisted by the country folk. They formed unions of labourers to guard their interests. There were escapes of villeins from the estates, like those of the slaves from the Southern states of America in the 1850s. Some landlords in their embarrassment offered to commute the labour services they claimed and to procure obedience by granting leases to small-holders. On some manors the serfs were enfranchised in a body and a class of free tenants came into being. But this feature was rare. The greatest of all landlords was the Church. On the whole the Spiritual Power stood up successfully against the assault of this part of its flock. When a landlord was driven, as was the Abbot of Battle, on the manor of Hutton, to lease vacant holdings this was done on the shortest terms, which at the first tactical opportunity were reduced to a yearly basis. A similar attempt in eighteenth-century France to revive obsolete feudal claims aroused the spirit of revolution.

The turmoil through which all England passed affected the daily life of the mass of the people in a manner not seen again in our social history till the

Industrial Revolution of the nineteenth century. Here was a case in which a Parliament based upon property could have a decided opinion. In England, as in France, the Crown had more than once in the past interfered with the local regulation of wages, but the Statute of Labourers (1351) was the first important attempt to fix wages and prices for the country as a whole. In the aggravated conditions following the pestilence Parliament sought to enforce these laws as fully as it dared. "Honorary justices of labour", drawn from the rural middle classes and with fixed salaries, were appointed to try offenders. Between 1351 and 1377 nine thousand cases of breach of contract were tried before the Common Pleas. In many parts the commissioners, who were active and biased, were attacked by the inhabitants. Unrest spread wide and deep.

Throughout the summer of 1381 there was a general ferment.[1] Beneath it all lay organisation. Agents moved round the villages of Central England, in touch with a "Great Society" which was said to meet in London. In May violence broke out in Essex. It was started by an attempt to make a second and more stringent collection of the poll-tax which had been levied in the previous year. The turbulent elements in London took fire, and a band under one Thomas Faringdon marched off to join the rebels. Walworth, the mayor, faced a strong municipal opposition which was in sympathy and contact with the rising. In Kent, after an attack on Lesnes Abbey, the peasants marched through Rochester and Maidstone, burning manorial and taxation records on their way. At Maidstone they released the agitator John Ball from the episcopal prison, and were joined by a military adventurer with gifts and experience of leadership, Wat Tyler.

The royal Council was bewildered and inactive. Early in June the main body of rebels from Essex and Kent moved on London. Here they found support. John Horn, fishmonger, invited them to enter; the alderman in charge of London Bridge did nothing to defend it, and Aldgate was opened treacherously to a band of Essex rioters. For three days the city was in confusion. Foreigners were murdered; two members of the Council, Simon Sudbury, the Archbishop of Canterbury and Chancellor, and Sir Robert Hales, the Treasurer, were dragged from the Tower and beheaded on Tower Hill; the Savoy palace of John of Gaunt was burnt; Lambeth and Southwark were sacked. This was the time for paying off old scores. Faringdon had drawn up proscription lists, and the extortionate financier Richard Lyons was killed. All this has a modern ring. But the loyal citizen body rallied round the mayor, and at Smithfield the young King faced the rebel leaders. Among the insurgents there seems to have been a general loyalty to the sovereign. Their demands were reasonable but disconcerting. They asked for the repeal of oppressive statutes, for the abolition of villeinage, and for the division of Church property. In particular they asserted that no man ought to be a serf or do labour services to a *seigneur*, but pay fourpence an acre a year for his land and

1   The Peasants' Revolt.

not have to serve any man against his will, but only by agreement. While the parley was going on Tyler was first wounded by Mayor Walworth and then smitten to death by one of the King's esquires. As the rebel leader rolled off his horse, dead in the sight of the great assembly, the King met the crisis by riding forward alone with the cry, "I will be your leader. You shall have from me all you seek. Only follow me to the fields outside." But the death of Tyler proved a signal for the wave of reaction. The leaderless bands wandered home and spread a vulgar lawlessness through their counties. They were pursued by reconstructed authority. Vengeance was wreaked.

The rising had spread throughout the South-West. There were riots in Bridgwater, Winchester, and Salisbury. In Hertfordshire the peasants rose against the powerful and hated Abbey of St Albans, and marched on London under Jack Straw. There was a general revolt in Cambridgeshire, accompanied by burning of rolls and attacks on episcopal manors. The Abbey of Ramsey, in Huntingdonshire, was attacked, though the burghers of Huntingdon shut their gates against the rioters. In Norfolk and Suffolk, where the peasants were richer and more independent, the irritation against legal villeinage was stronger. The Abbey of Bury St Edmunds was a prominent object of hatred, and the Flemish woollen-craftsmen were murdered in Lynn. Waves of revolt rippled on as far north as Yorkshire and Cheshire, and to the west in Wiltshire and Somerset.

But after Tyler's death the resistance of the ruling classes was organised. Letters were sent out from Chancery to the royal officials commanding the restoration of order, and justices under Chief justice Tresilian gave swift judg-ment upon insurgents. The King, who accompanied Tresilian on the punitive circuit, pressed for the observance of legal forms in the punishment of rebels. The warlike Bishop le Despenser, of Norwich, used armed force in the Eastern Counties in defence of Church property, and a veritable battle was fought at North Walsham. Nevertheless the reaction was, according to modern examples, very restrained. Not more than a hundred and fifty executions are recorded in the rolls. There was nothing like the savagery we have seen in many parts of Europe in our own times. Law re-established ruled by law. Even in this furious class reaction no men were hanged except after trial by jury. In January 1382 a general amnesty, suggested by Parliament, was proclaimed. But the victory of property was won, and there followed the unanimous annulment of all concessions and a bold attempt to re-create intact the manorial system of the early part of the century.

Yet for generations the upper classes lived in fear of a popular rising and the labourers continued to combine. Servile labour ceased to be the basis of the system. The legal aspect of serfdom became of little importance, and the development of commutation went on, speaking broadly, at an accelerated pace after 1349. Such were the more enduring legacies of the Black Death. The revolt, which to the historian is but a sudden flash of revealing light on medieval conditions among the poorer classes, struck with lasting awe the imagination of its contemporaries. It left a hard core of bitterness among the peasantry, and called forth a vigorous and watchful resistance from authority. Henceforth a fixed desire for the division of ecclesiastical property was conceived. The spread of Lollardy after the revolt drew upon it the hostility of the intimidated victors. Wyclif's "poor preachers" bore the stigma of having fomented the troubles, and their persecution was the revenge of a shaken system.

In the charged, sullen atmosphere of the England of the 1380s Wyclif's doctrines gathered wide momentum. But, faced by social revolution, English society was in no mood for Church reform. All subversive doctrines fell under censure, and although Wyclif was not directly responsible or accused of seditious preaching the result was disastrous to his cause. The landed classes gave silent assent to the ultimate suppression of the preacher by the Church. This descended swiftly and effectively. Wyclif's old opponent, Courtenay, had become Archbishop after Sudbury's murder. He found Wyclif's friends in control of Oxford. He acted with speed. The doctrines of the reformer were officially condemned. The bishops were instructed to arrest all unlicensed preachers, and the Archbishop himself rapidly became the head of a system of Church discipline; and this, with the active support of the State in Lancastrian days, eventually enabled the Church to recover from the attack of the laity. In 1382 Courtenay descended upon Oxford and held a convocation in the chapter house of what is now Christ Church. The chief Lollards were sharply summoned to recant. The Chancellor's protest of university privilege was brushed aside. Hard censure fell upon Wyclif's followers. They blenched and bowed. Wyclif found himself alone. His attack on Church doctrine as distinct from Church privilege had lost him the support of Gaunt. His popular preachers and the beginnings of English Bible-reading could not build a solid party against the dominant social forces.

Wyclif, who died in 1384, had appealed to the conscience of his age. Baffled, though not silenced, in England, his inspiration stirred a distant and little-known land, and thence disturbed Europe. Students from Prague had come to Oxford, and carried his doctrines, and indeed the manuscripts of his writings, to Bohemia. From this sprang the movement by which the fame of John Huss eclipsed that of his English master and evoked the enduring national consciousness of the Czech people.

By his frontal attack on the Church's absolute authority over men in this world, by his implication of the supremacy of the individual conscience, and by his challenge to ecclesiastical dogma Wyclif had called down upon himself the thunderbolts of repression. But his protest had led to the first of the Oxford Movements. The cause, lost in his day, impelled the tide of the Reformation. Lollardy, as the Wyclif Movement came to be called, was driven beneath the surface. The Church, strengthening its temporal position by alliance with the State, brazenly repelled the first assault; but its spiritual authority bore henceforward the scars and enfeeblement resulting from the conflict.

The King was now growing up. His keen instincts and precocious abilities were sharpened by all that he had seen and done. In the crisis of the Peasants' Revolt the brunt of many things had fallen upon him, and by his personal action he had saved the situation on a memorable occasion. It was the King's Court and the royal judges who had restored order when the feudal class had lost their nerve. Yet the King consented to a prolonged tutelage. John of Gaunt, Viceroy of Aquitaine, quitted the realm to pursue abroad interests which included personal claims to the kingdom of Castile. He left behind him his son, Henry Bolingbroke, a vigorous and capable youth, to take charge of his English estates and interests.

It was not till he was twenty that Richard determined to be complete master of his Council, and in particular to escape from the control of his uncles. No King had been treated in such a way before. His grandfather had been obeyed when he was eighteen. Richard at fourteen had played decisive parts. His Household and the Court around it were deeply interested in his assumption of power. This circle comprised the brains of the Government, and the high Civil Service. Its chiefs were the Chancellor, Michael de la Pole, Chief Justice Tresilian, and Alexander Neville, Archbishop of York. Behind them Simon Burley, Richard's tutor and close intimate, was probably the guide. A group of younger nobles threw in their fortunes with the Court. Of these the head was Robert de Vere, Earl of Oxford, who now played a part resembling that of Gaveston under Edward II. The King, the fountain of honour, spread his favours among his adherents, and de Vere was soon created Duke of Ireland. This was plainly a political challenge to the magnates of the Council. Ireland was a reservoir of men and supplies, beyond the control of Parliament and the nobility, which could be used for the mastery of England.

The accumulation of Household and Government offices by the clique around the King and his effeminate favourite affronted the feudal party, and to some extent the national spirit. As so often happens, the opposition found in foreign affairs a vehicle of attack. Lack of money, fear of asking for it, and above all no military leadership, had led the Court to pacific courses. The nobility were at one with the Parliament in decrying the unmartial Chancellor Pole and the lush hedonism of the Court. "They were", they jeered, "rather knights of Venus than of Bellona." War must be waged with France; and on this theme in 1386 a coherent front was formed against the Crown. Parliament was led to appoint a commission of five Ministers and nine lords, of whom the former Councillors of Regency were the chiefs. The Court bent before the storm of Pole's impeachment. A purge of the Civil Service, supposed to be the source alike of the King's errors and of his strength, was instituted; and we may note that Geoffrey Chaucer, his equerry, but famous for other reasons, lost his two posts in the Customs.

When the commissioners presently compelled the King to dismiss his personal friends Richard in deep distress withdrew from London. In North Wales he consorted with the new Duke of Ireland, at York with Archbishop Neville, and at Nottingham with Chief Justice Tresilian. He sought to marshal his forces for civil war at the very same spot where Charles I would one day unfurl the royal standard. Irish levies, Welsh pikemen, and above all Cheshire archers from his own earldom, were gathering to form an army. Upon this basis of force Tresilian and four other royal judges pronounced that the pressure put upon him by the Lords Appellant, as they were now styled, and the Parliament was contrary to the laws and Constitution of England. This judgment, the legal soundness of which is undoubted, was followed by a bloody reprisal. The King's uncle, Gloucester, together with other heads of the baronial oligarchy, denounced the Chief Justice and those who had acted with him, including de Vere and the other royal advisers, as traitors to the realm. The King – he was but twenty – had based himself too bluntly upon his royal authority. The lords of the Council were still able to command the support of Parliament. Moreover, they resorted to arms. Gloucester, with an armed power, approached London. Richard, arriving there first, was welcomed by the people. They displayed his red and white colours, and showed attachment to his person, but they were not prepared to fight the advancing baronial army. In Westminster Hall the three principal Lords Appellant, Gloucester, Arundel, and Warwick, with an escort outside of three hundred horsemen, bullied the King into submission. He could do no more than secure the escape of his supporters.

De Vere retired to Chester and raised an armed force to secure the royal rights. With this, in December 1387, he marched towards London. But now appeared in arms the Lords Appellant, and also Gaunt's son Henry. At Radcot Bridge, in Oxfordshire, Henry and they defeated and broke de Vere. The favourite fled overseas. The King was now at the mercy of the proud faction which had usurped the rights of the monarchy. They disputed long among themselves whether or not he should be deposed and killed. The older men were for the extreme course; the younger restrained them. Richard was brutally threatened with the fate of his great-grandfather, Edward II. So severe was the discussion that only two of the Lords Appellant consented to remain with him for supper. It was Henry, the young military victor, who pleaded for moderation, possibly because his father's claim to the throne would have been overridden by the substitution of Gloucester for Richard.

The Lords Appellant, divided as they were, shrank from deposing and killing the King; but they drew the line at nothing else. They forced him to yield at every point. Cruel was the vengeance that they wreaked upon the upstart nobility of his circle and his legal adherents. The Estates of the Realm were summoned to give countenance to the new régime. On the appointed day the five Lords Appellant, in golden clothes, entered Westminster Hall arm-in-arm. "The Merciless Parliament" opened its session. The most obnoxious opponents were the royal judges, headed by Tresilian. He had promulgated at Nottingham the doctrine of the Royal Supremacy, with its courts and lawyers, over the nobles who held Parliament in their hand. To this a sombre answer was now made, which, though, as so often before, it asserted the fact of feudal power, also proclaimed the principle of Parliamentary control. The fact vanished in the turbulence of those days, but the principle echoed down into the seventeenth century.

Chief Justice Tresilian and four of the other persons responsible for the Nottingham declaration were hanged, drawn, and quartered at Tyburn. The royal tutor, Burley, was not spared. The victory of the old nobility was complete. Only the person of the King was respected, and that by the narrowest of margins. Richard, forced not only to submit but to assent to the slaughter of his friends, buried himself as low as he could in retirement.

We must suppose that this treatment produced a marked impression upon his mind. It falls to the lot of few mortals to endure such ordeals. He brooded upon his wrongs, and also upon his past mistakes. He saw in the triumphant lords men who would be tyrants not only over the King but over the people. He laid his plans for revenge and for his own rights with far more craft than before. For a year there was a sinister lull.

On May 3, 1389, Richard took action which none of them had foreseen. Taking his seat at the Council, he asked blandly to be told how old he was. On being answered that he was three-and-twenty he declared that he had certainly come of age, and that he would no longer submit to restrictions upon his rights which none of his subjects would endure. He would manage the realm himself; he would choose his own advisers; he would be King indeed. This stroke had no doubt been prepared with the uncanny and abnormal cleverness which marked many of Richard's schemes. It was immediately successful. Bishop Thomas, the Earl of Arundel's brother, and later Archbishop of Canterbury, surrendered the Great Seal at his demand. Bishop Gilbert quitted the Treasury, and the King's sympathisers, William of Wykeham and Thomas Brantingham, were restored to their posts as Chancellor and Treasurer. King's nominees were added to those of the Appellants on the judicial bench. Letters from the King to the sheriffs announced that he had assumed the government, and the news was accepted by the public with an unexpected measure of welcome.

Richard used his victory with prudence and mercy. In October 1389 John of Gaunt returned from Spain, and his son, Henry, now a leading personage, was reconciled to the King. The terrible combination of 1388 had dissolved. The machinery of royal government, triumphant over faction resumed its sway, and for the next eight years Richard governed England in the guise of a constitutional and popular King.

The patience and skill with which Richard accomplished his revenge are most striking. For eight years he tolerated the presence of Arundel and Gloucester, not, as before, as the governors of the country, but still in high positions. There were moments when his passion flared. In 1394, when Arundel was late for the funeral of the Queen, Anne of Bohemia, and the whole procession was delayed, he snatched a steward's wand, struck him in the face and drew blood. The clergy raised a cry that the Church of Westminster had been polluted. Men raked up an old prophecy that God's punishment for the murder of Thomas Becket would not be exacted from the nation until blood was shed in that sacred nave. Yet after a few weeks we see the King apparently reconciled to Arundel and all proceeding under a glittering mask.

While the lords were at variance the King sought to strengthen himself by gathering Irish resources. In 1394 he went with all the formality of a Royal Progress to Ireland, and for this purpose created an army dependent upon himself, which was to be useful later in overawing opposition in England. When he returned his plans for subduing both the baronage and the Estates to his authority were far advanced. To free himself from the burden of war, which would make him directly dependent upon the favours of Parliament, he made a settlement with France. After the death of his wife, Anne, he had married in 1396 the child Isabelle, daughter of Charles VI of France. Upon this a truce or pact of amity and non-aggression for thirty years was concluded. A secret clause laid down that if Richard were in future to be menaced by any of his subjects the King of France would come to his aid. Although the terms of peace were the subject of complaint the King gained immensely by his liberation from the obligation of making a war, which he could only sustain by becoming the beggar and drudge of Parliament. So hard had the Estates pressed the royal power, now goading it on and now complaining of results, that we have the unique spectacle of a Plantagenet king lying down and refusing to pull the wagon farther over such stony roads. But this did not spring from lack of mental courage or from narrowness of outlook. It was a necessary feature in the King's far-reaching designs. He wished beyond doubt to gain absolute power over the nobility and Parliament. Whether he also purposed to use this dictatorship in the interests of the humble masses of his subjects is one of the mysteries, but also the legend, long linked with his name. His temperament, the ups and downs of his spirits, his sudden outbursts, the almost superhuman refinements of his calculations, have all been abundantly paraded as the causes of his ruin. But the common people thought he was their friend. He would, they imagined, had he the power, deliver them from the hard oppression of their masters, and long did they cherish his memory.

The Irish expedition had been the first stage towards the establishment of a despotism; the alliance with France was the second. The King next devoted himself to the construction of a compact, efficient Court party. Both Gaunt and his son and Mowbray, Earl of Norfolk, one of the former Appellants, were now rallied to his side, partly in loyalty to him and partly in hostility to Arundel and Gloucester. New men were brought into the Household. Sir John Bushy and Sir Henry Greene represented local county interests and were unquestioning servants of the Crown. Drawn from the Parliamentary class, the inevitable arbiter of the feuds between Crown and aristocracy, they secured to the King the influence necessary to enable him to face the Estates of the Realm. In January 1397 the Estates were summoned to Westminster, where under deft and at the same time resolute management they showed all due submission. Thus assured, Richard decided at last to strike.

Arundel and Gloucester, though now somewhat in the shade, must have considered themselves protected by time and much friendly intercourse from the consequences of what they had done in 1388. Much had happened since then, and Chief Justice Tresilian, the tutor Burley, and other victims of that blood-bath seemed distant memories. It was with amazement that they saw the King advancing upon them in cold hatred rarely surpassed among men. Arundel and some others of his associates were declared traitors and accorded only the courtesy of decapitation. Warwick was exiled to the Isle of Man. Gloucester, arrested and taken to Calais, was there murdered by Richard's agents; and this deed, not being covered by constitutional forms, bred in its turn new retributions. A stigma rested henceforward on the King similar to that which had marked John after the murder of Arthur. But for the moment he was supreme as no King of all England had been before, and still his wrath was unassuaged.

Parliament was called only to legalise these events. It was found to be so packed and so minded that there was nothing it would not do for the King. Never has there been such a Parliament. With ardour pushed to suicidal lengths, it suspended almost every constitutional right and privilege gained in the preceding century. It raised the monarchy upon a foundation more absolute than even William the Conqueror, war-leader of his freebooting lieutenants, had claimed. All that had been won by the nation through the crimes of John and the degeneracy of Edward II, all that had been conceded or established by the two great Edwards, was relinquished. And the Parliament, having done its work with this destructive thoroughness, ended by consigning its unfinished business to the care of a committee of eighteen persons. As soon as Parliament had dispersed Richard had the record altered by inserting words that greatly enlarged the scope of the committee's work. If his object was not to do away with Parliament, it was at least to reduce it to the rôle it had played in the early days of Edward I, when it had been in fact as well as in name the "King's Parliament".

The relations between Gaunt's son, Henry, the King's cousin and contemporary, passed through drama into tragedy. Henry believed himself to have saved the King from being deposed and murdered by Gloucester, Arundel, and Warwick in the crisis of 1388. Very likely this was true. Since then he had dwelt in familiarity and friendship with Richard; he represented a different element from the old nobility who had challenged the Crown. These two young men had lived their lives in fair comradeship; the one was King, the other, as son of John of Gaunt, stood near the throne and nearer to the succession.

A quarrel arose between Henry and Thomas Mowbray, now Duke of Norfolk. Riding back from Brentford to London, Mowbray voiced his uneasiness. The King, he said, had never forgiven Radcot Bridge nor the former Appellant party to which he and his companion had both belonged. They would be the next victims. Henry accused Mowbray of treasonable language. Conflicting reports of what had been said were laid before Parliament. Each, when challenged, gave the lie to the other. Trial by battle appeared the correct solution. The famous scene took place in September 1398. The lists were drawn; the English world assembled; the champions presented themselves; but the King, exasperating the spectators of all classes who had gathered in high expectation to see the sport, cast down his wardour, forbade the combat, and exiled Mowbray for life and Henry for a decade. Both lords obeyed the royal commands. Mowbray soon died; but Henry, astounded by what he deemed ingratitude and injustice, lived and schemed in France.

During 1398 there were many in the nation who awoke to the fact that a servile Parliament had in a few weeks suspended many of the fundamental rights and liberties of the realm. For some time they had had no quarrel with the King. They now saw him revealed as a despot. Not only the old nobility, who in the former crisis had been defeated, but all the gentry and merchant classes were aghast at the triumph of absolute rule. Nor did their wrath arise from love of constitutional practices alone. They feared, perhaps with many reasons not known to us, that the King, now master, would rule over their heads, resting himself upon the submissive shoulders of the mass of the people. They felt again the terror of the social revolution which they had tasted so recently in the Peasants' Revolt. A solid amalgamation of interest, temper, and action united all the classes which had raised or found themselves above the common level. Here was a King, now absolute, who would, as they muttered, let loose the mob upon them.

In February of 1399 died old John of Gaunt, "time-honoured Lancaster". Henry, in exile, succeeded to vast domains, not only in Lancashire and the North but scattered all over England. Richard, pressed for money, could not refrain from a technically legal seizure of the Lancaster estates in spite of his promises. He declared his cousin disinherited. This challenged the position of every property-holder. And forthwith, by a fatal misjudgment of his strength and of what was stirring in the land, the King set forth in May upon a punitive expedition, which was long overdue, to assert the royal authority in Ireland. He left behind him a disordered administration, deprived of troops, and a land violently incensed against him. News of the King's departure was carried to Henry. The moment had come; the coast was clear, and the man did not tarry. In July Henry of Lancaster, as he had now become, landed in Yorkshire, declaring that he had only come to claim his lawful rights as heir to his venerated father. He was immediately surrounded by adherents, particularly from the Lancaster estates, and the all-powerful Northern lords, led by the Earl of Northumberland. The course of his revolt followed exactly that of Isabella and Mortimer against Edward II seventy-two years before. From York Henry marched across England, amid general acclamation, to Bristol, and just as Isabella had hanged Hugh Despenser upon its battlements, so now did Henry of Lancaster exact the capital forfeit from William Scrope, Earl of Wiltshire, Bushy, and Greene, King Richard's Ministers and representatives.

It took some time for the news of Henry's apparition and all that followed so swiftly from it to reach King Richard in the depths of Ireland. He hastened back, though baffled by stormy seas. Having landed in England on July 27, he made a rapid three weeks' march through North Wales in an attempt to gather forces. What he saw convinced him that all was over. The whole structure of his power, so patiently and subtly built up, had vanished as if by enchantment. The Welsh, who would have stood by him, could not face the advancing power of what was now all England. At Flint Castle he submitted to Henry, into whose hands the whole administration had now passed. He rode through London as a captive in his train. He was lodged in the Tower. His abdication was extorted; his death had become inevitable. The last of all English kings whose hereditary right was indisputable disappeared for ever beneath the portcullis of Pontefract Castle.[1] Henry, by and with the consent of the Estates of the Realm and the Lords Spiritual and Temporal, ascended the throne as Henry IV, and thereby opened a chapter of history destined to be fatal to the medieval baronage. Although Henry's lineage afforded good grounds for his election to the Crown, and his own qualities, and still more those of his son, confirmed this decision, a higher right in blood was to descend through the house of Mortimer to the house of York, and from this the Wars of the Roses later broke out upon England.

---

1   The popular belief (certainly Shakespeare's) is that Richard II was murdered at Pontefract Castle. But the evidence for this is circumstantial.

CHAPTER EIGHTEEN

HENRY BOLINGBROKE
AND HENRY V

Henry IV – Parliament strengthens financial powers – De Heretico
Comburendo published – heretics burned alive – Owen Glendower – Henry
kills Hotspur at the Battle of Shrewsbury – the Percy rebellion –
Archbishop Scrope of York beheaded – Henry IV dies in Westminster
Abbey – Henry V – Henry conquers Harfleur – the Battle of Agincourt –
the Treaty of Troyes – Henry marries Catherine of Valois – Henry V dies
of dysentery aged thirty-five

ALL POWER and authority fell to King Henry IV,[1] and all who had run risks to place him on the throne combined to secure his right, and their own lives. From the outset Henry depended upon Parliament to make good by its weight the defects in his title, and rested on the theory of the elective, limited kingship rather than on that of absolute monarchy. He was therefore alike by mood and need a constitutional King. Great words were used at his accession. "This honourable realm of England, the most abundant angle of riches in the whole world", said Archbishop Arundel, "has been reduced to destruction by the counsels of children and widows. Now God has sent a man, knowing and discreet, for governance, who by the aid of God will be governed and counselled by the wise and ancient of his realm." Henry would not act by his own will nor of his own "voluntary purpose or singular opinion, but by common advice, counsel, and consent". Here we see a memorable advance in practice. Parliament itself must not however be deemed a fountain of wisdom and virtue. The instrument had no sure base. It could be packed or swayed. Many of the Parliaments of this period were dubbed with epithets: "the Good Parliament", "the Mad Parliament", "the Merciless Parliament", were fresh in memory. Moreover, the stakes in the game of power played by the great nobles were far beyond what ordinary men or magnates would risk. Who could tell that some sudden baronial exploit might not overset the whole structure upon which they stood?

---

1   Henry Bolingbroke (see above) was the eldest surviving son of John of Gaunt and Blanche of Lancaster, through whom John inherited the Dukedom of Lancaster. It is important to remember this for an understanding of the Wars of the Roses.

As each change of power had been attended by capital vengeance upon the vanquished there arose in the Commons a very solid and enduring desire to let the great lords cut each other's throats if they were so minded. Therefore the Commons, while acting with vigour, preferred to base themselves upon petition rather than resolution, thus throwing the responsibility definitely upon the most exalted ruling class.

Seeking further protection, they appealed to the King not to judge of any matter from their debates or from the part taken in them by various Members, but rather to await the collective decision of the House. They strongly pressed the doctrine of "grievances before supply", and although Henry refused to accept this claim he was kept so short of money that in practice it was largely conceded. During this time therefore Parliamentary power over finance was greatly strengthened. Not only did the Estates supply the money by voting the taxes, but they began to follow its expenditure, and to require and to receive accounts from the high officers of the State. Nothing like this had been tolerated by any of the Kings before. They had always condemned it as a presumptuous inroad upon their prerogative. These great advances in the policy of England were the characteristics of Lancastrian rule, and followed naturally from the need the house of Lancaster had to buttress its title by public opinion and constitutional authority. Thus Parliament in this early epoch appears to have gained ground never held again till the seventeenth century.

But although the spiritual and lay Estates had seemed not only to choose the sovereign but even to prescribe the succession to the Crown, and the history of these years furnished precedents which lawyers of the Stuart period carefully studied, the actual power of Parliament at this time must not be overstated. The usurpation of Henry IV, the establishment of the rival house in the person of Edward IV, the ousting of Edward V by his uncle, were all acts of feudal violence and rebellion, covered up by declaratory statutes. Parliament was not the author, or even the powerful agent, in these changes, but only the apprehensive registrar of these results of martial and baronial struggles. Elections were not free: the pocket borough was as common in the fifteenth as in the eighteenth century, and Parliament was but the tool and seal of any successful party in the State. It had none the less been declared upon Parliamentary authority, although at Henry's instance, that the crown should pass to the King's eldest son, and to his male issue after him. Thus what had been the English usage was overridden by excluding an elder line dependent on a female link. This did not formally ban succession in the female line, but such was for a long time the practical effect.

On one issue indeed, half social, half religious, King and Parliament were heartily agreed. The Lollards' advocacy of a Church purified by being relieved of all worldly goods did not command the assent of the clergy. They resisted with wrath and vigour. Lollardy had bitten deep into the minds not only of the poorer citizens but of the minor gentry throughout the country. It was in essence a challenge first to the Church and then to the wealthy. The

Lollards now sought to win the lay nobility by pointing out how readily the vast treasure of the Church might provide the money for Continental war. But this appeal fell upon deaf ears. The lords saw that their own estates stood on no better title than those of the Church. They therefore joined with the clergy in defence of their property. Very severe laws were now enacted against the Lollards. The King declared, in full agreement with the Estates, that he would destroy heresies with all his strength. In 1401 a terrible statute, *De Heretico Comburendo,* condemned relapsed heretics to be burnt alive, and left the judgment solely to the Church, requiring sheriffs to execute it without allowing an appeal to the Crown. Thus did orthodoxy and property make common cause and march together.

But the Estates of the Realm considered that their chief immediate safeguard lay in the blotting out of the eclipsed faction. They were the hottest against Richard and those who had been faithful to him. Henry might have been able to stem this tide of cowardly retribution but for a sinister series of events. He and most of his Court fell violently ill through something they had eaten, and poison was suspected. The Welsh, already discontented, under the leadership of Owen Glendower,[1] presently espoused Richard's cause. The slowness of communication had enabled one set of forces to sweep the country while the opposite had hardly realised what was happening. Now they in their turn began to move. Five of the six former Lords Appellant, finding themselves in the shade, formed with friends of Richard II a plot to seize the usurping prince at Windsor. Recovered from his mysterious sickness, riding alone by dangerous roads, Henry evaded their trap. But armed risings appeared in several parts of the country. The severity with which these were quelled mounted to the summit of Government. The populace in places joined with the Government forces. The townsfolk at Cirencester beheaded Lord Lumley and the Earls of Kent and Salisbury, the last a Lollard. The conspiracy received no genuine support. All the mercy of Henry's temper could not moderate the prosecutions enforced by those who shared his risks. Indeed in a year his popularity was almost destroyed by what was held to be his weakness in dealing with rebellion and attempted murder. Yet we must understand that he was a braver, stronger man than these cruel personages below him.

The unsuccessful revolt, the civil war which had begun for Richard after his fall, was fatal to the former King. A sanctity dwelt about his person, and all the ceremonial and constitutional procedure which enthroned his successor could not rob him of it. As he lay in Pontefract Castle he was the object of many sympathies both from his adherents and from the suppressed masses. And this chafed and gnawed the party in power. Richard's death was announced in February 1400. But far and wide throughout England spread the tale that he had escaped, and that in concealment he awaited his hour to bring the common people of the time to the enjoyment of their own.

1 Owen Glendower or Owain Glyndwr (1354–c.1416) planned to split the kingdom between himself, the Percys and Edmund Mortimer.

All this welled up against Henry Bolingbroke. He faced continual murder plots. The trouble with the Welsh deepened into a national insurrection. Owen Glendower, who was a remarkable man, of considerable education, carried on a war which was the constant background of English affairs till 1409. The King was also forced to fight continually against the Scots. After six years of this harassment we are told that his natural magnanimity was worn out, and that he yielded himself to the temper of his supporters and of his Parliament in cruel deeds. It may well be so.

His most serious conflict was with the Percys. These lords of the Northern Marches, the old Earl of Northumberland and his fiery son Hotspur, had for nearly three years carried on the defence of England against the Scots unaided and almost entirely at their own expense. They also held important areas for the King in North Wales. They could no longer bear the burden. They demanded a settlement of the account. The Earl presented a bill for £60,000. The King, in bitter poverty, could offer but £40,000. Behind this was a longer tale. The Percys had played a great part in placing Henry on the throne. But Edmund Mortimer, Hotspur's brother-in-law, had joined Glendower in rebellion, and the family were now under suspicion. They held a great independent power, and an antagonism was perhaps inevitable. Hotspur raised the standard of revolt. But at Shrewsbury on July 21, 1403, Henry overcame and slew him in a small, fierce battle. The old Earl, who was marching to his aid, was forced to submit, and pardon was freely extended to him. Parliament was at pains to absolve him from all charges of treason and rebellion and declared him guilty of trespass alone. This clemency was no doubt due to the necessities of the Border and to lack of any other means of defending it against the Scots. The Earl therefore addressed himself to this task, which secured his position at the head of strong forces.

But two years later, with his son's death at heart, he rebelled again, and this time the conspiracy was far-reaching. Archbishop Scrope of York and Thomas Mowbray, Earl of Nottingham, were his principal confederates. The programme of the rebellion was reform, and all personal issues were avoided. Once again Henry marched north, and once again he was successful. Northumberland was driven across the Border, where for some years he remained a menace. Scrope and Mowbray fell into the hands of the King's officers, and Henry, in spite of the appeals of the Archbishop of Canterbury, allowed them to be beheaded after a summary trial. Scrope's execution caused a profound shock throughout the land, and many compared it with the murder of Thomas Becket. At the same time the King's health failed. He was said to be smitten with leprosy, and this was attributed to the wrath of God. The diagnosis at least was incorrect. He had a disfiguring affection of the skin, and a disease of the heart, marked by fainting fits and trances. He was physically a broken man. Henceforward his reign was a struggle against death as well as life.

He still managed to triumph in the Welsh war, and Owen Glendower was forced back into his mountains. But Parliament took all advantages from the

King's necessities. Henry saw safety only in surrender. He yielded himself and his burdens to the Estates with the constitutional deference of a modern sovereign. They pressed him hard, and in all the ways most intimately galling. Foreigners, not even excepting the Queen's two married daughters, were to be expelled. A Council must be nominated by the King which included the Parliamentary leaders. The accounts of Government expenses were subjected to a Parliamentary audit. The King's own Household was combed and remodelled by unfriendly hands. The new Council demanded even fuller powers. The King pledged himself to govern only by their advice. By these submissions Henry became the least of kings.

But there can be no doubt that the dying sovereign still gripped convulsively the reins of power. Misgovernment and decrepitude remained for a while successfully enthroned. In 1412, when the King could no longer walk and scarcely ride, he was with difficulty dissuaded by his Council from attempting to command the troops in Aquitaine. He lingered through the winter, talked of a Crusade, summoned Parliament in February, but could do no business with it. In March, when praying in Westminster Abbey, he had a prolonged fit, from which he rallied only to die in the Jerusalem Chamber on March 20, 1413.

Upon his death a new personality, built upon a grand historic scale, long hungry for power, ascended without dispute the throne not only of England, but very soon of almost all Western Christendom. A gleam of splendour falls across the dark, troubled story of medieval England. Henry V was King at twenty-five. He felt, as his father had never done, sure of his title. He had spent his youth in camp and Council; he had for five or six years intermittently conducted the government of the kingdom during his father's decline. The romantic stories of his riotous youth and sudden conversion to gravity and virtue when charged with the supreme responsibility must not be pressed too far. It may well be true that "he was in his youth a diligent follower of idle practices, much given to instruments of music, and fired with the torches of Venus herself". But if he had thus yielded to the vehement ebullitions of his nature this was no more than a pastime, for always since boyhood he had been held in the grasp of grave business.

In the surging realm, with its ailing King, bitter factions, and deep social and moral unrest, all men had for some time looked to him; and succeeding generations have seldom doubted that according to the standards of his day he was all that a king should be. His face, we are told, was oval, with a long, straight nose, ruddy complexion, dark, smooth hair, and bright eyes, mild as a dove's when unprovoked, but lion-like in wrath; his frame was slender, yet well-knit, strong, and active. His disposition was orthodox, chivalrous, and just. He came to the throne at a moment when England was wearied of feuds and brawl and yearned for unity and fame. He led the nation away from internal discord to foreign conquest; and he had the dream, and perhaps the prospect, of leading Western Europe into the high championship of a leading Crusade. Council and Parliament alike showed themselves suddenly bent on war with France. As was even then usual in England, they wrapped this up in phrases of opposite import. The lords knew well, they said, "that the King will attempt nothing that is not to the glory of God, and will eschew the shedding of Christian blood; if he goes to war the cause will be the renewal of his rights, not his own wilfulness". Bishop Beaufort opened the session of 1414 with a sermon upon "Strive for the truth unto death" and the exhortation "While we have time, let us do good to all men". This was understood to mean the speedy invasion of France.

The Commons were thereupon liberal with supply. The King on his part declared that no law should be passed without their assent. A wave of reconciliation swept the land. The King declared a general pardon. He sought to assuage the past. He negotiated with the Scots for the release of Hotspur's son, and reinstated him in the Earldom of Northumberland. He brought the body, or reputed body, of Richard II to London, and reinterred it in Westminster Abbey, with pageantry and solemn ceremonial. A plot formed against him on the eve of his setting out for the wars was suppressed, by all appearance with ease and national approval, and with only a handful of executions. In particular he spared his cousin, the young Edmund Mortimer, Earl of March, who had been named as the rival King, and through whose family much that was merciless was to follow later.

In 1407 Louis, Duke of Orleans, the decisive power at the Court of the witless French King, Charles VI, had been murdered at the instigation of the Duke of Burgundy, and the strife of the two parties which divided France became violent and mortal. To this the late King of England had owed the comparative relief from foreign menace which eased the closing years of his reign. At Henry V's accession the Orleanists had gained the preponderance in France, and unfurled the Oriflamme against the Duke of Burgundy. Henry naturally allied himself with the weaker party, the Burgundians, who, in their distress, were prepared to acknowledge him as King of France.

The English army of about ten thousand fighting men sailed to France on August 11, 1415, in a fleet of small ships, and landed without opposition at the mouth of the Seine. Harfleur was besieged and taken by the middle of September. The King now invited the Dauphin to end the war by single combat. The challenge was declined. The attrition of the siege, and disease, which levied its unceasing toll on these medieval camps, had already wrought havoc in the English expedition. The main power of France was now in the field. The Council of War, on October 5, advised returning home by sea.

But the King, leaving a garrison in Harfleur, and sending home several thousand sick and wounded, resolved, with about a thousand knights and men-at-arms and four thousand archers, to traverse the French coast in a hundred-mile march to his fortress at Calais, where his ships were to await him. All the circumstances of this decision show that his design was to tempt the enemy to battle. This was not denied him. Marching by Fécamp and Dieppe, he had intended to cross the Somme at the tidal ford, Blanchetaque, which his great-grandfather had passed before Crécy. Falsely informed that the passage would be opposed, he moved by Abbeville; but here the bridge was broken down. He had to ascend the Somme to above Amiens by Boves and Corbie, and could only cross at the ford of Béthencourt. All these names are well known to our generation. On October 20 he camped near Péronne. He was now deeply plunged into France. It was the turn of the Dauphin to offer the grim courtesies of chivalric war. The French heralds came to the English camp and inquired, for mutual convenience, by which route His Majesty would desire to proceed. "Our path lies straight to Calais", was Henry's answer. This was not telling them much, for he had no other choice. The French army, which was already interposing itself, by a right-handed movement across his front fell back before his advance-guard behind the Canche river. Henry, moving by Albert, Frévent, and Blangy, learned that they were before him in apparently overwhelming numbers. He must now cut his way through, perish, or surrender. He lay for the night at the village of Maisoncelles, maintaining utter silence and the strictest discipline. The French headquarters were at Agincourt, and it is said that they kept high revel and diced for the captives they should take.

The English victory of Crécy was gained against great odds upon the defensive. Poitiers was a counter-stroke. Agincourt ranks as the most heroic of all the land battles England has ever fought. It was a vehement assault. The French, whose numbers have been estimated at about twenty thousand, were drawn up in three lines of battle, of which a proportion remained mounted. With justifiable confidence they awaited the attack of less than a third their number, who, far from home and many marches from the sea, must win or die. Mounted upon a small grey horse, with a richly jewelled crown upon his helmet, and wearing his royal surcoat of leopards and lilies, the King drew up his array. The archers were disposed in six wedge-shaped formations, each supported by a body of men-at-arms. At the last moment Henry sought to avoid so desperate a battle. Heralds passed to and fro. He offered to yield Harfleur and all his prisoners in return for an open road to Calais. The French prince replied that he must renounce the crown of France. On this he resolved to dare the last extremity. The whole English army, even the King himself, dismounted and sent their horses to the rear; and shortly after eleven o'clock on St Crispin's Day, October 25, he gave the order, "In the name of Almighty God and of Saint George, Avaunt Banner in the best time of the year, and Saint George this day be thine help." The archers kissed the soil in reconciliation to God, and, crying loudly, "Hurrah! Hurrah! Saint George and Merrie England!" advanced to within three hundred yards of the heavy masses in their front. They planted their stakes and loosed their arrows.

The French were once again unduly crowded upon the field. They stood in three dense lines, and neither their cross-bowmen nor their battery of cannon could fire effectively. Under the arrow storm they in their turn moved forward down the slope, plodding heavily through a ploughed field already trampled into a quagmire. Still at thirty deep they felt sure of breaking the line. But once again the long-bow destroyed all before it. Horse and foot alike went down; a long heap of armoured dead and wounded lay upon the ground, over which the reinforcements struggled bravely, but in vain. In this grand moment the archers slung their bows, and, sword in hand, fell upon the reeling squadrons and disordered masses. Then the Duke of Alençon rolled forward with the whole second line, and a stubborn hand-to-hand struggle ensued, in which the French prince struck down with his own sword Humphrey of Gloucester. The King rushed to his brother's rescue, and was smitten to the ground by a tremendous stroke; but in spite of the odds Alençon was killed, and the French second line was beaten hand to hand by the English chivalry and yeomen. It recoiled like the first, leaving large numbers of unwounded and still larger numbers of wounded prisoners in the assailants' hands.

Now occurred a terrible episode. The French third line, still intact, covered the entire front, and the English were no longer in regular array. At this moment the French camp-followers and peasantry, who had wandered round the English rear, broke pillaging into the camp and stole the King's crown, wardrobe, and Great Seal. The King, believing himself attacked from behind, while a Superior force still remained unbroken on his front, issued the dread order to slaughter the prisoners. Then perished the flower of the French nobility, many of whom had yielded themselves to easy hopes of ransom. Only the most illustrious were spared. The desperate character of this act, and of the moment, supplies what defence can be found for its ferocity. It was not in fact a necessary recourse. The alarm in the rear was soon relieved; but not before the massacre was almost finished. The French third line quitted the field without attempting to renew the battle in any serious manner. Henry, who had declared at daybreak, "For me this day shall never England ransom pay," now saw his path to Calais clear before him. But far more than that: he had decisively broken in open battle at odds of more than three to one the armed chivalry of France. In two or at most three hours he had trodden underfoot at once the corpses of the slain and the will-power of the French monarchy.

When in 1416 the Holy Roman Emperor Sigismund visited London in an effort to effect a peace he recognised Henry as King of France. But there followed long, costly campaigns and sieges which outran the financial resources of the Island and gradually cooled its martial ardour. A much larger expedition crossed the Channel in 1417. After a hard, long siege Caen was taken; and one by one every French stronghold in Normandy was reduced in successive years. After hideous massacres in Paris, led by the Burgundians, hot-headed supporters of the Dauphin murdered the Duke of Burgundy at Montereau in 1419, and by this deed sealed the alliance of Burgundy with England. Orleanist France was utterly defeated, not only in battle, but in the war. In May 1420, by the Treaty of Troyes, Charles VI recognised Henry as heir to the French kingdom upon his death and as Regent during his life. The English king undertook to govern with the aid of a Council of Frenchmen, and to preserve all ancient customs. Normandy was to be his in full sovereignty, but on his accession to the French throne would be reunited to

France. He was accorded the title "King of England and Heir of France". To implement and consolidate these triumphs he married Charles's daughter Catherine, a comely princess, who bore him a son long to reign over impending English miseries.

He induced the Queen of Naples to adopt his eldest brother, John of Bedford, as her heir. The King of Castile and the heir of Portugal were descended from his father's sisters. Soon after his death the youngest of his brothers, Humphrey of Gloucester, married Jacqueline of Holland and Hainault, who possessed other lands as well. "The pedigrees of Southern and Western Europe alike met in the house of Lancaster, the head of which thus seemed to be the common head of all." It seemed to need only a Crusade, a high, sacred common cause against the advancing Ottoman power, to anneal the bonds which might have united, for a space at least, all western Europe under an Englishman. The renewal of strife between England and France consumed powerful contingents which could have been used in defending Christendom against the Turkish menace.

This was the boldest bid the Island ever made in Europe. Henry V was no feudal sovereign of the old type with a class interest which overrode social and territorial barriers. He was entirely national in his outlook: he was the first King to use the English language in his letters and his messages home from the front; his triumphs were gained by English troops; his policy was sustained by a Parliament that could claim to speak for the English people. But glory was, as always, dearly bought. The imposing Empire of Henry V was hollow and false. Where Henry II had failed his successor could not win. When Henry V revived the English claims to France he opened the greatest tragedy in our medieval history.

Fortune, which had bestowed upon the King all that could be dreamed of, could not afford to risk her handiwork in a long life. In the full tide of power and success he died at the end of August 1422 of a malady contracted in the field, probably dysentery, against which the medicine of those times could not make head. When he received the Sacrament and heard the penitential psalms, at the words "Build thou the walls of Jerusalem" he spoke, saying, "Good Lord, thou knowest that my intent has been and yet is, if I might live, to re-edify the walls of Jerusalem." This was his dying thought. He died with his work unfinished. He had once more committed his country to the murderous dynastic war with France. He had been the instrument of the religious and social persecution of the Lollards. Perhaps if he had lived the normal span his power might have become the servant of his virtues and produced the harmonies and tolerances which mankind so often seeks in vain. But Death drew his scythe across these prospects. The gleaming King, cut off untimely, went to his tomb amid the lamentations of his people, and the crown passed to his son, an infant nine months old.

CHAPTER NINETEEN

HENRY VI AND
THE WARS OF THE ROSES

*Henry VI — Joan of Arc — French triumphs — the foundation of Eton
and King's College, Cambridge — Henry marries Margaret of Anjou —
the overthrow and death of Gloucester — the secret of Maine — Jack Cade —
the Paston Letters — beginnings of the Wars of the Roses — the Shrewsbury
Declaration — madness of the King — the birth of Edward, Prince of
Wales — recovery of Henry — the Battle of Wakefield — Duke of York
killed — the sons of dead nobles seek revenge — the Battle of Mortimer's
Cross — Towton — the Duke of York crowned Edward IV — truce with
Scotland — Henry confined to the Tower — the siege of Harlech*

A BABY WAS King of England. Bedford and Gloucester, the uncles of the infant Henry VI, became Protectors, and with a Council comprising the heads of the most powerful families, attempted to sustain the work of Henry V. A peculiar sanctity enshrined the hero's son, and the glory of Agincourt played radiantly around his cradle. Nurses, teachers, and presently noble guardians, carefully chosen for the boy's education and welfare, were authorised to use "reasonable chastisement" when required. But this was little needed, for the child had a mild, virtuous, honest, and merciful nature. His piety knew no bounds, and was, with hunting and a taste for literature, the stay and comfort of his long, ignominious, and terrifying pilgrimage. Through his father he inherited the physical weakness of the house of Lancaster, and through his mother the mental infirmities of Charles VI. He was feeble alike in body and mind, unwise and unstable in his judgments, profuse beyond his means to his friends, uncalculating against his enemies, so tender-hearted that it was even said he would let common thieves and murderers live, yet forced to bear the load of innumerable political executions. Flung about like a shuttlecock between the rival factions; presiding as a helpless puppet over the progressive decay of English society and power; hovering bewildered on the skirts of great battles; three times taken prisoner on the field; now paraded with all kingly pomp before Parliaments, armies, and crowds, now led in mockery through the streets, now a captive, now a homeless fugitive, hiding, hungry; inflicted from time to time by phases of total or partial idiocy; he endured in the fullest measure for nearly fifty years the miseries of human existence, until the hand of murder dispatched him to a world which he was sure would be better, and could hardly have been worse than that he had known. Yet with all his shame of failure and incompetence, and the disasters these helped to bring upon his country, the English people recognised his goodness of heart and rightly ascribed to him the quality of holiness. They never lost their love for him; and in many parts of the country wherever the house of Lancaster was stubbornly defended he was venerated both as saint and martyr.

At the time of the great King's [Henry V] death the ascendancy of the English arms in France was established. In his brother, John, Duke of Bedford, who went to France as Regent and Commander-in-Chief, a successor of the highest military quality was found. The alliance with Burgundy, carrying with it the allegiance and the sympathies of Paris, persisted. The death, in October 1422, of the French king, who had signed the Treaty of Troyes, while it admitted the English infant to the kingship of France, nevertheless exposed his title to a more serious challenge. South of the Loire, except of course in Gascony, the Dauphin ruled and was now to reign. The English attempt to conquer all vast France with a few thousand archers led by warrior nobles, with hardly any money from home, and little food to be found in the ruined regions, reached its climax in the triumph of Verneuil. There seemed to the French to be no discoverable way to contend against these rugged, lusty, violent Islanders, with their archery, their flexible tactics, and their audacity, born of victories great and small under varying conditions and at almost any odds. Even five years later at the "Battle of the Herrings", gained in February 1429 by Sir John Falstaff, odds of six to one could not prevail. A convoy of four hundred wagons was bringing to the front the herrings indispensable to the English army during Lent. They were suddenly attacked on the road. But they formed their wagons into what we should now call a laager; the archers stood between and upon them, and at ranges greater than the muskets of Marlborough, Frederick the Great, or Napoleon could ever attain broke the whole assault. Yet the Dauphin, soon to be King Charles VII, stood for France, and everywhere, even in the subjugated provinces, a dull, deep sense of nationality, stirring not only in gentlefolk, but in all who could rise above the submerged classes, centred upon him.

There now appeared upon the ravaged scene Joan of Arc. In the poor, remote hamlet of Domrémy, on the fringe of the Vosges Forest, she served at the inn. She rode the horses of travellers, bareback, to water. She wandered on Sundays into the woods, where there were shrines, and a legend that some day from these oaks would arise one to save France. In the fields where she tended her sheep the saints of God, who grieved for France, rose before her in visions. St Michael himself appointed her, by right divine, to command the armies of liberation. Joan shrank at first from the awful duty, but when he returned attended by St Margaret and St Catherine, patronesses of the village church, she obeyed their command.

She convinced Baudricourt, governor of the neighbouring town, that she was inspired. He recommended her to a Court ready to clutch at straws. She made a perilous journey across France. She was conducted to the King's presence in the immense stone pile of Chinon. There, among the nobles and courtiers in the great hall, under the flaring torches, she at once picked out the King, who had purposely mingled with the crowd. "Most noble Lord Dauphin," she said, "I am Joan the Maid, sent on the part of God to aid you and the kingdom, and by His order I announce that you will be crowned in the city of Rheims." Alone with him, she spoke of State secrets which she must either have learned from the saints or from other high authority. She asked for an ancient sword which she had never seen, but which she described minutely before it was found. She fascinated the royal circle. When they set her astride on horseback in martial guise it was seen that she could ride. As she couched her lance the spectators were swept with delight.

Orleans in 1429 lay under the extremities of siege. A few thousand English, abandoned by the Burgundians, were slowly reducing the city by an incomplete blockade. The Maid now claimed to lead a convoy to the rescue. In armour plain and without ornament, she rode at the head of the troops. She restored their spirits; she broke the spell of English dominance. Upon her invocation the spirit of victory changed sides, and the French began an offensive which never rested till the English invaders were driven out of France.

Joan now was head indeed of the French army; it was dangerous even to dispute her decisions. The contingents from Orleans would obey none but her. She told Charles he must march on Rheims to be crowned upon the throne of his ancestors. The idea seemed fantastic: Rheims lay deep in enemy country. But under her spell he obeyed, and everywhere the towns opened their gates before them and the people crowded to his aid. With all the pomp of victory and faith, with the most sacred ceremonies of ancient days, Charles was crowned at Rheims. By his side stood the Maid, resplendent, with her banner proclaiming the Will of God. If this was not a miracle it ought to be.

Joan now became conscious that her mission was exhausted; her voices were silent; she asked to be allowed to go home to her sheep and the horses of the inn. But all adjured her to remain. The French captains who conducted the actual operations, though restive under her military interference, were deeply conscious of her value to the cause.

Up to this point she had championed the Orleanist cause. After her "twenty victories" the full character of her mission appeared. It became clear that she served God rather than the Church, and France rather than the Orleans party. Indeed, the whole conception of France seems to have sprung and radiated from her. Thus the powerful particularist interests which had hitherto supported her were estranged. Meanwhile she planned to regain Paris for France. When in May 1430 the town of Compiègne revolted against the decision of the King that it should yield to the English, Joan with only six hundred men attempted its succour. The enemy, at first surprised, rallied, and a panic among the French ensued. Joan, undaunted, was bridled from the field by her friends. She still fought with the rearguard. The two sides were intermingled. The fortress itself was imperilled. Its cannon could not fire upon the confused *mêlée*. Flavy, the governor, whose duty it was to save the town, felt obliged to pull up the drawbridge in her face and leave her to the Burgundian.

She was sold to the rejoicing English for a moderate sum. For a whole year her fate hung in the balance, while careless, ungrateful Charles lifted not a finger to save her. There is no record of any ransom being offered. Joan had recanted under endless pressure, and had been accorded all the mercy of perpetual imprisonment on bread and water. But in her cell the inexorable saints appeared to her again. Entrapping priests set her armour and man's clothes before her; with renewed exaltation she put them on. From that moment she was declared a relapsed heretic and condemned to the fire. Amid an immense concourse she was dragged to the stake in the market-place of Rouen. High upon the pyramid of faggots the flames rose towards her, and the smoke of doom wreathed and curled. She raised a cross made of firewood, and her last word was "Jesus!" History has recorded the comment of an English soldier who witnessed the scene. "We are lost," he said. "We have burnt a saint." All this proved true. Joan of Arc perished on May 30, 1431, and thereafter the tides of war flowed remorselessly against the English. All Northern France, except Calais, was reconquered.

As Henry VI grew up his virtues and simpleness became equally apparent. He was not entirely docile. In 1431, when he was ten years old, Warwick, his preceptor, reported that he was "grown in years, in stature of his person, and also in conceit and knowledge of his royal estate, the which causes him to grudge any chastising". At fifteen he was already regularly attending Council meetings. He was allowed to exercise a measure of prerogative both in pardons and rewards. When the Council differed it was agreed he should decide. He often played the part of mediator by compromise. Before he was eighteen he had absorbed himself in the foundation of his colleges at Eton and at Cambridge.[1] He was thought by the high nobles to take a precocious and unhealthy interest in public affairs which neither his wisdom nor experience could sustain. He showed a feebleness of mind and spirit and a gentleness of nature which were little suited to the fierce rivalries of a martial age. Opinion and also interests were divided upon him. Flattering accounts of his remarkable intelligence were matched by other equally biased tales that he was an idiot almost incapable of distinguishing between right and wrong. Modern historians confirm the less complimentary view. At the hour when a strong king alone could re-create the balance between the nation and the nobility, when all demanded the restraint of faction at home and the waging of victorious war without undue expense abroad, the throne was known to be

---

[1] Henry VI founded Eton as a preparatory school for (his) King's College, Cambridge.

occupied by a devout simpleton suited alike by his qualities and defects to be a puppet.

These were evil days for England. The Crown was beggarly, the nobles rich. The people were unhappy and unrestful rather than unprosperous. The religious issues of an earlier century were now dominated by more practical politics. The empire so swiftly gained upon the Continent was being cast away by an incompetent and self-enriching oligarchy, and the revenues which might have sent irresistible to beat the French were engrossed by the Church.

The princes of the house of Lancaster disputed among themselves. After Bedford's death in 1435 the tension grew between Gloucester and the Beauforts. Cardinal Beaufort, Bishop of Winchester, and one of the legitimatised sons of John of Gaunt's third union, was himself the richest man in England, and a prime master of such contributions as the Church thought it prudent to make to the State. From his private fortune, upon pledges which could only be redeemed in gold, he constantly provided the Court and often the Council, with ready money. Leaning always to the King, meddling little with the ill-starred conduct of affairs, the Beauforts and their associate, William de la Pole, Earl of Suffolk, maintained by peaceful arts and critical detachment an influence to which the martial elements were often forced to defer. The power of this faction was in 1441 turned in malice upon the Duke of Gloucester. He was now wedded, after the invalidation of his marriage with his wife Jacqueline, to the fair Eleanor Cobham, who had long been his mistress. As the weakest point in this array she was singled out for attack, and was accused with much elaboration of lending herself to the black arts. She had made, it was alleged, a wax figure of the King, and had exposed it from time to heat, which wasted it away. Her object, according to her accusers, was to cause the King's life to waste away too. She was declared guilty. Barefoot, in penitential garb, she was made to walk for three days through the London streets, and then consigned to perpetual imprisonment with reasonable maintenance. Her alleged accomplices were put to death. This was of course a trial of strength between the parties and a very real pang and injury to Gloucester.

The loss of France, as it sank in year by year, provoked a deep, sullen rage throughout the land. This passion stirred not only the nobility, but the archer class, with their admiring friends in every village. A strong sense of wounded national pride spread among the people. Where were the glories of Crécy and Poitiers? Where were the fruits of famous Agincourt? All were squandered, or indeed betrayed, by those who had profited from the overthrow and murder of good King Richard. There were not lacking agitators and preachers, priestly and lay, who prepared a national and social upheaval by reminding folks that the true line of succession had been changed by violence. All this was an undercurrent, but none the less potent. It was a background, shadowy but dominant. Exactly how these forces worked is unknown; but slowly, ceaselessly, there grew in the land, not only among the nobility and gentry, strong parties which presently assumed both shape and organisation.

At twenty-three it was high time that King Henry should marry. Each of the Lancastrian factions was anxious to provide him with a queen; but Cardinal Beaufort and his brothers, with their ally, Suffolk, whose ancestors, the de la Poles of Hull, had founded their fortunes upon trade, prevailed over the Duke of Gloucester, weakened as he was by maladministration and ill-success. Suffolk was sent to France to arrange a further truce, and it was implied in his mission that he should treat for a marriage between the King of England and Margaret of Anjou, niece of the King of France. This remarkable woman added to rare beauty and charm a masterly intellect and a dauntless spirit. Like Joan the Maid, though without her inspiration or her cause, she knew how to make men fight. Even from the seclusion of her family her qualities became well known. Was she not then the mate for this feeble-minded King? Would she not give him the force that he lacked? And would not those who placed her at his side secure a large and sure future for themselves?

Suffolk was well aware of the delicacy and danger of his mission. He produced from the King and the lords an assurance that if he acted to the best of his ability he should not be punished for ill consequences, and that any errors proved against him should be pardoned in advance. Thus fortified he addressed himself to his task with a zeal which proved fatal to him. The father of Margaret, René of Anjou, was not only cousin of the French King and his favourite counsellor, but in his own right King of Jerusalem and of Sicily. These magnificent titles were not sustained by practical enjoyments. Jerusalem was in the hands of the Turks, he did not own a square yard in Sicily, and half his patrimony of Anjou and Maine was for years held by the English army. Suffolk was enthralled by Margaret. He made the match and in his eagerness, by a secret article, agreed without formal authority that Maine should be the reward of France. So strong was the basic power of Gloucester's faction, so sharp was the antagonism against France, so loud were the murmurs that England had been betrayed in her wars, that the clause was guarded as a deadly secret. The marriage was solemnised in 1445 with such splendour as the age could afford. Suffolk was made a marquis, and several of his relations were ennobled. The King was radiantly happy, the Queen faithfully grateful. Both Houses of Parliament recorded their thanks to Suffolk for his public achievement. But the secret slumbered uneasily, and as the sense of defeat at the hands of France spread through ever-widening circles its inevitable disclosure boded a moral danger.

During the six years following the condemnation of his wife Eleanor in 1441 Gloucester had been living in retirement, collecting books for Oxford University Library, which he founded. His enemies at this grave juncture resolved upon his final overthrow. Suffolk and Edmund Beaufort, nephew of the Cardinal, supported by the Dukes of Somerset and Buckingham, with the Queen in their midst and the King in their charge, arrested Gloucester when he came to a Parliament summoned at St Edmondsbury, where an adequate royal force had been secretly assembled. Seventeen days Gloucester's corpse was displayed, so that all could see there was no wound upon it. But the manner of Edward II's death was too well known for this proof to be accepted. It was generally believed, though wrongly, that Gloucester had been murdered by the express direction of Suffolk and Edmund Beaufort. It has however been suggested that his death was induced by choler and amazement at the ruin of his fortunes.

It soon appeared that immense forces of retribution were on foot. When in 1448 the secret article for the cession of Maine became public through its occupation by the French, anger was expressed on all sides. England had paid a province, it was said, for a princess without a dowry; traitors had cast away much in the field, and given up the rest by intrigue. At the root of the fearful civil war soon to rend the Island there lay this national grief and wrath at the ruin of an empire. All other discontents fused themselves with this. The house of Lancaster had usurped the throne, had ruined the finances, had sold the conquests, and now had stained its hands with foul murder. From these charges all men held the King absolved alike by his good heart and silly head. But henceforward the house of York increasingly becomes a rival party within the State.

Edmund Beaufort, now Duke of Somerset, became commander of the army in France. Suffolk remained at home to face a gathering vengeance. The Navy was disaffected. Bishop Moleyns, Keeper of the Privy Seal, sent to Portsmouth to pay what could be paid to the Fleet, was abused by the sailors as a traitor to the country, and murdered in a riot of the troops about to reinforce Somerset in France. The officer commanding the fortresses which were to be ceded to France had refused to deliver them. The French armies advanced and took with a strong hand all that was now denied. Suffolk was impeached. The King and Margaret strove, as in honour bound, to save him. Straining his prerogative, Henry burked the proceedings by sending him in 1450 into a five years' exile. We now see an instance of the fearful state of indiscipline into which England was drifting. When the banished Duke was crossing the Channel with his attendants and treasure in two small vessels, the *Nicholas of the Tower*, the largest warship in the Royal Navy, bore down upon him and carried him on board. He was received by the captain with the ominous words "Welcome, traitor", and two days later he was lowered into a boat and beheaded by six strokes of a rusty sword. It is a revealing sign of the times that a royal ship should seize and execute a royal Minister who was travelling under the King's special protection.

In June and July a rising took place in Kent, which the Lancastrians claimed to bear the marks of Yorkist support. Jack Cade, a soldier of capacity and bad character, home from the wars, gathered several thousand men, all summoned in due form by the constables of the districts, and marched on London. He was admitted to the city, but on his executing Lord Say, the Treasurer, in Cheapside, after a mob trial, the magistrates and citizens turned against him, his followers dispersed under terms of pardon, and he himself was pursued and killed. This success restored for the moment the authority of the Government, and Henry enjoyed a brief interlude in which he devoted himself anew to his colleges at Eton and Cambridge, and to Margaret, who had gained his love and obedience.

As the process of expelling the English from France continued fortresses fell, towns and districts were lost, and their garrisons for the most part came home. The speed of this disaster contributed powerfully to shock English opinion and to shake not only the position of individual Ministers but the very foundations of the Lancastrian dynasty. Cash and ambition ruled and the land sank rapidly towards anarchy. The King was a helpless creature, respected, even beloved, but no prop for any man. Parliament, both Lords and Commons, was little more than a clearing house for the rivalries of nobles.

The force of law was appropriated by intrigue. Baronial violence used or defied legal forms with growing impunity. The Constitution was turned against the public. No man was safe in life or lands, or even in his humblest right, except through the protection of his local chief. The celebrated Paston Letters[1] show that England, enormously advanced as it was in comprehension, character, and civilisation, was relapsing from peace and security into barbaric confusion. The roads were insecure. The King's writ was denied or perverted. The royal judges were flouted or bribed. The rights of sovereignty were stated in the highest terms, but the King was a weak and handled fool.

It was upon this community that the agonies of the Wars of the Roses were now to fall. The claims and hopes of the opposition to the house of Lancaster were embodied in Richard, Duke of York. According to established usage he had a prior right to the crown. York was the son of Richard, Earl of Cambridge, and grandson of Edmund, Duke of York, a younger brother of John of Gaunt. As the great-grandson of Edward III he was the only other person besides Henry VI with an unbroken male descent from Edward III, but in the female line he had also a superior claim through his descent from Gaunt's elder brother, Lionel of Clarence. By the Act of 1407 the Beauforts – Gaunt's legitimatised bastards – had been barred from the succession. If Henry VI should succeed in annulling the Act of 1407 then Edmund Beaufort (Somerset) would have a better male claim with York. It was this that York feared. York had taken Gloucester's place as first Prince of the Blood. After Gloucester's death there survived no male of the legitimate house of Lancaster save Henry VI. Around York and beneath him there gathered an immense party of discontent, which drove him hesitantly to demand a place in the Government, and eventually, through Queen Margaret's increasing hostility, the throne itself.

A Yorkist network grew up in all parts of the country, but mainly in the South and West of England, in Kent, in London, and in Wales. It was significant that Jack Cade, at the head of the Kentish insurgents, had pretended to the name of Mortimer. It was widely believed that the Yorkists, as they began

[1] More than 1,000 letters within the Norfolk family of Paston. They give an insight to the way in which a middle-class family lived as well as a commentary of the Wars of the Roses. (They are now lodged in the British Library.)

to style themselves, had procured the murder of Bishop Moleyns at Portsmouth, and of Suffolk on the high seas. Blood had thus already flowed between the houses of Lancaster and York.

In these conditions the character of Richard of York deserves close study. He was a virtuous, law-respecting, slow-moving, and highly competent prince. Every office entrusted to him by the Lancastrian régime had been ably and faithfully discharged. He had given good service. He would have been content with the government of Calais and what was left of France, but being deprived of this for the sake of Somerset he accepted the government of Ireland. Not only did he subdue part of that island, but in the very process he won the goodwill of the Irish people. Thus on the one side a weak King with a defective title in the hands of personages discredited by national disaster, and now with blood-guilt upon them, and on the other an upright and wise administrator supported by a nation-wide party and with some superior title to the Crown.

Anyone who studies the argument which now tore the realm will see how easily honest men could convince themselves of either cause. All England was divided between these two conceptions. Although the Yorkists predominated in the rich South, and the Lancastrians were supreme in the warlike North, there were many interlacements and overlaps. While the townsfolk and the mass of the people, upon the whole, abstained from active warfare in this struggle of the upper classes and their armed retainers, and some thought "the fewer nobles the better", their own opinion was also profoundly divided. They venerated the piety and goodness of the King; they also admired the virtues and moderation of the Duke of York. The attitude and feeling of the public, in all parts and at all times, weighed heavily with both contending factions. Thus Europe witnessed the amazing spectacle of nearly thirty years of ferocious war, conducted with hardly the sack of a single town, and with the mass of the common people little affected and the functions of local government very largely maintained.

In 1450 the ferment of discontent and rivalries drew the Duke of York into his first overt act. He quitted his government in Ireland and landed unbidden in Wales. During the Parliamentary session of the following year a member of the Commons, one Young, boldly proposed that the Duke of York should be declared heir to the throne. This demand was formidable, not only for its backing, but for its good sense. The King had now been married for six years and had no child. The repute in which he stood made it seem unlikely that he would have any. Ought he not, men asked at this time, to designate his successor? If not York, whom then? It could only be Somerset or another representative of the Beaufort line. One can see how shrewdly this thrust was made. But the King, animated certainly by Margaret, repulsed it with unwonted vigour. He refused to abandon his hope of progeny, and, as soon as the Parliament had dispersed, sent the presumptuous Member to the Tower. At this time, also, he broke with the Duke of York, who retired to his castle at Ludlow, on the borders of Wales.

Disgusted by the Government's failure to restore order and justice at home and to prevent military disasters in France, York became more and more convinced that the Beaufort party, which dominated the weak-willed King, must be driven from power. Prayers and protests had failed; there remained the resort to arms. Accordingly, on February 3, 1452, York sent an address to the citizens of Shrewsbury, accusing Somerset of the disgrace in France and of "labouring continually about the King's Highness for my undoing, and to corrupt my blood and to disinherit me and my heirs and such persons as be about me. ... Seeing that the said Duke ever prevaileth and ruleth about the King's person, and advises him so ill that the land is likely to be destroyed, I may full conclude to proceed in all haste against him with the help of my kinsmen and friends." On this he marched from Shrewsbury towards London, with an army of several thousand men, including artillery. He moved into Kent, plainly expecting that those who had marched with Jack Cade would rally to his cause. The response was disappointing. London closed its gates against his emissaries. The King was carried by Margaret, Somerset, and the Lancastrian interests to Blackheath, with a superior force. Civil war seemed about to begin.

But York felt himself the weaker. He was constitutionally averse from violence. Norfolk was on his side, and other great nobles, but the Earl of Warwick, twenty-four years old, was with the King. Every effort was made to prevent bloodshed. Parleys were unending. In the event York dispersed his forces and presented himself unarmed and bareheaded before King Henry, protesting his loyalty, but demanding redress. His life hung by a thread. Few about the King's person would have scrupled to slay him. But all knew the consequences. York stood for a cause; he was supported by the Commons; half the nation was behind him; his youthful son, the Earl of March, had a second army on foot on the Welsh border. York declared himself "the King's liegeman and servant". Since he was supported by the Commons and evidently at the head of a great party, the King promised that "a sad and substantial Council" should be formed, of which he should be a member. The Court had still to choose between Somerset and York. The Queen, always working with Somerset, decided the issue in his favour. He was appointed Constable of Calais, garrisoned by the only regular troops in the pay of the Crown, and was in fact for more than a year at the head of affairs both in France and at home.

Then in quick succession a series of grave events occurred. The disasters culminated in France. Talbot's attempt to reconquer Gascony failed; he was defeated at Castillon in July 1453, and Bordeaux fell in October. Somerset, the chief commander, bore the burden of defeat. In this situation the King went mad. He had gone down to Wiltshire to spend July and August. Suddenly his memory failed. He recognised no one, not even the Queen. He could eat and drink, but his speech was childish or incoherent. He could not walk. When these terrible facts became known Queen Margaret aspired to be Protector. But the adverse forces were too strong for the Lancastrian party to make the challenge. Moreover, she had another preoccupation. On October 13 she gave birth to a son.[1] How far this event was expected is not clear, but, as long afterwards with James II, it inevitably hardened the hearts of all men. It seemed to shut out for ever the Yorkist claim. Now it seemed there would be a Lancastrian ascendancy for ever.

The insanity of the King defeated Somerset: he could no longer withstand York. Norfolk, one of York's supporters, presented a petition against him to the Council, and in December 1453 he was committed to the Tower. The strength of York's position bore him to the Protectorate. He moved by Parliamentary means and with great moderation, but he was not to be withstood. He obtained full control of the Executive, and enjoyed the support of both Houses of Parliament. He had not long to show his qualities, but an immediate improvement in the administration was recognised. He set to work with cool vigour to suppress livery and maintenance and to restore order on the roads and throughout the land. He did not hesitate to imprison several of his own most prominent adherents, among them the Earl of Devonshire, for levying a private war. If he refrained from bringing Somerset, who was still imprisoned, to trial, this was only from mercy. His party were astounded at his tolerance. When the Government was in his hands, when his future was marred by the new heir to the Crown, when his power or his life might be destroyed at any moment by the King's recovery, he kept absolute faith with right and justice. Here then is his monument and justification. He stands before history as a patriot ready to risk his life to protect good government, but unwilling to raise his hand against the State in any personal interest.

Surprises continued. When it was generally believed that Henry's line was extinct he had produced an heir. When he seemed to have sunk into permanent imbecility he suddenly recovered. At Christmas 1454 he regained all his faculties.

In the spring of 1455 the Red Rose of Lancaster bloomed again. York ceased legally to be Protector from the moment that the King's mental recovery was known; he made no effort to retain the power. Queen Margaret took the helm. Somerset was not only released but restored to his key position. York's government of Calais, which had been conferred upon him for seven years, was handed back to his rival. He was no longer invited to the King's Council board; and when a Great Council of peers was convened at Leicester he feared that he was summoned only to be tried. He retired to Sandal, in Yorkshire, and, being joined by the Earls of Warwick and Salisbury, together with a large company of nobles, strongly attended, he denounced Somerset as the man who, having lost Normandy and Guienne, was now about to ruin the whole kingdom. York's lords agreed upon a resort to arms. With three thousand men they marched south. At the same time the Duke of Norfolk appeared at the head of several thousand Yorkists, and Shrewsbury and Sir Thomas Stanley of a few thousands more. All these forces moved towards London, with St Albans

---

1   Edward, Prince of Wales, who was killed at the Battle of Tewkesbury in 1471.

as their point of concentration. The King, the Queen, Somerset, and the Court and Lancastrian party, with their power, which numbered less than three thousand men, moved to Watford to meet them.

St Albans was an open town. The ancient, powerful monastery there had prevented the citizens from "girding themselves about with a great wall", lest they should become presumptuous. For this reason it was a convenient rendezvous. Here the King's army arrived and the royal standard was unfurled in St Peter's Street and Hollowell Street. York, Salisbury, and Warwick did not wait for the heavy reinforcements that were approaching them. They saw that their forces had the advantage and that hours counted. This time there was a fight. It was a collision rather than a battle; but it was none the less decisive. Lord Clifford held for the King the barrier across the street which York attacked with archery and cannon; but Warwick, circling the town, came in upon him from behind, slew him, and put the royal troops to flight. Somerset was killed "fighting for a cause which was more his own than the King's". The Duke of Buckingham and his son were wounded by arrows; Somerset's son, the Earl of Dorset, was captured sorely wounded and carried home in a cart. The King himself was slightly wounded by an arrow. He did not fly, but took refuge in a tradesman's house in the main street. There presently the Duke of York came to him, and, falling upon his knees, assured him of his fealty and devotion. Not more than three hundred men perished in this clash at St Albans, but these included an extraordinary proportion of the nobles on the King's side. The rank and file were encouraged to spare one another; the leaders fought to the death. The bodies of Somerset and Clifford lay naked in the street for many hours, none daring to bury them. The Yorkist triumph was complete. They had now got the King in their hands. Somerset was dead. Margaret and her child had taken sanctuary. The victors declared their devotion to the royal person and rejoiced that he was rid of evil counsellors. Upon this Parliament was immediately summoned in the King's name.

We are however in the presence of the most ferocious and implacable quarrel of which there is factual record. The individual actors were bred by generations of privilege and war, into which the feudal theme had brought its peculiar sense of honour, and to which the Papacy contributed such spiritual sanction as emerged from its rivalries and intrigues. It was a conflict in which personal hatreds reached their maximum, and from which mass effects were happily excluded.

Needless causes of confusion may be avoided. Towns must not be confused with titles. The mortal struggle of York and Lancaster did not imply any antagonism between the two well-known English counties. York was in fact the stronghold of the Lancastrians, and the Yorkists founded their strength upon the Midlands and the south of England. Let us now set forth the facts as they occurred.

St Albans was the first shedding of blood in strife. The Yorkists gained possession of the King. But soon we see the inherent power of Lancaster. They had the majority of the nobles on their side, and the majesty of the

Crown. In a few months they were as strong as ever. Continual trials of strength were made. There were risings in the country and grim assemblies of Parliament. Legality, constitutionalism, and reverence for the Crown were countered, but not yet overthrown, by turbulent and bloody episodes. The four years from 1456 to 1459 were a period of uneasy truce. All seemed conscious of the peril to themselves and to their order. But Fate lay heavy upon them. There were intense efforts at reconciliation. The spectacle was displayed to the Londoners of the King being escorted to Westminster by a procession in which the Duke of York and Queen Margaret walked side by side, followed by the Yorkist and Lancastrian lords, the most opposed in pairs. Solemn pledges of amity were exchanged; the Sacrament was taken in common by all the leaders; all sought peace where there was no peace. Even when a kind of settlement was reached in London it was upset by violence in the North. In 1459 fighting broke out again. A gathering near Worcester of armed Yorkists dispersed in the presence of the royal army and their chiefs scattered. York returned to Ireland, and Warwick to his captaincy of Calais, in which he had succeeded Somerset.

War began in earnest in July 1460. York was still in Ireland; but the Yorkist lords under Warwick, holding bases in Wales and at Calais, with all their connections and partisans, supported by the Papal legate and some of the bishops, and, on the whole, by the Commons, confronted the Lancastrians and the Crown at Northampton. Henry VI stood entrenched, and new cannon guarded his line. But when the Yorkists attacked, Lord Grey of Ruthven, who commanded a wing, deserted him and helped the Yorkists over the breast-works. The royal forces fled in panic. King Henry VI remained in his tent, "sitting alone and solitary". The victors presented themselves to him, bowing to the ground. As after St Albans, they carried him again to London, and, having him in their power once more, ruled in his name. The so-called compromise in which all the Estates of the Realm concurred was then attempted. Henry was to be King for life; York was to conduct the Government and succeed him at his death. All who sought a quiet life for the nation hailed this arrangement. But the settlement defied the fact that Queen Margaret, with her son, the Prince of Wales, was at liberty at Harlech Castle, in Wales. The King in bondage had disinherited his own son. The Queen fought on.

With her army of the North and of North Wales Margaret advanced to assert the birthright of her son. The Duke of York, disdaining to remain in the security of Sandal Castle until his whole strength was gathered, marched against her. At Wakefield on December 30, 1460, the first considerable battle of the war was fought. The Lancastrians, with superior forces, caught the Yorkists by surprise, when many were foraging, and a frightful rout and massacre ensued. Here there was no question of sparing the common men; many hundreds were slaughtered; but the brunt fell upon the chiefs. No quarter was given. The Duke of York was killed; his son, the Earl of Rutland, seventeen years old, was flying, but the new Lord Clifford, remembering

St Albans, slaughtered him with joy, exclaiming, "By God's blood, thy father slew mine; and so will I do thee, and all thy kin." Henceforward this was the rule of the war. The old Earl of Salisbury, caught during the night, was beheaded immediately by Lord Exeter, a natural son of the Duke of Buckingham. Margaret's hand has been discerned in this severity. The heads of the three Yorkist nobles were exposed over the gates and walls of York. The great Duke's head, with a paper crown, grinned upon the landscape, summoning the avengers.

Hitherto the struggle had been between mature, comfortable magnates, deeply involved in State affairs and trying hard to preserve some limits. Now a new generation took charge. There was a new Lord Clifford, a new Duke of Somerset, above all a new Duke of York, all in their twenties, sword in hand, with fathers to avenge and England as the prize. When York's son, hitherto Earl of March, learned that his father's cause had devolved upon him he did not shrink. He fell upon the Earl of Wiltshire and the Welsh Lancastrians, and on February 2, 1461, at the Battle of Mortimer's Cross, near Hereford, he beat and broke them up. He made haste to repay the cruelties of Wakefield. "No quarter" was again the word. Among those executed after the battle was Owen Tudor, a harmless notable, who, with the axe and block before him, hardly believed that he would be beheaded until the collar of his red doublet was ripped off. His son Jasper lived, as will be seen to carry on the quarrel.

The victorious Yorkists under their young Duke now marched to help the Earl of Warwick, who had returned from Calais and was being hard pressed in London; but Queen Margaret forestalled him, and on February 17, at the second Battle of St Albans, she inflicted upon Warwick a bloody defeat. Warwick, who was at this time the real leader of the Yorkist party, with many troops raised abroad and with the latest firearms and his own feudal forces, had carried the captive King with him and claimed to be acting in his name. But Margaret's onset took him by surprise. "Their prickers [scouts] came not home to bring tidings how nigh the Queen was, save one came and said that she was nine mile off." Warwick and Norfolk escaped; half their army was slaughtered. King Henry had been carted to the scene. There, beneath a large tree, he watched what happened with legitimate and presently unconcealed satisfaction. Two knights of high renown in the French war, one the redoubtable Sir Thomas Kyriel, had been appointed as his warders and guardians. Above all they were to make sure no harm came to him. They therefore remained with him under his tree, and all were surrounded by the victorious army. Among the many captains of consequence whom Margaret put to death in cold blood the next morning these two cases needed special consideration. King Henry said he had asked them to bide with him and that they had done so for his own safety. Queen Margaret produced her son Edward, now seven years old, to whose disinheritance the King had perforce consented, and asked this child, already precociously fierce, to pronounce. "Fair son, with what death shall these two knights die whom you see there?" "Their heads should be cut off" was the ready answer. As Kyriel was being led away to his fate he exclaimed, "May the wrath of God fall on those who have taught a child to speak such words." Thus was pity banished from all hearts, and death or vengeance was the cry.

Margaret now had her husband safe back in her hands, and with him the full authority of the Crown. The road to London was open, but she did not choose to advance upon it. The fierce hordes she had brought from the North had already disgraced themselves by their ravages far and wide along their line of march. They had roused against them the fury of the countryside. We cannot judge the circumstances fully. Edward of York was marching with the triumphant army of Mortimer's Cross night and day to reach London. Warwick had joined him in Oxfordshire with the survivors of St Albans. Perhaps King Henry pleaded that the capital should not become a battlefield, but at any rate Margaret and her advisers did not dare to make it so. Flushed with victory, laden with spoil, reunited with the King, the Lancastrians retired through Dunstable to the North, and thus disguised the fact that their Scottish mercenaries were already jogging home with all that they could carry.

This was the turning-point in the struggle. Nine days after the second Battle of St Albans Edward of York entered London. The citizens, who might have submitted to Margaret and the King, now hailed the Yorkists with enthusiasm. The pretence of acting in the King's name could serve no longer. The Yorkists had become without disguise traitors and rebels against the Crown. But the mood of the youthful warrior who had triumphed and butchered at Mortimer's Cross recked little of this charge. As he saw it, his father had been ruined and killed through respect for the majesty of Henry VI. He declared himself King, and on March 4, 1461, was proclaimed at Westminster with such formalities as were possible. Henceforward he declared that the other side were guilty of treason, and that he would enforce upon them every penalty.

These assertions must now be made good, and King Edward IV marched north to settle once and for all with King Henry VI. Near York the Queen, with the whole power of Lancaster, confronted him not far from Tadcaster, by the villages of Saxton and Towton. Some accounts declare that a hundred thousand men were on the field, the Yorkists having forty and the Lancastrians sixty thousand; but later authorities greatly reduce these figures.

On March 28 the Yorkist advance-guard was beaten back at Ferry Bridge by the young Lord Clifford, and Warwick himself was wounded; but as heavier forces arrived the bridge was carried, Clifford was slain, and the Yorkist army passed over. The next day one of the most ruthless battles on English soil was fought. The Lancastrians held a good position on rising ground, their right flank being protected by the flooded stream of the Cock, in many places unfordable. Although Edward's army was not complete and the Duke of Norfolk's wing was still approaching, he resolved to attack. The battle began in a blinding snowstorm, which drove in the faces of the Lancastrians. Under this cover clumps of Yorkist spearmen moved up the slope. The wind gave superior range to the archery of the attack and the Lancastrian shafts fell short, while they themselves suffered heavily. Under this pressure the decision was taken to advance downhill upon the foe. For six hours the two sides grappled furiously, with varying success. At the height of the battle Warwick is said to have dismounted and slain his horse to prove to his men he would not quit them alive. But all hung in the balance until late in the afternoon, when the arrival of the Duke of Norfolk's corps upon the exposed flank of the Lancastrians drove the whole mass into retreat, which soon became a rout.

Now the Cock beck, hitherto a friend to Lancaster, became an enemy. The bridge towards Tadcaster was blocked with fugitives. Many thousands of men, heavily armoured, plunged into the swollen stream, and were drowned in such numbers that hideous bridges were formed of the corpses and some escaped thereby. The pursuit was carried on far into the night. Margaret and her son escaped to York, where King Henry had been observing the rites of Palm Sunday. Gathering him up, the imperious Queen set out with her child and a cluster of spears for the Scottish border. The bodies of thousands of English-men lay upon the field. Edward, writing to his mother, conceals his own losses, but claims that twenty-eight thousand Lancastrian dead had been counted. It is certain that the flower of the Lancastrian nobility and knighthood fell upon the field. For all prisoners there was but death. The Earl of Devonshire and "the bastard of Exeter" alone were spared, and only for a day. When Edward reached the town of York his first task was to remove the heads of his father and others of Margaret's victims and to replace them with those of his noblest captives. Three months later, on June 28, he was crowned King at Westminster, and the Yorkist triumph seemed complete. It was followed by wholesale proscriptions and confiscations. Parliament in November 1461 passed an Act of Attainder which, surpassing all previous severities, lapped a hundred and thirty-three notable persons in its withering sweep. Not only the throne but one third of the estates in England changed hands. It was measure for measure.

After Towton the Lancastrian Cause was sustained by the unconquerable will of Queen Margaret. Never has her tenacity and rarely have her vicissi-tudes been surpassed in any woman. Apart from the sullen power of Lancaster in the North, she had the friendly regard of two countries, Scotland and France. Both had felt the heavy arm of England in former reigns; both rejoiced at its present division and weakness. The hatred of the Scots for the English still excited by its bitterness the wonder of foreigners. When Louis XI succeeded his father, Charles VII, in 1461, the year of Towton, he found his own country almost a desert, horrible to see. The fields were untitled; the villages were clusters of ruined hovels. Amid the ruins, the weeds and brushwood – to use a term which recurs – of what were formerly cultivated and fertile fields, there dwelt a race of peasants reduced to the conditions and roused to the ferocity of wolves. All this was the result of the English invasion. Therefore it was a prime aim of Scottish and French policy, always moving hand-in-hand, to foster the internal strife of England and to sustain the weaker party there.

Margaret, as Queen of England and Princess of France, was an outstanding personage in the West of Europe. Her qualities of courage and combativeness, her commanding, persuasive personality, her fury against those who had driven her and her husband from the throne, produced from this one woman's will-power a long series of desperate, forlorn struggles after the main event had been decided, and after the lapse of years for one brief spell reversed it. English national interests did not enter her mind. She had paid her way with Scotland by the surrender of Berwick. She clinched her bargain with Louis XI by mortgaging Calais to him for 20,000 gold livres.

In 1462 Margaret, after much personal appeal to the Courts of France, Burgundy, and Scotland, found herself able to land with a power, and whether by treachery or weakness the three strongest Northern castles, Bamburgh, Alnwick, and Dunstanburgh, opened their gates to her. Louis XI had lent her the services of a fine soldier, Pierre de Brézé, who under her spell spent his large fortune in her cause. In the winter of 1462 therefore King Edward gathered his Yorkist powers, and, carrying his new train of artillery by sea to Newcastle, begin the sieges of these lost strongholds. The King himself lay stricken with measles at Durham, and Lord Warwick conducted the operations. The heavy cannon, each with its pet name, played havoc with the masonry of the castles. So vigorously were the sieges conducted that even Christmas leave was forbidden. Margaret, from Berwick, in vain attempted the relief of Alnwick. All three fortresses fell in a month.

The behaviour of Edward at this moment constitutes a solid defence for his character. This voluptuous young King, sure of his position, now showed a clemency unheard of in the Wars of the Roses. Not only did he pardon the Lancastrian nobles who were caught in the fortresses, but he made solemn pacts with them and took them into his full confidence. The Duke of Somerset and Sir Ralph Percy, on swearing allegiance, were not merely allowed to go free, but restored to their estates. Percy was even given the guardianship of two of the castles. Somerset, son of the eminent Minister slaughtered in the first Battle of St Albans, was admitted to even higher favour. Having made his peace, he was given a high command and a place in the inner councils of the royal army. In this new position at first he gave shrewd military advice, and was granted special pensions by the King.

Edward's magnanimity and forgiveness were ill repaid. When Margaret returned with fresh succours from France and Scotland in 1463 Percy opened the gates of Bamburgh to the Scots, and Alnwick was betrayed about the same time by a soured Yorkist officer, Sir Ralph Grey. Meanwhile Queen Margaret, with King Henry in her hands, herself besieged the castle of Norham, on the Tweed, near Berwick. Once again Edward and the Yorkists took the field, and the redoubtable new artillery, at that time esteemed as much among the leading nations as atomic weapons are today, was carried to the North. The great guns blew chunks off the castles. Margaret fled to France, while Henry buried himself amid the valleys and the pious foundations of Cumberland. This was the final parting of King Henry VI and his Queen – Queen she was. Margaret took the prince with her.

Edward's clemency had been betrayed by Percy, but he did not withdraw his confidence from Somerset. The King was a man capable of the most bloody deeds when compelled, as he thought, by necessity, and at the same time eager to practise not only magnanimity, but open-hearted confidence. The confidence he showed to Somerset must have led him into deadly perils. When in the autumn of 1463 he went to the North Somerset and two hundred of his own men were his bodyguard. At Northampton, where bitter memories of the battle lingered, the townsfolk were first astounded and then infuriated to see this bearer of an accursed name in company with their Yorkist sovereign. Only King Edward's personal exertions saved his new-found follower from being torn to pieces. After this he found it necessary to provide other employment for Somerset and his escort. Somerset was sent to Holt Castle, in Denbighshire. The brawl at Northampton we must suppose convinced him that even the King could not protect him from his Yorkist foes. At Christmas 1463 Somerset deserted Edward and returned to the Lancastrian side. The names of these great nobles were magnets in their own territories. The unstable Duke had hoped to gain possession of Newcastle, and many of his adherents on the report that he was in the neighbourhood came out to him; but he was driven away, and they were caught and beheaded.

Again the banner of Lancaster was raised. Somerset joined King Henry. Alnwick and Bamburgh still held out. Norham and Skipton had been captured, but now Warwick's brother Montagu with a substantial army was in the field. On April 25, 1464, at Hedgeley Moor, near Alnwick, he broke and destroyed the Lancastrian revolt. The leaders perished on the field, or afterwards on the block. Sir Ralph Percy fought to the death, and used the expression, remarkable for one who had accepted pardon and even office from King Edward, "I have saved the bird in my bosom." What was this "bird"? It was the cause of Lancaster, which might be dissembled or even betrayed under duress, but still remained, when occasion served, the lodestar of its adherents. There were many who had this bird in their bosoms, but could never have coined Percy's grand phrase or stooped to his baseness.

Edward's experiment of mercy in this quarrel was now at an end, and the former rigours were renewed in their extreme degree. Somerset, defeated with a small following at Hexham on May 15, 1464, was beheaded the next morning. Before the month was out in every Yorkist camp Lancastrian nobles and knights by dozens and half-dozens were put to death. There was nothing for it but to still these unquiet spirits. John Tiptoft, Earl of Worcester, Constable of England, versed in the civil law, and with Italian experience, presided over drumhead courts-martial, and by adding needless cruelties to his severities justified a vengeance one day to be exacted.

Meanwhile the diplomacy of the English Crown had effected a fifteen years' truce with the King of Scotland, and was potent both at the Courts of France and Burgundy. Margaret remained helpless at Bar-le-Duc. Poor King

Henry was at length tracked down near Clitheroe in Lancashire, and conveyed to London. This time there was no ceremonial entry. With his feet tied by leather thongs to the stirrups, and with a straw hat on his head, the futile but saintly figure around whom such storms had beaten was led three times round the pillory, and finally hustled to the Tower, whose gates closed on him – yet not, this time, for ever.

With the fall of Alnwick only one fortress in the whole kingdom still resisted. The castle of Harlech, on the western sea, alone flaunted the Red Rose. Harlech stood a siege of seven years. When it surrendered in 1468 there were found to be but fifty effective men in the garrison. With two exceptions, they were admitted to mercy. Among them was a child of twelve, who had survived the rigours of the long blockade. He was the nephew of Jasper, the grandson of Owen Tudor, and the future founder of the Tudor dynasty and system of government. His name was Richmond, later to become King Henry VII.

CHAPTER TWENTY

EDWARD IV

*Edward IV – the Neville family rule England – the King marries
Elizabeth Woodville – cross purposes with France – the King and the
Nevilles collide – the northern rebellion – the slaughter of Edgcott –
Edward IV held at Middleham – Henry VI still in the Tower – nobles
behead Queen's father – Edward IV released – execution of Lancastrians
– Warwick and Clarence accused of treason – Warwick and Margaret of
Anjou plot the overthrow of Edward – the Battle of Barnet – the Battle of
Tewkesbury – death of the Prince of Wales – Richard of Gloucester orders
the murder of Henry VI – Edward IV and Louis XI sign the Treaty of
Picquigny – the death of Clarence*

KING EDWARD IV had made good his right to the Crown upon the
field. He was a soldier and a man of action. But he was at this time
a fighting man and little more, and when the fighting stopped he
had no serious zest for sovereignty. The land was fair; the blood of
youth coursed in his veins; all his blood debts were paid. With ease and
goodwill he sheathed his sharp sword. It had won him his crown; now to enjoy
life. The successes of these difficult years had been gained for King Edward
by the Neville family. Warwick, and Montagu, now Earl of Northumberland,
with George Neville, Archbishop of York, had the whole machinery of
government in their hands. The King had been present only at some of the
actions. He could even be reproached for his misguided clemency, which had
opened up again the distresses of civil war. His magnanimity had been at
length sternly repressed by his counsellors and generals. In the first part of his
reign England was therefore ruled by the two brothers, Warwick and
Northumberland. They believed they had put the King on the throne, and
meant him to remain there while they governed. The King did not quarrel
with this. In all his reign he never fought but when he was forced; then he was
magnificent. History has scolded this prince of twenty-two for not possessing
immediately the statecraft and addiction to business for which his office called.
Edward united contrasting characters. He loved peace; he shone in war. But he
loved peace for its indulgences rather than its dignity. His pursuit of women,
in which he found no obstacles, combined with hunting, feasting, and drinking
to fill his life. Were these not the rightful prizes of victory? Let Warwick and

Northumberland and other anxious lords carry the burden of State, and let the King be merry. For a while this suited all parties. The victors divided the spoil; the King had his amusements and his lords their power and policy.

Thus some years slipped by, while the King, although gripping from time to time the reins of authority, led in the main his life of ease. One day the King a-hunting was carried far by the chase. He rested for the night at a castle. In this castle a lady of quality, niece of the owner, had found shelter. Elizabeth Woodville, or Wydvil, was the widow of a Lancastrian knight, Sir John Grey, "in Margaret's battle at St Albans slain". Her mother, Jacquetta of Luxembourg, had been the youthful wife of the famous John, Duke of Bedford, and after his death she had married his steward, Sir Richard Woodville, later created Earl Rivers. This condescension so far below her station caused offence to the aristocracy. She was fined £11,000 as a deterrent to others. Nevertheless she lived happily ever after, and bore her husband no fewer than thirteen children, of whom Elizabeth was one. There was high as well as ordinary blood in Elizabeth's veins. She was an austere woman, upright, fearless, chaste and fruitful. She and her two sons were all under the ban of the attainder which disinherited the adherents of Lancaster. The chance of obtaining royal mercy could not be missed. The widow bowed in humble petition before the youthful conqueror, and, like the tanner's daughter of Falaise, made at first glance the sovereign her slave. He spurned the counsels of prudence and worldly wisdom. Why conquer in battles, why be a king, if not to gain one's heart's desire? But he was well aware of the dangers of his choice. His marriage in 1464 with Elizabeth Woodville was a secret guarded in deadly earnest. The statesmen at the head of the Government, while they smiled at what seemed an amorous frolic, never dreamed it was a solemn union, which must shake the land to its depths.

Warwick's plans for the King's future had been different. Isabella of the house of Spain, or preferably a French princess, were brides who might greatly forward the interests of England. A royal marriage in those days might be a bond of peace between neighbouring states or the means of successful war. Warwick used grave arguments and pressed the King to decide. Edward seemed strangely hesitant, and dwelt upon his objections until the Minister, who was also his master, became impatient. Then at last the truth was revealed to all: he had for five months been married to Elizabeth Woodville. Here then was the occasion which sundered him from the valiant King-maker, fourteen years older, but also in the prime of life. Warwick had deep roots in England, and his popularity, whetted by the lavish hospitality which he offered to all classes upon his many great estates, was unbounded. The Londoners looked to him. He held the power. But no one knew better than he that there slept in Edward a tremendous warrior, skilful, ruthless, and capable when roused of attempting and of doing all.

The King too, for his part, began to take more interest in affairs. Queen Elizabeth had five brothers, seven sisters, and two sons. By Royal decree he raised them to high rank, or married them into the greatest families. He went so far as to marry his wife's fourth brother, at twenty, to the Dowager Duchess of Norfolk, aged eighty. Eight new peerages came into existence in the Queen's family: her father, five brothers-in-law, her son, and her brother Anthony. This was generally thought excessive. It must be remembered that at this time there were but sixty peers, of whom not more than fifty could ever be got to Parliament on one occasion. All these potentates were held in a tight and nicely calculated system. The arrival of a new nobility who had done nothing notable in the war and now surrounded the indolent King was not merely offensive, but politically dangerous to Warwick and his proud associates.

But the clash came over foreign policy. In this sad generation England, lately the master, had become the sport of neighbouring states. Her titled refugees, from one faction or the other, beset the Courts of Western Europe. The Duke of Burgundy had been shocked to learn one morning that a Duke of Exeter and several other high English nobles were actually begging their bread at the tail of one of his progresses. Ashamed to see such a slight upon his class, he provided them with modest dwellings and allowances. Similar charities were performed by Louis XI to the unhappy descendants of the victors of Agincourt. Margaret with her retinue of shadows was welcomed in her pauper stateliness both in Burgundy and in France. At any moment either Power, now become formidable as England had waned, might support the exiled faction in good earnest and pay back the debts of fifty years before by an invasion of England. It was the policy of Warwick and his connection to make friends with France, by far the stronger Power, and thus obtain effectual security. In this mood they hoped to make a French match for the King's sister. Edward took the opposite line. With the instinct which afterwards ruled our Island for so many centuries, he sought to base English policy upon the second strongest state in Western Europe. He could no doubt argue that to be the ally of France was to be in the power of France, but to be joined with Burgundy was to have the means of correcting if not of controlling French action. Amid his revelries and other hunting he nursed a conqueror's spirit. Never should England become a vassal state; instead of being divided by her neighbours she would herself, by dividing them, maintain a balance. At this time these politics were new; but the stresses they wrought in the small but vehement world of English government can be readily understood nowadays.

The King therefore, to Warwick's chagrin and alarm, in 1468 married his sister Margaret to Charles the Bold, who had in 1467 succeeded as Duke of Burgundy. Thus not only did these great lords, who at the constant peril of their lives and by all their vast resources had placed him on the throne, suffer slights and material losses by the creation of a new nobility, but they had besides to stomach a foreign policy which they believed would be fatal to England, to the Yorkist party, and to themselves. What help could Burgundy give if France, joined to the house of Lancaster, invaded England? What would happen to them, their great estates, and all who depended upon them, in such a catastrophe? The quarrel between the King and Warwick, as head of the Nevilles, was not therefore petty, or even, as has often been suggested, entirely personal.

The offended chiefs took deep counsel together. The Nevilles were at length ready to try conclusions with him. Warwick's plan was singular in its skill. He had gained the King's brother, Clarence, to his side by whispering that but for this upstart brood of the Woodvilles he might succeed Edward as King. As bond it was secretly agreed that Clarence should marry Warwick's daughter Isabella. When all was ready Warwick struck. A rising took place in the North. Thousands of men in Yorkshire under the leadership of various young lords complained in arms about taxation. The "thrave", a levy paid since the days of Athelstan, became suddenly obnoxious. But other grievances were urged, particularly that the King was swayed by "favourites". At the same time in London the House of Commons petitioned against lax and profuse administration. The King was now forced to go to the North. Except his small bodyguard he had no troops of his own, but he called upon his nobles to bring out their men. He advanced in July to Nottingham, and there awaited the Earls of Pembroke and Devon, both new creations of his own, who had marshalled the levies of Wales and the West. As soon as the King had been enticed northwards by the rebellion Warwick and Clarence, who had hitherto crouched at Calais, came to England with the Calais garrison. Warwick published a manifesto supporting the Northern rebels, "the King's true subjects" as he termed them, and urged them "with piteous lamentations to be the means to our Sovereign Lord the King of remedy and reformation". Warwick was joined by many thousands of Kentish men and was received with great respect in London. But before he and Clarence could bring their forces against the King's rear the event was decided. The Northern rebels intercepted Pembroke and Devon, and at Edgcott, near Banbury, defeated them with a merciless slaughter, a hundred and sixty-eight knights, squires, and gentlemen either falling in the fight or being executed thereafter. Both Pembroke and later Devon were beheaded.

The King, trying to rally his scattered forces at Olney, in Buckinghamshire, found himself in the power of his great nobles. His brother, Richard of Gloucester, known to legend as "Crookback" because of his alleged deformity, seemed his only friend. At first he attempted to rally Warwick and Clarence to their duty, but in the course of conversation he was made to realise that he was their captive. With bows and ceremonies they explained that his future reign must be in accordance with their advice. He was conveyed to Warwick's castle at Middleham, and there kept in honourable but real restraint under the surveillance of the Archbishop of York. At this moment therefore Warwick the King-maker had actually the two rival Kings, Henry VI and Edward IV, both his prisoners, one in the Tower and the other at Middleham. This was a remarkable achievement for any subject. To make the lesson even plainer, Lord Rivers, the Queen's father, and John Woodville, her brother, were arrested and executed at Kenilworth without any pretence of trial. Thus did the older nobility deal with the new.

But the relations between Warwick and the King did not admit of such simple solutions. Warwick had struck with suddenness, and for a while no one realised what had happened. As the truth became known the Yorkist nobility viewed with astonishment and anger the detention of their brave, victorious sovereign, and the Lancastrians everywhere raised their heads in the hopes of profiting by the Yorkist feud. The King found it convenient in his turn to dissemble. He professed himself convinced that Warwick and Clarence were right. He undertook to amend his ways, and after he had signed free pardons to all who had been in arms against him he was liberated. Thus was a settlement reached between Warwick and the Crown. King Edward was soon again at the head of forces, defeating Lancastrian rebels and executing their leaders, while Warwick and all his powerful connections returned to their posts, proclaimed their allegiance, and apparently enjoyed royal favour. But all this was on the surface.

In March 1470, under the pretence of suppressing a Lancastrian rebellion in Lincolnshire, the King called his forces to arms. At Losecoat Field he defeated the insurgents, who fled; and in the series of executions which had now become customary after every engagement he obtained a confession from Sir Robert Welles which accused both Warwick and Clarence of treason. The evidence is fairly convincing; for at this moment they were conspiring against Edward, and shortly afterwards refused to obey his express order to join him. The King, with troops fresh from victory, turned on them all of a sudden. He marched against them, and they fled, astounded that their own methods should be retorted upon themselves. They sought safety in Warwick's base at Calais; but Lord Wenlock, whom he had left as his deputy, refused to admit them. Even after they had bombarded the sea-front he made it a positive favour to send a few flagons of wine to Clarence's bride, who, on board ship, had just given birth to a son. The King-maker found himself by one sharp twist of fortune deprived of almost every resource he had counted upon as sure. He in his turn presented himself at the French Court as a suppliant.

But this was the best luck Louis XI had ever known. He must have rubbed his hands in the same glee as when he visited his former Minister, Cardinal Jean Balue, whom he kept imprisoned in an iron cage at Chinon because he had conspired with Charles the Bold. Two years earlier Edward as the ally of Burgundy had threatened him with war. Now here in France were the leaders of both the parties that had disputed England for so long. Margaret was dwelling in her father's Anjou. Warwick, friend of France vanquished in his own country, had arrived at Honfleur. With gusto the stern, cynical, hard-pressed Louis set himself to the task of reconciling and combining these opposite forces. At Angers he confronted Margaret and her son, now a fine youth of seventeen, with Warwick and Clarence, and proposed brutally to them that they should join together with his support to overthrow Edward. At first both parties recoiled. Nor can we wonder. A river of blood flowed between them. All that they had fought for during these cruel years was defaced by their union. Warwick and Margaret had slain with deliberation each other's dearest friends and kin. She had beheaded his father Salisbury, slain his uncle York and his cousin Rutland. He for his part had butchered the two Somersets, father and son, the Earl of Wiltshire, and many of her devoted adherents. The common people who had fallen in their quarrel, they were uncounted. In 1459 Margaret had declared Warwick attainted, a terrible outlawry. In 1460 he had branded her son as bastard or changeling. They had done each other the gravest human injuries. But they had one bond in common. They hated Edward and they wanted to win. They were the champions of a generation which could not accept defeat. And here, as indeed for a time it proved, appeared the means of speedy triumph.

Warwick had a fleet, commanded by his nephew, the bastard of Fauconberg. He had the sailors in all the seaports of the south coast. He knew he had but to go or send his summons to large parts of England for the people to take arms at his command. Margaret represented the beaten, disinherited, proscribed house of Lancaster, stubborn as ever. They agreed to forgive and unite. They took solemn oaths at Angers upon a fragment of the Holy Cross, which luckily was available. The confederacy was sealed by the betrothal of Margaret's son, the Prince of Wales, to Warwick's younger daughter, Anne. Edward had been staggered by his brother's conduct. He did not however allow his personal resentment to influence his action. A lady in attendance upon the new Duchess of Clarence proved to be a discreet and accomplished emissary of the King. She conveyed to Clarence soon after he fled from England that he had only to rejoin his brother for all to be pardoned and forgotten. The new agreement between Warwick and Margaret decided Clarence to avail himself of this fraternal offer, but not immediately.

King Edward was by now alarmed and vigilant, but he could scarcely foresee how many of his supporters would betray him. Warwick repeated the process he had used a year before. Fitzhugh, his cousin, started a new insurrection in Yorkshire. Edward gathered some forces and, making little of the affair, marched against the rebels. Warned by Charles of Burgundy, he even expressed his wish that Warwick would land. He seems to have been entirely confident. But never was there a more swift undeception. Warwick and Clarence landed at Dartmouth in September 1470. Kent and other southern counties rose in his behalf. Warwick marched to London. He brought the miserable Henry VI from his prison in the Tower, placed a crown on his head, paraded him through the capital, and seated him upon the throne.

At Nottingham Edward received alarming news. The major part of his kingdom seemed to have turned against him. Suddenly he learned that while the Northern rebels were moving down upon him and cutting him from his Welsh succours, and while Warwick was moving northward with strong forces, the Marquis of Montagu, Warwick's brother, hitherto faithful, had made his men throw up their caps for King Henry. When Edward heard of Montagu's desertion, and also of rapid movements to secure his person, he deemed it his sole hope to fly beyond the seas. He had but one refuge – the Court of Burgundy; and with a handful of followers he cast himself upon his brother-in-law. Charles the Bold was also cautious. He had to consider the imminent danger of an attack by England and France united. Until he was sure that this was inevitable he temporised with his royal refugee relation. But when it became clear that the policy of Warwick was undoubtedly to make war upon him in conjunction with Louis XI he defended himself by an obvious manoeuvre. He furnished King Edward with about twelve hundred trustworthy Flemish and German soldiers and the necessary ships and money for a descent. These forces were collected secretly in the island of Walcheren.

Meanwhile the King-maker ruled England, and it seemed that he might long continue to do so. He had King Henry VI a puppet in his hand. But while these violent transformations were comprehensible to the actors, and the drama proceeded with apparent success, the solid bulk of England on both sides was incapable of following such too-quick movements and reconciliations. Almost the whole population stood wherever it had stood before. Their leaders might have made new combinations, but ordinary men could not believe that the antagonism of the Red and the White Rose was ended. It needed but another shock to produce an entirely different scene. It is significant that, although repeatedly urged by Warwick to join him and her husband, King Henry, in London, and although possessed of effective forces, Margaret remained in France, and kept her son with her.

In March 1471 Edward landed with his small expedition at Ravenspur, a port in Yorkshire now washed away by the North Sea, but then still famous for the descent of Henry of Bolingbroke in 1399. The King, fighting for his life, was, as usual, at his best. York shut its gates in his face, but, like Bolingbroke, he declared he had only come to claim his private estates, and bade his troops declare themselves for King Henry VI. Accepted and nourished on these terms, he set forth on his march to London. Montagu, with four times his numbers, approached to intercept him. Edward, by extraordinary marches, manoeuvred past him. All Yorkist lords and adherents in the districts through which he passed joined his army. At Warwick he was strong enough to proclaim himself King again. The King-maker, disconcerted by the turn of events, sent repeated imperative requests to Margaret to come at once, and at Coventry stationed himself in King Edward's path. Meanwhile his brother Montagu followed Edward southward, only two marches behind. In this dire strait Edward had a resource unsuspected by Warwick. He knew Clarence was his man. Clarence was moving from Gloucestershire with considerable forces, ostensibly to join Warwick; but Edward, slipping round Warwick's flank, as he had out-marched and outwitted Montagu, placed himself between Warwick and London, and in the exact position where Clarence could make his junction with him.

Both sides now concentrated all their strength, and again large armies were seen in England. Edward entered London, and was cordially received by the bewildered citizens. Henry VI, who had actually been made to ride about the streets at the head of six hundred horsemen, was relieved from these exertions and taken back to his prison in the Tower. The decisive battle impended on the

North Road, and at Barnet on April 14, 1471, Edward and the Yorkists faced Warwick and the house of Neville, with the new Duke of Somerset, second son of Edmund Beaufort, and important Lancastrian allies.

Throughout England no one could see clearly what was happening, and the Battle of Barnet, which resolved their doubts, was itself fought in a fog. The lines of battle overlapped; Warwick's right turned Edward's left flank, and *vice versa*. The King-maker, stung perhaps by imputations upon his physical courage, fought on foot. The new Lord Oxford, a prominent Lancastrian, whose father had been beheaded earlier in the reign, commanding the overlapping Lancastrian left, found himself successful in his charge, but lost in the mist. Little knowing that the whole of King Edward's rear was open to his attack, he tried to regain his own lines and arrived in the rear of Somerset's centre. The badge of a star and rays on his banners was mistaken by Warwick's troops for the sun and rays of King Edward. Warwick's archers loosed upon him. The mistake was discovered, but in those days of treason and changing sides it only led to another blunder. It was assumed that he had deserted. The cry of treason ran through Warwick's hosts. Oxford, in his uncertainty, rode off into the gloom. Somerset, on the other flank, had already been routed. Warwick, with the right wing, was attacked by the King and the main Yorkist power. Here indeed it was not worth while to ask for mercy. Warwick, outnumbered, his ranks broken, sought to reach his horse. He would have been wise in spite of taunts to have followed his usual custom of mounting again on the battle day after walking along the lines; for had he escaped this zigzag story might have ended at the opposite point. But north of the town near which the main struggle was fought the King-maker, just as he was about to reach the necessary horse, was overtaken by the Yorkists and battered to death. He had been the foremost champion of the Yorkist cause. He had served King Edward well. He had received ill-usage from the youth he had placed and sustained upon the throne. By his depraved abandonment of all the causes for which he had sent so many men to their doom he had deserved death; and for his virtues, which were distinguished, it was fitting that it should come to him in honourable guise.

On the very day of Barnet Margaret at last landed in England. Somerset, the fourth Duke, with his father and his elder brother to avenge, fresh from the disaster at Barnet, met her and became her military commander. On learning that Warwick was slain and his army beaten and dispersed the hitherto indomitable Queen had her hour of despair. Sheltering in Cerne Abbey, near Weymouth, her thought was to return to France; but now her son, the Prince of Wales, nearly eighteen, in whose veins flowed the blood of Henry V, was for fighting for the crown or death. Margaret rallied her spirits and appeared once again unbroken by her life of disaster. Her only hope was to reach the Welsh border, where strong traditional Lancastrian forces were already in arms. The King-maker aberration had been excised. The struggle was once again between Lancaster and York. Edward, near London, held interior lines. He strove to cut Margaret off from Wales. Both armies marched incessantly.

In their final march each covered forty miles in a single day. The Lancastrians succeeded in reaching the goal first, but only with their troops in a state of extreme exhaustion. Edward, close behind, pressed on, and on the 4th of May brought them to battle at Tewkesbury.

The Lancastrians were scattered or destroyed. Somerset and many other notables who thought themselves safe in sanctuary were dragged forth and decapitated. Margaret was captured. The Prince of Wales, fighting valiantly, was slain on the field, according to one chronicler, crying in vain for succour to his brother-in-law, the treacherous Clarence. Margaret was kept for a show, and also because women, especially when they happened to be queens, were not slaughtered in this fierce age. She remained in captivity, moved from place to place, until ransomed by Louis XI. Eleven years after Tewkesbury she died in poverty in her father's Anjou.

After the battle Richard of Gloucester had hastened to London. He had a task to do at the Tower. As long as the Prince of Wales lived King Henry's life had been safe, but with the death of the last hope of Lancaster his fate was sealed. On the night of May 21 the Duke of Gloucester visited the Tower with full authority from the King, where he probably supervised the murder of the melancholy spectator who had been the centre of fifty years of cruel contention.

The rest of the reign of Edward IV may be told briefly. The King was now supreme. His foes and his patrons alike were dead. He was now a matured and disillusioned statesman. He had every means of remaining complete master of the realm while leading a jolly life. Even from the beginning of his reign he had been chary of calling Parliaments. They made trouble; but if money were needed they had to be called. Therefore the cry in those days which sobered all sovereigns was, "The King should live of his own." But this doctrine took no account of the increasing scope of government. How could the King from his paternal estates, together with certain tolls and tithes, fifteenths, and a few odd poundages, and the accidents of people dying intestate or without adult heirs, or treasure-trove and the like, maintain from these snips an administration equal to the requirements of an expanding society? Still less on this basis could full-blooded wars be waged against France as was expected.

Edward was resolved to have as little to do with Parliament as possible, and even as a boy of twenty in the stress of war he tried hard and faithfully to "live of his own". Now that he was victorious and unchallenged, be set himself to practise the utmost economy in everything except his personal expenses, and to avoid any policy of adventure abroad which might drive him to beg from Parliament. He had a new source of revenue in the estates of the attainted Lancastrians. The Crown had gained from the Wars of the Roses. Many were the new possessions which yielded their annual fruit. Thus so long as there was peace the King could pay his way. But the nobility and the nation sought more. They wanted to reconquer France. They mourned the loss of the French provinces. They looked back across their own miseries to the glories of Agincourt, Poitiers, and Crécy. The King, the proved warrior, was expected to produce results in this sphere. It was his intention to do the least possible. He had never liked war, and had had enough of it. Nevertheless he obtained from the Parliament considerable grants for a war in alliance with Burgundy against France.

In 1475 he invaded France, but advanced only as far as Picquigny, near Amiens. There he parleyed. Louis XI shared his outlook. He too saw that kings might grow strong and safe in peace, and would be the prey and tool of their subjects in war. The two kings sought peace and found it. Louis XI offered Edward IV a lump sum of 75,000 crowns, and a yearly tribute of 50,000. This was almost enough to balance the royal budget and make him independent of Parliament. Edward closed on the bargain, and signed the Treaty of Picquigny. But Charles the Bold, his ally of Burgundy, took it amiss. At Péronne, in full assembly, with all the English captains gathered, he declared that he had been shamefully betrayed by his ally. A most painful impression was created; but the King put up with it. He went back home and drew for seven successive years this substantial payment for not harrying France, and at the same time he pocketed most of the moneys which Parliament had voted for harrying her.

At this date the interest of these transactions centres mainly upon the character of Edward IV, and we can see that though he had to strive through fierce deeds and slaughter to his throne he was at heart a Little-Englander and a lover of ease. It by no means follows that his policy was injurious to the realm. He made his administration live thriftily, and on his death he was the first King since Henry II to leave not debts but a fortune.

There came a day when he had to call Parliament together. This was not however to ask them for money. When in January 1478 Edward called the Parliament, he had no other business but to condemn Clarence. He adduced a formidable catalogue of crimes and affronts to the Throne, constituting treason. The Parliament, as might be expected, accepted the King's view. By a Bill of Attainder they adjudged Clarence worthy of death, left the execution in the hands of the King, and went home relieved at not having been asked to pay any more taxes. Clarence was already in the Tower. How he died is much disputed. Some say the King gave him his choice of deaths. Certainly Edward did not intend to have a grisly public spectacle. According to Shakespeare the Duke was drowned in a butt of Malmsey wine. This was certainly the popular legend believed by the sixteenth century. Why should it not be true? At any rate no one has attempted to prove any different tale.

Queen Elizabeth over the course of years had produced not only five daughters, but two fine boys, who were growing up. In 1483 one was twelve and the other nine. The succession to the Crown seemed plain and secure. The King himself was only forty. In another ten years the Yorkist triumph would have become permanent. But here Fate intervened, and with solemn hand reminded the pleasure-loving Edward that his account was closed. His main thought was set on securing the crown to his son, the unfledged Edward V; but in April 1483 death came so suddenly upon him that he had no time to take the necessary precautions. Although always devoted to Queen Elizabeth, he had lived promiscuously all his life. She was in the Midlands, when, after only ten days' illness, this strong King was cut down in his prime. The historians assure us that this was the penalty of debauchery. It may well have been appendicitis, an explanation as yet unknown. He died unprepared except by the Church, and his faithful brother Richard saw himself suddenly confronted with an entirely new view of his future.

CHAPTER TWENTY-ONE

RICHARD III

Twelve-year-old Edward succeeds his father as Edward V – Richard,
Duke of Gloucester seizes boy-King and confines him to the Tower –
beheading starts with Lord Hastings – Prince Richard, Duke of York,
taken to the Tower with his brother – the Shaw Sermon – Richard of
Gloucester enthroned as Richard III – the death of the "Princes in the
Tower" – Buckingham centre of conspiracy – death of the Prince of
Wales – Henry, Earl of Richmond, lands at Milford Haven – Stanley's
Test – the Battle of Bosworth Field – the death of Richard III – end of
the Wars of the Roses

A PROTECTORATE WAS inevitable.[1] There could be no doubt about the protector. Richard of Gloucester, the King's faithful brother, renowned in war, grave and competent in administration, enriched by Warwick's inheritance and many other great estates, in possession of all the chief military offices, stood forth without compare, and had been nominated by the late King himself. Around him gathered most of the old nobility. They viewed with general distaste the idea of a King whose grandfather, though a knight, had been a mere steward to one of their own order. They deplored a minority and thereafter the rule of an unproved, inexperienced boy-King. They were however bound by their oaths and by the succession in the Yorkist line that their own swords had established.

One thing at least they would not brook: Queen Elizabeth and her low-born relations should no longer have the ascendancy. On the other hand, Lord Rivers at Ludlow, with numerous adherents and family supporters, had possession of the new King. For three weeks both parties eyed one another and parleyed. It was agreed in April that the King should be crowned at the earliest moment, but that he should come to London attended by not more than two thousand horsemen. Accordingly this cavalcade, headed by Lord Rivers and his nephew, Grey, rode through Shrewsbury and Northampton. They had reached Stony Stratford when they learned that Gloucester and his ally, the Duke of Buckingham, coming to London from Yorkshire, were only ten miles behind them. They turned back to Northampton to greet the two

---

1 The new king was the twelve-year-old eldest surviving son of Edward IV and Elizabeth Woodville and therefore nephew of Richard of Gloucester, Edward IV's brother.

Dukes, apparently suspecting no evil. Richard received them amicably; they dined together. But with the morning there was a change.

When he awoke Rivers found the doors of the inn locked. He asked the reason for this precaution. Gloucester and Buckingham met him with scowling gaze and accused him of "trying to set distance" between the King and them. He and Grey were immediately made prisoners. Richard then rode with his power to Stony Stratford, arrested the commanders of the two thousand horse, forced his way to the young King, and told him he had discovered a design on the part of Lord Rivers and others to seize the Government and oppress the old nobility. On this declaration Edward V took the only positive action recorded of his reign. He wept. Well he might.

The next morning Duke Richard presented himself again to Edward. He embraced him as an uncle; he bowed to him as a subject. He announced himself as Protector. He dismissed the two thousand horsemen to their homes; their services would not be needed. To London then! To the coronation! Thus this melancholy procession set out. The Queen, who was already in London, had no illusions. She took sanctuary at once with her other children at Westminster, making a hole through the wall between the church and the palace to transport such personal belongings as she could gather. The King arrived in London only on May 4, and the coronation, which had been fixed for that date, was necessarily postponed. He was lodged at the Bishop of London's palace, where he received the fealty of all the lords, spiritual and temporal. But the Protector and his friends felt that it was hardly becoming that he should be the guest of an ecclesiastic, and when the Queen's friends suggested that he might reside at the Hospital of the Knights of St John in Clerkenwell Richard argued that it would be more fitting to the royal dignity to dwell in one of his own castles and on his own ground. The Tower was a residence not only commodious but at the same time safe from any popular disorder. To this decision the lords of the Council gave united assent, it not being either easy or safe for the minority to disagree. With much ceremony and protestations of devotion the child of twelve was conducted to the Tower and its gates closed behind him.

London was in a ferment, and the magnates gathered there gazed upon each other in doubt and fear. The next step in the tragedy concerned Lord Hastings. He had played a leading part in the closing years of Edward IV. After the King's death he had been strong against the Woodvilles; but he was the first to detach himself from Richard's proceedings. It did not suit him, nor some of the other magnates, that all power should rapidly be accumulating in Richard's hands. He began to be friendly with the Queen's party, still in the sanctuary of Westminster Abbey. Of what happened next all we really know is that Hastings was abruptly arrested in council at the Tower on June 13 and beheaded without trial on the same day. Sir Thomas More late in the next reign wrote his celebrated history. His book was based of course on information given him under the new and strongly established régime. His object seems to have been less to compose a factual narrative than a moralistic drama. In it

Richard is evil incarnate, and Henry Tudor, the deliverer of the kingdom, all sweetness and light. The opposite view would have been treason. Not only is every possible crime attributed by More to Richard, and some impossible ones, but he is presented as a physical monster, crookbacked and withered of arm. No one in his lifetime seems to have remarked these deformities, but they are now very familiar to us through Shakespeare's play. Needless to say, as soon as the Tudor dynasty was laid to rest defenders of Richard fell to work, and they have been increasingly busy ever since.

More's tale however has priority. We have the famous scene at the Council in the Tower. It was Friday, June 13. Richard arrived in the Council chamber about nine, apparently in good humour. "My lord," he said to Bishop Morton, "you have very good strawberries in your garden at Holborn. I pray you let us have a mess of them." The Council began its business. Richard asked to be excused for a while; when he returned between ten and eleven his whole manner was changed. He frowned and glared upon the Council, and at the same time clusters of armed men gathered at the door. "What punishment do they deserve," demanded the Protector, "who conspire against the life of one so nearly related to the King as myself, and entrusted with the government of the realm?" There was general consternation. Hastings said at length that they deserved the punishment of traitors. "That sorceress my brother's wife," cried Richard, "and others with her see how they have wasted my body with sorcery and witchcraft." So saying, he is supposed to have bared his arm and showed it to the Council, shrunk and withered as legend says it was. In furious terms he next referred to Jane Shore, with whom Hastings had formed an intimacy on the late King's death. Hastings, taken aback, replied, "Certainly if they have done so heinously they are worthy of a heinous punishment." "What?" cried Crookback. "Dost thou serve me with 'ifs' and 'ands'? I tell thee they have done it, and that I will make good upon thy body, traitor!" He struck the Council table with his fist, and at this signal the armed men ran in, crying "Treason!", and Hastings, Bishop Morton, and the Archbishop of York with some others were seized. Richard bade Hastings prepare for instant death. "I will not dine until I have his head." There was barely time to find a priest. Upon a log of wood which lay by chance in the Tower yard Hastings was decapitated. Terror reigned.

Richard had ordered his retainers in the North to come to London in arms under his trusted lieutenant, Sir Richard Ratcliffe. On the way south Ratcliffe collected Lords Rivers, Vaughan, Grey, and the commanders of the two thousand horse from the castles in which they were confined, and at Pomfret cut off their heads a few days after Hastings had suffered. These executions are undisputed fact.

Meanwhile the Queen and her remaining son[1] still sheltered in sanctuary. Richard felt that it would be more natural that the two brothers should be together under his care, and he moved the purged Council to request the

1   Richard, the young Duke of York.

Queen to give him up. The Council contemplated the use of force in the event of a refusal. Having no choice, the Queen submitted, and the little prince of nine was handed over in Westminster Hall to the Protector, who embraced him affectionately and conducted him to the Tower, which neither he nor his brother was ever to leave again.

Richard's Northern bands were now approaching London in considerable numbers, many thousands being expected, and he felt strong enough to take his next step. The coronation of Edward V had been postponed several times. Now a preacher named Shaw, brother of the Lord Mayor of London, one of Richard's partisans, was engaged to preach a sermon at St Paul's Cross. Taking his text from the Book of Wisdom, "Bastard slips shall not take root", he impugned Edward IV's marriage with Elizabeth Woodville upon a number of grounds, including sorcery, violation of the alleged previous betrothal to Eleanor Butler, and the assertion that the ceremony had been performed in an unconsecrated place. He argued from this that Edward's children were illegitimate and that the crown rightly belonged to Richard. The suggestion was even revived that Edward IV himself had not been his father's son. Richard now appeared, accompanied by Buckingham, evidently expecting to be publicly acclaimed; but, says More, "the people were so far from crying 'King Richard!' that they stood as if turned into stones for wonder of this shameful sermon". Two days later the Duke of Buckingham tried his hand, and according to an eye-witness he was so eloquent and well rehearsed that he did not even pause to spit; but once again the people remained mute, and only some of the Duke's servants threw up their caps, crying, "King Richard!"

Nevertheless on June 25 Parliament met, and after a roll declaring that the late King's marriage with Elizabeth was no marriage at all and that Edward's children were bastard it petitioned Richard to assume the crown. A deputation, headed by the Duke of Buckingham, waited on Richard, who was staying at the house of his mother, whose virtue he had aspersed. With becoming modesty Richard persistently refused; but when Buckingham assured him of their determination that the children of Edward should not rule, and that if he would not serve the country they would be forced to choose some other noble, he overcame his conscientious scruples at the call of public duty. The next day he was enthroned, with much ceremony

The King now had a title acknowledged and confirmed by Parliament, and upon the theory of the bastardy of Edward's children he was also the lineal successor in blood. Thus the whole design seemed to have been accomplished. Yet from this very moment there began that marked distrust and hostility of all classes towards King Richard III which all his arts and competence could not allay. It is contended by the defenders of King Richard that the Tudor version of these events has prevailed. But the English people who lived at the time and learned of the events day by day formed their convictions two years before the Tudors gained power, or were indeed a prominent factor. Richard III held the authority of government. He told his own story with what facilities were available and he was spontaneously and almost universally disbelieved. Indeed, no fact stands forth more unchallengeable than that the overwhelming majority of the nation was convinced that Richard had used his power as Protector to usurp the crown and that the princes had disappeared in the Tower. It will take many ingenious books to raise this issue to the dignity of a historical controversy.

No man had done more to place Richard upon the throne than the Duke of Buckingham, and upon no one had the King bestowed greater gifts and favours. Yet during these first three months of Richard's reign Buckingham from being his chief supporter became his mortal foe. His motives are not clear. Perhaps he shrank from becoming the accomplice in what he foresaw would be the closing act of the usurpation. Perhaps he feared for his own safety, for was he not himself of royal blood? He was descended both through the Beauforts and Thomas of Woodstock from Edward III. It was believed that when the Beaufort family was legitimatised by letters patent under King Richard II, confirmed by Henry IV, there had been a reservation rendering them incapable of inheriting the crown. But this reservation had not been a part of the original document, and had only been written in during the reign of Henry IV. The Duke of Buckingham, as a Beaufort on his mother's side, possessed the original letters patent under the Great Seal, confirmed in Parliament, in which no such bar was mentioned. Although he guarded this secret with all needful prudence he must now look upon himself as a potential claimant to the crown, and he must feel none the safer if Richard should so regard him. Buckingham's mind was troubled by the knowledge that all the ceremony and vigour with which Richard's ascent to the throne had been conducted did not affect the general feeling that he was a usurper. In his castle at Brecknock he began to talk moodily to his prisoner, Bishop Morton; and the Bishop, who was a master of the persuasive arts and a consummate politician, undoubtedly gained a great hold upon him.

Meanwhile King Richard began a progress from Oxford through the Midlands. At every city he laboured to make the best impression, righting wrongs, settling disputes, granting favours, courting popularity. Yet he could not escape the sense that behind the displays of gratitude and loyalty which naturally surrounded him there lay an unspoken challenge to his Kingship. There was little concealment of this in the South. In London, Kent, and throughout the Home Counties feeling already ran high against him, and on all men's lips was the demand that the princes should be liberated. Richard did not as yet suspect Buckingham, who had parted from him at Gloucester, of any serious disaffection. But he was anxious for the safety of his crown. How could he maintain it while his nephews lived to provide a rallying point for any combination of hostile forces against him?

So we come to the principal crime ever afterwards associated with Richard's name. His interest is plain. His character was ruthless. It is certain that the helpless children in the Tower were not seen again after the month of July 1483. Yet we are invited by some to believe that they languished in captivity, unnoticed and unrecorded, for another two years, only to be done to death by Henry Tudor. According to Sir Thomas More's story, Richard resolved in July to extirpate the menace to his peace and sovereignty presented by the princes. He sent a special messenger, by name John Green, to Brackenbury, the Constable of the Tower, with orders to make an end of them. Brackenbury refused to obey. "Whom should a man trust," exclaimed the King when Green returned with this report, when those who I thought would most surely serve at my command will do nothing for me?" A page who heard this outburst reminded his master that Sir James Tyrell, one of Richard's former companions in arms, was capable of anything. Tyrell was sent to London with a warrant authorising Brackenbury to deliver to him for one night all the keys of the Tower. Tyrell discharged his fell commission with all dispatch. One of the four gaolers in of the princes, Forest by name, was found willing, and with Dighton, Tyrell's own groom, did the deed. When the princes were asleep these two assassins pressed the pillows hard down upon their faces till they were suffocated, and their bodies were immured in some secret corner of the Tower. There is some proof that all three murderers were suitably rewarded by the King. But it was not until Henry VII's reign, when Tyrell was lying in the Tower under sentence of death for quite a separate crime, that he is alleged to have made a confession upon which, with much other circumstantial evidence, the story as we know it rests.

In the reign of Charles II, when in 1674 the staircase leading to the chapel in the White Tower was altered, the skeletons of two young lads whose apparent ages fitted the two princes, were found buried under a mass of rubble. They were examined by the royal surgeon and the antiquaries reported that they were undoubtedly the remains of Edward V and the Duke of York. Charles accepted this view, and the skeletons were reburied in Henry VII's Chapel at Westminster with a Latin inscription laying all blame upon their perfidious uncle, "the usurper of the realm". This has not prevented various writers, among whom Horace Walpole is notable, from endeavouring to clear Richard of the crime, or from attempting to cast it, without any evidence beyond conjecture, upon Henry VII. However, in our own time an exhumation has confirmed the view of the disinterested authorities of King Charles's reign.

Buckingham had now become the centre of a conspiracy throughout the West and South of England against the King. He had reached a definite decision about his own claims to the crown. He seems to have assumed from his knowledge of Richard that the princes in the Tower were either dead or doomed. He met at this time Margaret, Countess of Richmond, survivor of the Beaufort line, and recognised that even if the house of York were altogether set aside both she and her son Henry Tudor, Earl of Richmond, stood between him and the crown. The Countess of Richmond, presuming him to be still Richard's right-hand man, asked him to win the King's consent to a marriage between her son Henry of Richmond and one of King Edward's daughters, Elizabeth, still in sanctuary with their mother at Westminster.

Richard would never have entertained such a project, which was indeed the extreme opposite to his interests. But Buckingham saw that such a marriage would unite the claims of York and Lancaster, bridge the gulf that had parted England for so long, and enable a tremendous front to be immediately formed against the usurper.

The popular demand for the release of the princes was followed by a report of their death. When, how, and by whose hand the deed had been done was not known. But as the news spread like wildfire a kind of fury seized upon many people. Although accustomed to the brutalities of the long civil wars, the English people of those days still retained the faculty of horror; and once it was excited they did not soon forget. A modern dictator with the resources of science at his disposal can easily lead the public on from day to day, destroying all persistency of thought and aim, so that memory is blurred by the multiplicity of daily news and judgment baffled by its perversion. But in the fifteenth century the murder of the two young princes by the very man who had undertaken to protect them was regarded as an atrocious crime, never to be forgotten or forgiven. In September Richard in his progress reached York, and here he created his son Prince of Wales, thus in the eyes of his enemies giving confirmation to the darkest rumours.

All Buckingham's preparations were for a general rising on October 18. He would gather his Welsh forces at Brecknock; all the Southern and Western counties would take up arms; and Henry, Earl of Richmond, with the aid of the Duke of Brittany, would land with a force of five thousand men in Wales. But the anger of the people at the rumoured murder of the princes deranged this elaborate plan. In Kent, Wiltshire, Sussex, and Devonshire there were risings ten days before the appointed date; Henry of Richmond was forced to set sail from Brittany in foul weather on October 12, so that his fleet was dispersed; and when Buckingham unfurled his flag at Brecknock the elements took sides against him too. A terrific storm flooded the Severn valley, and he found himself penned on the Welsh border in a district which could not supply the needs of his army, and unable, as he had planned, to join the rebels in Devonshire.

King Richard acted with the utmost vigour. He had an army and he marched against rebellion. The sporadic risings in the South were suppressed. Buckingham's forces melted away, and he himself hid from vengeance. Richmond reached the English coast at last with only two ships, and sailed westwards towards Plymouth, waiting for a sign which never came. Such was the uncertainty at Plymouth that he warily made further inquiries, as a result of which he sailed back to Brittany. Buckingham, with a high price on his head, was betrayed to Richard, who lost not an hour in having him slaughtered. The usual crop of executions followed. Order was restored throughout the land, and the King seemed to have established himself securely upon his throne and he proceeded in the new year to inaugurate a series of enlightened reforms in every sphere of Government.

A terrible blow now fell upon the King. In April 1484 his only son, the

Prince of Wales, died at Middleham, and his wife, Anne, the daughter of the King-maker, whose health was broken could bear no more children. Henry Tudor, Earl of Richmond now became obviously the rival claimant and successor to the throne. Richmond, "the nearest thing to royalty the Lancastrians party possessed", was a Welshman, whose grandfather, Owen Tudor, executed by the Yorkists in 1461, had married, if indeed he married, Henry V's widow, Catherine of France, and whose father Edmund had married the Lady Margaret Beaufort. Thus Richmond could trace his descent through his mother from Edward III, and on his father's side had French royal blood in his veins as well as a shadowy claim to descent from Cadwallader and the legendary ancient kings of Britain, including King Arthur. His life had been cast amid ceaseless trouble. For seven years of childhood he had been besieged in Harlech Castle. At the age of fourteen, on the defeat of the Lancastrians at Tewkesbury, he was forced to flee to Brittany. Thereafter exile and privation had been his lot. These trials had stamped themselves upon his character, rendering him crafty and suspicious. This, however, did not daunt a proud spirit nor cloud a wise and commanding mind. Nor did it cast a shadow over his countenance, which was, we are told, "smiling and able, especially in his communications".

All hopes in England were now turned towards Richmond, and it was apparent that the marriage which had been projected between him and Edward IV's eldest daughter Elizabeth offered a prospect of ending for ever the cruel dynastic strife of which the land was unutterably weary. After the failure of Buckingham's rebellion Richmond and his expedition had returned to Brittany. The Duke of Brittany, long friendly, again accorded shelter and subsistence to the exile and his band of perhaps five hundred Englishmen of quality. But King Richard's diplomacy was active. He offered a large sum of money for the surrender of his rival. During the illness of the Duke of Brittany the Breton Minister, Landois, was disposed to sell the valuable refugee. Richmond however, suspecting the danger, escaped in the nick of time by galloping hell for leather into France, where, in accordance with the general policy of keeping English feuds alive, he was well received by the French regent, Anne. Meanwhile the Duke of Brittany, recovering, reproved his Minister and continued to harbour the English exiles. In France Richmond was joined by the Earl of Oxford, the leading survivor of the Lancastrian party, who had escaped from ten years' incarceration and plunged once again into the old struggle.

As the months passed many prominent Englishmen, both Yorkist and Lancastrian, withdrew themselves from Richard's baleful presence, and made their way to Richmond, who from this time forth stood at the head of a combination which might well unite all England. His great hope lay in the marriage with the Princess Elizabeth. But in this quarter Richard had not been idle. Before the rebellion he had taken steps to prevent Elizabeth slipping out of sanctuary and England. In March 1484 he made proposals to the Dowager Queen, Dame Elizabeth Grey as he called her, of reconciliation. The unhappy

Queen did not reject his overtures. Richard promised in a solemn deed "on his honour as a King" to provide maintenance for the ex-Queen and to marry her daughters suitably to gentlemen. This remarkable document was witnessed not only by the Lords Spiritual and Temporal, but in addition by the Lord Mayor of London and the Aldermen. In spite of the past the Queen had to trust herself to this. She quitted sanctuary. She abandoned the match for her daughter with Richmond. She and the elder princesses were received at Richard's Court and treated with exceptional distinction. At the Christmas Court at Westminster in 1484 high revels were held. It was noticed that the changes of dress provided for Dame Elizabeth Grey and her daughters were almost royal in their style and richness. The stigma of bastardy so lately inflicted upon Edward's children, and the awful secret of the Tower, were banished. Although the threat of invasion was constant, gaiety and dancing ruled the hour. "Dame Elizabeth" even wrote to her son by her first marriage, the Marquis of Dorset, in Paris, to abandon Richmond and come home to share in the new-found favour.

More surprising still, Princess Elizabeth seems to have been by no means hostile to the attentions of the usurper. In March 1485 Queen Anne died, probably from natural causes. Rumours were circulating that Richard intended to marry his niece himself, in order to keep her out of Richmond's way. This incestuous union could have been achieved by Papal dispensation, but Richard disavowed all intention of it, both in Council and in public. And it is indeed hard to see how his position could have been strengthened by marrying a princess whom he had declared illegitimate. However that may be, Richmond was thereby relieved of a great anxiety.

All through the summer Richmond's expedition was preparing at the mouth of the Seine, and the exodus from England of substantial people to join him was unceasing. The suspense was wearing to Richard. He felt he was surrounded by hatred and distrust, and that none served him but from fear or hope of favour. His dogged, indomitable nature had determined him to make for his crown the greatest of all his fights. He fixed his headquarters in a good central position at Nottingham. Commissions of muster and array were ordered to call men to arms in almost every county. Departing perforce from the precepts he had set himself in the previous year, he asked for a "benevolence", or "malevolence" as it was described, of thirty thousand pounds. He set on foot a disciplined regular force. He stationed relays of horsemen every twenty miles permanently along the great roads to bring news and carry orders with an organised swiftness hitherto unknown in England. This important development in the postal system had been inaugurated by his brother. At the head of his troops Richard ceaselessly patrolled the Midland area, endeavouring by strength to overawe and by good government to placate his sullen subjects. He set forth his cause in a vehement proclamation, denouncing "... one, Henry Tydder, son of Edmund Tydder, son of Owen Tydder", of bastard blood both on his father's and mother's side, who of his ambition and covetousness pretended to the crown, "to the disinheriting and destruction of all the noble and worshipful blood of his realm for ever". But this fell cold.

On August 1 Richmond embarked at Harfleur with his Englishmen, Yorkist as well as Lancastrian, and a body of French troops. A fair wind bore him down the Channel. He evaded the squadrons of "Lovell our dogge",[1] doubled Land's End, and landed at Milford Haven on the 7th. Kneeling, he recited the psalm *Judica me, Deus, et decerne causam meam*. He kissed the ground, signed himself with the Cross, and gave the order to advance in the name of God and St George. He had only two thousand men; but such were his assurances of support that he proclaimed Richard forthwith usurper and rebel against himself. The Welsh were gratified by the prospect of one of their race succeeding to the crown of mighty England. It had been for ages a national dream. The ancient Britons would come back into their own. Richard's principal chieftain and Officer, Rhys ap Thomas, considered himself at first debarred by his oath of allegiance from aiding the invader. He had declared that no rebels should enter Wales, "except they should pass over his belly". He had however excused himself from sending his only son to Nottingham as a hostage, assuring Richard that nothing could bind him more strongly than his conscience. This now became an obstacle. However, the Bishop of St David's offered to absolve him from his oath, and suggested that he might, if still disquieted, lay himself upon the ground before Richmond and let him actually step over his belly. A more dignified but equally satisfactory procedure was adopted. Rhys ap Thomas stood under the Molloch Bridge near Dale while Henry of Richmond walked over the top. Anything like a scandalous breach of faith was thus avoided. The Welsh gentry rallied in moderate numbers to Richmond, who displayed not only the standard of St George, but the Red Dragon of Cadwallader. With five thousand men he now moved eastwards through Shrewsbury and Stafford.

For all his post-horses it was five days before the King heard of the landing. He gathered his army and marched to meet his foe. At this moment the attitude of the Stanleys became of decisive importance. They had been entrusted by the King with the duty of intercepting the rebels should they land in the West. Sir William Stanley, with some thousands of men, made no attempt to do so. Richard thereupon summoned Lord Stanley, the head of the house, to his Court, and when that potentate declared himself "ill of the sweating sickness" he seized Lord Strange, his eldest son, to hold him answerable with his life for his father's loyalty. This did not prevent Sir William Stanley with the Cheshire levies from making friendly contact with Richmond. But Lord Stanley, hoping to save his son, maintained till the last moment an uncertain demeanour.

The city of York on this occasion stood by the Yorkist cause. The Duke of Norfolk and Percy, Earl of Northumberland, were Richard's principal

---

1   1st Viscount Francis Lovell (Lovel), Richard III's Lord Chamberlain and one of the King's servants name-called in a popular verse. See also note on page 219.

adherents. "The Catte and the Ratte"[1] had no hope of life but in their master's victory. On August 17, thus attended, the King set forth towards Leicester at the head of his army. Their ordered ranks, four abreast, with the cavalry on both flanks and the King mounted on his great white charger in the centre, made a formidable impression upon beholders. And when on Sunday, the 21st, this whole array came out of Leicester to meet Richmond near the village of Market Bosworth it was certain that a decisive battle impended on the morrow.

Appearances favoured the King. He had ten thousand disciplined men under the royal authority against Richmond's hastily gathered five thousand rebels. But at some distance from the flanks of the main army, on opposite hill-tops, stood the respective forces, mainly from Lancashire and Cheshire, of Sir William Stanley and Lord Stanley, the whole situation resembling, as has been said, four players in a game of cards. Richard, according to the Tudor historians, although confessing to a night of frightful dreams and demon-hauntings, harangued his captains in magnificent style. "Dismiss all fear. ... Every one give but one sure stroke and the day is ours. What prevaileth a handful of men to a whole realm? As for me, I assure you this day I will triumph by glorious victory or suffer death for immortal fame." He then gave the signal for battle, and sent a message to Lord Stanley that if he did not fall on forthwith he would instantly decapitate his son. Stanley, forced to this bitter choice, answered proudly that he had other sons. The King gave orders for Strange's execution. But the officers so charged thought it prudent to hold the stroke in suspense till matters were clearer. "My lord, the enemy is past the marsh. After the battle let young Stanley die."

But even now Richmond was not sure what part Lord Stanley and his forces would play. When, after archery and cannonade, the lines were locked in battle all doubts were removed. The Earl of Northumberland, commanding Richard's left, stood idle at a distance. Lord Stanley's force joined Richmond. The King saw that all was lost, and, shouting "Treason! Treason!" hurled himself into the thickest of the fray in the desperate purpose of striking down Richmond with his own hand. He actually slew Sir William Brandon, Richmond's standard-bearer, and laid low Sir John Cheney, a warrior renowned for his bodily strength. He is said even to have reached Richmond and crossed swords with him. But at this moment Sir William Stanley's three thousand, "in coats as red as blood", fell upon the struggling Yorkists. The tides of conflict swept the principals asunder. Richmond was preserved, and the King, refusing to fly, was borne down and slaughtered as he deserved.

Richard's crown, which he wore to the last, was picked out of a bush and placed upon the victor's head. The Duke of Norfolk was slain fighting bravely; his son, Lord Surrey, was taken prisoner; Ratcliffe was killed; Catesby, after being allowed to make his will, was executed on the field; and Henry Tudor became King of England. Richard's corpse, naked, and torn by

1   The Rat, the Cat, and Lovel the Dog was a political rhyme about Richard III's three main supporters: the Rat (Sir Richard Ratcliffe) and Cat (Sir John Catesby), and Lovel (Viscount Lovell).

wounds, was bound across a horse, with his head and long hair hanging down, bloody and hideous, and in this condition borne into Leicester for all men to see.

Bosworth Field may be taken as closing a long chapter in English history. Though risings and conspiracies continued throughout the next reign the strife of the Red and the White Rose had in the main come to an end. Neither won. A solution was reached in which the survivors of both causes could be reconciled. The marriage of Richmond with the adaptable Princess Elizabeth produced the Tudor line, in which both Yorkists and Lancastrians had a share. The revengeful ghosts of two mingled generations were laid for ever. Richard's death also ended the Plantagenet line. For over three hundred years this strong race of warrior and statesmen kings, whose gifts and vices were upon the highest scale, whose sense of authority and Empire had been persistently maintained, now vanished from the fortunes of the Island. The Plantagenets and the proud, exclusive nobility which their system evolved had torn themselves to pieces.

CHAPTER TWENTY-TWO

THE ROUND WORLD

*The sixteenth century begins — the Renaissance — Erasmus — printing —
Luther — Calvin — the Reformation — the explorers: Diaz, da Gama,
Columbus, Cabot — the New World — Henry VII and the Tudors —
North–South divide — Simnel and Warbeck, pretenders to the throne —
Irish rivals — Poynings' Law — the rule of Kildare — a royal marriage with
Scotland — the King's Council — the death of Henry VII*

W E HAVE now reached the dawn of what is called the sixteenth
century which covers a period in which extraordinary changes
affected the whole of Europe. For two hundred years or more
the Renaissance had been stirring the thought and spirit of
Italy — and now came forth in the vivid revival of the traditions of ancient
Greece and Rome, in so far as these did not affect the foundations of the
Christian faith. The Popes had in the meanwhile become temporal rulers, with
the lusts and pomps of other potentates, yet they claimed to carry with them
the spiritual power as well. The revenues of the Church were swelled by the
sale of "Indulgences" to remit Purgatory both for the living and the dead. The
offices of bishop and cardinal were bought and sold, and the common people
taxed to the limit of their credulity. At the same time literature, philosophy,
and art flowered under classical inspiration, and the minds of men to whom
study was open were refreshed and enlarged. These were the humanists, who
attempted a reconciliation of classical and Christian teachings, among the
foremost of whom was Erasmus of Rotterdam.[1] To him is due a considerable
part of the credit for bringing Renaissance thought to England. Printing
enabled knowledge and argument to flow through the many religious societies
which made up the structure of medieval Europe and from about 1450
onwards printing presses formed the core of a vast ever-growing domain.
There were already sixty universities in the Western world, from Lisbon to

---

1 Desiderius Erasmus (c.1466–1536) was a Dutch humanist who became a travelling Augustinian
monk. He came to England and was for three years Lady Margaret Reader at Cambridge
University, where he lectured in Greek. He wrote a new Latin version of the New Testament
(*Novum Instrumentum*) and, among other works, a satire against theologians inspired by Sir
Thomas More (*Encomium Moriae*).

Prague, and in the early part of the new century these voluntarily opened up broader paths of study and intercourse which rendered their life more fertile and informal. In the Middle Ages education had largely been confined to training the clergy; now it was steadily extended, and its purpose became to turn out not only priests but lay scholars and well-informed gentlemen. The man of many parts and accomplishments became the Renaissance ideal.

This quickening of the human spirit was accompanied by a questioning of long-held theories. For the first time, in the course of the fifteenth century men began to refer to the preceding millennium as the Middle Ages. Though much that was medieval survived in their minds, men felt they were living on the brink of a new and modern age. It was an age marked not only by splendid achievements in art and architecture, but also by the beginnings of a revolution in science. Vast new perspectives were opening. The urge to inquire, to debate, and seek new explanations spread from the field of classical learning into that of religious studies. Greek and even Hebrew texts, as well as Latin, were scrutinised afresh. Inevitably this led to the questioning of accepted religious beliefs. The Renaissance bred the Reformation.

In 1517, at the age of thirty-four, Martin Luther, a German priest, denounced the sale of Indulgences, nailed his theses on this and other matters on the door of Wittenberg Castle church, and embarked on his venturesome intellectual foray with the Pope. What began as a protest against Church practices soon became a challenge to Church doctrine. In this struggle Luther displayed qualities of determination and conviction at the peril of the stake which won him his name and fame. He started or gave an impulse to a movement which within a decade swamped the Continent, and proudly bears the general title of the Reformation. It took different forms in different countries, particularly in Switzerland under Zwingli and Calvin.[1] The latter's influence spread from Geneva across France to the Netherlands and Britain, where it was most strongly felt in Scotland.

The Reformation added to the confusion and uncertainty of an age in which men and states were tugging unwillingly and unwittingly at the anchors that had so long held Europe. After a period of ecclesiastical strife between the Papacy and the Reformation, Protestantism was established over a great part of the Continent under a variety of sects and schools, of which Lutheranism covered the larger area. The Church in Rome, strengthened by the heart-searching Catholic revival known as the Counter-Reformation and in the more worldly sphere by the activities of the Inquisition, proved able to maintain itself through a long series of religious wars. The division between the assailants and defenders of the old order threatened the stability of every state in modern Europe and wrecked the unity of some. England and France came out of the struggle scarred and shaken but in themselves united. A new

---

1 Ulrich Zwingli (1484–1531), the Swiss reformer, was ordained as a Roman Catholic priest but led the Reformation in Switzerland. Jean Calvin or Cauvin (1509–64), the French-born reformer, was leader of the Reformation in Geneva, where he established a rigorously Presbyterian theocracy.

barrier was created between Ireland and England, a new bond of unity forged between England and Scotland. The Holy Roman Empire of the German people dissolved into a dust of principalities and cities; the Netherlands split into what we now know as Holland and Belgium. Dynasties were threatened, old loyalties forsworn. By the middle of the century the Calvinists were the spearhead of the Protestant attack, the Jesuits the shield and sword of Catholic defence and counterattack. Not for another hundred years would exhaustion and resignation put an end to the revolution that began with Luther. It ended only after Central Europe had been wrecked by the Thirty Years War, and the Peace of Westphalia in 1648 terminated a struggle whose starting-point had been almost forgotten. It was not until the nineteenth century that a greater sense of toleration based upon mutual reverence and respect ruled the souls of men throughout the Christian world.

While the forces of Renaissance and Reformation were gathering strength in Europe the world beyond was yielding its secrets. Italian geographers and navigators had for some time been trying to find a new sea-route to the Orient which would be unhampered by the infidel. Portugal was the first to discover a new path. Helped by English Crusaders, she had achieved her independence in the twelfth century, gradually expelled the Moors from her mainland, and now reached out to the African coastline. Prince Henry the Navigator, grandson of John of Gaunt, had initiated a number of enterprises. Exploring began from Lisbon. All through the later fifteenth century Portuguese mariners had been pushing down the west coast of Africa, seeking for gold and slaves, slowly extending the bounds of the known world, till, in 1487, Bartholomew Diaz rounded the great promontory that marked the end of the African continent. He called it "the Cape of Storms", but the King of Portugal with true insight renamed it "the Cape of Good Hope". The hope was justified; in 1498 Vasco da Gama dropped anchor in the harbour of Calicut; the sea-route was open to the wealth of India and the Farther East.

An event of greater moment for the future of the world was meanwhile taking shape in the mind of a Genoese named Christopher Columbus. Brooding over the dreamlike maps of his fellow-countrymen, he conceived a plan for sailing due west into the Atlantic beyond the known islands in search of yet another route to the East. He married the daughter of a Portuguese sailor who had served with the Navigator, and from his father-in-law's papers he learnt of the great oceanic ventures. In 1486 he sent his brother Bartholomew to seek English backing for the enterprise. Bartholomew was captured by pirates off the French coast, and when he finally arrived in England and won the notice of Henry Tudor, the new King, it was too late. Christopher, however, had gathered the support of the joint Spanish sovereigns, Ferdinand of Aragon and Isabella of Castile, and under their patronage in 1492 he set sail into the unknown from Palos, in Andalusia. After a voyage of three months he made landfall in one of the islands of the Bahamas.

It was nearly a hundred years before England began to exert her potential sea-power. Her achievements during this period were by comparison meagre. The merchants of Bristol tried to seek a north-west passage beyond the Atlantic to the Far East, but they had little success or encouragement. Their colleagues in London and Eastern England were more concerned with the solid profits from trade with the Netherlands. Henry Tudor, however, appreciated private enterprise, provided it did not involve him in disputes with Spain. He financed an expedition by John Cabot, who was a Genoese like Columbus and lived in Bristol. In 1497 Cabot struck land near Cape Breton Island. But there was little prospect of trade, and an immense forbidding continent seemed to block further advance. On a second voyage Cabot sailed down the coast of America in the direction of Florida, but this was too near the region of Spanish efforts. Upon Cabot's death the cautious Henry abandoned his Atlantic enterprise.

The arrival of the Spaniards in the New World, and their discovery of precious metals, had led them into wordy conflict with the Portuguese. As one of the motives of both countries was the spreading of the Christian faith into undiscovered heathen lands they appealed to the Pope, in whose hands the gift of new countries was at this time conceived to lie. By a series of Bulls in the 1490s the Borgia Pope Alexander VI drew a line across the world dividing the Spanish and Portuguese spheres. This remarkable dispensation stimulated the conclusion of a treaty between Spain and Portugal. A north-south line 370 leagues west of the Azores was agreed upon, and the Portuguese felt entitled to occupy Brazil. Although the Portuguese were first in the field of oceanic adventure their country was too small to sustain such efforts. It is said that half the population of Portugal died in trying to hold their overseas possessions. Spain soon overtook them. In the year of Columbus's first voyage, Granada, the only Moorish city which survived on Spanish soil, had fallen to the last great Crusading army of the Middle Ages. Henceforward the Spaniards were free to turn their energies to the New World. In less than a generation a Portuguese captain, in Spanish pay, Magellan, set out on the voyage to South America and across the Pacific that was to take his ship round the globe. Magellan was killed in the Philippines, but his chief officer brought his ship home round the Cape of Good Hope. The scattered civilisations of the world were being drawn together, and the new discoveries were to give the little kingdom in the northern sea a fresh importance. Into this new world stepped the Tudors.

In 1485, in the person of Henry VII, a new dynasty now mounted the throne, and during the twenty-four years of careful stewardship that lay before him a new era in English history began. Henry's first task was to induce magnates, Church, and gentry to accept the decision of Bosworth and to establish himself upon the throne. He was careful to be crowned before facing the representatives of the nation, thus resting his title first upon conquest, and only secondly on the approbation of Parliament. At any rate, Parliament was committed to the experiment of his rule. Then he married, as had long been planned, the heiress of the rival house, Elizabeth of York.

Lack of money had long weakened the English throne, but military victory now restored to Henry most of the Crown lands alienated during the fifteenth century by confiscation and attainder, and many other great estates besides. He already possessed a valuable nucleus in the inheritance of the Lancastrian kings, whose heir he was. The North Country estates of Richard, Duke of Gloucester, were his by right of conquest, and later the treason and execution of Sir William Stanley, who had been discontented with his rewards after Bosworth, brought spacious properties in the Midlands into the royal hands. Henry was thus assured of a settled income.

But this was not enough. It was essential to regulate the titles by which land was held in England. The rapid succession of rival monarchs had produced a feeling of insecurity and legal chaos among the landowners. Execution and death in battle had shattered the power of the great feudal houses. The survivors and the mass of smaller landed gentry were in constant danger of losing their estates by actions in the law-courts started by personal enemies and based on past allegiances or treacheries. It was difficult to find a man whose family had not supported a losing side at some point or other during the civil wars. All this was extremely dangerous to Henry, for if the landowners were uncertain and insecure about the legal possession of their property they might follow another usurper if one should appear. Legislation was therefore passed stating that all who gave their allegiance to the King for the time being – that is, to the King upon the throne – should be secure in their lives and property. This idea of an actual King as distinct from a rightful King was characteristic of the new ruler. Sure of himself, Henry did not shrink from establishing his power upon a practical basis.

Then there were the frontiers. Throughout the history of medieval England there runs a deep division between North and South. In the South a more fully advanced society dwelt in a rich countryside, with well-developed towns and a prosperous wool trade with Flanders and Italy. The Wars of the Roses had been a serious threat to this organised life, and it was in the South that Henry found his chief support. He put down disorder in the countryside, and representatives of the merchant classes co-operated with him in Parliament. Henry's careful attention to this body sprang from a real community of interests, the need for settled government. If this was despotism, it was despotism by consent.

The North was very different. Great feudal houses like the Percys dominated the scene. The land was mountainous and barren, the population lawless and turbulent. Communications were slow, and the King's authority was often ignored and sometimes flouted. Richard, Duke of Gloucester, had been popular in these parts. His spirit was in harmony with the surroundings. In a rough-and-ready fashion he had governed well, and the city of York remained faithful to his memory even after Bosworth. Henry had not only to preserve order and authority in these regions, but also to establish a secure frontier against the Scots. As the new owner of the Gloucester estates he had acquired a strategic base in the North. It was impossible to govern England from London in the fifteenth century. The machinery of administration was too primitive, and it was essential to delegate authority. Councils were accordingly established to administer the Northern parts and the Welsh marches. Trusted servants were given wide powers of administration, and new officials who owed everything to their master and were trained in the law now began to play a decisive part in the work of government. They had always been active in the King's household and the courts of law. Now for the first time they had the ascendancy over the old nobles of the feudal age. Such were men like Henry Wyatt, the King's trusted agent in the North and captain of the key castle of Berwick, and Edmund Dudley in the South; and from them and their like the Sidneys, Herberts, Cecils, and Russells were descended.

The threat of internal disorder marched with the menace from beyond the sea. Henry had to keep ceaseless watch for the invasion of pretenders supported by foreign aid. The Court of Burgundy was a centre of plots against him, the Duchess being the sister of Richard III, and twice she launched pretenders against the Tudor régime. The first was Lambert Simnel, who finished ingloriously as a scullion in the royal kitchens. The second and more formidable was Perkin Warbeck, the son of a boatman and collector of taxes at Tournai, put forward as the younger of the princes murdered in the Tower. Backed by discontented Yorkist nobles in Ireland, by Burgundian money, Austrian and Flemish troops, and Scottish sympathy, Warbeck remained at large for seven years, plotting openly. Thrice he attempted to seize the English throne. But the classes who had backed the King since Bosworth were staunch. Warbeck's invasion of Kent was repulsed by the yokels before the military arrived, his attack from Scotland penetrated only four miles across the Border, and a Cornish rising in 1497 which he joined melted away. He fled to sanctuary, whence he was taken to London and kept in custody. Two years later, after two attempts at escape, he was executed, after confessing his guilt, on the scaffold at Tyburn.

Henry had many reasons to feel his throne shake a little beneath him. The Wars of the Roses had weakened English authority in Wales, but it was in Ireland that their effects were most manifest. The dynastic struggle had been eagerly taken up in Ireland; there were Lancastrians and Yorkists among the great Anglo-Irish families, and there were Lancastrian and Yorkist cities in the English Pale around Dublin and among remote outposts of the Englishry like Limerick and Galway. But all this turmoil was a mere continuation of clan feuds. The Butler family, under its hereditary chief, the Earl of Ormonde, was Lancastrian, because it had always been more loyal to the King of England than the rival house of Fitzgerald. The Fitzgeralds, led by the Earl of Kildare in Leinster and the Earl of Desmond in Munster, both having close alliances of blood and marriage with the native chiefs, were Yorkist in sympathy, because they thus hoped to promote their own aggrandisement.

In Munster the Desmond Fitzgeralds were already "more Irish than the Irish". In the Pale, Kildare, who was called "Garret More", or Great Earl, might perform his feudal duties and lead the English, but on his remoter lands on the Shannon a different rule prevailed. Lords Deputy from England found it profitless to assert their legal powers in face of Kildare's dominating local position and island-wide alliances. There was even a chance, unknown since the defeat and death of Edward Bruce, that his great house might provide a dynasty for all Ireland. But even if Kildare remained loyal to England would he adhere to a Yorkist king or a Lancastrian king? His kinsman Desmond supported Lambert Simnel; there was good reason to suspect that he himself supported Perkin Warbeck. Sir Edward Poynings, appointed Lord Deputy of Ireland in 1494, tried to limit his powers of mischief. He persuaded the Irish Parliament at Drogheda to pass the celebrated Poynings' Law, subordinating the Irish Parliament to the English, which was not repealed for three hundred years and remained a grievance till the twentieth century.

Kildare was attainted and sent over to London; but Henry was too wise to apply simple feudal justice to so mighty an offender, with his fighting clan on the outskirts of Dublin, and cousins, marriage-kin, and clients all over the island. The charges against the Great Earl were serious enough apart from his suspect favour to Perkin Warbeck. Had he not burned down the cathedral of Cashel? The Earl admitted it, but excused himself in a fashion that appealed to the King. "I did, but I thought that the Archbishop was inside." Henry VII accepted the inevitable with a dictum that is famous, if not authentic. "Since all Ireland cannot govern the Earl of Kildare, let the Earl of Kildare govern all Ireland." Kildare was pardoned, freed, married to the King's cousin, Elizabeth St John, and sent back to Ireland, where he succeeded Poynings as Lord Deputy.

Power in Ireland still rested on the ability to call out and command a sufficiency of armed men. In this the English King exercised a potent and personal influence. He could clothe with the royal insignia and status of Deputy any great noble who could muster and control the fighting men. On the other hand, by raising Butlers and Burkes the King could make it impossible for even a Kildare to control the great clan chiefs. This precarious and shifting balance was for a while the only road to establishing a central Government. No English king had yet found how to make his title of "Lord of Ireland" any more real than his title of "King of France".

Henry's dealings with Scotland are characteristic of his shrewd judgment. His first move was to shake the position of the Scottish King, James IV, by shipping armaments through Berwick to the baronial opponents of the Crown and by continual intrigues with the opposing factions. Border raids, as often in the past, troubled the peaceful relations of the two kingdoms, and an ugly situation arose when James lent his support to the Pretender Perkin Warbeck. But Henry's ultimate aims were constructive. He signed a truce with James which was confirmed by treaty. Although not obviously a man of imagination, he had his dreams. He may even have looked to the time when the everlasting fight between Scots and English would end and the ceaseless danger of a Franco-Scottish alliance which had threatened medieval England so often should be for ever broken. At any rate, Henry took the first steps to unite

England and Scotland by marrying his daughter Margaret to James IV in 1502, and there was peace in the North until after his death.

With France too his policy was eminently successful. He realised that more could be gained by the threat of war than by war itself. Henry summoned Parliament to consent to taxation for a war against France, and proceeded to gather together a small army, which crossed to Calais in 1492 and besieged Boulogne. At the same time he entered into negotiations with the French King, who, unable to face Spain, the Holy Roman Emperor, and England simultaneously, was compelled to buy him off. Henry gained both ways. Like Edward IV, he pocketed not only a considerable subsidy from France, which was punctually paid, but also the taxes collected in England for war.

The most powerful new monarchy in Europe was Spain, recently forged into a strong state by the united efforts of Ferdinand of Aragon and Isabella of Castile and their successful warfare against the Moors. Their marriage marked the unification of the country. From 1489, when Henry's eldest son, Arthur, was betrothed to their daughter, the Infanta Catherine, England and Spain worked steadily together to secure booty from France – Spain in the form of territory, Henry as an annual tribute in cash, which amounted in the earlier years to about a fifth of the regular revenues of the Crown.

Henry VII as a statesman was imbued with the new, ruthless political ideas of Renaissance Europe. He strove to establish a strong monarchy in England, moulded out of native institutions. Like his contemporary, Lorenzo de'Medici, in Florence, Henry worked almost always by adaptation, modifying old forms ever so slightly, rather than by crude innovation. Without any fundamental constitutional change administration was established again on a firm basis. The King's Council was strengthened. It was given Parliamentary authority to examine persons with or without oath, and condemn them, on written evidence alone, in a manner foreign to the practice of the Common Law.

The main function of the King's Council was to govern rather than to judge. The choice of members lay with the monarch. Even when chosen they could not attend of right; they could be dismissed instantly; meanwhile they could stop any action in any court in England and transfer it to themselves, arrest anyone, torture anyone. A small inner committee conducted foreign affairs. Another managed the finances, hacking a new path through the cumbrous practices of the medieval Exchequer; treasurers were now appointed who were answerable personally to the King. And at the centre was the King himself, the embodiment of direct personal government, often authorising or auditing expenditure, even the most trifling, with great sprawling initials which may still be seen at the Record Office in London. Henry VII was probably the best businessman to sit upon the English throne.

He was also a remarkably shrewd picker of men. Few of his Ministers came from the hereditary nobility; many were Churchmen; almost all were of obscure origin. Richard Fox, Bishop of Winchester, Chief Minister, and the most powerful man in England after the King, had been a schoolmaster at

Hereford before he met Henry in Paris and they became companions in exile. Edmund Dudley was an under-sheriff of the City of London, who came under the King's notice in connection with the regulation of the Flanders wool trade. John Stile, who invented the first diplomatic cipher, and was appointed Ambassador to Spain, began his career as a grocer or a mercer. Richard Empson was the son of a sieve-maker. Henry was at first not yet strong enough to afford mistakes. Daily, in all his leisure, he made notes on political affairs, on matters which required attention, "especially touching persons", whom to employ, to reward, to imprison, to outlaw, exile, or execute.

Like the other princes of his age, his main interest, apart from an absorbing passion for administration, was foreign policy. He maintained the first permanent English envoys abroad. Diplomacy, he considered, was no bad substitute for the violence of his predecessors, and early, accurate, and regular information was essential to its conduct. A spy system was organised even in England. Also, like other princes, Henry built and altered. His chapel at Westminster and his palace at Richmond are superb monuments of his architectural taste. Though personally frugal, he maintained a calculated pageantry; he wore magnificent clothes, superb jewels, rich and glittering collars, and moved in public under a canopy of state, waited upon by noblemen, with a Court where about seven hundred persons dined daily in the Tower at his expense, entertained by jesters, minstrels, huntsmen, and his famous leopards.

When he died in 1509, Henry VII had ruled for nearly a quarter of a century. His skill and wisdom in transmuting medieval institutions into the organs of modern rule have not been questioned. His achievement was indeed massive and durable. He built his power amid the ruins and ashes of his predecessors. He thriftily and carefully gathered what seemed in those days a vast reserve of liquid wealth. He trained a body of efficient servants. He magnified the Crown without losing the co-operation of the Commons. He identified prosperity with monarchy. Among the princes of Renaissance Europe he is not surpassed in achievement and fame by Louis XI of France or Ferdinand of Spain.

CHAPTER TWENTY-THREE

KING HENRY VIII

*Henry VIII – Defender of the Faith – the Habsburgs – the death of
Prince Arthur – marriage to Catherine of Aragon – the rise of Wolsey –
war with France – the Battle of the Spurs – Flodden Field – peace with
France – Anne Boleyn – the self-aggrandisement of Wolsey – Star
Chamber at work – local government reforms – Henry's navy – Wolsey's
diplomatic service – the Field of the Cloth of Gold – the discarding of
Catherine of Aragon – the fall of Wolsey – the rise of Cranmer*

THE AGE in which the young King Henry VIII grew up was, when
seen from the perspective of later centuries, one in which an old
order was dying. But it scarcely seemed so to those who lived in it.
The change most visible to the eyes of a ruler was the creation of
the modern European state system. This novelty, menacing and baffling, was
no remote phenomenon. Across the Channel the new French monarchy had
emerged much strengthened from the Hundred Years War. Louis XI and his
son, Charles VIII, were no longer mere heads of a loosely integrated group of
feudal principalities. They ruled a united and populous France from the
Channel to the Mediterranean.

The Holy Roman Empire was visibly in dissolution. But for two generations past the Emperor had been the head of the house of Habsburg, and what
arms could not do diplomacy and luck did. As Emperor, Maximilian was for
ever illustrating the difference between reach and grasp, but he had married
the greatest heiress in Europe. The house of Austria thus began to act on the
maxim of gaining its major victories by marriage. In the next generation the
counsel was followed with even more brilliant results, for the Archduke Philip,
heir of Maximilian and Mary, married an even greater heiress than his mother,
the Infanta Joanna, heir to Castile, Aragon, Sicily, and Naples. It was her sister
who had accelerated the rise of the house of Tudor by marrying Prince Arthur
and after him King Henry VIII.

In this world of growing power the King of England had to move and act
with far fewer resources than his neighbours. His subjects numbered not many
more than three millions. He had smaller revenues, no standing army, no state
apparatus answerable only to the royal will. And yet by the mere proximity of

France and the Imperial Netherlands England was forced to play a part in European politics. Her King was involved in wars and negotiations, shifts in alliances, and changes in the balance of power, of which he had had little experience, and could only in a secondary degree affect.

Until the death of his elder brother, Prince Arthur, Henry had been intended for the Church. He had therefore been brought up by his father in an atmosphere of learning. Much time was devoted to serious studies – Latin, French, Italian, theology, music – and also to bodily exercise, to the sport of jousting, at which he excelled, to tennis, and hunting the stag. Henry in his maturity was a tall, red-headed man who preserved the vigour and energy of ancestors accustomed for centuries to the warfare of the Welsh marches. His massive frame towered above the throng, and those about him felt in it a sense of concealed desperation, of latent force and passion. Bursts of restless energy and ferocity were combined with extraordinary patience and diligence. Deeply religious, Henry regularly listened to sermons lasting between one and two hours, and wrote more than one theological treatise of a high standard. He was accustomed to hear five Masses on Church days, and three on other days, served the priest at Mass himself, was never deprived of holy bread and holy water on Sunday, and always did penance on Good Friday. His zeal in theological controversy earned him from the Pope the title of "Defender of the Faith". An indefatigable worker, he digested a mass of dispatches, memoranda, and plans each day without the help of his secretary. He wrote verses and composed music. Profoundly secretive in public business, he chose as his advisers men for the most part of the meanest origin: Thomas Wolsey, the son of a poor and rascally butcher of Ipswich, whose name appears on the borough records for selling meat unfit for human consumption; Thomas Cromwell, a small attorney; Thomas Cranmer, an obscure lecturer in divinity. Like his father he distrusted the hereditary nobility, preferring the discreet counsel of men without a wide circle of friends.

Almost his first act, six weeks after the death of his father in 1509, was to marry his brother Arthur's widow, Princess Catherine of Aragon. He was aged eighteen and she was five years and five months older. She had made great efforts to fascinate him, and succeeded so well that while Ferdinand and Henry VII had made plans for the match long beforehand, and had obtained from the Pope a dispensation for a marriage within the degrees of affinity prohibited by the Church, there can be no doubt that Henry was eager to complete the proceedings. Catherine was at Henry's side during the first twenty-two years of his reign, while England was becoming a force in European affairs, perilous for foreign rulers to ignore. Until she reached the age of thirty-eight she remained, apart from three or four short lapses, the mistress of his affections, restrained his follies, and in her narrow way helped to guide public affairs between the intervals of her numerous confinements. Henry settled down to married life very quickly, in spite of a series of misfortunes which would have daunted a less robust character. The Queen's first baby was born dead, just after Henry's nineteenth birthday;

another died soon after birth a year later. In all there were to be five such disappointments.

The King continued the standing alliance with his father-in-law, Ferdinand of Aragon, which had brought honour and wealth to England. He supported the Pope, and was sent the Golden Rose, the highest distinction which could be conferred on any Christian prince. He deliberated with his father's grave counsellors William Warham, Lord Chancellor and Archbishop of Canterbury; Richard Fox, Bishop of Winchester; Thomas Ruthal, Bishop of Durham and royal Secretary – and under their guidance pursued for a short time the policy which his father had always favoured – isolation, provided that France continued to pay tribute. But Henry was on the edge of the vortex of Europe's new politics. Frontiers were altering almost from month to month. Ferdinand of Aragon, Catherine's father, had conquered the Kingdom of Naples, and the two French border provinces of Cerdagne and Roussillon. Other princes had done nearly as well. Amid the alluring vistas of conquest which opened up before Henry his father's aged counsellors remained obstinately men of peace. Henry VII had only once sent English levies abroad, preferring to hire mercenaries who fought alongside foreign armies. Henry VIII now determined that this policy should be reversed.

For some time he had been watching Dean Wolsey of Lincoln, a discovery of the Marquess of Dorset, whose sons had been to Magdalen College School at Oxford when Wolsey was the master there. Dorset had liked Wolsey well enough to invite him to stay for the Christmas holidays, and had provided him with several livings. The young priest then obtained a post as chaplain to the Governor of Calais. Besides academic learning Wolsey possessed a remarkable aptitude for negotiation and finance – he had been bursar of Magdalen College – and Henry VII, sensing his abilities, had taken him over from the Governor and employed him on minor official business abroad. He was promoted by Henry VIII to the Council Board in November 1509, with the office of almoner to the royal household. He was then aged thirty-six.

Two years later Wolsey's growing influence may be perceived in the decision to join the Holy League against France, for it was in the same week that Wolsey signed his first documents as an executive member of the Council. He was put in charge of preparations for the war, and his former pupil, the young Marquis of Dorset, was Commander-in-Chief. France was preoccupied with Italian adventures, and Henry planned to reconquer Bordeaux, lost sixty years before, while King Ferdinand invaded Navarre, an independent kingdom lying athwart the Pyrenees, and the Pope and the republic of Venice operated against the French armies in Italy. The year was 1512, and this was the first time since the Hundred Years War that an English army had campaigned in Europe.

But the English found that the style of warfare they had learned in the Wars of the Roses, with long-bows and ponderously armed mounted men, had become obsolete on the Continent. Both Ferdinand and the French employed professional infantry, Swiss and Austrian, who advanced at a great pace in solid squares with eighteen-foot pikes bristling in every direction. The primitive firearms of the day, known as arquebuses, were too heavy and slow-firing to inflict serious damage on these fast-moving squares. Ferdinand sent a great deal of military advice to Henry, and suggested that he should use his gathered wealth to procure an overwhelming professional force of his own. But before Henry could adopt this plan, Dorset's army, as unaccustomed to Gascon wine as to French tactics, and ravaged by dysentery, disintegrated. The troops refused to obey their officers and boarded the transports for home. Dorset abandoned a fruitless campaign and followed them. After negotiations lasting throughout the winter of 1512–13 Ferdinand and the Venetians deserted Henry and the Pope and made peace with France. The Holy League, they concluded, although high-sounding in name, had proved futile as a political combination.

In England the responsibility for these failures was cast on the new adviser, Wolsey. In fact it was in the hard work of administration necessitated by the war that he had first shown his abilities and immense energy. The lay members of the Council, however, had from the beginning opposed a war policy managed by a priest and had intrigued to get rid of him. But Henry VIII and the Pope never wavered. Pope Julius II, who had been besieged by a French force in Rome, had excommunicated the entire French army, and now grew a beard, an adornment then out of fashion, and swore he would not shave until he was revenged on the King of France. Henry, not to be outdone, also grew a beard. It was auburn, like his hair. He arranged to hire the Emperor Maximilian, with the Imperial artillery and the greater part of the Austrian army, to serve under the royal standard of England.

These arrangements, though costly, were brilliantly successful. Under Henry's command, the English, with Austrian mercenaries, routed the French in August 1513 at the Battle of the Spurs, so called because of the rapidity of the French retreat. Bayard, the most famous knight in Europe, was captured, together with a host of French notables. Tournai, the richest city of all North-East France, surrendered at the mere sight of the Imperial artillery, and was occupied by an English garrison. To crown all, Queen Catherine, who had been left behind as Regent of England, sent great news from the North.

To aid their French ally the Scots in the King's absence had crossed the Tweed in September and invaded England with an army of fifty thousand men. Thomas Howard, Earl of Surrey, son of Richard III's Duke of Norfolk, slain at Bosworth, and still under the family attainder, was none the less entrusted with the command. This skilful veteran, the only experienced general left in England after Dorset's failure, knowing every inch of the ground, did not hesitate to march round the Scottish army, and, although outnumbered by two to one, placed himself between the enemy and Edinburgh. At Flodden Field a bloody battle was fought on September 9, 1513. Both armies faced their homeland. The whole of Scotland, Highland and Lowland alike, drew out with their retainers in the traditional schiltrons, or circles of spearmen, and around the standard of their King. The English archers once again directed upon these redoubtable masses a long, intense, and murderous arrow storm. Moreover, the bills or axes in the hands of English infantry were highly effective against the Scottish spears in hand-to-hand assault, while the English cavalry awaited the chance of piercing the gaps caused by slaughter. When night fell the flower of the Scottish chivalry lay in their ranks where they had fought, and among them King James IV. This was the last great victory gained by the long-bow. Surrey was rewarded by the restoration of the Norfolk dukedom. In Scotland a year-old child succeeded to the throne as James V. His mother, the Regent, was Henry's sister Margaret, and peace now descended on the Northern border for the greater part of the reign.

Henry had every intention of renewing his campaign in France in 1514, but his successes had not been to the liking of Ferdinand of Spain. Ferdinand now set about making a separate peace with France, into which he also tried to draw the Emperor Maximilian. Faced with the defection of his allies, Henry was quick to launch a counter-stroke. First he looked to the defences of the realm, and took measures to strengthen his navy. Then he sought and obtained a favourable peace treaty with France, thereby securing exactly double the amount of annual tribute that had been paid to his father. The crowning event of the peace was the marriage between Henry's young sister, Mary, and Louis XII himself. She was seventeen, he was fifty-two. The story runs that she extracted from her brother the promise that if she married this time for diplomacy she would be free next time to marry for love. Promise or no promise, that is what she did. She was Queen of France for three months; then, as Queen Dowager, and to Henry's displeasure, she cut short her widowhood by marrying Charles Brandon, Duke of Suffolk. But in this case the royal wrath subsided and Henry VIII joined in the wedding festivities. The marriage ultimately bore tragic fruit: a grandchild was the Lady Jane Grey, who was for ten days to be Queen of England.

Among those who had crossed with the bridal retinue to France was a young girl named Mary Boleyn. She was one of three nieces of the Duke of Norfolk, all of whom successively engaged the dangerous and deadly love of Henry VIII. Mary and her sister Anne had been educated in France at an expensive academy attached to the French Court. On her return to England Mary married William Carey, a Gentleman of the Bedchamber, and before long became the King's mistress. Her father was upon this favour created Lord Rochford, while her sister, Anne, continued her studies in France.

Wolsey was richly rewarded for the foreign successes. He received the Bishopric of Lincoln during the course of the negotiations; then, after the peace terms were settled, the Archbishopric of York; and, a year later, after long negotiation by the King on his behalf, in September 1515, a cardinal's hat. This shower of ecclesiastical honours did not, however, give Wolsey sufficient civil authority, and in December 1515 Henry created him Lord Chancellor in place of Warham, whom he forced to resign the Great Seal. For fourteen years Wolsey in the King's name was the effective ruler of the realm. At the height of his influence Wolsey enjoyed an income equivalent to about £500,000 a year in early twentieth-century money. He kept a thousand servants, and his palaces surpassed the King's in splendour. He loaded profitable favours upon his relations, including his illegitimate son, who held eleven Church appointments, and their incomes, while still a boy. These counts against him gradually added up in the course of years. But for the time being – and it was for a long time, as Chief Ministers go – he successfully held in his grasp an accumulation of power that has probably never been equalled in England.

Successes abroad enabled Wolsey to develop Henry VII's principles of centralised government. During the twelve years that he was Lord Chancellor Parliament met only once, for two sessions spreading over three months in all. The Court of Star Chamber grew more active.[1] It evolved new and simple methods copied from Roman law, by which the Common Law rules of evidence were dispensed with, and persons who could give evidence were simply brought in for interrogation, one by one, often without even the formality of an oath. Justice was swift, fines were heavy, and no one in England was so powerful that he could afford to flout the Star Chamber. When a common soldier of the Calais garrison once sent his wife to complain of his treatment by the Lord Deputy of Calais she received a full hearing. The new generation grown up after the Wars of the Roses was accustomed to royal law and order, and determined that it should prevail.

Thus it was that this system of arbitrary government, however despotic in theory, however contrary to the principles believed to lie behind Magna Carta, in fact rested tacitly on the real will of the people. Henry VIII, like his father found an institution ready to his hand in the unpaid Justice of the Peace, the local squire or landlord, and taught him to govern. Rules and regulations of remarkable complexity were given to the Justice to administer; and later in the century Justices' manuals were produced, which ran through innumerable editions and covered almost every contingency which could arise in country life.

The Tudors were indeed the architects of an English system of local government which lasted almost unchanged until Victorian times. Unpaid local men, fearless and impartial, because they could rely on help from the King, dealt with small matters, sitting in the villages often in twos and threes. Bigger matters such as roads and bridges and sheep-stealing came before quarter sessions in the appropriate town. It was a rough justice that the country gentlemen meted out, and friendship and faction often cut across the interests of both the nation and the Crown. If in the main they carried the directions of the Crown to the people, the Justices could also on occasion, by turning a deaf ear to official advice, express popular resistance to the royal will.

Within a few years of his accession Henry embarked upon a programme

---

1   The court of law developed from the King's Council and that which heard petitions. Its name comes from the room in which it met, the Star Chamber, in the Palace of Westminster.

of naval expansion, while Wolsey concerned himself with diplomatic manoeuvre. Henry had already constructed the largest warship of the age, the *Great Harry*, of 1,500 tons, with seven tiers one above the other, and an incredible array of guns. The fleet was built up under the personal care of the sovereign, who ordered the admiral to send word to him in minute detail "how every ship did sail", and was not content until England commanded the Narrow Seas. Wolsey's arrangements for the foreign service were hardly less remarkable. A system of couriers and correspondents was organised over Western Europe, through whom news was received in England as quickly as during the wars of Marlborough or Wellington. The dispatches of this period, at the height of the Renaissance, are as closely knit and coloured as any in history; each event, the size of armies, rebellions in Italian cities, movements within the College of Cardinals, taxes in France, is carefully weighed and recorded. For some years at least Wolsey was a powerful factor and balancing weight in Europe.

The zenith of this brilliant period was reached at the Field of the Cloth of Gold in June 1520, when Henry crossed the Channel to meet his rival, Francis I of France, for the first time. Henry's main perplexity was, we are told, about his appearance; he could not decide how he would look best, in his beard as usual or clean-shaven. At first he yielded to Catherine's persuasion and shaved. But directly he had done so he regretted the step and grew the beard again. It reached its full luxuriance in time to create a great impression in France.

At the Field of the Cloth of Gold, near Guisnes, the jousting and feasting, the colour and glitter, the tents and trappings, dazzled all Europe. It was the last display of medieval chivalry. Many noblemen, it was said, carried on their shoulders their mills, their forests, and their meadows. But Henry and Francis failed to become personal friends. Henry, indeed, was already negotiating with Francis's enemy, the new Emperor Charles V, who had lately succeeded his grandfather, Maximilian. Within a month he had concluded an alliance with the Emperor, thus forfeiting the French tribute. When the Emperor declared war on Francis English wealth was squandered feverishly on an expedition to Boulogne and subsidies to mercenary contingents serving with the Emperor. Wolsey had to find the money. When Kent and the Eastern Counties rose against a species of capital levy imposed by Wolsey in the second year of war, and absurdly misnamed the "Amicable Grant", the King pretended he did not know of the taxation. The Government had to beat a retreat, the campaign was abandoned, and Wolsey got the King's consent to make secret overtures for peace to Francis.

These overtures were Wolsey's fatal miscalculation; only six weeks later the Imperial armies won an overwhelming victory over the French at Pavia, in Northern Italy. After the battle the entire peninsula passed into the hands of the Emperor. Italy was destined to remain largely under Habsburg domination until the invasions of Napoleon. But although Francis himself was taken prisoner and crushing terms of peace were imposed on France, England did not share in the spoils of victory. Henry could no longer turn the scales in Europe. The blame was clearly Wolsey's, and the King decided that perhaps the Cardinal had been given too free a hand. He insisted on visiting the great new college which Wolsey was building at Oxford, Cardinal College, destined to become Christ Church, the largest and most richly endowed in the university. When he arrived he was astonished at the vast sums which were being lavished upon the masonry. "It is strange", he remarked to the Cardinal, "that you have found so much money to spend upon your college and yet could not find enough to finish my war."

Up till now he had been inseparable from Wolsey. But after Pavia Henry began to have second thoughts. Perhaps, he decided, Wolsey would have to be sacrificed to preserve the popularity of the monarch. Then there was Queen Catherine. In 1525 she was aged forty. A typical Spanish princess, she had matured and aged rapidly; it was clear that she would bear Henry no male heir. Either the King's illegitimate son, the Duke of Richmond, now aged six, would have to be appointed by Act of Parliament, or perhaps England might accept Catherine's child, Mary, now aged nine, as the first Queen of England in her own right since Matilda. It was still doubtful if a woman could succeed to the throne by English law. Would England tolerate being ruled by a woman? Might Mary not turn out very like her Spanish mother, narrow and bigoted, a possible queen perhaps in Spain, or France, or Austria, countries full of soldiers, but not acceptable to the free English, who had obeyed Henry VII and Henry VIII because they wished to obey, and although there was no central army except the Beefeaters in the Tower? Would Mary be able to rule in the Tudor manner, by favour and not by force?

The long clash of the Wars of the Roses had been a nightmare to the nation which a disputed succession might revive. To the monarch these great questions of State were also questions of conscience, in which his sensual passions and his care for the stability of the realm were all fused together. They perplexed Henry for two more years. The first step, clearly, was to get rid of Catherine. In May 1527 Cardinal Wolsey, acting as Papal Legate and with the collusion of the King, held a secret ecclesiastical court at his house in Westminster. He summoned Henry to appear before him, charged with having married his deceased brother's wife within the degrees of affinity prohibited by the laws of the Church. Henry's authority had been a Bull of dispensation obtained by Ferdinand and Henry VII in 1503, which said in effect that since the marriage between Catherine and Arthur had not been consummated Catherine was not legally Henry's deceased brother's wife and Henry could marry Catherine. Although Catherine, on the advice of successive Spanish ambassadors, maintained to her dying day that her marriage with Arthur had not been consummated nobody was convinced. She had lived under the same roof with Prince Arthur for seven months.

After hearing legal argument for three days the court decided that the point should be submitted to a number of the most learned bishops in England. Several bishops replied, however, that provided Papal dispensation had been secured such a marriage was perfectly lawful. Henry then tried to persuade Catherine herself that he and she had never been legally married, that they had lived in mortal sin for eighteen years. He added that as he intended to abstain from her company in future he hoped she would retire far from Court. Catherine burst into tears and firmly refused to go away.

About a fortnight later Wolsey crossed the Channel to conduct prolonged negotiations for a treaty of alliance with France. While Wolsey was away Henry became openly infatuated with Anne Boleyn. Since she had returned from school in France Anne had grown into a vivacious, witty woman of twenty-four, very slender and frail, with beautiful black eyes and thick black hair, so long that she could sit on it, which she wore flowing loose over her shoulders.

Henry had been carefully guarded by Wolsey and Catherine. He had had mistresses before, but never openly. The appearance at Court of a lady with whom he spent hours at a time created an extraordinary stir. Together Anne and Henry arranged to send a special royal ambassador to Pope Clement VII, independently of the resident ambassador chosen by Wolsey, to seek not only annulment of the King's marriage, but also a dispensation to marry again at once. Dr William Knight, now over seventy, was brought forth from retirement to undertake this delicate mission. Two entirely different sets of instructions were prepared for Knight. One made no mention of the proposed new marriage and was to be shown to Wolsey as he passed through Compiègne on his way to Rome; the other was the one on which Knight was to act. Wolsey was shown the dummy instructions as arranged, and at once saw that they had been drafted by ignorant laymen. He hurried home to have the instructions altered, and thus learned all. But although he now took over the management of the negotiations every expedient proved fruitless. The Papal Legate, Cardinal Campeggio, who was sent to England to hear the case used all possible pretexts to postpone a decision. Now that Italy had fallen to the Habsburgs the Pope was at the mercy of the Imperial soldiery. In 1527 they shocked Europe by seizing and sacking Rome. The Pope was now practically a prisoner of Charles V, who was determined that Henry should not divorce his aunt.

This broke Wolsey. New counsellors were called in. A follower of the Duke of Norfolk, Dr Stephen Gardiner, was appointed Secretary to the King. Soon after this appointment Dr Cranmer, a young lecturer in divinity at Cambridge and a friend of the Boleyns, made a helpful new suggestion to Gardiner, that the question whether the King had ever been legally married should be withdrawn from the lawyers and submitted to the universities of Europe. The King at once took up the idea. Cranmer was sent for and complimented. Letters and messengers were dispatched to all the universities in Europe. At the same time the King had the writs sent out for a Parliament, the first for six years, to strengthen his hand in the great changes he was planning. Norfolk and Gardiner, not Wolsey, completed the arrangements. Wolsey retired in disgrace to his diocese of York, which he had never visited.

On October 9, 1529, Wolsey's disgrace was carried a step farther by an indictment in the King's Bench under one of the Statutes of Praemunire, passed in the reign of Richard II. While the proceedings were going forward in the King's Bench, Norfolk and Suffolk came to Wolsey to take away the Great Seal as a mark that he was no longer Lord Chancellor. But Wolsey protested, saying that he had been made Chancellor for life. Next day they came again, bearing letters signed by the King. When they had gone with the seal the great Cardinal broke down, and was found seated, weeping and lamenting his misfortunes. The charge under Praemunire was supplemented by a charge of traitorous correspondence with the King of France, conducted without the King's knowledge.

As Wolsey journeyed back to London, where the cell in the Tower used by the Duke of Buckingham before his execution was again being placed in readiness, he fell ill, and when he neared Leicester Abbey for the night he told the monks who came out to greet him, "I am come to leave my bones among you." About eight in the morning two days later he sank into a last decline, murmuring to those gathered at the bedside, "If I had served God as diligently as I have done the King He would not have given me over in my grey hairs." Soon afterwards he died; and they found next to his body a shirt of hair, beneath his other shirt, which was of very fine linen holland cloth. This shirt of hair was unknown to all his servants except his chaplain.

CHAPTER TWENTY-FOUR

THE BREAK WITH ROME

*The Reformation – the mood against the Church – Divorce – Annates
Bill – Sir Thomas More resigns – Henry marries Anne Boleyn – Cranmer
becomes Archbishop of Canterbury – the birth of the future Elizabeth I –
the execution of Fisher and More – Queen Catherine dies – Anne Boleyn
executed – Henry marries Jane Seymour – the dissolution of the
monasteries – Thomas Cromwell – the Tyndale and Coverdale
Bibles – the Pilgrimage of Grace – Henry marries Anne of Cleves –
Cromwell executed – Norfolk and the reaction against the Reformation –
Henry marries Catherine Howard – Catherine's affair with Culpeper –
Catherine Howard's execution – Henry marries Catherine Parr – war
in Scotland – the Battle of Solway Moss – the siege of Boulogne –
Ancrum Moor – the French land on the Isle of Wight – the death of
Henry VIII*

C RANMER'S IDEA of an appeal to the universities about Henry's
marriage to Catherine had proved a great success, and the young
lecturer was rewarded with an appointment as Ambassador to the
Emperor. Even the University of Bologna, in the Papal States,
declared that the King was right and that the Pope could not set aside so
fundamental a law. The King determined to mark his displeasure with the
Pope by some striking measure against the power of the Church of England.
Why, he asked, was the right of sanctuary allowed to obstruct the King's
justice? Why were parsons permitted to live far away from their parishes and
hold more than one living while underpaid substitutes did the work for the
absentees? Why did Italians enjoy the revenues of English bishoprics? Why
were the clergy demanding fees for probate on wills and gifts on the death of
every parishioner? The King would ask his learned Commons to propose
reforms.

A committee was formed of all the lawyers in the House, and they drafted
the necessary Bills in record time. The House of Lords, where the bishops and
abbots still had more votes than the lay peers, agreed to the Bills reforming
sanctuaries and abolishing mortuary fees, which affected the lower clergy

only, but when the Probate Bill came up to the Lords the Archbishop of Canterbury "in especial", and all the other bishops in general, both frowned and grunted. Fisher, Bishop of Rochester, a representative of the old school, warned the Lords that religious innovation would bring social revolution in its train. He pointed to the national Czech revolt led by John Huss.[1]

"My lords," he said, "you see daily what Bills come here from the Commons house, and all is for the destruction of the Church. For God's sake see what a realm the kingdom of Bohemia was; and when the Church went down, then fell the glory of the kingdom. Now with the Commons is nothing but *down with the Church*, and all this meseemeth is for lack of faith only."

The Commons soon heard of this bold speech, and Members pointed out the implication of the last words – that laws the Commons made were laws made by pagans and heathen people and not worthy to be kept. Sharp exchanges took place before the Probate Bill could be forced through the Lords, and rancour grew. Thus from the outset the Reformation House of Commons acquired a corporate spirit, and during its long life, longer than any previous Parliament, eagerly pursued any measure which promised revenge against the bishops for what it deemed their evasion and duplicity over the Probate Bill. Hostility to the Episcopate smouldered, and marked the Commons for more than a hundred years.

The King was already delighted with what they had done. But he made it clear that he remained fully orthodox in matters of doctrine, that he was merely adhering to the principle of Colet[2] and other leading divines whom he had known in his youth, that men could be Catholic though critical of Papal institutions. "If Luther", he declared, "had confined himself to denouncing the vices, abuses, and errors of the clergy, instead of attacking the sacraments of the Church and other divine institutions, we should all have followed him and written in his favour." After this blunt though reasoned statement the negotiations in Rome for annulling the King's marriage encountered even greater obstacles.

During December 1530 the Attorney-General charted the whole body of the clergy with breaking the fourteenth-century Statutes of Praemunire and Provisors which had been passed to limit the powers of the Pope. This they had done by acquiescing in Wolsey's many high-handed actions in his rôle as Papal Legate. Henry, after defeating the bishops in the matter of probate by enlisting the support of Parliament, knew that Convocation would not defy him. On February 7, 1531, the clergy acknowledged that the King was "their especial Protector, one and supreme lord, and, as far as the law of Christ allows, even supreme head".

Parliament, which had been prorogued from month to month since the great doings about probate in 1529, was now recalled to hear and disseminate

---

1   John Huss (1373?–1415). Rector of Prague University, defender of Wycliffe (Wyclif), rejector of Papal authority and burned at the stake.
2   Henry would have been twenty-eight when John Colet (c.1467–1519), the Dean of St Paul's Cathedral and English humanist and church reformer, died.

the royal view on the divorce. Lord Chancellor More came down to the House and said, "There are some who say that the King is pursuing a divorce out of love for some lady, and not out of any scruple of conscience; but this is not true," and he read out the opinions of twelve foreign universities and showed a hundred "books" drawn up by doctors of strange regions, all agreeing that the King's marriage was unlawful. Then the Lord Chancellor said, "Now you of this Commons house may report in your counties what you have seen and heard, and then all men shall openly perceive that the King hath not attempted this matter of will or pleasure, as some strangers report, but only for the discharge of his conscience and surety of the succession of his realm."

Throughout these proceedings Queen Catherine remained at Court. The King, although he rode and talked openly with Anne, left Catherine in charge of his personal wardrobe, including supervision of the laundry and the making of his linen. When he required clothes he continue to apply to Catherine, not Anne. Anne was furiously jealous, but for months the King refused to abandon his old routine. A new attempt was then made by the Boleyn party to persuade Catherine to renounce her rights. On June 1, 1531, she was waited on by Norfolk, Suffolk, and Gardiner, Anne's father, now Earl of Wiltshire, Northumberland, and several others. As before she refused to renounce anything. Finally, about the middle of July, Anne took the King on a long hunting expedition, away from Windsor Castle, longer than any they had ever made together. Catherine waited, day after day, until a month had gone by, but still there was no news of the King's return. At last the messenger came: the King would come back. But his Majesty did not wish to see the Queen; she was commanded to retire instantly to Wolsey's former palace at Moor, in Hertfordshire. Henceforward she and her daughter Mary were banished from Court.

The winter of 1531–2 was marked by the tensest crisis of Henry's reign. A form of excommunication, or even interdict, had been drafted in Rome, ordering the King to cast off his concubine Anne within fifteen days, only the penalties being left blank. The shadow of Papal wrath hung over England. Opposition merely confirmed the King in his plans. The Annates Bill was drafted as a fighting measure, in case the worst occurred. It armed the King for a greater struggle with the Papacy than had preceded Magna Carta. If the Court of Rome, its preamble ran, endeavoured to wield excommunication, interdict, or process compulsory in England, then all manner of sacraments and divine service should continue to be administered, and the interdict should not by any prelate or minister be executed or divulged. If any one named by the King to a bishopric were restrained by Bulls from Rome from accepting office he should be consecrated by the Archbishop, or any one named to in Archbishopric. And the Annates, a mainstay of the Papal finances, were limited to 5 per cent of their former amount.

This was the most difficult Bill which Henry ever had to steer through Parliament. He was obliged to go down to the House of Lords himself at least three times, and even then seemed likely to fail, until he thought of an entirely new expedient – the first public division of the House.[1] With considerable amendment the Bill was passed.

The next step was to make the clergy submit to the royal supremacy. Henry got the Commons to prepare a document called the Supplication against the Ordinaries, directed against the authority of Church courts. "Ordinaries" was the legal term for bishops and their deputies who enjoyed rights of jurisdiction. Although Convocation was truculent at first, making submission only in vague and ambiguous terms, Henry refused to compromise, and at the third attempt they agreed to articles of his own, making him effective master of the Church in England. On the very afternoon these articles were submitted for the royal consent, May 16, 1532, Sir Thomas More resigned the Lord Chancellorship as a protest against royal supremacy in spiritual affairs. He had tried to serve his sovereign faithfully in everything; now he saw that Henry's courses must inevitably conflict with his own conscientious beliefs.

Thus the English Reformation was a slow process. An opportunist King measured his steps as he went, until England was wholly independent of administration from Rome. The death in August of old Archbishop Warham, principal opponent of the King's divorce, opened further possibilities and problems. Henry did not hasten to appoint a successor. He had to consider how far he could go. If there were a struggle could any of his bishops be trusted to forget the oath which they had sworn to the Pope at their consecration? Would there be a rebellion? Would the Emperor, Queen Catherine's nephew, invade England from the Low Countries? Could the King rely on French neutrality?

In order to weigh these factors at first hand the King went over to Boulogne with only a few friends, including Anne Boleyn, for personal discussion with Francis I. He returned reassured. Confident that he could carry through even the most startling appointment to Canterbury, he recalled Cranmer from his embassy. Cranmer had been married twice, the second time in Germany after ordination, in the new German fashion for priests, to the niece of a well-known Lutheran. Since the marriage of priests was still illegal in England, Cranmer's wife went ahead in disguise. Cranmer himself took leave of the Emperor at Mantua on November 1, 1532, and left the following day, arriving in London in the middle of December. A week later he was offered the Archbishopric of Canterbury. He accepted. Henceforward, until Henry died, Cramner's wife was always hidden, and if she accompanied him was obliged, according to popular repute, to travel with the luggage in a vast chest specially constructed to conceal her.

A month later Henry secretly married Anne Boleyn. Historians have never discovered for certain who performed the ceremony, or where. Cramner himself was not the priest. Both he and the Imperial Ambassador reported subsequently that the marriage had taken place in January 1533. Undoubtedly,

---

1   Those "for the King's welfare" would stand on one side, those in opposition, on the other. It would take a brave man to publicly oppose.

in the eyes of the Roman Catholic world, Henry VIII committed bigamy, for he had been married nearly twenty-five years to Catherine of Aragon, and his marriage had not yet been annulled in Rome, or even in England, by any court or any public act. He simply assumed he had never been legally married at all, and left the lawyers and clergy to put the matter right afterwards.

Cranmer became Archbishop in the traditional manner. At the King's request Bulls had been obtained from Rome by threatening the Papacy with a rigorous application of the Act of Annates. Cranmer swore to obey the Pope with the usual oath, though reservations were made before and afterwards, and he was consecrated with the full ceremonial. This was important: the man who was to carry through the ecclesiastical revolution had thus been accepted by the Pope and endowed with full authority. Two days afterwards, however, a Bill was introduced into Parliament vesting in the Archbishop of Canterbury the power, formerly possessed by the Pope, to hear and determine all appeals from the ecclesiastical courts in England. Future attempts to use any foreign process would involve the drastic penalties of Praemunire. The judgments of the English courts were not to be affected by any Papal verdict or by excommunication, and any priest who refused to celebrate divine service or administer the sacraments was made liable to imprisonment. This momentous Bill, the work of Thomas Cromwell, which abolished what still remained of Papal authority in England, passed through Parliament in due course, and became known as the Act of Appeals. The following month Henry himself wrote a letter, describing his position as "King and Sovereign, recognising no superior in earth but only God, and not subject to the laws of any earthly creature." The breach between England and Rome was complete.

Having established his supremacy, Henry proceeded to exploit it. In March 1533 Convocation was asked two questions: was it against the Law of God, and not open to dispensation by the Pope, for a man to marry his brother's wife, he being dead without issue, but having consummated the marriage? Answer by the prelates and clergy present: Yes. By Bishop Fisher of Rochester: No. Was Prince Arthur's marriage with Queen Catherine consummated? Answer by the clergy: Yes. By the Bishop: No. Thereupon the Bishop was arrested and committed to the Tower. About ten days later the Duke of Norfolk with royal commissioners waited on Queen Catherine at Ampthill. Every sort of reason was advanced why she should renounce her title voluntarily. She refused to resign. A fortnight later Cranmer opened a court at Dunstable, and sent a proctor to Ampthill citing Catherine to appear. She refused. In her absence the Archbishop pronounced judgment. Catherine's marriage with Henry had existed in fact but not in law; it was void from the beginning; and five days afterwards the marriage with Anne was declared valid. Queen Anne Boleyn was crowned on June 1 in Westminster Abbey.

The following month it became clear that the new Queen was expecting a child. As the confinement approached Henry remained with her at Greenwich, and took the greatest care she should not be disturbed. A magnificent and valuable bed, which had lain in the Treasury since it had formed part of a

French nobleman's ransom, was brought forth, and in it on September 7, 1533, the future Queen Elizabeth was born. Although bonfires were lighted there was no rejoicing in Henry's heart. A male heir had been his desire. After he had defied the whole world, perhaps committed bigamy, and risked deposition by the Pope and invasion, here was only a second daughter. He galloped at once away from Greenwich, away from Anne, and in three days had reached Wolf Hall, in Wiltshire, the residence of a worthy old courtier, Sir John Seymour, who had a clever son in the diplomatic service and a pretty daughter, a former Maid of Honour to Queen Catherine. Jane Seymour was about twenty-five, and although she was attractive no one considered her a great beauty. But she was gay, and generally liked, and Henry fell in love with her.

After the birth of Elizabeth criticism of the King and his ecclesiastical measures could no longer be stifled. If the choice was between two princesses, men said, then why not choose Mary, the legitimate one? But the King would have none of this argument. An Act was passed vesting the succession in Elizabeth. In March 1534 every person of legal age, male or female, through-out the kingdom was forced to swear allegiance to this Act and renounce allegiance to all foreign authority in England. The clergy were prohibited from preaching unless specially licensed; a Bidding prayer[1] was prescribed for use in all churches, containing the words, "Henry VIII being immediately next unto God, the only and supreme head of this Catholic Church of England, and Anne his wife, and Elizabeth daughter and heir to them both, our Princess." To publish or pronounce maliciously by express words that the King was a tyrant or heretic was made high treason. As the brutality of the reign increased many hundreds were to be hanged, disembowelled, and quartered on these grounds.

Fisher and Sir Thomas More, who both refused the oath, were confined in the Tower for many months. At his trial More offered a brilliant defence, but the King's former trust in him had now turned into vengeful dislike. Under royal pressure the judges pronounced him guilty of treason. While Fisher was in the Tower the Pope created seven cardinals, of whom one was "John, Bishop of Rochester, kept in prison by the King of England". Directly Henry heard the news he declared in anger several times that he would send Fisher's head to Rome for the Cardinal's hat. Fisher was executed in June 1535 and More in July. For their fate the King must bear the chief responsibility; it is a black stain on his record. Shortly afterwards Henry was excommunicated and in theory deprived of his throne by the Pope.

In January 1536 Queen Catherine died. If the King was minded to marry again he could now repudiate Queen Anne without raising awkward questions about his earlier union. It was already rumoured by the Seymour party that in her intense desire for an heir Queen Anne had been unfaithful to the King soon after the birth of Elizabeth, with several lovers. If proved, this offence

---

1 A Bidding prayer was one requested of the congregation in favour of certain persons or objects nominated by the King. [Churchill]

was capital. The Queen had accordingly been watched, and one Sunday two young courtiers, Henry Norris and Sir Francis Weston, were seen to enter the Queen's room, and were, it was said, overheard making love to her. Next day a parchment was laid before the King empowering a strong panel of counsellors and judges, headed by the Lord Chancellor, or any four of them, to investigate and try every kind of treason. The King signed. On Tuesday the Council sat all day and late into the night, but as yet there was not sufficient evidence. The following Sunday a certain Smeaton, a gentleman of the King's chamber, who played with great skill on the lute, was arrested as the Queen's lover. Smeaton subsequently under torture confessed to the charge. On Monday Norris was among the challengers at the May Day tournament at Greenwich, and as the King rode to London after the jousting he called Norris to his side and told him what was suspected. Although Norris denied everything he also was arrested and taken to the Tower.

The following morning the Queen was requested to come before the Council. Although her uncle, the Duke of Norfolk, presided at the examination, no Queen of England, Anne complained afterwards, could have been treated with such brutality. At the conclusion of the proceedings she was placed under arrest, and kept under guard until the tide turned to take her up-river to the Tower.

On Friday morning the special commissioners of treason appointed the previous week, including Anne Boleyn's father, the Earl of Wiltshire, and the entire bench of judges except one, formed the court for the trial of Anne's lovers. A special jury consisting of twelve knights had been summoned, and found the prisoners guilty. They were sentenced to be hanged, drawn and quartered, but execution was deferred until after the trial of the Queen. This opened the following Monday in the Great Hall of the Tower. She was charged with being unfaithful to the King; promising to marry Norris after the King was dead; giving Norris poisoned lockets for the purpose of poisoning Catherine and Mary; and other offences, including incest with her brother. The Queen denied the charges vigorously, and replied to each one in detail. The peers retired, and soon returned with a verdict of guilty. Norfolk pronounced sentence: the Queen was to be burnt or beheaded, at the King's pleasure.

Anne received the sentence with calm and courage. She declared that if the King would allow it she would like to be beheaded like the French nobility, with a sword, and not, like the English nobility, with an axe. Her wish was granted; but no executioner could be found in the King's dominions to carry out the sentence with a sword, and it was found necessary to postpone the execution from Thursday to Friday while an expert was borrowed from St Omer, in the Emperor's dominions.

On May 19, 1536, the headsman was already waiting, leaning on his heavy two-handed sword, when the Constable of the Tower appeared, followed by Anne in a beautiful night robe of heavy grey damask trimmed with fur, showing a crimson kirtle beneath. "Pray for me," she said, and knelt down while one of the ladies-in-waiting bandaged her eyes. Before there was time to say a Paternoster she bowed her head, murmuring in a low voice, "God have pity on my soul." "God have mercy on my soul" she repeated, as the executioner stepped forward and slowly took his aim. Then the great blade hissed through the air, and with a single stroke his work was done.

As soon as the execution was known Henry appeared in yellow, with a feather in his cap, and ten days later was privately married to Jane Seymour at York Place. Jane proved to be the submissive wife for whom Henry had always longed. Anne had been too dominating and too impulsive. Jane was the opposite, gentle though proud; and Henry spent a happy eighteen months with her. She was the only Queen whom Henry regretted and mourned, and when she died, still aged only twenty-seven, immediately after the birth of her first child, the future Edward VI, Henry had her buried with royal honours in St George's Chapel at Windsor. He himself lies near her.

Though all had been bliss at Court while Jane was Queen rural England was heavy with discontents. Henry was increasingly short of revenue and Church properties offered a tempting prize. Just before Anne's trial he had gone down to the House of Lords in person to recommend a Bill suppressing those smaller monasteries which contained fewer than twelve monks. There were nearly four hundred of them, and the combined rent of their lands amounted to a considerable sum. The religious orders had for some time been in decline, and parents were becoming more and more averse to handing over their sons to the cloisters. Monks turned to the land in search of recruits, and often waived the old social distinctions, taking the sons of poor tenant farmers. But the number of novices was rarely sufficient. At some houses the monks had given up all hope of carrying on, and squandered the endowments, cutting down woods, pawning the plate, and letting the buildings fall into disrepair or ruin. Grave irregularities had been discovered by the ecclesiastical Visitors over many years. The idea of suppression was not altogether new: Wolsey had suppressed several small houses to finance his college at Oxford, and the King had since suppressed over twenty more for his own benefit. Parliament made little difficulty about winding up the smaller houses, when satisfied that their inmates were either to be transferred to large houses or pensioned off. During the summer of 1536 royal commissioners toured the country, completing the dissolution as swiftly as possible.

The King had now a new chief adviser. Thomas Cromwell, in turn mercenary soldier in Italy, cloth agent, and money-lender, had served his apprenticeship in statecraft under Wolsey, but he had also learned the lessons of his master's downfall. Ruthless, cynical, Machiavellian, Cromwell was a man of the New Age. His ambition was matched by his energy and served by a penetrating intelligence. When he succeeded Wolsey as the King's principal Minister he made no effort to inherit the pomp and glory of the fallen Cardinal. Nevertheless his were more solid achievements in both State and Church. In the administration of the realm Cromwell devised new methods to replace the institutions he found at hand. Before his day Government policy had for centuries been both made and implemented in the royal household. Though Henry VII had improved the system he had remained in a sense a medieval king. Thomas Cromwell thoroughly reformed it during his ten years of power, and when he fell in 1540 policy was already carried out by Government departments, operating outside the household. Perhaps his greatest accomplishment, though not so dramatic as his other work, was his inception of the Government service of modern England. Cromwell is the uncommemorated architect of our great departments of State.

As First Minister Cromwell handled the dissolution of the monasteries with conspicuous, cold-blooded efficiency. It was a step which appealed to the well-to-do. The high nobility and country gentry acquired on favourable terms all kinds of fine estates. Sometimes a neighbouring merchant, or a syndicate of City men and courtiers, bought or leased the confiscated lands. Many local squires had long been stewards of monastic lands, and now bought properties which they had managed for generations. Throughout the middle classes there was great irritation at the privileges and wealth of the Church. They resented the undue proportion of the national income engrossed by those who rendered no economic service. The King was assured of the support of Parliament and the prosperous classes. Most of the displaced monks, nearly ten thousand in all, faced their lot with relief or fortitude, assisted by substantial pensions. Some even married nuns, and many became respectable parish clergy.

English agriculture, to meet the demands of a growing population and an expanding cloth industry, was turning from arable farming to pasture. Hence the broad acres on the ecclesiastical estates were now fertilised by the ideas and the money of their new owners, the country gentlemen and merchants. The Reformation is sometimes blamed for all the evils attributed to the modern economic system. Yet these evils, if such they were, had existed long before Henry VIII began to doubt the validity of his marriage to Catherine of Aragon. Thomas More, who did not live to see events run their course, had already in *Utopia* outlined to his contemporaries the sharp features of the new economy.

In the field of religious belief the Reformation brought profound change. The Bible now acquired a new and far-reaching authority. The older generation considered that Holy Writ was dangerous in the hands of the unlearned and should only be read by priests. But complete printed Bibles, translated into English by Tyndale and Coverdale, had appeared for the first time late in the autumn of 1535, and were now running through several editions.

In the autumn, when the new taxes came to be assessed after Michaelmas, farmers and yokels collected in large numbers throughout the North of England and Lincolnshire, swearing to resist the taxes and maintain the old order in the Church. The revolt, which took the name of "the Pilgrimage of Grace", was spontaneous. Its leader, a lawyer named Robert Aske, had his position thrust upon him. The nobles and higher clergy took no part. Although the rebels greatly outnumbered the loyal levies, and the King had no regular troops except the Yeomen of the Guard, Henry at once showed what

Wolsey had called his "royal stomach". He refused to compromise with rebellion. When his Commissioners of Taxes were taken prisoners by the rebels in Lincolnshire he sent a terrifying message:

"This assembly is so heinous that unless you can persuade them to disperse and send a hundred of their ringleaders with halters round their necks to the Lieutenant to do with them as shall be thought best ... we see no way to save them. For we have already sent ... the Duke of Suffolk, our Lieutenant, ... with a hundred thousand men,[1] horse and foot, in harness, with munitions and artillery. ... We have also appointed another great army to invade their territories as soon as they are out of them, and to burn, spoil, and destroy their goods, wives, and children with all extremity."

After this the Commissioners reported that the common people as a whole were prepared to recognise the King as Supreme Head of the Church and to allow him for this once to have the first-fruits and the tenths from the clergy, together with the subsidy he was demanding. In early 1537 the rebellion collapsed as quickly as it had arisen, but Henry determined to make examples of the ringleaders. Seventy were hanged as traitors at Carlisle Assizes alone, and when Norfolk, the victorious general, seemed inclined to clemency the King sent word that he desired a large number of executions. Altogether some two hundred and fifty of insurgents were put to death.[2]

As a further blow to the old school the Government commissioned in Paris a great printing of English Bibles, more sumptuous than any previous edition, and in September 1538 directed that every parish in the country should purchase a Bible of the largest volume in English, to be set up in each church, where the parishioners might most commodiously resort to the same and read it. Six copies were set up in St Paul's, in the City of London, and multitudes thronged the cathedral all day to read them, especially, we are told, when they could get any person that had an audible voice to read aloud. This Bible has remained the basis of all later editions, including the Authorised Version prepared in the reign of James I.

Up to this point Thomas Cromwell had consistently walked with success. But he now begin to encounter the conservatism of the older nobility. They were more than content with the political revolution, but they wanted the Reformation to stop with the assertion of the royal supremacy, and they opposed the doctrinal changes of Cranmer and his following. The Duke of Norfolk headed the reaction, and the King, who was rigidly orthodox, except where his lusts or interests were stirred, agreed with it. Stephen Gardiner, Bishop of Winchester and later Queen Mary's adviser, was the brain behind the Norfolk party. Its leaders took pains to point out that France and the Emperor might invade England and execute the sentence of deposition which the Pope had pronounced. The King himself was anxious to avoid a total religious cleavage with the European Powers. The Catholic front seemed

---

1   There is no sure evidence for this figure.
2   Aske was executed at York in 1537.

overwhelmingly strong, and the only allies which Cromwell could find abroad were minor German princelings. With these large issues in their keeping, Norfolk's faction vigilantly awaited their chance. It came, like so much of the action of this memorable reign, as a result of the conjugal affairs of the King.

The King was now a widower. One Continental house he considered marrying into was the Duchy of Cleves, which to some extent shared his own attitude in religion, hating the Papacy, yet restricting Lutheranism. Then news arrived of a startling diplomatic development. The French and Imperial Ambassadors waited together on the King to inform him that Francis I had invited the Emperor Charles V, who was in his Spanish dominions, to pass through Paris on his way to put down a revolt at Ghent, and the Emperor had accepted. The two sovereigns had resolved to forget old grudges and make common cause. An alliance with the princes of Northern Germany against the two Catholic monarchs now seemed imperative, and negotiations for a marriage between Henry and Anne, the eldest Princess of Cleves, were hurried on. Anne's charms, Cromwell reported, were on everybody's lips. "Everyone," he announced, "praises her beauty both of face and body. One says she excels the Duchess of Milan as the golden sun does the silver moon." Anne spoke only German, spent her time chiefly in needlework, and could not sing or play any instrument. She was thirty years old, very tall and thin, with an assured and resolute countenance, slightly pockmarked, but was said to possess wit and animation, and did not over-indulge in beer.

Anne spent Christmas at Calais, waiting for storms to abate, and on the last day of the year 1539 arrived at Rochester. Henry had sailed down in his private barge, in disguise, bearing a fine sable fur among the presents. On New Year's Day he hurried to visit her. But on seeing her he was astonished and abashed. Embraces, presents, compliments, all carefully arranged on the voyage, were forgotten. He mumbled a few words and returned to the barge, where he remained silent for many minutes. At last he said very sadly and pensively, "I see nothing in this woman as men report of her, and I marvel that wise men should have made such report as they have done."

But the threat from abroad compelled the King to fulfil his contract. Since he now knew as much about the Canon Law on marriage as anyone in Europe, he turned himself into the perfect legal example of a man whose marriage might be annulled. The marriage was never consummated. He told his intimate counsellors that he had gone through the form of it from political necessity, against his true desire, and without inward consent, for fear of making a ruffle in the world and driving Anne's brother the Duke into the hands of the Emperor and the King of France.

Norfolk and Gardiner now saw their chance to break Cromwell, as Wolsey had been broken, with the help of a new lady. Yet another of Norfolk's nieces, Catherine Howard, was presented to Henry at Gardiner's house, and captured his affections at first sight. The Norfolk faction soon felt strong enough to challenge Cromwell's power. In June 1540 the King was persuaded to get rid of Cromwell and Anne together. Cromwell was condemned under a Bill of

Attainder charging him principally with heresy and "broadcasting" erroneous books and implicitly with treason. Anne agreed to have her marriage annulled, and Convocation pronounced it invalid. She lived on in England, pensioned and in retirement, for another seventeen years. A few days after Cromwell was executed on July 28 Henry was privately married to his fifth wife, Catherine Howard.

Catherine, about twenty-two, with auburn hair and hazel eyes, was the prettiest of Henry's wives. His Majesty's spirits revived, his health returned, and he went down to Windsor to reduce weight. But wild, tempestuous Catherine was not long content with a husband nearly thirty years older than herself. Her reckless love for her cousin, Thomas Culpeper, was discovered, and she was executed in the Tower in February 1542 on the same spot as Anne Boleyn.

Henry's sixth wife, Catherine Parr, was a serious little widow from the Lake District, thirty-one years of age, learned, and interested in theological questions, who had had two husbands before the King. She married Henry at Hampton Court on July 12, 1543, and until his death three years later made him an admirable wife, nursing his ulcerated leg, which grew steadily worse and in the end killed him. She contrived to reconcile Henry with the future Queen Elizabeth; both Mary and Elizabeth grew fond of her, and she had the fortune to outlive her husband.

The pain from his leg made Henry ill-tempered; he suffered fools and those who crossed him with equal lack of patience. Suspicion dominated his mind and ruthlessness marked his actions. At the time of his marriage with Catherine Parr he was engaged in preparing the last of his wars. The roots of the conflict lay in Scotland. Hostility between the two peoples still smouldered, ever and again flickering into flame along the wild Border. Reviving the obsolete claim to suzerainty, Henry denounced the Scots as rebels, and pressed them to relinquish their alliance with France. The Scots successfully defeated an English raid at Halidon Rig. Then in the autumn of 1542 an expedition under Norfolk had to turn back at Kelso, principally through the failure of the commissariat, which, besides its other shortcomings, left the English army without its beer, and the Scots proceeded to carry the war into the enemy's country. Their decision proved disastrous. Badly led and imperfectly organised, they lost more than half their army of ten thousand men in Solway Moss and were utterly routed. The news of this second Flodden killed James V, who died leaving the kingdom to an infant of one week, Mary, the famous Queen of Scots.

At once the child became the focus of the struggle for Scotland. Henry claimed her for the bride of his own son and heir. But the Scots Queen-Mother was a French princess, Mary of Guise. The pro-French Catholic party, led by Cardinal Beaton, resisted, repudiated Henry's terms, and began negotiations for marrying Mary to a French prince. Such a marriage could never be accepted by England. The Imperial Ambassador, who sought Henry's aid in the Emperor's struggle with France, found himself eagerly welcomed at

Court. Once again England and the Empire made common cause against the French, and in May 1543 a secret treaty was ratified between Charles V and Henry. Throughout the year, and well into the spring of 1544, the preparations continued. While Scotland was left to Edward Seymour, brother of Queen Jane, and now Earl of Hertford, the King himself was to cross the Channel and lead an army against Francis in co-operation with an Imperial force from the north-east.

The plan was excellent, but the execution failed. Henry and Charles distrusted each other; each suspected the other of seeking a separate peace. Wary of being drawn too deep into the Emperor's plans, Henry sat down to besiege Boulogne. The town fell on September 14, and Henry was able to congratulate himself on at least one tangible result from his campaign. Five days later the Emperor made his peace with Francis, and refused to listen to Henry's complaints and exhortations. Meanwhile the English in Scotland, after burning Edinburgh and laying waste much country, ceased to make headway, and in February 1545 were defeated at Ancrum Moor.

Henry's position was extremely grave. Without a single ally, the nation faced the possibility of invasion from both France and Scotland. The crisis called for unexampled sacrifices from the English people; never had they been called upon to pay so many loans, subsidies, and benevolences. To set an example Henry melted down his own plate and mortgaged his estates. At Portsmouth he prepared for the threatened invasion in person. A French fleet penetrated the Solent and landed troops in the Isle of Wight; but they were soon driven off, and the crisis gradually passed. Next year a peace treaty was signed, which left Boulogne in English hands for eight years, at the end of which time France was to buy it back at a heavy price. Scotland was not included in the settlement. The war in the North smouldered on, bursting into flame for a time at the assassination of Cardinal Beaton, but yielding no definite results. Henry completely failed in Scotland. He would make no generous settlement with his neighbours, yet he lacked the force to coerce them. For the next fifty years they were to tease and trouble the minds of his successors.

In 1546 Henry was as yet only fifty-five. In the autumn he made his usual progress through Surrey and Berkshire to Windsor, and early in November he came up to London. He was never to leave his capital alive again. In these last few months one question dominated all minds: the heir to the kingdom was known, a child of nine, but who would be the power behind the throne? Norfolk or Hertford? The party of reaction or the party of reform?

A sudden and unexpected answer was given. On December 12, 1546, Norfolk and his son Surrey, the poet, were arrested for treason and sent to the Tower. Surrey's foolish conduct had made trouble inevitable. He talked wildly of the time when the King should be dead, and, inconveniently remembering his descent from Edward I, he had quartered the royal arms with his own, despite the heralds' prohibitions. The King remembered that years before Norfolk had been put forward as a possible heir to the throne, and Surrey had been suggested as a husband for Princess Mary. His suspicions aroused, he acted swiftly; in mid-January Surrey was executed.

Parliament assembled to pass a Bill of Attainder against Norfolk. On Thursday the 27th the royal assent was given and Norfolk was condemned to death. But that same evening the King himself was dying. The physicians dared not tell him so, for prophesying the King's death was treason by Act of Parliament. Then, as the long hours slowly passed, Sir Anthony Denny, "boldly coming to the King, told him what case he was in, to man's judgment not like to live; and therefore exhorted him to prepare himself for death." The King took the grim news with fortitude. Urged to summon the Archbishop, he replied that first he would "take a little sleep; and then, as I feel myself, I will advise upon the matter." While he slept Hertford and Paget walked the gallery outside, scheming and contriving how to secure their power. Shortly before midnight the King awoke. He sent for Cranmer. When he came Henry was too weak to speak; he could only stretch out his hand to Cranmer. In a few minutes the Supreme Head had ceased to breathe.

CHAPTER TWENTY-FIVE

THE PROTESTANT STRUGGLE

Edward VI – Cranmer's and Edward Seymour's religious revolution – the
Book of Common Prayer – wool profits and land enclosures – Latimer's
Sermon of the Plough – East and West rebellions – the hanging of Robert
Ket – the rise of Dudley, Earl of Warwick and "The Lords in London" –
the execution of Somerset – Lady Jane Grey – the death of Edward VI –
Jane Grey proclaimed Queen – Mary Tudor claims her throne – the
emergence of William Cecil – the restoration of the Roman Mass –
Mary betrothed to Philip of Spain – Protestant protest – the execution of
Sir Thomas Wyatt – Princess Elizabeth confined to Woodstock –
Protestant Martyrs – the death of Bloody Mary

I T WAS Jane, daughter of the Protestant house of Seymour, who had
produced the future Edward VI. Nevertheless the Catholic Norfolks
retained much of their power and influence. While Henry lived they
constituted a check and barrier to the Reforming party. Henry had
restrained Cranmer's doctrinal innovations, and in the main upheld the whole
Norfolk interest, represented in religion by Stephen Gardiner, Bishop of
Winchester. Henry wanted his own way but he saw no need to change the faith
or even the ritual to which his subjects had been born.

With the new reign a deeper and more powerful tide began to flow. The
guardian and chief counsellor of the child-King[1] was his uncle, Edward
Seymour, now Duke of Somerset. He and Cranmer proceeded to transform
the political reformation of Henry VIII into a religious revolution. Foreign
scholars from Germany and Switzerland, and even from distant Poland, were
given chairs in the Universities of Oxford and Cambridge to educate the new
generation of clergy in the Reformed doctrines. The Book of Common
Prayer, in shining English prose, was drawn up by Cranmer and accepted by
Parliament in 1549. Then followed, after Somerset's fall, the Forty-two
Articles of Religion, and a second Prayer Book, until, on paper at least,
England became a Protestant State. Somerset and Cranmer were both men of
sincerity; they believed in the religious ideas which they intended their

---

1   Edward VI was ten when he became King in 1546; he died six years later.

countrymen to accept; but the mass of the people neither knew nor cared about theological warfare, and there were many who actively opposed the imported foreign creeds.

Somerset himself was merely one of the regents appointed under Henry's will, and his position as Protector, at once dazzling and dangerous, had little foundation in law or precedent. Rivals crowded jealously upon him. His brother, Thomas Seymour, Lord High Admiral, had his own ambitions. The pale child Edward VI, who was constitutionally consumptive, might not live long. The next Protestant heir was Princess Elizabeth. She was living with Lady Catherine Parr, last and most fortunate of Henry's wives, and Catherine Parr was now married to the Admiral. He thought fit to make advances to the young princess even before the death of his wife, and girlish romps took place in her bedroom that led to scandal. Proofs were discovered of Thomas Seymour's plots against his brother, and the Protector was forced in January 1549 to dispose of him by Act of Attainder and the block on Tower Hill. Thus Somerset surmounted the first crisis of the new reign.

Far more serious than such personal threats were the distresses and discontents in the countryside. The life and economy of medieval England were fast dissolving. Landlords saw that vast fortunes could be made from wool, and the village communal strips barred their profits. Warfare had been going on for decades between landowner and peasantry. Slowly and surely the rights and privileges of the village communities were infringed and removed. Common land was seized, enclosed, and turned to pasture for flocks. Dissolution of the monasteries removed the most powerful and conservative element in the old system, and for a time gave fresh impetus to a process already under way. The multiplication of enclosures caused distress throughout the realm. In some counties as much as one-third of the arable land was turned over to grass, and the people looked in anger upon the new nobility, fat with sacrilegious spoil, but greedy still.

Somerset had thus to face one of the worst economic crises that England has endured. The popular preachers were loud in denunciation. The Sermon of the Plough, preached by Hugh Latimer at Paul's Cross in 1548, is a notable piece of Tudor invective. "In times past men were full of pity and compassion; but now there is no pity; for in London their brother shall die in the streets for cold; he shall lie sick at the door between stock and stock [that is, between the door-posts], and then perish for hunger. In times past, when any rich man died in London, they were wont to help the scholars at the universities with exhibition. When any man died they would bequeath great sums of money toward the relief of the poor. ... Charity is waxen cold; none helpeth the scholar nor yet the poor; now that the knowledge of God's Word is brought to light, and many earnestly study and labour to set it forth, now almost no man helpeth to maintain them."

Somerset was surrounded by men who had made their money by the methods which Latimer denounced. He himself sympathised with the yeoman and peasantry, and appointed commissions to inquire into the enclosures. But this increased the discontent, and encouraged the oppressed to take matters into their own hands. Two rebellions broke out. The Catholic peasantry in the South-West rose against the Prayer Book, and the yokels of the Eastern Counties against the enclosing landlords. This gave a fine handle to Somerset's enemies. In Germany in 1524–26 the Reformation had been followed by the bloody Peasants' War, in which the poorer classes in the countryside and the towns rose with the blessing of the reformer Zwingli against their noble oppressors. The same thing seemed about to happen in the England of 1549. Foreign mercenaries suppressed the Western rebellion. But in Norfolk the trouble was more serious. A tannery-owner named Robert Ket took the lead. He established his headquarters outside Norwich on Mousehold Hill, where about sixteen thousand peasants gathered in a camp of turf huts roofed with boughs. Under a large oak tree Ket, day after day, tried country gentlemen charged with robbing the poor. No blood was shed, but property acquired by enclosing common land was restored to the public, and the rebels lived upon the flocks and herds of the landowners. The local authorities were powerless, and Somerset was known to recognise the justice of their grievances. The disorders spread to Yorkshire, and presently reverberated in the Midlands.

John Dudley, Earl of Warwick, son of the man who had been Henry VII's agent, now seized his opportunity. He had proved an able soldier in the French campaigns of Henry VIII, and had been careful to hide his real character and motives. He was a self-seeking, vigorous man, and the champion of wealth and property. Now he was given command of the troops to suppress the rising. The Government felt itself so militarily weak that followers of the rebels were offered a free pardon. Ket was not unmoved. The herald came to his camp, but a small incident brought disaster. While Ket was standing by the oak tree, meditating an interview with Warwick, a small urchin drew the attention of the herald's party "with words as unseemly as his gesture was filthy", and he was immediately shot with an arquebus. The murder enraged Ket's followers. Fighting began. Warwick's best troops were German mercenaries, whose precise fire-drill shattered the peasant array. Three thousand five hundred were killed. There were no wounded. A few made a stand for their lives behind a barricade of farm carts and surrendered. Ket was taken prisoner, and hanged at Norwich Castle. Warwick had by accident made his mark as a strong man.

Somerset's enemies claimed the credit for restoring order. They blamed the rising in the East on his enclosure commissions and his sympathy for the peasants, and the rebellion in the West on his religious reforms. His foreign policy had driven the Scots into alliance with France, and he had lost Henry's one conquest, Boulogne. Warwick became the leader of the Opposition. "The Lords in London", as Warwick's party were called, met to take measures against the Protector. No one moved to support him. They quietly took over the Government. After a spell in the Tower, Somerset, now powerless, was for some months allowed to sit in the Council, but as conditions got worse so the danger grew of a reaction in his favour. In January 1552, splendidly garbed as for a state banquet, he was executed on Tower Hill. This handsome, well-meaning man had failed completely to heal the dislocation of Henry's reign and fell a victim to the fierce interests he had offended.

The nominal King of England, Edward VI, was a cold, priggish invalid of fifteen. In his diary he noted his uncle's death without a comment. The Government of Warwick, now become Duke of Northumberland, was held together by class resistance to social unrest. His three years of power displayed to the full the rapacity of the ruling classes. Doctrinal reformation was a pretence for confiscating yet more Church lands, and new bishops paid for their consecration with portions of the episcopal estates. The so-called grammar schools of Edward VI were but the beginning of spacious plans carried out in Elizabeth's reign for endowing education out of the confiscated lands of the monasteries. Thomas More's definition of government as "a conspiracy of rich men procuring their own commodities under the name and title of a commonwealth" fitted England very accurately during these years.

Under the Succession Act of 1543 the next heir to the throne was Princess Mary, the Catholic daughter of Catherine of Aragon. Northumberland might well tremble for the future. For a moment he thought of substituting Elizabeth for her half-sister; but Elizabeth, now aged nineteen and wise for her years, had no intention of committing herself to such an arrangement. A desperate scheme was evolved. The younger daughter of Henry VII had married the Duke of Suffolk, and their heirs had been named in Henry VIII's will as next in line of succession after his own children. The eldest grandchild in this Suffolk line was Lady Jane Grey, a girl of sixteen. Northumberland married this girl to his son, Guildford Dudley. Nothing remained but to effect a military *coup* when the young King died. But Princess Mary, now aged thirty-six, took care to avoid Northumberland's advances. When Edward fell ill she took refuge on the estates of the Duke of Norfolk, ignoring a summons to appear at her brother's deathbed.

On July 6, 1553, Edward VI expired, and Lady Jane Grey was proclaimed Queen in London. The only response to this announcement was gathering resistance: Northumberland was too much hated throughout the land. The common people flocked to Mary's support. The Privy Counsellors and the City authorities swam with the tide. Northumberland was left without an ally. In August Mary entered London with Elizabeth at her side. Lady Jane and her husband were consigned to the Tower. In vain Northumberland grovelled. He asserted that he had always been a Catholic, with shattering effect on the Protestant party. But nothing could save him from an ignominious death.

The woman who now became Queen was probably the most unhappy and unsuccessful of England's sovereigns. Mary Tudor, the only surviving child of Catherine of Aragon and Henry VIII, had been brought up in the early years of her father's reign with all the ceremony due to the heiress to the throne. She had been betrothed at different times to the heirs both of France and the Empire. As with her mother, religion dominated her being, and Catherine's divorce and the break with Rome brought tragic and catastrophic change. Mary had been declared illegitimate by Act of Parliament; she was pressed to forsake her religion, and endured bitter conflicts between her duty to her father and her conscience. Her half-sister and half-brother overshadowed her at Court. She had clung to her confessors and her chapel throughout the reign of Edward VI, and was naturally feared by the ruling group of Protestant politicians in London. The Spanish blood in her was strong. She entered into close and confidential relations with Renard, the Imperial Ambassador. Her accession portended a renewal of the Roman connection and a political alliance with the Empire.

We are assured that, except in matters of religion, Mary was by nature merciful. She certainly accepted the allegiance of the counsellors and officials who came meekly to her. The most adroit among them, William Cecil, was to keep close to Government circles throughout her reign, and great was to be his future under her successor. Secure upon the throne, Mary proceeded to realise the wish of her life – the restoration of the Roman communion. In Stephen Gardiner, Bishop of Winchester, one of Norfolk's circle in the later years of Henry VIII, she found an able and ardent servant. The religious legislation of the Reformation Parliament was repealed. But one thing Mary could not do. She could not restore to the Church the lands parcelled out among the nobility. The Tudor magnates were willing to go to Mass, but not to lose their new property. Even so there was trouble. Mary never realised that the common people, particularly in London, coupled Catholicism with foreign influence. They had indeed been taught to do so under Henry VIII, but the feeling was older than that. The English Bible and the English Prayer Book were in their hands, and there was a wide, if superficial, attachment to the Reformed Faith. Protestant leaders fled to Geneva and the German Rhineland towns. There was rioting in the capital. Gardiner's life was threatened. He wore a mail shirt throughout the day and was guarded by a hundred men at night.

The most urgent question was whom Mary should marry. The Commons supported an English candidate, Edward Courtenay, Earl of Devon, a descendant of the house of York. But Mary's eyes were fixed overseas. Renard, envoy of the Emperor Charles V, worked fast, and she promised to wed the Emperor's son, the future Philip II of Spain. Sir Thomas Wyatt, son of the poet of Henry VIII's reign, formed a plot to prevent the marriage by force, and Courtenay gathered a conspiracy against her in the West. News of the Spanish betrothal filtered through the Court and reached the people. Ugly stories of the Inquisition and the coming of Spanish troops passed from mouth to mouth. The Commons came in deputation to beg the Queen not to violate the feelings of the nation. But Mary had all the obstinacy of the Tudors and none of their political sense. She was now on the threshold of her dreams – a Catholic England united in intimate alliance with the Catholic Empire of the Habsburgs.

All eyes turned to Princess Elizabeth, in watchful retirement at Hatfield. The English succession was vital to the Courts of Europe. The French

Ambassador, Noailles, began to be active. The stakes were high. In the rivalry of Valois and Habsburg which tormented Europe England's support might mean victory or defeat. Elizabeth was suspected of turning for advice to the Frenchman. It was suggested that she might marry Courtenay. But events began to move fast. In the West Courtenay precipitated a rising. Soon after the Spanish match was proclaimed rebellion broke out yet again in Southern England. Sir Thomas Wyatt raised his standard in Kent and marched slowly towards London, gathering men as he came. The capital was in alarm. The citizens went in fear of the sack of their houses. But Mary, bitter and disappointed with her people, and knowing she had failed to win their hearts, showed she was not afraid. If Wyatt entered the capital her ambitions as a Catholic Queen were doomed. In a stirring speech at Guildhall she summoned the Londoners to her defence. There was division among the rebels. Wyatt was disappointed by Courtenay, whose rising was a pitiable failure. The Kentish rebels hoped to force terms from the Queen, not to depose her. Straggled fighting took place in the streets, and the Queen's men cut up the intruders. Wyatt was executed. This sealed the fate of Lady Jane Grey and her husband. In February 1554 the two walked calmly to their death on Tower Green.

Elizabeth's life was now in great danger. Though Wyatt had exonerated her she was the only rival claimant to the throne, and the Spaniards demanded her execution before their prince was committed to marrying the Queen. But Mary had shed blood enough and Renard could not persuade her to sign away the life of her half-sister. Every argument was used. Elizabeth indeed had very little hope, and had determined to ask, like her mother, that she might be beheaded with the sword. But, fearlessly and passionately, she denied all disloyal dealings with Courtenay or Wyatt. Perhaps Mary believed her. At any rate, after some months she was released and sent to Woodstock, where, in quiet and pious seclusion, she awaited the turn of fortune.

As summer came Philip sailed northwards across the seas. Mary journeyed to Winchester to greet her bridegroom. With all the pomp of sixteenth-century royalty the marriage was solemnised in July 1554 according to the rites of the Catholic Church. Gardiner was now dead; but a successor was found in the English cardinal Reginald Pole. Pole had been in exile throughout the reign of Henry VIII, his family having been lopped and shorn in Henry's judicial murders. This representative of the Pope was not only a Prince of the Church, but practically a Prince of the Blood, a second cousin of the Queen and a grandson of "false, fleeting, perjured Clarence".

Mary has been for ever odious in the minds of a Protestant nation as the Bloody Queen who martyred her noblest subjects. Generations of Englishmen in childhood learnt the sombre tale of their sacrifice from Foxe's *Book of Martyrs*, with its gruesome illustrations. These stories have become part of the common memory of the people – the famous scenes at Oxford in 1555, the faggots which consumed the Protestant bishops, Latimer and Ridley, the pitiful recantation and final heroic end in March 1556 of the frail, aged

Archbishop, Cranmer. Their martyrdom rallied to the Protestant faith many who till now had shown indifference.

In vain the Queen strove to join English interests to those of the Spanish state. She had married to make England safe for Catholicism, and she had sacrificed what little personal happiness she could hope for to this dream. As the wife of the King of Spain, against the interests of her kingdom, and against the advice of prudent counsellors, among them Cardinal Pole, she allowed herself to be dragged into war with France, and Calais, the last possession of the English upon the Continent, fell without resistance. This national disgrace, this loss of the symbol of the power and glory of medieval England, bit deep into the hearts of the people and into the conscience of the Queen. Hope of a child to secure the Catholic succession was unfulfilled. Philip retired to the Netherlands and then to Spain, aloof and disappointed at the barrenness of the whole political scheme. Surrounded by disloyalty and discontent, Mary's health gave way. In November 1558 she died, and a few hours later, in Lambeth Palace, her coadjutor, Cardinal Pole, followed her. The tragic interlude of her reign was over. It had sealed the conversion of the English people to the Reformed Faith.

CHAPTER TWENTY-SIX

GLORIANA

Elizabeth I — Mary Queen of Scots — Matthew Parker, Robert Dudley
and Nicholas Bacon — the emergence of the Puritans — John Knox — the
question of Royal marriage — Mary marries Darnley — Walsingham
as ambassador — Catholic conspiracy — Mary Queen of Scots held in
captivity — the Pope excommunicates Elizabeth — the St Bartholomew's
Eve massacre — Mary executed at Fotheringay — plundering the Spanish
treasure ships — war with Spain — Hawkins and Drake — Cadiz —
the Armada — the East India Company — Raleigh and Essex — the death
of Drake — insurrection in Ireland — Hugh O'Neill — Shakespeare —
the execution of Essex — Mountjoy puts down Irish rebellion —
the end of the Tudors

LIZABETH WAS twenty-five years old when, untried in the affairs of State, she succeeded her half-sister on November 17, 1558. There could be no doubt who her father was. A commanding carriage, auburn hair, eloquence of speech, and natural dignity proclaimed her King Henry's daughter. She could speak six languages, and was well read in Latin and Greek. As with her father and grandfather, a restless vitality led her hither and thither from mansion to mansion, so that often none could tell where in a week's time she might be sleeping. When to keep silence, how to bide her time and husband her resources, were the lessons she learnt from her youth. The times demanded a politic, calculating, devious spirit at the head of the State, and this Elizabeth possessed. She had, too, a high gift for picking able men to do the country's work. It came naturally to her to take the credit for their successes, while blaming them for all that went wrong.

Few sovereigns ever succeeded to a more hazardous inheritance than she. England's link with Spain had brought the hostility of France and the loss of Calais. Tudor policy in Scotland had broken down. The old military danger of the Middle Ages, a Franco-Scottish alliance, again threatened. In the eyes of Catholic Europe Mary, the Queen of Scots, and wife of the Dauphin of France who became King Francis II in 1169 had a better claim to the English throne than Elizabeth, and with the power of France behind her she stood a good chance of gaining it. Mary of Guise, the Regent and Queen-Mother of

Scotland, pursued a pro-French and pro-Catholic policy, and in Edinburgh and Paris the Guises held the keys of power. Even before the death of Henry VIII England's finances had been growing desperate. English credit at Antwerp, the centre of the European money market, was so weak that the Government had to pay 14 per cent for its loans. The coinage, which had been debased yet further under Edward VI, was now chaotic. England's only official ally, Spain, suspected the new régime for religious reasons.

Elizabeth had been brought up a Protestant. She was a paragon of the New Learning. Around her had gathered some of the ablest Protestant minds: Matthew Parker,[1] who was to be her Archbishop of Canterbury; Nicholas Bacon,[2] whom she appointed Lord Keeper of the Great Seal; Roger Ascham,[3] the foremost scholar of the day; and, most important of all, William Cecil, the adaptable civil servant who had already held office as Secretary under Somerset and Northumberland. Of sixteenth-century English statesmen Cecil was undoubtedly the greatest. He possessed a consuming thirst for information about the affairs of the realm and immense industry in the business of office. Cautious good judgment marked all his actions. Elizabeth, with sure instinct, summoned him to her service. Their close and daily collaboration was to last, in spite of shocks and jars, until Cecil's death, forty years later.

Religious peace at home and safety from Scotland were the foremost needs of the realm. England became Protestant by law, Queen Mary's Catholic legislation was repealed, and the sovereign was declared supreme Governor of the English Church. But this was not the end of Elizabeth's difficulties. New ideas were in debate on the very nature and foundations of political power. Ever since the days of Wyclif in the 1380s there had been, running in secret veins under the surface of society in England, a movement of resistance to the Church order. With the Reformation the notion that it might be a duty to disobey the established order on the grounds of private conviction became for

[1] Matthew Parker (1504–75), who was Archbishop of Canterbury from 1559 until his death, had been Anne Boleyn's tutor. As an evangelical, he fell from Queen Mary's favour. As Archbishop of Canterbury in Elizabeth's reign, Parker oversaw the revision of the Forty-two Articles of the Church doctrine, which became the Thirty-nine Articles. But Parker's deeper interest was the concept of theology which arose, as E.J. Bicknell in his "Introduction to the Thirty-nine Articles" wrote, "from man's effort to understand his own life". This reflected what Parker saw as his true role. He was never the political courtier some think but was probably happiest when left to his scholarship, particularly Anglo-Saxon studies. The expression "Nosey Parker" is said to derive from the archbishop's inquisitiveness (although it may equally come from park keepers snooping on lovers). A street at Westminster named after him, recently housed a branch of the Intelligence services and was known as Nosey Parker Street.

[2] Nicholas Bacon (1509–79) was Cecil's brother-in-law and father of the courtier and philosopher, Francis Bacon.

[3] Roger Ascham (1515–68) was a Cambridge classicist who became tutor to the teenage Elizabeth from 1548. Despite being a Protestant, he retained favour under both Edward VI and Mary I and was appointed Latin secretary to the Catholic Queen Mary, returning to Elizabeth's service as her secretary when she became Queen. He is best known as author of *Toxophilus* (1545) a treatise on archery, and of *The Scholemaster* (1570), on classical education. These were remembered for their prose, not then a common literary form.

the first time since the conversion to Christianity of the Roman Empire the belief of great numbers. But so closely were Church and State involved that disobedience to the one was a challenge to the other.

It is at this point that the party known as the Puritans, who were to play so great a rôle in the next hundred years, first enter English history. Democratic in theory and organisation, intolerant in practice of all who differed from their views, the Puritans challenged the Queen's authority in Church and State, and although she sought for freedom of conscience and could maintain with sincerity that she "made no windows into men's souls", she dared not let them organise cells in the body religious or the body politic. She realised that unless the Government controlled the Church it would be too weak to survive the Counter-Reformation now gathering head in Catholic Europe. So Elizabeth had soon to confront not only the Catholic danger from abroad, but Puritan attack at home, led by fanatical exiles of Mary's reign who now streamed back from Geneva and from the Rhineland towns.

Nevertheless the Reformation in Europe took on a new aspect when it came to England. All the novel questions agitating the world – the relation of the National Church to Rome on one side and to the national sovereign on the other; its future organisation; its articles of religion; the disposal of its property, and the property of its monasteries – could only be determined in Parliament, where the Puritans soon formed a growing and outspoken Opposition. The gentry in Parliament were themselves divided. On two points alone perhaps were they heartily in accord: once they had got their share of abbey lands they did not mean to part with them, and anything was better than having the Wars of the Roses over again. Otherwise they fell into two great divisions, those who thought things had gone far enough, and those who wanted to go a step farther. It was the future distinction of Cavalier and Puritan, Churchman and Dissenter, Tory and Whig.

The immediate threat lay north of the Border. French troops supported the French Queen Mother in Scotland. A powerful Puritan party among the Scottish nobility, abetted by the persecuted preachers, were in arms against them, while John Knox raised his harsh voice against foreign rule and from exile in Geneva poured forth his denunciations of "the monstrous regiment of women". He meant of course that rule by women seemed to him unnatural. Elizabeth watched these doings with interest and anxiety. If the French party got control of Scotland their next move would be against her throne. Want of money forbade a major military effort, but the Fleet was sent to blockade the Scottish ports and prevent reinforcements arriving from France. Arms and supplies were smuggled across the Border to the Protestant party. Knox was permitted to return to his native land by way of Leith, and his preachings had a powerful effect. A small English army intervened on the Scottish Protestant side, and at this moment Mary of Guise died. Elizabeth's efforts had been modest, but they prevailed. By the Treaty of Leith in 1560 the Protestant cause in Scotland was assured for ever. France herself now plunged into religious strife, and was obliged at the same time to concentrate her forces against the

Habsburg Empire. Elizabeth gained a respite and could look squarely to the future.

One thing seemed certain to all contemporaries. The security of the English State depended in the last resort on an assured succession. If Elizabeth married an Englishman her authority might be weakened, and there would be fighting among the suitors. The perils of such a course were borne in on her as she watched the reactions of her Court to her long and deep affection for the handsome, ambitious Robert Dudley, a younger son of Northumberland, whom she made Earl of Leicester. This was no way out. During the first months of her reign she had also to consider the claims of her brother-in-law, Philip II of Spain. A Spanish marriage had brought disaster to her sister, but marriage to Philip might buy a powerful friend; refusal might drive his religious animosity into the open. Marriage into one of the reigning houses of Europe would mean entangling herself in its European policy and facing the hostility of her husband's rivals. In vain the Houses of Parliament begged their Virgin Queen to marry and produce an heir. Elizabeth was angry. She would admit no discussion.

Meanwhile there was Mary Stuart, Queen of Scots. Her young husband, King Francis II, had died shortly after his accession, and in December 1560 she returned to her own kingdom. Her mother's uncles, the Guises, soon lost their influence at the French Court, and her mother-in-law, Catherine de Médicis, replaced them as Regent for King Charles IX. Thus in the last half of the sixteenth century women for a time controlled three countries – France, England, and Scotland. Mary Stuart was a descendant of Henry VIII; she lived in an age when it was a novelty for a woman to be the head of a state; and she was now unmarried. Her presence in Scotland disturbed the delicate balance which Elizabeth had achieved by the Treaty of Leith. The Catholic English nobility, particularly in the North, were not indifferent to Mary's claims. Some of them dreamed of winning her hand. But Elizabeth knew her rival. She knew that Mary was incapable of separating her emotions from her politics. Mary had only been a few years in Scotland when she married her cousin, Henry Stuart, Lord Darnley, a weak, conceited youth who had both Tudor and Stuart blood in his veins. The result was disaster. The old feudal factions, now sharpened by religious conflict, seized Scotland in their grip. Mary's power melted slowly and steadily away. Favourites brought from the cultured French Court to cheer her in this grim land were unpopular, and one of them, David Riccio, was seized in her chamber and stabbed to death. Her husband became a tool of her opponents. In desperation she connived at his murder, and in 1567 married his murderer, a warlike Border lord, James Hepburn, Earl of Bothwell, whose unruly sword might yet save her throne and her happiness. But defeat and imprisonment followed, and in 1568 she escaped into England and threw herself upon the mercy of the waiting Elizabeth.

Mary in England proved even more dangerous than Mary in Scotland. She became the focus of plots and conspiracies against Elizabeth's life. The survival of Protestant England was menaced by her existence. Secret emissaries of Spain crept into the country to nourish rebellion and claim the allegiance of Elizabeth's Catholic subjects. The whole force of the Counter-Reformation was unloosed against the one united Protestant country in Europe. If England were destroyed it seemed that Protestantism could be stamped out in every other land. Assassination was to be the first step. But Elizabeth was well served. Francis Walsingham, Cecil's assistant and later his rival in the Government, tracked down Spanish agents and English traitors. This subtle intellectual and ardent Protestant, who had remained abroad throughout the reign of Mary Tudor, and whose knowledge of European politics surpassed that of anyone in Elizabeth's counsel, created the best secret service of any Government of the time. But there was always a chance that someone would slip through; there was always a danger so long as Mary lived that public discontent or private ambition would use her and her claims to destroy Elizabeth. In 1569 the threat became a reality.

In the North of England society was much more primitive than in the fertile South. Proud, independent, semi-feudal nobles now felt themselves threatened not only by Elizabeth's authority but by a host of new gentry like the Cecils and the Bacons, enriched by the dissolution of the monasteries and hungry for political power. Moreover there was a deep religious division between North and South. The South was largely Protestant; the North remained dominantly Catholic. The idea was now advanced that Mary should marry the Duke of Norfolk, senior of the pre-Tudor nobility, and his somewhat feeble head was turned at the prospect of gambling for a throne. He repented in time. But in 1569 the Earls of Northumberland and Westmorland led a rising in the North. Mary was confined at Tutbury in the care of Lord Hunsdon, Elizabeth's soldier cousin on the Boleyn side, a trustworthy servant throughout her reign, and one of her few relations. Before the rebels could seize her she was conveyed hurriedly southwards. In the South the Catholic lords made no move. The first act of the widespread Catholic conspiracy against Elizabeth was over. After twelve years of very patient rule she was unchallenged Queen of all England.

Rome was prompt to retaliate. In February 1570 Pope Pius V, a former Inquisitor-General, issued a Bull of excommunication against Elizabeth. From this moment Spain, as head of Catholic Europe, was supplied with a spiritual weapon should the need for attack arise. Elizabeth's position was weakened. She entered into negotiations with Catherine de Médicis, and a political alliance was concluded at Blois in April 1572. Both women distrusted the Spanish power, since Catherine realised that Catholic France had as much to fear from Spain as Protestant England. For a short time events ran with Elizabeth. Spain's weakness centred in the Netherlands, where a robust population with immense taxable resources had long fretted under Philip's rule. The whole territory was on the edge of rebellion. Elizabeth now had a potential new ally on the Continent. She even thought of marrying one of Queen Catherine's younger sons, on condition that France did not take advantage of the turmoil to expand into the Netherlands. But a terrible event in Paris dashed such prospects. By a sudden massacre of the Huguenots on the eve of the feast of St Bartholomew, August 23, 1572, the Guises, pro-Spanish and ultra-Catholic, recaptured the political power they had lost ten years earlier. Feeling ran high in London. The English Ambassador, Francis Walsingham, was recalled. When the French Ambassador came to explain away the event Elizabeth and her Court, clothed all in black, received him in silence. Having thus done her duty as a Protestant Queen, Elizabeth stood godmother to the French king's baby and continued her matrimonial negotiations with his brother.

Walsingham, now Secretary of State, and second only to Cecil in the Queen's Council, was far from content. Exile in Mary's reign and service as Ambassador in Paris had convinced him that Protestantism would only survive in Europe if England gave it unlimited encouragement and aid. In the long run there could be no compromise with the Catholics. Sooner or later war would come, and he urged that everything should be done to preserve and secure potential allies before the final clash. Opposed to all this was Cecil, now Lord Burghley. Friendship with Spain, symbolised in the marriage of Catherine of Aragon and nourished by commercial interests, had been a Tudor tradition since the days of Henry VII, and good relations with the Power that still controlled a large part of the Netherlands could alone preserve the great market for English wool and cloth. Queen Mary's marriage with Philip had been widely unpopular in England; but in Burghley's view this was no time to go to the opposite extreme and intervene in the Netherlands on the side of Philip's rebels. Such a step would inflame the Puritan extremists and inject a dangerous fanaticism into foreign policy. When Burghley became Lord Treasurer in 1572 his attitude hardened. Aware of the slender resources of the State, deeply concerned for the loss of trade with Spain and the Netherlands, he maintained that Walsingham's policy would founder in bankruptcy and disaster.

Elizabeth was inclined to agree. But Walsingham's case had been strengthened by the Massacre of St Bartholomew, and the Queen was compelled to move into a cold war in the Netherlands, and an undeclared war at sea, until she was confronted with the massive onslaught of an Armada. These happenings had their effect on politics in England. Most of the Puritans had at first been willing to conform to Elizabeth's Church Settlement in the hope of transforming it from within, but they now strove to drive the Government into an aggressive Protestant foreign policy, and at the same time secure their own freedom of religious organisation. Their position in the country was strong. They had allies at Court and Council, like Walsingham, with whom the Queen's favourite, Leicester, was now closely associated. In defiance of the Church Settlement they began to form their own religious communities, with their own ministers and forms of worship. Their aim and object was nothing less than the establishment of a theocratic despotism. Like the Catholics they held that Church and State were separate and independent. To such men the Elizabethan Settlement, the Anglican Church, with its historic liturgy and ceremonial, its comprehensive articles and its episcopal government, were abhorrent as unscriptural, as Calvin interpreted Scripture. A crack was opening in the surface of English society, a crack which would widen into a gulf. The Lutheran Church fitted well enough with monarchy, even with absolutism, but Calvinism, as it spread out over Europe, was a dissolving agency, and a violent interruption of historic continuity.

The Catholic onslaught also gathered force. Throughout the 1570s numbers of Catholic priests were arriving in England from the English seminaries at Douai and St Omer, charged with the task of nourishing Catholic sentiment and maintaining connection between the English Catholics and Rome. Their presence at first aroused little apprehension in Government circles. Elizabeth was slow to believe that any of her Catholic subjects were traitors, and the failure of the 1569 rising had strengthened her confidence in their loyalty. But about the year 1579 missionaries of a new and formidable type began to slip into the country. These were the Jesuits, the heralds and missionaries of the Counter-Reformation. Their lives were dedicated to re-establishing the Catholic faith throughout Christendom. Foremost among them were Edmund Campion and Robert Parsons. Their movements were carefully watched by Walsingham's spies, and a number of plots against Elizabeth's life were uncovered. The Government was forced to take more drastic measures. Queen Mary had burnt some three hundred Protestant martyrs in the last three years of her reign. In the last thirty years of Elizabeth's reign about the same number of Catholics were executed for treason.

The conspiracies naturally focused upon the person of Mary Queen of Scots, long captive. She was the heir to the English throne in the event of Elizabeth's removal from the world. Elizabeth herself was reluctant to recognise the danger to her life, yet the plots sharpened the question of who should succeed to the English throne. The death of Mary would make her son James the heir to the crown of England, and James was in safe Calvinist hands in Scotland. To avoid having another Catholic Queen it was only necessary to dispose of Mary before the Catholics, or their allies, disposed of Elizabeth. Walsingham and his party in the Council now concentrated their efforts on persuading the Queen that Mary must die. Plying her with evidence of Mary's complicity in the numerous conspiracies, they pressed hard on Elizabeth's conscience; but she shrank from the calculated shedding of royal blood.

In the midsummer of 1584 William the Silent, leader of the Dutch Protestant revolt against Spain, was fatally wounded by a Spanish agent in his house at Delft. Walsingham's arguments against Mary were overwhelmingly strengthened by this assassination, and English opinion reacted vehemently. At the same time Spanish feeling against England, already embittered, by the raids, conducted with Elizabeth's connivance, of the English privateers, blazed into startling hostility. The Netherlands, once Spanish order had been restored, were to be a base for a final attack upon the Island, and Elizabeth was compelled to send Leicester with an English army to Holland to prevent the complete destruction of the Dutch. A voluntary association of Protestant gentry was formed in 1585 for the defence of Elizabeth's life. In the following year evidence of a conspiracy, engineered by one Anthony Babington, an English Catholic, was laid before the Council by Walsingham. One of his agents had mingled with the conspirators for over a year. Mary's connivance was undeniable. Elizabeth was at last persuaded that her death was a political necessity. After a formal trial Mary was pronounced guilty of treason. Parliament petitioned for her execution, and Elizabeth at last signed the death warrant. Within twenty-four hours she regretted it and tried, too late, to stop the execution. She had a natural horror of being responsible for the judicial murder of a fellow sovereign. Although she knew it was essential for the safety of her country, she was anxious that the supreme and final decision should not rest upon her.

In the early morning of February 8, 1587, Mary was summoned to the great hall of Fotheringay Castle. Accompanied by six of her attendants, she awaited the servants of the English Queen. From the neighbouring countryside the gentry gathered to witness the sentence. Mary appeared at the appointed hour soberly clad in black satin. In the quietness of the hall she walked with stately movements to the cloth-covered scaffold erected by the fireplace. The solemn formalities were smoothly completed.

War was now certain. The chances were heavily weighted in favour of Spain. From the mines of Mexico and Peru there came a stream of silver and gold which so fortified the material power of the Spanish Empire that King Philip could equip his forces beyond all known scales. The treasure must therefore be arrested at its source or captured from the ships which conveyed it across the oceans. In the hope of strengthening her own finances and harassing the enemy's preparations against the Netherlands and ultimately against herself, Elizabeth had accordingly sanctioned a number of unofficial expeditions against the Spanish coasts and colonies in South America. Gradually these expeditions had assumed an official character, and the Royal Navy surviving from the days of Henry VIII was rebuilt and reorganised by John Hawkins, son of a Plymouth merchant, who had formerly traded with the Portuguese possessions in Brazil. Hawkins had learnt his seamanship in slave-running on the West African coast and in shipping negroes to the Spanish colonies. In 1573 he was appointed Treasurer and Controller of the Navy. He had moreover educated an apt pupil, a young adventurer from Devon, Francis Drake.

This "Master Thief of the unknown world", as his Spanish contemporaries called Drake, became the terror of their ports and crews. His avowed object was to force England into open conflict with Spain, and his attacks on the Spanish treasure ships, his plundering of Spanish possessions on the western coast of the South American continent on his voyage round the world in 1577, and raids on Spanish harbours in Europe, all played their part in driving Spain to war. From their experiences on the Spanish Main the English seamen knew they could meet the challenge so long as reasonable equality was maintained.

With the ships that Hawkins built they could fight and sink anything the Spaniards might send against them.

Most of the King of Spain's ships came from his Italian possessions and were built for use in the Mediterranean. They were unsuited to a voyage round the western coasts of Europe and up the Channel. The galleons constructed for the trade routes to the Spanish colonies in South America were too unwieldy. But in the year 1580 Philip II had annexed Portugal, and the Portuguese naval constructors had not been dominated by the Mediterranean. They had experimented with classes of ships for action in the South Atlantic, and Portuguese galleons therefore formed the basis of the fleet which was now concentrated in the harbour of Lisbon. Preparations were delayed for a year by Drake's famous raid on Cadiz in 1587. In this "singeing of the King of Spain's beard" a large quantity of stores and ships was destroyed. Nevertheless in May 1588 the Armada was ready.

A hundred and thirty ships were assembled, carrying 2,500 guns and more than 30,000 men, two-thirds of them soldiers. Twenty were galleons, forty-four were armed merchantmen, and eight were Mediterranean galleys. The rest were either small craft or unarmed transports. Their aim was to sail up the Channel, embark the expeditionary corps of 16,000 veterans from the Netherlands under Alexander of Parma, and land it on the south coast of England.[1]

The renowned Spanish Admiral Santa Cruz was now dead, and the command was entrusted to the Duke of Medina-Sidonia, who had many misgivings about the enterprise. His tactics followed the Mediterranean model of grappling with the enemy ships and gaining victory by boarding. His fleet was admirably equipped for carrying large numbers of men; it was strong in heavy short-range cannon, but weak in long-distance culverins – which was why the English kept out of range until the last battle. The seamen were few in proportion to the soldiers. These were recruited from the dregs of the Spanish population and commanded by army officers of noble families who had no experience of naval warfare. Many of the vessels were in bad repair; the provisions supplied under a corrupt system of private contract were insufficient and rotten; the drinking water leaked from butts of unseasoned wood. Their commander had no experience of war at sea, and had begged the King to excuse him from so novel an adventure.

It was uncertain where the attack would fall, but the prevailing westerly winds made it likely that the Armada would sail up the Channel, join Parma, and force a landing on the Essex coast. The nation was united in the face of the Spanish preparations. Leading Catholics were interned in the Isle of Ely, but as a body their loyalty to the Crown was unshaken. An army was assembled at Tilbury which reached twenty thousand men, under the command of Lord Leicester. This, with the muster in the adjacent counties, constituted a force which should not be underrated.

---

1   Troops were not the difficulty. If order were maintained for a while in the Netherlands an expeditionary force could be detached from the Spanish army. A corps was deemed sufficient.

Hawkins's work for the Navy was now to be tested. He had begun over the years to revise the design of English ships from his experience of buccaneering raids in colonial waters. The castles which towered above the galleon decks had been cut down; keels were deepened, and design was concentrated on sea-worthiness and speed. Most notable of all, heavier long-range guns were mounted. Cannon were traditionally deemed "an ignoble arm", fit only for an opening salvo to a grappling fight, but Hawkins, with ships built to weather any seas, opposed hand-to-hand fighting and advocated battering the enemy from a distance with the new guns. The English sea-captains were eager to try these novel tactics against the huge overmasted enemy galleons, with their flat bottoms and a tendency to drift in a high wind. In spite of Hawkins's efforts only thirty-four of the Queen's ships, carrying six thousand men, could put to sea in 1588. As was the custom, however, all available privately owned vessels were hastily collected and armed for the service of the Government, and a total of a hundred and ninety-seven ships was mustered; but at least half of them were too small to be of much service.

The Queen had urged her seamen to "keep an eye upon Parma", and she was nervous of sending the main fleet as far west as Plymouth. Drake was for bolder measures. In a dispatch of March 30, 1588, he proposed sending the main body to attack a port on the Spanish coast – not Lisbon, which was well fortified, but somewhere near by, so as to force the Armada to sea in defence of the coastline. Thus, it was argued, the English would be certain of engaging the Spanish fleet and there would be no danger of its slipping past them on a favourable wind into the Channel.

The Government preferred the much more perilous idea of stationing isolated squadrons at intervals along the south coast to meet all possible lines of attack. They insisted on concentrating a small squadron of the Queen's ships at the eastern end of the Channel to keep watch on Parma. Drake and his superior, Lord Howard of Effingham, the commander of the English fleet, were alarmed and impatient, and with the greatest difficulty prevented a further dispersion of their forces. A southerly gale stopped their attacking the Spanish coast, and they were driven into Plymouth with their supplies exhausted and scurvy raging through the ships. In the event they had plenty of time to consider their strategy. The Armada left the Tagus on May 20, but was smitten by the same storms which had repulsed Howard and Drake. Two of their 1,000-ton ships were dismasted. They put in to refit at Corunna, and did not set sail again until July 12. News of their approach off the Lizard was brought into Plymouth harbour on the evening of July 19. The English fleet had to put out of the Sound the same night against light adverse winds which freshened the following day. A sober nautical account of the operation is preserved in Howard's letter to Walsingham of July 21:

> Although the wind was very scant we first warped out of harbour that night, and upon Saturday turned out very hardly, the wind being at south-west; and about three o'clock of the afternoon descried the Spanish fleet, and did what we

could to work for the wind, which [by this] morning we had recovered, descryng their fleet to consist of 120 sail, whereof there are four galleases [galleys] and many ships of great burden. At nine of the clock we gave them fight, which continued until one.[1]

If Medina-Sidonia had attacked the English vessels to leeward of his ships as they struggled to clear the land on the Saturday there would have been a disaster. But his instructions bound him to sail up the Channel, unite with Parma, and help transport to England the veteran troops assembled near Dunkirk. By difficult, patient, precarious tacking the English fleet got to windward of him, and for nine days hung upon the Armada as it ran before the westerly wind up the Channel, pounding away with their long-range guns at the lumbering galleons. They had gained the weather gauge. On July 23 the wind sank and both fleets lay becalmed off Portland Bill. The Spaniards attempted a counter-attack with Neapolitan galleys, rowed by hundreds of slaves, but Drake, followed by Howard, swept in upon the main body, and, as Howard reported, "the Spaniards were forced to give way and flocked together like sheep".

A further engagement followed on the 25th off the Isle of Wight. It looked as if the Spaniards planned to seize the island as a base. But as the westerly breeze blew stronger the English still lay to windward and drove them once more to sea in the direction of Calais, where Medina, ignorant of Parma's movements, hoped to collect news. The Channel passage was a torment to the Spaniards. The guns of the English ships raked the decks of the galleons, killing the crews and demoralising the soldiers. The English suffered hardly any loss.

Medina then made a fatal mistake. He anchored in Calais Roads. The Queen's ships which had been stationed in the eastern end of the Channel joined the main fleet in the straits, and the whole sea-power of England was now combined. A council of war held in the English flagship during the evening of July 28 resolved to attack. The decisive engagement opened. After darkness had fallen eight ships from the eastern squadron which had been filled with explosives and prepared as fire-ships – the torpedoes of those days – were sent against the crowded Spanish fleet at anchor in the roads. Lying on their decks, the Spanish crews must have seen unusual lights creeping along the decks of strange vessels moving towards them. Suddenly a series of explosions shook the air, and flaming hulks drifted towards the anchored Armada. The Spanish captains cut their cables and made for the open sea. Collisions without number followed. One of the largest galleys, the *San Lorenzo*, lost its rudder and drifted aground in Calais harbour, where the Governor interned the crew. The rest of the fleet, with a south-south-west wind behind it, made eastwards to Gravelines.

Medina now sent messengers to Parma announcing his arrival, and by dawn on July 29 he was off the sandbanks of Gravelines expecting to find Parma's

1   Laughton, *Defeat of the Spanish Armada* (Navy Records Society, 1894), vol. i, p. 273. [Churchill]

troops ready shipped in their transports. But there was no sail to be seen. The tides in Dunkirk harbour were at the neap. It was only possible to sail out with a favourable wind upon a spring tide. Neither condition was present. The army and the transports were not at their rendezvous. The Spaniards turned to face their pursuers. A long and desperate fight raged for eight hours, a confused conflict of ships engaging at close quarters. The official report sent to the English Government was brief: "Howard in fight spoiled a great number of the Spaniards, sank three and drove four or five on the banks." The English had completely exhausted their ammunition, and but for this hardly a Spanish ship would have got away. Yet Howard himself scarcely realised the magnitude of his victory. "Their force is wonderful great and strong," he wrote on the evening after the battle, "yet we pluck their feathers by little and little."

The tormented Armada now sailed northwards out of the fight. Their one aim was to make for home. The horrors of the long voyage round the north of Scotland began. Not once did they turn upon the small, silent ships which followed them in their course. Neither side had enough ammunition. The homeward voyage of the Armada proved the qualities of the Spanish seamen. Facing mountainous seas and racing tides, they escaped from their pursuers. The English ships, short of food and shot, their crews grumbling at their wretched outfits, were compelled to turn southwards to the Channel ports. The weather helped the Spaniards. The westerly wind drove two of the galleons as wrecks upon the coast of Norway; but then it shifted. As Medina recorded, "We passed the isles at the north of Scotland, and we are now sailing towards Spain with the wind at north-east." Sailing southwards, they were forced to make for the western coast of Ireland to replenish their supplies of water. They had already cast their horses and mules into the sea. The decision to put in on the Irish coast was disastrous. Their ships had been shattered by the English cannonades and now were struck by the autumn gales. Seventeen went ashore. The search for water cost more than five thousand Spanish lives. Nevertheless over sixty-five ships, about half of the fleet that had put to sea, reached Spanish ports during the month of October.

The English had not lost a single ship, and scarcely a hundred men. But their captains were disappointed. For the last thirty years they had believed themselves superior to their opponents. They had now found themselves fighting a much bigger fleet than they had imagined the Spaniards could put to sea. Their own ships had been sparingly equipped. Their ammunition had run short at a crucial moment. The gunnery of the merchant vessels had proved poor and half the enemy's fleet had got away. There were no boastings; they recorded their dissatisfactions. But to the English people as a whole the defeat of the Armada came as a miracle.

England had emerged from the Armada year as a first-class Power. She had resisted the weight of the mightiest empire that had been seen since Roman times. Her people awoke to a consciousness of their greatness, and the last years of Elizabeth's reign saw a welling up of national energy and enthusiasm focusing upon the person of the Queen. In the year following the Armada the first three books were published of Spenser's *Faerie Queene*, in which Elizabeth is hymned as Gloriana. Poets and courtiers alike paid their homage to the sovereign who symbolised the great achievement. Elizabeth had schooled a generation of Englishmen.

The success of the seamen pointed the way to wide opportunities of winning wealth and fame in daring expeditions. In 1589 Richard Hakluyt published his magnificent book, *The Principal Navigations, Traffics and Discoveries of the English Nation*. Here in their own words the audacious navigators tell their story. Hakluyt speaks for the thrusting spirit of the age when he proclaims that the English nation, "in searching the most opposite corners and quarters of the world, and, to speak plainly, in compassing the vast globe of the earth more than once, have excelled all the nations and peoples of the earth". Before the reign came to a close another significant enterprise took its beginning. For years past Englishmen had been probing their way through to the East, round the Cape of Good Hope and overland across the expanses of the Middle East. Their ventures led to the founding of the East India Company. At the start it was a small and struggling affair, with a capital of only £72,000. Dazzling dividends were to be won from this investment. The British Empire in India, which was to be painfully built up in the course of the next three centuries, owes its origins to the charter granted by Queen Elizabeth to a group of London merchants and financiers in the year 1600.

But there was no way of delivering a decisive stroke against Spain. The English Government had no money for further efforts. The total revenues of the Crown hardly exceeded £300,000 a year, including the fruits of taxation granted by Parliament. Out of this sum all expenses of Court and Government had to be met. The cost of defeating the Armada is reckoned to have amounted to £160,000, and the Netherlands expeditionary force at one stage was calling for £126,000 a year. The lights of enthusiasm slowly faded out. In 1595 Walter Raleigh again tried his hand, this time in search of Eldorado in Guiana. But his expedition brought no profits home. At the same time Drake and the veteran Hawkins, now in his sixties, set out on a last voyage. Hawkins fell ill, and as his fleet was anchoring off Porto Rico he died in his cabin. Drake, cast down by the death of his old patron, sailed on to attack the rich city of Panama. With a dash of his former spirit he swept into the bay of Nombre de Dios. But conditions were now very different. The early days had gone for ever. Spanish government in the New World was well equipped and well armed. The raid was beaten off. The English fleet put out to sea, and in January 1596 Francis Drake, having assumed his armour to meet death like a soldier, expired in his ship. As the conflict with Spain drew inconclusively on, and both sides struck at each other in ever-growing, offensive exhaustion, the heroic age of sea fights passed away.

Victory over Spain was the most shining achievement of Elizabeth's reign, but by no means the only one. The repulse of the Armada had subdued religious dissension at home. Events which had swung England towards Puritanism while the Catholic danger was impending swung her back to the Anglican settlement when the peril vanished in the smoke of the burning Armada at Gravelines. A few months later, in a sermon at St Paul's Cross, Richard Bancroft, who was later to be Archbishop of Canterbury, attacked the Puritan theme with the confidence of a man who was convinced that the Anglican Church was not a political contrivance, but a divine institution. He took the only line on which the defence of the Church could be sustained with an enthusiasm equal to that of its assailants: it was not "the religion set forth by Her Majesty", but the Church of the Apostles still subsisting by virtue of the episcopal succession. But Bancroft saw also that to maintain the cause a better type of clergy was needed, men of "solid learning", and such he set himself to provide.

The Church Elizabeth had nursed to strength was a very different body from the half-hearted and distracted community of her early years: more confident, more learned, far less inclined to compromise with dissidents within or separatists without; strong in the attachment of thousands to whom its liturgy had become dear by habit and who thought of it as the Church into which they had been baptised. Their devotion to the Church of England as a sacred institution was as profound and sincere as the attachment of the Calvinist to his presbytery or the Independent to his congregation.

By now the men who had governed England since the 1550s were passing from power and success to their graves. War with Spain had set a premium on martial virtues. Young and eager men like Walter Raleigh and Robert Devereux, Earl of Essex, quarrelled for permission to lead enterprises against the Spaniards. The Queen hesitated. She knew that the security she had striven for all her life was very fragile. She knew the danger of provoking the might of Spain, backed as it was by all the wealth of the Indies. She was growing old and out of touch with the younger generation, and her quarrel with Essex marked and revealed her changing mood. Essex was Leicester's[1] stepson, and Leicester brought him into the circle of the Court. He found the Government in the hands of the cautious Cecils, William, Lord Burghley, and his son Robert. The Queen's favour had lighted upon the hard, handsome, and ambitious Captain of the Guard, Sir Walter Raleigh. Essex was the younger and the more fiery, and he soon displaced the Captain in the affections of Elizabeth. He too was ambitious, and set out to create his own party in Court and Council and subdue the influence of the Cecils. He found support in the Bacon brothers, Anthony and Francis, sons of the Lord Keeper, Nicholas Bacon, who had earlier in the reign been a colleague and brother-in-law of Burghley's. The young nephews were discontented with their uncle's lack of attention. They were dangerous enemies, and Essex was a convenient figurehead for thrusting a more forward policy upon the Queen. They had

---

[1] Robert Dudley, Earl of Leicester (c.1532–88) a favourite of Elizabeth. His wife, Amy Robsart was found dead with her neck broken in 1560. Some believed she'd been murdered to further the chance of Dudley marrying the Queen. In 1578, he married the widow of the first Earl of Essex.

both served in the Embassy in Paris, and, like Walsingham, had built up an admirable intelligence service. It was with their help that Essex became an expert on foreign affairs and showed the Queen that he had ability as well as charm. In 1593 he was made a Privy Counsellor. Relations with Spain were again becoming tense. Essex soon headed the war party in the Council; and once the old Lord Treasurer pulled a Prayer Book out of his pocket and, shaking a finger at his young opponent, read out the verse, "Bloodthirsty and deceitful men shall not live out half their days." In 1596 an expedition was sent against Cadiz under the joint command of Essex and Raleigh. In the sea fight for the harbour Raleigh was the outstanding leader. The Spanish fleet was burned and the town lay open to the English crews. Essex was the hero of the shore fight. It was a brilliant combined operation, and Cadiz was held by the English for a fortnight. The fleet returned home triumphant, but, to Elizabeth's regret, little the richer. During its absence Robert Cecil had become Secretary of State.

Victory at Cadiz heightened the popularity of Essex among the younger members of the Court and throughout the country. The Queen received him graciously, but with secret misgiving. Was he the incarnation of the spirit of this new generation, whose rash eagerness she feared? Would the younger men look to him rather than to her as their leader? For the moment all went well. Essex was made Master of the Ordnance. He was given command of an expedition to intercept a further Armada now gathering in the ports of Western Spain. In the summer of 1597 it seemed that another "Enterprise of England" was about to sail. The English ships headed south-west and made for the Azores. There was no sign of the great fleet whose passage they were to bar, but the islands made a convenient base where they could await the treasure ships from the New World. Raleigh too was in the expedition. The English failed to take any of the island ports; the Spanish Treasure Fleet eluded them; the Armada put out into the Bay of Biscay with the seas clear of defending ships to the north. Once again the winds saved the Island. The badly manned galleons tottered into a northern gale scattered and sinking. The disorganised fleet crept back into its ports. King Philip was kneeling in his chapel in the Escorial praying for his ships. Before the news of their return could reach him he was seized with a paralytic stroke, and the tale of their failure was brought to him on his deathbed.

Essex came home to find a sovereign still vigorous and dominating. The muddle and quarrelling which had marred the Azores expedition enraged Elizabeth. She declared she would never send the Fleet out of the Channel again, and this time she kept her word. Essex retired from Court, and was sure he was misunderstood. There was a plaintive correspondence. Wild thoughts went surging through his mind. A little group gathered round him and schemed to force the sun of the royal favour into the heavens again. Troubles in Ireland, which now came to a head, seemed to offer him the chance of recovering both the Queen's goodwill and his own prestige. The Counter-Reformation revived and reanimated opposition to Protestant England. For the Queen's Government in London this meant strategic anxieties, since any Power hostile to England could readily take advantage of Irish discontents. In the first thirty years of Elizabeth's reign Ireland was shaken by three major rebellions. Now in the 1590s a fourth rising had erupted into a wearing and expensive war.

With Spanish backing, Hugh O'Neill, Earl of Tyrone, was threatening the whole English dominance of Ireland. If Essex became Lord Deputy and destroyed the rebellion he might recover his power in England. It was a perilous gamble. In April 1599 Essex was allowed to go to Ireland, at the head of the largest army that England had ever sent there. He accomplished nothing and was on the verge of ruin. But he planned a dramatic stroke. Disobeying the express orders of the Queen, he deserted his command and rode in haste to London unannounced. Robert Cecil had quietly waited for his rival to overreach himself. Angry scenes followed between Essex and the Queen, and the Earl was confined to his house. Weeks dragged by, and a desperate plot was made by Essex and his younger companions, including Shakespeare's patron, the Earl of Southampton. There was to be a rising in the City, a concentration upon Whitehall, and a seizure of the Queen's person. To symbolise the result a new play, which culminated in a royal dethronement, was to be produced at Southwark – Shakespeare's *Richard II*.[1] The scheme failed, and the end came in February 1601 with Essex's death within the Tower. Elizabeth well understood the issues at stake. This was not yet an age of party politics, but of patronage and clientage. In destroying Essex she saved England from the consumption of civil war.

In Ireland, Essex was succeeded by Lord Mountjoy, a tenacious and energetic commander, who soon had the rebellion under control. When a Spanish force, some four thousand strong, landed at Kinsale in 1601 they were too late. Mountjoy routed their Irish allies and compelled the Spaniards to surrender. Even Tyrone finally made his submission. Ireland had at last, though only temporarily, been conquered by English arms.

If Essex challenged the political power of Elizabeth, more significant was the challenge to her constitutional power in the Parliament of 1601. Throughout the reign the weight and authority of Parliament had been steadily growing. Now the issue turned on monopolies. For some time the Crown had eked out its slender income by various devices, including the granting of patents of monopolies to courtiers and others in return for payment. Some of these grants could be justified as protecting and encouraging inventions, but frequently they amounted merely to unjustified privileges, involving high prices that placed a burden upon every citizen. In 1601 grievances flared up into a full-dress debate in the House of Commons. An angry Member read out a list extending from a patent for iron manufacture to a patent for drying pilchards. If the Commons pushed their proposals to a division the whole basis

---

1   Essex's "rebellion" took place on February 8, 1601. Shakespeare's *Richard II* had been first performed six years earlier, in 1595, and the first quarto dates from 1597. The assertion of a connection between the play and Essex should, therefore, be viewed with some caution.

of her constitutional authority would be under fire. She acted swiftly. Some monopolies were abolished forthwith. All, she promised, would be investigated. So she forestalled the direct challenge, and in a golden speech to a large gathering of her Commons summoned to her chamber she told them, "Though God hath raised me high, yet this I account the glory of my crown, that I have reigned with your loves." It was to be her last appearance in their midst.

In the early hours of the morning of March 24, 1603, Queen Elizabeth died. Thus ended the Tudor dynasty. For over a hundred years, with a handful of bodyguards, the Tudors had maintained their sovereignty, kept the peace, baffled the diplomacy and onslaughts of Europe, and guided the country through changes which might well have wrecked it. Parliament was becoming a solid affair based on a working harmony between Sovereign, Lords and Commons, and the traditions of English monarchical government had been restored and gloriously enhanced. But these achievements carried no guarantee of their perpetuation. The monarchy could only govern if it was popular. The Crown was now to pass to an alien Scottish line, hostile in political instincts to the class which administered England. The good understanding with Parliament which the Tudors had nourished came to a fretful close.

CHAPTER TWENTY-SEVEN

THE UNITED CROWNS

King James — the Royal prerogative — the Puritans' Petition — No Bishop, No King — the Gunpowder Plot — the Authorised Version of the Bible — Chief Justice Coke — alliance with Spain — Princess Elizabeth weds the Elector Frederick — the execution of Raleigh — George Villiers, Duke of Buckingham — the death of James I — the Pilgrim Fathers and the New World

KING JAMES VI of Scotland was the only son of Mary Queen of Scots. He had been subjected from his youth to a rigid Calvinist upbringing which was not much to his taste. With little money and strict tutors he had long coveted the throne of England, but till the last moment the prize had seemed elusive. But now all appeared settled. Cecil was his ally and skilful manager in the tense days after the Queen died. James was proclaimed King James I of England without opposition, and in April 1603 began a leisurely journey from Holyrood to London. He had fixed ideas about kingship and the divine right of monarchs to rule. He was a scholar with pretensions of being a philosopher, and in the course of his life published numerous tracts and treatises, ranging from denunciations of witchcraft and tobacco to abstract political theory. He came to England with a closed mind, and a weakness for lecturing. But England was changing. The habit of obedience to a dynasty had died with the last of the Tudors. Spain was no longer a threat, and the Union of the Crowns deprived foreign enemies of an ally, or even a foothold, in the Island.

The country gentlemen on whom the Tudors relied to maintain a balance against the old nobility, and on whom they had devolved the whole business of local government, were beginning to feel their strength. England was secure, free to attend to her own concerns, and a powerful class was now eager to take a hand in their management. On the other hand, James's title to the Crown was not impeccable, and the doctrine of Divine Right, originally devised to justify the existence of national sovereignties against a universal Church or Empire, was called in to fortify his position. But how to reconcile a King claiming to rule by Divine Right and a Parliament with no other basis than ancient customs?

His first Parliament at once raised the question of Parliamentary privilege and Royal Prerogative. In dutiful but firm language the Commons drew up an Apology reminding the King that their liberties included free elections, free speech, and freedom from arrest during Parliamentary sessions. James, like his son after him, treated these expressions of national grievance contemptuously, brushing them aside as personal insults to himself and mere breaches of good manners. Hitherto James had been straitened; now he thought he was rich. The "beggarly Scotsmen" who had come South with him also enriched themselves. The expenses of the Court increased at an alarming rate. To his surprise James very soon found himself pressed for money. This meant frequent Parliaments. Frequent Parliaments gave members the opportunity to organise themselves, and James neglected to control Parliamentary sessions through his Privy Counsellors, as Elizabeth had done. Robert Cecil, now Earl of Salisbury, had no direct contact with the Commons. The King indulged his taste for lecturing, and frequently reminded them of his Divine Right to rule and their solemn duty to supply his needs.

It was an ancient and obstinate belief that the King should "live of his own", and that the traditional revenues from the Crown lands and from the customs should suffice for the upkeep of the public services. Parliament normally voted customs duties to each monarch for life, and did not expect to have to provide more money except in emergencies. To meet his needs James had to stress and revive the prerogative rights of taxation of the medieval kings, and he soon irritated a House which remembered its recent victory over Elizabeth upon monopolies. Fortunately the judges ruled that the ports were under the King's exclusive jurisdiction and that he could issue a "book of rates" – that is, impose extra customs duties – as he thought fit. This gave James a revenue that, unlike the old feudal grants, rose with the increasing national wealth and the higher prices. The Commons questioned the judges' ruling, and James made matters worse by turning the argument into a technical one about Royal Prerogative. Here, but only for a time, the matter rested.

The King had decided views on religion. He was greeted upon his accession with a petition from the Puritans, whose organisation Elizabeth had broken in the 1590s. These opponents of the episcopal State Church now hoped that the new King from Calvinist Scotland would listen to their case; a milder party would have been satisfied with some modification of ceremony. But James had had enough of the Kirk. He realised that Calvinism and monarchy would quarrel in the long run and that if men could decide for themselves about religion they could also decide for themselves on politics. In 1604 he held a conference at Hampton Court between the Puritan leaders and those who accepted the Elizabethan system. His prejudice was soon manifest. In the middle of the debate he accused the Puritans of aiming "as a Scottish presbytery which agreeth as well with the monarch as God and the Devil". James made it clear there would be no changes in the Elizabethan Church Settlement. His slogan was "No Bishop, no King".

The Catholics were also anxious and hopeful. After all, the King's mother had been their champion. Their position was delicate. If the Pope would allow them to give their secular allegiance to the King, James might let them practise their own religion. But the Pope would not yield. A European controversy was raging about the nature of obedience, and James plunged into the argument. The Jesuits who had assailed Elizabeth were all-powerful at Rome, and replied with many volumes attacking his right to the throne. The air seemed charged with plots. James, although inclined to toleration, was forced to act. Catholics were fined for refusing to attend the services of the Established Church and their priests were banished.

Disappointment and despair led a small group of Catholic gentry to an infernal design for blowing up James and his whole Parliament by gunpowder while they were in session at Westminster.[1] They hoped that this would be followed by a Catholic rising and that in the confusion a Catholic régime might be re-established with Spanish help. The chief plotter was Robert Catesby, assisted by Guy Fawkes, a veteran of the Spanish wars against the Dutch. One of their followers warned a relative who was a Catholic peer. The story reached Cecil, and the cellars of Parliament were searched. Fawkes was taken on the spot, and there was a storm of excitement in the City. James went down to open Parliament, and made an emotional speech upon what an honourable end it would have been to die with his faithful Commons. The House displayed an incomprehensible indifference, and, turning to the business of the day, discussed the petition of a Member who had asked to be relieved of his Parliamentary duties owing to an attack of gout. The conspirators were hunted down, tortured, and executed.[2]

At this time a splendid and lasting monument was created to the genius of the English-speaking peoples. All the Puritan demands had been rejected, but towards the end of the Hampton Court conference a Puritan divine, Dr John Reynolds, President of the Oxford College of Corpus Christi, had asked seemingly on the spur of the moment, if a new version of the Bible could be produced. The idea appealed to James. Till now the clergy and laity had relied on a number of different translations – Tyndales's, Coverdale's, the Geneva Bible, the "Bishop's Bible" of Queen Elizabeth. Their texts varied. Some were disfigured by marginal notes and glosses upholding and advocating partisan interpretations of Scripture and extremist theories of ecclesiastical organisation. Each party and sect used the version which best suited its own views and doctrines. Here, thought James, was the chance to rid the Scriptures of propaganda and produce a uniform version which could be entrusted to all. Within a few months committees or "companies" were set up, two each in Oxford, Cambridge, and Westminster, comprising in all about fifty scholars and divines. They were selected for this work without regard to their theological or ecclesiastical bias. Directions were issued with speed. Each committee was assigned a portion of the text, and their draft was to be scrutinised by all the other committees and finally revised by a committee of

1   5 November 1606.
2   The Thanksgiving Service for the deliverance of November 5 was not removed from the Prayer Book until 1854. [Churchill]

twelve. Tendentious renderings were forbidden, and marginal notes or glosses were prohibited except for cross-references or to explain the meaning of Greek or Hebrew words which were difficult to translate. About three years passed in preliminary research, and the main work did not get under way till 1607, but it was then accomplished with remarkable swiftness. In an age without an efficient postal service or mechanical methods of copying and duplicating texts, the committees, though separated by considerable distances, finished their task in 1609. Nine months sufficed for the scrutiny of the supervisory committee, and in 1611 the Authorised Version of the Bible was produced by the King's Printer. It won an immediate and lasting triumph. Copies could be bought for as little as five shillings. It superseded all other versions. No new revision was deemed necessary for nearly three hundred years.

James and his Parliaments grew more and more out of sympathy as the years went by. James saw himself as the schoolmaster of the whole Island. In theory there was a good case for absolute monarchy. The whole political development of the sixteenth century was on his side. He found a brilliant supporter in the person of Francis Bacon, the ambitious lawyer who had dabbled in politics with Essex, and crept back to obedience when his patron fell. Bacon held a succession of high legal offices, culminating in the Lord Chancellorship. He maintained that the absolute and enlightened rule of the King with the help of his judges was justified by its efficiency, but his theories were unreal and widely unpopular.

The subsequent conflict centred on the nature of the Royal Prerogative and the powers of an Act of Parliament. The modern view had not yet emerged that an Act of Parliament is supreme and unalterable unless repealed or amended, and that the sovereign power of the State can be exercised in no other way. The Tudor statutes had indeed been the instruments of profound changes in the Church and State, and there seemed little they could not do. But statutes required both the assent of Parliament and the approval of the King. No Parliament could meet without the summons of the King, or sit after he had dismissed it. Little else but financial necessity could compel the King to call a Parliament. If money could be raised elsewhere he might govern for years at a time without one. Moreover, a certain undefined prerogative power the King assuredly had; the exigencies of government required it. Who was to say what he could and could not do? If the King chose, on grounds of public interest, to make an ordinance dispensing with a statute, who could say he was acting illegally? At this point the Common Lawyers, headed by Chief Justice Coke, stepped to the forefront of English history.

Coke, one of the most learned of English judges, gave a blunt answer to these controversies. He declared that conflict between Prerogative and statute should be resolved not by the Crown but by the judges. It was a tremendous assertion, for if the judges were to decide which laws were valid and which were not they would become the ultimate lawgivers in the State. They would form a Supreme Court, assessing the legality of both royal and Parliamentary enactments. Coke's high claims were not without foundation. They rested on the ancient tradition that law declared in the courts was superior to law published by the central authority. Coke himself was reluctant to admit that law could be made, or even changed. It existed already, merely awaiting revelation and exposition. If Acts of Parliament conflicted with it they were invalid. Thus at the beginning of his career Coke was not fighting on the same side as Parliament. In England his main assertions on behalf of fundamental law were overruled.

James had a very different view of the function of judges. They might have the duty of deciding between the conflicting claims of statute and Prerogative, but if so they were bound to decide in the Crown's favour. Their business, as Bacon put it, was to be "lions under the throne". As judges were appointed by the King and held office during his good pleasure, they should obey him like other royal servants. The controversy was embittered by personal rivalry between Bacon and Coke, who now found himself in an untenable position. No judge could be impartial about the King's Prerogative if he were liable to instant dismissal on the King's command. James first tired to muzzle Coke by promoting him from the Court of Common Pleas to the King's Bench. Unsuccessful in this, he dismissed him in 1616. The remaining members of the Bench sided with the King. Five years later Coke entered the House of Commons and found that the most active lawyers of the day were in agreement with him. Their leadership was readily accepted. Few of the country gentlemen sitting in the Commons had any deep knowledge of Parliamentary history, or could produce any coherent theory to justify the claims of Parliament. They simply felt a smouldering injustice at the arbitrary conduct and jarring theories of the King. For all its stirring movements, this was an age of profound respect for precedents and constitutional forms. If the lawyers had remained solid for the Crown and the whole weight of legal opinion been thrown into the royal scale the Commons's task would have been much harder. With all the force of interpreted precedent against them, they would have had to break with the past and admit they were revolutionaries. But the adherence of the lawyers freed them from an agonising choice. Coke, Selden,[1] and others, including Pym, who had read law at the Middle Temple even if he had not practised, formed a group of able leaders, who took and held the initiative. Learned in the law, and not always too scrupulous in the interpretations they twisted from it, they gradually built up a case on which Parliament could claim with conviction that it was fighting, not for something new, but for the traditional and lawful heritage of the united and disciplined opposition which Pym was to lead against King Charles.

James's foreign policy perhaps met the needs of the age for peace, but often clashed with its temper. The main struggle had already shifted from the high

---

1   John Selden (1584–1654) a Middle Temple lawyer and oriental scholar. Imprisoned for questioning King James's claim that Parliamentary Privileges were gifts of the monarchy. In 1628 he was one of the authors of the Petition of Right. Although opposed to Charles I, he took no part in Laud's prosecution and disapproved of the execution of Charles I.

seas to Europe. The house of Habsburg, at the head of the Holy Roman Empire, still dominated the Continent from Vienna. The territories of the Emperor and of his cousin the King of Spain now stretched from Portugal to Poland, and their power was backed by the proselytising fervour of the Jesuits. The Commons and the country remained vehemently hostile to Spain, and viewed with alarm and anxiety the march of the Counter-Reformation. But James was unmoved. He regarded the Dutch as rebels against the Divine Right of Kings. The Spanish Ambassador, Count Gondomar, financed a pro-Spanish party at the new Court; learning nothing from Tudor experience, James proposed not merely an alliance with Spain but a Spanish match for his son.

His daughter, however, was already in the opposite camp. The Princess Elizabeth had married one of the Protestant champions of Europe, Frederick, the Elector Palatine of the Rhine,[1] and Frederick was soon projected into violent revolt against the Habsburg Emperor Ferdinand. Habsburg attempts to recover for the Catholic faith those areas in Germany which the law of the Empire had recognised as Protestant provoked the vehement opposition of the Protestant princes. The storm-centre was Bohemia, where a haughty, resolute Czech nobility obstructed the centralising policy of Vienna both in religion and politics. In the fifteenth-century days of John Huss they had set up their own Church and fought both Pope and Emperor. Now they defied Ferdinand. In 1618 their leaders flung the imperial envoys from the windows of the royal palace in Prague. This action, later known as the Defenestration, started a war which was to ravage Germany for thirty years. The Czechs offered Frederick the throne of Bohemia. Frederick accepted and became the recognised leader of the Protestant revolt.

Although his daughter was now Queen of Bohemia, James showed no wish to intervene on her behalf. He was resolved to keep out of the conflict in Europe at all costs, and judged he could best help his son-in-law's cause through friendship with Spain. Parliament was indignant and alarmed. He reminded them that these matters were beyond their scope. No taunts of personal timidity moved him. He stuck to his convictions and kept the peace. Whether this was wise and far-sighted is not easy to measure; it was certainly unpopular.

The Elector Frederick was soon driven out of Bohemia, and his hereditary lands were occupied by Habsburg troops. So short had been his reign that he is known to history as "the Winter King". The House of Commons clamoured for war. Private subscriptions and bands of volunteers were raised for the defence of the Protestants. James contented himself with academic discussions upon Bohemian rights with the Spanish ambassador. To pose as Protestant champion in the great war now begun might gain a fleeting popularity with his subjects, but would also deliver him into the hands of the

---

1   The Hanoverian monarchs, from George I onwards, were among the descendants of this marriage.

House of Commons. Puritan forces in the country would make themselves heard in louder tones. Besides, the fortunes of war were notoriously uncertain. James seems genuinely to have believed in his mission as the Peacemaker of Europe, and he also had a deep-rooted nervous dislike of fighting, founded in the tumultuous experiences of his youth in Scotland. He ignored the demand for intervention, and continued his negotiations for the Spanish match.

In the midst of these turmoils Sir Walter Raleigh was executed in Palace Yard to please the Spanish government. Raleigh had been imprisoned at the beginning of the reign for conspiring to supplant James by his cousin, Arabella Stuart. This charge was probably unjust, and the trial certainly so. Raleigh's dream of finding gold on the Orinoco River, which had cheered his long confinement, ended in disaster in 1617. This last expedition of his for which he was especially released from the Tower, had merely affronted the Spanish governors of South America. The old capital sentence was now revived against him. His death on October 29, 1618, was intended to mark the new policy of appeasement and prepare the way for ever between King James and the English people.

James was much addicted to favourites, and his attention to handsome young men resulted in a noticeable loss of respect for the monarchy. One of his favourites, Robert Carr, created Earl of Somerset by the King's caprice, was implicated in a murder by poison, of which his wife was undoubtedly guilty. Carr was succeeded in the King's regard by a good-looking, quick-witted, extravagant youth, George Villiers, soon ennobled as Duke of Buckingham. This young man quickly became all-powerful at court, and in the affections of James. He formed a deep and honourable friendship with Charles, Prince of Wales. He accepted unhesitatingly the royal policy of a Spanish marriage, and in 1623 staged a romantic trip to Madrid for the Prince and himself to view the bride. Their unorthodox behaviour failed to impress the formal and ceremonious Court of Spain. Moreover, the Spaniards demanded concessions for the English Catholics, which James knew Parliament would never grant. They refused to intercede with the Emperor for the restoration of the Palatinate lands to Frederick. In the end the King's better feelings triumphed. "I like not," he declared, "to marry my son with a portion of my daughter's tears." The negotiations with Spain foundered.

But the King and his Council had gone too far on this path not to be smitten and shaken by its sudden closing. The Council, deeply committed, told the King that Buckingham had spoiled the affair by his impatience and conceit. They cleared the Spanish court from the charge of discourtesy and justified the Spanish attitude towards the Palatinate. But Buckingham and Charles were now eager for war. James at first wavered. He was, he said, an old man who once knew something about politics. Now the two beings he loved best in the world urged him upon a course directly contrary to his judgment and past action.

In this sharp pinch Buckingham with remarkable agility turned himself from a royal favourite into a national, if short-lived, statesman. While using all his personal address to over-persuade the sovereign, he sought and obtained the support of Parliament and people. But now came the question of raising funds for the war that was to follow. James and Prince Charles had in mind campaigns in Europe that would seek to regain the Palatinate. Parliament urged a purely naval war with Spain, in which great profits from the Indies might be won. Suspicious of the King's intentions, the Commons voted less than half the sum for which he asked, and laid down stringent conditions as to how it should be spent. Buckingham trimmed his sails and for the moment preserved his new Parliamentary prestige. This he used to break his rival, Lord Treasurer Cranfield. The Treasurer, now Earl of Middlesex, was one of the outstanding "new men" in the kingdom. He was a merchant who had risen to great wealth and high office. He was now dismissed and imprisoned by the Parliamentary engine of impeachment. This weapon had already been used against Bacon, who was found guilty of corruption in 1621, dismissed from the Chancellorship, fined, and banished. It was never to be laid aside until many great issues, already alive, but little comprehended by Buckingham or by his dear friend Charles, had been settled once and for all.

No sooner was the Spanish match broken off than Buckingham turned to France for a bride for Charles. When he and the Prince of Wales had passed through Paris on their way to Madrid Charles had been struck by the charm of Marie de Médicis's daughter, Henrietta Maria, sister of Louis XIII and then in her fourteenth year. Buckingham found the negotiations agreeable to the French Court, and especially to Queen Marie. A marriage with a Protestant princess would have united the Crown and Parliament. But this was never the intention of the governing circle. A daughter of France seemed to them the only alternative to the Infanta. How could England face Spain alone. The old King wanted to see his son married. He said he lived only for him. He ratified the marriage treaty in December 1624. Three months later the first King of Great Britain[1] was dead.

The struggle with Spain had long absorbed the energies of Englishmen, and in the last years of Queen Elizabeth few fresh enterprises had been carried out upon the oceans. For a while little was heard of the New World. The novel idea of founding colonies also received a setback. Gilbert, Raleigh, and Grenville had been its pioneers. Their bold plans had come to nothing, but they left behind them an inspiring tradition. Now after a lapse of time their endeavours were taken up by new figures, less glittering, more practical and luckier.

Though the general standard of living improved during the sixteenth century, a wide range of prices rose sixfold, and wages only twofold. Industry was oppressed by excessive Government regulation. The medieval system of craftsmen's guilds, which was still enforced, made the entry of young apprentices harsh and difficult. The squirearchy, strong in its political alliance

1   The title, King of Great Britain, was assumed by James because Parliament could not make up
    its mind to bring about the Union that, de facto, existed when James VI of Scotland became James
    I of England.

with the Crown, owned most of the land and ran all the local-government. The march of enclosures which they pursued drove many English peasants off the land. The whole scheme of life seemed to have contracted and the framework of social organisation had hardened. There were many without advantage, hope, or livelihood in the New Age. Colonies, it was thought, might help to solve these distressing problems.

The Government was not uninterested. Trade with lively colonies promised an increase in the customs revenue on which the Crown heavily depended. Merchants and the richer landed gentry saw new opportunities across the Atlantic for profitable investment, and an escape from cramping restrictions on industry and the general decline of European trade during the religious wars. Capital was available for overseas development. Raleigh's attempts had demonstrated the ill-success of individual effort, but a new method financing large-scale trading enterprises was evolving in the shape of the joint stock company. In 1606 a group of speculators acquired a royal charter creating the Virginia company.

A plan was carefully drawn up in consultation with experts such as Hakluyt, but they had little practical experience and under-estimated the difficulties of the profoundly novel departure they were making. After all, it is not given to many to start a nation. It was a few hundred people who now took the first step. A settlement was made at Jamestown, in the Chesapeake Bay, on the Virginian coast, in May 1607. By the following spring half the population was dead from malaria, cold, and famine. After a long and heroic struggle the survivors became self-supporting, but profits to the promoters at home were very small. Captain John Smith, a military adventurer from the Turkish wars, became the dictator of the tiny colony, and enforced harsh discipline. The marriage of his lieutenant John Rolfe with Pocahontas, the daughter of an Indian chief, caused a sensation in the English capital. But the London company had little control and the administration of the colony was rough-and-ready. The objects of the directors were mixed and ill-defined. Some thought that colonisation would reduce poverty and crime in England. Others looked for profit to the fisheries of the North American coast, or hoped for raw materials to reduce their dependence on the exports from the Spanish colonies. All were wrong, and Virginia's fortune sprang from a novel and unexpected source. By chance a crop of tobacco was planted and the soil proved benevolent. Tobacco had been introduced into Europe by the Spaniards and the habit of smoking was spreading fast. Demand for tobacco was great and growing, and the profits on the Virginia crop were high. Smallholders were bought out, big estates were formed, and the colony began to stand on its own feet. As it grew and prospered its society came to resemble the Mother Country, with rich planters in the place of squires.

Beneath the drab exterior of Jacobean England, with favouritism at Court and humiliation in Europe, other and more vital forces were at work. The Elizabethan bishops had driven the nobler and tougher Puritan spirits out of the Established Church. But though they destroyed the organisation of the party small illegal gatherings of religious extremists continued to meet. There was no systematic persecution, but petty restrictions and spyings obstructed their peaceful worship. A congregation at Scrooby, in Nottinghamshire, led by one of their pastors, John Robinson, and by William Brewster, the Puritan bailiff of the manor of the Archbishop of York, resolved to seek freedom of worship abroad. In 1607 they left England and settled at Leyden, hoping to find asylum among the tolerant and industrious Dutch. For ten years these Puritan parishioners struggled for a decent existence. They were small farmers and agricultural workers, out of place in a maritime industrial community, barred by their nationality from the guilds of craftsmen, without capital and without training. The only work they could get was rough manual labour. They were persistent and persevering, but a bleak future faced them in Holland. They were too proud of their birthright to be absorbed by the Dutch. The authorities had been sympathetic, but in practice unhelpful. The Puritans began to look elsewhere.

Emigration to the New World presented itself as an escape from a sinful generation. There they might gain a livelihood unhampered by Dutch guilds, and practise their creed unharassed by English clerics. Throughout the winter of 1616–17, when Holland was threatened with a renewal of war with Spain, there were many discussions among the anxious community. A mortal risk and high adventure lay before them. To the perils of the unknown, to famine, and the record of past failures were added gruesome tales of the Indians; how they flayed men with the shells of fishes and cut off steaks which they broiled upon the coals before the eyes of the victim. Their plan was to settle in Guiana, but then they realised it was impossible to venture out upon their own. Help must come from England. They accordingly sent agents to London to negotiate with the only body interested in emigration, the Virginia company. One of the members of its council was an influential Parliamentarian, Sir Edwin Sandys. Supported by the London merchant backers of the company, he furthered the project. Here were ideal settlers, sober, hardworking, and skilled in agriculture. They insisted upon freedom of worship, and it would be necessary to placate the Anglican bishops. Sandys and the emissaries from Holland went to see the King. James was sceptical. He asked how the little band proposed to support itself in the company's territory in America. "By fishing," they replied. This appealed to James. "So God have my soul," he exclaimed in one of his more agreeable remarks, "'tis an honest trade! It was the Apostles' own calling."

The Leyden community was granted a licence to settle in America, and arrangements for their departure were hastened on. Thirty-five members of the Leyden congregation left Holland and joined sixty-six West Country adventurers at Plymouth, and in September 1620 they set sail in the *Mayflower*, a vessel of 180 tons. After two and a half months of voyaging across the winter ocean they landed outside the jurisdiction of the Virginia company. This invalidated their patent from London. Before they landed there was trouble among the group about who was to enforce discipline. Those who had joined the ship at Plymouth were no picked band of saints, and had no intention of submitting to the Leyden set. There was no possibility of appealing to England. Yet, if they were not all to starve, some agreement must be reached.

Forty-one of the more responsible members thereupon drew up a solemn compact which is one of the remarkable documents in history, a spontaneous covenant for political organisation. "In the name of God, Amen. We whose names are under-written ... do by these presents solemnly and mutually in the presence of God, and one of another, covenant and combine ourselves together into a civil body politic, for our better ordering and preservation and furtherance of the ends aforesaid; and by virtue hereof to enact, constitute, and frame such just and equal laws, ordinances, acts, constitutions, and offices, from time to time, as shall be thought most meet and convenient for the general good of the colony, unto which we promise all due submission and obedience."

In December on the American coast in Cape Cod Bay these men founded the town of Plymouth. The same bitter struggle with nature that had taken place in Virginia now began. There was no staple crop. But by toil and faith they survived. The financial supporters in London reaped no profits. In 1627 they sold out and the Plymouth colony was left to its own resources. Such was the founding of New England.

For ten years afterwards there was no more planned emigration to America; but the tiny colony of Plymouth pointed a path to freedom. In 1629 Charles I dissolved Parliament and the period of so-called Personal Rule began. As friction grew between Crown and subjects, so opposition to the Anglican Church strengthened in the countryside. Absolutism was commanding the Continent, and England seemed to be going the same way. Many people of independent mind began to consider leaving home to find freedom and justice in the wilds. Just as the congregation from Scrooby had emigrated in a body to Holland, so another Puritan group in Dorset, inspired by the Reverend John White, now resolved to move to the New World. After an unhappy start this venture won support in London and the Eastern Counties among backers interested in trade and fishing as well as in emigration. Influential Opposition peers lent their aid. After the precedent of Virginia a chartered company was formed, eventually named "The Company of the Massachusetts Bay in New England". News spread rapidly and there was no lack of colonists. An advance party founded the settlement of Salem, to the north of Plymouth. In 1630 the Governor of the company, John Winthrop, followed with a thousand settlers. The wilderness that Winthrop chose lay on the Charles river, and to this swampish site the capital of the colony was transferred. Here from modest beginnings arose the city of Boston, which was to become in the next century the heart of resistance to British rule and long remain the intellectual capital of America.

The Massachusetts Bay company was by its constitution a joint stock corporation, organised entirely for trading purposes, and the Salem settlement was for the first year controlled from London. But by accident or intent there was no mention in the charter where the company was to hold its meeting. Some of the Puritan stock-holders realised that there was no obstacle to transferring the company, directors and all, to New England. A general court of the company was held, and this momentous decision taken. From the joint stock company was born the self-governing colony of Massachusetts. Between 1629 and 1640 the colonists rose in numbers from three hundred to fourteen thousand.

The leaders and ministers who ruled in Massachusetts, however, had views of their own about freedom. It must be the rule of the godly. They understood toleration as little as the Anglicans, and disputes broke out about religion. By no means all were rigid Calvinists, and recalcitrant bodies split off from the parent colony when such quarrels became strident. Outside of the settlement were boundless beckoning lands. In 1635 and 1636 some of them moved to the valley of the Connecticut river, and founded the town of Hartford near its banks. They were joined by many emigrants direct from England. This formed the nucleus of the settlement of the River Towns, later to become the colony of Connecticut. There, three thousand miles from home, enlightened rules of government were drawn up. A "Fundamental Order" or constitution was proclaimed, similar to the *Mayflower* compact about fifteen years before. A popular government, shared in by all the freemen of the colony, was set up, and maintained itself in a modest way until its position was formally regularised after the Restoration of the Stuart monarchy.

By 1640 five main English settlements had been established in North America: Virginia, technically under the direct rule of the Crown, and administered, somewhat ineffectually, by a standing committee of the Privy Council since the company's charter was abrogated in 1624; the original Pilgrim settlement at Plymouth, which, for want of capital, had not expanded; the flourishing Massachusetts Bay Colony, and its two offshoots, Connecticut and Rhode Island.

Two other ventures, both essentially commercial, established the English-speaking peoples in the New World. Since Elizabethan days they had often tried to get a foothold in the Spanish West Indies. In 1623, on his way back from a fruitless expedition to Guiana, a Suffolk gentleman named Thomas Warner explored one of the less inhabited West Indian islands. He deposited a few colonists on St Christopher, and hurried home to get a royal patent for a more extensive enterprise. This achieved, he returned to the Caribbean, and, though much harassed by Spanish raids, he established the English in this disputed sea. By the 1640s Barbados, St Christopher, Nevis, Montserrat, and Antigua were in English hands and several thousand colonists had arrived. Sugar assured their prosperity, and the Spanish grip on the West Indies was shaken. There was much competition and warfare in the succeeding years, but for a long time these island settlements were commercially much more valuable to England than the colonies in North America.

Another settlement of this period was sponsored by the monarchy. In theory all land settled by Englishmen belonged to the King. He had the right to grant such portions as he chose either to recognised companies or to individuals. Just as Elizabeth and James had granted industrial and commercial monopolies to courtiers, so now Charles I attempted to regulate colonial settlement. In 1632 George Calvert, Lord Baltimore, a Roman Catholic courtier who had long been interested in colonisation, applied for a patent for settling in the neighbourhood of Virginia. It was granted after his death to his son. The terms of the patent resembled the conditions under which land was already held in Virginia. It conferred complete proprietary rights over the new area, and tried to transport the manorial system to the New World. The government of the colony was vested in the Baltimore family, who had supreme power of appointment and regulation. Courtiers and merchants subscribed to the venture, and the new colony was named Maryland in honour of Charles's Queen, Henrietta Maria. Although the proprietor was a Roman Catholic there was a tolerant flavour about its government from the beginning, because Baltimore had only obtained his patent by proclaiming the religion of the Established Church as the official creed of the new settlement. The aristocratic nature of the régime was much modified in practice, and the powers of the local administration set up by Baltimore increased at the expense of his paper rights.

In these first decades of the great emigration over eighty-thousand English-speaking people crossed the Atlantic. From the beginning its leaders were out of sympathy with the Government at home. The creation of towns and settlements from the wilderness, warfare with the Indians, and the remoteness and novelty of the scene widened the gulf with the Old World.

CHAPTER TWENTY-EIGHT

CHARLES I AND THE
PERSONAL RULE

The Puritan gentry — Charles I weds Henrietta Maria of France — war
with Spain — Cardinal Richelieu — the Petition of Right — the
assassination of Buckingham — Arminianism — Personal Rule —
Wentworth — the Navy debate — John Hampden tests the King's law — the
rise of William Laud — the Prayer Book, the Scots and the origins of the
Civil War — at war with the bishops — Wentworth's Irish solution — the
Pacification of Berwick — 1640 and the end of Personal Rule — the Short
Parliament — Pym leads Parliamentary opposition — the Scots enter
Newcastle

GREAT POLITICAL and religious crisis was overhanging England. Already in King James's time Parliament had begun to take the lead, not only in levying taxes but increasingly in the conduct of affairs, and especially in foreign policy. It is remarkable to see how far-reaching was the interest shown by the educated part of the English nation in Europe; and as they thought and moved so did the great mass of people behind them. Events in Prague or Ratisbon seemed as important to Englishmen as what happened in York or Bristol. The frontiers of Bohemia, the conditions in the Palatinate, ranked as high as many domestic questions. This wide outlook was no longer due, as in the days of the Plantagenets, to dynastic claims of Continental sway. The furious winds of religious strife carried men's thoughts afar. The English people felt that their survival and their salvation were bound up for ever with the victory of the Reformed Faith, and they watched with straining, vigilant eyes every episode which marked its advance or misfortune. An intense desire for England to lead and champion the Protestant cause wherever it was assailed drove forward the Parliamentary movement with a force far greater than would ever have sprung merely from the issues which were now opening at home.

Tudor authority had been accepted as a relief from the anarchy of the Wars of the Roses, and had now ceased to fit either the needs or the temper of a continually growing society. Men looked back to earlier times. Great lawyers like Coke and Selden had directed their gaze to the rights which they thought

Parliament possessed under the Lancastrian kings. Ranging farther, they spoke with pride of the work of Simon de Montfort, of Magna Carta, and even of still more ancient rights in the mists of Anglo-Saxon monarchy. From these studies they derived the conviction that they were the heirs of a whole structure of fundamental law inherent in the customs of the Island, and now most apt and vital to their immediate problems. The past seemed to them to provide almost a written Constitution, from which the Crown was threatening to depart. But the Crown also looked back, and found many precedents of a contrary character, especially in the last hundred years, for the most thorough exercise of the Royal Prerogative. Both King and Parliament had a body of doctrine upon which they dwelt with sincere conviction. This brought pathos and grandeur to the coming struggle.

A society more complex than that of Tudor England was coming into existence. Trade, both foreign and internal, was expanding. Coal-mining and other industries were rapidly developing. Larger vested interests were in being. The men at the head of this strenuous and, to our time, invaluable movement were notable figures. Coke had taught the later Parliaments of James I the arguments upon which they could rest and the methods by which they might prevail. His knowledge of the Common Law was unique. He unearthed an armoury of precedents, and set many to work upon their furbishing and sharpening. Two country gentlemen stand with him: one from the West, Sir John Eliot, a Cornishman; the other, Thomas Wentworth, a Yorkshire squire. Both these men possessed the highest qualities of force and temper. For a time they were rivals, for a time they were foes. By opposite paths both reached the extremity of sacrifice. Behind them, lacking nothing in grit, were leaders of the Puritan gentry, Denzil Holles, Arthur Hazelrigg, John Pym. Pym was eventually to go far and to carry the cause still farther. He was a Somerset man, a lawyer, strongly anti-High-Church, and with an interest in colonial ventures. Here was a man who understood every move in the political game, and would play it out remorselessly.

The Parliaments of James, and now those of Charles, were for war and intervention in Europe. They sought to use the money-power, of which they were the masters, to induce the King and his Ministers to tread these dangerous paths. They knew well, among other things, that the stresses of war would force the Crown to come to them. They saw that their power would grow with the adoption of their policy, which was also their faith. The pacifism of James I, often ignominious, had upon the whole avoided this trap. But King Charles and Buckingham were high-spirited men in the ardour of youth. The King was affronted by the manner in which his father's overtures for a Spanish match, and he himself, had been slighted in Madrid. He was for war with Spain. He at once carried through his marriage with the French princess Henrietta Maria. Her arrival at Dover surrounded by a throng of French Papists and priests was the first serious shock to Charles's popularity. The new Parliament granted supplies against Spain; but their purpose to review the whole question of indirect taxation was plain when they resolved that the customs duties of tonnage and poundage without which the King could not live, even in peace, should for the first time for many reigns be voted, not for the King's life, but only for one year.

The war with Spain went badly. Buckingham led an expedition to Cadiz in an attempt to emulate the feats of Queen Elizabeth's days, but it accomplished nothing. On his return Parliament resolved to unseat the glittering, profuse, incompetent Minister. Buckingham was impeached, and to save his friend the King hastily dissolved Parliament. A new complication was now added to the scene. France showed no desire to fight for the recovery of the Palatinate on England's behalf. Disputes also arose over the fulfilment of Charles's treaty of marriage with Queen Henrietta Maria, and the breach was widened by the cause of the Huguenots. The new, powerful French Minister, Cardinal Richelieu,[1] was determined to curb the independence of the Huguenots in France, and in particular to reduce their maritime stronghold of La Rochelle. English sympathies naturally lay with these French Protestants whom they had helped to sustain in the days of Henry of Navarre, and the two countries drifted into war.

The King was torn between the grinding need of finding money for the war and the danger that Parliament would again impeach his friend. In his vexation, and having the war on his hands, he resorted to dubious methods of raising money. He demanded a forced loan; and when many important persons refused to pay he threw them into prison. Five of these prisoners, known as the Five Knights, appealed against these proceedings. But King's Bench ruled that *habeas corpus* could not be used against imprisonments "by special command of the King". From the agitation this aroused sprang the famous Petition of Right.

Forced loans could not suffice to replenish the Treasury, and having secured a promise that the impeachment of Buckingham would not be pursued the King agreed to summon Parliament. The country was now in a ferment. The election returned men pledged to resist arbitrary exactions. The Parliament which assembled in March 1628 embodied the will of the natural leaders of the nation. It wished to support the war, but it would not grant money to a King and Minister it distrusted.

It must not be supposed that all the wrongdoing was on one side. Parliament, which had approved the wars, was playing a hard game with the King, confronting him with the shame to his princely honour of deserting the Huguenots, or else yielding the Prerogative his predecessors had so long enjoyed. Their tactics were artful, and yet justified by their convictions and by the facts. They offered no fewer than five subsidies, amounting to £300,000, all to be paid within twelve months. Here was enough to carry on the war; but

---

1   Armand Jean du Plessis de Richelieu (1585–1642) became chief minister to Louis XIII in 1624, the year before Charles I became King. Richelieu remained the most powerful man in France until his death in 1642, the year the English Civil War started. During this period he enhanced the powers of the French monarch, consistently outwitted his enemies (and friends) and was responsible for France's victory in the Thirty Years' War.

before they would confirm this in a Bill they demanded their price. The following four resolutions were passed unanimously: that no freeman ought to be restrained or imprisoned unless some lawful cause was expressed; that the writ of *habeas corpus* ought to be granted to every man imprisoned or restrained, even though it might be at the command of the King or of the Privy Council; that if no legal cause for imprisonment were shown the party ought to be set free or bailed; that it was the ancient and undoubted right of every freeman to have a full and absolute property in his goods and estates, and that no tax, loan, or benevolence ought to be levied by the King or his Ministers without common consent by Act of Parliament.

At Coke's prompting the Commons now went on to frame the Petition of Right. Its object was to curtail the King's Prerogative. The Petition complained against forced loans, imprisonment without trial, billeting, and martial law. These and others of the King's proceedings were condemned "as being contrary to the rights and liberties of the subjects, and the laws and statutes of the nation". Unless the King accepted the Petition he would have no subsidies, and must face the wars to which Parliament had incited him as best he could. Charles, resorting to manoeuvre, secretly consulted the judges, who assured him that even his consent to these liberties would not affect his ultimate Prerogative. When his first evasive answer was delivered a howl went up from the great majority of all assembled. He fell back upon the opinion of the judges and gave full consent. The Commons voted all the subsidies, and believed that a definite bargain had been struck.

We reach here, amid much confusion, the main foundation of English freedom. The right of the Executive Government to imprison a man, high or low, for reasons of State was denied. At the back of the Parliament movement in all its expressions lay a deep fear. Everywhere in Europe they saw the monarchies becoming more autocratic. The States-General, which had met in Paris in 1614, had not been summoned again; it was not indeed to be summoned until the clash of 1789. The rise of standing armies, composed of men drilled in firearms and supported by trains of artillery, had stripped alike the nobles and the common people of their means of independent resistance. Rough, as the times had been in the earlier centuries, "bills and bows" were a final resource which few kings had cared to challenge. But now on the Parliamentary side force as yet was lacking.

Both sides pressed farther along their paths. The King, having got his money, dwelt unduly upon assurances that he had received from the judges that his Prerogative was intact. The Commons came forward with further complaints against the growth of Popery and Arminianism – the form of High Church doctrine most directly opposed to Calvinism – about the mismanagement of the war, and about injury to trade and commerce from naval weakness in the Narrow Seas. They renewed their attack on Buckingham, asking the King whether it was consistent with his safety, or the safety of the realm, that the author of so many calamities should continue to hold office or remain near his sacred person. But now the King and Buckingham hoped that a second and successful expedition would relieve the Huguenots in La Rochelle. Charles dismissed the Houses. Far better to rescue Protestants abroad than to persecute Catholics at home.

Buckingham himself was deeply conscious of the hatreds of which he was the object, and it is clear that in putting himself at the head of a new expedition to La Rochelle he hoped to win again for himself some national backing, which would at least divide his pursuers. But at the moment he was about to embark at Portsmouth, he was stabbed to death by a fanatical naval lieutenant. The death of Buckingham was a devastating blow to the young King. At the same time it immensely relieved his public difficulties, for much of the anger of the Parliament died with the favourite; and it brought for the first time a unity into his married life. Hitherto he had been morally and mentally dominated by "Steenie", the beloved friend of his boyhood and youth, to whom he confided his innermost thoughts. The death of Buckingham was the birth of his love for his wife.

Though the Commons had granted the five subsidies, they held tonnage and poundage in reserve. When the year lapsed for which this had been voted the Parliamentary party throughout the country were angered to find that the King continued to collect the tax by his officers. In all this was seen the King's contempt for the Petition of Right. When copies of the Petition were printed it was found that the King's first evasive answer was appended, and not his later plain acceptance in the ancient form. The expedition to La Rochelle, which had sailed under another commander, miscarried and eventually the Huguenots in despair surrendered the city to the King of France. This collapse caused shock and grief throughout England. Thus when Parliament met again at the beginning of 1629 there was no lack of grievances both in foreign and domestic policy. Yet it was upon questions of religion that the attack began. The Commons showed themselves to be in a most aggressive mood, and worked themselves into a passion by long debates upon the indulgence and laxity with which the laws against Popery were enforced. This brought the great majority of them together; and the zealots, who, however intolerant, were ardent to purify what they deemed a corrupt Church, joined with the patriots who were laying the foundations of English freedom.

In a comprehensive resolution the Commons declared that whoever furthered Popery or Arminianism, whoever collected or helped to collect tonnage and poundage before it was granted, or even paid it, was a public enemy. The personal censures formerly heaped on Buckingham were now transferred to the Lord Treasurer, Richard Weston, who was denounced as a Papist, if not indeed a Jesuit, engaged in exacting taxes illegally. All this was embodied in a single Remonstrance. The Speaker, who had been gained to the King's side, announced on March 2 that the King adjourned the House till the 10th, thus frustrating the carrying of the Remonstrance. A wave of wrath swept through the assembly. When the Speaker rose to leave he was forced back and held down on his chair by two resolute and muscular Members, Holles and Valentine. The doors were bared against Black Rod, and the Remonstrance, recited from memory by Holles, was declared carried by acclamation. The doors were then opened and the Members poured forth tumultuously. It was a long time before any of them met in their Chamber again. It had become plain to all that King and Commons could not work together on any terms. The next week Parliament was dissolved and the period of King Charles's Personal Rule began.

The Personal Rule of the King was not set up covertly by degrees. Charles openly proclaimed his intention. "We have showed", he said, "by our frequent meeting our people, our love to the use of Parliaments; yet, the late abuse having for the present driven us unwillingly out of that course, we shall account it presumption for any to prescribe at any time unto us for Parliaments, the calling, continuing, and dissolving of which is always in our own power, and shall be more inclinable to meet in Parliament again, when our people shall see more clearly into our interests and actions and when such as have bred this interruption shall have received their condign punishment."

This policy required other large measures. First, there must be peace with France and Spain. Without the support of Parliament Charles had not the strength to carry on foreign wars. It was not difficult to obtain peace. Indeed both the French and Spanish Governments showed their contempt of English exertions when they voluntarily returned the prisoners they had taken at La Rochelle and in the Netherlands. The second condition was the gaining of some at least of the Parliamentary leaders. Sir Henry Savil, Thomas Digges, and Wentworth were deemed both possible and serviceable acquisitions. Digges had proved himself willing to endure prison for the Parliamentary cause; he thawed somewhat readily in the royal sunshine. But Wentworth was the man of all others most worth winning.

To Wentworth therefore the King turned. In December 1628 he became Lord President of the Council of the North and a member of the Privy Council. From this moment he not only abandoned all the ideas of which he had been the ablest exponent, but all the friends who had fought on his side. He sailed on in power and favour while Eliot, his rival but for long his comrade, was condemned for contempt of the King's Government and languished to his death in the Tower. The very force of Wentworth's practical mind led him to a theme which was the exact contrary of all he had previously espoused. Elaborate explanations have been offered to mitigate the suddenness of this transformation. We are invited to regard him as the only man who could have achieved the reunion of Parliament and the monarchy. Allowance must be made for the different values assigned in those days to royal favour and public duty.

His natural inclination was, as he once avowed, to live not under the frown but under the smile of his sovereign. A hatred centred upon Wentworth different from that which even incompetence attracted to other Ministers. He was "the Satan of the Apostasy", "the lost Archangel", "the suborned traitor to the cause of Parliament". No administrative achievements, no address in business, no eloquence, no magnitude of personality, could atone to his former friends for his desertion. And they had eleven years to think about it all. Savile and Digges had already accepted office; and a couple of eminent lawyers whose opinions had been adverse to the Crown were also persuaded to sing the opposite tune. The lesser figures of the Parliamentary movement either suffered ill-usage at the Royal hands or, like Holles, Hazelrigg, and Pym, were allowed to brood and fume in obscurity.

But the third and least sentimental condition of the Personal Rule was dominant – money. First, an extreme frugality must be practised by the executive – no wars, no adventures of any kind, no disturbances; all State action reduced to a minimum; quietness by all means. The Crown had to make shift with what it could scrape from old taxes. The wealth gained by national toil fructified in the pockets of the people. Peace reigned throughout the land. No large questions could be stirred. The King, with his elegant, dignified Court, whose figures are portrayed by the pencil of Van Dyck, whose manners and whose morals were an example to all, reigned on the smallest scale. He was a despot, but an unarmed despot. No standing army enforced his decrees. There was more tolerance towards religious differences in the King's circle than anywhere else in the land. He sincerely believed, his judges vehemently asserted, and his people found it difficult to deny, that he was ruling according to many of the old customs of the realm. It is a travesty to represent this period of Personal Rule as a time of tyranny in any effective sense. In later years, under the yoke of Cromwell's Major-Generals, all England looked back to these placid thirties as an age of ease and tranquillity.

Meanwhile Wentworth, now Lord-Lieutenant of Ireland, had, by a combination of tact and authority, reduced that kingdom to a greater submission to the British Crown than ever before or since. He assuaged internal feuds; he established order and prosperity; and with an undoubted measure of general acquiescence he produced an Irish army and a substantial Irish subvention for the upkeep of Charles's crown. His repute in history must rest upon his Irish administration. At the end of seven years he stood at the head of a country which he had disciplined and exploited, but which, without any apparent violent measures or bloodshed, lay docile in his hands.

By all these means under a modest frugal régime King Charles managed to do without a Parliament. Hungry forces still lay in shadow. All the ideas which they cherished and championed stirred in their minds, but they had no focus, no expression. Many who would have been vehement if the chance had come their way were content to live their life from day to day. Harvests were now abundant and the rise in prices had almost ceased. There was no longer a working-class problem. The Poor Law was administered with exceptional humanity.[1] Ordinary gentlefolk might have no share in national government, but they were still lords on their own estates. In quarter sessions they ruled the

[1]   As early as 1536, a law ordered relief for the poor but insisted that fit and "sturdy beggars" should be put to work. The first important Poor Law Act appeared in 1601. This taxed property owners with paying towards poor relief in parishes. Half a century earlier, parish registers had recorded names of the needy, from which came variations of the expression "on the parish".

shires, and as long as they kept clear of the law and paid their taxes with a grunt they were left in peace.

Presently Charles's lawyers and sleuth-hounds drew attention to an anomaly which had grown with the passage of years. According to the immemorial laws of England, perhaps of Alfred the Great, the whole land should pay for the upkeep of the Fleet. However, for a long time only the maritime counties had paid for the Navy. Yet was not this Navy the shield of all the peace and freedom which thrived in Britain? Why should not all pay were all benefited? The project commended itself to the King. In August 1635 he levied "Ship Money" upon the whole country.

Forthwith a Buckinghamshire gentleman, a former Member of Parliament, solidly active against the Crown, stood forth among many others and refused to pay. His assessment was no more than twenty shillings; but upon the principle that even the best of taxes could be levied only with the consent of Parliament he faced the distraint and imprisonment which were the penalties of contumacy. John Hampden's refusal was selected by both sides as a test case. The Parliamentarians, who had no other means of expression, saw in it a trial upon which all eyes would be directed, and welcomed a martyr whose sacrifice would disturb the public tameness. They wished to hear the people groan at tyranny. The Crown, on the other hand, was encouraged by the logic of its argument. The case of Hampden therefore became famous at once and for ever. An obelisk at Princes Risborough records to this day his valiant assertion that the inland counties have no concern for the royal Navy, except so far as Parliament shall require them to pay. The Crown prevailed. But the grievance ran far and wide. Ninety per cent of "Ship Money" was eventually collected for the year 1637, but only 20 per cent for 1639. Everywhere persons of property looked up from their pleasant life and began to use again the language of the Petition of Right.

Yet this alone would not have sufficed to rouse the country. The Parliamentary party therefore continued to foster religious agitation as the surest means of waking England from its apathy. Here emerges the figure of the man who of all others was Charles's evil genius – William Laud, Archbishop of Canterbury. He was a convinced Anglican, whole-hearted in his opposition both to Rome and to Geneva, and a leader in the movement away from Calvinism. Among his innovations was the railing off of the altar, and a new emphasis on ceremony and the dignity of the clergy. The gulf between clergy and congregation was widened and the role of authority visibly enhanced. Thus the King's religious ideas marched in step with his politics and resentments multiplied.

Laud now found a new source of revenue for the Crown. Under the statues of Elizabeth everyone was obliged to go to Church; they might think as they liked, but they must conform in public worship. This practice had fallen into widespread disuse. Now all over England men and women found themselves hauled before the justices for not attending church, and fined one shilling at a time. Here indeed was something that ordinary men and women could understand. This was no question for lawyers and judges in the court of the Exchequer; it was something new and something teasing. The Puritans, already chafed, regarded it as persecution. The Parliamentary agitation which had been conducted during all these years with so much difficulty gained a widespread accession of strength at a time when the King's difficulties had already massed themselves into a stack.

It is by no means certain that, left to herself, England would have broken into revolt. It was in Scotland, the home of the Stuarts and Charles's birthplace, that the torch was lighted which began the vast conflagration. Laud was dissatisfied with the spiritual conditions prevailing in the Northern Kingdom, and he moved the King to make some effort to improve them. The Scots must adopt the English Prayer Book, and enter broadly into communion with their English brethren. Besides the desire for uniformity in religious ceremonies throughout the whole Island, King Charles had practical and secular aims. Charles on his accession had alienated the nobles by an Act which sought to take away from them all the Church lands they had acquired since the Reformation. Furthermore, he was determined to reform the system of collecting tithes, which had largely fallen into their hands. The burden on the smaller landholders was to be reduced and the stipends of the clergy increased. Charles's plans for reinforcing episcopacy in Scotland thus drove the Scottish nobles in to opposition.

The bishops, for their part, as agents of the distant King, found themselves increasingly disliked by their own clergy as well as by the landowners. In order to strengthen the hands of the Scottish bishops a new exposition of Canon Law was framed emphasising the position of the Crown, and a new Prayer Book or Liturgy was drawn up in London to regulate the forms of public worship in Scotland. These books were promulgated in the year 1636. No one appears to have foreseen the circumstances. Charles and his advisers had no thought of challenging doctrine, still less of taking any step towards Popery. They desired to assert the Protestant High Church view. They defined with new stress the Royal Supremacy, and they prescribed, especially in the sacrament of the Lord's Supper, a somewhat more elaborate ritual. Thus in their course they affronted at the same time the property interests of the powerful, the religious convictions of all classes, and the independent spirit of the Scottish nation. The resentment excited was general, and was immediately turned into the channels of most violent prejudice.

The Scottish people believed, and were told by their native leaders to believe, that they were to be forced by the royal authority to take the first fatal steps towards Roman Catholicism. Every tenet, every word, of the new Prayer Book was scanned with profound suspicion. Was not the King married to a Popish wife, who practised idolatry in her private chapel? When in July 1637 the dignitaries of Scottish Church and State were gathered in St Giles's Church in Edinburgh for the first solemn reading of the new Prayer Book the ceremony became a riot. A surge of passion swept the ancient capital before which the episcopal and royal authorities trembled. Edinburgh had defied the

Crown, and no force was found to resist it. King Charles was startled by the news. He tried to reassure his Scottish subjects. He dwelt in forcible terms upon his hatred of Popery, and professed himself willing to amend the new Prayer Book. But this was in vain; only the immediate withdrawal of the offensive book could have availed. Instead a long argument on minor points began, with repeated concessions on the part of the King and growing anger throughout Scotland. Once again we see in a long period of wordy contention and legal interchanges the prelude to a violent convulsion. The Scots, shrewdly advised by their men of law, cast their resistance into the form of a Petition, a Grand Supplication, under the pressure of which the new Prayer Book was withdrawn. But too late. A tempest was blowing which bore men forward. Respect and loyalty were still professed to the King; the blast beat upon the bishops. At length the whole original policy of the King was withdrawn. It had served only to raise a counter-movement, which grew in intensity.

At the beginning of 1638 the Petition was abandoned for the signing of a Covenant. Much of it merely repeated the confession of faith agreed upon by all fifty years before under the reign of King James VI. On February 28, 1638, the Covenant was read in Greyfriars churchyard in Edinburgh. The Earl of Sutherland, the first to sign his name thereto, was followed by a long list of notables who felt themselves borne forward upon what is described as the "demoniacal frenzy" of the populace. The scroll was signed in the church by many who cut a vein for their ink, and copies were taken for signature to nearly every town and village. It embodied the unalterable resolve of a whole people to perish rather than submit to Popery.

The Marquis of Hamilton, an experienced Scottish statesman, who was to follow his King to the scaffold, was sent North as lay commissioner, with the supreme aim of making friends again. Hamilton fought for nothing more than some show of dignity to cover the temporary royal retreat. He was expostulating with a whirlwind. It was agreed that a General Assembly should be convoked. The Committee of the Covenanters, sitting in Edinburgh, set themselves to organise the elections as elections have never been managed before. The Assembly which met in St Mungo's Cathedral in Glasgow was found to be dominated by the religious convictions of the Northern kingdom, supported by a formidable lay element, who, surrounded by fervent adherents of all classes, sat armed with sword and dagger in the middle of the church. Before Charles sent Hamilton to Scotland they had had a significant conversation. The King had said that if the reconciliation failed Hamilton should collect troops and put down rebellion. "But," said Hamilton, "what if there be not enough troops found in the country for this purpose?" "Then," answered Charles, "power shall come from England, and I will myself come in person with them, being resolved to hazard rather my life than to suffer the supreme authority to be contemned." This occasion now arose. He ordered the dissolution of the Assembly. That body declared itself resolved to continue in permanent session. They took this step with full knowledge of what it meant.

The refusal of the General Assembly of Scotland in November 1638 to dissolve upon the demand of the King's commissioner has been compared to that of the French National Assembly in 1789, when for the first time they resisted the royal will. The facts and circumstances no doubt were different; but both events led by unbroken chains of causation to the same end, namely, the solemn beheading of the King.

Laud in England and Wentworth in Ireland were in constant correspondence, and to stamp out defiance while time remained was the mood of both. That mood prevailed, and both King and Covenanters looked about for arms and means of war. The King's Council turned its eyes to Wentworth's troops in Ireland, and even to Spain. There was talk of hiring two thousand Spanish infantry to form the nucleus around which the well-affected in Scotland, of whom there were many, especially in the Eastern Highlands, might gather. But the Convenanters had far better resources overseas. The famous part played by the Scots brigades and by Scottish generals under Gustavus Adolphus in Germany had left Scotland with an incomparable military reserve. Alexander Leslie had risen in the Thirty Years War to the rank of Field-Marshal. He felt himself called upon to return to fight the same quarrel on his native soil. To him it was but a flanking operation in the vast conflict of the Protestants with the Catholic Church. The nobles of Scotland bowed to Leslie's military reputation. They obeyed his orders. In a few months, and long before any effective preparations could be made in the South, Scotland had the strongest armed force in the Island. It was inspired with earnest, slowly roused, and now fanatical religious passion. They still had reverence for the King. They would even on occasion cheer his name. But their banners displayed the motto "For Christ's Crown, and the Covenant". The lines of antagonism were drawn with cold, pedantic, inflexible resolve. In May 1639 this army, about twenty thousand strong, stood upon the Scottish Border opposite the weaker, ill-disciplined, and uncertain forces which Charles and his advisers had gathered.

It was clear from the first that in the King's camp there was no united desire to make war upon the Scots; on the contrary, parleys were set on foot in a good spirit, and on June 18 the so-called "Pacification of Berwick" was agreed. The Scots promised to disband their army and restore the royal castles, which they had seized. The King agreed to the summoning in the following August both of a General Assembly and of a Parliament; that these should henceforward be regularly summoned, and that one should have the decision of ecclesiastical and the other temporal affairs. He declined to recognise the enactments of the Assembly at Glasgow, because they reflected upon his duty as a sovereign; but for the time being he accepted the abolition of the Episcopacy. So far had he travelled since the gay plan of a High Church Liturgy. Charles, however, thought of the Pacification as a device to gain time, and the Covenanters were soon convinced of this. The spirit of independence was now aroused throughout Scotland. Wrath was expressed at the restoration of the royal fortresses, and fears at the dispersal of the Scottish army.

Hamilton, returning to Scotland, found himself in a world of rising antagonism. The Scottish Parliament, which met in Edinburgh at the end of August 1639, claimed forthwith that the King's Privy Council should be responsible to it, and that the King should follow its advice in appointing commanders of troops, and especially of fortresses. They repudiated the jurisdiction of the Treasury, particularly in the coinage, which was being debased; and they even required that honours and dignities should be bestowed in accordance with their wishes. When these intentions became apparent Hamilton could only at first temporise by adjournments, and finally by a prorogation until June 1640. Before the Assembly dispersed it left in full authority a powerful and representative committee, which was in fact the Government of Scotland.

In the complicated pattern of Western Europe the Scots were not only the ardent partisans of Protestantism, but the friends of France against the Austro-Spanish combination. They viewed the neutral and isolationist foreign policy of King Charles as unduly favouring the Catholic interest. They sought to revive in an intimate form their traditional association with France. By the end of 1639 Charles saw himself confronted with an independent State and Government in the North, which, though it paid formal homage to him as King, was resolved to pursue its own policy both at home and abroad. It thus challenged not only the King's Prerogative, but the integrity of his dominions. He felt bound to fight. But how?

Wentworth was now summoned from Ireland to strengthen the Council. His repute at Court stood high. He had restored not only order but the appearance of loyalty throughout Ireland. Irish sympathies lay upon the Catholic side. Ruling as an enlightened despot, the Lord Deputy had raised and was paying and training an Irish army of eight thousand men. He believed himself capable of enforcing upon Scotland, and later upon England, the system of autocratic rule which had brought him success in the sister island. Wentworth saw clearly enough that the royal revenues were not sufficient to support the cost of the campaign. He concluded therefore that Parliament must be summoned. In his over-confidence he thought that the Commons would prove manageable. He was wrong. But a momentous step was taken. After nearly eleven years of Personal Rule the King issued writs for a new Parliament, and elections were held throughout England. This opened the famous struggle of Parliament against the King.

The Parliamentary forces, though without public expression, had been neither impotent nor idle. Under a mild despotism they had established a strong control of local government in many parts of the country. They presented the issues of 1629 with the pent-up anger and embitterment of eleven years of gag and muzzle. Charles had now to come back cap in hand to those very forces which he had disdainfully dismissed. Parliament met on April 13, 1640. The membership had been changed by time and fortune. Only a quarter of the former Members reappeared. Eliot was dead in the Tower; Wentworth was now Earl of Strafford, and the King's First Minister. But of the old lot one man stood forth, competent, instructed, and avenging. From the moment when the new, afterwards called the Short, Parliament met, Pym was the central figure. In a long, majestic oration he restated the main case and the added griefs. Charles and his chief counsellors, Strafford and Laud, found no comfort from the new assembly. On the contrary, they were met by such a temper that by an act of extreme imprudence it was dissolved on May 5 after a few days. Its calling had only served to excite and engage the whole of England in the controversy.

The expedient of calling Parliament had clearly failed. The Scottish army was on the border and, only weak, ill-disciplined forces could be mustered against it. To place armed men in the field both money and a cause were needed. Neither could be found. The Scots crossed the Tweed in good order. The cavalry stood upstream to break the current while the foot waded across. They met with no opposition until they reached the Tyne. Then, as before the Pacification of Berwick, the two hosts faced one another. The Scottish leaders were encouraged in their invasion by the Parliamentary and Puritan movements throughout England, and in the centre of this combination stood Pym. For some days little happened, but one morning a Scottish horseman, watering his horse in the river, came too near the English outposts. Some one pulled a trigger; the shot went home; the imprudent rider was wounded; all the Scots cannon fired and all the English army fled. A contemporary wrote that "Never so many ran from so few with less ado". The English soldiers explained volubly that their flight was not due to fear of the Scots, but to their own discontents, mentioning especially that they had had no pay. This did not prevent the Scottish army arriving swiftly before the gates of Newcastle. Here the Scots generals declared that they stood for the liberties of England, and appealed for aid from all who agreed with the Parliamentary and Puritan cause. The magistrates, however, were only induced to open their gates on the blunt reminder that Newcastle was in fact a conquered city. Meanwhile Strafford at York was frantically striving to form a front against the invasion, vainly hoping that the insult to English soil would produce the longed-for revival of the national spirit, trying without success to gain a majority upon the Council for the importation of Irish troops.

At this time many of the lords who were now meeting in London pressed on the King the proposal to summon a Magnum Concilium, which was an assembly of the Peers without the Commons. Centuries had passed since it had been convoked, but was not here a crisis which demanded it? Charles agreed, but this antique body could only recommend that Parliament should be called. The King could not defend the country himself. Only Parliament could save the land from what had now become an act of Scottish aggression. At this moment King Charles's moral position was at its worst. He had plumbed the depths of personal failure. His enemies, while compassing and finally achieving his destruction, now built and rebuilt for him a party and a cause for which any man could die.

CHAPTER TWENTY-NINE

THE REVOLT OF PARLIAMENT

*Buying off the Scots – the Long Parliament – Strafford and Laud
impeached – the Root and Branch Petition – Charles forced to sign Bill of
Attainder – Strafford executed – Charles seeks reconciliation with Scots –
slaughter in Ireland – the Grand Remonstrance – Charles tries to arrest
Pym and his supporters – London rises against the royal breach of
Parliamentary privilege – Charles I quits London and raises his standard
in Nottingham – the Battle of Edgehill starts the Civil War – the Queen
runs Parliamentary blockade – the Battle of Marston Moor – Cromwell
takes charge of army – Laud executed – the Battle of Naseby*

INEXORABLE FORCES compelled the King to do what he most feared.
The Scottish army had possession of Durham and Northumberland.
Their leaders were in close correspondence with the Parliamentary and
Puritan party in England. They put forward not only demands which
affected the Northern kingdom, but others which they knew would rever-
berate in the South. The Privy Council addressed itself to making a truce with
the Scots, who demanded forty thousand pounds a month to maintain their
army on English soil until their claims should be met. By haggling this was
reduced to £850 a day. Thus the two armies, facing each other with sheathed
swords, were each to be maintained during an indefinite period of negotiation
at the cost of the Crown, which was penniless. The so-called "Bishops' War"
was over; the real war had yet to begin.

There now arose from all quarters a cry that Parliament should be
summoned. At least half the lords had remained in London. A group of them,
headed by the Earl of Bedford, who was in close touch with Pym, waited on
the Privy Council and called for a Parliament. It was even implied that if the
King would not issue the writs himself a Parliament would be convened without him. The King recognised that his theory of monarchy must be modified.
In summoning the new Parliament he accepted a different relationship
between the people and the Crown. The calling of Parliament relieved for a
space the severe tension, and the choosing of Members employed the zeal of
partisans. But it was only after long begging, supported by the very lords who
were opposing the King, and on their personal security, that the City of

London consented to advance £50,000, pending the meeting of Parliament, to keep the Scottish army in victorious possession of the North of England and the English army from dissolving in mutiny.

There is no surer way of rousing popular excitement than the holding of General Elections in quick succession. Passions ran high; beer flowed. Three-fifths of the Members of the Short Parliament, 294 out of 493, were returned, and nearly all the newcomers were opponents of the Government. Of the men who had made a name in Opposition not one was rejected. The King could count on less than a third of the House. Thus on November 3, 1640, was installed the second longest and most memorable Parliament that ever sat in England.[1] It derived its force from a blending of political and religious ideas. It was upborne by the need of a growing society to base itself upon a wider foundation than Tudor paternal rule. It used for tactical purposes the military threat of the invaders from Scotland. Scottish commissioners and divines arrived in London. They were astonished at the warmth of their welcome, and were hailed as the deliverers of England. They found themselves outpaced in their hostility to the bishops by some of their English Parliamentary allies. The negotiations were protracted from week to week at an expense to the Crown which could only be defrayed by Parliament. Demands in both kingdoms for far-reaching changes in the civil and religious government which had lasted for centuries were pooled and set forth again with combined force. The accession of James I had involved the union of the Crowns of England and Scotland; but now in a manner very different from what James or his son had conceived there was a union of the dominant political parties in both countries, and they strove together for a common cause. Here then was an explosive charge, pent in a strong cannon and directed upon King Charles and those who were his trusted Ministers.

Of these the first and most obnoxious was Strafford. Pym and Hampden, the leading figures in the new House of Commons, were immediately in command of a large and indignant majority. The Crown now made no resistance to the principle that redress of grievances should precede supply; but the grievances of the Commons could be satisfied only by vengeance. Strafford possessed convincing proofs of the correspondence carried on by Pym and others with the invading Scots. This was plain treason if the King's writ ran. It was believed that Strafford meant to open this formidable case; but Pym struck first. All the rage of the Parliamentary party, all the rancour of old comradeship forsworn, all that self-preservation dictated, concentrated upon "the wicked Earl" a blast of fury such as was never recorded in England before or since. On the morning of November 11 the doors of St Stephen's Chapel were locked; the key placed upon the table; no strangers might enter, no Member might leave. Late in the afternoon Pym and Hampden, attended by three hundred Members, carried the articles of Strafford's impeachment up to

---

1   The Long Parliament met until 1653 when Cromwell, having dismissed the Rump of the Long Parliament and the Barebones Parliament, presided as Protector. Hence, the first Protectorate Parliament met in 1654.

the House of Lords. At the King's request Strafford had come to London. In the morning he had been greeted with respect by the peers. Hearing what was afoot, he returned to the Chamber. But now all was changed. He was received with a hollow murmur. Shouts were raised that he should withdraw while the issue was being debated. He was forced to do so. In less than an hour the powerful Minister saw himself transformed into an accused prisoner. He found himself to his own and the general surprise kneeling at the Bar to receive the directions of his peers. He was deprived of his sword and taken into custody by Black Rod. As he went through the crowd on his journey to Black Rod's house the hostility of the populace was terrible.

The proscription extended to all the Ministers, as they would now be called, of the King. Archbishop Laud, impeached in the Lords, silenced when he sought to reply, was removed by water to the Tower. Sir Francis Windebanke, the Secretary of State, and some others escaped to the Continent. Lord Keeper Sir John Finch, leaving the Woolsack, appeared before the House of Commons in his robes of office bearing the Great Seal of England in his embroidered bag, and defended himself in such moving words that all were hushed. Nevertheless this produced no longer delay than was necessary for him to flee the country. All this was done by the fierce anger of the Commons, supported by the Londoners and by the distant military forces of Scotland, and accepted by the Peers.

The Commons were harassed by fears and rumours. They had been careful to pay the Scottish army for invading England; it was the English troops who had gone short. There were tales of mutinies and military plots. Pym, with cold-blooded skill, played upon these alarms, which indeed needed but a tremor of Parliamentary weakness to become real. The aggressive tendencies of the majority in the Commons shaped themselves into a demand for the abolition of Episcopacy. The Scots, now so influential in London and masters in the North, sought to establish the Presbyterian system of Church government. This was indeed turning the tables. A petition signed by fifteen thousand was presented to the House, and caught up by the majority, seeking to extirpate the Episcopate "root and branch". But now for the first time effective counter-forces appeared. A second petition signed by seven hundred clergymen hostile to the principles of the King and the Archbishop proposed the restriction of the bishops' power to spiritual matters, and limited them at certain points in these. Here was a line of resistance upon which the other side could form.

Meanwhile the trial of Strafford had begun. Proceeding as they did upon admittedly rival interpretations of law and justice, the Commons at once found difficulty in establishing a case against the hated Minister. That he was the arch-enemy of all that the majority championed, and indeed of the rights and liberties of the nation, was apparent. But to prove him guilty of the capital offence of treason was not possible. Within the large wooden structure erected in Westminster Hall the leaders of the nation, its magnates and politicians and divines, assembled. One-third of the floor was thronged with the public. The

King and Queen sat daily in their special box, hoping by their presence to restrain the prosecution. Strafford defended himself with magnificent ability. Each morning he knelt to the Lord Steward and bowed to the lords and to the assembly. Each day by logic and appeal he broke up the heads of accusation. He successfully derided the theory of "cumulative treason" to which the managers of the impeachment were soon reduced. How could a number of alleged misdemeanours be made to add up to treason? He drove home the massive doctrine of English liberty, "No law, no crime." What law had he broken? With every art of the orator, or, as his foes said, of the actor, he wrought not only upon the minds but upon the sentiments of the audience. The King worked night and day upon the peers. There was nothing he would not concede to save Strafford. He had assured him on his kingly word that he should not suffer in liberty or life. The sympathy not only of the galleries, crowded with the wives of all the leading men, but of the peers themselves, was gradually gained. On the thirteenth day the prisoner's hopes stood high.

Now Pym and his colleagues made a deadly stroke. Sir Henry Vane, Secretary of the Privy Council, had a son who was ardent for the popular cause. This son, by an act of bad faith which after many stormy years was to cost him his life, purloined a note which his father had preserved of the discussion in the King's Council on May 5, 1640. The cryptic sentiments ascribed to Strafford were: "Everything is to be done as power will admit, and that you are to do. They refused, you are acquitted towards God and man. You have an army in Ireland you may employ here to reduce this kingdom. Confident as anything under Heaven, Scotland shall not hold out five months."

The Commons declared that this convicted Strafford of advising the use of an Irish army to subdue England. The words in their context seem to mean that Scotland was intended, and Scotland at the time of their utterance was in rebellion against the King. Vane the elder, Secretary of the Council, in cross-examination could not, or would not, say whether the words "this kingdom" meant England or Scotland. The other members of the Council who were examined declared that they had no recollection of the words; that the debate regarded the means of reducing Scotland, not England; and that they had never heard the slightest hint of employing the Irish army anywhere but in Scotland. It must have been present in all minds that if an Irish army had been successfully used in Scotland it would assuredly have found other employment thereafter; but this was not the point in question. Strafford's answer covered all issues. "What will be the end," he said, "if words which are spoken in the King's Privy Council, half understood or misunderstood by its members, are to be turned into crime? No one will any longer have the courage to speak out his opinion plainly to the King." The lawyers also declared themselves on his side. There was no doubt that he had won his case.

The Commons, baffled, claimed to advance new evidence. Strafford demanded that if this were admitted he should have an equal right. The lords decided in his favour. And then suddenly there arose from the mass of Members gathered in the court loud cries of "Withdraw! Withdraw!" The Commons trooped back to St Stephen's Chapel and again locked their doors. Was this enemy of English rights to escape by legal processes? They knew he was their foe, and they meant to have his blood. They would dispense with a trial and have him declared guilty by Act of Parliament. Pym and Hampden did not themselves put forward the plan of a Bill of Attainder. They had it moved by one of their principal followers; but when it was launched they threw their weight behind it, and the weight of the angry, tumultuous City outside.

The Bill of Attainder passed the House of Commons on April 21, 1641, by 204 votes to 59. Among the minority was Lord Digby, who had come to Parliament as one of the leading opponents of the Crown. With all his gifts, which were exceptional, he pleaded against his own party. He gained nothing but the suspicion of being a renegade. A surge of panic and of wrath convulsed the assembly. When a board creaked overhead they thought of the Gunpowder Plot. The names of the fifty-nine were spread abroad as traitors defending a traitor. The aspect of the multitude which daily beset the approaches to Parliament became more than ever threatening. The peers deemed to be favourable to Strafford were cowed by the frenzy they saw around them. When Oliver St John urged the case for the Attainder in a great conference between the Houses he used arguments not of law but of revolution. Parliament was not bound, like inferior tribunals, by existing laws, but was justified in making new ones to suit circumstances. Its only guide should be care for the public weal: it was the political body, embracing all, from the King to the beggar, and could deal with individuals for the good of the whole, could open a vein to let out the corrupted blood. It had been said that the law must precede the offence; that where no law was there could be no transgression. But that plea could not avail for the man who had desired to overthrow all laws.

Only half the lords who had been present at the impeachment dared to vote upon the Bill of Attainder, and these in great preponderance sent Strafford to his doom. They had become convinced that if they let him go the King would use him to make war upon the Houses; and, as the Earl of Essex, the discontented son of Queen Elizabeth's favourite, brutally observed, "Stone-dead hath no fellow." The King tried to gain control of the Tower and of the prisoner. But the Governor, Sir William Balfour, closed his gates. He also spurned an immense bribe offered him by Strafford. The cry for "Justice!" rang through London streets. A mob of several thousand, many of them armed, appeared before the palace roaring for Strafford's head. In Parliament it was bruited that they would now impeach the Queen.

This was the agony of Charles's life, to which none of his other sufferings compared. But his real release came from Strafford himself. In a noble letter, written before the vote in the Lords, he had urged the King not to let any promise to him endanger the monarchy or the peace of the realm. At last

Charles made the surrender which haunted him to the last moment of his life. He gave his assent to the Bill of Attainder.

In the crash of the Strafford trial and execution the King let various matters slip. The Triennial Bill providing for the summoning of Parliament at least once in three years, if necessary, in spite of the Crown, put a final end to the system of Personal Rule over which Charles had so far presided. The grant of tonnage and poundage for one year only was accompanied by a censure upon the exaction of Ship Money, and reparation to all who had suffered for their resistance to it. The King perforce subscribed to all this. But he must have been completely broken for the moment when he assented to a measure designed "to prevent inconvenience that may happen by the untimely prorogation or dissolving of this present Parliament" except by its own consent. He accepted this on the same day as the Bill of Strafford's Attainder. It was in fact a law making this Parliament, since called the Long Parliament, perpetual. Many other changes necessary to the times and remedial to the discontents were made. The judges, whose tenure had hitherto been dependent upon the pleasure of the Crown, now held office on good behaviour. The Court of Star Chamber, which Henry VII had used to curb the baronage, but which had in the lapse of time become oppressive to the people, was abolished. So was the Court of High Commission, which had striven to impose religious uniformity. The jurisdiction of the Privy Council was strictly and narrowly defined. The principles of the Petition of Right about personal liberty, particularly freedom from arbitrary arrest, were now finally established. Charles endorsed these great decisions. He had realised that in his trusteeship of the rights of monarchy he had grasped too much. The whole Tudor system which the Stuarts had inherited was shaken from its base.

From the day when Strafford's head fell beneath the axe there began a conservative reaction, partial but nation-wide. Charles, who at the meeting of the Parliament had been almost alone with his cluster of hated Ministers, found himself increasingly sustained by strong and deep currents of public feeling. If he had only allowed these to have their flow he might have reached a very good establishment. The excesses and fanaticism of the Puritan party, their war upon the Church, their confederacy with the Scottish invaders, roused antagonisms of which the hitherto helpless Court was but a spectator, but from which the Crown might by patience and wisdom emerge, curtailed certainly but secure. Henceforward the quarrel was no longer between King and people, but between the two main themes and moods which have until the confusion of the modern age disputed for mastery in England. The twentieth century was to dawn before men and women became unable to recognise their political ancestors in this ancient conflict.

Charles now felt that his hope lay in a reconciliation with Scotland. The interplay of the Scots army in the North with the Puritan faction at Westminster was irresistible. He resolved to go to Scotland himself and open a Parliament in Edinburgh. Pym could hardly object to this. Charles accepted everything he had most abhorred. He strove to win the hearts of the

Covenanters. He listened devoutly to their sermons and sang the psalms in the manner of the Kirk. He assented to the establishment of total Presbyterianism in Scotland. But all was in vain. Charles was accused of complicity in an ill-starred attempt of Royalist partisans to kidnap the Scottish leader, the Marquess of Argyll. The Scots were confirmed in their obduracy, and the King returned to England crestfallen.

Upon this melancholy scene a hideous apparition now appeared. The execution of Strafford liberated all the elemental forces in Ireland which his system had so successfully held in restraint. The Irish Parliament in Dublin, formerly submissive, had hastened to voice their complaints against his rule. At the same time a Roman Catholic Celtic people regarded the English Protestantism with the utmost aversion. Strafford's disciplined Irish army was disbanded. Some efforts were made by Charles's Ministers to enlist the religious convictions of the Irish in the royal cause. But all this fused into inextricable ruin. The passions of the original inhabitants and of the hungry, downtrodden masses, bursting from all control, were directed upon the gentry, the landowners, and the Protestants, both within and without the Pale. A veritable Jacquerie,[1] recalling the dark times in France, broke upon the land in the autumn of 1641. The propertied classes, their families and dependants, fled to the few garrisoned towns. Cruelties unspeakable were reported on all sides, and the Government, under the Lords Justices, struck back without mercy. A general slaughter of males and a policy of devastation were proclaimed throughout large parts of the countryside. The Puritan party saw, or declared that they saw, in the Irish outrage the fate to which they would be consigned if the Popish tendencies of the bishops were armed with the sword of an absolute sovereign. They regarded the native Irish as wild beasts to be slain at sight, and the cruelties which they in their turn were to wreak in their hour of triumph took their impulse from this moment.

During September and October conservative reaction had become a tide. Who could accuse the Court of army plots when the English and Irish armies had both been disbanded? Englishmen, irrespective of religious and constitutional convictions, were ill disposed to be taxed for the upkeep of invading Scottish troops. Presbyterianism made little appeal to the bulk of the English people, who, so far as they were not satisfied with the Elizabethan Church tradition, sought spiritual comfort or excitement in the more vehement sects which had sprung up in the general turmoil of the Reformation, or in the Puritan body itself, such as Anabaptism and Brownism,[2] both of which were as much opposed to Presbytery as to Bishops. The House of Commons at the end of 1641 had travelled far. Pym and his supporters were still dominant and more extreme.

But there was an opposition equally resolute. The Lords were now at

1 Jacquerie, old French term for peasants and usually refers to the fourteenth-century rising of northern French peasants.
2 Brownism, after Robert Browne (c.1550–1633) who was against the establishment church and whose followers were the forerunners of the Congregationalists.

variance with the Commons, and a large majority, when they attended, sided with the King. From being the servants of the national cause the Puritans had become an aggressive faction. It was in this stormy weather that Pym and Hampden sought to rally their forces by bringing forward what was called the "Grand Remonstrance". This long document, on which committees had been at work for many months, was in fact a party manifesto. It was intended to advertise all that had so far been accomplished by Parliament in remedying old grievances, and to proclaim the future policy of the Parliamentary leaders. Pym's hope was to re-establish the unity of his diverse followers and so the more extreme demands for religious reform were dropped. The power of bishops was to be curtailed, but they were not to be abolished.

Nevertheless the growing body of Conservatives, or "Episcopalian Party", as they were sometimes named, were affronted by the Remonstrance and determined to oppose it. They did not like the way that Pym was going. They wanted "to win the King by the sweeter way of concealing his errors than by publishing of them". Pym, however, was preparing to carry the struggle further; he would appeal to the people and win complete control for Parliament over the King's Ministers. Here was a sweeping challenge to royal authority. But the King now had at his side very different counsellors from those of a year before. Many of his former opponents, chief among them Digby and his father, the Earl of Bristol, were hostile to Pym. Bishop Williams, foremost of Laud's critics, now stood against Laud's accusers. Falkland and Colepeper ranged themselves against the violence of the majority and were soon to take office in the King's Government. Edward Hyde, later famous as the historian Clarendon, opened the debate by insisting that the aim must now be peace: if the Remonstrance as a whole were carried, and especially if it were published, the disputes would be embittered and prolonged.

The debate was long and earnest, vehement with restrained passion. At last at midnight the Remonstrance, somewhat amended, was put to the vote. When Parliament had met a year earlier the King's party could not count on a third of its members. Now the Grand Remonstrance was carried only by eleven votes. A motion was put forward by the majority that it should be printed forthwith. On this the Commons rose to a clash of opposing wills. About one o'clock in the morning a lawyer of the Middle Temple, Mr Geoffrey Palmer, demanded that the clerk should record the names of all who protested. The procedure of protest by a minority was, and long continued to be, customary in the House of Lords, but the principle of the Commons was that the vote of the majority was the vote of the House. Palmer seemed to ask who was prepared to protest. A great crowd rose to their feet with the cry, "All! All!" Plumed hats were waved, men laid their hands upon their swords, some even drew them and rested their hands upon the pommels. Only Hampden's suave, timely intervention prevented a bloody collision. But here the pathway of debate was broken, and war alone could promise further stepping-stones.

A hitherto little-noticed Member for Cambridge, Oliver Cromwell, rather rough in his manners, but an offshoot of Thomas Cromwell's line said to Falkland as they left the House, "If the Remonstrance had been rejected I would have sold all that I had next morning, and never have seen England any more; and I know there are many honest men of the same resolution." The King who, in spite of his failure in Scotland and the Irish catastrophe, had been conscious of ever-gathering support, was now drawn into various contradictory blunders. At one moment he sought to form a Ministry dependent upon the majority faction which ruled the House of Commons. Still seeking desperately for a foothold, Charles invited Pym himself to become Chancellor of the Exchequer. Such a plan had no contact with reality. Colepeper took the post instead, and Falkland became Secretary of State. Next, in violent revulsion, Charles resolved to prosecute five of his principal opponents in the Commons for high treason. Upon this wild course he was impelled by Queen Henrietta Maria. She taunted him with cowardice, and exhorted him, if he would ever see her again, to lay strong hands upon those who spent their nights and days seeking his overthrow and her life. He certainly convinced himself that Pym meant to impeach the Queen.

Thus goaded, Charles, accompanied by three or four hundred swordsmen – "Cavaliers" we may now call them – went down to the House of Commons. It was January 4, 1642. Never before had a king set foot in the Chamber. When his officers knocked at the door and it was known that he had come in person members of all parties looked upon each other in amazement. His followers beset the doors. All rose at his entry. The Speaker, William Lenthall, quitted his chair and knelt before him. The King, seating himself in the chair, after professing his goodwill to the House, demanded the surrender of the five indicted Members – Pym, Hampden, Holles, Hazelrigg, and Strode. But a treacherous message from a lady of the Queen's Bedchamber had given Pym a timely warning. The accused Members had already embarked at Westminster steps and were safe amid the train-bands and magistrates of the City. Speaker Lenthall could give no information. "I have only eyes to see and ears to hear as the House may direct," he pleaded. The King, already conscious of his mistake, cast his eyes around the quivering assembly. "I see that the birds are flown," he said lamely, and after some civil reassurances he departed at the head of his disappointed, growling adherents. But as he left the Chamber a low, long murmur of "Privilege" pursued him.[1]

Upon this episode the wrath of London became uncontrollable. The infuriated mobs who thronged the streets and bellowed outside the palace caused Charles and his Court to escape from the capital to Hampton Court. He never saw London again except to suffer trial and death. Within a week of his intrusion into the House the five Members were escorted back to Parliament from the City. Their progress was triumphal. Over two thousand armed men

---

1   Until recently the Members of Parliament for the City of London took their places on the Treasury bench at the opening of a session in perpetual acknowledgment of the services rendered by the City in protecting the five men.

accompanied them up the river, and on either bank large forces, each with eight pieces of cannon, marched abreast of the flotilla. Henceforth London was irretrievably lost to the King. By stages he withdrew to Newmarket, to Nottingham, and to York. Here he waited during the early months of 1642, while the tireless antagonisms which rent England slowly rebuilt him an authority and an armed force. There were now two centres of government. Pym, the Puritans, and what was left of the Parliament ruled with dictatorial power in London *in the King's name*. The King, round whom there gathered many of the finest elements in Old England, freed from the bullying of the London mob, became once again a prince with sovereign rights. About these two centres there slowly assembled the troops and resources for the waging of civil war.

On June 1, 1642, Parliament presented nineteen Propositions to the King. This ultimatum demanded that the Council, the King's Great Officers of State, and his children's tutors should be appointed by Parliament; that Parliament should be given complete control over the Militia, and over the army required for the reconquest of Ireland – that is to say, "the power of the sword"; and that a Church Settlement should be determined by the wishes of Parliament. In brief, the King was invited to surrender his whole effective sovereignty over Church and State. But underlying the apparently clear-cut constitutional issue was a religious and class conflict. The Puritans were predominant in Parliament, High Churchmen at Court. The "new Classes" of merchants and manufacturers and the substantial tenant farmers in some counties were claiming a share of political power, which had hitherto been almost monopolised by the aristocracy and the hereditary landlords.

Yet when the alignment of the parties on the outbreak of the Civil War is surveyed no simple divisions are to be found. Brother fought against brother, father against son. The Royalists' appeal was negative, but none the less potent. Against loyalty to Parliament they invoked loyalty to the Crown; against Puritan ardour Anglican unity. On both sides men went into the fight doubtfully, but guided by their belief in high-souled ideals. On both sides were others – dissolute courtiers, ambitious politicians spoiling for a fight, out-of-work mercenaries, ready to profit from the national dissensions; but, broadly, the contest now became a tragic conflict of loyalties and ideals.

The arrogant tone and ever-growing demands of the Parliamentary party shaped the lines of the struggle and recruited the forces of the King. The greater part of the nobility gradually rallied to the Royalist cause; the tradesmen and merchants generally inclined to the Parliament; but a substantial section of the aristocracy were behind Pym, and many boroughs were devotedly Royalist. The gentry and yeomen in the counties were deeply divided. Those nearer London generally inclined to Parliament, while the North and West remained largely Royalist.

Both sides fought in the name of the King, and both upheld the Parliamentary institution. The Roundheads always spoke "of King and Parliament". The orders given to their first Commander-in-Chief, the Earl of

Essex, directed him to "rescue" the King and princes, if necessary by force, from the evil counsellors into whose power they had fallen. Charles vowed himself to live as a constitutional monarch and to respect the laws of the realm. Behind all class and political issues the religious quarrel was the driving power. For more than seventy years absolute peace had reigned in England. Except for a few officers who had seen service on the Continent, no one knew anything about military matters. At first the Cavaliers, trained in fencing, inured to the chase, with their gamekeepers and dependants, had a military advantage over the Roundheads. From York the King looked to Hull, where the weapons of his disbanded army against the Scots had been stored. The Prince of Wales and the Duke of York, who were but boys aged twelve and nine, paid a visit to Hull and were courteously received, but when the King himself sought entry the Governor, Sir John Hotham, closed the gates and manned the ramparts against him. As he had only a few thousand local levies or train-bands the King had to accept the rebuff. It was more, it was a heavy blow. Arms were vital. At Nottingham, where town and county alike had proclaimed devotion, Charles set up his standard on August 22 and called his loyal subjects to his aid. This was the ancient signal for feudal duty, and its message awoke ancestral memories throughout the land.

At Nottingham the King had only eight hundred horse and three hundred foot, and at first it seemed doubtful whether any royal army could be raised. But the violence of Parliament served him well. By the end of September he had with him two thousand horse and six thousand foot. A few weeks later their numbers were more than doubled, and other forces were raised for him all over the country. The Queen, who had found refuge in Holland, sent arms and trained officers, procured by the sale of the Crown jewels. But the Navy, which Charles had quarrelled with his subjects to sustain, adhered to Parliament and the blockade was hard to run. The great nobles supplied the King with money. The Marquess of Newcastle is said to have spent nearly a million pounds upon the Royalist cause, and the Marquess of Worcester seven or eight hundred thousand. The University of Oxford melted their plate, and this example was followed in many a hall and manor. When Cambridge University was found in the same mood Cromwell intervened with armed force. Meanwhile the Roundheads, sustained by ample funds from the wealth and regular taxation of London, levied and trained an army of twenty-five thousand men under Lord Essex. As on the Royalist side, most of the regiments were raised personally by prominent people. But whereas the King could give only a commission to raise a regiment or a troop Parliament could provide the equipment as well. The quality of the Parliamentary forces was inferior, but they made up in zeal what they lacked in discipline and military skill. The London militia, drilled by German instructors, were already to be respected.

The King, skilfully avoiding Essex's army, now moved west to join his Welsh reinforcements, and then struck south for the Thames valley and London. There was a panic in the capital when this became evident. An address was hastily dispatched to the King, proposing that he should return to his Parliament, and at the same time Essex was enjoined to overtake him. Charles did not dare to be caught between the troops in London and those who followed hard upon him.

At Edgehill, in Warwickshire, on October 23, 1642, the royal army turned on its pursuers and attacked them before their rearguard, who was approaching the village of Kineton, had come in. The battle was marked by abundant ignorance and zeal on both sides. Prince Rupert of the Rhine, the King's nephew, who, with his younger brother, Prince Maurice, both fresh from the European wars, had hastened to his side and taken command of the cavalry, charged and overthrew all the Parliamentary horse on their left wing. Carried away by his own ardour or the indiscipline of his troopers, he pursued the Roundheads into Kineton village, where he plundered the baggage train. Meanwhile the King and the royal infantry, unsupported by any cavalry of his own, had to withstand the assault of the Parliamentary foot and several strong bodies of horse. After confused and bloody fighting even Charles's own guards were broken. His cannon were captured. The royal standard was for a time taken, and its bearer, Sir Edmund Verney, was cut down. But the approach of the Parliamentary rearguard under Hampden drove Rupert and his cavalry from the baggage train. They returned to the battlefield in time to avert defeat. Both sides retired to their morning positions and gazed at each other in doubt and confusion. At least five thousand Englishmen lay upon the field; twelve hundred were buried by the vicar of Kineton.

Edgehill, which might so easily have ended the war in the King's favour, was judged a drawn battle. Essex rightly resumed his march to cover London, which was in fact, however, a retreat. The King occupied Banbury, and in triumph entered Oxford, which now became his headquarters and remained so to the very end. Fighting and pillage spread throughout the country. The constitutional issue, the religious quarrel, and countless local feuds were combined in a new surge of party hatred. The cleavages of the great Civil War dominated English life for two centuries.

From the beginning of 1643 the war became general. Classes and interests as well as parties and creeds did their best against one another. The ports and towns, the manufacturing centres, mostly adhered to the Parliament; what might be called Old England rallied to Charles. In the North Queen Henrietta Maria arrived from Holland. Braving the blockade, she brought a considerable shipload of cannon and munitions to Bridlington, on the Yorkshire coast. The Parliamentary warships were hard upon her wake. Coming as close inshore as the ebb tide would permit, they fired their guns upon the house where she was sleeping. Her men assured the Queen that her ship and its priceless cargo would be defended, and in barefoot haste she sheltered from the whistling shot in the village. This personal cannonade upon the Queen, by the Parliamentary admiral Batten, was deemed unwarrantable and indecent in an age where sex, rank, and chivalry still counted. Henrietta Maria entered York amid intense rejoicing. Enormous crowds of loyal people cheered the imposing train of cannon which followed behind her. Some had thought that she, a woman, would urge the King to peace. On the contrary, she brought with her a spirit of war as tameless and indomitable as Margaret of Anjou.

Parliament was already in some doubts about the capacity of Essex as a general. The peace party favoured him, but the fancy of those who wanted all-out war was Sir William Waller, now sent to command the Parliamentary army in the West. The Cornishmen, however, showed a lively devotion to the royal cause and uncommon nimbleness and courage in fighting. Here also the most sagacious and skilful of the Royalist generals, Sir Ralph Hopton, commanded. Three fierce battles on a small scale were fought by Hopton and Waller. A warm personal friendship subsisted between them, but, as Waller wrote to his opponent, "each had to bear his part in a matter of honour and fidelity". At Lansdowne, outside Bath, Hopton's Cornishmen stormed Waller's position. The feature of Waller's army was the London cavalry. These were so completely encased in armour that they looked like "moving fortresses", and were called by both sides "the Lobsters". The Lobsters were charged uphill by the Royalists, who wrought great havoc among them. Waller was defeated, but Hopton's losses were so severe that he took refuge in Devizes. Hopton himself was wounded by the explosion of almost the only powder wagon in his army. His horsemen, under Prince Maurice, ran away. But the Prince, returning by a rapid march with fresh cavalry from Oxford, found Waller drawn up to receive him on Roundway Down. The Royalists attacked and drove the Lobsters headlong down the steep slopes, while Hopton moved out from the town and completed the victory with his infantry.

Fired with these successes, Rupert, with the Oxford army joined to Hopton's forces, summoned, assaulted, and procured the surrender of the city of Bristol. This was the second city in the kingdom, and on the whole its inhabitants were Royalist. They had undermined the resistance of the Parliamentary garrison; they looked upon Rupert as a deliverer. The warships in the port declared for the King, and hope dawned of a royal squadron which could command the Bristol Channel. King Charles was master in the West.

His cause had also prevailed in Yorkshire. Here Lord Fairfax and his son, Sir Thomas, led the Parliamentary forces. Sir Thomas besieged York; but the Marquess of Newcastle, a man of no military aptitude, rich, corpulent, proud, but entirely devoted, led his territorial retainers, the valiant "white-coats", to its relief, and later in the summer overwhelmed the Fairfaxes at Adwalton Moor. Upon the Parliamentary side there now appeared numbers of peasants armed with scythes or bludgeons – "the Clubmen", as they were called. These shared in the slaughter to the full. The defeat left Parliament with Hull as their only stronghold in the North. The Governor of Scarborough, Hugh Cholmley, a distinguished Member of Parliament, had already deserted the Roundheads, carrying over his forces and bringing about the surrender of the town. Meanwhile in the Midlands also the Royalists made head. The Hastings family had the upper hand in Leicestershire and the Cavendishes in Lincolnshire, though Charles Cavendish himself was defeated and slain in a sharp fight near Gainsborough by Colonel Cromwell, who for the first time brought into the field the mounted troops of the Eastern Counties Association, which he had organised and trained.

Charles possessed a certain strategic comprehension. He had not that intense clarity of view and promptitude to act which are the qualities of great commanders, but his military outlook took all things in, and he was brave in action. From the beginning of 1643 his design was for a general advance on London. Hopton from the West, Newcastle from the North, himself from Oxford, would converge on the capital and break the prime centre of rebellion. Till midsummer the results of the fight seemed to favour this decisive plan; but the King had neither the resources nor the authority for so large a combination. Thus the King, in the zenith of his military fortune, resolved to besiege Gloucester.

Meanwhile in London Pym, the master of the Parliament, the heart and soul of the Roundhead war, was in grievous straits. So far all had gone ill and every hope had been broken. Strong currents of Royalism now flowed in the capital. These joined themselves to the peace movement. The Common Council of the City was unyielding; but Royalist opinion was too strong to be silenced. At one time seventy merchants were in prison for refusing to pay taxes which they judged illegal. On another occasion hundreds of women crowded to Westminster to present a petition for peace. When the troopers rode in among them the frantic women tried to drag them from their saddles. "Let us throw the dog Pym into the Thames," they cried. But the soldiers drew their swords and slashed the women with extreme brutality, chasing them round Palace Yard, so that many were injured before they could escape. Pym's life was ebbing to its close. He had cancer. His greatest colleague, Hampden, had died of wounds early in the year after a clash with Rupert's cavalry at Chalgrove Field. The ruin of his cause and the approach of death in an array of disaster seemed to be the only reward of Pym's struggles. Undaunted, he bore up against all; and the last impulse of his life may well have turned the scale. All the Puritan forces in London were roused to repudiate peace. The preachers exhorted their congregations, and warlike crowds beset Westminster. The relief of Gloucester was the cry.

The Earl of Essex had fallen into just disrepute as a general, and was suspected of political lukewarmness. Now, however, he was ordered and conjured to relieve Gloucester. He accepted the duty, perhaps hoping this would give him strength to stop England tearing herself to pieces. At Gloucester Governor Massey had failed the King. The violent Puritanism within his walls left him no choice of treacheries. The King's resources, indeed the art of war in England at this time, afforded no satisfactory method of making a siege. Compared with the gigantic systematised operations of later times the sieges of the English Civil War were feeble and primitive. A few batteries of cannon, with scanty powder and ball tried to make a hole in the wall in which both sides could fight with sword and musket until food ran short or the inhabitants in fear of sack forced a capitulation. The King had made no progress against

Gloucester when, in the early days of September, Essex and the London army drew near in superior numbers. There was no choice but to raise the siege and retire upon Oxford.

Essex entered Gloucester in triumph, but found himself immediately short of supplies and food, with a formidable enemy between him and home. Both armies headed for London, and on September 20 they clashed at Newbury, in Berkshire. There was a long and bitter conflict. Once again Rupert's cavalry beat their opponents; but they could make no impression on the London pikemen and musketeers. A third of the troops were casualties, and on the Royalist side many nobles fell. Among them Lord Falkland found in death the release he had for some time sought from a world and a quarrel which he could no longer endure. The battle was undecided when darkness fell. Essex had no choice but to renew it at dawn; but the King withdrew, stricken by the loss of so many personal friends and short of powder, and the London road lay open to the Roundheads.

The King's large plan for 1643 had failed. Nevertheless the campaign had been very favourable to him. He had gained control of a great part of England. His troops were still, on the whole, better fighting-men than the Roundheads. Much ground lost at the beginning of the war had been recovered. A drift of desertion to the royal camp had begun. All could see how even were the forces which rent the kingdom. On both sides men's thoughts turned to peace. Not so the thoughts of Pym; he looked to the Scots; by substantial money payments he induced a Scots army of not less than eleven thousand men to intervene. He led Parliament on September 25 into signing a Solemn League and Covenant among themselves and with the Scots to wage war with untiring zeal. It was a military alliance expressed in terms of a religious manifesto. Then on December 8 Pym died, uncheered by success, but unwearied by misfortune. He had neglected his private affairs in the public cause, and his estate would have been bankrupt had not Parliament, as some expression of their grief and gratitude, paid his debts. He remains the most famous of the old Parliamentarians, and the man who more than any other saved England from absolute monarchy and set her upon the path she has since pursued.

There was a lull during the winter. Charles was encouraged by the death of the great French Minister, Richelieu, which restored power to his Queen's brother, Louis XIII, and by the friendly aid of the King of Denmark. In Ireland the Earl of Ormonde, Lord-Lieutenant, had made a truce with the Catholics, who, in spite of all atrocities committed and suffered, still accepted the monarchy. The Royalist camp even considered bringing Irish Papists into England, and rumours of this did harm to the King's cause. But the "Cessation" in Ireland, as it was called, enabled Irish Protestant regiments and other royal troops to be brought to England, where they played a recognisable part.

Charles had never dissolved the Parliament which was warring against him, because in so doing he would have invalidated his assent not only to the Act which he had unwisely accepted in 1641, making it virtually perpetual, but many other laws which counted with his own supporters. Declaring therefore that the Parliament at Westminster was no longer a free Parliament, he summoned all who had been expelled or who had fled from it to a Counter-Assembly. The response was remarkable. Eighty-three peers and a hundred and seventy-five Members met in Oxford on January 22, 1644. But these advantages were overwhelmed by the arrival in England of a Scottish army of eighteen thousand foot and three thousand horse who crossed the Tweed in January. For this succour the London Parliament paid £31,000 a month and the cost of equipment. But the Scots, though in a sense hired, had other objects besides money. They now aspired to outroot the Episcopacy and impose by armed force the Presbyterian system of Church government upon England. They had the best of both worlds; they were invited to invade a wealthy country at its own expense in the cause of Almighty God and their own particular style of public worship. Punctual cash payments and assured salvation awaited them across the Border.

It was now that Oliver Cromwell came into prominence. The Member for Cambridge was deemed the best officer on the Parliamentary side, though he had not yet held a supreme command. At the head of the troops of the Eastern Counties Association, he had triumphed at Gainsborough in a dark hour. His regiment had a discipline and quality surpassing, as it seemed, any formation on either side. He could not be ignored. He could not be suppressed. The rise of Cromwell to the first rank of power during 1644 sprang both from his triumphs on the battlefield and his resistance to the Presbyterians and the Scots at Westminster. Except for Papists and Episcopalians, he declared for liberty of conscience. All the obscurer Protestant sects saw in him their champion.

The Scottish Commissioners and divines nor their English colleagues could afford to quarrel with Cromwell and his Independents while the Royalists were unsubdued. They thought it better for their Army to penetrate deeply into England and become involved in the war before dealing with these "dissenting brethren" as they deserved. Thus not for the first or last time theology waited upon arms; and in the long run it was the alliance of the Anglican and Presbyterian against their common enemy the Independent that restored both the monarchy and the Established Church.

In the North the Marquess of Newcastle had now to contend with the Scottish army on one side and the two Fairfaxes on the other. He made the military movements usual under such conditions. In the spring he marched north against the Scots and left Lord Bellasis to ward off the Roundheads. Bellasis was overwhelmed at Selby on April 11 by the Fairfaxes. Newcastle's rear was thereby exposed, and he could do no more than maintain himself in York, where he was presently vigorously besieged.

The King now wrote Rupert a letter which contained the following passage: "If York be lost I shall esteem my crown little less, unless supported by your sudden march to me, and a miraculous conquest in the South, before the effects of the Northern power can be found here. ... Wherefore I command

and conjure you, by the duty and affection which I know you bear me, that, all new enterprises laid aside, you immediately march according to your first intention, with all your force, to the relief of York; but if that be lost ... that you immediately march with your whole strength directly to Worcester to assist me and my army, without which, or your having relieved York by beating the Scots, all the successes you can afterwards have most infallibly will be useless to me."[1]

Rupert needed no spur, and took these involved sentences as an order to fight an immediate battle on the first chance. "Before God," said Colepeper to Charles when he heard that the letter had been sent, "you are undone, because upon this peremptory order he will fight whatever comes on't." So it fell out. Rupert saved York at its last gasp: the mine was sprung; the walls were already breached. The Scots and Roundheads withdrew together westwards covering Leeds and joining the forces from East Anglia under Lord Manchester and Cromwell. The three Puritan armies were thus combined, and numbered twenty thousand foot and seven thousand horse.

Their outposts lay upon a ridge at Marston Moor. Rupert met the Marquess of Newcastle, and their united forces reached eleven thousand foot and seven thousand horse. The Marquess was against fighting. He regarded the Northern theatre as relieved for the time being. He expected reinforcements from Durham. He was vexed that Rupert should have command over him. He would have been content to see the Prince march back southwards to join the King, but Rupert said he " had a letter from the King with a positive and absolute command to fight the enemy". "Happen what will," said the Marquess to his friends, "I will not shun to fight, for I have no other ambition than to live and die a loyal subject of his Majesty." Accordingly the Royalist army followed the enemy to Marston Moor, and on July 2 found themselves near their encampments.

The whole day passed in alternating rain and sunshine, with both armies in close contact. Rupert imagined that it rested with him to begin the battle on the morrow, but at six o'clock in the evening he was himself attacked by the whole force of the Roundheads, who out-numbered his infantry by nearly two to one. A heavy column of steel-clad cavalry was seen approaching at a fast trot. It was Cromwell and his Ironsides. The royal army, who, though drawn up, were preparing to eat their evening meal, had neither the advantage of a defensive position nor the impulsion of attack. None the less they made a glorious fight. Goring's cavalry of the left wing beat the Roundhead right, and, falling upon the Scots in the centre, threw them into disorder and retreat. The veteran Alexander Leslie, now Lord Leven, quitted the field, declaring all was lost, and was arrested by a constable ten miles away. But Cromwell, with the help of the remaining Scots under David Leslie, restored the day. Now for the first time the heroic, dreaded Cavaliers met their match, and their master.

---

1   Gardiner, *History of the Great Civil War* (1901), vol. i, p. 571. [Churchill]

Marston Moor was the largest and also the bloodiest battle of the war. Little quarter was given and there were four thousand slain. Newcastle's "white-coats" fought to the death, and fell where they stood. They had boasted they would dye these white coats with the blood of the foe. They were indeed reddened, but with their own blood. Night alone ended the pursuit. A disaster of the first magnitude had smitten the King's cause. His Northern army was shattered and the whole of the North was lost. The prestige of Rupert's cavalry was broken. The Marquess, broken-hearted, fled into exile. Rupert, whom nothing could appal, gathered up the remnants of his army and led them safely south to Shrewsbury.

The success of the King's campaign in the South veiled, at least for a time, the disaster at Marston Moor. Charles revealed unexpected qualities as a general. He had begun to like the life of a camp, with its stir and movement of war. By May Charles could only gather ten thousand men to meet the two armies of Essex and Waller, who each had as many. He hoped that the ill-feeling between the Roundhead generals would give him a chance to strike at them separately. But instead they moved in concert upon Oxford. The city was ill supplied for a siege, and could certainly not maintain the Royalist field army as well as its garrison. It was expected, not only by the Parliament, but in his own circles, that the King would be caught in Oxford and compelled to surrender. However, after providing for the defence of the city, Charles, with great skill, eluded both of the converging armies and reached Worcester.

The two Roundhead generals were then forced to divide their forces, as he had foreseen. Waller manoeuvred against the King, who gradually moved northwards, while Essex broke into the Royalist West. Then, turning east, the King inflicted a severe check on Waller at Cropredy Bridge, in Oxfordshire, on June 6, capturing all his artillery. He was undaunted by Marston Moor. Outmarching and outwitting Waller, he suddenly during August began to march westward, with the intention of taking Essex in the rear. Essex had made some progress, and had relieved both Lyme and Plymouth from siege; but he found himself obstinately opposed in districts where the whole countryside was hostile to the Roundheads. Now the King himself came suddenly upon him. Essex was outnumbered, his supplies were cut off, and after rejecting a proposal for surrender he sailed with his officers to Plymouth, ordered his cavalry to cut their way out of the trap, and left the rest of his army to its fate. All the infantry and artillery, to the number of eight thousand men, surrendered at Lostwithiel, in Cornwall, on September 2.[1]

The main forces of the Parliament were now thrown against the King. Manchester and Waller were reinforced by Cromwell. Once again, on October 27, the armies met at Newbury and once again there was a drawn battle, followed by a Royalist retirement. It was late in November before active warfare paused. Charles re-entered Oxford in triumph. The campaign had been his finest military achievement. In the teeth of adversity he had

1 1644.

maintained himself with little money or supplies against odds of two or three to one. Moreover, on the side of the Parliament there lay always the hard weight of a greatly superior artillery.

Cromwell rode in from the Army to his duties as a Member of Parliament. His differences with the Scots and his opposition to Presbyterian uniformity were already swaying Roundhead politics. He now made a vehement and organised attack on the conduct of the war, and its mismanagement by lukewarm generals of noble rank, namely Essex and Manchester. Essex was discredited enough after Lostwithiel, but Cromwell also charged Manchester with losing the second Battle of Newbury by sloth and want of zeal. He himself was avid for the power and command which he was sure he could wield; but he proceeded astutely. While he urged the complete reconstitution of the Parliamentary army upon a New Model similar to his own in the Eastern Counties, his friends in the House of Commons proposed a so-called "Self-denying Ordinance", which would exclude Members of either House from military employment. The handful of lords who still remained at Westminster realised well enough that this was an attack on their prominence in the conduct of the war, if not on their social order; but there were such compelling military reasons in favour of the measure that neither they nor the Scots, who already dreaded Cromwell, could prevent its being carried. Essex and Manchester, who had fought the King from the beginning of the quarrel, who had raised regiments and served the Parliamentary cause in all fidelity, were discarded. They pass altogether from the story.

During the winter months the Army was reconstituted in accordance with Cromwell's ideas. The old personally-raised regiments of the Parliamentary nobles were broken up and their officers and men incorporated in entirely new formations. These, the New Model, comprised eleven regiments of horse, each six hundred strong, twelve regiments of foot, twelve hundred strong, and a thousand dragoons, in all twenty-two thousand men. Compulsion was freely used to fill the ranks. In one district of Sussex the three conscriptions of April, July, and September 1645 yielded a total of 149 men. A hundred and thirty-four guards were needed to escort them to the colours.

At the King's headquarters it was thought that these measures would demoralise the Parliamentary troops; and no doubt at first this was so. But the Roundhead faction now had a symmetrical military organisation led by men who had risen in the field and had no other standing but their military record and religious zeal. Sir Thomas Fairfax was appointed Commander-in-Chief. Cromwell, as Member for Cambridge, was at first debarred from serving. However, it soon appeared that his Self-denying Ordinance applied only to his rivals. The urgency of the new campaign and military discontents which he alone could quell forced even the reluctant Lords to make an exception in his favour. In June 1645 he was appointed General of the Horse, and was thus the only man who combined high military command with an outstanding Parliamentary position. From this moment he became the dominant figure in both spheres.

Amid these stresses Archbishop Laud, who languished ailing in the Tower, was brought to the scaffold. Roundheads, Scots, and Puritans alike could all combine upon this act of hatred. The House of Commons upon a division rejected his appeal to be decapitated rather than hanged, drawn, and quartered. Overnight however this barbarous decision was mitigated, and after he had uttered an unyielding discourse the old man's head was chopped off in a dignified manner.

The desire of all Englishmen for an end to the unnatural strife forced itself upon the most inflamed partisans. "Clubmen" reappeared. Large numbers of farmers and their labourers, together with townsfolk, assembled in many parts of the country with such weapons as they could find, protesting against the exactions and pillage of the contending forces. They now showed themselves rather more favourable to the King than to the Parliament. Largely to please the Scots, a parley for a peace settlement was set on foot at Uxbridge, near London, and on this many hopes were reposed, though not by the die-hards in Parliament. But neither King Charles nor the Roundhead executive had the slightest intention of giving way upon the two main points – Episcopacy and the control of the armed forces.

The antagonism of the Scots towards Cromwell and the pressure to enforce by law Presbyterian conformity against independent sectarianism were now at their height. Echoes of Marston Moor mingled with doctrinal differences. Leven and a part of the Scottish army had run away, while Cromwell and his Ironsides had remained to conquer. The Scots retorted by accusing Cromwell of personal cowardice in action; but this theme did not carry conviction. Their unwarrantable and intolerant interference in English life, though well paid, had drawn upon them a formidable animosity, and their main object of enforcing Presbyterianism was now frustrated by forces hitherto unimagined but wielding a sharp and heavy sword.

At the same time the Marquess of Montrose sprang upon the scene. He had been a Covenanter, but having quarrelled with Argyll went over to the King. Now he made himself known to history as a noble character and brilliant general. He pledged his faith to Charles, and distracted all Scotland by a series of victories gained against much larger forces, although sometimes his men had only stones to throw before falling on with the claymore. Dundee, Aberdeen, Glasgow, Perth, and Edinburgh were at one time or another in his power. He wrote to Charles assuring him that he would bring all Scotland to his rescue if he could hold out. But a decisive battle impended in the South.

On June 14, 1645, the last trial of strength was made. Charles, having taken Leicester, which was sacked, met Fairfax and Cromwell in the fine hunting country about Naseby. The Cavaliers had so often saved themselves by the offensive spirit, which Rupert embodied to the eclipse of other military qualities, that they did not hesitate to attack uphill the Roundhead army of twice their numbers. The action followed what had almost become the usual course. Rupert shattered the Parliamentary left, and though, as at Edgehill, his troopers were attracted by the Parliamentary baggage column, he returned to strike heavily at the central Roundhead infantry. But Cromwell on the other flank drove all before him, and also took control of the Roundhead reserves. The royal foot, beset on all sides by overwhelming numbers, fought with devotion. The King wished himself to charge to their rescue with the last reserve which stood about his person. He actually gave the order; but prudent hands were laid upon his bridle by some of his staff, and the royal reserves wheeled to the right and retreated above a mile. Here they were joined by Rupert, who had seen nothing but success, the Royalist cavalry quitting the field intact. The foot were killed or captured. Quarter was given, and the butchery was less than at Marston Moor. A hundred Irish women who were found in the Royalist camp were put to the sword by the Ironsides on grounds of moral principle as well as of national prejudice. Naseby was the expiring effort of the Cavaliers in the open field. There still remained many sieges, with reliefs and manoeuvrings, but the final military decision of the Civil War had been given.

CHAPTER THIRTY

THE AXE FALLS

*Charles I surrenders to the Scots – the Scots hand him to the Parliamentary
Commissioners – the army demands wages and rights – Charles escapes
to Carisbrooke Castle – the Second Civil War – Pride's Purge – Charles I
executed – the Republic – the Council of State – assault on the
Levellers – Gerard Winstanley and the Diggers – Cromwell sacks
Drogheda – Montrose executed – Charles II's declaration of loyalty –
the Engagers – war with Scotland – the Battle of Worcester – the
Boscobel oak – Charles II flees – Navigation Act – war against the
Dutch – the Rump Parliament – war with Spain – the Barebones
Parliament – Cromwell the Protector – the major generals – Cromwell
refuses the Crown – the death of the Lord Protector*

BY THE spring of 1646 all armed resistance to the Parliamentary Army
was beaten down. Charles was now ready to yield upon the control
of the armed forces, but for the sake of the Episcopal establishment
of the Church of England he was prepared to continue the struggle
single-handed. Montrose had been defeated in the autumn of 1645 at
Philiphaugh, near the Border, by detachments from the regular Scottish army
in England. Yet it was to the Scots Government that Charles thought of
turning. He saw the deep division which was now open between Scotland and
the Ironsides. He hoped that his Sovereign Majesty, though stripped of power,
might yet raise, from what seemed a most adverse quarter, a new resource for
his unquenchable purpose. He also had expectations of aid from France, where
Queen Henrietta Maria had taken refuge. In the event all her efforts on his
behalf came to nothing, and she never saw her husband again.

The King resolved to place himself in the hands of the Scots. A French
agent obtained from them a verbal promise that the King should be secure in
his person and in his honour, and that he should not be pressed to do anything
contrary to his conscience. On this he resorted to the headquarters of the
Scottish army, which, with the Roundheads, was besieging Newark. Newark
fell, and the Scots immediately turned northwards. The King had persuaded
himself he was a guest; but he soon found he was a prisoner. Although treated
with ceremony, he was closely guarded, deprived of all intercourse with his

personal followers, and his windows were watched lest an uncensored letter should be thrown into the street. Kept at Newcastle in these hard circumstances, he entered upon nearly a year's tenacious bargainings on the national issues at stake. Parliament's plan was to keep Charles captive till they had built him a constitutional and religious cage, and meanwhile to use his name and sign manual for all that they wished to do in their party interest. He was to subscribe to the Covenant; the bishops were to be abolished. The Fleet and militia were for twenty years to be in the hands of Parliament. An immense catalogue of pains and penalties, described as "branches" and "qualifications", flung all his faithful friends and supporters into a kind of attainder as wholesale as that which had smitten the house of Lancaster after Towton.

In February 1647 the Scots, having been paid an instalment of half the sum due to them for their services in England, handed over Charles under guarantee for his safety to Parliamentary Commissioners and returned to their own country. This transaction, though highly practical, wore and still wears a sorry look. When the Scots had taken their payment Charles was led with the greatest deference to Holmby House in Northamptonshire by his new owners. His popularity became at once manifest. From Newcastle southwards the journey was a progress of cheering crowds and clashing bells. To greet the King, to be freed from the cruel wars, to have the Old England back again, no doubt with some important changes, was the national wish. Completely broken in the field, as previously in the Parliamentary struggle, Charles was still incomparably the most important figure in England. Every one was for the King, provided he would do what they wished. Stripped of all material weapons, he was more than ever conscious of the power of the institution which he embodied. But a third and new partner had appeared upon the English scene. The Ironside Army, twenty-two thousand strong, was not yet the master, but was no longer the servant, of those who had created it. At its head stood its renowned and trusted generals: Thomas Fairfax, Commander-in-Chief; Oliver Cromwell, its sun of glory; Henry Ireton, its brain and in a large degree its conscience. Beneath them, upon the grim parades, stirred political and religious controversies sufficient in themselves for civil and social wars far more embittered than that which had been finished.

Now that the war was won most Members of Parliament and their leaders had no more need of the Army. A large number of regiments should be employed in Ireland to avenge the Irish massacres of 1641. Suitable garrisons must be maintained in England. As for the rest, let them go to their homes with the thanks of the House of Commons to cheer them in their later life. But here a matter very awkward on such occasions obtruded itself. The pay of the Army was in arrear. In March 1647 the foot were owed for eighteen weeks and the horse for forty-three. At Westminster in this once great Parliament it was felt that a six weeks' payment should efface the debt. The soldiers did not look upon all this in the same way.

In the first phase of the dispute Parliament assumed it had the power to give orders. Cromwell, as Member for Cambridge, assured them in the name of

Almighty God that the Army would disband when ordered. But he must have used a different language in the other quarter, because when the Army received the Parliamentary decisions they responded by a respectful petition from the officers. In this document, drawn up probably by Ireton, they asked for themselves and their men arrears of pay, indemnity for acts done in the war, guarantees against future conscription, and a pension for disabled men, widows, and children. They sought a guarantee which would be national and permanent, and for all the tight-knit majority organisation at Westminster this guarantee the kingly office could alone supply.

Here is the salient fact which distinguishes the English Revolution from all others: that those who wielded irresistible physical force were throughout convinced that it could give them no security. Deep in the nature of the men who had broken the King's power was the conviction that law in his name was the sole foundation on which they could build. The Parliamentary leaders received the officers' petition with displeasure. They seemed to imagine themselves in full control. Eventually they ordered each regiment to proceed to a different station in order that they might be separately disbanded or sent to Ireland. The reply of the Army was to concentrate at Newmarket. There they made a Solemn Engagement not to disband until their desires were met. As the balance between authority and physical force seemed fairly even both sides sought allies. The Presbyterians in Parliament looked to the Scots and the Army leaders looked to the King. The generals – Cromwell, Ireton, and Fairfax, Commander-in-Chief, to put them in their order of power – saw themselves about to be reduced to something lower than the venomous faction politicians, who thought the victory was their own property and that all they had to do was to enjoy and distribute its spoils in a narrowly selected circle. Up to this point the Army, generals, officers, and men were at one.

Cromwell and Ireton felt that if they could get hold of the King physically, and before Parliament did so, it would be much. If they could gain him morally it would be all. Ireton was already secretly in touch with the King. Now in early June on his and Cromwell's orders Cornet Joyce, with near four hundred Ironside troopers, rode to Holmby House, where the King, surrounded by his household and attended by the Parliamentary Commissioners, was agreeably residing. The colonel of the Parliamentary guard fled. Charles, convinced of his personal inviolability, passed the night in calm serenity. In the morning Cornet Joyce intimated with due respect that he had come to remove the King. Charles made no protest. The King found Newmarket attractive. The Army at any rate lay there. For three days the King lay at Childerley, near Newmarket. Cambridge University flocked out with loyal addresses, which had been lacking in the Civil War. Soon arrived Cromwell, Ireton and Fairfax. The royal captive was removed to Hatfield, thence to Hampton Court, where the officers of the household were astonished to see the King walking up and down the garden for hours conversing and laughing with the rebel generals, all apparently in the highest good-humour. Eventually the following royal message was framed: "His Majesty conceives the Propositions of Parliament as being destructive to the main principal interests of the Army, and of all those whose affections concur with them; and His Majesty, having seen the Proposals of the Army, ... believes his two Houses will think with him that they much more conduce to the satisfaction of all interests and may be a fitter foundation for a lasting peace than the Propositions now tendered by Parliament. He therefore propounds (as the best way in his judgment in order to peace) that his two Houses would instantly take into consideration those Proposals."[1]

Charles was never wholly sincere in his dealings with the Army leaders; he still pinned his hopes on help from the Scots. Parliament for their part rejected the military and royal proposals. They stood by faction and the party policy, and they too hoped that the Scots might be brought to put down the warriors who had saved them in their need. Here were checks. But another came from the Army itself. Hitherto the generals had held the officers, and the officers had held the men; but all was boiling with force and thought, surging upwards upon religious passion. The generals wished to make a good arrangement for the country, for the King, and for themselves. The rank and file had deeper-cutting convictions. The only chance for the arrangement between Charles and Cromwell was that it should be carried swiftly into effect. Instead there was delay. The main preoccupation of the generals was to hold their men. But the old harangues did not seem effective in a military assembly which already looked upon the King as "the Man of Blood", and were astonished that their honoured leaders should defile themselves.

The Presbyterian party in the House of Commons now realised they could not quell the Army. But the City of London, its apprentices and its mob, as yet unconvinced, held them to their duty. They were forced by riot and violence to rescind the conciliatory resolutions which, much against their will, they had offered to the Army. In fear of the London mob, the Speaker and fifty or sixty Members resorted to Army headquarters at Hounslow, claiming the protection of Cromwell. This was granted. On August 6, the Army marched on London, occupied Westminster, entered the City, and everything except their problems fell prostrate before them. At Putney in the autumn of 1647 the Army held keen debate. All sorts of new figures sprang up: Sexby, Rainborow, Wildman, Goffe the preaching colonel. These spoke with fervour and power, and every time they hit the bull's-eye. "A man is not bound to a system of government which he hath not had any hand in setting over him."

The doctrine of natural right to political equality shocked Ireton as much as it would have shocked Burke or Fox. He sought rigidly the middle course between a Parliament which could not be dissolved and the rank and file of an Army which would not be disbanded. His precise arguments commanded Cromwell's intellectual assent, but not his political judgment. When General Ireton dwelt upon the principle that only those should vote who had what is now called "a stake in the country" his audience became thoughtful. When he

---

1   G.M. Young, *Charles I and Cromwell*, p. 67. [Churchill]

pointed out that a claim for political equality based on the law of God or the law of Nature would affect the rights of property, when he said, "By the same right of Nature he hath an equal right in any goods he sees", the soldiers did not recoil in horror from this conclusion. Their ideas were soon abreast of those of the Chartists in the nineteenth century – manhood suffrage at twenty-one, equal electoral districts, biennial Parliaments, and much more in prospect.

Cromwell heard all this and brooded over it. His outlook was Elizabethan. He thought such claims would lead to anarchy. Ireton's would-be calming arguments only opened up new vistas of subversion. Apart from all this political talk, Cromwell had to think of discipline. He still held power. He used it without delay. He carried a resolution that the representative officers and agitators should be sent back to their regiments. He replaced the General Council of the Army by a General Council of his officers. The political conceptions of the Putney Ironsides were only to be realised in our own day.

Late in this autumn of 1647 Cromwell and Ireton came to the conclusion that even with the pay and indemnity settled they could not unite King and Army. They could not carry the troops. Religious notions which Pym and Hampden would have detested, a Republicanism which the Long Parliament had persistently eschewed, and behind these questions of property, manhood suffrage, and, in terms then unknown, Socialism and Communism, all seethed in the conclaves and conventicles of the soldiers. It remained only to find occasion to break the dangerous, glittering contacts which had been made. There was no difficulty. Royalist England, beaten in arms, mulcted in estate, still lived and breathed, watching for its chance. Parliament continued to formulate its solidly based political aims. The Scots, imbued with religious fervour and personal cupidity, hung on the Border. Charles, who was aware of all these movements, began to look elsewhere. Under these stresses the combination between the defeated King and the victorious generals finally splintered. It was easy for an Ironside colonel, by the directions of his chiefs, to hint to Charles that his life was in danger, that meetings were held openly at which his assassination in the public interest was debated by ruthless men. At the same time no restriction was placed upon his movements.

In November the King, convinced that he would be murdered by the soldiery, whom their officers could no longer restrain, rode off in the night, and by easy stages made his way to Carisbrooke Castle, in the Isle of Wight. Here, he dwelt for almost a year, defenceless, sacrosanct, a spiritual King, a coveted tool, an intriguing parcel, an ultimate sacrifice. There still resided in him a principle which must be either exploited or destroyed; but in England he no longer had the power to make a bargain. There remained the Scots. With them he signed a secret Engagement by which Royalism and Presbyterianism were to be allied. From this conjunction there shortly sprang the Second Civil War.

The Second Civil War was very different in cause and conditions from the first. The parts played by almost all the principals were altered, or even reversed. The King and his Prerogative were now seen, not as obstacles to Parliamentary right, but as the repository of ordinary English freedom. The story of the Second Civil War is short and simple. King, Lords and Commons, landlords and merchants, the City and the countryside, bishops and presbyters, the Scottish army, the Welsh people, and the English Fleet, all now turned against the New Model Army. The Army beat the lot. They marched to Wales; they marched to Scotland, and none could withstand them. A mere detachment sufficed to quell a general rising in Cornwall and the West. They broke the Royalist forces at Colchester; and here a new rigour became apparent. The Royalist commanders, Lucas and Lisle, contrary to all previous conventions, were by Fairfax's order shot outside the walls after the surrender. Cromwell, having subdued the Welsh rising, moved swiftly to the North, picked up his forces, and fell on the Scottish army as it was matching through Lancashire. The trained Scottish forces, under Lord Leven, stood aside. The invaders were cut off, caught, and destroyed at Preston. The Fleet, which had been so potent a few years back against a struggling King, could do little against this all-mastering, furious army which stalked the land in rags, almost barefoot, but with bright armour, sharp swords, and sublime conviction of its wrongheaded mission.

By the end of 1648 all was over. Cromwell was Dictator. King Charles, at Carisbrooke Castle, where the donkey treads the water-wheel, was left to pay the bill. It was mortal. The execution of Charles Stuart, "the Man of Blood", could alone satisfy the soldiers and enable their leaders to hold their obedience. He was brought to the mainland and confined in Hurst Castle. Here the new severities of the Second Civil War marked the rules to which he was subjected. Hitherto his personal dignity and comfort had always been consulted. Now, with scarcely a personal attendant, he found himself shut in the candleless gloom of a small tower prison. There was still a further interlude of negotiations; they were nothing but parleyings with a doomed man. And in this darkness the King rose to his greatest height. His troublous, ill-starred reign had shown him in many wrong attitudes; but at the end he was to be granted by Fate the truly magnificent and indisputable rôle of the champion of English – nay, British, for all the Island was involved – rights and liberty. After some delay he was during the Christmas season brought towards London.

It must have been a vivid contrast with the privations of Hurst Castle when the King rested for nearly a week at Windsor. Here all again was respect and ceremony. A nucleus of the staff and household were in attendance. The King dined every night in ancient state, served on the knee. The Parliamentary officers joined him at table, saluted, and quitted him with the deepest bows. A strange interlude! But now forward to London. London lay locked under the guard and countersign of the Army. Some Parliamentary time-server had stood by Colonel Thomas Pride when the Members sought to take their seats in the House of Commons, and had ticked off all those not likely to obey the Army's will. Members were arrested, and out of a total of over five hundred three hundred did not take their seats again. This was "Pride's Purge".[1] The great trial of "the Man of Blood" was to be presented to the nation and to the world. English law and precedent were scoured from the most remote times, but no sanction or even cover for such a proceeding could be found. The slaying of princes had many examples. Edward II at Berkeley Castle, Richard II at Pontefract, had met terrible fates; but these were deeds wrapped in secrecy, disavowed by authority, covered at the time by mystery or the plea of natural causes. Here the victorious Army meant to teach the English people that henceforward they must obey; and Cromwell who eighteen months before might have been King Charles's Viceroy of Ireland, now saw in his slaughter his only chance of supremacy and survival. In vain did Fairfax point out that the stroke which killed the captive King would make his son in Holland the free possessor of all his rights.

No English jurist could be found to frame the indictment or invent the tribunal. A Dutch lawyer, Isaac Dorislaus, who had long lived in England, was able to deck what was to be done in the trappings of antiquity. The language of the order convening the court had no contact with English history; it looks back to the classical age, when the ruin of tyrants was decreed by the Senate or the Praetorian Guard. An ordinance passed by the docile remnant of the Commons created a court of a hundred and thirty-five Commissioners, of whom barely sixty would serve, to try the King. The carpenters fitted Westminster Hall for its most memorable scene. This was not only the killing of a king, but the killing of a king who at that time represented the will and the traditions of almost the whole British nation.

The more detail in which the famous trial has been described the greater is the sense of drama. The King, basing himself upon the law and Constitution he had strained and exploited in his years of prosperity, confronted his enemies with an unbreakable defence. He eyed his judges, as Morley says, "with unaffected scorn". He refused to acknowledge the tribunal. To him it was a monstrous illegality. John Bradshaw, the president of the court, could make no logical dint upon this. Cromwell and the Army could, however, cut off the King's head, and this at all costs they meant to do. The overwhelming sympathy of the great concourse gathered in Westminster Hall was with the King. When, on the afternoon of the final sitting, after being refused leave to speak, he was conducted from the Hall it was amid a low, intense murmur of "God save the King". But the soldiers, primed by their corporals, and themselves in high resolve, shouted, "Justice! Justice! Execution! Execution!"

Personal dignity and convenience were consulted to the last. Every facility was accorded the King to settle his temporal affairs and to receive the consolations of religion. This was not a butchery, but a ceremony, a sacrifice, or, if we may borrow from the Spanish Inquisition, "an act of faith". On the morning of January 30, 1649, Charles was conducted from St James's, whither

---

1 Colonel Pride's men expelled those Members of Parliament – the most Presbyterian – who wanted further negotiations with the King. Those "approved" Members who remained, the Rump, voted to bring Charles I to trial.

he had been removed from his comfortable lodgings by the river, to Whitehall. Snow fell, and he had put on his warm underclothes. He walked briskly amid the Ironside guard, saying, "Step out now", across the half-mile which led him to the Banqueting House. There, no attempt was made to interfere with his wishes so far as they did not conflict with what had been resolved. But most of those who had signed the death warrant were aghast at the deed of which they were to bear the weight, and the ultimate vengeance. Cromwell had found great difficulty in holding together enough of his signatories. Fairfax, no mean person, still Commander-in-Chief, was outraged. He had to be mastered. Ireton and Harrison remained in the building with the doomed King. Cromwell was there, and wherever else was necessary.

At one o'clock in the afternoon Charles was informed that his hour had come. He walked through a window of the Banqueting House on to the scaffold. Masses of soldiers, many ranks deep, held an immense multitude afar. The King looked with a disdainful smile upon the cords and pulleys which had been prepared to fasten him down, upon the fantastic assumption that he would carry his repudiation of the tribunal which had condemned him even to physical lengths. He resigned himself to death, and assisted the executioner in arranging his hair under a small white satin cap. He laid himself upon the block, and upon his own signal his head was struck off at a single stroke. His severed head was shown to the people, and someone cried, "This is the head of a traitor!" An incalculable multitude had streamed to the spot, swayed by intense though inarticulate emotions. When they saw the severed head "there was such a groan by the thousands then present", wrote a contemporary diarist, "as I never heard before and desire may never hear again."[1]

A strange destiny had engulfed this King of England. None had resisted with more untimely stubbornness the movement of his age. He had been in his heyday the convinced opponent of all we now call our Parliamentary liberties. Yet as misfortunes crowded upon him he increasingly became the physical embodiment of the liberties and traditions of England. His mistakes and wrong deeds had arisen not so much from personal cravings for arbitrary power as from the conception of kingship to which he was born and which had long been the settled custom of the land. In the end he stood against an Army which had destroyed all Parliamentary government, and was about to plunge England in a tyranny at once more irresistible and more petty than any seen before or since.

The English Republic had come into existence even before the execution of the King. On January 4, 1649, the handful of Members of the House of Commons who served the purposes of Cromwell and the Army resolved that "the people are, under God, the original of all just power, ... that the Commons of England in Parliament assembled, being chosen by and representing the people, have the supreme power in this nation." On the 9th it was voted that the name of a single person should no longer be mentioned in

---

1   The young Samuel Pepys witnessed the execution.

legal transactions under the Great Seal. A new seal was presented, bearing on one side a map of England and Ireland and on the other a picture of the House of Commons, with the inscription "In the first year of freedom, by God's blessing restored." A statue of Charles I was thrown down, and on the pedestal were inscribed the words "Exit the tyrant, the last of the Kings." On February 5 it was declared that the House of Lords "is useless and dangerous and ought to be abolished." Thereafter it ceased to meet. Vengeance was wrought upon a number of peers taken prisoner in the Second Civil War, and Lords Hamilton and Holland, statesmen of high intellectual qualities and long record, were beheaded.

The country was now to be governed by a Council of State chosen annually by Parliament. Its forty-one members included peers, judges, and Members of Parliament, among them most of the principal regicides. It was found to be fearless, diligent, and incorrupt. The judiciary hung for a time in the balance. Six of the twelve judges refused to continue, but the rest, their oath of allegiance being formally abrogated, agreed to serve the Commonwealth. The highly conservative elements at the head of the Army held firmly to the maintenance of the Common Law and the unbroken administration of justice in all non-political issues.

The accession of the lawyers to the new régime was deemed essential for the defence of privilege and property against the assaults of the Levellers,[1] agitators, and extremists. This had now become the crucial issue. Fierce and furious as was the effort of the Levellers, there was no hesitation among the men in power to put them down. Even Ireton was excluded from the new Council of State, with which all power rested. Cromwell and his colleagues were familiar with the extremists' demands. They had originally been put forward by five cavalry regiments who had signed the "Agreement of the People", promoted by John Lilburne at the time of the abortive negotiations between Cromwell and the King in 1647.

It was essential to divide and disperse the Army, and Cromwell was willing to lead the larger part of it to a war of retribution in the name of the Lord Jehovah against the idolatrous and bloodstained Papists of Ireland. It was thought that an enterprise of this character would enlist the fanaticism of the rank and file. Lots were drawn which regiments should go to Ireland, and were drawn again and again until only the regiments in which the Levellers were strongest were cast. A pamphlet on *England's New Chains* spread through the Army. Mutinies broke out. Many hundreds of veteran soldiers appeared in bands in support of "the sovereignty of the people", manhood suffrage, and annual Parliaments. This mood was not confined to the soldiers.

Behind these broad principles the idea of equal rights in property as well as in citizenship was boldly announced by a group led by Gerard Winstanley, which came to be known as "the Diggers". Numbers of persons appeared upon the common lands in Surrey and prepared to cultivate them on a

---

1   Led by John Lilburne (c.1614–57), the Levellers got their name because they wanted to "level" people – that is, to make everyone the same – by democratic means.

communal basis. These "Diggers" did not molest the enclosed lands, leaving them to be settled by whoever had the power to take them; but they claimed that the whole earth was a "common treasury" and that the common land should be for all. They argued further that the beheaded King traced his right to William the Conqueror, with whom a crowd of nobles and adventurers had come into England, robbing by force the mass of the people of their ancient rights in Saxon days. Historically the claim was overlaid by six centuries of custom and was itself highly disputable; but this was what they said. The rulers of the Commonwealth regarded all this as dangerous and subversive nonsense. No one was more shocked than Cromwell. He cared almost as much for private property as for religious liberty. The Council of State chased the would-be cultivators off the common land, and hunted the mutinous officers and soldiers to death without mercy.

Cromwell's campaign of 1649 in Ireland was equally cold-blooded, and equally imbued with those Old Testament sentiments which dominated the minds of the Puritans. The spirit and peril of the Irish race might have prompted them to unite upon Catholic toleration and monarchy, and on this they could have made a firm affiance with the Protestant Royalists, who, under the Marquess of Ormonde, had an organised army of twelve thousand men. But the arrival of the Papal Nuncio Rinuccini had aggravated the many forces of incoherence and strife. Ormonde's army was grievously weakened before Cromwell landed. He had already in 1647 ceded Dublin to a Parliamentary general; but he had later occupied the towns of Drogheda and Wexford and was resolved to defend them. Upon these Cromwell marched with his ten thousand veteran troops. Ormonde would have done better to have kept the open field with his regulars and allowed the severities of the Puritan invaders to rally the Irish nation behind him. Instead he hoped that Cromwell would break his teeth upon a long siege of Drogheda, in which he placed a garrison of three thousand men, comprising the flower of the Irish Royalists, and English volunteers. Cromwell saw that the destruction of these men would not only ruin Ormonde's military power, but spread a helpful terror throughout the island. He therefore resolved upon a deed of "frightfulness" deeply embarrassing to his nineteenth-century admirers and apologists.

Having unsuccessfully summoned the garrison to surrender, he breached the ramparts with his cannon, and at the third assault, which he led himself, stormed the town. There followed a massacre so all-effacing as to startle even the opinion of those fierce times. All were put to the sword. None escaped; every priest and friar was butchered. The corpses were carefully ransacked for valuables. The ferreting out and slaughter of those in hiding lasted till the third day. The war continued in squalid, murderous fashion for two years after Cromwell had left Ireland. In his hatred of Popery, which he regarded as a worldwide conspiracy of evil, he sought to identify the Royalist garrison of Drogheda with the Roman Catholic Irish peasantry who had massacred the Protestant landlords in 1641. He ought to have known that not one of them had the slightest connection with that eight-year-old horror. Cromwell in

Ireland, disposing of overwhelming strength and using it with merciless wickedness, debased the standards of human conduct and sensibly darkened the journey of mankind. The consequences of Cromwell's rule in Ireland have distressed and at times distracted English politics down even to the present day. Upon all of us there still lies "the curse of Cromwell".

At the moment when the axe severed the head of Charles the First from his body his eldest son became, in the opinion of most of his subjects and of Europe, King Charles the Second. Within six days, as soon as horsemen could bear the tidings northward, the Scottish Estates proclaimed him King of Great Britain, France, and Ireland. Charles II sheltered at The Hague. The predominant sentiment in Holland was friendly to him, and shocked by his father's execution.

Montrose, when his army fell to pieces, had on the advice of the late King quitted Scotland, believing at first that the Whitehall execution robbed his life of all purpose. His spirit was revived by a priest who preached to him a duty of revenge. With a handful of followers he landed in Caithness, was defeated by the Government forces and betrayed for a paltry bribe into their power. He was dragged through many Scottish towns, and hanged at Edinburgh on a specially high gallows amid an immense agitated concourse. Uplifted by his commanding spirit above physical misfortune, he regarded his sufferings as glorious martyrdom, abashed his fiercest foes by his noble gaze, and has left a name long cherished in Scottish ballad and romance. His body, cut into an unusual number of pieces, was distributed for an example through the scenes of his triumphs. Yet at the same time that Argyll and the Covenanters inflicted this savage punishment upon an unorthodox Royalist they themselves prepared for war with England in the cause of monarchy and entered into urgent treaty with the young King.

Hard courses were laid before Charles II. If, said the Scottish Government, you will embrace the Covenant and become the champion of the Presbyterian cause not only will we bring all Scotland under your sovereignty, but we will march with you into England, where Presbyterians and Royalists alike will join to re-establish the sacred majesty of the Crown against Republicans and regicides. Here at the darkest moment was the proclamation of the continuance of the monarchy. But the price was extortionate and deadly. Charles II must bind himself to destroy the Episcopacy and enforce upon England a religious system odious to all who had fought for his father. He had been carefully and strictly brought up, and was versed in the religious and political controversies of the times. He hesitated long before taking the grim decision of selling his soul to the Devil, as he conceived it, for the interest of the Crown and betraying the cause to save its life.

The fulfilment of the contract was as harsh as the signing. On the ship before the King landed in Scotland the most precise guarantees were extracted. When the King looked out from the windows of the house in which he was lodged at Aberdeen a grisly object met his view. It was the shrivelled hand of Montrose, his devoted servant and friend, nailed to the wall. He found himself virtually a prisoner in the hands of those who had besought him to be their sovereign. He listened to endless sermons, admonitions, and objurgations. He bowed the knee in what was to him the temple of Baal. We may admire as polished flint the convictions and purposes of the Scots Government and its divines, but one must be thankful never to have been brought into contact with any of them.

It was the essence of Scottish policy to separate their new war with England from the invasion which had so lamentably failed at Preston two years before. All those who had taken part in that ill-starred attempt – "the Engagers", as they were called, after the name of the agreement with Charles I – were barred from the new venture. A purge of the Army stripped it of three or four thousand of its most experienced officers and men; their places were filled with "ministers' sons, clerks, and such other sanctified creatures, who hardly ever saw or heard of any sword but that of the spirit". Still there was again an army to fight for the Crown, and both Cardinal Mazarin[1] in France and Prince William of Orange[2] in Holland lent their aid to Scotland.

The unhappy young King was forced, by the need to fight and the desire to win, to issue a declaration in which he desired to be "deeply humbled before God because of his father's opposition to the Solemn League and Covenant; and because his mother had been guilty of idolatry, the toleration of which in the King's house could not but be a high provocation to a jealous God visiting the sins of the fathers upon the children". Charles wondered whether he would dare to look his mother in the face again, and in fact she told him she would never again be his political adviser. On this strange foundation a large Scottish army gathered on the Border.

The menace in the North brought Cromwell back from Ireland. Fairfax, thoroughly estranged from his former colleagues, refused to invade Scotland, and the Council of State at last appointed Cromwell Commander-in-Chief in form as he had long been in fact. The English troops had invaded the Lowlands, hugging the coast, where they could be victualled from the sea by their Fleet. The armies manoeuvred against each other. David Leslie[3] was no mean opponent, and his army far more numerous. Cromwell was forced back upon Dunbar, dependent on wind and weather for his daily bread. He might still escape south by sea, picking up supplies at the East Coast ports. But this was no culmination to a career of unbroken success. In the Scottish camp there were two opinions. The first, held by Leslie, was for letting Cromwell go. The second was urged by the six leading ministers of religion; now was the time

---

1   Jules Mazarin (1601–61), Richelieu's nominated successor as Minister of France. Survived the death of Louis XIII and prospered under the patronage of the Queen-regent, Anne of Austria who appears to have been in love with him.

2   William of Orange (1626–50), Stadholder of the Netherlands, by his marriage to Mary, son-in-law of Charles I and father of the future William III of England (1650–1702).

3   David Leslie (1601–82) should not be confused with Alexander Leslie, 1st Earl of Leven (c.1580–1661) who led the Scots in the Bishops' War and accepted Charles I's surrender at Newark. But both Leslies were at Dunbar in 1650, and both were eventually captured by Cromwell's forces.

to wreak the Lord's vengeance upon those guilty ones who would bring spiritual anarchy into the Reformed Church. Bigotry prevailed over strategy. The pious Scottish army descended from their blockading heights and closed down upon Cromwell and his saints to prevent their embarkation. Both sides confidently appealed to Jehovah; and the Most High, finding so little to choose between them in faith and zeal, must have allowed purely military factors to prevail. It was again September 3.[1] Once the battle was joined among these politico-religious warriors the end was speedy. The Scots fled, leaving three thousand dead on the field. Nine thousand were prisoners in Oliver's hungry camp, and the Army of the Presbyters was broken.

The disaster carried Scots policy out of the trammels of dogma. National safety became the cry. All haste was made to conciliate the Engagers and reinforce the depleted ranks with the officers and men so improvidently cashiered. The services of English Royalists were gratefully accepted. The King was crowned at Scone. Political ideas supervened upon the religious war. The plan of marching south, leaving Cromwell behind in Edinburgh, which he had occupied, and rousing the Royalist forces in England, captivated the majority of the Scots Council. But the religious, and what would later be called Radical, influences still retained enough strength to spoil this. The six Presbyterian ministers who professed to know what would be pleasing to the Almighty spread about the belief that the defeat at Dunbar was due to the estrangement of the Lord Jehovah from an army which espoused the cause of the son of an Uncovenanted King. Upon this reason or pretext many quitted the ranks.

A Scottish army now invaded England in 1651 upon a Royalist rather than a Presbyterian enterprise. It is proof of Cromwell's political and military sagacity that he allowed them to pass. He could by timely marches have over-taken them almost at the Border, but his intention was to cut them off from their supplies. The event justified his calculation. On September 3, sixteen thousand Scots were brought to battle at Worcester, not only by the twenty thousand veterans of the New Model, but by the English militia, who rallied in large numbers against this fresh inroad of the hated and interfering Scots. Charles acquitted himself with distinction. He rode along the regiments in the thick of the fighting, encouraging them in their duty. The struggle was one of the stiffest contests of the civil wars, but it was forlorn, and the Scots and their Royalist comrades were destroyed as a military force. Few returned to Scotland. Charles II escaped with difficulty from the stricken field; a thousand pounds was set upon his head. The land was scoured for him. He hid for a whole day in the famous oak tree at Boscobel, while his pursuers passed by. On every side were men who would have rejoiced to win the price of catching him. But also on every side were friends, if they could be found, secret, silent,

---

1 Siege of Drogheda began in September 1649 (the massacre took place on September 11), the Battle of Dunbar, September 3, 1650, the Battle of Worcester September 3, 1651. Cromwell was to die on September 3, 1658.

unflinching. Thus after six weeks of desperate peril did the King find himself again in exile. His most faithful surviving supporter, Lord Derby, paid the last forfeit of loyalty on the scaffold. Lady Derby, who had gallantly defended her home at Lathom House, still hoped to keep the royal standard flying in the Isle of Man, the independence of which the Derbys had proclaimed; but Parliamentary ideas and later Parliamentary troops reduced this last asylum of Royalism. The valiant chieftainess was long imprisoned, and afterwards dwelt in penury. This was the end of the Civil War or Great Rebellion. England was mastered; Ireland was terrorised; Scotland was conquered. The three kingdoms were united under a Government in London which wielded autocratic power. The most memorable chapter in English history was closed by irresistible forces, which ruled absolutely for a while, but settled nothing.

The monarchy had gone; the Lords had gone; the Church of England was prostrate; of the Commons there remained nothing but the few survivors contemptuously named the Rump. The Rump sat high in its own estimation. It was the surviving embodiment of the Parliamentary cause. Its members felt that the country would need their guidance for many a long year. It was nationalistic, at once protectionist and bellicose. Their Navigation Act forbade all imports not carried either in English ships or in those of the country of origin. Their rivalry with the Dutch, who controlled the Baltic trade and the spice trade with the Indies, and dominated the herring fisheries, provoked against a sister Protestant republic the first war in English history which was fought for primarily economic reasons.[1]

The Rump prospered only so long as their Lord General was at the wars. When he returned victorious he was struck by their unpopularity. He was also shocked at their unrepresentative character. Above all he observed that the Army, hitherto occupied about God's business in other directions, looked sourly on their civilian masters and paymasters. He laboured to mediate between the shrunken Parliament and its gigantic sword, but even he could not withhold his criticism.

He accordingly went to the House on April 20, 1653, accompanied by thirty musketeers. He took his seat and for a time listened to the debate. Then, rising in his place, he made a speech which grew in anger as it proceeded. "Come, come," he concluded, "I will put an end to your prating. You are no Parliament." He called in his musketeers to clear the House and lock the doors. Here sank for the moment all the constitutional safeguards and processes built and treasured across the centuries, from Simon de Montfort to the Petition of Right. One man's will now ruled.

Cromwell, although crafty and ruthless as occasion claimed, was at all times a reluctant and apologetic dictator. He recognised and deplored the arbitrary character of his own rule, but he had no difficulty in persuading himself that his authority sprang both from Above and below. Was he not the new Moses,

---

1   The First Dutch War, 1652, is not to be confused with the "Battle of the Herrings", which was fought in 1429 during the Hundred Years' War.

the chosen Protector of the people of God, commanded to lead them into the Promised Land, if that could indeed be found? Cromwell only desired personal power in order to have things settled in accord with his vision, not of himself or his fame but of the England of his youthful dreams. He was a giant laggard from the Elizabethan age.

Cromwell's successes and failures in foreign policy bore consequences throughout the reign of Charles II. He sought to advance the world-interests of Protestantism and the particular needs of British commerce and shipping. In 1654 he ended the sea war against the Dutch which had begun two years earlier. He made ardent proposals for an alliance between the republics of England and Holland, which should form the basis of a Protestant League, capable not only of self-defence but of attacking the Catholic Powers. The Dutch leaders were content to wind up with the least cost to their trading prospects a war in which they knew they were beaten.

Conflict between France and Spain was meanwhile proceeding. Cromwell could choose his side. In spite of grave arguments to the contrary urged by the Council, he sent a naval expedition to the West Indies in September 1654 and Jamaica was occupied. This act of aggression led slowly but inevitably to war between England and Spain, and a consequent alliance between England and France. In June 1658 six thousand veteran English soldiers in Flanders under Marshal Turenne defeated the Spaniards at the Battle of the Dunes and helped to capture the port of Dunkirk. The blockade of the Spanish coasts disclosed the strength of Britain's sea-power. Cromwell's imperial eye rested long upon Gibraltar. He examined schemes for capturing the marvellous rock. This was reserved for the days of Marlborough, but England retained Dunkirk and Jamaica as a result of Cromwell's war with Spain.

Cromwell found no difficulty in reconciling the predatory aims of the Spanish war with his exertions for a European Protestant League. He was ever ready to strike against the religious persecution of Protestants abroad. When in 1655 he heard that Protestant sect in the valleys north of Piedmont called the Vaudois were being oppressed and massacred by order of the Duke of Savoy he suspended his negotiations with France and threatened to send the Fleet against the Savoyard port of Nice. When he learnt that war had begun between such good Protestant neighbours as the Swedes and the Danes he tried to persuade the Dutch to take part in joint mediation, and for a time arranged a truce. In the main, however, Cromwell's foreign policy was more successful in helping British trade and shipping than in checking or reversing the Counter-Reformation. The Mediterranean and Channel were cleared of pirates, foreign trade expanded, and the whole world learnt to respect British seapower.

But how to find a worthy, docile Parliament, with the fear of God and the root of the matter in their hearts, to aid and comfort the Lord Protector in his task? He sought a Parliament whose authority would relieve him from the reproach of a despotism similar to that which he had punished in "the Man of Blood", which would sustain, and within respectful limits correct, his initiative, without of course diverging from his ideals or hampering his sword or signet. But such Parliaments do not exist. Parliaments are awkward things. They have a knack of developing collective opinions of their own, which they derive from those who elect them. Cromwell sought the right kind of Parliament to limit his own dictatorship without crossing his will, and he boxed the compass in his search. He had expelled the Rump in the cause of an overdue popular election. He replaced it not by an elected but by a hand-picked body of Puritan notables, who became known to history as "Barebone's Parliament", after one of their members, Praise-God Barebone. This was to be a Parliament of Saints, with trustworthy political records.

The independent or congregational Churches drew up a panel, from which the Council of Officers chose a hundred and twenty-nine English representatives and – thus revealing their sense of proportion – five Scottish and six Irish nominees. The political behaviour of the Saints was a sad disappointment to their convoker. With breath-taking speed they proceeded to sweep the board clear of encumbrances in order to create a new Heaven and earth. They sought to disestablish the Church and abolish tithes without providing any livelihood for the clergy. In a single day's debate they abolished the Court of Chancery. They threatened rights of property and proclaimed Levelling ideas. With a temerity justified only by spiritual promptings, they reformed taxation in a manner which seemed to weaken the security for the soldiers' pay. This was decisive. The Army bristled. Cromwell, to whose advice the Saints no longer hearkened, saw them as a set of dangerous fools. He afterwards referred to his action in convening them as "a story of my own weakness and folly". The Army leaders, wishing to avoid the scandal of another forcible ejection, persuaded or compelled the more moderate Saints to get up very early one morning before the others were awake and pass a resolution yielding back their power to the Lord General from whom it had come.

His high place, for all its apparent strength, depended on the precarious balance of Parliament and Army. He could always use the Army against Parliament; but without a Parliament he felt himself very much alone with the Army. The whole cluster of these serious, practical, and hitherto triumphant revolutionaries needed to set up a Parliament, if only to have something to pull down. Ireton had died in Ireland, but Lambert and other Army leaders of various ranks drew up an "Instrument of Government", which was in fact the first and last written English Constitution. Cromwell gratefully accepted the Instrument and assumed the title of Lord Protector. But once again all went wrong with the Parliament. It no sooner met in September 1654 than it was seen to contain a fierce and lively Republican group, which, without the slightest gratitude to the Army leaders or to the Protector for their apparent deference to Republican ideas, set themselves to tear the new Constitution to pieces. Cromwell at once excluded the Republicans from the House. But even then the remaining Parliamentary majority sought to limit the degree of religious toleration guaranteed by the Instrument, to restrict the Lord Protector's control of the Army, and to reduce both its size and pay. This was carrying the farce too far. At the earliest moment allowed by the Instrument Cromwell dissolved the Commons.

Military dictatorship supervened, naked if not wholly unashamed. A Royalist colonel named Penruddock managed to capture Salisbury in March 1655. The rising was easily suppressed. But the outbreak, combined with the discovery by Thurloe,[1] who directed the highly efficient secret service, of a number of abortive plots, convinced the Protector of great danger. He now proceeded to divide England and Wales into eleven districts, over each of which a Major-General was placed, with the command of a troop of horse and a reorganised militia. The Major-Generals were given three functions – police and public order, the collection of special taxes upon acknowledged Royalists, and the strict enforcement of Puritan morality. For some months they addressed themselves with zeal to their task.

None dared withstand the Major-Generals; but the war with Spain was costly and the taxes insufficient. Like Charles I, Cromwell was driven again to summon a Parliament. The Major-Generals assured him of their ability to pack a compliant House. But Levellers, Republicans, and Royalists were able to exploit the discontent against the military dictatorship, and a large number of Members who were known enemies of the Protector were returned. By a strained use of a clause in the Instrument of Government Cromwell managed to exclude a hundred of his opponents from the House, while another fifty or sixty voluntarily withdrew in protest. Even after this purge his attempt to obtain a confirmation of the local rule of the Major-Generals met with such vehement opposition that he was compelled to do without it. Indeed, many of the remaining Members "were so highly incensed against the arbitrary acting of the Major-Generals" that they "searched greedily for any powers that will be ruled and limited by law".

It was at this stage that a group of lawyers and gentry decided to offer Cromwell the crown. "The title of Protector," said one of them, "is not limited by any rule or law; the title of King is." Thus the "Humble Petition and Advice" in 1657 which embodied the proposed Constitution provided not only for the restoration of kingship, but also for the firm re-establishment of Parliament, including a nominated Upper House and a substantial reduction in the powers of the Council of State. But the Army leaders and still more the soldiers showed at once their inveterate hostility to the trappings of monarchy, and Cromwell had to content himself with the right to nominate his successor to the Protectoral throne. In May 1657 he accepted the main provisions of the new Constitution without the title of King.

The Republicans rightly foresaw that this virtual revival of the monarchy opened the way for a Stuart restoration. Under the terms of the "Humble Petition" Cromwell had agreed to allow the Members whom he had excluded

---

1 John Thurloe (1616–68), diplomat and lawyer, was secretary of the Council of State and seventeenth-century "spy-master". His correspondence is still used as a primary source of historical research.

to return to Westminster, while his ablest supporters were taken away to fill the new Upper House. The Republicans could therefore act both inside and outside Parliament against the new régime. Cromwell, in the exaggerated belief that a hostile design was on foot against him, suddenly, in January 1658, dissolved the most friendly Parliament which he had ever had.

The maintenance of all privilege and authority in their own hands at home and a policy of aggression and conquest abroad absorbed the main energies of Cromwell and his Council. They were singularly barren in social legislation. Their treatment of the Poor Law has been called "harshness coupled with failure". Much better conditions and more improvements were established under the personal rule of Charles I between 1629 and 1640 than under those who claimed to rule in the name of God and the sovereignty of the Saints. They considered that poverty should be punished rather than relieved. The English Puritans, like their brethren in Massachusetts, concerned themselves actively with the repression of vice. All betting and gambling were forbidden. In 1650 a law was passed making adultery punishable by death, a ferocity mitigated by the fact that nothing would convince the juries of the guilt of the accused. Drunkenness was attacked vigorously and great numbers of ale-houses were closed. Swearing was an offence punishable by a graduated scale of fines: a duke paid 30s. for his first offence, a baron 20s., and a squire 10s. Common people could relieve their feelings at 3s. 4d. Not much was allowed for their money; one man was fined for saying "God is my witness," and another for saying "Upon my life." These were hard times. The feast days of the Church, regarded as superstitious indulgences, were replaced by a monthly fast day. Christmas excited the most fervent hostility of these fanatics. Parliament was deeply concerned at the liberty which it gave to carnal and sensual delights. Soldiers were sent round London on Christmas Day before dinner-time to enter private houses without warrants and seize meat cooking in all kitchens and ovens. Everywhere was prying and spying.

All over the country the May-poles were hewn down, lest old village dances around them should lead to immorality or at least to levity. Walking abroad on the Sabbath, except to go to church, was punished, and a man was fined for going to a neighbouring parish to hear a sermon. It was even proposed to forbid people sitting at their doors or leaning against them on the Sabbath. Bear-baiting and cock-fighting were effectually ended by shooting the bears and wringing the necks of the cocks. All forms of athletic sports, horse-racing, and wrestling were banned, and sumptuary laws sought to remove all ornaments from male and female attire.

But behind all this apparatus of cant and malignity stood an army of disciplined sectaries, who constantly extorted increases both of their numbers and their pay, and against whom none could make head. Their generals and colonels soon engrossed to themselves rich landed estates carved out of the Crown lands: Fleetwood became the owner of Woodstock Manor, Lambert of Wimbledon, Okey of Ampthill, and Pride of Nonesuch. Hazelrigg and Birch secured large holdings from the bishoprics of Durham and Hereford. To the mass of the nation, however, the rule of Cromwell manifested itself in the form of numberless and miserable petty tyrannies, and thus became hated as no Government has ever been hated in England before or since. What wonder that under the oak-eaves, broad and far throughout the countryside, men dreamed fondly of what they called the good old times and yearned for the day when "the King shall enjoy his own again"?

Liberty of conscience as conceived by Cromwell did not extend to the public profession of Roman Catholicism, Prelacy, or Quakerism. He banned open celebration of the Mass and threw hundreds of Quakers into prison. But such limitations to freedom of worship were caused less by religious prejudice than by fear of civil disturbance. Religious toleration challenged all the beliefs of Cromwell's day and found its best friend in the Lord Protector himself. Believing the Jews to be a useful element in the civil community, he opened again to them the gates of England, which Edward I had closed nearly four hundred years before.

Although a very passionate man when fully roused, he was frequently harassed by inner doubts and conflicts. His strict Puritan upbringing and the soul-stressing of his youth had left him, even though convinced that he belonged to the Chosen People of God, without any certainty as to his own righteousness. Though he attributed his political and military victories to the special interventions of Providence, he could write to a friend that he feared he was liable to "make too much" of "outward dispensations". This uncertainty about himself excused opportunism, and reflected itself in his famous utterance, "No man goes so high as he who knows not where he is going." His doubts about political objectives became increasingly marked in his last years, and he grew more and more dependent on the advice and opinions of others. And thus there was ever a conflict in the man between his conviction of his divine right to rule for the good of the people and a genuine Christian humility at his own unworthiness. "Is it possible to fall from grace?" he inquired of his chaplain on his deathbed. On being reassured, he said, "Then I am saved, for I know that once I was in grace." On September 3, 1658, the anniversary of the Battles of Dunbar and Worcester and of the siege of Drogheda, in the crash and howling of a mighty storm, death came to the Lord Protector.

CHAPTER THIRTY-ONE

THE RESTORATION

*Tumbledown Dick – end of the Protectorate – Charles Fleetwood and
John Lambert – Royalists defeated at Winnington Bridge – the army
hands over power – the Declaration of Breda – Restoration of the
Monarchy – the executioner settles scores – Cromwell's body exhumed –
the Cavalier Parliament – the Clarendon Code – royal mistresses – the rise
of John Churchill – war with the Dutch – the Battles of Lowestoft and
North Foreland – the Great Plague – the Fire of London – Wren begins
rebuilding St Paul's – England acquires New York – the fall of Clarendon
– the Cabal – the rise of France – the Spanish Succession – the Triple
Alliance – the Treaty of Dover – the Battle of Sole Bay – the rise of
William of Orange*

I T PROVED impossible to fill the void which the death of the Lord
Protector had created. In his last hours Cromwell had in terms "very
dark and imperfect" nominated his eldest son, Richard, to succeed him.
"Tumbledown Dick", as his enemies nicknamed him, was a respectable
person with good intentions, but without the force and capacity required by
the severity of the times. His brother, Henry, who was both able and energetic,
strove like Richard to strengthen the civil power even at the expense of the
monarchical attributes of the Protector's office. Army leaders were, however,
determined to preserve their independent power. They complained of the
conduct of the Commons and that the "good old cause" was endangered.

In their conflict with the Army Parliament became willing to entrust the
chief command to the Protector. This brought the dispute to a head. Within
four months of succeeding to his august office Richard Cromwell found
himself deserted even by his personal guard. The Army was master, with
Fleetwood[1] and Lambert[2] rivals at its head. Even in this hour of bloodless and
absolute triumph the soldiery felt the need of some civil sanction for their acts.

---

1   Charles Fleetwood (*c.*1618–92), Oliver Cromwell's son-in-law, was Lord Deputy of Ireland and
    later one of the Major-Generals. He was deprived of his office at the Restoration.

2   John Lambert (1619–84) was one of the organisers of the downfall of the Barebones Parliament.
    He often opposed Cromwell, but after the Restoration he was tried and kept in prison until his
    death.

But where could they find it? At length an expedient was suggested to them. They declared that they recollected that the members of the Parliamentary assembly which sat in April 1653 had been "champions of the good old cause and had been throughout favoured with God's assistance". They went to the house of the former Speaker, Lenthall, and invited him and his surviving colleagues of 1653 to renew the exercise of their powers, and in due course, to the number of forty-two, these astonished Puritan grandees resumed the seats from which they had been expelled six years earlier. Thus was the Rump of the Long Parliament exhumed and exhibited to a bewildered land.

A Council of State was formed in which the three principal Republican leaders, Vane, Hazelrigg, and Scott, sat with eight generals and eighteen other Members of Parliament. Provision was made for Oliver Cromwell's sons, whose acquiescence in the abolition of the Protectorate was desired. Their debts were paid; they were provided with residences and incomes. Richard accepted these proposals at once, and Henry after some hesitation. Both lived unharmed to the end of their days. The Great Seal of the Protectorate was broken in two. The Army declared that they recognised Fleetwood as their Commander-in-Chief, but they agreed that the commissions of high officers should be signed by the Speaker in the name of the Commonwealth. A Republican Constitution based on the representative principle was set up, and all the authorities in the land submitted themselves to it.

While these stresses racked the Republican administration in London a widespread Royalist movement broke out in the country. In the summer of 1659 Cavaliers, strangely consorting with Presbyterian allies, appeared in arms in several counties. At Winnington Bridge, on August 19, the Royalists were chased from the field. The revolt was so swiftly crushed that Charles II, fortunately for himself, had no chance of putting himself at its head. At this moment Lambert became the most prominent figure. He had returned to London from the victory at Winnington Bridge with most of his troops. In October, when Parliament, offended at his arrogance, sought to dismiss him and his colleagues from their commands, he took the lead in bringing his regiments to Westminster and barred all the entrances to St Stephen's Chapel. Even Speaker Lenthall, who had signed the generals' commissions, was prevented from entering. When he asked indignantly "did they not know him" the soldiers replied that they had not noticed him at Winnington Bridge. No blood was shed, but the chief power passed for the moment into Lambert's hands.

Lambert was a man of high ability, with a military record second only to Oliver Cromwell's and a wide knowledge of politics. He did not attempt to make himself Lord Protector. Far different were the ideas that stirred him. His wife, a woman of culture and good family, cherished Royalist sympathies and family ambitions. A plan was proposed, to which she and the General lent themselves, for the marriage of their daughter to Charles II's brother, the Duke of York, as part of a process by which Lambert, if he became chief magistrate of the Republic, would restore the King to the throne. This protectorate was seriously entertained on both sides; and the extreme lenience shown to all the Royalists taken prisoner in the recent rising was a part of it. Lambert seems to have believed that he could satisfy the Army, both in politics and religion, better under a restored monarchy than under either the Rump or a Protectorate. His course was secret, tortuous, and full of danger. Already Fleetwood's suspicions were aroused, and a deep antagonism grew between these two military chiefs. At the same time the Army, sensing its own disunity, began to have misgivings about its violent actions against Parliament.

The schism in the rank and file was beginning to destroy the self-confidence of the troops and put an end to the rule of the sword in England. At Christmas the Army resolved to be reconciled with Parliament. "Let us live and die with Parliament," they shouted. They marched to Chancery Lane and drew up before the house of Speaker Lenthall. Instead of the disrespect with which they had so recently treated him, the soldiers now expressed their penitence for having suspended the sittings of the House. They submitted themselves to the authority of Parliament and hailed the Speaker as their general and the father of their country. But obviously this could not last. Someone must set in train the movement which would produce in England a Government which stood for something old or new. It was from another quarter that deliverance was to come.

The Cromwellian commander in Scotland, though very different in temperament from Lambert, was also a man of mark. Once again England was to be saved by a man who was not in a hurry. George Monk,[1] a Devonshire gentleman, who had in his youth received a thorough military training in the Dutch wars, had come back to England at the beginning of the Great Rebellion equipped with rare professional knowledge. He was a soldier of fortune, caring more for plying his trade than for the causes at stake. He had fought for Charles I in all three kingdoms. After being captured and imprisoned by the Roundheads he went over to their side, and soon gained an important command. He fought in Ireland, and at sea against the Dutch. He had steered his way through all the hazardous channels and storms, supporting in turn and at the right moment Parliament, the Commonwealth, and the Protectorate.

He brought Scotland, in Oliver Cromwell's day, into complete subjection, but without incurring any lasting animosity. He ranged himself from the first against the violence of the Army in London. Moving with the sentiments of the Scottish people, he gained from a Convention supplies to maintain his army without causing offence. He purged his command of all officers whom he could not trust.

Monk was one of those Englishmen who understand to perfection the use of time and circumstance. It is a type which has thriven in our Island. During the autumn of 1659 General Monk in his headquarters on the Tweed with his

1   Often written as Monck. George Monk (1608–70), later 1st Duke of Albemarle, had participated in the Battle of Dunbar and in the First Dutch War.

well-ordered army of about seven thousand men was the object of passionate solicitations from every quarter. They told him he had the future of England in his hands, and all appealed for his goodwill. The General received the emissaries of every interest and party in his camp. He listened patiently, as every great Englishman should, to all they had to urge, and with that simple honesty of character on which we flatter ourselves as a race he kept them all guessing for a long time what he would do.

At length when all patience was exhausted Monk acted. He crossed the Tweed from Coldstream on the cold, clear New Year's Day of 1660. At York he received what he had long hoped for, the invitation of the House of Commons, the desperate Rump, to come to London. He marched south through towns and counties in which there was but one cry – "A free Parliament!" When Monk and his troops reached London he was soon angered by the peremptory orders given him by the Rump, including one to pull down the City gates in order to overawe the capital. For the City was now turning Royalist and collecting funds for Charles II. Unlike Cromwell and Lambert, Monk decided to tame the Rump by diluting, not by dissolving it. In February he recalled the Members who had been excluded by Pride's Purge. These were mainly Presbyterians, most of whom had become at heart Royalists. The restoration of the monarchy came into sight. On the night of the return of the excluded Members Samuel Pepys saw the City of London "from one end to another with a glory about it, so high was the light of the bonfires and so thick round it. … and the bells rang everywhere." The restored Parliament as their first act declared invalid all Acts and transactions since Pride's Purge in 1648. They declared Monk Commander-in-Chief of all the forces. The Rump of the Long Parliament was dissolved by its own consent. Monk was satisfied that a free Parliament should be summoned, and that such a Parliament would certainly recall Charles II. He was genuinely convinced after his march from Scotland that the mass of the English people were tired of constitutional experiments and longed for the return of the monarchy.

But there was a vast pother of matters which must be settled. This was no time for vengeance. Monk sent word to Charles II advising him to offer a free and general pardon, subject only to certain exceptions to be fixed by Parliament; to promise full payment of the soldiers' arrears, and to confirm the land sales. Here was an England where a substantial part of the land, the main source of wealth and distinction, had passed into other hands. These changes had been made good in the field. They could not be entirely undone. Monk's advice was accepted by Charles's faithful Chancellor, Edward Hyde,[1] who had shared his master's exile and was soon to be rewarded with the Earldom of Clarendon. Hyde drafted Charles's manifesto called the Declaration of Breda. In this document the King promised to leave all thorny problems for future Parliaments to settle. It was largely due to Hyde's lawyerly concern for Parliament and precedent that the Restoration came to

1   Edward Hyde, 1st Earl of Clarendon (1609–74), politician and loyal adviser to the king, was the
     author of one of the most important accounts of the period, *History of the Great Rebellion*.

stand for the return of good order and the revival, after Cromwell's experiments, of the country's ancient institutions.

While the negotiations reached their final form the elections for a new Parliament were held. Nominally those who had borne arms against the Republic were excluded, but the Royalist tide flowed so strongly that this ban had no effect. Lambert, escaping from the Tower, in which he had been confined, prepared to dispute the quarrel in the field. His men deserted him, and he was recaptured without bloodshed. This fiasco sealed the Restoration. Monk, the bulk of his army, the City militia, the Royalists throughout the land, the great majority of the newly elected House of Commons, the peers, who assembled again as if nothing had happened, were all banded together, and knew that they had the power. The Lords and Commons were restored. It remained only to complete the three Estates of the Realm by the recall of the King.

Parliament hastened to send the exiled Charles a large sum of money for his convenience, and soon concerned itself with the crimson velvet furniture of his coaches of State. The Fleet, once so hostile, was sent to conduct him to his native shores. Immense crowds awaited him at Dover. There on May 25, 1660,[1] General Monk received him with profound reverence as he landed. The journey to London was triumphal. All classes crowded to welcome the King home to his own. They cheered and wept in uncontrollable emotion. They felt themselves delivered from a nightmare. They now dreamed they had entered a Golden Age. Charles, Clarendon, Nicholas,[2] the well-tried secretary, and a handful of wanderers who had shared the royal misfortunes gazed about them in astonishment. Could this be the same island from which they had escaped so narrowly only a few years back? Still more must Charles have wondered whether he slept or waked when on Blackheath he saw the dark, glistening columns of the Ironside Army drawn up in stately array and dutiful obedience. This was not only the Restoration of the monarchy; it was the restoration of Parliament. Indeed, it was the greatest hour in Parliamentary history. The House of Commons had broken the Crown in the field; it had at length mastered the terrible Army it had created for that purpose. It had purged itself of its own excesses, and now stood forth beyond all challenge, or even need of argument, as the dominant institution of the realm. All that was solid in the constitutional claims put forward against Charles I had become so deeply rooted that it was not even necessary to mention it. All the laws of the Long Parliament since Charles I quitted London at the beginning of 1642, all the statutes of the Commonwealth or of the Protectorate, now fell to the ground. But there remained the potent limitations of the Prerogative to which Charles I had agreed. The statutes to which he had set his seal were valid. The work of 1641 still stood. Above all, everyone now took it for granted that the

1 The year in which Samuel Pepys started his diary. It ended in 1669 (Pepys died in 1703).
2 Sir Edward Nicholas who had stood by Charles I through the Civil War and then served Charles II.

Crown was the instrument of Parliament and the King the servant of his people. A new conception of sovereignty had now been born.

Of about sixty men who had signed the late King's death warrant a third were dead, a third had fled, and a bare twenty remained. King Charles strove against his loyal Parliament to save as many as possible. Feeling ran high. The King fought for clemency for his father's murderers, and Parliament, many of whose Members had abetted their action, clamoured for retribution. In the end nine suffered the extreme penalty of treason. They were the scapegoats of collective crime. Nearly all of them gloried in their deed. Harrison and other officers stepped upon the scaffold with the conviction that posterity would salute their sacrifice. Hugh Peters, the fiery preacher, alone showed weakness, but the example of his comrades and a strong cordial sustained him, and when the executioner, knife in hand, covered with blood, met him in the shambles with "How does that suit you, Dr Peters?" he answered steadfastly that it suited him well enough.

The numbers of those executed fell so far short of the public demand that an addition was made to the bloody scene which at any rate cost no more life. The corpses of Cromwell, Ireton, and Bradshaw were pulled out of their coffins in Westminster Abbey, where they had been buried a few years earlier in solemn state, drawn through the streets on hurdles to Tyburn, hanged upon the three-cornered gibbet for twenty-four hours, their heads spiked up in prominent places, and the remains cast upon the dunghill. Pym and twenty other Parliamentarians, were also disinterred and buried in a pit. Such ghoulish warring with the dead was enforced by the ferocity of public opinion, to which the King was glad to throw carcasses instead of living men.

Only two other persons in England were condemned to death, General Lambert and Sir Harry Vane. Lambert had a wild career behind him, and in the last year of the Republic might at any moment have laid his hands upon supreme power. We have seen the plans which he had indulged for his daughter's marriage. He had imagined himself as the Constable of the Restoration, forestalling Monk, or alternatively as a successor of His Highness the Lord Protector after destroying Monk. He was a man of limitless audacity and long experience in military revolution. But all just failed. Now Lambert, the Ironside general, hero of a dozen fields, humbled himself before his judges. He sought mercy from the King. He found in the King's brother, the Duke of York, a powerful advocate. He was pardoned, and lived the rest of his life in Guernsey, "with liberty to move about the island," and later in Plymouth, consoling himself with painting and botany.

Vane was of tougher quality. He scorned to sue for mercy, and so spirited was his defence, so searching his law and logic, that he might well have been indulged. But there was one incident in his past which now proved fatal to him. It was remembered that twenty years before he had purloined, and disclosed to Pym, his father's notes of the Privy Council meeting, alleging that Strafford had advised the bringing of an Irish army into England, thus sealing Strafford's fate. He met his death with the utmost alacrity and self-confidence, and the blare of trumpets drowned the cogent arguments he sought to offer to the hostile crowd.

Almost the only notable in Scotland to suffer death at the Restoration was the Marquess of Argyll. He came to London to join in the royal welcome, but was immediately arrested. Charles, wishing to be rid of the burden, sent him back to Scotland to be tried by his peers and fellow-countrymen. In all therefore, through Charles's exertions, and at some expense to his popularity, less than a dozen persons were put to death in this intense Counter-Revolution.

The longest Parliament in English history now began. It lasted eighteen years. It has been called the Cavalier Parliament – or, more significantly, the Pension Parliament. It was composed at first of men well past their prime and of broken veterans of the war, but when it was eventually dissolved all except two hundred of them had been replaced at by-elections, often by Roundheads or their heirs. From the moment when it first met it showed itself more Royalist in theory than in practice. It rendered all honour to the King. It had no intention of being governed by him. The many landed gentry who had been impoverished in the royal cause were not blind monarchists. They did not mean to part with any of the Parliamentary rights which had been gained in the struggle. They were ready to make provision for the defence of the country by means of militia; but the militia must be controlled by the Lord-Lieutenants of the counties. They vehemently asserted the supremacy of the Crown over the armed forces; but they took care that the only troops in the country should be under the local control of their own class. Thus not only the King but Parliament was without an army. The repository of force had now become the county families and gentry. Having established this as the result of bitter experiences and long meditation, the Cavalier Parliament addressed itself to religion, with special regard to the political and social aspects, and to its own interests.

Since Clarendon as Lord Chancellor was the chief Minister, and Preponderant in the Government, his name is identified with the group of Acts which re-established the Anglican Church and drove the Protestant sects into enduring opposition. Charles would have preferred to take the way of toleration, Clarendon that of comprehension. But the zeal of the Cavalier Parliament, of the followers of Laud, now returned from exile, and of some recalcitrant Presbyterian leaders, baffled them both. Parliament recognised that there were religious bodies definitely outside the National Church, and determined, if not to extirpate them, at least to leave them outside under grievous disabilities. In so doing it consolidated Nonconformity as a political force with clear objectives: first, toleration, which was secured at the Revolution of 1688; and thereafter the abolition of the privileged status of the Church. But this latter was only attained, and that partially, when in the nineteenth century the vote of the commercial and industrial middle class became a decisive factor in political combinations. An exact assessment of the influence of Nonconformity on English political thought would be difficult to make. It carried forward much of the old Puritan austerity and stubbornness, with much of its narrowness. Its learning was often great. Perhaps a comprehensive Church with wide terms of subscription would best have served the cause of religion. But it is also possible that the variety of religious thought which Nonconformity provided could not have been contained within a State Church however broadly based, and that the Three Bodies, as they came to be called – Presbyterians with their rationalism, Congregationalists with their independence, Baptists with their fervour were expressions of deeply seated and divergent tendencies of the English mind.

For good or for ill, the "Clarendon Code" was a parting of the ways. It destroyed all chance of a United National Church. The Cavalier Parliament accepted the schism, and rejoiced in belonging to the larger, richer, and more favoured section. They built upon their system not a nation but a party. The country gentlemen and landowners who had fought for God and King should have their own Church and bishops, as they now had their own militia and their own Commission of the Peace. The Clarendon Code of 1662 went some way beyond the ideas of Clarendon himself. He had hoped for a union in Church and State, inspired by the heart-melting of the Restoration. Neither did Charles will this great separation. He walked by the easy path of indifference to the uplands of toleration. He was certainly not spiritually minded. If a gentleman was going to be religious perhaps Rome would give him the greatest satisfaction.

The Cavalier Parliament sternly corrected this deplorable laxity. The Clarendon Code consisted of a series of statutes: the Corporation Act of 1661 required all persons holding municipal office to renounce the Solemn League and Covenant – a test which excluded many of the Presbyterians; to take the oath of non-resistance which excluded Republicans; and to receive the Sacrament according to the rites of the Church of England – which excluded Roman Catholics and some of the Nonconformists. The object of this Act was to confine municipal office, closely connected with the election of Members of Parliament, to Royalist Anglicans. The Act of Uniformity of 1662 imposed upon the clergy the Prayer Book of Queen Elizabeth, with some excisions and certain valuable additions. It required from them a declaration of unfeigned assent and consent to all and everything contained in the Prayer Book, and exacted from them and from all teachers in schools and universities a declaration "to conform to the Liturgy of the Church of England as it is now by law established". One-fifth of the clergy, nearly two thousand ministers, refusing to comply, were deprived of their livings. These sweeping decisions were followed by other measures of enforcement. The Conventicle Act of 1664 sought to prevent the ejected clergy from preaching to audiences of their own, and the Five-Mile Act of 1665 forbade them to go within five miles of any "City or Town Corporate or Borough or any parish or place where they had preached or held a living".

This Code embodied the triumph of those who had been beaten in the field and who had played little part in the Restoration. Its echoes divide the present-day religious life of England. It potently assisted the foundation of parties. As Macaulay wrote, and later writers have confirmed his view, "there was a great line which separated the official men and their friends and dependants, who were sometimes called the Party, from those who were sometimes honoured with the appellation of the Country party." Those who enjoyed official patronage, or hoped to do so, naturally had different interests from those who did not. But alongside this distinction another cleavage was opening. The lines were being drawn in political life between the Conservative and Radical traditions which have persisted down to our own day.

For these far-reaching fissures Charles II had no responsibility. Throughout his reign he consistently strove for toleration. In May 1663 he tried to suspend the operation of the Act of Uniformity for three months; but the reinstated bishops and the constitutional lawyers frustrated him. In December he issued his first Declaration of Indulgence, claiming to exercise a dispensing power inherent in the Crown to relieve Dissenters from the laws enforcing religious conformity or requiring oaths; but the Commons, unconscious that it was what they themselves were doing, protested vehemently against any scheme for "establishing schism by a law". In March 1671 he ran great risks with a second Declaration of Indulgence, which sought to suspend "the execution of all manner of penal laws in matters ecclesiastical against whatsoever classes of Nonconformists and Recusants", as the Roman Catholics were called. "Penal statutes in matters ecclesiastical", rejoined the House of Commons severely, "cannot be suspended but by Act of Parliament."

But Charles II had need of an Act of Indulgence for himself. Court life was one unceasing flagrant and brazen scandal. His two principal mistresses, Barbara Villiers, created Countess of Castlemaine, and Louise de Kérouaille – "Madame Carwell", as the English called her – created Duchess of Portsmouth, beguiled his leisure and amused themselves with foreign affairs. His marriage with Catherine of Braganza, who brought a rich dowry of eight hundred thousand pounds and the naval bases of Tangier and Bombay, in no way interrupted these dissipations. His treatment of his wife was cruel to an extreme degree: he forced her to accept Barbara as her Lady-in-Waiting. The refined, devout Portuguese princess on one occasion was so outraged that the blood gushed from her nostrils and she was borne swooning from the Court. It was with relief that the public learned that the King had taken a mistress from the people, the transcendently beautiful and good-natured Nell Gwynn, who was lustily cheered in the streets as "the Protestant whore". But these were only the more notorious features of a life of lust and self-indulgence which disgraced a Christian throne, and in an Asiatic Court would have been veiled in the mysteries of the seraglio.

It is inevitable that after a period of intense effort there should follow one of exhaustion and disarray. But this was a fleeting view. The race endured, and in Charles's Court, at his side, there was already a young man, an ensign in his Guards, a partner in his games at tennis, an intruder, as he learned with some displeasure, in the affections of Lady Castlemaine, who would one day grasp a longer and a brighter sword than Cromwell's and wield it in wider fields only against the enemies of British greatness and freedom. A Dorsetshire squire, Winston Churchill, along with his father, had fought in the Royalist ranks and had been wounded, mulcted, and expropriated by the Roundheads. The King could do little for his faithful adherent. He tried without success to persuade Clarendon to include Sir Winston in his private committee of Parliamentary managers. But he found a place at Court for his son as one of his own pages, and for his daughter Arabella in the household of the Duchess of York. Both improved their advantage. John Churchill[1] obtained a commission in the Guards; Arabella became the mistress of the Duke of York, and bore him a son, James Fitz James, afterwards famous as the warrior Duke of Berwick.

Two personalities of force and capacity, vividly contrasted in character, Clarendon and Ashley, afterwards Earl of Shaftesbury, swayed the Privy Council. Shaftesbury had plunged into the Revolution in the Short Parliament when he was but eighteen. "I no sooner perceived myself in the world but I found myself in a storm." He had fought on the Roundhead side. He had worked with Cromwell. As a leader of the Presbyterians he had influenced and aided Monk in bringing about the Restoration. It took him time to rise, but he was still young, and he had deeply ingrained convictions. No one understood better the anatomy of the convulsive forces which had devastated the country, but had at length for the time being worn themselves out upon each other. Shaftesbury was the most powerful representative of the vanished domination. Although he had headed the Presbyterians against the Army in the year of anarchy no one knew more about the spirit of the Independents. He was therefore the foremost advocate of toleration in the Council, and no doubt fortified the King in all he did to that end. He was always conscious of the fierce Ironside dogs who now seemed to sleep so quietly. He knew where they lay and how to put his hands on them. His other care was the City of London, of whose decisive weight on great occasions he had a lively recollection. Throughout the reign he stood by the City of London, and the City stood by him. The legislation of the Cavalier Parliament vexed the King almost as much as Shaftesbury, but neither could withstand in practice or in principle the obstinate will-power of a large Parliamentary majority.

For the first seven years of the reign Clarendon continued First Minister. This wise, venerable statesman wrestled stoutly with the licentiousness of the King and Court, with the intrigues of the royal mistresses, with the inadequacy of the revenue, and with the intolerance of the House of Commons. He was also confronted with the intrigues of Henry Bennett, Charles's favourite, who was made Secretary of State and Earl of Arlington. An important and sometimes sinister part in the politics of the reign was played by this flamboyant figure. Clarendon's daughter had won the heart of the Duke of York, and in spite of all that could be done to prevent it the marriage had been solemnised. The Chief Minister was now father-in-law to

---

1   John Churchill (1650–1722) was created 1st Duke of Marlborough in 1702.

the King's brother. His grandchildren might succeed to the throne. The jealousy of the nobles was inflamed and Clarendon's sense of his own greatness was inflated by this royal connection. But for the moment, other matters needed the attention of those who governed the Island.

The rivalry of England and Holland upon the seas in fishery and in trade had become intense, and the strength of the Dutch had revived since Cromwell's war. The commerce of the East Indies flowed to Amsterdam, that of the West Indies to Flushing; that of England and Scotland passed to the Continent through Dort and Rotterdam. The herrings caught off Scottish coasts produced rich revenues for the States-General. The Dutch East India Company gathered the wealth of the Orient. Great Dutch fleets, heavily laden, doubled the Cape of Good Hope several times a year. On the West African coast the Dutch also prospered, and their colonies and trading stations grew continually. They had a settlement on the Hudson, thrust among the colonies of New England. It was too much. Parliament was moved by the merchants; the King was roused to patriotic ardour, the Duke of York thirsted for naval glory. The great sum of over two and a half millions was voted. More than a hundred new ships were built, armed with new and heavier cannon. Former Cavalier and Cromwellian officers joined hands and received commissions from the King. Rupert and Monk commanded divisions of the Fleet. War at sea began off the West African coast in 1664, and spread to home waters in the following year.

In June the English fleet of more than 150 ships, manned by 25,000 men and mounting 5,000 guns, met the Dutch in equal strength off Lowestoft, and a long, fierce battle was fought, in which many of the leaders on both sides perished. The old Cromwellian admiral, John Lawson, who used to dress like a common sailor, was mortally wounded. By the side of the Duke of York his friends Lords Falmouth and Muskerry were killed by a single cannon-ball. But the Dutch admiral Kortenaer and their Commander-in-Chief, Opdam, shared their fate. At the height of the action the *Royal Charles* (formerly the *Naseby*[1]), with the Duke on board, engaged the Dutch flagship at close quarters. Opdam, cool and resolute, was directing the battle from a chair on his quarter-deck when a lucky salvo from the English fired the magazine and blew him and his ship into the air. The English artillery was markedly superior in weight and skill, and the Dutch withdrew worsted though undismayed.

An even greater battle than Lowestoft was fought in June 1666. Louis XIV had promised to aid Holland if she were attacked. Although Charles protested that the Dutch were the aggressors, France declared war on England. For four days the English and Dutch fleets battled off the North Foreland. De Ruyter commanded the Dutch, whose ships now mounted heavier cannon. The sound of the guns was heard in London, and men realised with dismay that Rupert, having to watch for the French fleet in the Channel, was separated from Monk. At the close of the second day's cannonading the English were outmatched;

1   The *Naseby* had brought Charles II back to England from his exile in Holland.

then Rupert, arriving on the third day, restored the balance. But the fourth day was adverse, and Monk and Rupert, with heavy losses, retired into the Thames.

But other calamities drained the strength of the Island. From the spring of 1665 the Great Plague had raged in London. Never since the Black Death in 1348 had pestilence spread such ravages. In London at the climax about seven thousand people died in a single week. The Court retired to Salisbury, leaving the capital in the charge of Monk, whose nerves were equal to every kind of strain. The worst of the plague was over when in September 1666 the Great Fire engulfed the tormented capital. It broke out near London Bridge, in a narrow street of wooden houses, and, driven by a strong east wind, the flames spread with resistless fury for four whole days. Wild suspicions that the fire was the work of Anabaptists, Catholics, or foreigners maddened the mob. The King, who had returned to London, acquitted himself with courage and humanity. When the fire was at length stopped outside the City walls by blowing up whole streets more than thirteen thousand dwelling-houses, eighty-nine churches, and St Paul's Cathedral had been devoured. The warehouses containing the merchandise for months of trade and many warlike stores were destroyed. The yield of the chimney tax, then so important to the revenue, was ruined. Yet the fire extinguished the plague, and to later times it seems that the real calamity was not so much the destruction of the insanitary medieval city as the failure to carry through Wren's plan for rebuilding it as a unity of quays and avenues centred on St Paul's and the Royal Exchange. The task of reconstruction was none the less faced with courage, and from the ashes of the old cathedral rose the splendid dome of St Paul's as it stands today.

Although the war dragged on till 1667 Charles now sought peace both with France and Holland. Want of money prevented the English battle fleet from keeping the sea, and while the negotiations lingered the Dutch, to spur them, sailed up the Medway under Admiral De Ruyter, victor at the Battle of North Foreland in the previous year, broke the boom which guarded Chatham harbour, burnt four ships of the line, and towed away the battleship *Royal Charles*, which had destroyed Admiral Opdam in the Battle of Lowestoft. The sound of enemy cannon, this time loud and clear, rolled up the Thames. In the general indignation and alarm even Cavaliers remarked that nothing like this had happened under Cromwell.

Peace, of which both sides had equal need, was made on indifferent terms. England's chief gain in the war was New Amsterdam, now renamed New York. But recriminations began. The Court asked how the country could be defended when Parliament kept the King so short of money. Parliament retorted that he had spent too much on his mistresses and luxuries. Clarendon, expostulating with all sides, was assailed by all. He had fallen out with Parliament, rebuked the mistresses, and, worst of all, bored the King. An impeachment was launched against him, and he went into exile, there to complete his noble *History of the Rebellion*, which casts its broad and lasting illumination on the times through which he lived. The growing discontents of the Cavalier Parliament at the morals and expense of the Court made it necessary to broaden the basis of the Government, and from 1668 five principal personages began to be recognised as the responsible Ministers. There had been much talk of Cabinets and Cabals; and now, by chance, the initials of these five men, Clifford, Arlington, Buckingham, Ashley, and Lauderdale, actually spelt the word "CABAL".

The dominant fact on the continent of Europe, never realised by Cromwell, was the rise of France at the expense of Spain and Austria. Among men born to a throne few have outshone Louis XIV in natural capacity. He was now in his youthful prime. The French people, consolidated under the sagacious government of Cardinal Mazarin, were by far the strongest nation in Europe. They numbered twenty millions, four times as many as the population of England. The Thirty Years War, which had ended only in 1648, had broken the Imperial power in Germany. The house of Habsburg presided in a spiritual and historical sense over a loose association of divided Germanic principalities, without exerting authority or receiving more than ceremonial allegiance. Even in his own hereditary Austrian lands the Holy Roman Emperor was distracted by the hostility of the Magyars of Hungary and the unceasing threat of Turkish invasion. Thus along the French frontiers stood no strong state nor solidly joined confederation. Flanders, Brabant, Liège, Luxembourg, Lorraine, Alsace, Franche-Comté, and Savoy, all lay open to the ambition, force, and diplomacy of France.

At the same time to the southward the evident decay of Spain and of the Spanish ruling family cast a lengthening shadow of disturbance upon the world. Mazarin had schemed to unite, if not at first the Crowns, at least the royal families of France and Spain, with all that that promised in world dominion. He had induced Louis XIV to marry the Infanta of Spain; but though as Queen of France she had had to renounce her rights in the Spanish succession the renunciation was conditional on the payment of a large sum of money included in her dowry. The Spaniards could not pay, and Louis already looked to the union of the two Crowns of France and Spain as the main goal of his life.

But King Philip of Spain married a second time, and when he died in 1665 he left a sickly son, who as Charles III of Spain lingered for thirty-five years as a flickering obstruction to the French design. Louis, his claims postponed indefinitely, resolved to compensate himself in the Netherlands. He declared that by the ancient custom of the Duchy of Brabant children of a first marriage should suffer no loss if their father married again, and that the Queen of France accordingly had sovereignty over the Spanish Netherlands, of which Brabant formed a large part. These pretensions were asserted in the first war into which Louis led his people.

The Spanish Government did not greatly resent, and could not at all resist, the French demands upon the Belgic provinces. But if Belgium fell to France the Dutch Republic could not survive. John De Witt, at the head of the Dutch oligarchy, had been willing to fight England at sea, but a war on land against

France was beyond the strength of the Republic. Moreover, it might reinforce the Orange party, who were De Witt's rivals. Their head, Prince William, was aged seventeen and was astonishingly able.[1]

De Witt tried to negotiate; he offered large concessions. But Louis XIV sent Marshal Turenne into Flanders, occupied a large part of the Spanish Netherlands, and placated the Emperor by a partition treaty which to some extent safe guarded Imperial interests. Thus harassed, De Witt made peace with England.

Charles and the Cabal, aided by their envoy Sir William Temple at The Hague, concluded a triple alliance with Holland and Sweden against France. The Protestant combination was hailed with delight by the whole country. The King and Ministers found themselves for a time borne up by public favour. This, the first of the long series of coalitions against France, checked Louis XIV for a while. He was forced to make peace with Spain. Louis XIV was determined to buy off one of the two maritime powers before resuming war. He addressed himself to England and in 1670 began secret negotiations with Charles II. Above all things Charles needed money. He pointed out to Louis that Parliament would give him ample funds to oppose France; how much would Louis pay him not to do so? If he paid enough Charles would have no need to call the dreaded Parliament together. Here was the basis of the shameful Treaty of Dover.

Besides the clauses which were eventually made public, there was a secret clause upon which Arlington and Clifford were Charles's only confidants. "The King of Great Britain, being convinced of the truth of the Catholic Faith, is determined to declare himself a Catholic ... as soon as the welfare of his realm will permit. His Most Christian Majesty promises to further this action by giving to the King of Great Britain two million livres tournois ... and to assist His Britannic Majesty with six thousand foot-soldiers." The King was also to receive a subvention of £166,000 a year. Charles undertook to betray his country for money, some of which he devoted to his pleasures and mistresses. But it is doubtful if he ever intended to keep so unnatural a promise. At any rate he made no attempt to do so, and spent most of the cash on the Fleet.

The Treaty of Dover contemplated a third Dutch war, in which France and England would combine when Louis XIV felt the moment opportune. In March 1672 Louis claimed fulfilment of the pact. There was no lack of pretexts for quarrel between England and Holland. In a great battle at Sole Bay on May 28, 1672, De Ruyter surprised the English and French, who were ten ships stronger, as they lay at anchor. Grievous and cruel was the long battle. The Suffolk shores were crowded with frantic spectators, and the cannonade was heard many miles away. The French squadron put out to sea, but the wind prevented them from engaging. The Duke of York's flagship, the *Prince*, was beset on every side. Upon her decks stood the first company of the Guards, in which Ensign Churchill was serving. She became such a wreck that the Duke,

[1] Future William III of England.

who fought with his usual courage, was forced to shift his flag to the *St Michael*, and, when this ship was in turn disabled, to the *London*. Lord Sandwich, in the second flagship, perished when the *Royal James* sank, burnt almost to the water's edge. Nevertheless the Dutch drew off with very heavy losses of their own.

On land Louis struck with terrible force at the hard-pressed Republic. Suddenly, without cause or quarrel, his cavalry swam the Rhine and his armies invaded Holland. A hundred and twenty thousand French troops, armed for the first time with a bayonet which fitted around instead of blocking the muzzle of the musket, were irresistible. Four Dutch provinces were occupied and many strongholds opened their gates. The Dutch people, faced with extermination, turned in their peril to William of Orange. The great-grandson of William the Silent, now Captain-General, did not fail them. He uttered the famous defiance, "We can die in the last ditch." The sluices in the dykes were opened; the bitter waters rolled in a deluge over the fertile land, and Holland was saved. At The Hague a revolution took place and William of Orange became Stadtholder. De Witt resigned. He and his brother were torn to pieces by an Orange mob in the capital.

CHAPTER THIRTY-TWO

THE POPISH PLOT

The Test Act – the Duke of York, heir to the throne, splits loyalty to the monarchy – Lord Shaftesbury leads Opposition – Danby becomes the King's Chief Minister – the marriage of the Duke of York's Protestant daughter, Mary, to William of Orange – the Popish Plot – Titus Oates – the end of the Cavalier Parliament – Danby sent to the Tower – the Exclusion Bill – the King's bastard heir –the origin of Whigs and Tories – George Savile, the Trimmer – the fall of Shaftesbury – the Rye House Plot – Russell and Sidney executed – Charles II dies

THE MEETING of Parliament in February of 1673 had apprised Charles of his subjects' loathing for the war against the Dutch Protestant Republic, in which he had allowed himself to become engaged, not as the champion of English commerce, but as the lackey of Louis XIV. Resentment of the Dutch affronts at sea and jealousy of their trade were overridden by fear and hatred of Papist France and her ever-growing dominance in Europe. Whispers ran afoot through London that the King and his Ministers had been bribed by France to betray the freedom and the faith of the Island. The secret article in the Dover Treaty had only to be known to create a political explosion of measureless violence. Shaftesbury, though not privy to it, must have had his suspicions. Early in 1673 Arlington seems to have confessed the facts to him.

With dexterity and promptitude Shaftesbury withdrew himself from the Government, and became the leader of an Opposition which was ultimately as violent as that of Pym. The growing antagonism of the Commons to France, the fear of the returning tides of Popery, the King's "laxity towards Papists", the conversion of the Duke of York[1] to Rome, all stirred a deep and dangerous agitation throughout the whole country, in which the dominant Anglican forces were in full accord with Presbyterian and Puritan feeling. Everywhere there was the hum of political excitement. Coffee-houses buzzed; pamphlets circulated; by-elections were scenes of uproar. A Bill was forced upon the King for a Test. No man could hold office or a King's commission afloat or ashore who would not solemnly declare his disbelief in the doctrine of

---

1   James, Duke of York (1633–1701) was the King's younger brother and the future James II.

Transubstantiation. This purge destroyed the Cabal. Clifford, a Catholic, refused to forswear himself; Arlington was dismissed because of his unpopularity; Buckingham had a personal quarrel with the King. Shaftesbury had already voted for the Test Act, and was the leader of the Opposition. Lauderdale alone remained, cynical, cruel, and servile, master of Scotland.

All eyes were now fixed upon James, Duke of York. His marriage, after the death of his first wife, Anne Hyde, to the Catholic princess Mary of Modena had rendered him suspect. Would he dissemble or would he give up his offices? Very soon it was known that the heir to the throne had laid down his post of Lord High Admiral rather than submit to the Test. This event staggered the nation. The Queen was unlikely to give King Charles an heir. The crown would therefore pass to a Papist King, who showed that for conscience sake he would not hesitate to sacrifice every material advantage. The strength of the forces now moving against the King and his policy rose from the virtual unanimity which prevailed between the Anglicans and the Dissenters, between the swords which had followed Rupert and the swords which had followed Cromwell. All the armed forces were in the hands of the Royalist gentry, and there were many thousands of Cromwell's old soldiers in London alone. They were all on the same side now, and at their head was the second great Parliamentary tactician of the century, Shaftesbury. This was of all combinations the most menacing to the King.

The power of the Cavalier Parliament had been made plain in every dispute with the Crown. It had exerted itself in foreign policy, had completely controlled domestic affairs, and had compelled the King to change his advisers by the hard instruments of the Test Act or Impeachment. A new departure was now made. Sir Thomas Osborne, a Yorkshire landowner, had gathered great influence in the Commons, and was to a large extent forced upon the King for his own salvation. His policy was the union into one strong party with a popular programme of all those elements which had stood by the monarchy in the Civil War and were now deeply angered with the Court. Economy, Anglicanism, and independence from France were the principal ideals of this party, and Osborne now carried them to the King's Council. He was very soon raised to the peerage as Earl of Danby, and began an administration which was based on a party organisation possessing a small but effective majority in the House of Commons.

In foreign affairs the new Minister publicly differed from his master. He opposed French ascendancy and interference, and gained general support thereby; but he was forced to become privy to the King's secret intrigues with Louis XIV, and, holding strongly to the Cavalier idea that the King should have considerable personal power, he was lured into asking the French monarch for money on Charles's behalf.

The height of Danby's precarious popularity was reached when he contrived a marriage between Mary, the Duke of York's daughter by his first wife, and the now famous Protestant hero, William of Orange. This match was of the highest consequence. Dread of a Papist King had already turned all eyes to the formidable, gleaming figure of the Stadtholder of Holland, Charles I's grandson by his daughter. William's inflexible Protestantism, grave demeanour, high gifts, and noble ancestry had raised him already to a position of eminence in Europe. Married now to the daughter of the Duke of York, the English heir presumptive, he seemed to offer an alternative succession to the Crown. This was by no means the outlook of King Charles II, still less of his brother, James. They did not regard the danger as serious. Charles was led to believe that Shaftesbury's opposition might be diminished by such a marriage, and the Duke of York's self-confidence was proof against so remote a menace to his title. Thus the marriage was made, and the two maritime nations, which had recently contended in fierce, memorable battles in the Narrow Seas, became united by this remarkable tie. Since then the Dutch and English peoples have seldom been severed in the broad course of European events.

It was at this moment that Louis XIV, dissatisfied with his English investments and indignant at a marriage which threatened to carry England into the Dutch system and was a strong assertion of Protestant interests, resolved to ruin Danby. He revealed to the Opposition, most of whom took his bribes while opposing his interests, that the English Minister had been asking for French money. The revelation was made in the House of Commons with careful preparation, and in the most dramatic fashion. It exploded at a frightful moment. The tale of dark designs to subjugate Protestant England to Rome was on every lip. Rumours about a secret treaty with the French king and the bugbear of the Duke of York's seemingly inevitable succession were now inflamed and fanned by what was called the "Popish Plot".

A renegade priest of disreputable character, Dr Titus Oates, presented himself as the Protestant champion. He had acquired letters written by Catholics and Jesuits in England to their co-religionists in St Omer and other French Catholic centres. From these materials he accused the Duchess of York's private secretary, Coleman, of a conspiracy to murder the King, bring about a French invasion, and cause a general massacre of Protestants. Many responsible men in both Houses of Parliament believed Oates's accusations, or pretended that they did. An order was issued for Coleman's arrest. It is certain that he had no intent against Charles, but he was a centre of Catholic activity and correspondence. He succeeded in burning the bulk of his papers; but those that were seized contained indiscreet references to the restoration of the Old Faith, and to the Catholic disappointment at Charles's attitude, which in the rage of the hour gave colour to Oates's accusations.

Meanwhile Shaftesbury, long versed in revolutions, saw his opportunity to ride the storm. Montagu, a former Ambassador to France, in collusion with the Whig and Puritan leaders, had exposed letters written by Danby in which there was mention of six million livres as the price of English assent to the proposed Treaty of Nimwegen between the French and the Dutch, and also the King's desire to be independent of Parliamentary grants. By this treaty the French were to make considerable gains. Danby, in reply, read other letters which mitigated but did not overturn the crude facts. His impeachment was resolved. Even Strafford had not been in a more perilous plight. Indeed, it seemed hardly possible that he could save his head. Charles, wishing to stay the capital proceedings instituted against his Minister, partly unjustly, and anyhow for actions which Danby had taken only to please the King, at length, in December 1678, dissolved the Cavalier Parliament.

This Parliament had sat, with intervals, for eighteen years. It was born in the Cavalier fervour of the Restoration; it ended when the King was convinced it would reduce him to the status of a Venetian Doge. Charles, in breaking this prop which had so long sustained him, did not intend to put his trust in a different party. He hoped that the new set of Members would be less rigid, less grooved and opinionated than the old. He supposed that the country was more friendly to him than the London hive in which Shaftesbury was now supreme. But all this was illusion. The trusty followers of the Court, who hitherto had mustered a hundred and fifty, now returned barely thirty. Charles II yielded to the wish of the nation; he bowed to the hostile Parliament. Danby, threatened by attainder, was glad to be forgotten for five years in the Tower. He had still a part to play.

The brunt fell upon James, Duke of York. The Duke retired to the Low Countries, carrying with him on his staff the very young captain in the British and colonel in the French Army, John Churchill, his trusted aide-de-camp and man of business. Charles, thus relieved at home, faced the fury of the anti-Popish hurricane. Oates and other perjurers who followed in his train instituted a reign of terror against the English Catholic notables. By perjury and suborned evidence they sent a number of blameless Catholics to the scaffold. The King made every effort in his power to protect them. Not for mean motives he endured the horrible ordeal which his subjects imposed upon him, of signing the death warrants of men he knew were guiltless. He abandoned his easy, indolent detachment from politics. He saw that his life and dynasty were at stake. The last five years of his reign are those most honourable to his memory. His mortal duel with Shaftesbury was a stirring episode. It was diamond cut diamond. At the beginning the King seemed at the mercy of this terrible subject; but by using time and letting passions find their vent, as well as by strokes of demonic ingenuity, Charles II emerged the victor.

The struggle centred upon the Exclusion Bill. To keep the Papist heir from the throne was the main object of the majority of the nation. Anything rather than that. But who then should succeed? Shaftesbury looked to William of Orange; but he also looked, with more favour, upon the Duke of Monmouth, Charles's illegitimate son by Lucy Waters. Here was a young man, charming, romantic, brave, gleaming, our beloved Protestant Duke – was he born in wedlock or was he a bastard? Some form of marriage it was widely believed had been solemnised between the King and Lucy. There was a "black box" in which the marriage lines were said to repose. It had been spirited away by emissaries of the Pope. What had now become the more powerful party in England longed to establish Monmouth's legitimacy. They wanted a King, a

Protestant King, an Anglican King bred in constitutional ways, with a strain of common blood to give him sense, and a clear-cut policy of organising Protestantism against the Catholic overlordship of Europe which Louis XIV was trying to achieve. Only one man could decide this issue. Charles had merely to recognise Monmouth as his heir to free himself from every trouble and assure the future of his country. Nothing would induce the King to betray the succession. Sensualist, libertine, agnostic, dilettante, he had one loyalty – the royal blood, the legitimate succession. However painful it might be for himself and his realm, he conceived it his sacred duty to pass the crown to a brother whose virtues and whose vices alike rendered him of all others the man, as he knew well, least fitted to wear it. Nevertheless the legend of the "black box" has persisted, and in our own time we have been told how a Duke of Buccleuch, descended from the unfortunate Monmouth, discovered and destroyed, as dangerous to the monarchy, the marriage certificate of Lucy Waters.

The new House of Commons met more fierce than the old one had parted. There was an overwhelming anti-Catholic majority. It proceeded immediately to impeach, and, when this lagged, to attaint Danby. It concentrated its efforts upon the Exclusion Bill. There was grave logic behind this measure. When Papists were excluded by law from every post in the realm, how should the kingly power and prerogative be wielded by one of the proscribed faith? Charles laboured to prescibe a compromise. He could not admit that Parliament should alter the lineal succession to the Crown. Out of such courses had sprung the Wars of the Roses. But he offered remarkable limitations which, were they accepted, and could they be enforced, would create a narrowly limited constitutional monarchy in England. All ecclesiastical patronage would be withdrawn from a Popish sovereign. No Papist should sit in either House of Parliament, or hold any office or place of trust. The Parliament sitting at the King's death should remain sitting for a certain time, or reassemble without further summons if it was not in session. The judges should only be appointed with the consent of Parliament. Finally, he formally abandoned the claim for which his father had fought so long – the power of the sword. Lord-Lieutenants who controlled the militia, their deputies, and the officers of the Navy would be nominated by Parliament. But in the prevailing temper no one would believe that any restrictions could be imposed upon a Popish King. The Exclusion Bill passed its second reading by an overwhelming vote, and the King descended upon the Parliament with another dissolution.

The Protestant tide again swept the country, and in all parts men voted against the Duke of York becoming King. Earnest and venerable divines tried to induce James to return to the Church of his fathers and his future subjects. He remained obdurate. To the warrior quality of his nature was added the zeal of a convert. As soon as the King saw that the election gave him no relief he prorogued the meeting of the resulting Parliament for almost another year. And it is in this interval that we first discern the use of those names Whig and

Tory which were to divide the British Island for nearly two hundred years.

During this year 1680, before the new Parliament had met, the gentry, who had the main power in the land, began to be disturbed at the violence of the Protestant Movement. The Royalist-Anglican elements increasingly recognised in Shaftesbury's agitation the terrible lineaments of Oliver Cromwell. The loathed memory of the Civil War and the so-called "Commonwealth" obsessed the older generation. If petitions for the exclusion of the Duke of York were signed by many thousands in the cities and towns, so also abhorrence of these demands upon the Crown was widespread in the country. But no parties could live under such labels as Petitioners and Abhorrers. Instead of naming themselves they named each other.

The term "Whig" had described a sour, bigoted, canting, money-grabbing Scots Presbyterian. Irish Papist bandits ravaging estates and minor-houses had been called "Tories". Neither side was lacking in power of abuse. "A Tory is a monster with an English face, a French heart, and an Irish conscience." The Whig, "talks of nothing but new light and prophecy. ... he prays for the King, but with more distinctions and mental reservations than an honest man would in taking the Covenant."[1] Yet the names Whig and Tory not only stuck, but became cherished and vaunted by those upon whom they were fastened. They gradually entered into the whole life of the nation, and represented in successive forms its main temperamental types. They were adorned by memorable achievements for the welfare of England, and both had their share in the expansion and greatness which were to come. Party loyalties and names came to be transmitted by families across the generations, though the issues changed with the times, and the party groupings varied. Orators and famous writers, sure of their appeal, pointed to them in terms of pride.

The harassed King, rather than face his fourth Parliament, adopted an expedient which recalls the futile *Magnum Consilium* to which his father had been drawn forty years before. Sir William Temple, envoy at The Hague, a leading advocate of an anti-French policy and architect of the triple alliance which had checked Louis XIV at Aix-la-Chapelle, proposed a plan for a Privy Council, reduced in numbers but clothed with power. Thirty magnates of both parties, half office-holders, half independent, would replace the old secret Cabal or Cabinet which had connived at the Treaty of Dover. For good or ill the royal policy should be open; there was to be an end, it was thought, of secret diplomacy. Charles was now in full breach with Louis XIV, who scattered his bribes widely among the Opposition. He accepted the plan. A glorified Privy Council assembled. Shaftesbury, the leader of the Opposition, was appointed its president by the King. These well-meant endeavours came to nought. The stresses were too great, and inside the Council of thirty there soon developed an inner ring which conducted all the business. Shaftesbury was in no wise placated by his re-admission to official life. He did not abandon the movement and party of which he was head. On the contrary, he used his

1   David Ogg, *England in the Reign of Charles II* (1934). [Churchill]

position to advance their interests. When Parliament met in October 1680 he again championed the Exclusion Bill, and at this moment he reached his zenith. He seemed to combine in himself the power of a Minister of the Crown and the popularity of a leader of incipient revolt. The Exclusion Bill was carried through the Commons, and the struggle was fought out in the Lords.

That it ended bloodlessly was largely due to the statesman who has rendered the word "Trimmer" illustrious. George Savile, Marquess of Halifax, was the opponent alike of Popery and of France. He was one of those rare beings in whom cool moderation and width of judgment are combined with resolute action. Halifax, who had been so hot against Danby, broke the Exclusion Bill in the House of Lords. His task was rendered easier by the difficulty of advancing an alternative successor to the Crown. Of those who were against James some were for his eldest daughter, Mary, wife of the renowned Prince of Orange, in whose veins the royal blood of England also flowed. Shaftesbury had played with this idea, but in the end decided for the bastard Monmouth. He procured his admission to the Privy Council. He wove him into the texture of his party. The Whigs propagated the fiction that he was legitimate after all. But this complaisant solution, which Charles would never tolerate, did not appeal to an assembly every man of which owned lands, wealth, and power through the strictest interpretations of hereditary right. The Anglican Church refused to resist Popery by crowning bastardy. By sixty-three votes to thirty the Peers rejected the Exclusion Bill.

Presently it was learned that Parliament was to meet in Oxford, where the King could not be bullied by the City of London and Shaftesbury's gangs of apprentices called "White Boys". To Oxford then both sides repaired. Charles moved his Guards to the town, and occupied several places on the roads from London with troops. The Whig lords arrived with bodies of armed retainers, who eyed the Household Cavalry and gallants of the Court with the respectful hostility of gentlemen upon a duelling-ground. The Members came down in parties of forty or fifty, the London M.P.s being escorted by armed citizens. A trial of strength impended, and none, could tell that it would not take a bloody form. The large majority of the Commons was still resolved upon the Exclusion Bill.

It would seem that the King kept two courses of action open, both of which he had prepared. He had caused Lawrence Hyde, Clarendon's son, the Duke of York's brother-in-law, a competent financier, to examine precisely the state of the normal revenue granted to the Crown for life. Could the King by strict economies "live of his own"? Hyde reported that it was impossible to discharge the royal services upon the original grant of customs and excise and such further taxes as Parliament had conceded. With strict economy, however, the deficit would not be large. Hyde was next employed in negotiating with Louis XIV, and eventually a hundred thousand pounds a year was obtained upon the understanding that England would not act contrary to French ambitions on the Continent. With this aid it was thought the King could manage independently of the ferocious Parliament.

England had now reached a point in its history as low as when King John, in not dissimilar stresses, had made it over as a fief to the Pope. Moreover, the King did not intend to adopt this ignominious policy which he had in his pocket, or almost in his pocket, unless he found no hope in Parliament. He made a show of going to extreme lengths to meet the national fear of a Popish King. The sacred principle of hereditary succession must not be destroyed, but short of this every security should be given. James, when he succeeded, should be King only in name. The kingdom would be governed by a Protector and the Privy Council. The accident of the conversion of the heir presumptive to Rome should not strip him of his royalty, but should deprive him of all power. The administration should rest in Protestant hands. If a son was born to James he would be educated as a Protestant and ascend the throne on coming of age. In default of a son, James's children, the two staunch Protestant princesses, Mary and after her Anne, would reign. The Protector meanwhile was to be no other than William of Orange.

There is no doubt that the King might have agreed to such a settlement, and could then have defied France and made an alliance with the Dutch and the Protestant princes of Germany. No one can lightly censure this scheme, and the fact that it was framed reveals the grinding conflicts in Charles's mind. But Shaftesbury thought otherwise. He and all his party were set upon Monmouth for the Crown. Parliament had no sooner met than its hostile temper was apparent. The King in his speech deplored the factious, unreasonable behaviour of its predecessor. The House of Commons re-elected the old Speaker, who hinted in his humble address that they saw no need for change in their demeanour. Shaftesbury, still a member of the Privy Council, in a sense part of the Government held a hard conversation with the King in the presence of many awestruck notables. A paper was handed to Charles demanding that Monmouth should be declared successor. Charles replied that this was contrary to law and also to justice.

The sitting of the Commons two days later, on March 26, 1681, was decisive. A private Member of importance unfolded to the House the kind of plan for a Protestant Protectorate during James's reign which the King had in mind. Charles would perhaps have been wise to let this discussion proceed. But Oxford was a camp in which two armed factions jostled one another. At any moment there might be an outbreak. Just as James would sacrifice all for his religious faith, so Charles would dare all for the hereditary principle. There was no risk he would not run to prevent his beloved son, Monmouth, from ousting a brother who was the main source of all his troubles.

The Commons passed a resolution for excluding the Duke of York. On the Monday following two sedan chairs made their way to Parliament.[1] In the first was the King, the crown hidden beneath his feet; in the second, which was closed, were the sceptre and the robes of State. Thus Charles wended his way to the House of Lords, installed in the Geometry School of the university. The

---

1   The Parliament had been called in 1681 and was still sitting at Oxford.

Commons were debating a question of jurisdiction arising out of a Crown prosecution for libel, and a Member was declaiming about the bearing of Magna Carta upon the point, when Black Rod knocked at the door and summoned them to the Peers. Most Members thought that this portended some compliance by the King with their wishes. They were surprised to see him robed, upon his throne, and astounded when the Lord Chancellor declared in his name that Parliament was again dissolved.

No one could tell what the consequences would be. Forty years before the Scottish Assembly had refused to disperse upon the warrant of the Crown. A hundred years later the National Assembly of France was to resort to the tennis-court at Versailles to affirm its continued existence. But the dose of the Civil War still worked in the Englishmen of 1681. Their respect for law paralysed their action. Charles had hazarded rightly. On one day there was a Parliament regarding itself as the responsible custodian of national destiny, ready to embark upon dire contention; the next a jumble of Members scrambling for conveyances to carry them home.

From this time Shaftesbury's star waned and the sagacious Halifax entered the ascendant. The reaction against the execution of the Catholic lords and others was now apparent, and the submission of Parliament to a third dissolution gave it substance. Within two months the King felt strong enough to indict Shaftesbury for fomenting rebellion. This strange man was now physically almost at the last gasp. His health, though not his spirit, was broken. His appearance – he could hardly walk – dismayed his followers. The Middlesex Grand jury, faithful to his cause, wrote "Ignoramus" across the bill presented against him. This meant that they found the evidence insufficient. He was liberated according to law. But meanwhile one of his followers had been hanged at Oxford on charges similar to those which Shaftesbury had escaped in London. He could no longer continue the struggle. He counselled insurrection; and it seemed that a royal murder would be one of its preliminaries. Shaftesbury at this point fled to Holland, hoping perhaps for Dutch support, and died at The Hague in a few weeks.

The absorbing question now was whether there would be civil war. All the Cromwellian forces were astir; indeed, there was a terror in men's hearts that if James came to the throne they would have to choose between turning Papist and being burnt at the stake. Their fears increased when James returned from exile in May 1682. An ex-officer of the Roundheads, "Hannibal" Rumbold, dwelt in the Rye House by the Newmarket Road, where it ran through a cutting. Fifty zealous Ironsides could easily overpower the small travelling escort of the King and the Duke of York on their return from their pastime of horse-racing. The lucky accident of a fire in Newmarket, by which much of the town was destroyed, led Charles and James to return some days before the expected date. They passed the Rye House in safety, and a few weeks later the secret of the plot was betrayed. It compromised the much wider circles in which armed resistance had been considered. It transformed everything. Hitherto the Whigs had exploited the Popish Plot and made common folk believe that the King was about to be butchered by the Roman Catholics. Here was the antidote. Here was a Whig or Puritan Plot from the other side to kill the King.

Two famous men were engulfed. Neither William Lord Russell nor Algernon Sidney had sought the King's life; but Russell had been privy to preparations for revolt, and Sidney had been found with an unpublished paper, scholarly in character, justifying resistance to the royal authority. The Tory Cavalier party, relieved of its fears and now roused in its turn, clamoured for vengeance. Charles classed Russell, and to a lesser extent Sidney, with Sir Harry Vane as enemies of the monarchy. After public trial both went to the scaffold. Russell refused to attempt the purchase of his life by bowing to the principle of non-resistance. Sidney affirmed with his last breath the fundamental doctrines of what had now become the Whig Party. Intense discussion was held by Church and State with both these indomitable men. Nothing was yielded by them. These executions were of lasting significance. Martyrs for religion there had been in plenty. Great Ministers of State and public men had fallen in the ruin of their policies. But here were the first martyrs for the sake of Party.

The power of Charles at home remained henceforth unchallenged. He was able to make a counter-attack. The Whig strongholds were in the boroughs and cities. These depended on their charters for the control of local government and the benches of magistrates. Influence at Parliamentary elections was also at stake. By pressure and manipulation Tory sheriffs were elected in London, and henceforth through that agency City juries could be trusted to deal severely with Whig delinquents. Nothing like Shaftesbury's acquittal could occur again. Success in London was followed up in the Provinces. The Whig corporations were asked by writs of *Quo Warranto* to prove their title to their long-used libertines. These titles were found in many cases, to the satisfaction of the royal judges, to be defective. Under these pressures large numbers of hitherto hostile corporations threw themselves on the mercy of the Crown and begged for new charters in accordance with the royal pleasure. The country gentlemen, ever jealous of the privileges of the boroughs, lent their support to the Government. Thus the Whigs, overborne in the countryside, now saw their power crippled in the towns as well. It is remarkable that they should have survived as a political force and that the course of events should so soon have restored them to predominance.

Against his own wishes the triumphant King followed meekly the foreign policy which his French paymaster prescribed. He lived with increasing frugality; his mistresses became concerned for their future, and scrambled for pensions solidly secured upon the revenues of the Post Office. Only the Fleet was nursed. Louis continued his aggressions and waged war upon freedom and the Protestant faith. His armies overran the Spanish Netherlands; he laid his hands on Strasbourg; he made inroads upon the German principalities. He ruled splendid and supreme in Europe. England, which under Elizabeth and Cromwell had played a great European part, for a while shrank, apart from domestic politics, to a quiescent and contented community, busy with commerce and colonies, absorbed in its own affairs and thankful they were easier.

Across the seas widespread thrusts were taking place, often on the initiative of the men on the spot rather than by planned direction from London. English commerce was expanding in India and on the West Coast of Africa. The Hudson's Bay Company, launched in 1669, had set up its first trading posts and was building up its influence in the northern territories of Canada. On the coasts of Newfoundland English fishermen had revivified the earliest colony of the Crown. On the American mainland the British occupation of the entire eastern seaboard was almost complete. The capture of New York and the settlement of New Jersey had joined in contiguity the two existing groups of colonies that lay to the north and south. Inland the state of Pennsylvania was beginning to take shape as an asylum for the persecuted of all countries under the guidance of its Quaker proprietor, William Penn. To the south the two Carolinas had been founded and named in honour of the King. At the end of Charles's reign the American colonies contained about a quarter of a million settlers, not counting the increasing number of slaves, transhipped from Africa. The local assemblies of the colonists were sturdily asserting traditional English rights against the interventions of the King's Ministers from London. Talk of excluding James from the throne died away. He had now become the vehement supporter of French aims in Europe. Unchastened by the past, he dreamed of reconverting England to Rome under the sword of France. In all but name he became again Lord High Admiral. He dilated to Charles, who had no illusions, upon the proved efficacy of a strong policy. He braced himself and hardened his heart for the mission which lay before him.

The King was only fifty-six, and in appearance lively and robust, but his exorbitant pleasures had undermined his constitution. To represent him as a mere voluptuary is to underrate both his character and his intellect. His whole life had been an unceasing struggle. The tragedy he had witnessed and endured in his youth, the adventures and privations of his manhood, the twenty-five years of baffling politics through which he maintained himself upon the throne, the hateful subjugations forced on him by the Popish Plot, now in his last few years gave place to a serene experience. All the fires of England burned low, but there was a genial glow from the embers at which the weary King warmed his hands. Halifax, now more than ever trusted, still urged him to the adventure of a new Parliament, and Charles might have consented, when suddenly in February 1685 an apoplectic stroke laid him low. With that air of superiority to death for which all mortals should be grateful he apologised for being "so unconscionable a time in dying". James was at hand to save his soul. Old Father Huddleston, the priest who had helped him in the days of the Boscobel oak, was brought up the backstairs to rally him to Rome and give the last sacrament. Apart from hereditary monarchy, there was not much in which Charles believed in this world or another. He wanted to be King, as was his right, and have a pleasant life.

CHAPTER THIRTY-THREE

THE BLOODLESS REVOLUTION

The Catholic James II — Monmouth's rebellion — Judge Jeffreys — the King prorogues a recalcitrant Parliament — Catholics given high offices — William of Orange supports the King's opponents — clergy refuse to proclaim James's Declaration of Indulgence — bishops sent to Tower — Not Guilty verdicts free bishops — Shrewsbury and supporters send for William of Orange — Lilliburlero — James agrees to reverse pro-Catholic laws — William of Orange lands at Torbay — James allowed to escape abroad

J AMES WAS a convert to Rome. He was a bigot, and there was no sacrifice he would not make for his faith. He lost his throne in consequence, and his son carried on after him the conscientious warfare, to his own exclusion. Toleration was the natural first step to the revival of Catholicism. The King was determined that the Catholics should not be persecuted, and for tactical reasons, at a later date, he extended his protection to the Dissenters. It is possible that he fortified himself inwardly by asserting that all he wanted was toleration, and by the enlightened use of the dispensing power to be the true father of all his people. Afterwards in exile he entered into a correspondence, of which sixty letters have been preserved, with Rancé, the Prior of the Trappists, in which devotion to the Catholic faith is combined with toleration. But by then toleration was the most he could hope for if he ever returned to England. The English Protestant nation would have been very foolish to trust themselves to the merciful tolerances of James II once he had obtained the absolute power he sought.

The sudden death of Charles II came as a shattering blow to his well loved bastard, Monmouth. He was in Holland, a gay prince, dancing and skating, happy with his beautiful mistress, Lady Wentworth. Thus he beguiled the time till Protestant feeling in England and his father's love should win him what he believed was his birthright. Suddenly he found that he must deal henceforward not with a father who would forgive anything, but with an uncle who forgave nothing, and had a long score in his ledger. William of Orange had entertained him agreeably at The Hague, but on the day when Charles's death was known reasons of State supervened and he ordered him to leave the country. He gave him good advice to take a commission from the Emperor against the Turks.

But Monmouth was in the grip of the exiles. Around him were the desperate fugitives from the Rye House Plot. "Claim your rights," they said. "Now or never!" Monmouth might well have been content to lead a happy life with Lady Wentworth, but these morose and frantic men drove him to his doom. They all thought of the England they had quitted in 1681. Before Monmouth's eyes, too, there shone the scenes of his progress through the West Country. Would not all England rise for "our beloved Protestant Duke" against a Popish King? Three little ships with Argyll, son of the Covenanting Earl, and "Hannibal" Rumbold were prepared for Scotland. Three others, with other Rye House conspirators or followers of Shaftesbury, would carry Monmouth upon his perilous challenge.

James's public practice of the Roman faith immediately disquieted the Anglican clergy; but its effect did not reach the country for some time. The royal proclamation was generally accepted. The calling of a Parliament to vote such revenues as expired with Charles II was indispensable. The electors returned a House of Commons loyal and friendly to the new King. They voted him a revenue for life which, with the growth of trade, amounted to nearly £2,000,000 a year. Sir Edward Seymour, High Tory, who was out of temper with the management of the elections in his own West Country, alone warned the House of its imprudence and urged delay.

It was at this moment on June 11, 1685, that Monmouth landed. He had been nineteen days at sea, using up his luck in escaping the English warships. He entered the harbour of Lyme Regis, not far from Portland Bill. He was at once welcomed by the populace. He issued a proclamation asserting the validity of his mother's marriage and denouncing James as a usurper who had murdered Charles II. In one day fifteen hundred persons signed the rolls of enlistment in his army. But when the messengers brought the news at a gallop to Whitehall James was found in the first flush of his power. He had no large army; but there were the Household Cavalry and a regiment of Dragoons under his long-trusted officer and agent, Lord Churchill. There were also two regiments of regular infantry under Colonel Kirke which had been withdrawn from Tangier when that outpost was abandoned. All the ruling forces rallied round the Crown. Parliament swore to live and die with the King. Monmouth was attainted and a price was placed upon his head. Extraordinary supplies were voted. The militia was called out, and almost everywhere responded. A French emigrant, Louis Duras, long resident in England, who had been created Earl of Feversham, was placed in command of the royal troops; but Churchill by forced marches had already reached the spot. Monmouth and his rebels, who by then amounted to six or seven thousand ardent men, made a long march through Taunton and Bridgwater towards Bristol, which closed its gates against him, then circled back by Bath and Frome, and finally, a month after his landing, reached Bridgwater again. Churchill, now joined by Kirke, hung close upon him from day to day, while Feversham and the royal army approached.

Despite the enthusiasm for his cause among the common people the unhappy Duke knew that he was doomed. He had learned that Argyll and Rumbold, landing in Scotland, had been overpowered and captured. Their execution was imminent. One last chance remained – a sudden night attack upon the royal army. Feversham was surprised in his camp at Sedgemoor; but an unforeseen deep ditch, called the Bussex Rhine, prevented a hand-to-hand struggle. Churchill, vigilant and active, took control. The West Country peasantry and miners, though assailed by sixteen pieces of artillery and charged in flank and rear by the Household troops, fought with Ironside tenacity. They were slaughtered where they stood, and a merciless pursuit, with wholesale executions, ended their forlorn endeavour. Monmouth escaped the field only to be hunted down a few days later. He could claim no mercy, and none did he receive. Chief Justice Jeffreys was sent into the West to deal with the large number of prisoners. This cruel, able, unscrupulous judge made his name for ever odious by "the Bloody Assize". Between two and three hundred persons were hanged, and about eight hundred transported to Barbados, where their descendants still survive. The ladies of the Court scrambled for the profits of selling these poor slaves, and James marked the ruthless judge for advancement to Lord Chancellor.

The conduct of William of Orange showed his statecraft. He was under treaty to send three regiments of infantry to James's aid. He fulfilled his obligation with alacrity. He even offered to come in person to command them. On the other hand, he did not try too hard to stop Monmouth's expedition from sailing. If the Duke won there would be a Protestant King of England, who would certainly join a coalition against Louis XIV. If he failed the last barrier which stood between William and his wife Mary and the succession to the English throne would be for ever removed. Of the two alternatives that which he most desired came to pass.

James was now at the height of his power. The defeat of the rebels and the prevention of another civil war had procured a nation-wide rally to the Crown. Of this he took immediate advantage. As soon as Jeffreys "'campaign", as James called it, was ended he proposed to his Council the repeal of the Test Act and the Habeas Corpus Act. These two hated relics of his brother's reign seemed to him the main objects of assault. In the emergency he had given many commissions to Catholic officers. He was determined to retain them in his new, tripled army. Halifax, as Lord President of the Council, pointed to the statutes which this would affront; Lord Keeper North warned his master of the dangers he was incurring. Halifax was removed, not only from the Presidency of the Council, but from the Privy Council altogether; and when North died soon after, Chief Justice Jeffreys, red-handed from "the Bloody Assize", was made Lord Chancellor in his stead. Robert Spencer, Earl of Sunderland, later in the year became Lord President in the place of Halifax, as well as Secretary of State, and, was henceforward James's Chief Minister. Sunderland is a baffling figure who served in turn Charles, James, and later William III. He throve by changing sides. Now he had become a Papist to please his master. No one knew better than he the politics and inclinations of the leading families in the country, and that is what made him indispensable to successive sovereigns.

Parliament met for its second session on November 9,[1] and the King laid his immediate purpose before it. In his blunt way he declared, with admitted reason, that the militia was useless. They had twice run away before Monmouth's half-armed peasantry. A strong standing Army was indispensable to the peace and order of the realm. He also made it plain that he would not dismiss his Catholic officers on the morrow of their faithful services. These two demands shook the friendly Parliament to its foundations. Its most hideous nightmare was a standing Army, its dearest treasure the Established Church. While the old loyalties, revived by recent dangers, still inspired the Tory nobles and country gentlemen, the doctrine of non-resistance dominated the Church. Both were prepared to condone the breach of the Test Act committed by Catholic officers during the rebellion. The Commons offered an additional grant of £700,000 to strengthen the royal forces. They only asked, with profuse expressions of devotion, for reassurance that Acts of Parliament should not be set aside by the Prerogative, and for comforting words about the security of the Protestant religion. The King gave a forbidding answer.

In the House of Lords Devonshire, the hardy Whig, Halifax, the renowned ex-Minister, Bridgewater and Nottingham, actually members of the Privy Council, and, not the least, Henry Compton, Bishop of London, son of a father who had died for Charles I at Newbury, asserted the rights of the nation. A day was fixed for further discussion, and the judges were invited to pronounce upon the lawfulness of the King's proceedings. James had not yet packed the Bench with his partisans. He saw plainly that the declaration which must now be expected from the judges and the House of Lords would constitute a massive obstacle to that very dispensing power for the relief and preferment of the Catholics upon which his heart was set. He therefore repeated the stroke by which Charles II had dispersed the Parliament at Oxford in 1681. On November 20 he suddenly appeared in the House of Lords, summoned the Commons to the Bar, and prorogued Parliament. It never met again while he was King.

Freeing himself from Parliamentary opposition by repeated prorogations, King James proceeded throughout 1686 to relieve his fellow-religionists. First he desired to dispense with the Test against Catholics in the Army. The judges whom he consulted were adverse, but after various dismissals and appointments the Bench assumed a new complexion. Roman Catholic peers were admitted to the Privy Council. He set up an Ecclesiastical Commission, almost identical with the old Court of High Commission destroyed by the Long Parliament, the main function of which was to prevent Anglican clergy from preaching against Catholicism. Bishop Compton had already been dismissed from the Privy Council. He was now suspended from his functions as Bishop of London. These actions disturbed the whole realm. The methods of absolutism were being used to restore the Catholic religion, more dreaded than absolutism itself. Lawyers discerned that a direct conflict between statutory law and Royal Prerogative had arisen.

By the end of the year James had driven away many of his most faithful friends and disquieted everybody. Halifax, who had saved him from the Exclusion Bill, was brooding in the country. Danby only liberated from the Tower in 1684, had perforce abandoned his dream of Church and King. He saw it could never be realised with a Papist sovereign. Albemarle, son of General Monk, had quitted the royal service. The Church, the bulwark of legitimacy, the champion of non-resistance, seethed with suppressed alarms, and only the powerful influence of Lawrence Hyde, now Earl of Rochester, upon the bishops and clergy prevented a vehement outburst. It was plain that the King, with all the downright resolution of his nature, was actively and of set purpose subverting the faith and Constitution of the land.

During the whole of 1686 and 1687 James held Parliament in abeyance, and used his dispensing power to introduce Roman Catholics into key positions. Whigs and Tories drew closer together. James was uniting the party that had challenged his brother with the party that had rallied so ardently to his brother's defence. He now embarked upon a political manoeuvre at once audacious, crafty, and miscalculated. Hitherto he had striven only to relieve his Catholic subjects. He would now bid for the aid of the Dissenters, who were equally oppressed. If Whigs and Tories were combined he would match them by a coalition of Papists and Nonconformists under the armed power of the Crown. In William Penn, the Quaker courtier and founder of the state of Pennsylvania across the seas, influential in both this and the former reign, he found a powerful and skilled agent. Thus did the King break down the national barriers of his throne and try to shore it up with novel, ill-assorted, and inadequate props.

In January 1687 came the fall of the Hydes. For a long time both had been unhappy in their offices. Clarendon, the elder brother, in Ireland, had been overawed by James's faithful follower, the Roman Catholic Earl of Tyrconnel; Rochester, in Whitehall, was subdued by Sunderland. On January 7, 1687, Rochester was dismissed from the Treasury, and three days later Clarendon was replaced by Tyrconnel. The friend of the Hydes who governed Scotland in His Majesty's name was superseded by two Catholics. These changes marked another definite stage in the reign of James II. The prorogation of Parliament at the end of 1685 had been the beginning of Cavalier and Anglican discontent against the Crown. With the dismissal of Rochester began the revolutionary conspiracy. Meanwhile James was raising and preparing his Army. Charles II's forces of about seven thousand men had cost £280,000 a year. Already James was spending £600,000 upon the upkeep of more than twenty thousand men. The Duke of Berwick, now eighteen years old, was made Governor of Portsmouth, and Catholics commanded at both Hull and Dover. Eventually a Catholic admiral ruled the Channel Fleet.

William of Orange watched the King's proceedings with close attention. Soon after the dismissal of the Hydes, Dykevelt, a Dutchman of the highest character, arrived in London as his envoy, partly to exhibit William as pleading with James to moderate his measures, and partly to sound the Opposition leaders. Dykevelt saw all the statesmen opposed to the Court, and made it clear that they could count upon William and Mary for help. The provocations of the royal policy continued. The first Declaration of Indulgence was issued. It did precisely what James's Parliament had objected to in advance: it set aside statutory Act by Royal Prerogative. Defenders of James's conduct are concerned to exaggerate the number of English Catholics. It is even claimed that one-eighth of the population still adhered, in spite of generations of persecution, to the Old Faith. The old Catholic families in England however, apart from favoured individuals, were deeply apprehensive of the headlong adventure upon which the King was launching them. The Pope himself, in accordance with the policy of the Holy See, deprecated James's excessive zeal, and his Legate in England urged caution and prudence. But the King hardened his heart and strengthened his Army.

The national fear and hatred of Catholicism were inflamed by the daily landing on the British shores of miserable victims of Catholic "toleration" as practised in France by the most powerful sovereign in the world. All classes and parties knew the close sympathy and co-operation of the French and English Courts. They saw all they cared for in this world and the next threatened. They therefore entered, not without many scruples and hesitations, but with inexorable resolve, upon the paths of conspiracy and rebellion. In England during the autumn of 1688 everything pointed, as in 1642, to the outbreak of civil war. But now the grouping of the forces was far different from the days when Charles I unfurled his standard at Nottingham. The King had a large, well-equipped regular Army, with a powerful artillery. He believed himself master of the best, if not at the moment the largest, Navy afloat. He could call for powerful armed aid from Ireland and from France. He held the principal seaports and arsenals under trusty Catholic governors. He enjoyed substantial revenues. He assumed that the Church of England was paralysed by its doctrine of non-resistance, and he had been careful not to allow any Parliament to assemble for collective action. Ranged against him on the other hand were not only the Whigs, but almost all the old friends of the Crown. The men who had made the Restoration, the sons of the men who had fought and died for his father at Marston Moor and Naseby, the Church whose bishops and ministers had so long faced persecution for the principle of Divine Right, the universities which had melted their plate for King Charles I's coffers and sent their young scholars to his armies, the nobility and landed gentry whose interests had seemed so bound up with the monarchy – all, with bent heads and burning hearts, must now prepare themselves to outface their King in arms. Never did the aristocracy or the Established Church face a sterner test or serve the nation better than in 1688. They never flinched; they never doubted.

In this wide and secret confederacy there were two main divisions of policy. The moderates, led by Halifax and Nottingham, urged caution and delay. There had been no widespread conversions to Catholicism, as James had hoped, and he would never get a Parliament to support him. On the other hand stood the party of action, headed by Danby. He was the first man of great position who definitely set himself to bring William and a foreign army into England. With Danby were the Whig leaders – Shrewsbury, Devonshire, and some others. As early as the spring of 1688 they invited William to come over; and William replied that if he received at the right moment a formal request from leading English statesmen he would come, and that he would be ready by September.

Much now turned upon the Army. If the troops obeyed orders and fought for the King England would be torn by civil war, the end of which no man could foresee. But if the Army refused to fight, or was prevented from fighting by any means, then the great issues at stake would be settled bloodlessly. The supreme object of all the conspirators, civil or military, was to coerce the King without using physical force. And now events struck their hammer-blows. At the end of April James had issued a second Declaration of Indulgence. He ordered that the Declaration should be read in all the churches. On May 18 seven bishops, headed by the Primate, the venerable William Sancroft, protested against this use of the dispensing power. The clergy obeyed their ecclesiastical superiors and the Declaration was left unread. James, furious at disobedience, and apparently scandalised at this departure by the Church he was seeking to undermine, from its doctrine of non-resistance, demanded that the bishops should be put on trial for seditious libel. His Minister, Sunderland, now thoroughly alarmed, endeavoured to dissuade him from so extreme a step. Even Lord Chancellor Jeffreys told Clarendon that the King was going too far. But James persisted, the trial was ordered, and the bishops, all of whom refused the proffered bail, were committed to the Tower.

Up to this moment there always lived the hope that the stresses which racked the nation would die with the King. The accession of either Mary, the heir-presumptive, or Anne, the next in order, promised an end to the struggle between a Catholic monarch and a Protestant people. Peaceable folk could therefore be patient until the tyranny was past. The doctrine of non-resistance did not seem a principle of despair. But on June 10, while the trial of the bishops was still pending, the Queen gave birth to a son. Thus there lay before the English people the prospect of a Papist line, stretching out indefinitely upon the life of the future. The bishops, formerly detested, never popular, now became the idols of the nation. As they stepped on board the barge for the Tower they were hailed by immense crowds with greetings in which reverence and political sympathy were combined. For the first time the Episcopacy found itself in alliance with the population of London. The same scenes were repeated when they were brought back to Westminster Hall on June 15, and at their trial on June 29. The sitting lasted until late in the evening, and the jurors remained together throughout the night. When on the following day the bishops were declared "Not Guilty" the verdict was acclaimed with universal joy. As they left the court masses of people, including lifelong foes of the Episcopacy, knelt down and asked their blessing. But the attitude of the Army was more important. The King had visited them at Hounslow, and as he departed heard loud cheering. "What is that clamour?" he asked. "Sire, it is nothing: the soldiers are glad that the bishops are acquitted." "Do you call that nothing?" said James.

On the same night, while cannon and tumults proclaimed the public joy, the seven leaders of the party of action met at Shrewsbury's town house, and there and then signed and dispatched their famous letter to William. It was cool and businesslike in tone. "If the circumstances stand so with your Highness," it said, "that you believe you can get here time enough, in a condition to give assistance this year, ... we, who subscribe this, will not fail to attend your Highness upon your landing." The signatories were Shrewsbury, Danby, Russell, Bishop Compton, Devonshire, Henry Sidney and Lumley. The letter was conveyed to The Hague by Admiral Herbert, disguised as a common sailor, and its signatories spread throughout the Island for the purpose of levying war upon the King. Shrewsbury, a former Catholic, converted Protestant, after mortgaging his estates to raise £40,000, crossed the seas to join William. Danby undertook to raise Yorkshire; Compton toured the North "to see his sisters". Devonshire, who had lain since 1685 in obscurity at Chatsworth, formed his tenantry into a regiment of horse. William, stricken in his ambition by the birth of a male Stuart heir, exclaimed, "Now or never!" and began to prepare his expedition.

The birth of the baby prince struck so cruel a blow to the hopes of the nation that it was received with general incredulity, sincere or studiously affected. From the beginning doubts had been thrown upon the belated pregnancy of the Queen. The prayers and intercessions of the Catholics, and their confident predictions that a son would be born as a result, led to a widespread conviction that a trick had been practised. The legend that a child had been smuggled into St James's Palace in a warming-pan was afoot even before the ashes of the official bonfires had been cleared from the streets. By the King's improvidence the majority of persons present at the birth were Papists, the wives of Papists, or foreigners. The Archbishop of Canterbury was absent; he had that day been conducted to the Tower. Neither of the Hydes had been summoned, though as Privy Counsellors, brothers-in-law of the King, and uncles to the two princesses, whose rights to the Crown were involved, their presence would have been natural. The Dutch Ambassador, who had a special duty to William, was not invited. It is more important, perhaps, that Princess Anne was not there. She was at Bath with the Churchills. It was vital to the nation to prove that the child was an impostor. Sincerely attached to the principle of legitimacy, the English Protestants had no other means of escape from the intolerable fact of a Papist heir.

Churchill in August renewed his pledge to William, given fifteen months before, and wrote in his own handwriting a signed letter, still extant, which if betrayed would have cost him his life. "Mr Sidney will let you know how I intend to behave myself; I think it is what I owe to God and my country. My honour I take leave to put into your Royal Highness's hands, in which I think it safe. If you think there is anything else that I ought to do, you have but to command me, and I shall pay an entire obedience to it, being resolved to die in that religion that it has pleased God to give you both the will and power to protect." Nevertheless this extraordinary man, who at this time played only a subordinate part, continued to hold all his offices and commands in the Army, and no doubt intended to use all his influence with the troops against James when the time came. He hoped in this way either to compel the King to submit or to deprive him of all means of resistance. His sincerity of purpose and duplicity of method were equal. He acted as if he was conducting a military operation. Moreover, deceit is inseparable from conspiracy.

Across the sea, watching from day to day the assembled armies of France, lay William of Orange with the troops and Fleet of Holland. But before he could invade England he had to obtain the sanction of the States-General. At a moment when the whole of the French Army was massed and ready for immediate advance it was not easy to persuade the anxious burghers of Holland or the threatened princes of Germany that their best chance of safety lay in sending a Dutch army into England. However, William convinced Frederick III of Brandenburg, and received from him a contingent under Marshal Schomberg. The other German princes acquiesced in the Prussian view. Most of Catholic Spain set political above religious considerations and made no difficulty about attempting to dethrone a Catholic king. The Emperor's religious scruples were removed by the Pope. All these diverse interests and creeds were united in a strategy so far-seeing and broad-minded as is only produced by an overpowering sense of common danger.

All, however, turned upon the action of France. If the French armies marched against Holland William and the whole Dutch strength would be needed to face them, and England must be left to her fate. If, on the other hand, Louis struck upon the Rhine at Brandenburg and the German coalition, then the expedition could sail. Louis XIV kept all in suspense till the last moment. Had James been willing to commit himself finally to a French alliance Louis would have invaded Holland. But James had patriotic pride as well as religious bigotry. To the last he wavered so that in Holland they thought he was allied to France, and in France to Holland. Louis therefore decided that the best he could hope for would be an England impotent through civil war. At the end of September he turned his armies towards the middle Rhine, and from that moment William was free to set forth. The States General granted him authority for his English enterprise and James's hour was come.

The King's attempt to bring in some of the Irish Roman Catholic regiments which Tyrconnel had raised for him produced symptoms so menacing that the project was abandoned. The hatred and fears of all classes found expression in an insulting, derisive ballad against the Irish and the Papists. *Lilliburlero* like *Tipperary* in our own times, was on all lips, in all ears, and carried a cryptic message of war to all hearts.[1] Everyone watched the weathercock. All turned on the wind. Rumour ran riot. The Irish were coming. The French were coming. The Papists were planning a general massacre of Protestants. The kingdom was sold to Louis. Nothing was safe, and no one could be trusted. The laws, the Constitution, the Church – all were in jeopardy. But a deliverer would appear. He would come clad with power from over the seas to rescue England from Popery and slavery – if only the wind would blow from the east.

The scale and reality of William's preparations and the alarming state of feeling throughout England had terrified Sunderland and Jeffreys. These two Ministers induced the King to reverse his whole policy. Parliament must be called without delay. All further aggressive Catholic measures must be stopped and a reconciliation made with the Episcopal Church. On October 3 James agreed to abolish the Ecclesiastical Commission, to close the Roman Catholic schools, to restore the Protestant Fellows of Magdalen College, to put the Act of Uniformity into force against Catholics and Dissenters. The dismissed Lord-Lieutenants were invited to resume their functions in the counties. Their charters were restored to the recalcitrant municipalities. The bishops were begged to let bygones be bygones. The Tory squires were urged to take their old places in the magistracy. In the last few months of his reign James was compelled to desert the standard he had himself set up and try in vain by the sacrifice of all his objectives to placate the furies he had aroused. But it was too late.

On October 19 William set out upon the seas. His small army was a microcosm of Protestant Europe-Dutch, Swedes, Danes, Prussians, English, and Scotch, together with a forlorn, devoted band of French Huguenots, to the number of fourteen thousand, embarked upon about five hundred vessels, escorted by sixty warships. William had planned to land in the North, where Danby and other nobles were in readiness to join him. But after he had once been driven back by a gale the wind carried him through the Straits of Dover, which he passed in full view of the crowded coasts of England and France. On November 5 he landed at Torbay, on the coast of Devon. James was not at first greatly alarmed at the news. He hoped to pen William in the West and to hamper his communications by sea. The troops which had been sent to Yorkshire were recalled to the South, and Salisbury was fixed as the point of assembly for the royal army. At this crisis the King could marshal as large an army as Oliver Cromwell at his height. Still, twenty-five thousand men, or nearly double the number of William's expedition, were around Salisbury

---

1   The satirical anti-Catholic ballad *Lilliburlero, Bullen-a-la* was written by Thomas Wharton, 1st Marquess of Wharton (1648–1714), who was a Whig Member of Parliament and Lord Lieutenant of Ireland (1708–10). The ballad poked fun at Irish Catholics. The theme 'Lero, lero, lilli burlero' was said to have been used by the Irish Catholics when they massacred the Protestants in 1641.

when the King arrived on November 19. This was the largest concentration of trained full-time troops that England had ever seen.

But now successive desertions smote the unhappy prince. Lord Cornbury, eldest son of the Earl of Clarendon, an officer of the Royal Dragoons, endeavoured to carry three regiments of horse to William's camp. James, warned from many quarters, meditated Churchill's arrest. On the night of November 23, having failed to carry any large part of the Army with them, Churchill and the Duke of Grafton, with about four hundred officers and troopers, quitted the royal camp. At the same time the Princess Anne, attended by Sarah Churchill, and guided by Bishop Compton, fled from Whitehall and hastened northwards. And now revolt broke out all over the country. Danby was in arms in Yorkshire, Devonshire in Derbyshire, Delamere in Cheshire. Lord Bath delivered Plymouth to William. Byng,[1] later an admiral, representing the captains of the Fleet, arrived at his headquarters to inform him that the Navy and Portsmouth were at his disposal. City after city rose in rebellion. By one spontaneous, tremendous convulsion the English nation repudiated James.

The King, finding resistance impossible, assembled such peers and Privy Counsellors as were still in London, and on their advice entered into negotiations with the Prince of Orange. Meanwhile the invading army moved steadily forward towards London. James sent his wife and son out of the kingdom, and on the night of December 11 stole from the palace at Whitehall, crossed the river, and rode to the coast. He endeavoured to plunge his realm into anarchy. He threw the Great Seal into the Thames, and sent orders to Feversham to disband the Army, and to Dartmouth to sail to Ireland with what ships he could. The wildest rumours of Irish massacres spread through the land. The London mob sacked the foreign embassies, and a panic and terror, known as "Irish Night", swept the capital. James in his flight had actually got on board a ship, but, missing the tide, was caught and dragged ashore by the fishermen and townsfolk. He was brought back to London, and after some days of painful suspense was allowed to escape again. This time he succeeded and left English soil for ever.

---

1   George Byng, 1st Viscount Torrington (1663–1733) was the father of Admiral John Byng, famously shot for neglect of duty in 1757.

CHAPTER THIRTY-FOUR

WILLIAM OF ORANGE

William and Mary – Danby's return – the Convention Parliament – war with France – Churchill created Earl of Marlborough – Louis XIV supports the exiled James II – James lands in Ireland – the siege of Londonderry – the French beat Dutch and English fleets off Beachy Head – the Battle off the Boyne – split between Queen and Sarah Churchill – Marlborough dismissed – the Battle of Cape La Hogue – English débâcle against French – Charles Montagu opens the Bank of England – Queen Mary dies from smallpox – the Treaty of Ryswick – the rise of Robert Harley – the Act of Settlement – the War of Spanish Succession – William and Marlborough re-united – the death of James II – Louis recognises the Pretender – the second Grand Alliance – the death of William III

ROM HIS earliest years the extraordinary Prince who in the general interest robbed his father-in-law of the British throne had dwelt under harsh and stern conditions. William of Orange was fatherless and childless. His life was loveless. His marriage was dictated by reasons of State. He was brought up by a termagant grandmother, and in his youth was regulated by one Dutch committee after another. His childhood was unhappy and his health bad. He had a tubercular lung. He was asthmatic and partly crippled. But within this emaciated and defective frame there burned a remorseless fire, fanned by the storms of Europe, and intensified by the grim compression of his surroundings. His greatest actions began before he was twenty-one. From that age he had fought constantly in the field, and toiled through every intrigue of Dutch domestic politics and of the European scene. For four years he had been the head of the English conspiracy against the Catholic King James II.

Women meant little to him. For a long time he treated his loving, faithful wife with indifference. Later on, towards the end of his reign, when he saw how much Queen Mary had helped him in the English sphere of his policy, he was sincerely grateful to her, as to a faithful friend or Cabinet officer who had maintained the Government. His grief at her death was unaffected.

In religion he was of course a Calvinist; but he does not seem to have derived much spiritual solace from the forbidding doctrines of the sect. As a sovereign and commander he was entirely without religious prejudices. No agnostic could have displayed more philosophic impartiality. Protestant, Catholic, Jew, or infidel were all the same to him. He dreaded and hated Gallican Catholicism less because it was to him idolatrous than because it was French. He employed Catholic officers without hesitation when they would serve his purpose. He used religious questions as counters in his political combinations. While he beat the Protestant drum in England and Ireland, he had potent influence with the Pope, with whom his relations were at all times a model of comprehending statesmanship. It almost seemed that a being had been created for the sole purpose of resisting the domination of France and her "Great King".

It was the natural consequence of such an upbringing and of such a mission that William should be ruthless. Although he had not taken part in the conspiracy to murder the Dutch statesmen, the De Witts, in 1672, he had rejoiced at it, profited by it, and protected and pensioned the murderers. The darkest stain upon his memory was to come from Scotland. A Highland clan whose chief had been tardy in making his submission was doomed to destruction by William's signed authority. Troops were sent to Glencoe "to extirpate that den of thieves". But the horror with which this episode has always been regarded arises from the treacherous breach of the laws of hospitality by which it was accomplished. The royal soldiers lived for weeks in the valley with the clansmen, partaking of their rude hospitality under the guise of friendship. Suddenly, on a freezing winter night, they turned upon their hosts and murdered them by the score while they slept or fled from their huts. The King had not prescribed the method, but he bears the indelible shame of the deed.

The whole British nation had been united in the expulsion of James. But there was now no lawful Government of any kind. A Convention Parliament was summoned by the Prince on the advice of the statesmen who had made the Revolution. Personal ambitions and party creeds shot through the complicated manoeuvres which led to the final constitutional arrangements. King Charles's former Minister, the Earl of Danby, had much to hope for from these weeks of chaos. It was he who had created the Tory Party from the Anglican gentry and the Established Church after the breakdown of the Cabal. The intrigues of Charles with France and the Popish Plot had wrecked his political career. To save him from the malice of his enemies the King had incarcerated him in comfort in the Tower. He had been released towards the end of the reign, and now in the 1688 Revolution he saw his chance to remake his fortunes. His position as a great landowner in the North had enabled him to raise the gentry and provide a considerable military force at a critical and decisive moment. With the prestige of this achievement behind him he had arrived in London.

Loyal Tories were alarmed by the prospect of disturbing the Divine Right in the Stuart succession. Danby got in touch with Princess Mary. An obvious solution which would please many Tories was the accession of Mary in her own right. In this way the essential basis of the Tory creed could be preserved, and for this Danby now fought in the debates of the hastily assembled Lords. But other Tories, including Mary's uncle, the Earl of Clarendon, favoured the appointment of William as Regent, James remaining titular King. This cleavage of ideas helped the Whigs to prevail. The Whigs looked on the Revolution as the vindication of their own political belief in the idea of a contract between Crown and people. It now lay with Parliament to settle the succession. The whole situation turned upon the decision of William. Would he be content with the mere tide of honorary consort to his wife? If so the conscience of the Tories would not be violated and the Whig share in the Revolution would be obscured. The Whigs themselves had lost their leaders in the Rye House Plot, and it was a single politician who played their game for them and won, while they reaped the benefit.

George Savile, Marquis of Halifax, "the Trimmer" as he was proud to be called, was the subtlest and most solitary statesman of his day. His strength in this crisis lay in his knowledge of William's intention. The suggestion that William should be Regent on behalf of James was rejected in the Lords, but only by 51 votes to 49. After protracted debates in the Convention Halifax's view was accepted that the Crown should be jointly vested in the persons of William and Mary. His triumph was complete, and it was he who presented the Crown and the Declaration of Rights to the two sovereigns on behalf of both Houses. But his conception of politics was hostile to the growing development of Party. In a time of high crisis he could play a decisive rôle. He possessed no phalanx of partisans behind him. His moment of power was brief; but the Whig Party owed to him their revival in the years which followed.

Step by step the tangle had been cleared. By the private advice of John and Sarah Churchill, Princess Anne, Mary's younger sister, surrendered in favour of William her right to succeed to the throne should Mary predecease him. Thus William gained without dispute the Crown for life. He accepted this Parliamentary decision with good grace. Many honours and promotions at the time of the coronation rewarded the Revolutionary leaders. Churchill, though never in William's immediate circle, was confirmed in his rank of Lieutenant-General, and employed virtually as Commander-in-Chief to reconstitute the English Army. He was created Earl of Marlborough, and when in May 1689 war was formally declared against France, and William was detained in England and later embroiled in Ireland, Marlborough led the English contingent of eight thousand men against the French in Flanders.

William's paramount interest was in the great war now begun throughout Europe, and in the immense confederacy he had brought into being. He had regarded the English adventure as a divagation, a duty necessary but tiresome, which had to be accomplished for a larger purpose. He never was fond of England, nor interested in her domestic affairs. He required the wealth and power of England by land and sea for the European war. Once securely seated on the English throne he scarcely troubled to disguise these sentiments. It was not surprising that such manners, and still more the mood from which they evidently arose gave deep offence. William's unsociable disposition, his greediness at table, his silence and surliness in company, his indifference to women, his dislike of London, all prejudiced him with polite society. The ladies voted him "a low Dutch bear". The English Army too was troubled in its soul. Neither officers nor men could dwell without a sense of humiliation upon the military aspects of the Revolution. They did not like to see all the most important commands entrusted to Dutchmen. They eyed sourly the Dutch infantry who paced incessantly the sentry-beats of Whitehall and St James's, and contrasted their shabby blue uniforms with the scarlet pomp of the 1st Guards and Coldstreamers, now banished from London. As long as the Irish war continued, or whenever a French invasion threatened, these sentiments were repressed; but at all other times they broke forth with pent-up anger. As soon as he learned on the afternoon of December 23, 1688, that by King James's flight he had become undisputed master of England the Prince of Orange took the step for which he had come across the water. The French Ambassador was given twenty-four hours to quit the Island and England was committed to the general coalition against France. This opened a war which, with an uneasy interlude, gripped Europe for twenty-five years, and was destined to bring low to the ground the power of Louis XIV.

The exiled James was received by Louis with every mark of consideration and sympathy which the pride and policy of the Great King could devise. Ireland presented itself as the obvious immediate centre of action. James, sustained by a disciplined French contingent, many French officers, and large supplies of French munitions and money, had landed in Ireland in March. He was welcomed as a deliverer. He reigned in Dublin, aided by an Irish Parliament, and was soon defended by a Catholic army which may have reached a hundred thousand men. The whole island except the Protestant settlements in the North passed under the control of the Jacobites, as they were henceforth called. While William looked eastward to Flanders and the Rhine the eyes of his Parliament were fixed upon the opposite quarter. When he reminded Parliament of Europe they vehemently drew his attention to Ireland. The King made the time-honoured mistake of meeting both needs inadequately. The defence of Londonderry and its relief from the sea was the one glorious episode of the campaigning season of 1689.[1]

Cracks speedily appeared in the fabric of the original National Government. The Whigs considered that the Revolution belonged to them. Their judgment, their conduct, their principles, had been vindicated. Ought they not then to have all the offices? But William knew that he could never have gained the Crown of England without the help of the Cavaliers and High Churchmen, who formed the staple of the Tory Party. At the election of February 1690 the Tories won. It may seem strange that the new King should have turned to the inscrutable personality of the Earl of Sunderland, who had

---

[1] The defence of Londonderry lasted from 17 April to 30 July 1689. Some 30,000 Protestants were trapped in Londonderry by James II's forces, and the anniversary of the siege remains an important date in the Ulster calendar.

been King James's chief adviser. But James and Sunderland had now irrevocably quarrelled, and the Jacobites held the Earl mainly responsible for the Revolution. Sunderland was henceforth bound to William's interest, and his knowledge of the European political scene was invaluable to his sovereign's designs. After a brief interval he reappeared in England, and gained a surprising influence. He did not dare seek office for himself, but he made and marred the greatest fortunes. The actual government was entrusted to the statesmen of the middle view – the Duke of Shrewsbury, Sidney Godolphin, and Marlborough, and, though now, as always, he stood slightly aloof from all parties, Halifax. All had served King James. Of these men it was Godolphin during the next twenty years who stood closest to Marlborough. Great political dexterity was combined in him with a scrupulous detachment. He never thrust forward for power, but he was seldom out of office. He served under four sovereigns, and with various colleagues, but no one questioned his loyalty. He knew how to use a well-timed resignation, or the threat of it, to prove his integrity. Awkward, retiring, dreamy by nature, he was yet heart and soul absorbed by the business of government.

Had William used his whole strength in Ireland in 1689 he would have been free to carry it to the Continent in 1690; but in the new year he found himself compelled to go in person with his main force to Ireland, and by the summer took the field at the head of thirty-six thousand men. Thus the whole power of England was diverted from the main theatre of the war. The Prince of Waldeck, William's Commander in the Low Countries, suffered a crushing defeat at the skilful hands of Marshal Luxembourg in the Battle of Fleurus. At the same time the French Fleet gained a victory over the combined fleets of England and Holland off Beachy Head. The command of the Channel temporarily passed to the French under Admiral Tourville, and it seemed that they could at the same time land an invading army in England and stop William returning from Ireland.

Queen Mary's Council, of which Marlborough was a member, had to face an alarming prospect. They were sustained by the loyalty and spirit of the nation. The whole country took up what arms they could find. With a nucleus of about six thousand regular troops, and the hastily improvised militia and yeomanry, Marlborough stood ready to meet the invasion. However, on July 1, 1690, King William gained a decisive victory at the Boyne[1] and drove King James out of Ireland back to France. The end of 1690 therefore saw the Irish War ended and the command of the sea regained. William was thus free after two years to proceed in person to the Continent with strong forces and to assume command of the main armies of the Alliance. He took Marlborough with him at the head of the English troops. But no independent scope was given to Marlborough's genius, already discerned among the captains of the Allies, and the campaign, although on the greatest scale, was indecisive. Thereafter a divergence grew between the King and Marlborough.

1   Although James II and his army escaped, this battle established William of Orange's control over Ireland. Ulster Orangemen still celebrate July 12 (the "old" date of the battle).

When the commands for the next year's campaign were being assigned William proposed to take Marlborough to Flanders as Lieutenant-General attached to his own person. Marlborough demurred at this undefined position. He did not wish to be carried round Flanders as a mere adviser, offering counsel that was not taken, and bearing responsibility for the failures that ensued. He asked to remain at home unless required to command the British troops, as in the past year. But the King had offered them to one of his Dutch generals, Baron Ginkel, fresh from Irish victories at Aughrim and Limerick. In the Commons a movement was on foot for an address on the employment of foreigners. Marlborough was known to be sympathetic, and he proposed himself to move a similar motion in the House of Lords. Widespread support was forthcoming, and it even appeared at one time likely that the motion would be carried by majorities in both Houses. Moreover, Marlborough's activities did not end with Parliament. He was the leading British general, and many officers of various ranks resorted to him and loudly expressed their resentment at the favour shown to the Dutch.

At this time almost all the leading men in England resumed relations with James, now installed at Saint-Germain, near Paris. Godolphin also cherished sentiments of respectful affection towards the exiled Queen. Shrewsbury, Halifax, and Marlborough all entered into correspondence with James. King William was aware of this. He still continued to employ these men in great offices of State and confidence about his person. He accepted their double-dealing as a necessary element in a situation of unexampled perplexity. He tolerated the fact that his principal English counsellors were reinsuring themselves against a break-up of his Government or his death on the battle-field. He knew, or at least suspected, that Shrewsbury was in touch with Saint-Germain through his mother; yet he insisted on his keeping the highest offices. He knew that Admiral Russell had made his peace with James; yet he kept him in command of the Fleet. If he quarrelled with Marlborough it was certainly not because of the family contacts which the General preserved with his nephew, King James's son, the Duke of Berwick, or his wife Sarah with her sister, the Jacobite Duchess of Tyrconnel. The King probably knew that Marlborough had obtained his pardon from James by persuading the Princess Anne to send a dutiful message to her father. There was talk of the substitution of Anne for William and Mary, and at the same time the influence of the Churchills with Princess Anne continued to be dominating. Any rift between Anne and her sister, Queen Mary, must sharpen the already serious differences between the King and Marlborough. The ill-feeling between the royal personages developed rapidly. William treated Anne's husband, Prince George of Denmark, with the greatest contempt. He excluded him from all share in the wars. He would not take him to Flanders, nor allow him to go to sea with the Fleet. Anne, who dearly loved her husband, was infuriated by these affronts.

As often happens in disputes among high personages, the brunt fell on a subordinate. The Queen demanded the dismissal of Sarah Churchill from

Anne's household. Anne refused with all the obstinate strength of her nature. The talk became an altercation. The courtiers drew back distressed. The two sisters parted in the anger of a mortal estrangement. The next morning at nine o'clock Marlborough, discharging his functions as Gentleman of the Bedchamber, handed the King his shirt, and William preserved his usual impassivity. Two hours later the Earl of Nottingham, Secretary of State, delivered to Marlborough a written order to sell[1] at once all the offices he held, civil and military, and consider himself as from that date dismissed from the Army and all public employment and forbidden the Court. No reasons were given officially for this important stroke.

Marlborough took his dismissal with unconcern. His chief associates, the leading counsellors of the King, were offended. Shrewsbury let his disapproval be known; Godolphin threatened to retire from the Government. Admiral Russell, now Commander-in-Chief of the Navy, went so far as to reproach King William to his face with having shown ingratitude to the man who had "set the crown upon his head". The Queen now forbade Sarah to come to Court, and Anne retorted by quitting it herself. She left her apartments in the Cockpit at Whitehall and retired to Syon House, offered her by the Duke of Somerset. No pressure would induce Anne to part with her cherished friend, and in these fires of adversity and almost persecution links were forged upon which the destinies of England were presently to hang.

No sooner had King William set out upon the Continental war than the imminent menace of invasion fell upon the Island he had left denuded of troops. Louis XIV now planned a descent upon England. King James was to be given his chance of regaining the throne. It was not until the middle of April 1692 that the French designs became known to the English Government. Fevered but vigorous preparations were made for defence by land and sea. On May 19–20 the English and Dutch Fleets met Tourville with the main French naval power in the English Channel off Cape La Hogue. Russell's armada, which carried forty thousand men and seven thousand guns, was the stronger by ninety-nine ships to forty-four. Both sides fought hard, and Tourville was decisively beaten. Russell and his admirals, all of whom were counted on the Jacobite lists as pledged and faithful adherents of King James, followed the beaten Navy into its harbours. During five successive days the fugitive warships were cut out under the shore batteries by flotillas of English rowboats. The whole apparatus of invasion was destroyed under the very eyes of the former King whom it was to have borne to his native shore. The Battle of Cape La Hogue, with its consequential actions, effaced the memories of

---

1   All officers on a point of resignation offered their commissions for sale. Until the late nineteenth century, commissions were bought. Many offices of state carried with them the right to take a percentage of trade and commissions associated with that office. For example, Pepys made much of his fortune by taking commissions in the naval dockyards. In the case of Marlborough, Churchill is using the term sale as resignation and means that, publicly, no profit could any longer be made from title and position.

Beachy Head. It broke decisively for the whole of the wars of William and Anne all French pretensions to naval supremacy. It was the Trafalgar of the seventeenth century.

On land the campaign of 1692 unrolled in the Spanish Netherlands, which we now know as Belgium. It opened with a brilliant French success. Namur fell to the French armies. But worse was to follow. In August William marched by night with his whole army to attack Marshal Luxembourg. The French were surprised near Steinkirk in the early morning. Their advanced troops were overwhelmed and routed, and for an hour confusion reigned in their camp. But Luxembourg was equal to the emergency and managed to draw out an ordered line of battle. The British infantry formed the forefront of the Allied attack. Eight splendid regiments, under General Mackay, charged and broke the Swiss in fighting as fierce as had been seen in Europe in living memory. Luxembourg now launched the Household troops of France upon the British division, already strained by its exertions, and after a furious struggle, fought mostly with cold steel, beat it back. Meanwhile from all sides the French advanced and their reinforcements began to reach the field. Count Solms, the Dutch officer and William's relation, who had replaced Marlborough in command of the British contingent, had already earned the cordial dislike of its officers and men. With the remark, "Now we shall see what the bulldogs can do!" he refused to send Mackay the help for which he begged. The British lost two of their best generals and half their numbers killed and wounded, and would not have escaped but for the action of a subordinate Dutch general, Overkirk, afterwards famous in Marlborough's campaigns. William, who was unable to control the battle, shed bitter tears as he watched the slaughter, and exclaimed, "Oh, my poor English!" By noon the whole of the Allied army was in retreat, and although the losses of seven or eight thousand men on either side were equal the French proclaimed their victory throughout Europe.

The Continental ventures of William III now forced English statesmen to a reconstruction of the credit and finances of the country. The first war Government formed from the newly organised Whig Party possessed in the person of Charles Montagu a first-rate financier. It was he who was responsible for facing this major problem. The English troops fighting on the Continent were being paid from day to day. The reserves of bullion were being rapidly depleted and English financial agents were obsessed by the fear of a complete breakdown. The first essential step was the creation of some national organ of credit. In collaboration with the Scottish banker William Paterson, Montagu, now Chancellor of the Exchequer, started the Bank of England in 1694 as a private corporation. This institution, while maintaining the principle of individual enterprise and private joint-stock company methods, was to work in partnership with the Government, and was to provide the necessary means for backing the Government's credit.

Montagu was not content merely to stop here. With the help of the philosopher John Locke, and William Loundes of the Treasury, he planned a complete overhaul of the coinage. Within two years the recoinage was carried out, and with this solidly reconstructed financial system the country was able in the future not only to bear the burden of King William's wars, but to face the prolonged ordeal of a conflict over the Spanish Succession. It is perhaps one of the greatest achievements of the Whigs.

At the end of 1694 Queen Mary had been stricken with smallpox, and on December 28 she died, unreconciled to her sister Anne, mourned by her subjects, and lastingly missed by King William. Hitherto the natural expectation had been that Mary would long survive her husband, upon whose frail fiery life so many assaults of disease, war, and conspiracy had converged. An English Protestant Queen would then reign in her own right. Instead of this, the crown now lay with William alone for life, and thereafter it must come to Anne. This altered the whole position of the Princess, and with it that of the redoubtable Churchills, who were her devoted intimates and champions. From the moment that the Queen had breathed her last Marlborough's interests no longer diverged from William's. He shared William's resolve to break the power of France; he agreed with the whole character and purpose of his foreign policy. A formal reconciliation was effected between William and Anne. Marlborough remained excluded for four more years from all employment, military or civil, at the front or at home; but with his profound gift of patience and foresight upon the drift of events he now gave a steady support to William.

In 1695 the King gained his only success. He recovered Namur in the teeth of the French armies. This event enabled the war to be brought to an inconclusive end in 1696. It had lasted for over seven years. England and Holland – the Maritime Powers as they were called – and Germany had defended themselves successfully, but were weary of the struggle. Spain was bellicose but powerless, and only the Habsburg Emperor Leopold, with his eyes fixed on the ever-impending vacancy of the Spanish throne, was in earnest in keeping the anti-French confederacy in being. The Grand Alliance began to fall to pieces. The Treaty of Ryswick marked the end of the first period in this world war. William and Louis interchanged expressions of the highest mutual regard. Europe was temporarily united against Turkish aggression. Many comforted themselves with the hope that Ryswick had brought the struggle against the exorbitant power of France to an equipoise. This prospect was ruined by the Tories and their allies. The moment the pressure of war was relaxed they had no idea but to cast away their arms. England came out of the war with an army of eighty-seven thousand regular soldiers. The King considered that thirty thousand men and a large additional number of officers was the least that would guarantee the public safety and interest. His Ministers did not dare to ask for more than ten thousand, and the House of Commons would only vote seven thousand. The Navy was cut down only less severely. Officers and men were cast upon the streets or drifted into outlawry in the countryside. England, having made every sacrifice and performed prodigies of strength and valour, now fell to the ground in weakness and improvidence when a very little more perseverance would have made her, if not supreme, at least secure.

The apparent confusion of politics throughout William's reign was largely due to the King's great reluctance to put himself at the disposal of either of the two main party groups. He wished for a national coalition to support a national effort against France, and he was constitutionally averse from committing himself. But as the months passed he was forced to realise the differing attitudes of Whigs and Tories to the Continental war, and a familiar pattern of English politics began to emerge. The Whigs were sensitive to the danger of the French aggression in Europe. The Tories, on the other hand, resented the country being involved in Continental commitments and voiced the traditional isolationism of the people. The political story of the reign is thus a continuous see-saw. The Whigs managed two or three years of war, and then the Tories would return to power upon a rising tide of war-weariness. In 1697 the Whig administration was driven from office and Robert Harley,[1] now the rising hope of Toryism, created his power and position in the House of Commons.

This singularly modern figure whom everyone nowadays can understand, born and bred in a Puritan family, originally a Whig and a Dissenter, speedily became a master of Parliamentary tactics and procedure. In the process of opposing the Court he gradually transformed himself from Whig to Tory and from Dissenter to High Churchman. He it was who conducted the reckless movement for the reduction of the armed forces. He it was who sought to rival the Whig Bank of England with a Tory Land Bank. All the time, however, he dreamed of a day when he could step above Parliamentary manoeuvrings and play a part upon the great world stage of war and diplomacy. Harley was supported by Sir Edward Seymour, the pre-eminent "sham good-fellow" of the age, who marshalled the powerful Tories of Cornwall and the West. In the Lords he was aided by Nottingham and the Earl of Rochester. Together these four men exploited those unworthy moods which from time to time have seized the Tory Party. They froze out and hunted into poverty the veteran soldiery and faithful Huguenot officers. They forced William to send away his Dutch Guards. They did all they could to belittle and undermine the strength of their country. In the name of peace, economy, and isolation they prepared the ground for a far more terrible renewal of the war.

William was so smitten by the wave of abject isolationism which swept the governing classes of the Island that he contemplated an abdication and return to Holland. He would abandon the odious and intractable people whose religion and institutions he had preserved and whose fame he had lifted to the head of Europe.

William's distresses led him to look again to Marlborough, with whom the future already seemed in a great measure to rest. The King's life and strength

---

1   Robert Harley, 1st Earl of Oxford (1661–1724), chief minister to Queen Anne (1711–14) and
     negotiator of the Treaty of Utrecht (1713).

were ebbing, Anne would certainly succeed, and with the accession of Anne the virtual reign of Marlborough must begin. Marlborough patiently awaited this unfolding of events. Anne's sole surviving son, the Duke of Gloucester, was now nine years old, and it was thought fitting to provide the future heir apparent to the Crown with a governor of high consequence and with an establishment of his own. In the summer of 1698 William invited Marlborough to be governor of the boy prince "Teach him my lord," he said, "but to know what you are, and my nephew cannot want for accomplishments." At the same time Marlborough was restored to his rank in the Army and to the Privy Council.

While helping the King in many ways, he was most careful to keep a hold upon the Tory Party, because he knew that in spite of its many vices it was the strongest force in England and representative of some of the deepest traits in the English character. The Princess Anne too was a bigoted Tory and Churchwoman. The untimely death in 1700 of the little Duke of Gloucester, who succumbed to the fatal, prevalent scourge of smallpox, deprived Marlborough of his office. He still remained in the closest association with Sidney Godolphin and at the very centre of the political system.

There was now no direct Protestant heir to the English and Scottish thrones. By an Act of Settlement the house of Hanover, descended from the gay and attractive daughter of James I who had briefly been Queen of Bohemia, was declared next in succession after William and Anne. The Act laid down that every sovereign in future must be a member of the Church of England. It also declared that no foreign-born monarch might wage Continental wars without the approval of Parliament; he must not go abroad without consent, and no foreigners should sit in Parliament or on the Privy Council. Thus were recorded in statute the English grievances against William III. Parliament had seen to it that the house of Hanover was to be more strictly circumscribed than he had been. But it had also gone far to secure the Protestant Succession.

No great war was ever entered upon with more reluctance on both sides than the War of the Spanish Succession. Europe was exhausted and disillusioned. Over Europe hung the long-delayed, long-dreaded, ever-approaching demise of the Spanish Crown. William was deeply conscious of his weakness. He was convinced that nothing would make England fight again, and without England Holland could expect nothing short of subjugation. The King therefore cast himself upon the policy of partitioning the Spanish Empire, which included the southern Netherlands, much of Italy, and a large part of the New World. There were three claimants.

The first was France, represented either by the Dauphin or, if the French and Spanish Crowns could not be joined, by his second son, the Duke of Anjou. The next was the Emperor, who claimed as much as he could, but was willing to transfer his claims to his second son by his second wife, the Archduke Charles. Thirdly, there was the Emperor's grandson by his first marriage, the Electoral Prince of Bavaria. The essence of the new Partition

Treaty of September 24, 1698, was to give the bulk of the Spanish Empire to the candidate who, if not strongest in right, was at least weakest in power. Louis and William both promised to recognise the Electoral Prince as heir to Charles II of Spain. Important compensations were offered to the Dauphin. This plan concerted between Louis XIV and William III was vehemently resented by the Emperor. As it became known it also provoked a fierce reaction in Spain. Spanish society now showed that it cared above all things for the integrity of the Spanish domains and that the question of the prince who should reign over them all was secondary.

But now a starting event occurred. The Treaty of Partition had been signed at William's palace at Loo in Holland in September 1698. In February 1699 the Electoral Prince of Bavaria, heir to prodigious domains, the child in whose chubby hands the greatest states had resolved to place the most splendid prize, suddenly died. William and Louis arranged a second Treaty of Partition on June 11, 1699, by which the Archduke Charles was made heir-in-chief. To him were assigned Spain, the overseas colonies and Belgium, on the condition that they should never be united with the Empire. The Dauphin was to have Naples and Sicily, the Milanese, and certain other Italian possessions.

Meanwhile the feeble life-candle of the childless Spanish King burned low in the socket. To the ravages of deformity and disease were added the most grievous afflictions of the mind. The royal victim believed himself to be possessed by the Devil. His only comfort was in the morbid contemplation of the tomb. All the nations waited in suspense upon his failing pulses and deepening mania. He had however continued on the verge of death for more than thirty years, and one by one the great statesmen of Europe who had awaited this event had themselves been overtaken by the darkness of night. Charles had now reached the end of his torments. The rival interests struggled for access to his death-chamber. In the end he was persuaded to sign a will leaving his throne to the Duke of Anjou. The will was completed on October 7, and couriers galloped with the news from the Escorial to Versailles. On November 1 Charles II expired.

Louis XIV had now reached one of the great turning-points in the history of France. Should he reject the will, stand by the treaty, and join with England and Holland in enforcing it? But would England stir? On the other hand, should he repudiate the treaty, endorse the will, and defend his grandson's claims in the field against all comers? Would England oppose him? Apart from good faith and solemnly signed agreements upon which the ink was barely dry, the choice, like so many momentous choices, was nicely balanced. The Emperor had refused to subscribe to the Second Partition Treaty. Was it valid? Louis found it hard to make up his mind. A conference was held in Madame de Maintenon's room on November 8. It was decided to repudiate the treaty and stand upon the will.

Confronted with this event, William felt himself constrained to recognise the Duke of Anjou as Philip V of Spain. The House of Commons was still in a mood far removed from European realities. Neither party would believe that they could be forced into war against their decision – still less that their decision could change. They had just completed the disarmament of England. They eagerly accepted Louis XIV's assurance that, "content with his power, he would not seek to increase it at the expense of his grandson". The supreme event which roused all England to an understanding of what had actually happened in the virtual union of the Crowns of France and Spain was a tremendous military operation effected under the guise of brazen legality. Philip V had been acclaimed in Madrid. The Spanish Netherlands rejoiced in his accession. A line of fortresses in Belgium, garrisoned under treaty rights by the Dutch, constituted the main barrier of the Netherlands against a French invasion. Louis resolved to make sure of these barrier fortresses. During the month of February 1701 strong French forces arrived before all the Belgian cities. The Spanish commanders welcomed them with open gates. They had come, it was contended, only to help protect the possessions of His Most Catholic Majesty. The Dutch garrisons, overawed by force, and no one daring to break the peace, were interned. Antwerp and Mons; Namur – King William's famous and solitary conquest – Leau, Venloo, and a dozen secondary strongholds, all passed in a few weeks, without a shot fired, by the lifting of a few cocked hats, into the hands of Louis XIV. Others, like Liège, Huy, and its neighbouring towns, fell under his control through the adhesion to France of their ruler, the Prince-Bishop of Liège. Citadels defended during all the years of general war, the loss or capture of any one of which would have been boasted as the fruits of a hard campaign, were swept away in a month. All that the Grand Alliance of 1689 had defended in the Low Countries in seven years of war melted like snow at Easter.

Europe was roused, and at last England was staggered. Once more the fighting men came into their own. The armies newly dissolved, the officers so lightly dismissed and despised, became again important. Once more the drums began to beat, and smug merchants and crafty politicians turned to the martial class, whom they had lately abused and suppressed. The insular structure in which England had sought to dwell cracked about her ears. In June the House of Commons authorised the King to seek allies; ten thousand men at any rate should be guaranteed to Holland. William felt the tide had set in his favour. By the middle of the year the parties in opposition to him in his two realms, the Tory majority in the House of Commons and the powerful burgesses of Amsterdam were both begging him to do everything that he "thought needful for the preservation of the peace of Europe" – that is to say, for war.

This process united William and Marlborough. On May 31 he proclaimed Marlborough Commander-in-Chief of the English forces assembling in Holland. In June he appointed him Ambassador Extraordinary to the United Provinces. Discretion was given him not only to frame, but, if need be, to conclude treaties without reference to King or Parliament. The formation of the Grand Alliance had begun. It was now, in this deadly atmosphere, that the flash came which produced the British explosion.

On September 16, 1701, James II died. Louis visited in state his deathbed at Saint-Germain, and announced to the shadow Court that he recognised James's son as King of England and would ever sustain his rights. He was soon astounded by the consequences of his act. All England was roused by the insult to her independence. The Act of Settlement had decreed the succession of the Crown. The Treaty of Ryswick had bound Louis, not only in formal terms, but by a gentleman's agreement, to recognise and not to molest William III as King. Whigs and Tories vied with one another in Parliament in resenting the affront. The whole nation became resolute for war. Marlborough's treaties, shaped and presented with much knowledge of Parliamentary susceptibilities, were acclaimed; ample supplies were tendered to the Crown. King William was able to sever diplomatic relations with France. The Emperor had already begun the war and his famous general, Prince Eugene of Savoy, was fighting in the North of Italy.

The second Grand Alliance now formed must have seemed a desperate venture to those whose minds were seared by the ill-fortune of William's seven-years war. France had gained without a shot fired all the fortresses and territory so stubbornly disputed. The widest Empire of the world was withdrawn from the Alliance and added to the resources of its antagonists. Spain had changed sides, and with Spain not only the Indies, South America, and a great part of Italy, but the cockpit of Europe – Belgium and Luxembourg. Savoy, a deserter, still rested with France, though her greatest prince was an Austrian general. The Archbishopric of Cologne was also now a French ally. Bavaria, constant to the end in the last war, was to be with France in the new struggle. The Maritime Powers had scarcely a friendly port beyond their coasts. The New World, except in the North, was barred against them. The Mediterranean had become in effect a French lake. South of Plymouth no fortified harbour lay open to British and Dutch ships. They had their superior fleets, but no bases which would carry them to the inland sea.

On land the whole Dutch barrier had passed into French hands. Instead of being the rampart of Holland, it had become the sallyport of France. Louis, occupying the cities of Cologne and Treves, was master of the Meuse and of the Lower Rhine. He held all the Channel ports, and had entrenched himself from Namur through Antwerp to the sea. His winter dispositions disclosed his intention in the spring campaign to renew the invasion of Holland along the same routes which had led almost to its subjugation in 1672. A terrible front of fortresses, bristling with cannon, crammed with troops and supplies, betokened the approaching onslaught. The Dutch sheltered behind inundations and their remaining strongholds. Finally the transference of Bavaria to the side of France laid the very heart of the Habsburg domains open to French invasion. The Hungarians were in revolt against Austrian rule and the Turks were once more afoot. In every element of strategy by sea or by land, as well as in the extent of territory and population, Louis was twice as strong at the beginning of the War of the Spanish Succession as he had been at the Peace of Ryswick. Even the Papacy had changed sides. Clement XI had abandoned the policy of Innocent XI. He espoused the cause of the Great King and his tremendous armies. Such was the prospect, as it seemed, of overwhelming adversity which had opened upon the English people largely as the result of their faction and their fickle moods.

At this moment death overtook King William. On February 20, 1702, William was riding in the park round Hampton Court on Sorrel, a favourite horse. Sorrel stumbled in the new workings of a mole, and the King was thrown. The broken collar-bone might well have mended, but in his failing health the accident opened the door to a troop of lurking foes. Complications set in, and after a fortnight it was evident to him and to all who saw him that death was at hand. William died at fifty-two, worn out by his labours. Marlborough at the same age strode forward against tremendous odds upon the ten years of unbroken victory which raised the British nation to a height in the world it had never before attained.

CHAPTER THIRTY-FIVE

THE WAR OF THE
SPANISH SUCCESSION

Queen Anne – the Cockpit government – the age of Defoe, Swift,
Newton, Vanbrugh – Marlborough created Duke – Whigs banished from
power – nadir of the Grand Alliance – the Battle of Blenheim – England
wins Gibraltar – the Battle of Ramillies – the Act of Union with Scotland
– split between the Queen and Sarah Churchill – failure in France – the
Battle of Oudenarde – English capture Minorca – Whigs back in control –
the siege of Tournai – slaughter at Malplaquet

T HE AGE of Anne is rightly regarded as the greatest manifestation of
the power of England which had till then been known. The genius
of Marlborough in the field and his sagacity in counsel enabled the
growing strength of the nation to make its full effect on Europe.
The intimate, long-developed friendships of the Cockpit[1] circle now found
their expression in the smallest and most efficient executive which has ever
ruled England. Sarah managed the Queen, Marlborough managed the war,
and Godolphin[2] managed the Parliament. The Queen, for five glorious years,
threw herself with happiness and confidence into these capable hands.

There was at that time an extraordinary wealth of capacity in the English
governing class. All the offices of the State, military or political, could have
been filled two or three times over by able, vigorous, daring, ambitious
personalities. It was also the Augustan Age of English letters. Addison, Defoe,
Pope, Steele, Swift, are names which shine today. There was a vehement
outpouring of books, poems, and pamphlets. Art and science flourished. The
work of the Royal Society, founded in Charles II's reign, now bore a largesse
of fruit. Sir Isaac Newton in mathematics, physics, and astronomy completed

1 The Cockpit was a building close to today's Downing Street, which had a pit for cock fights.
  Although the original building was pulled down in 1675, its name was given to houses and Privy
  Council offices overlooking St James's park. In one of these houses lived Queen Anne, and
  around her she gathered her closest advisers. Thus the Queen's group is called, by Churchill, the
  Cockpit circle.
2 Sidney Godolphin, 1st Earl of Godolphin (1645–1712) was the Lord Treasurer who funded
  Marlborough (his patron) during the War of the Spanish Succession. Although he was influential
  in forming the Act of the Union, he was later (1710) dismissed in favour of Harley.

the revolution of ideas which had begun with the Renaissance. Architecture was led to noble achievements by Wren, and to massive monuments by Vanbrugh.

All the time controversy ran to extremes. The religious passions of former years now flowed into the channels of political faction. Never was the strife of party groups so hot, so fiercely maintained, or more unscrupulous. Men and parties, conscious of their message and of the magnitude of the opportunity, strove furiously against one another for the control of the State or for a share in its governance. They carried their rivalry to all lengths; but in the earlier years of the reign there was a common purpose of beating France. This was no small undertaking, for at that time England had but five million inhabitants, while the towering French monarchy was master of near twenty millions, united under the Great King.

In March 1702 Anne ascended the throne. She presented herself to the Houses of Parliament in robes and insignia which revived memories of Queen Elizabeth. "I know my own heart," she said, "to be entirely English." She accepted Marlborough's impulse upon the whole policy of the State. In the first momentous days of her reign he was not only her chief but her sole guide. Marlborough was made Captain-General of her armies at home and abroad. He acted immediately. No sooner had the Queen met the Privy Council on March 8 than he informed the Imperial Ambassador, Wratislaw, that the Queen, like the late King, would support unswervingly the interests of the Emperor. That same night he sent a personal message of reassurance to Antonie Heinsius, the Grand Pensionary or Chief Minister of Holland, offering in the name of the Queen resolute prosecution of the war and adherence to the treaties, and at the earliest moment when he could be spared he sailed for The Hague.

This was the great period of the Dutch Republic. The union of the seven provinces which had been forged in the fires of Spanish persecution and tempered by heroic war on land against France and on sea against England had now become a wonderful instrument and force in Europe. But the death of William III shook the entire structure of the Dutch oligarchy. He left no direct heir of the house of Orange whom all the United Provinces would accept as their leading Stadtholder. Who would lead their army against the gathering foes? Who would preserve the common cause of the sea-Powers? Queen Anne cherished the idea that her husband, Prince George, would become Generalissimo of the armies of the sea-Powers. There were forces in Holland which thought of a native commander for its troops. But all fell into Marlborough's hands. The office of Stadtholder and Commander-in-Chief was allowed to pass into abeyance and Marlborough was appointed Deputy Captain-General of Holland. He was thus in supreme command of the armies of the two Western Powers. Prussia, which had lately become a kingdom, and the Germanic States of the Rhine soon naturally associated themselves with this system. But although the highest title and general deference were accorded to the English General his authority could only assert itself at every stage by infinite patience and persuasiveness. Marlborough and the able Lord Treasurer, Godolphin, who fulfilled many of the duties of a Prime Minister, worked closely and harmoniously together. But in drawing up their plans both men had to consider the party stresses at Westminster and the powerful influence in the country of political grandees. Unquestioned authority was never granted to them; they always had to walk warily. Marlborough's reputation as a soldier was good upon the Continent, but he had never hitherto commanded a large army, and a dozen Dutch and German generals who must now work under him had seen far more service in the recent wars. The General of the Empire, Prince Eugene, at this time carrying on his successful campaign in Italy, stood forth as the foremost soldier of the Allies.

For the year 1702 Louis had decided to set his strongest army against Holland. He knew the division and uncertainty into which the Republic had been thrown by the death of King William. He regarded Marlborough as a favoured Court personage, able no doubt, and busy with intrigue, but owing his influence entirely to the Queen's affection for his wife. The French High Command therefore did not hesitate to place their main army, as soon as the campaigning season began, within twenty miles of Nimwegen, at the point where the valleys of the Meuse and the Rhine divide.

In May Marlborough made for Nimwegen. He found widespread despondency among the Allied troops and jealousy among the generals. But when his hand was felt upon the Army and its operations a different mood prevailed. In a brilliant campaign the new Captain-General conquered all the fortresses of the Meuse, and thus the whole river channel was freed. The hitherto aggressive French were seen baffled, hesitating, and in retreat. When after the storm of Liège Marlborough, narrowly escaping an ambuscade upon the Meuse, returned to The Hague he was received with intense public joy by the Dutch, and on his arrival in England he was created Duke by the Queen. In his very first year the tide of the war was set flowing in the opposite direction, and the whole Alliance, which had seemed about to collapse, was knit together by new bonds of constancy and hope.

The other English venture of 1702 was a naval expedition to Cadiz. William III had realised the importance to England of the Mediterranean and the harbours guarding its entrance. English trade with the Levant was seriously threatened by French ambition, and the French enthronement in Spain jeopardised English commercial interests. A powerful fleet and army sailed for Cadiz at the end of July under the Duke of Ormonde and Admiral Sir George Rooke. The commanders lacked the nerve to force the harbour upon the first surprise, and yielded themselves to what seemed the easier course. Troops were landed to capture the forts on the shore, and a prolonged series of desultory operations ensued, accompanied by pillage and sacrilege, tales of which spread far and wide throughout Spain. Meanwhile the defence grew continually stronger. A boom was placed across the entrance and ships were sunk in the channel by the enemy. After a month it was decided to re-embark the soldiers and sail for home.

The ignominy was relieved by a lucky windfall. As Rooke and Ormonde, on the worst of terms and each blaming the other, were returning disconsolately home news was brought that the Spanish Treasure Fleet with millions from the Indies aboard had run into Vigo Bay. Excited councils of war ensued. It was decided to raid the harbour. The lure of gold and the sting of Cadiz inspired the leaders, and at last they let loose their brave men, who fought with indomitable fury. By sundown they were masters of Vigo Bay. The entire enemy fleet was sunk, burned, or captured. Not one ship escaped. The treasures of the Indies were frantically carried inland on mules before the action, but enough remained for the victors to bear home a million sterling to sustain the Treasury and appease Parliament. In spite of this a searching inquiry was ordered into the conduct of Rooke and Ormonde at Cadiz. Marlborough, who had approved the expedition, and looked upon the capture of Cadiz as a stepping-stone to the entry to the Mediterranean and the seizure of Minorca, intervened to protect the impugned commanders. Had they shown at Cadiz one-half of the spirit of Vigo Bay the sea-Powers would have been masters of the Mediterranean in 1703.

The beginning of Queen Anne's reign seemed to open a period of Tory prosperity. All King William's Whig Ministers were banished from power. In Godolphin's administration Rochester, the Queen's uncle, and Nottingham, King William's High Tory Minister, played substantial and grandiose parts. But from the very outset a deep division opened between Marlborough, to whom Godolphin was inseparably bound, and their Tory colleagues. The traditional Tory view was that England should not aspire to play a leading part in the Continental struggle. Her true policy was to intervene only by seapower, and amid the conflicts of Europe to gain many territories overseas in the outer world.

The Whigs, on the other hand, though banished from office, were ardent advocates of the greatest military efforts. They supported Marlborough in all his courses. They derided the false strategy of colonial expeditions, and declared that no British interest was safe without victory in the main and decisive theatre. This dash of opinion, in which on both sides there was massive argument, governed the politics of the reign. Marlborough and Godolphin found themselves continually at variance with their other Tory colleagues upon the crucial question of how the war should be fought. If England did not join wholeheartedly in the Continental war Louis XIV would win it. The issue was radical, and much to his regret Marlborough found it necessary to use his paramount influence with the Queen against the leaders of the Tory Party. Moreover, there was a religious complication. Queen Anne, Marlborough, and Godolphin were all Tories born and bred, and all were Anglicans. Anne had long ago abandoned the conviction that her father's son, the exiled Prince of Wales, was not her brother. The Prince lived under French protection. He is known to British history as the "Old Pretender", but more gallantly in French annals as the Chevalier of St George. Queen Anne felt herself in her innermost conscience a usurper, and she was also gnawed by the feeling that she had treated her dead father ill. Her one justification against these self-questionings was her absolute faith in the Church of England. It was her duty to guard and cherish at all costs this sacred institution, the maintenance of which was bound up with her own title and the peace of her realm. To abdicate in favour of her Papist brother would be not only to betray her religion, but to let loose the horrors of civil war upon the land she ruled, loved, and in many ways truly represented.

For the campaign of 1703 Marlborough was able to concentrate the "Grand Army" of the Alliance around Maastricht, eighty miles south of Nimwegen, the starting-point of the previous year. He had set his heart on the capture of Ostend and of Antwerp. Ostend would give him a new communication with England; Antwerp controlled the waterways of the Scheldt, the Lys, and the canals, which, with the Meuse, formed the principal lines of advance to the French fortress zone. The "great design", as he called it, did not succeed because the Dutch were not willing to consent to the very severe offensive battle which Marlborough wished to fight. On the Danube and the Upper Rhine the armies of the Emperor suffered constant misfortune. They were defeated in the field in Bavaria, and the loss of the famous fortified cities of Augsburg, Ratisbon, and above all Landau, gave the French control of Southern German and the Upper Rhine.

Both at home and abroad the fortunes of the Grand Allies sank to a low ebb in the winter of 1703. Queen Anne here rose to her greatest height. "I will never forsake," she wrote to Sarah, using the private names which were current in the Cockpit circle, "your dear self, Mr Freeman [Marlborough], nor Mr Montgomery [Godolphin], but always be your constant faithful servant; and we four must never part till death mows us down with his impartial hand." With this support Marlborough during the winter months planned the supreme stroke of strategy which turned the whole fortune of the war. But before he could proceed to the Continent it was essential to reconstitute the Government of the High Tories. Rochester was already dismissed and Nottingham was soon to go. A new figure was required to fill the void. Harley, whom we have seen so active in reducing the armed forces and opposing King William's foreign policy had been Speaker, leader of the moderate Tories, and virtually Leader of the House of Commons. He was now invited to become a Secretary of State, and the inner circle of the Government was widened to admit him. The combination became Marlborough, Godolphin, and Harley, with the Queen and Sarah as before. In Harley's train Henry St John, a young Member who had made himself conspicuous by his brilliant speeches in favour of the Occasional Conformity Bill and was in high favour with the Tories, became Secretary at War, a post which brought him into close contact with Marlborough. All this being arranged, and a Parliamentary majority composed of the moderate Tories and the Whigs being procured, the Duke sailed for Holland.

The Elector of Bavaria, as we have seen, had abandoned the Emperor and was now the ally of France. A French army under Marshal Marsin had been sent to his aid, and Vienna, the Emperor's capital, would evidently be exposed to mortal peril in the coming year. By subtle arts of persuasion and deceit Marlborough, with the complicity of Heinsius alone, obtained the assent of the Dutch States-General for a campaign upon the Moselle with British troops and those in British pay. Disengaging himself from the main armies left to guard Holland, he marched rapidly through Bonn to Coblenz. At this point, when friend and foe alike expected him to turn right-handed and southwards up the Moselle towards Trarbach and Treves, the first part of his true intention was revealed. The long column of redcoats passed the confluence of the rivers, crossed the Rhine upon a floating bridge, and marched day after day with extreme rapidity through Mainz and Heidelberg into the heart of Germany. Beyond the Neckar Marlborough was joined by the contingents of Prussia and other German states, and on June 11 he met the Margrave, Prince Louis of Baden, commanding the Imperial Army of the Rhine, and Prince Eugene, who, though he had no actual command, represented the supreme military control of the Empire. Here for the first time began that splendid comradeship of the Duke and Eugene which for seven years continued without jealousy or defeat.

The annals of the British Army contain no more heroic episode than Marlborough's march from the North Sea to the Danube. All the French plans for the campaign were held in suspense while it proceeded. As Marlborough quitted the Low Countries Marshal Villeroy moved to meet him on the Moselle. When he reached Heidelberg the French generals expected a campaign on the upper Rhine. Only when he was already within reach of the Danube did they realise that he meant to strike at Bavaria and rescue Vienna. Marshal Tallard, with a second French army, was forthwith sent to reinforce the Elector and the French troops under Marshal Marsin. Marlborough and the Margrave, having arrived upon the Danube, in a bloody assault stormed the strong entrenchments of the Schellenberg, drove their defenders into the river, and forced an entry into Bavaria. As the Elector would not yield Marlborough delivered the country to military execution, and grievous devastation followed.

Meanwhile Eugene fell back before Tallard's superior strength and manoeuvred so as to join hands with Marlborough. The two armies, French and Bavarian, now united, recrossed the Danube, and Tallard conceived himself able to force the Allies into a disastrous retreat. Marlborough persuaded the Margrave, whose counsels were obstructive, to occupy himself with the siege of Ingolstadt, and marched suddenly to join Eugene. The twin captains – "one soul in two bodies" as they were described – fell upon the French and Bavarian army at Höchstädt, on the Danube, early in the morning of August 13. The French were somewhat more numerous, and had the advantage of a far more powerful artillery and of a strong position protected by the marshy streams of the Nebel. The battle was fought with the greatest fury on both sides. Eugene commanded the right and Marlborough the left and centre. The English attack upon the village of Blindheim – Blenheim, as it has been called in history – was repulsed, and for several hours the issue hung in the balance; but Marlborough about half-past five in the afternoon, after a series of intricate manoeuvres, crossed the Nebel and concentrated an overwhelming force of cavalry, supported by infantry and guns, against the French centre, which had gradually been denuded to withstand the attacks on either wing. At the head of eighty squadrons he broke the centre, routed the French cavalry, drove many thousands to death in the Danube, cut to pieces the remaining squares of French infantry, surrounded the great mass of French troops crowded into the village of Blenheim, and, as dusk fell on this memorable day, was able to write his famous letter to his wife: "I have not time to say more, but to beg you will give my duty to the Queen, and let her know her army has had a glorious victory. Monsieur Tallard and the two other Generals are in my coach and I am following the rest."

The victory of Blenheim almost destroyed the French and Bavarian armies on the Danube. Over forty thousand men were killed, wounded, captured, or dispersed. The remnant retreated through the Black Forest towards the Upper Rhine. One-third of both armies lay stricken on the field. Thirteen thousand unwounded prisoners, including the most famous regiments of France, passed the night of the 13th in the hands of the British infantry. Ulm surrendered after a brief siege, and Marlborough marched rapidly westward to the angle of the Rhine, where he was soon able to concentrate nearly a hundred thousand men. With Eugene and the Margrave he drove the French along the left bank towards Strasbourg and set siege to Landau, which surrendered in November. Finally, unwearied by these superb exertions, the Duke marched during October from the Rhine to the Moselle, where he closed a campaign ever a classic model of war by the capture of Treves and Trarbach.

All Europe was hushed before these prodigious events. Louis XIV could not understand how his finest army was not merely defeated, but destroyed. From this moment he thought no more of domination, but only of an honourable exit from the war he had provoked. The same year had seen remarkable successes at sea. A recent treaty of alliance with Portugal made possible effective English intervention in the Mediterranean, since the harbour of Lisbon was now at the disposal of the English Navy. In May 1704 a powerful Anglo-Dutch fleet under Admiral Rooke entered the inland sea. This was the prelude to a lasting naval triumph. Reinforced by a squadron under Sir Cloudesley Shovell, Rooke turned his attention in July to the Rock of Gibraltar. This fortress was then little more than a roadstead, but the possibilities of its commanding position at the gateway of the Mediterranean were already recognised. After bombardment the Rock was taken on August 4, in the same month as Blenheim, by a combined assault, led on land by Prince George of Hesse-Darmstadt. The French and Spanish Governments were both perturbed by this eruption of a new Power into the Mediterranean. The naval balance of the war was threatened, and the whole French Fleet came out to offer battle. A long and bloody engagement, fought off Malaga, failed to give them the advantage. The French therefore decided that Gibraltar must be recovered by siege. Throughout the winter of 1704–5 the Anglo-Dutch garrison, under Darmstadt, withstood an arduous attack by heavy forces. Failure to take the Rock brought sour quarrels over strategy between France and Spain. But Gibraltar remained in English hands, and proved a sure key to maritime power.

In this war a curious rhythm now recurs. When the fortunes of the Allies fell all obeyed Marlborough and looked to him to find the path to safety; but when he produced, infallibly, as it seemed, a new victorious scene the bonds of fear and necessity were relaxed and he was again hampered and controlled. Just as the brilliant campaign of 1702 was succeeded by the disappointments of 1703, so the grand recovery of 1704 gave place to disunity in 1705. For this year Marlborough planned an advance up the Moselle and a march to Paris.

The Dutch were overjoyed to see their Captain-General back in their home theatre. The French had constructed the famous lines of Brabant, covering the sixty miles from Antwerp to Namur, and these they now guarded with an equal army under Marshal Villeroy. Marlborough knew that he could not persuade the Dutch field deputies or their generals to contemplate a direct assault; but by a profound stratagem, which again deceived both sides, he feinted towards Namur, and then, by a long, sudden night-march, the purpose of which none but he understood, surprised the French and traversed the dreaded lines in the neighbourhood of Tirlemont without the loss of a single man. A brilliant cavalry action, in which he in person led the charge, drove back the French who were hurrying to the scene, and enabled him to establish himself amid the fortresses of Belgium. He now attempted a still more remarkable manoeuvre. Filling his wagons with eight days' supplies and separating himself from his base, he marched round Villeroy's right flank, and on August 18 confronted him with superior forces on what was one day to be called the Field of Waterloo. Marlborough believed a victory was in his hands, but the Dutch generals and deputies, headed by one of Marlborough's bitter rivals, General Slangenberg, delayed and prevented the battle, and Marlborough, being nearly at the end of his wagon-borne supplies, was forced to return to his base. Thus the campaign of 1705 ended again in disappointment and recriminations between the Allies.

Wearied with the difficulties of co-operating with the Dutch and with the Princes of the Rhine, Marlborough planned through the winter an even more daring repetition of his march to the Danube in 1704. He had succeeded in procuring from the King of Prussia, with whom he had immense personal influence, a strong Prussian force to aid Prince Eugene in Northern Italy. He now schemed to march across Europe with about twenty-five thousand British and British-paid troops by Coblenz, Stuttgart, and Ulm, through the passes of the Alps, to join Eugene in Northern Italy. There amid the vineyards and the olive trees the two great captains would gain another Blenheim and strike into France from the south. The States-General showed much more imagination and confidence than they had done in 1704. Their terms were simple. If Marlborough went he must take no Dutch troops. The Queen and the English

Cabinet gave full approval, and on this basis he perfected his plans, even ordering six hand-mills for every British battalion for grinding corn in this novel theatre.

But the earliest events of the campaign of 1706 destroyed the Italian project. The French forestalled the Allies in the field both on the Rhine and in Italy. At Calcinato Marshal Vendôme inflicted a severe minor defeat on the Imperial forces. In Germany Villars fell upon the Margrave and chased him over the Rhine. The key fortress of Landau was threatened. Marlborough's hopes were dashed. But now Fortune, whom Marlborough had so ruefully but sternly dismissed, returned importunate, bearing her most dazzling gift. Louis XIV had convinced himself, after the forcing of the lines of Brabant and Marlborough's threat to Brussels, that a defensive war could not be maintained against such an opponent. In robust mood he authorised Marshal Villeroy to seek a battle at the beginning of the campaign, and furnished him with the best-equipped army of France, all clothed in new uniforms and in perfect order.

At dawn on May 23 the two armies were in presence near the village of Ramillies. Marlborough, having deployed, about noon began a heavy but feigned attack upon the French left with the British troops. Availing himself of the undulations of the ground, he hurled the whole mass of the Dutch, British, and Danish cavalry, over 25,000 strong, upon the French horse between the villages of Taviers and Ramillies. Here stood the finest cavalry of France, including the famous Household troops. Casting aside his veil of secrecy and manoeuvre, Marlborough exclaimed, "I have five horses to two." Actually he had first four to three and finally five to three. But it was enough. After furious fighting, in which forty thousand horsemen were engaged, he broke the French line, drove their right from the field, and compromised their centre. Forgetting his duty as Commander-in-Chief, he charged into the cavalry battle, sword in hand. He was unhorsed and ridden over by the enemy. His equerry, Colonel Bingfield, while helping him to mount a second charger, had his head carried off by a cannonball which passed close to Marlborough's leg as he threw it over the saddle. But he soon resumed his full control of the tremendous event. His main infantry attack now broke upon the village of Ramillies, while his victorious cavalry, forming at right angles to the original front, swept along the whole rear of the French line. All the Allied troops now advanced, and the French army fled from the field in utter ruin. In this masterpiece of war, fought between armies almost exactly equal in strength and quality, the military genius of the English General, with a loss of less than five thousand men, destroyed and defeated his opponents with great slaughter and thousands of captives.

The consequences of Ramillies were even more spectacular than those which had followed Blenheim. If, as was said, Blenheim had saved Vienna, Ramillies conquered Belgium. Fortresses, the capture of any one of which would have rewarded the efforts of a long campaign, fell by the dozen. Antwerp and Brussels surrendered, and the astonished Dutch saw themselves again possessors of almost the whole barrier which had been lost in the last year of King William's reign. These immense successes were enhanced by the victories of Prince Eugene in Northern Italy. Marching across the broad base of the peninsula, he relieved Turin in a wonderful action against heavy odds, and thereafter drove the French completely out of Northern Italy.

While in the field Marlborough and Eugene carried all before them, a series of English party and personal rivalries prepared a general reversal of fortune. The Whigs, who were the main prop of the war, and upon whose votes the Queen's Government depended, demanded a share of public office. They chose the Earl of Sunderland, the son of James II's erratic Minister, an orthodox, opinionated man of high ability, as the thin end of the wedge by which they would force their way into the controlling circle of the Government. According to modern ideas their majority in both Houses of Parliament gave them the right, and even at this time it gave them the power, to acquire predominance in public affairs. But Sunderland had married Marlborough's daughter. "Therefore," reasoned the chief of the Whigs, "he could not take their move as an attack upon himself." But they let Godolphin know that if he could not make the Queen accept Sunderland they would use their power in Parliament both against the Government and personally against him. Marlborough and Godolphin, confronted with the vital need of obtaining from the House of Commons supplies to carry on the war, pressed the inclusion of Sunderland upon the Queen. She resisted tenaciously. It took the Battle of Ramillies to persuade her.

Britain's military prowess and the sense of the Island being at the head of mighty Europe now bore more lasting fruit. The Union with Scotland was approaching its closing stage. It had been debated, sometimes acrimoniously, ever since the Queen's accession. At last England was prepared to show some financial generosity to the Scots, and they in turn were willing to accept the Hanoverian succession. Marlborough, who was one of the Commissioners concerned, regarded the measure as vital to the strength of the realm. Not only the two nations but their Parliaments were joined together. If Scotland on the death of Queen Anne were to choose a different dynasty from England, all the old enmities of the Middle Ages might revive. Both sides judged it well worth some sacrifices to avoid such a breach between the two kingdoms. The Act of Union was finally passed in 1707, and in spite of some friction was generally accepted.

About this time Sarah's relations with the Queen entered on a perilous phase. She had to bear the brunt of her mistress's repugnance to a Whig infusion in the Cabinet. Anne loathed the Whigs from the bottom of her heart, but her Ministers could not see how it was possible to carry on the war without the Whigs and with only half the Tory Party at their back. Sarah wore out her friendship with the Queen in her duty of urging upon her an administration in harmony with Parliament. At the same time an interloper appeared. As Sarah grew older, and as all the affairs of a great lady with much more than the power of a Cabinet Minister pressed upon her, she sought some relief from the constant strain of personal attendance upon the Queen, which had been her life for so many years. Anne's feminine friendships were exacting. She wanted her companion to be with her all day long and playing cards far into the night. Gradually Sarah sought to lighten the burden of this perpetual intercourse. In a poor relation, Abigail Hill, she found an understudy.[1] She brought her into the Queen's life as a "dresser" or lady's maid. The Queen, after a while, took kindly to her new attendant. Sarah experienced relief, went more to the country and lived her family life. Abigail, by the beginning of 1707, had acquired an influence of her own with the Queen destined to deflect the course of European history.

Abigail was a cousin of Sunderland's. She was at the same time a cousin of Harley's. Harley was much disconcerted by the arrival of the Whig Sunderland in the Cabinet. He saw with the eye of a skilled politician that it was the prelude to a much larger Whig incursion. He felt embarrassed in his position as leader of the moderate Tories. One day a gardener handed him a secret letter from the Queen. She appealed for his help. No greater temptation could have been cast before an eighteenth-century statesman. Moreover, it harmonised with Harley's deep political calculations and his innate love of mystery and subterranean intrigue. Forthwith he set himself to plan an alternative Government based on the favour of the Queen, comprising Tories and moderate Whigs and sheltered by the renown and, he hoped, the services of Marlborough. This plan implied the ruin of Godolphin. Harley imagined that this would be no obstacle; but Marlborough when he became conscious of what was afoot would tolerate no severance between himself and his faithful colleague and friend. Thus Harley's intrigue became of necessity hostile to Marlborough. At the same time Sarah's influence with the Queen had plainly suffered a final eclipse.

Everything went wrong in 1707. Marlborough's design was that Eugene, aided by the Prussian contingent and all the reinforcements he could send him, should debouch from Italy into France and capture Toulon. From this sure naval base the Duke purposed not only to gain the command of the Mediterranean but to invade France in great strength in the following year. He used all his power, then at its height, to further this far-reaching plan, and after innumerable objections and divergences an Imperial army under Eugene marched along the Riviera to attack Toulon. Meanwhile Marlborough faced and held the superior forces of Marshal Vendôme in the main theatre of the Low Countries. But Vendôme always managed to avoid battle except on terms of a direct assault, which Marlborough was not strong enough to make. The campaign in the north thus reduced itself to stalemate.

Great misfortunes happened in Spain. The year, had closed with King Philip once more propped up in Madrid, but with the Allies firmly in possession of the eastern quarter of Spain. Now in 1707 the Allied generals

1   Abigail Hill was Sarah Churchill's cousin. In 1707 ambitious Abigail married Samuel Masham and quickly got him a peerage, which is why she is known as Abigail Hill and Abigail or Lady Masham.

fatally divided their forces. They advanced with only a part of them in the direction of Madrid. They were met and engaged in battle at Almanza by a greatly superior Franco-Spanish army under the Duke of Berwick. The French commander was a Catholic Englishman, the British commander a Protestant Frenchman. In such curious ways did loyalties divide. A bloody defeat was sustained by the Allies, and the whole Spanish scene, so nearly triumphant in 1706, was now completely reversed. On the Rhine the Margrave was surprised by Marshal Villars in the celebrated Lines of Stollhofen, and all these tremendous works, which constituted the effective defence of Germany, fell in a night into the hands of the enemy. The invasion and pillage of large parts of Germany followed.

The great enterprise against Toulon, to which Marlborough had subordinated all other interests, also ended in failure. This was the only occasion in the long wars when Eugene does not seem to have maintained his high standard, and the Duke of Savoy, who nominally commanded the Army, was even less enterprising. Eugene was a land animal. He never liked a plan which depended so much upon the sea. A magnificent English armada met him on the coast. Admiral Shovell was deeply imbued with Marlborough's strategies. He helped and fed Eugene's army along the coast, turning the flank of the enemy's successive positions with the fire of the Fleet. Arrived before Toulon, he landed thousands of sailors and marines and hundreds of cannon. All the time he assured the illustrious Prince that if his communications were cut the Fleet would embark and carry all his men wherever he wanted.

The French concentrated powerful forces not only to defend but to relieve Toulon. After several costly assaults the siege failed. The Imperial army retreated upon Italy. The British Fleet, after bombarding and largely destroying the harbour of Toulon and sinking the French warships which were clustered there, sailed for home or for winter harbours. One final disaster remained. Sir Cloudesley Shovell, making the winter passage home, was wrecked in thick and violent weather upon the sharp rocks of the Scillies. Two great ships and a frigate were dashed to pieces, fifteen hundred sailors were drowned, and, worst of all, Britain's finest admiral, Marlborough's trusted naval leader, perished on the shore.

Marlborough returned from these tribulations to a furious party storm in England. Harley's designs were now apparent, and his strength nourished itself upon the military misfortunes. Marlborough and Godolphin together resolved to drive him from the Cabinet. An intense political crisis supervened. At this time Harley was weakened by the fact that a clerk in his office named Greg had been caught betraying the most secret dispatches into the hands of the French Government. Harley had certainly been negligent in the management of his high correspondence, and the Whigs, in their natural wrath at being excluded from rightful power, made every effort to convict him of treason. Greg however, while confessing his own guilt, died at Tyburn avowing the innocence of his chief. It was alleged he could have saved his life by incriminating him.

Upon all this Marlborough demanded Harley's dismissal from his Secretaryship of State. Anne, now completely estranged from Sarah and with Abigail at her elbow, fought a stubborn fight for her favourite Minister. When Marlborough refused to sit another day in Cabinet with Harley and tendered his resignation the Queen answered that "he might as well draw his dagger and stab her then and there as do such a thing". But a true Stuart and daughter of James II would not let Harley go. Marlborough returned to his home at St Albans. When the Cabinet met and Harley rose to read some paper one of the Ministers roughly asked the Queen how they would do business in the absence of the General and the Treasurer. Harley was unconcerned. The Queen, nearly suffocating with emotion, left the room, and the Cabinet broke up in confusion. The news spread far and wide that Marlborough and Godolphin had been dismissed. Both Houses of Parliament decided to conduct no business until they were better informed. The City was in consternation. Anne's husband, the Prince George, perturbed by what he heard and saw of the public mood, and strengthened by what he felt himself, implored his wife to bow to the storm. Even then it was Harley and not the Queen who gave way. He advised the Queen to accept his resignation. She wept, and he departed. With him went Henry St John, whom Marlborough had regarded almost as an adopted son.

This struggle gave Marlborough a final lease of power. He had to a large extent lost the Queen. He had lost the moderate Tories. He must now increasingly throw himself into the hands of the Whigs, and at every stage of this process make wider the breach with the Queen. It was on these perilous foundations that he embarked upon the campaign of 1708. The plan was in principle a renewal of the double invasion of the previous year. For the only time in the Duke's career he bent and bowed under the convergent strains at home and in the field. Eugene, arriving with only a cavalry escort, found him near Brussels in the deepest depression. He was prostrated by fever and so ill that he had to be bled. For a few hours he seemed unable to recover from the strategic injury of the loss of the fruits of Ramillies, the Ghent and Bruges waterways which were the railways of those times. Here Eugene sustained his comrade. Marlborough rose from his sickbed, mounted his horse, and the Army was set in motion. By a tremendous march they reached Lessines, on the Dyle. At dawn on July 11 they set out towards the fortress and bridgehead of Oudenarde, on the Scheldt, which Vendôme intended to seize. The French had not contemplated the possibility of a battle, and their great army was crossing the river in a leisurely manner at Gavre. By half-past ten General Cadogan with the English vanguard, had reached the high ground north of Oudenarde. Including the bridges of the fortress, nine bridges in all were prepared. Behind Cadogan the whole Army, eighty thousand strong, came on in a state of extraordinary wrath and enthusiasm.

Vendôme could not at first believe that the Allies were upon the scene in force. He rode out to see for himself, and was drawn into action by degrees. The pace of the battle and its changes prevented all set arrangement. The

French fought desperately but without any concerted plan, and a large part of their army was never engaged. The shadows of evening had fallen upon a battlefield of hedges, enclosures, villages, woods, and watercourses, in which the troops were locked in close, fierce fighting, when the Dutch, under the veteran Overkirk, at length traversed the Oudenarde bridges and swung round upon the heights to the north. At the same time Eugene, with magnificent courage, broke through on the right. The opposite wings of the Allies almost met. The French army was now utterly confused and divided into two parts. More than forty thousand men were virtually surrounded by the Allies; the other forty thousand stood baffled on the ridge above the battle. It was pitch-dark when the fighting stopped. So intermingled were the combatants that orders were given to the Allies to cease firing and lie upon their arms. But the weapons of those days did not enable an encircling net to be thrown round field troops on such a scale. Most of the surrounded French escaped during the night. In furious anger and consternation Vendôme ordered a retreat on Ghent. A quarter of his army was destroyed or dispersed. Seven thousand prisoners, many high officers, and a wealth of standards and trophies were in Marlborough's hands when on the morning of July 12 he and his great companion rode their horses into the fine old square of Oudenarde.

This great victory altered the posture of the war. The Allies had recovered the initiative. Marlborough wished to march forward into France, leaving the great fortress of Lille behind him. He had already prepared in the Isle of Wight a force of seven thousand men with transports wherewith to seize Abbeville and establish a new base there behind the French barrier, from which he could march directly upon Paris. But he could not persuade Eugene. The "old Prince", as he was called, though younger than Marlborough, felt it too dangerous to leave Lille behind him, and was over-distrustful of operations dependent upon the sea. It was resolved to attack Lille, the strongest fortress of France. A brilliant action pierced the gloom of the autumn months. The long line of English communications stretching to Ostend was threatened by a powerful thrust of over twenty thousand French troops. The Allied convoys moving southwards upon Lille were in peril. General Webb, a Jacobite Tory and a competent soldier, was dispatched by Marlborough to meet the danger with an inferior force. A frontal attack upon Webb's position in the woods hard by the Château of Wynendael failed with heavy loss through the magnificent fire discipline of the English soldiers. The citadel of Lille fell in December. Bruges was recaptured at the end of December, and Ghent in the first days of January. Thus ended a campaign of struggle and hazard of which Prince Eugene said, "He who has not seen this has seen nothing."

At the same time the capture of Minorca, with its fine harbour at Mahon, gave to the English Navy at last a secure, permanent base in the Mediterranean. Thus the year which had opened in such dismal fashion ended in complete victory for the Allies. Louis XIV made far-reaching offers of peace to the Dutch, and Marlborough himself entered into secret negotiations with his nephew Berwick for the same purpose. The Great King was humbled. A terrible frost laid its grip upon tortured Europe. The seed froze in the ground; the cattle died in the fields, and the rabbits in their burrows. The misery of the French people reached the limit of endurance. All sought peace, and all failed to find it.

Meanwhile in England the Whigs had at last achieved their long purpose. They had compelled Marlborough and Godolphin to rest wholly upon them. They overbore the Queen. They drove the remaining Tories from the Cabinet, and installed a single-party administration, above which still sat the two super-Ministers, Marlborough and Godolphin. Hitherto, for all the differences upon methods, the war had had a common purpose. It was now a party policy. The Whigs, ardent, efficient masters of the Parliamentary arts, arrived in power at the very moment when their energy and war spirit were least needed. Marlborough and Godolphin, estranged from the Queen, must now conform to the decisions of a Whig Cabinet, while the Tories, sullen and revengeful in their plight, looked forward to their former leaders' downfall. Harley, by his gifts and his craft, by his injuries and his eminence, became their natural leader. To him rallied the elder statesmen, Rochester and Nottingham. Strong in the favour of the Queen, maintained up the backstairs by Abigail, Harley reached out to Shrewsbury, now back in English politics after a long retirement, and ready to play an ambitious and powerful middle part.

Marlborough's reign was ended. Henceforward he had but to serve. His paramount position in Europe and with the armies made him indispensable to either party as long as the war continued. First he served the Whigs and afterwards the Tories. He served the Whigs as plenipotentiary and General and later he served the Tories as General only. His great period, from 1702 to 1708, was over.

When we look upon the long years of terror and spoliation to which the princes of the Grand Alliance had been subjected by Louis XIV great allowances must be made for their suspicions in the hour of victory. After all, the war had been fought about the Spanish Succession, and none of the victories of Marlborough and Eugene had settled that issue. The Spanish people from high to low had accepted the claims and espoused the cause of the Duke of Anjou. In the fierceness of the struggle they had abandoned their hopes of preserving the Spanish inheritance in its integrity. They now set their hearts only upon having a king of their own choice. Philip V declared he would rather die than abandon the Spanish people who had rallied to his aid. Torcy, the French Foreign Minister and son of the great Colbert, asked what it was the Allies expected his master to do. Louis was willing to dissociate himself entirely from Philip, to withdraw all French troops from the Peninsula, even to yield important French fortresses as a guarantee. The Allied negotiators believed that he had only to give the order and Philip would abdicate. But this is by no means certain.

The negotiations broke on the article that Louis must himself become responsible for expelling his grandson from Spain on the pain of having the

Allies renew the war against him from the bases and fortresses he was to surrender in guarantee. The Great King, old and broken, amid the ruin of his ambitions and the misery of his people, might have yielded; but the Dauphin with indignation demanded that his son should not be robbed of his kingdom by his own kin.

Marlborough had laboured faithfully for peace, but he had not asserted to the full the still gigantic remnants of his personal power. He had misgivings, but upon the whole he expected the French to yield. "Are there no counter-proposals?" he asked in surprise when the courier brought the rejection of the Allied ultimatum. With Eugene he made some last efforts; but nothing availed. The disappointment of the Allies found vent in a vain and furious clamour that they had once again been tricked and fooled by Louis XIV. The drums beat in the Allied camps, and the greatest armies those war-worn times had seen rolled forward to the campaign of 1709 and the carnage of Malplaquet. From this time forth the character of the war was profoundly affected. From this moment France, and to a lesser degree Spain, presented national fronts against foreign inroad and overlordship. There was a strange invigoration in the patriotic spirit both of the French and Spanish peoples.

The Allied army had meanwhile been raised to its highest strength, and Marlborough and Eugene, concentrating south of Ghent, began the siege of Tournai. After a large and serious operation the city and citadel surrendered at the end of August. Marlborough now looked to Mons as the next objective. All this time the negotiations had been going forward behind the scenes, and both sides still felt that the little that separated them might at any moment be removed. But suddenly an explosion of war fury, an access of mental rage, took possession of both Governments and both armies down to the private soldiers. They discarded calculation, they flung caution to the winds; the King gave Villars full freedom for battle. Marlborough and Eugene responded with equal zeal. A terrible ardour inspired all ranks. They thirsted to be at each other's throats and slay their foes, and thus bring the long war to an end.

By swift movements Marlborough and Eugene invested Mons, and, advancing south of it, found themselves confronted by Villars in the gap between the woods in which the village of Malplaquet stands, almost along the line of the present French frontier. On September 11 a hundred and ten thousand Allied troops assaulted the entrenchments, defended by about ninety thousand French. The battle was fought with extreme severity, and little quarter was asked or given. Marlborough in the main repeated the tactics of Blenheim. He first attacked both French wings. The Dutch were repelled with frightful slaughter on the left. The right wing, under Eugene, broke through the dense wood, and eventually reached the open country beyond. Under these pressures Villars and his second in command, the valiant Boufflers, were forced to thin their centre. The moment came for which Marlborough was waiting. He launched the English corps under Orkney upon the denuded redoubts, and, having seized them, brought forward his immense cavalry masses, over thirty thousand strong, which had been waiting all day close at hand. With the "Grey" Dragoons and the Scots Greys in the van, the Allied cavalry passed the entrenchments and deployed in the plain beyond. Villars had been grievously wounded, but the French cavalry came forward in magnificent spirit, and a long series of cavalry charges ensued. At length the French cavalry were mastered. Their infantry were already in retreat.

Europe was appalled at the slaughter of Malplaquet. The Allies had lost over twenty thousand men, and the French two-thirds as many. There were hardly any prisoners. The victors camped upon the field, and Mons, the local object of the battle, was besieged and taken. But the event presented itself to all men as a terrible judgment upon the failure of the peace negotiations. The Dutch Republic was staggered by the slaughter of its finest troops. In England the Whigs, still for war on the most ruthless scale, proclaimed by oratory and pamphleteering that a decisive victory had been won. But the Tories accused them, and also Marlborough, of having thrown away the chance of a good peace to produce a fruitless carnage, the like of which Europe could not remember. Indeed Malplaquet, the largest and bloodiest battle of the eighteenth century, was surpassed only by Napoleon's barren victory at Borodino a hundred years later.

CHAPTER THIRTY-SIX

THE LAST OF THE STUARTS

Godolphin dismissed – Harley and St John take power – creation of the
South Sea Company – Marlborough accused of financial wrong-doing –
the English army retreats to Dunkirk – the Treaty of Utrecht and the
spoils of war – Marlborough goes into exile – Harley and St John in
mortal squabble – the death of Queen Anne

WHILE MARLBOROUGH was at these toils the political crisis of
Queen Anne's reign moved steadily to its climax. The church
of England was astir, and the Tory clergy preached against
the war and its leaders, especially Godolphin. Dr Sacheverell,
a High Church divine, delivered a sermon in London in violent attack upon
the Government, the Whigs, and the Lord Treasurer. With great unwisdom
the Government ordered a State prosecution in the form of an impeachment.
Not only the Tories but the London mob rallied to Sacheverell, and scenes
were witnessed recalling those which had attended the trial of the Seven
Bishops a quarter of a century before. By narrow majorities nominal penalties
were inflicted upon Sacheverell. He became the hero of the hour.

Queen Anne, advised by Harley, now felt strong enough to take her
revenge for what she considered the insult inflicted on her by the Whig
intrusion in to her Council. During a year by successive steps the whole
character of the Government was altered. First Sunderland was dismissed;
then in August Queen Anne ordered Godolphin to break his staff of office and
quit her service, adding, "but I will give you a pension of four thousand a
year". Godolphin spurned the pension and retired into a straitened private life.
The Whig Ministers of less consequence were also relieved of office. Harley
formed a predominantly Tory Government, and at his side Henry St John[1]
became Secretary of State. The new Government was largely built around the

---

1   Henry St John, 1st Viscount Bolingbroke (1678–1751), Secretary for War (1704–8), and Foreign
     Secretary (1710), laid the foundations for the nineteenth-century Tory party in such books as
     The Idea of a Patriot King (1738) and *A Dissertation upon Parties* (1735).
         Robert Harley, later 1st Earl of Oxford and Mortimer later quarrelled with Henry St John and
     was sacked in 1714. His library was purchased by the British Museum and was catalogued as the
     Harleian Collection.
         St John was later dismissed by George I and for a time went into exile. He returned in 1725
     and was a leading opponent of Walpole's government.

Duke of Shrewsbury, and found the support of many notables of high degree, outstanding abilities, and hungry ambition. The General Election, aptly launched, produced a substantial Tory majority in the House of Commons.

Marlborough returned from his ninth campaign to find England in the control of his political and personal foes. Yet in spite of all this Marlborough remained the most precious possession of the hostile Government and vengeful Queen. Before the Tories became responsible Ministers they thought they could have peace on victorious terms merely by intimating their willingness for it. They now realised that the downfall of Marlborough was also the revival of Louis XIV. From every quarter therefore, even the most unfriendly, Marlborough was urged, implored, or conjured to serve. Defeated Whigs, exultant Tories, Harley and St John, the Queen, the States-General, the King of Prussia, the Princes of the Rhine, and most fervent of all, the Emperor, called upon him to stand by the common cause. Terms were made between the Tory ministers and Marlborough for the proper upkeep of the armies at the front, and the Captain-General for the tenth year in succession took the field.

Harley and St John were now in full cry. Having dispatched Marlborough to the wars, they pursued with consistency, craft, and vigour the whole policy of the Tory Party. St John sent a large, ill-managed, ill-starred expedition to take Quebec from the French. Harley, as Chancellor of the Exchequer, was deep in financial plans for the creation of a great South Sea Company, which was to take over a part of the National Debt, and add to its revenues by importing slaves and merchandise into South America. From this the South Sea Bubble was later to be blown. But above all he sought peace with France. By secret channels, unknown to the Allies, he established contact with Torcy. Finding the French painfully stiff, he brought St John into the negotiations, which proceeded throughout 1711 without the knowledge of Parliament or of any of the confederate states. The method was treacherous, but the object reasonable.

In spite of the secret purpose they nursed in common, Harley and St John were soon estranged. Their rivalry had already become apparent when in March a French refugee, who had been discovered in treasonable correspondence with the enemy, stabbed Harley with a penknife while under examination in the Council Chamber. Harley was not seriously hurt, but his popularity throughout the country rose with a bound. The Queen now bestowed upon him the proud titles of Earl of Oxford and Mortimer, and appointed him to the office of Lord Treasurer, which had been in commission since the fall of Godolphin. He was at the height of his career.

Marlborough hoped again to make the campaign of 1711 in company with Eugene, and he concentrated no fewer than a hundred and forty thousand men in the neighbourhood of Douai. But at the end of April an event occurred which affected every aspect of the war. The Emperor Joseph died of smallpox. The Archduke Charles, then maintaining himself stubbornly in Barcelona, succeeded to the hereditary domains of the house of Austria, and was certain to be elected Emperor. To interrupt the election at Frankfort Louis XIV moved a large detachment of Villars's army to the angle of the Rhine. This entailed a corresponding movement of Eugene's army, which in May quitted Marlborough's camp, leaving the Duke with ninety thousand men facing Villars, whose army was still a hundred and twenty thousand strong. By subtle arts and stratagems he convinced Villars that he intended to make another frontal attack on the scale of Malplaquet south of Arras.

The great armies formed against each other and the lines of battle were drawn. Everyone expected an onslaught. The Allied generals were deeply distressed. On August 4 the Duke in person conducted a reconnaissance along the whole of Villar's front. Marlborough's soldiers had blind faith in a leader who had never led them wrong. But the high command was full of aches and fears. They did not notice that General Cadogan had silently slipped away from the great reconnaissance. They wondered at the absence of the artillery. They were not informed of the movements behind Marlborough's front. They knew nothing of his heavy concentration at Douai. At length tattoo beat and darkness fell. Orders came to strike tents and stand to arms. Soon staff officers arrived to guide the four columns, and in less than half an hour the whole army was on the march to the left. All through the moonlit night they marched eastward. They traversed those broad undulations between the Vimy Ridge and Arras which two centuries later were to be dyed with British and Canadian blood. The march was pressed with severity; only the briefest halts were allowed. But a sense of excitement filled the troops. It was not after all to be a bloody battle. The "Old Corporal" was up to something of his own. Before five o'clock on the morning of the 5th they reached the Scarpe near Vitry. Here the Army found a series of pontoon bridges already laid, and as the light grew they saw the long columns of their artillery now marching with them.

At daybreak Marlborough, riding in the van at the head of fifty squadrons, met a horseman who galloped up from Cadogan. He bore the news that Cadogan and the Prussian general Hompesch, with twenty-two battalions and twenty squadrons, had crossed the causeway at Arleux at 3 a.m. and were in actual possession of the enemy's lines. Marlborough now sent his aides-de-camp and staff officers down the whole length of the marching columns with orders to explain to the officers and soldiers of every regiment what he was doing and what had happened, and to tell them that all now depended upon their marching qualities. "My Lord Duke wishes the infantry to step out." In the result Marlborough formed a front beyond the lines, which Villars, arriving piecemeal, was unable to attack. There was, and is, a controversy whether Marlborough should not have attacked himself. Certainly both Blenheim and Oudenarde had confronted him with graver risks. But instead of forcing a battle he moved rapidly to his left, crossed the Scheldt, and cast his siege-grip on the fortress of Bouchain. Villars, with an army equal to Marlborough's whole strength, strove vehemently to interrupt the operation. The siege train arrived from Tournai on August 21, and the batteries began to fire on the 30th. While Marlborough bombarded Bouchain Villars bombarded him. It was a siege within a siege, with the constant possibility of a battle at adverse odds to the besiegers. There is no finer example of Marlborough's skill. Bouchain capitulated at the beginning of September. A hostile army as large as his own watched its powerful garrison marched out as prisoners of war. The Duke still wished to continue the campaign and he besieged Quesnoy. The physical forces were not lacking, but all the leaders were now morally worn out. The armies went into winter quarters and Marlborough returned home. For ten years he had led the armies of the Grand Alliance, and during all that period he never fought a battle he did not win or besieged a town he did not take. Nothing like this exists in the annals of war.

It was now impossible to conceal any longer the secret peace negotiations which had all this while been in progress. They came as a shock to the vehement London world. Harley – to use his former style – commanded a solid Tory majority in the Commons, but the Whigs still controlled the House of Lords. The Tory leaders were sure they could carry the peace if Marlborough would support it. To bend him to their will they had during the campaign set on foot an inquiry into the accounts of the armies, with the object of establishing a charge of peculation against him. If he would join with them in making peace and forcing it upon the Allies, or in making a separate peace, these charges would be dropped, and he would still enjoy "the protection of the Court". If not, they thought they had enough to blacken his character. The Duke, who was in close association with the Elector George of Hanover, the heir to the throne, and still enjoyed the support of the King of Prussia and the Princes of the Grand Alliance, would not agree to a separate peace in any circumstances.

Parliament opened in the winter of 1711 in intense crisis. The two great parties faced one another upon all the issues of the long war. The Whigs used their majority in the House of Lords. They carried a resolution, hostile to the Government, by a majority of twelve. But Harley, strong in the support of the House of Commons, and using to the full the favour of the Queen, met this assault with a decisive rejoinder. He loosed the charges of peculation upon Marlborough, and procured from the Queen an extraordinary creation of twelve peers to override the adverse majority in the Lords. These heavy blows succeeded. Marlborough was dismissed from all his offices and exposed to the censure of the House of Commons. The salaries and emoluments he had enjoyed as Captain-General of England, as Deputy Captain-General of Holland, and from many other posts and perquisites had enabled him, with his thrift and acquisitiveness, to build up a large fortune. He was now charged chiefly with converting to his own use during his ten years' command the 21 per cent levied upon the pay of all foreign contingents in the Allied army.

His defence was convincing. He produced Queen Anne's signed warrant of 1702 authorising him to make this deduction, which had always been customary in the Grand Alliance from the days of King William. He declared that all the money – nearly a quarter of a million – had been expended upon the Secret Service and Intelligence of the Army, which it was not denied had been the most perfect ever known. This did not prevent the Tories in the House of Commons from impugning his conduct by a majority of 276 against 165. A State prosecution was set on foot against the dismissed General for the repayment of very large sums. But all the princes of the Alliance, headed by the Elector of Hanover and the King of Prussia, solemnly affirmed in State documents "that they had freely granted 2.5 per cent to the Duke of Marlborough for the purposes of Secret Service and without expecting any rendering of account".

Harley and St John could not avoid the campaign of 1712. They appointed the Duke of Ormonde, the splendid magnifico who had failed at Cadiz, to the command. They assured the Dutch of their fidelity. Eugene was sent by the Emperor to the Low Countries. In exasperation at the behaviour of the London Cabinet he was betrayed into an over-audacious campaign. He laid siege to Quesnoy, and called upon Ormonde to aid him. But the English Government was now on the verge of a separate peace. St John sent secret restraining orders to Ormonde not to "partake in any siege in a way to hazard a battle" – as if such tactics were possible.

Upon a dark day the British Army, hitherto the most forward in the Allied cause and admired by all, marched away from the camp of the Allies in bitter humiliation and amid the curses of their old comrades. Many of Marlborough's veterans flung themselves on the ground in shame and fury. The outraged Dutch closed the gates of their cities in the face of the deserting Ally. Villars, advancing rapidly, fell upon Eugene's magazines at Denain and inflicted upon him a cruel defeat in which many of his troops were driven into the Scheldt and drowned. Upon this collapse Villars captured all the advanced bases of the Allies and took Douai, Quesnoy, and Bouchain. Thus he obliterated the successes of the past three years, and at the end of the terrible war emerged victorious. The English Army, under Ormonde, in virtue of a military convention signed with France, retreated upon Dunkirk, which was temporarily delivered to them. After these shattering defeats all the states of the Grand Alliance were compelled to make peace on the best terms possible.

What is called the Treaty of Utrecht was in fact a series of separate agreements between individual Allied states with France and with Spain. The Empire continued the war alone. In the forefront stood the fact that the Duke of Anjou, recognised as Philip V, held Spain and the Indies, thus flouting the unreasonable declaration to which the English Parliament had so long adhered. With this out of the way the British Government gained their special terms; the French Court recognised the Protestant succession in Britain, and agreed to expel the Pretender from France, to demolish the fortifications of Dunkirk, and to cede various territories in North America and the West Indies, to wit, Hudson Bay, Newfoundland, Nova Scotia, which had been captured by an expedition from Massachusetts, and St Christopher.

With Spain the terms were that England should hold Minorca and Gibraltar, thus securing to her, while she remained the chief sea-Power, the entry and control of the Mediterranean. Commercial advantages, one day to provoke another war, were obtained in Spanish South America, and in particular the Asiento, or the sole right for thirty years to import African negroes as slaves into the New World. A renunciation was made both by France and Spain of the union of their two Crowns. This, through many strange deaths in the French royal family, hung for its validity upon the frail child since known to history as Louis XV. The Catalans, who had been called into the field by the Allies, and particularly by England, and who had adhered with admirable tenacity to the Archduke whom they called Charles III, were delivered over under polite diplomatic phrases to the vengeance of the victorious party in Spain.

The Dutch secured a restricted barrier, which nevertheless included, on the outer line, Furnes, Fort Knocke, Ypres, Menin, Tournai, Mons, Charleroi, and Namur; Ghent, for communication with Holland; and certain important forts guarding the entrance to the Scheldt. Prussia obtained Guelderland at the expense of Dutch claims. All other fortresses in the Low Countries beyond the barrier were restored to France, including particularly Lille. The Duke of Savoy gained Sicily and a strong frontier on the Alps. Portugal was rewarded for feeble service with trading rights upon the Amazon. The frontiers on the Rhine and the fate of Bavaria and the Milanese were left to the decision of further war. Such were the settlements reached at Utrecht in the spring of 1713.

Marlborough was so much pursued by the Tory Party and harassed by the State prosecutions against him for his alleged peculation that at the end of 1712 he left the country and lived in self-imposed exile in Holland and Germany till the end of the reign. The final phase of the Tory triumph was squalid. St John, raised to the peerage as Viscount Bolingbroke, became involved in a mortal quarrel with Harley, Earl of Oxford. His scandalous life and his financial inroads upon the public exposed him to indictment at Harley's merciless hands; but, having procured the aid of Abigail by bribes, he supplanted Oxford in the Queen's favour. Anne was now broken with gout and other ailments. For many months her life hung upon a thread. She who had seen so much glory now drew towards an ignominious end. No one knows whether she wished to make her half-brother, the Pretender, her heir or not. Once again the two Englands which had contended since the Great Rebellion faced each other under different guises and upon an altered scene, but with the same main antagonisms. The Whigs, strong in the Act of Succession and in the Protestant resolve of the nation, prepared openly to take arms against a Jacobite restoration. The Elector of Hanover, supported by the Dutch and aided by Marlborough, gathered the forces to repeat the descent of William of Orange.

The closing months of 1714 were laden with forebodings of civil war. But Bolingbroke, although in the ascendant, had not the nerve or the quality to play this deadly game. Many accounts converge upon the conclusion that the final scene in the long duel between Oxford and Bolingbroke at the Cabinet Council of July 27 brought about the death of Queen Anne. Already scarcely capable of standing or walking, she nevertheless followed the intense political struggles proceeding around her with absorbed attention. She notified Oxford by gesture and utterance that he must surrender the Lord Treasurer's White Staff. The sodden, indolent, but none the less tough and crafty politician who had overthrown Marlborough and changed the history of Europe had his final fling at his triumphant rival. In savage tones across the table, both men being within six feet of the Queen, he denounced Bolingbroke to her as a rogue and a thief, and in terms of vague but none the less impressive menace made it plain that he would denounce him to Parliament. Anne was deeply smitten. She was harassed beyond endurance. She had taken all upon herself, and now she did not know which way to turn. She was assisted and carried from this violent confrontation, and two days later the actions which had hitherto tormented her body moved towards her brain.

Bolingbroke remained master of the field and of the day – but only for two days. On July 30, while the Queen was evidently at the point of death, the Privy Council met in the palace. They were about to transact business when the door opened and in marched the Duke of Somerset and Argyll. Both were Privy Counsellors, but neither had received a summons. They declared that the danger to the Queen made it their duty to proffer their services. Shrewsbury, the Lord Chamberlain, who had certainly planned this stroke, thanked them for their patriotic impulse. Bolingbroke, like Oxford some years before, blenched before the challenge. The Council pressed upon the deathbed of the Queen; they urged her to give to Shrewsbury the White Staff of Lord Treasurer, which Oxford had delivered. This would make Shrewsbury virtually head of the Government. With fleeting strength Anne, guided by the Lord Chancellor, passed the symbol to him, and then sank into a coma. The Council sat far into the night. Vigorous measures were taken to ensure the Hanoverian succession. Everything was prepared to secure the accession of the Elector of Hanover as George I. When Queen Anne breathed her last at half-past seven on August 1 it was certain that there would be no Popery, no disputed succession, no French bayonets, no civil war. Thus ended one of the greatest reigns in English history.

CHAPTER THIRTY-SEVEN

THE HOUSE OF HANOVER

George I – the German "gang" at court – Jacobite rising at Perth –
reading the Riot Act – the Battle of Sheriffmuir – the South Sea Bubble –
the first Prime Minister – patronage of Princess Caroline – the coming
men – Walpole and Newcastle – Bolingbroke's grab for power – the death
of George I – George II against Walpole – the War of Jenkins's Ear –
Rule Britannia composed – Walpole resigns – the War of Austrian
Succession – Pelham and Newcastle government – the return of Carteret –
the rise of William Pitt – the Battle of Dettingen – the '45 Jacobite
rebellion – the Battle of Culloden – Flora Macdonald – the not-so-bonny
prince flees – Pitt joins the Government – the death of Pelham –
war with France – England loses Minorca – Admiral Byng shot

URING THE late summer of 1714 all England awaited the coming of King George I. On September 18 he landed at Greenwich. This fortunate German prince, who could not speak English, viewed his new realms without enthusiasm. In accepting the throne of the United Kingdom he was conferring, as it seemed to him, a favour upon his new subjects. He was meeting the convenience of English politicians. In return he expected that British power and wealth would be made serviceable to his domains in Hanover and to his larger interests on the European scene. His royal duties would entail exile from home in an island he had only once previously visited and which he did not like. For years past, as heir presumptive, he had attentively watched the factious course of English politics. He had followed distastefully the manoeuvres of the party leaders, without understanding the stresses that gave rise to them or the principles that were at stake. Now on the banks of the Thames he looked about upon the nobles and Ministers who had come to greet him with suspicion and wariness, not unmingled with contempt. Here on English soil stood an unprepossessing figure, an obstinate and humdrum German martinet with dull brains and coarse tastes. As a commander in the late wars he had been sluggish and incompetent, and as a ruler of men he had shown no quickening ability or generosity of spirit. Yet the rigidity of his mind was relieved by a slow shrewdness and a brooding common sense. The British throne was no easy inheritance, especially for a foreign prince. King George took it up grudgingly, and it was ungraciously that he played his allotted part. He owed his crown to the luck of circumstance, but he never let it slip from his grasp.

Many holders of office under the previous reign nursed hopes of the new King. Others were filled with well-justified apprehension. Foremost among those now in acute anxiety was Bolingbroke. His fall was relentless and rapid. Upon the death of Anne he was still Secretary of State. But everyone suspected that if the Queen had lived a few weeks longer Bolingbroke would have laid the train for a Jacobite Restoration. He could expect little mercy. Nor was he left long in doubt. Soon a curt note of dismissal arrived for him from Hanover. Retiring to the country, he hovered aimlessly between regrets and fears. The first Parliament of the new reign demanded his impeachment. Bolingbroke fled to France disguised as a valet, his jauntiness utterly shattered. A few months later he took the plunge and became Secretary of State to the Pretender. The Court of Saint-Germain, with which he had long intrigued, was soon to disillusion him. Eight years of exile lay ahead. But this false, glittering figure has not yet passed out of our story. His great rival Robert Harley, Earl of Oxford, was meanwhile imprisoned in the Tower of London. No condign punishment was inflicted on him; but when he emerged from the Tower he was a broken man.

The political passions of the seventeenth century had spent themselves in the closing years of Queen Anne. The Tory Party was shattered, and England settled down, grumbling but safe, under the long rule of Whiggism. A rapid change in the atmosphere marked the decades following 1714. The wrath and venom of controversy were replaced by an apathetic tolerance. Great principles were no longer dominant. Political sentiment was replaced by political interest. Public life was degraded by materialism and politics became a mere striving for office and Crown patronage by rival groups of Whigs.

The monarchy too had lost its lustre. There was no pretence that the Hanoverian kings ruled by Divine Right. They held their position by the express sanction of Parliament. Even the symbolism of royalty was curtailed. The Court was no longer the centre of beauty, rank, and fashion. A certain dowdiness creeps into the ceremonial and the persons of the courtiers. Life in the royal palaces is dominated by the panoply and surroundings of a minor German princeling. The dreary names of the German women are ever present in the memoirs of the time – the Kielmansegges and the Wallmodens, the Platens and the Schulenbergs – all soon to deck themselves out with English titles and wealth. Much is heard in political circles of the influences of the German "gang" – Bernstorff and Bothmer, advisers whom the first George brought with him, and Roberthon, his Huguenot private secretary.

The men who led the Whig Party in the days of Queen Anne were fast retiring from the scene. Wharton, long the party's great organiser, died in 1715. Charles Montagu, now Lord Halifax, who had done so much to reconstruct English finances during King William's wars, followed his colleague in the same year, and Burnet, the diligent historian and the staunchest of Whig Churchmen, was also gone. Lord Somers, the former Lord Chancellor, dragged his life out paralysed and helpless for twelve months longer. And the greatest figure of them all, John Duke of Marlborough, lived on in splendid isolation in his houses at Blenheim and St Albans, stricken with a lingering paralysis, until he was released by death in 1722. His wife Sarah was doomed to live out her life for twenty years more, a croaking reminder of the high days of the Augustan Age. But she was alone.

A new generation of statesmen – Walpole, Stanhope, Carteret, and Townshend – were to ensure the peaceful transition from the age of Anne to the age of the Georges. Among this group Stanhope gradually became the leading Minister. He had commanded in Spain during the wars and had captured Minorca. Now his main interest lay in foreign affairs. In domestic matters he was less happy, and here the Government faced no tranquil task. The country had acquiesced in the imposition by Parliament of a German royal family. But there was strong feeling in many parts of England for the house of Stuart. In London, in Oxford, and in the West Country there were riots and shouting. The houses and meeting-places of the Dissenters were once more looted and wrecked as symbols of the new Whig régime. Portraits of King William were burnt in ceremony at Smithfield.

On September 6 the Earl of Mar raised the Jacobite Standard at Perth. Within a few weeks ten thousand men were in arms against Hanoverian rule in Scotland. But they had no proper plans and no solid link with the exiles in France. The Government in London acted at once. Parliament passed the Riot Act[1] to curb disturbances in the English towns. Oxford was occupied by a body of cavalry. Sellers of seditious pamphlets, talkers of seditious opinions, were swiftly arrested. *Habeas corpus* was suspended. A reward of £100,000 was posted for the apprehension of the Pretender, dead or alive. Dutch troops were demanded from Holland under the terms of the Barrier Treaty guaranteeing the Protestant succession in England, and the regular forces moved quietly northwards against the rebels. In the North of England a small band of gentry, led by Lord Derwentwater, rose in support of the Stuarts. They were unable to form effective contact with Mar; but, reinforced with four thousand Scots, they made a rash and forlorn attempt to raise help from the towns and countryside to the south of them. The Duke of Marlborough was consulted by the military authorities. "You will beat them", he said, marking Preston with his thumbnail on the map, "there". And on November 13 beaten there they were.

The Government forces in Scotland, led by the Whig Duke of Argyll, met the Jacobite army at Sheriffmuir on the same day. The battle was indecisive, but was followed by desertion and discouragement in the Jacobite ranks. With all hope of success gone, the Pretender landed in bad December weather upon

---

1   The Riot Act, which was passed in 1715, stated that if twelve or more people were in riotous assembly and refused to disperse when the Act was read to them, the penalty could be death. From this came the expression, to "read the Riot Act".

the Scottish coast. He brought neither money nor ammunition. Assembling the leaders, he evacuated them in a French vessel and returned to France. The collapse was followed by a batch of treason trials and about thirty executions. Despite the incompetence of the rising, the Government perceived and feared the unorganised opposition throughout the country to the new régime. They felt they must strengthen their grip on the administration. A Septennial Act prolonged the life of the existing House of Commons for another four years, and decreed septennial Parliaments henceforth. This was the boldest and most complete assertion of Parliamentary sovereignty that England had yet seen. Thus the Whigs established control of the Parliamentary machine. The 1715 rebellion made it even more easy for the Government to brand all Tories as Jacobites and disturbers of the peace. With political power and influence barred except to the favoured few, men turned to other pursuits and new adventures.

Financial speculation was encouraged. The Government was burdened with a war-debt of nearly fifty millions, and the idea of benefiting from the commercial prosperity of the world was not unattractive. In 1710 a Tory Ministry had granted a charter to a company trading with the South Seas, and had arranged for it to take over part of the National Debt. This connection had rapidly expanded the wealth of the South Sea Company, and in 1720 a group of Directors approached the Government with a plan to absorb the whole National Debt, then standing at about £30,000,000. The scheme soon came to stink of dishonesty, but the politicians were too greedy to reject it. There was a chance of wiping out the whole debt in twenty-five years. £1,250,000 is said to have been spent in bribes to Ministers, Members of Parliament, and courtiers. The Whig Chancellor of the Exchequer, John Aislabie, purchased £27,000 worth of South Sea stock before introducing the project to the House of Commons. The Bank of England, nervous of a growing financial rival, competed for the privilege of undertaking this gigantic transaction. But the South Sea Company outbid the Bank. In April 1720 the Bill sanctioning these proposals was brought before the House. It received a sober and savage attack at the hands of Robert Walpole, whose reputation was rising. But the Members were dazzled at the prospect of private gain. The House sleepily emptied even as Walpole spoke. The Bill was carried on April 2 by 172 votes to 35, and five days later an equally large majority secured its passage through the Lords, where Lord Cowper compared it to the wooden horse of Troy.

The mania for speculation broke loose. Stock soared in three months from 128 to 300, and within a few months more to 500. Amid the resounding cries of jobbers and speculators a multitude of companies, some genuine and some bogus, was hatched. By June 1721 the South Sea stock stood at 1050. Robert Walpole himself had the luck to make a handsome profit on his quiet investments. At every coffee-house in London men and women were investing their savings in any enterprise that would take their money. There was no limit to the credulity of the public. One promoter floated a company to manufacture an invention known as Puckle's Machine Gun, "which was to discharge round and square cannon-balls and bullets and make a total revolution in the art of war", the round missiles being intended for use against Christians and the square against the Turk. Other promoters invited subscriptions for making salt water fresh, for constructing a wheel of perpetual motion, for importing large jackasses from Spain to improve the breed of English mules, and the boldest of all was the advertisement for "a company for carrying on an undertaking of Great Advantage, but no one to know what it is". This amiable swindler set up a shop in Cornhill to receive subscriptions. His office was besieged by eager investors, and after collecting £2,000 in cash he prudently absconded.

The Government took alarm, and the process of suppressing these minor companies began. The South Sea Company was only too anxious to exterminate its rivals, but the pricking of the minor bubbles quickened and precipitated a slump. An orgy of selling began, and by October the South Sea stock stood at 150. Thousands were ruined. The porters and ladies' maids who had bought carriages and fineries found themselves reduced to their former station. Clergy, bishops, poets, and gentry found their life savings vanish overnight. There were suicides daily. The gullible mob whose innate greed had lain behind this mass hysteria and mania for wealth called for vengeance. The Postmaster-General took poison. His son, a Secretary of State, was snatched from his accusers by opportune smallpox. Stanhope, the chief Minister, died of strain. The Directors of the Company were arrested and their estates forfeited for the benefit of the huge army of creditors. A secret committee was appointed by the House of Commons to inquire into the nature and origins of these astonishing transactions. The books of the company were mutilated and incomplete. Nevertheless it was discovered that 462 members of the Commons and 122 peers were involved. Groups of frantic bankrupts thronged the Parliamentary lobbies. The Riot Act was read. There was a general outcry against the cupidity of the German ladies. "We are ruined by Trulls – nay, what is more, by old, ugly Trulls, such as could not find entertainment in the most hospitable hundreds of Old Drury." Walpole came to the rescue with a scheme for grafting a large section of the South Sea capital on to the Bank of England's stock and for reconstructing the National Debt. Apart from the estates of the Directors there were few assets for the mass of creditors. The brief hour of dreamed-of riches closed in wide-eyed misery. Bringing order to the chaos that remained was the first task of Britain's first Prime Minister.

One man only amid the crash and panic of 1721 could preserve the Whig monopoly. He was Robert Walpole, now established as the greatest master of figures of his generation. Soon he was to become a Knight of the Garter, one of the few Commoners to hold the honour. This Norfolk squire, who hunted five days a week, had risen to prominence as Secretary at War in the days of Marlborough. He had been imprisoned in the Tower after the Whig defeat of 1710, and since his release had been a leading figure of the Whig Party in the House of Commons. He had already been Chancellor of the Exchequer for three years, but he and his brother-in-law, Townshend, had resigned in 1717 in protest at the excessive pliancy of certain Whigs to the Hanoverian foreign policy of the King. Walpole had witnessed the disastrous effect on the Whig Party of the public impeachment of Sacheverell. He had no intention of repeating the mistake. The political crisis was quickly ended.

Walpole, on becoming head of the Government, immediately turned to financial reconstruction. He was First Lord, or Commissioner, of the Treasury, for the great office of Lord Treasurer had been abolished and its powers placed in the hands of a commission. The last sections of the National Debt taken over by the South Sea Company were portioned out between the Bank of England and the Treasury. The Sinking Fund he had instituted in 1717, whereby a sum of money was set aside from the revenue each year to pay off the National Debt, was put into operation. Within a few months the situation improved and England settled down again under another edition of Whig rule. With a business man at the head of affairs the atmosphere of national politics became increasingly materialistic. Walpole realised that the life of his Government depended on avoiding great issues that might divide the country. He knew that a mass of hostile opinion smouldered in the manor-houses and parsonages of England, and he was determined not to provoke it.

By careful attention to episcopal appointments, delicately handled by his friend Edmund Gibson, the Whig Bishop of London, Walpole increased the preponderance of his party in the House of Lords. He refused a comprehensive measure of toleration for the Dissenters, for this might have introduced religious strife into the world of politics. But while unwilling to legislate broadly on grounds of principle he took care that his Dissenting supporters who accepted office in local government in defiance of the Test Acts were quietly protected by annual Acts of Indemnity. Any sign of Tory activity was greeted by Walpole with the deadly accusation of Jacobitism. He had no illusions about the virtue of his supporters; but he knew there was a point beyond which corruption would not work. Walpole's object was to stabilise the Hanoverian régime and the power of the Whig Party within a generation. Taxation was low; the land tax, which was anxiously watched by the Tory squires, was reduced by economy to one shilling. The National Debt decreased steadily, and an overhaul of the tariff and the reduction of many irksome duties stimulated and expanded trade. By an *entente* with France and by rigid non-intervention in European politics Walpole avoided another war.

Bolingbroke[1] had offered an alliance, but Walpole had refused to allow him to regain his place in the House of Lords. The younger Whigs, like William Pulteney and John Carteret,[2] were too clever to be allowed to shine in Walpole's orbit. Not could they weaken his hold on the House of Commons while he exercised the patronage of the Crown. There was no hope except to

---

1   Walpole had allowed Bolingbroke to return from exile in 1726.
2   It was not until 1724 that Walpole got rid of Carteret, 1st Earl of Granville (1690–1763). He was made Lord-Lieutenant of Ireland until 1730 but returned to Government after Walpole's fall from power in 1742.

undermine his position with the King. A series of appeals to the German ladies by flattery and cash followed. Walpole was always quicker in satisfying their cupidity than his opponents. The Parliamentary Opposition gathered round the Prince of Wales. It was the Hanoverian family tradition that father and son should be on the worst of terms, and the future George II was no exception. The Government depended on the King; the Opposition looked to his son. All had an interest in the dynasty. But for the strong support of Caroline, Princess of Wales, Walpole would have been in serious danger.

George I died in 1727 and on the accession of George II Walpole suffered a brief eclipse. The new King dismissed him. But the Opposition leaders failed to form an alternative Government. The titular head of their stop-gap administration had to get Walpole to write the royal speech at the opening of George II's first Parliament. Secure in the confidence of Queen Caroline, Walpole returned to office and entrenched himself more firmly than before.

There had always been a danger that discontented, ambitious members of his Government would play on the King's interest in Hanoverian affairs. They would espouse the causes dear to the royal heart – the ancestral home, the great Continental scene, the Grand Alliance, the wars of Marlborough. This lure of European politics was too much for several of the men around Walpole. He meant to do as little as possible: to keep the peace, to stay in office, to juggle with men, to see the years roll by. But others responded to more lively themes. Walpole was forced to quarrel. His own brother-in-law, Charles Townshend, was dismissed at the end of 1729.[1] He [Walpole] then entered into close co-operation with a man of limited intelligence and fussy nature, but of vast territorial and electoral wealth – Thomas Pelham Holles, Duke of Newcastle.

Newcastle became Secretary of State. By his enemies Walpole was now mockingly called the "Prime Minister" – for this honourable title originated as a term of abuse. The chances of a successful Opposition seemed to be gone for ever. With every weapon of wit and satire at their command the brilliant young men who gathered round Bolingbroke and the surviving mistress of George I, the Duchess of Kendal, herself a subscriber to Bolingbroke's newspaper *The Craftsman*, could make no dint on the dull, corrupt, reasonable solidity of the administration. However, in 1733 a storm broke. Walpole proposed an excise on wines and tobacco, to be gathered by Revenue officers in place of a duty at the ports. The measure was aimed at the vast smuggling that rotted this source of the revenue. Every weapon at their command was used by the Opposition. Members of Parliament were deluged with letters. Popular ballads and pamphlets were thrust under the doors. National petitions and public meetings were organised throughout the land. Doleful images were

---

1   Walpole had taken command of Government foreign policy. This was Townshend's brief, and
    so although Churchill (and others) says that Townshend was dismissed, he also resigned when
    he found it impossible to work with Walpole. He went back to farming in East Anglia and
    became known as Turnip Townshend after he introduced turnips as part of his crop-rotation
    scheme.

raised of the tyranny of the Excisemen. Walpole's majority dwindled; his supporters deserted him like sheep straying through an open gate. Defeated by
one of the most unscrupulous campaigns in English history, Walpole withdrew his Excise reform. After a near division in the House of Commons he
uttered the famous saying, "This dance can no longer go." He crawled out of
the mess successfully, and the Opposition snatched no permanent advantage.

Bolingbroke now despaired of ever achieving political power, and in 1735
he retired once more to France. Those Whigs who were out of office grouped
themselves round Frederick, the new Prince of Wales. He in his turn became
the hope of the Opposition but all they could produce was an increased Civil
List for this ungifted creature. Their arrogance showed Walpole that people
were growing tired of his colourless rule. One of his sharpest critics was a
young Cornet of Horse named William Pitt. He was deprived of his
commission for his part in the attack. In 1737 Walpole's staunch ally, Queen
Caroline, died. There was steadily growing a reaction, both in the country and
in the House of Commons, to the interminable monopoly of political power
by this tough, unsentimental Norfolk squire, with his head for figures and his
horror of talent, keeping the country quiet, and, though it was only an incident, feathering his own nest.

At long last the Opposition discerned the foundation of Walpole's
ascendancy, namely, the avoidance of any controversy which might stir the
country as a whole. Their campaign against the Excise, which appealed to
popular forces outside Walpole's command, pointed the path to his final overthrow. Supreme in the narrow circle of the Commons and the Court,
Walpole's name angered many and inspired no one. The country was bored.

All that was needed to destroy the mechanism of Walpole's rule was an
issue that would stir the country, and which would in its turn stampede the
quiescent, half-squared Members of Parliament into a hostile vote against the
Minister. The crack came from a series of incidents in Spanish America. In
1713 the Treaty of Utrecht had granted the English the right to send one
shipful of negro slaves a year to the Spanish plantations in the New World.
Such was the inefficiency of Spanish administration that it was easy to run
contraband cargoes of negroes in defiance of what was called the "Asiento
contract", and the illicit trade grew steadily in the years of peace. But when the
Spanish Government at last began to reorganise and extend its colonial
government English ships trading unlawfully in the Spanish seas were stopped
and searched by the Spanish coastguards. Profits were high, and merchants in
London forced Walpole to challenge the right of search. A series of
negotiations followed with Madrid.

The Directors of the South Sea Company were interested in these regions.
Suppressing English interlopers was not in itself to their disadvantage, but
they were themselves involved in dispute with Spain over payments due to the
Spanish king under the Asiento contract for the annual ship. Driven to the
verge of bankruptcy, they hoped to use the anti-Spanish feeling in London to
avoid their obligations. The preliminary Convention of Prado was settled and

negotiated at Madrid in January 1739. Spain, also nearly bankrupt, was just as anxious to avoid war. She offered many concessions, and Walpole drastically reduced the claims of English merchants. But the Opposition would have none of it. The South Sea Company had been excluded from the preliminary Convention, and continued its quarrel with the Spanish Government independently of official negotiations. In May Spain suspended the Asiento and refused to pay any of the compensations agreed by the Prado Convention.

Meanwhile the Opposition in Parliament had opened a broad attack on the Government's negotiations with Spain. Much was heard of the honour of England. A captain trading with the Spanish possessions, one Jenkins, was brought before the House of Commons to produce his ear in a bottle, and to maintain that it had been cut off by Spanish coastguards when his ship was searched. Jenkins's ear caught the popular imagination and became the symbol of agitation. Whether it was in fact his own ear or whether he had lost it in a seaport brawl remains uncertain, but the power of this shrivelled object was immense. A vociferous group of orators led by Pulteney became known ironically as the "Patriots". Without troubling to study the terms of the preliminary agreement with Spain, the Opposition drove their attack home.

The Spaniards might have ignored the bellicose Opposition in the British Parliament. Walpole and Newcastle were not strong enough to do so. If the country demanded war with Spain the Ministers were prepared to ride with them rather than resign. Spain had disarmed her Fleet after signing the Convention of Prado as proof of her sincerity. English ships in the Mediterranean had been ordered home, but after the Storm at Westminster the orders were revoked in March. Walpole was further alarmed by the hostile attitude of France; but none the less he yielded ground slowly and steadily. On October 19, 1739, war was declared.[1] Now opened a mighty struggle, at first with Spain only, but later by the family compact between the Bourbon monarchs involving France. Thus began that final duel between Britain and her nearest neighbour which in less than a century was to see the glories of Chatham, the follies of Lord North, the terrors of the French Revolution and the rise and fall of Napoleon.

By sure degrees, in the confusion and mismanagement which followed, Walpole's power, as he had foreseen, slipped from him. The operations of the ill-manned Fleet failed. There were riots in London. The Prince of Wales appeared everywhere, to be cheered by opponents of the Government. A new tune was on their lips, with Thomson's resounding words, "Rule, Britannia".

In February 1741 an Opposition Member, Samuel Sandys, proposed an address to the King for the dismissal of Walpole. For the last time the old Minister outwitted his foes. He had made overtures to the Jacobite group in the Commons, even letting it be supposed that he would countenance a Jacobite

---

1 The war is often called the War of Jenkins's Ear. It was a famous year, which saw the founding of the Black Watch and the start of John Wesley's open-air preaching.

Restoration. To the amazement of all, the Jacobites voted for him. The Opposition, in the words of Lord Chesterfield, "broke in pieces". But under the Septennial Act elections were due. The Prince of Wales spent lavishly in buying up seats, and his campaign, managed by Thomas Pitt, brother of William, brought twenty-seven Cornish seats over to the Opposition. The electoral influence of the Scottish earls counted against Walpole, and when the Members returned to Westminster his Government was defeated on an election petition (contested returns were in those days decided by the House on purely party lines) and resigned. It was February 1742.

Sir Robert had governed England for twenty-one years. He was the first Chief Minister to reside at Number Ten. He had accomplished the work of his life, the peaceful establishment of the Protestant succession in England. He had soothed and coaxed a grumbling, irritated country into acquiescence in the new régime. He had built up a powerful organisation, fed and fattened on Government patronage. He had supervised the day-to-day administration of the country, unhampered by royal interference. The sovereign had ceased after 1714 to preside in person over the Cabinet save on exceptional occasions – a most significant event. George I could not speak English and had to converse with his Ministers in French or such dog-Latin as they remembered from Eton. Walpole had created for himself a dominating position in this vital executive committee, now deprived of its titular chairman. He tried to make himself supreme over his Ministers and establish in practice that rebellious colleagues were dismissed by the King. But he founded no convention of collective Ministerial responsibility. One of the charges against him after his fall was that he had sought to become "sole and Prime Minister". Now he went to the House of Lords as Earl of Orford. He was the first great House of Commons man in British history, and if he had resigned before the war with Spain he might have been called the most successful.

The war between Britain and Spain, which the Opposition had forced upon Walpole, was soon merged in a general European struggle. Britain had expected to fight naval and colonial campaigns in Spanish waters and on the Spanish Main. Instead she found herself engaged in a Continental war. Two royal deaths in 1740 set the conflict in motion. East of the Elbe the rising kingdom of Prussia acquired a new ruler. Frederick II, later called the Great, ascended his father's throne. He inherited a formidable army which he fretted to use. It was his ambition to expand his scattered territories and weld them into the strongest state in Germany. Military gifts and powers of leadership, a calculating spirit and utter ruthlessness, were his in equal portion. Almost immediately he had the chance to put them to the test. In October the Habsburg Emperor Charles VI died, leaving his broad domains, though not his Imperial title, to his daughter Maria Theresa. The Emperor had extracted solemn guarantees from all the Powers of Europe that they would recognise her accession in Austria, Hungary, Bohemia, and the Southern Netherlands. But these meant nothing to Frederick. He attacked and seized the Austrian province of Silesia, which lay to the south of his own territories. France, ever jealous of the Habsburgs, encouraged and supported him. Thus Europe was plunged into what is termed the War of the Austrian Succession.[1]

In England King George II was much beset by the problems that arose. His hereditary Electorate of Hanover was dearer to his heart than the Kingdom of Great Britain. He correctly measured the ambitions of his nephew, Frederick of Prussia. He was fearful that the next Prussian onslaught might engulf his own estates in Germany. In London, after Walpole's fall, King George's Government was managed by Henry Pelham, First Lord of the Treasury, and his brother, the Duke of Newcastle, long a Secretary of State.[2] Their great territorial wealth and electoral influence enabled them to maintain Whig dominion over the House of Commons. They were skilled in party manoeuvre, but inexpert in the handling of foreign or military affairs. George II turned for help and advice to the Pelhams' rival, Lord Carteret. Under Walpole Carteret had shared the fate of all men who were clever enough to be dangerous, and was dismissed to the Lord-Lieutenancy of Ireland. Sir Robert's fall restored him to public life at Westminster. By supporting the King's German interests he was now able to outbid the Pelhams for the royal favour. Carteret wanted Hanover and England to preserve and promote a balance of power in Europe. He thought he held the clue to the Continental maze. He spoke German and was an intimate of the sovereign. In 1742 he was appointed a Secretary of State. To meet the combination of France, Spain, and Frederick the Great he negotiated a treaty with Maria Theresa and renewed the traditional agreements with the Dutch. Financial help was promised to Austria, and preparations were made for raising an army to aid the Queen of Hungary, as Maria Theresa was proudly called.

Carteret, to his misfortune, lacked both the personal position and the political following to put his decisions to good effect. He was an individualist, with no gift for party organisation, depending essentially and only upon the favour of the Crown. Hostility soon gathered against him in Parliament. Foremost among his critics was William Pitt, Member for the ancient but uninhabited borough of Old Sarum. His grandfather had been Governor of Madras and owner of the famous Pitt diamond. From Eton Pitt had gone into the Army. His commanding officer, Lord Cobham, had been deprived of his regiment by Walpole for agitating against the Excise scheme. This had soon put an end to the young cornet's military career, and he followed his patron and colonel into Opposition politics. Lord Cobham was head of the Temple family and related to the Grenvilles and Lytteltons. In close political association with this group of disaffected Whigs Pitt began his political career. He played a noisy part in the Opposition campaign for war against Spain, and was a relentless critic of Newcastle's conduct of the operations.

---

1 The war lasted from 1740 until 1748.
2 Pelham and Newcastle did not govern immediately after Walpole's resignation as Churchill suggests. From January 1742 to July 1743 the nominal Prime Minister was Lord Wilmington, but during this eighteen-month period, the real leader of the Government was probably Carteret, who told Wilmington what to do.

Thirty thousand British troops, under the command of one of Marl-borough's old officers, the Earl of Stair, fought on the Continent. In the spring of 1743 the King himself, accompanied by his younger son, the Duke of Cumberland, left England to take part in the campaign. The Allied forces were concentrated upon the River Main, in the hope of separating the French from their German allies. Bavaria too had taken advantage of the turmoil to attack Queen Maria Theresa, and the Bavarian Elector, with French backing, had been declared Holy Roman Emperor. In the Empire this was the first departure from the Habsburg line in three hundred years. It proved to be a brief interlude. A superior French army under Marshal Noailles lay in the neighbourhood, with the object of cutting off his enemy from their bases in Holland and destroying them in open battle. At the village of Dettingen, near Aschaffenburg, the forces came into conflict. The French cavalry, impatient at delays, charged the Allied left wing. King George's horse bolted, but, dismounting, and sword in hand, he led the Hanoverian and British infantry into action against the French dragoons. They broke and fled, and many were drowned in trying to cross the Main. The French foot failed to retrieve the day, and after four hours' fighting the Allies were in possession of the field. They had lost barely two thousand men, the French twice as many. For the last time an English king had fought at the head of his troops. His son, the Duke of Cumberland, had also shown marked bravery in this sharp action. The witness was a young officer named James Wolfe.

The Battle of Dettingen raised a brief enthusiasm in London, but opinion slowly hardened against the continuance of a major European war. England was again the head and the paymaster of another Grand Alliance. A new Bourbon Family Compact had been signed between France and Spain, and Secret Service agents reported Jacobite intrigues in Paris. There was talk in London of a French invasion. Dutch troops were hastily brought over to Sheerness. At the end of 1744 Carteret, now Lord Granville, was driven from office. Newcastle again dominated the Government.

For the campaign of 1745 the King made Cumberland Captain-General of the Forces on the Continent. This young martinet had created the illusion of military capacity by his bravery at Dettingen. He had to face the most celebrated soldier of the day, Marshal Saxe. The French Army concentrated against the barrier fortress line, the familiar battleground of Marlborough's wars, now held by the Dutch. Having masked Tournai, Saxe took up a strong position centring upon the village of Fontenoy, near the Mons road. Cumberland drew up his army in battle order, and marched it under fire to within fifty paces of the French army. He was outnumbered by nearly two to one. Lieutenant-Colonel Lord Charles Hay, of the 1st (Grenadier) Guards, stepped from the front ranks, took out a flask, raised it in salute to the French Household troops, and declared, "We are the English Guards, and hope you will stand till we come up to you, and not swim the Scheldt as you did the Main at Dettingen." Cheers rang out from both sides. The English advanced, and at thirty paces the French fired. The murderous fusillade did not halt the Allied infantry, and they drove the enemy from their positions. For hours the French cavalry tried to break the Allied columns, and, watching the Irish Brigade of the French Army sweeping into action, Cumberland exclaimed, "God's curse on the laws that made those men our enemies." It is a more generous remark than is usually recorded of him. At the fall of darkness he withdrew in perfect order down the road to Brussels. At any rate England played no further part in the War of the Austrian Succession. In October 1745 Cumberland withdrew his men to meet the Young Pretender's invasion of England, and our Continental allies were beaten on every front. The only good news came from across the Atlantic. English colonists, supported by a naval squadron, captured the strongest French fortress in the New World, Louisburg, on Cape Breton.

Newcastle, "the impertinent fool" as King George called him, was in confusion. He had no war policy, and having ousted Carteret from the Government had now to "broaden the bottom of the administration",[1] as they said in the terms of those days. The Pelham régime, built up upon the support of Whig family groups, was artificial, but it had its merits. Henry Pelham was a good administrator, economical and efficient, but he was a lesser Walpole faced with a major European war. Newcastle, in his own whimsical way, looked upon the work of government as the duty of his class, but he had no clear ideas on how to discharge it. Lord Shelburne, later Prime Minister, describes these brothers: "They had every talent for obtaining Ministry, and none for governing the kingdom except decency, integrity, and Whig principles." But the war dominated everything. For ten years the Pelham brothers made constant and frantic efforts to create a stable Government. Fumbling and out of date in Europe, and unmindful of the great future overseas, the broad-bottomed Administration of the 1740s was a painful affair.

There had been much discontent in Scotland since the Union of 1707. In the inaccessible Highlands, where the writ of English government hardly ran, there was a persistent loyalty to the house of Stuart and the Jacobite cause. Living in their mountain villages like hill tribesmen, a law unto themselves, the immemorial zest for plunder and forays was still unslaked among the clans. The Union had not alleviated their poverty. While the rest of Scotland was gripped by the discipline of the Presbyterian Kirk, the Highlands were ruled by chiefs incapable of combining among themselves or of keeping the peace, but still preserving the tatters of warlike and romantic honour.

After the failure of the rising in 1715 the Jacobites had stayed quiet, but once England was involved in war upon the Continent their activities revived. The Old Pretender was now living in retirement, and his son, Prince Charles Edward, was the darling of the impecunious exiles who clustered round him in Rome and Paris. He sailed from Nantes in June 1745 with a handful of followers and landed in the Western Isles of Scotland. Thus began one of the most audacious and irresponsible enterprises in British history. Charles had

---

1   This government was called the "broad-bottom" administration because it was a broad political
     coalition. It lasted from November 1744 until March 1754.

made scarcely any preparations. He could command support only in the Highlands, which contained but a small proportion of the whole population of Scotland. The clans were always ready to fight, but never to be led. Arms and money were short, the Lowlands hostile, and the Highland troops were hated. The commercial classes regarded them as bandits. The cities had long accepted Hanoverian rule.

Twelve hundred men under Lord George Murray raised the Jacobite standard at Glenfinnan. About three thousand Government troops gathered in the Lowlands under Sir John Cope. The rebels marched southwards; Prince Charles entered the palace at Holyrood, and Cope was met and routed on the battlefield of Prestonpans. By the end of September Charles was ruler of most of Scotland in the name of his father, "King James VIII"; but his triumph was fleeting. The castle of Edinburgh held out for King George, and from time to time discharged a sullen shot. The mass of the Scottish people were apathetic. In London, however, there was panic; a run on the Bank was only met by paying out in sixpences. Most of the Army was still in Flanders.

With five thousand men the Young Pretender crossed the Border. Three forces were assembled against him. General Wade stood at Newcastle; Cumberland marched to block the London road at Lichfield and strike westwards if he tried to join the Jacobites in the Welsh mountains. A third, encamped on Finchley Common to protect London, still lives in Hogarth's satirical print. This the King did not like. He fancied himself as a warrior and thought it unbecoming to make fun of soldiers.

The Highlanders were quick on the move. Plundering as they went, they marched due south, occupying Carlisle, Penrith, Lancaster, and Preston. The number of English adherents that came in was depressingly small. They had hopes of getting reinforcements in Manchester. A drummer boy and a whore preceded them into the town as an inducement for recruits. Their combined efforts brought in two hundred men. Many Highlanders deserted and returned home during the southward march. Liverpool was staunchly Hanoverian, and equipped a regiment at its own expense. The chieftains demanded to return to Scotland. Charles knew of the panic in London, and hoped to profit by it, but he had no control over his followers. By brilliant tactics Lord George Murray had manoeuvred Cumberland away from the London road and the path to the capital was open. But it was December. The English commanded the sea; there was no hope from France; the Dutch and Hessians were sending troops to England. There was feverish recruitment in London. A six-pound bonus was paid to everyone who enlisted in the Guards.

At Derby Charles gave the signal to retreat. Two days later news came that the Jacobites in Wales were ready to rise. A winter march began to the fastnesses of Northern Scotland. The English forces followed like vultures, hanging upon the rear and wings of the rebel army. Murray showed great skill in the withdrawal, and in rearguard actions his troops were invariably successful. They turned and mauled their pursuers at Falkirk. But with Teutonic thoroughness the Duke of Cumberland concentrated the English armies for a decision, and in April 1746 on Culloden Moor the last chances of a Stuart restoration were swept into the past for ever. The Stuarts were to linger in men's memories as a sentimental, though ill-founded, legend of gracious and kindly kings. No quarter was given on the battlefield, where Cumberland earned his long-lived title of "Butcher". Charles Edward escaped over the moors with a few faithful servants. Disguised as a woman, he was smuggled across to the island of Skye by that heroine of romance, Flora Macdonald. Thence he sailed for the Continent, to drink out his life in perpetual exile. Flora Macdonald, for her gallant and virtuous part in this episode, was imprisoned for a time in the Tower of London. Ruthless repression measured the fears of the Hanoverian Government for their régime. The Highlanders were disarmed and the remnants of feudalism abolished. Jacobitism vanished from the political life of Great Britain.

In the crisis of the rebellion the Pelhams delivered their ultimatum. They must have Pitt or they would resign. In April 1746 Pitt became Paymaster of the Forces, an office of immense emolument in time of war. By a custom, openly avowed, the Paymaster was permitted to carry his balances to his private account and draw the interest on them. Further, he received commission on the subsidies paid to foreign allies for the maintenance of their troops in the field. Pitt refused to accept a penny beyond his official salary. The effect on public opinion was electric. By instinct rather than calculation he gained the admiration and confidence of the middle classes, the City, the rising mercantile towns, and the country freeholders. A born actor, by this gesture he caught the eye of the people, and held it as no statesman had held it before him. For nine years Pitt learnt the day-to-day work of administration. The dismal war on the Continent ended with the Treaty of Aix-la-Chapelle in 1748. Nothing was settled between Britain and France by this peace. The only gainer was Frederick the Great, who had stepped in and out of the war as it suited him. He kept Silesia.

Pitt now spent many hours in earnest discussion with Newcastle on the need for a new foreign policy. By acid and frequent attacks he had forced his way into the Government, only to find himself paralysed by the displeasure of the sovereign. In 1751 Frederick, Prince of Wales, the nominal head of the Opposition, died. Pitt and other young politicians had once entertained great hopes of achieving power when this nonentity should succeed to the throne. His death weakened the unity of a potential Ministry. In 1754 Henry Pelham expired and the flimsy administration tottered. Pitt was enveloped in the toils of group politics. He was now a powerful candidate for high office, backed by his political allies, the Cobhams and the Grenvilles, and what was left of the Prince of Wales's circle who met at Leicester House. But the King was relentless in his dislike of Pitt, and Cumberland, who had a political following of his own, succeeded in pushing into the Cabinet Pitt's most dangerous rival, Henry Fox. Breaking away from the constricted field of politics, which Newcastle managed by the methods of Walpole, Pitt was to revive and rekindle the national sentiment of the English which had been inspired by

Marlborough's wars. Appealing over the heads of petty groups to the nation at large, he was eventually to knock down the fragile structures of contemporary politicians and bring a driving wind of reality into politics. But the arrival of Fox in the Government, an avaricious expert in contemporary political method, made Pitt despair. After a great speech in the Commons he was dismissed from the Pay Office in November 1755.

Two months later a diplomatic revolution took place towards which the four main Powers of Europe had for some time been groping. A convention was signed between Britain and Prussia, shortly followed by a treaty between the French and the Austrians. Thus there was a complete reversal of alliances. A third war with France began with a new and vigorous ally on England's side, the Prussia of Frederick the Great, but with a fumbling Government at Westminster. The mismanagement of the early years of the struggle, which had been precipitated by the bellicose Cumberland gave Pitt his chance. The loss of the island of Minorca raised a national outcry. The Government, faced with this national disgrace, lost its nerve. Cumberland's favourite, Henry Fox, bolted into retirement. The Government shifted the blame on to Admiral Byng, whose ill-equipped fleet had failed to relieve the Minorca garrison. By one of the most scandalous evasions of responsibility that an English Government has ever perpetrated Byng was shot for cowardice upon the quarterdeck of his flagship. Pitt pleaded for him with the King. "The House of Commons, Sir, is inclined to mercy." "You have taught me", the King replied, "to look for the sense of my people elsewhere than in the House of Commons." Pitt's hour had almost come. But he had learnt by experience that weight in the country was not enough without Parliamentary influence, such as the Duke of Newcastle commanded. The Duke, thoroughly frightened by the general outcry, knew that all his connections, all his patronage, would not save him if the nation was determined to call him to account. The two men drew together. Pitt was ready to leave the jobbing to the Duke. And the Duke showed himself ready to lead a quiet life behind the glory of Pitt's achievements and the splendour of his eloquence.

CHAPTER THIRTY-EIGHT

PITT THE ELDER

Origins of the American colonies – the Navigation Laws – the migrants –
the Westward march – the first world war – Pitt and the battles of the
Americas – Loudon and the massacre of Fort William – Amherst and
Wolfe – the Heights of Abraham – the capture of Canada – the isolation
of the Great Commoner – the rise of the Earl of Bute – the death of
George II – the ambitions of George III – Pitt's resignation – war with
Spain – the Peace of Paris

PITT'S RISE to power and his victorious conduct of a world-wide war were to have a profound effect on the history of North America. Throughout the first half of the seventeenth century Englishmen had poured into the American continent. Legally the colonies in which they settled were chartered bodies subordinate to the Crown, but distracted by the Civil War the Mother Country left them alone, and although Cromwell's Commonwealth asserted that Parliament was supreme over the whole of the English world its decree was never put into practice, and was swept away by the Restoration. But after 1660 the home Government had new and definite ideas. For the next fifty years successive English administrations tried to enforce the supremacy of the Crown in the American colonies and to strengthen royal power and patronage in the overseas possessions. This led to unceasing conflict with the colonial assemblies, who resented the threat to royalise and unify colonial administration. Most of these assemblies were representative bodies of freeholders who claimed and exercised the same rights, procedure, and privileges as the Parliament at Westminster. The men who sat in them were many of them bred in a tradition hostile to the Crown. Their fathers had preferred exile to tyranny, and they regarded themselves as fighting for the same issues as had divided the English Parliament from Strafford and Charles I.

For a long time the English Parliament played no part in the conflict. The struggle lay between the colonies and the King's Ministers in the Privy Council. These officials were determined to call a halt to self-government in America. In 1682 they were asked to grant a charter for settling vacant lands on the borders of the Spanish possession of Florida. The Council refused, saying it was the policy of the Crown "not to constitute any new propriety in America nor to grant any further powers that might render the plantations less dependent on the Crown". Under James II these royalist tendencies were sharpened. New York became a royal province in 1685. The New England colonies were united into a "dominion of New England" on the French model in Canada. The main argument was the need for union against French expansion, but the move was fiercely resisted and the English Revolution of 1688 was a signal for the overthrow and collapse of the "dominion of New England".

How could the British Empire fight off the threat with a factious Parliament, fretful colonial assemblies, and a swarm of committees? The answer devised was an eminently practical one. British colonial trade must be planned and co-ordinated in London. One of its main objects must be to foster the British Merchant Navy, and to provide a reserve of ships and seamen in the event of war. The foundation of the whole system was the series of enactments known as the Navigation Laws. Colonial trade must travel only in British bottoms, with British crews and to British ports. The colonies were forbidden any outside trade of their own that might hinder the growth of British shipping. Moreover, the economic theories of the age supported this attack on colonial independence. The prevailing view of trade was based on the desire for self-sufficiency and on economic nationalism – or mercantilism as it was called. The wealth of a country depended upon its trade balance. An excess of imports over exports meant loss of bullion and economic weakness. National prosperity required the control of plentiful natural resources. Colonies were vital. They must produce essential raw materials, such as timber for the Navy, and afford a market for the growing manufactures of the home country. Colonial manufactures must be stifled to prevent competition inside it, and trade between the colonies themselves must be strictly regulated. Such, in brief, was the economic conception enshrined in the legislation of the seventeenth century.

No seventeenth-century Government could enforce such a code over thousands of miles. American assemblies grumbled but went their own way, ingeniously evading the Westminster restrictions. The English Revolution of 1688 changed the whole position. Hitherto the colonies had regarded the Parliament in England as their ally against the Crown. But the time was to come when Parliament, victorious over the Crown in the constitutional struggles at home, would attempt to enforce its own sovereignty over America. The clash was delayed by the War of the Spanish Succession. The long European struggle with France compelled the avoidance of fundamental issues elsewhere; and in the hope of marshalling the resources of the English-speaking peoples for the supreme conflict all efforts to impose the authority of the English Government in the New World were dropped. The Board of Trade and Plantations was allowed to subside and the colonies were largely left to themselves.

But in the course of time the colonists grew more and more resolved to press their advantage, and the middle years of the eighteenth century witnessed a vehement assault by the colonial Assemblies upon the authority of the Imperial Government. They were bent on making themselves into sovereign Parliaments, supreme in the internal government of the several colonies, and free of all restrictions or interference from London. Innumerable struggles took place between the Governors and the legislatures of the colonies. There were many complaints on both sides. The Crown looked upon posts overseas as valuable patronage for its servants, the Government for their supporters. Thus the whole colonial administration was tainted with the prevailing corruption of English public life.

The early eighteenth century saw the foundation of the last of the Thirteen Colonies. The philanthropist James Oglethorpe had been painfully moved by the horrible condition of the small debtors in English prisons. After much thought he conceived the idea of allowing these people to emigrate to a new colony. The Government, was approached, and in 1732 a board of trustees was created to administer a large tract of territory lying below South Carolina. The following year the first settlement was founded at Savannah. Small estates were created, and religious toleration was proclaimed for all except Catholics. The first settlers were English debtors, but the foundation promised a new life for the oppressed in many parts of Europe. Bands of Jews quickly arrived, followed by Protestants from Salzburg, Moravians from Germany, and Highlanders from Skye. The polyglot community, named Georgia, soon attracted ardent missionaries, and it was here that John Wesley began his ministering work.

The high moral atmosphere of these beginnings was soon polluted by mundane quarrels. The settlers, like their brethren in the other colonies, coveted both rum and slaves. The trustees of the community wearied of their task of government; and their prolonged bickering with the rising merchants of Savannah ended in the cancellation of the charter. In 1752 Georgia came under royal control. This colony was the last foundation of the Mother Country in the territories that were later to become the United States. Emigration from England had now dwindled to a trickle, but new settlers arrived from other parts. Towards the end of the seventeenth century there had been an influx of Scottish-Irish refugees, whose industrial and commercial endeavours at home had been stifled by the legislation of the English Parliament. They formed a strong English-hating element in their new homes. Pennsylvania received a steady flow of immigrants from Germany, soon to number over two hundred thousand souls. Hard-working and prosperous Huguenots arrived from France in flight from religious persecution. People were also moving from colony to colony. The oases of provincial life were linked up. The population was rapidly doubling itself. Limitless land to the West offered homes for the sons of the first generation. The abundance of territory to be occupied encouraged large families. Contact with primeval conditions created a new and daring outlook. A sturdy independent society was producing its own life and culture, influenced and coloured by surrounding conditions. The Westward march had begun, headed by the Germans and the Irish in Pennsylvania. The slow trail over the mountains in search of new lands was opening. There was a teeming diversity of human types. In Kentucky and on the Western farms which bordered the Indian country were rugged pioneers and sturdy yeomen farmers, and in the New England colonies assertive merchants, lawyers, and squires, and the sons of traders. This varied society was supported in the North by the forced labour of indentured servants and men smuggled away from the press-gangs in English towns, in the South by a mass of slaves multiplied by yearly shiploads from Africa.

Events in Europe, of which most Americans were probably scarcely conscious, now came to bear upon the destiny of the Thirteen Colonies. When Pitt first joined the Ministry as Secretary of State in November 1756 Frederick the Great declared, "England has long been in labour, but at last she has brought forth a man." Nothing like it had been seen since Marlborough. From his office in Cleveland Row Pitt designed and won a war which extended from India in the East to America in the West. The whole struggle depended upon the energies of this one man. He gathered all power, financial, administrative, and military, into his own hands. He could work with no one as an equal. His position depended entirely on success in the field. His political enemies were numerous. He would tolerate no interference or even advice from his colleagues in the Cabinet; he made no attempt either to consult or to conciliate, and he irritated Newcastle and the Chancellor of the Exchequer by interfering in finance. But in the execution of his military plans Pitt had a sure eye for choosing the right man. He broke incompetent generals and admirals and replaced them with younger men upon whom he could rely: Wolfe, Amherst, Conway, Howe, Keppel, and Rodney. Thus he achieved victory.

Pitt did not confine himself to a single field of operations. By taking the initiative in every quarter of the globe Britain prevented the French from concentrating their forces, confused their plan of campaign, and forced them to dissipate their strength. Unless France were beaten in Europe as well as in the New World and in the East she would rise again. Both in North America and in Europe she was in the ascendant. At sea she was a formidable enemy. In India it seemed that if ever a European Power established itself on the ruins of the Mogul Empire its banner would be the lilies and not the cross of St George. War with France would be a world war – the first in history; and the prize would be something more than a rearrangement of frontiers and a redistribution of fortresses and sugar islands.

Whether Pitt possessed the strategic eye, whether the expeditions he launched were part of a considered combination, may be questioned. Now, as at all times, his policy was a projection on to a vast screen of his own aggressive, dominating personality. In the teeth of disfavour and obstruction he had made his way to the foremost place in Parliament, and now at last fortune, courage, and the confidence of his countrymen had given him a stage on which his gifts could be displayed and his foibles indulged.

On the Continent Britain had one ally, Frederick of Prussia, facing the combined power of Austria, Russia, and France. Sweden too had old grudges to avenge, old claims to assert against him. Frederick, by a rapid march through Saxony into Bohemia, sought to break through the closing circle. But in 1757 he was driven back into his own dominions; Cumberland, sent to protect Hanover and Brunswick, was defeated by the French and surrendered both. Russia was on the march; Swedish troops were again seen in Pomerania. Minorca had already fallen. From Canada Montcalm was pressing against the American frontier forts. Never did a war open with darker prospects. Warfare had broken out in 1755. General Braddock was sent from England to re-establish British authority west of the Alleghanies, but his forces were cut to pieces by the French and Indians in Pennsylvania. In this campaign a young Virginian officer named George Washington learnt his first military lessons. The New England colonies lay open to attack down the easy path of invasion, the Hudson valley. A struggle began for a foothold at the valley head. There was little organisation. Each of the colonies attempted to repel Red Indian raids and French settlers with their own militias. They were united in distrusting the home Government, but in little else. Although there were now over a million British Americans, vastly outnumbering the French, their quarrels and disunion extinguished this advantage. Only the tactful handling of Pitt secured their co-operation, and even so throughout the war colonial traders continued to supply the French with all their needs in defiance of the Government and the common interest.

The year 1756 was disastrous for England in America, and indeed upon all fronts. Oswego, the only English fort on the Great Lakes, was lost. The campaign of 1757 was hardly more successful. The fortress of Louisburg, which commanded the Gulf of St Lawrence, had been taken by in Anglo-Colonial force in the 1740s and returned to France at the peace treaty of 1748 at Aix-la-Chapelle. English troops were now sent to recapture it. They were commanded by an ineffectual and unenterprising officer, Lord Loudon. Loudon prepared to attack by concentrating at Halifax such colonial troops from New England as the colonies would release. This left the Hudson valley open to the French. At the head of the valley were three small forts: Crown Point, Edward, and William Henry. The French, under the Governor of Canada, Montcalm, and his Red Indian allies, swept over the frontier through the wooded mountains and besieged Fort William Henry. The small colonial garrison held out for five days, but was forced to surrender. Montcalm was unable to restrain his Indians and the prisoners were massacred. The tragedy bit into the minds of the New Englanders. It was Loudon who was to blame. The British were not defending them; while New England was left exposed to the French, the troops which might have protected them were wasting time at Halifax. Indeed, by the end of July Loudon decided that Louisburg was impregnable and had given up the attempt.

Pitt now bent his mind to the American war. Throughout the winter he studied the maps and wrote dispatches to the officers and governors. A threefold strategic plan was framed for 1758. Loudon was recalled. His successor, Amherst, with Brigadier Wolfe, and naval support from Halifax, was to sail up the St Lawrence and strike at Quebec. Another army, under Abercromby, was to seize Lake George at the head of the Hudson valley and try to join Amherst and Wolfe before Quebec. A third force, under Brigadier Forbes, would advance up the Ohio valley from Pennsylvania and capture Fort Duquesne, one of a line of French posts along the Ohio and the Mississippi. The Fleet was so disposed as to stop reinforcements leaving France. Amherst and Wolfe hammered at the northern borders of Canada. In July Louisburg was captured. But Abercromby, advancing from Ticonderoga, became entangled in the dense woods; his army was badly beaten and his advance was halted. The Pennsylvanian venture was more successful. Fort Duquesne was taken and destroyed and the place renamed Pittsburg; but lack of numbers and organisation compelled the British force to retire at the end of the campaign.

Pitt was undaunted. He realised the need for a combined offensive along the whole frontier from Nova Scotia to the Ohio. Isolated inroads into French territory would bring no decision. On December 29, 1758, further instructions were accordingly sent to Amherst. The necessity for cutting across the French line of expansion was again emphasised. There was also much talk about the need of acquiring Red Indian allies. Amherst thought little of this. Several months earlier he had written to Pitt that a large number of Indians were promised him. "They are a pack of lazy, rum-drinking people and little good, but if ever they are of use it will be when we can act offensively. The French are much more afraid of them than they need be; numbers will increase their Terror and may have a good Effect." Nevertheless it was fortunate for the British that the Six Nations of the Iroquois, who occupied a key position between the British and French settlements near the Great Lakes, were generally friendly; they, like the American colonists, were alarmed at French designs on the Ohio and the Mississippi.

According to the new plan, in the coming year the Navy would attack the French West Indies, and the invasion of Canada up the St Lawrence would be pushed harder than ever in spite of the bitter experience of the past. Since the campaign of 1711 there had been several attempts to ascend the mighty river. Wolfe reported the Navy's "thorough aversion" to the task. It was indeed, hazardous. But it was to be backed by a renewed advance up the Hudson against the French fort of Niagara on the Great Lakes, the importance of which Pitt had emphasised in his instructions.

The plan succeeded. The year 1759 brought fame to British arms throughout the world. In May the Navy captured Guadeloupe, the richest sugar island of the West Indies. In July Amherst took Ticonderoga and Fort Niagara, thus gaining for the American colonies a frontier upon the Great Lakes. In September the expedition up the St Lawrence attacked Quebec. Wolfe conducted a personal reconnaissance of the river at night, and beguiled the officers by reciting Gray's "Elegy": "The paths of glory lead but to the grave." By brilliant co-operation between Army and Navy Wolfe landed his men, and led them by the unsuspected path, under cover of darkness, up the steep cliffs of the Heights of Abraham. In the battle that followed Montcalm was defeated and killed and the key fortress of Canada was secured. Wolfe, mortally wounded, lived until victory was certain, and died murmuring, "Now God be praised, I will die in peace."

But it needed another year's fighting to gain Canada for the English-speaking world. In May 1760 the British garrison in Quebec was relieved after a winter siege. With cautious and dogged organisation Amherst converged on Montreal. In September the city fell and the huge province of French Canada changed hands. Pitt had not only won Canada, with its rich fisheries and Indian trade, but had banished for ever the dream and danger of a French colonial empire stretching from Montreal to New Orleans. Little could he know that the extinction of the French menace would lead to the final secession of the English colonies from the British Empire.

Pitt's very success contributed to his fall. Just as Marlborough and Godolphin had been faced by a growing war-weariness after Malplaquet, so now Pitt, an isolated figure in his own Government, confronted an increasing dislike of the war after the great victories of 1759. To the people at large he was the "Great Commoner". This lonely, dictatorial man had caught their imagination. He had broken through the narrow circle of aristocratic politics, and his force and eloquence gained him their support. Contrary to the conventions of the age, he had used the House of Commons as a platform from which to address the country. His studied orations in severe classical style were intended for a wider audience than the place-holders of the Duke of Newcastle. Pitt had a contempt for party and party organisations. His career was an appeal to the individual in politics. His vast powers of work and concentration tired all who came in contact with him. Afflicted early in life with severe gout, he had to struggle with ill-health through the worst anxieties of war government. He hardly troubled to see his colleagues. All business was conducted from his office, except for weekly meetings with Newcastle and the Treasury Secretary to arrange the finances of his strategy, money and troops for Wolfe and Clive, subsidies for Frederick the Great. But his power was transient. There were not only enemies within the Government, stung by his arrogance and his secrecy, but also among his former political allies, the Princess of Wales and her circle at Leicester House. Here the young heir to the throne was being brought up amid the Opposition views of his mother and her confidant, the Earl of Bute. Pitt had been their chosen candidate for the sunshine days when the old King should die. They now deemed him a deserter. They branded his acceptance of office in 1746 as a betrayal. Bute, with his close position at this future Court, was the most dangerous of Pitt's opponents, and it was he who stimulated opinion and the Press against the war policy of the Minister.

Pitt's position was indeed perilous. It seemed as if Britain had achieved everything she desired. All that was left was the unpopular commitment to Prussia, and Bute found it only too easy to convert the feelings of weariness into an effective opposition to Pitt. The war had to be paid for. It was in vain that Pitt attempted to show that no lasting or satisfactory peace could be secured till France was defeated in Europe.

In October 1760 George II died. George III had very clear ideas of what he wanted and where he was going. He meant to be King, such a King as all his countrymen would follow and revere. Under the long Whig régime the House of Commons had become an irresponsible autocracy. Would not the liberties of the country be safer in the hands of a monarch, young, honourable, virtuous, and appearing thoroughly English, than in a faction governing the land through a packed and corrupt House of Commons? But in such a monarchy what was the place of a man like Pitt, who owed nothing to corruption, nothing to the Crown, and everything to the people and to his personal domination of the House of Commons? His profound reverence for the person and office of George II could not conceal from either of them the fact that Pitt was a very great man and the King a very limited man. Bute, "the Minister behind the curtain", was now all-powerful at Court. Newcastle, who had long chafed under the harsh, domineering ways of his colleague, was only too ready to intrigue against him. There was talk of peace. Negotiations were opened at The Hague, but broke down when Pitt refused to desert Prussia. The French War Minister, Choiseul, like Torcy fifty years before, saw his chance. He realised that Pitt's power was slipping. In 1761 he made a close alliance with Spain, and in September the negotiations with England collapsed. With the power of Spain behind her in the Americas, France might now regain her dominance in the New World.

Pitt hoped that war with Spain would rouse the same popular upsurge as in 1739. The chance of capturing more Spanish colonies might appeal to the City. His proposal for the declaration of war was put to the Cabinet. He found himself isolated. He had no choice but resignation.

William Pitt ranks with Marlborough as the greatest English man in the century between 1689 and 1789. He was not the first English statesman to think in terms of a world policy and to broaden on to a world scale the political conceptions of William III. But he is the first great figure of British Imperialism. Pitt too had brought the force of public opinion to bear upon politics, weakening the narrow monopoly of the great Whig houses. His heroic period was now over.

Unsupported by the fame of Pitt, the Duke of Newcastle was an easy victim, and the administration slid easily into the hands of Lord Bute. His sole qualification for office, apart from great wealth and his command of the Scottish vote, was that he had been Groom of the Stole to the King's mother. For the first time since the assassination of the Duke of Buckingham the government of England was committed to a man with no political experience.

Within three months of Pitt's resignation the Government were compelled to declare war on Spain. This led to further successes in the West Indies and elsewhere. The British Fleet seized the port of Havana, which commanded the trade routes of the Spanish Main and the movement of the Treasure Fleets. In the Pacific Ocean an expedition from Madras descended upon the Philippines and captured Manila. At sea and on land England was mistress of the outer world. These achievements were largely cast away.

Fifty years after the Treaty of Utrecht Britain signed a new peace with France. Bute sent the Duke of Bedford to Paris to negotiate its terms. The Duke thought his country was taking too much of the globe and would be in perpetual danger from European coalitions and attacks by dissatisfied nations. He believed in the appeasement of France and Spain and the generous return of conquests. Pitt, on the other hand, demanded the decisive weakening of the enemy. To his mind there would be no secure or permanent peace until France and Spain were placed at a lasting disadvantage. He could take no part in the negotiations, and he vehemently denounced the treaty as undermining the safety of the realm.

Britain's acquisitions under the terms of the Peace of Paris in 1763 were nevertheless considerable. In America she secured Canada, Nova Scotia, Cape Breton, and the adjoining islands, and the right to navigate the Mississippi, important for Red Indian trade. In the West Indies Grenada, St Vincent, Dominica, and Tobago were acquired. From Spain she received Florida. In Africa she kept Senegal. In India, as will be related, the East India Company preserved its extensive conquests, and although their trading posts were returned the political ambitions of the French in the sub-continent were finally extinguished. In Europe Minorca was restored to England, and the fortifications of Dunkirk were at long last demolished.

Historians have taken a flattering view of a treaty which established Britain as an Imperial Power, but its strategic weakness has been smoothly overlooked. It was a perfect exposition of the principles of the Duke of Bedford. The naval power of France had been left untouched. In America she received back the islands of St Pierre and Miquelon, in the Gulf of the St Lawrence, with the right to fish upon the shores of Newfoundland. These were the nursery of the French Navy, in which about fourteen thousand men were permanently employed. Their commercial value was nearly half a million pounds a year. They might form naval bases or centres for smuggling French goods into Canada. In the West Indies the richest prize of the war, the sugar island of Guadeloupe, was also handed back, together with Martinique, Belle Isle, and St Lucia. Guadeloupe was so rich that the English Government even considered keeping it and in exchange returning Canada to the French. These islands were also excellent naval bases for future use against England.

Spain regained the West Indian port of Havana, which controlled the maritime strategy of the Caribbean. She also received back Manila, an important centre for the China trade. If the English had retained them the fleets of France and Spain would have been permanently at their mercy. In Africa, in spite of Pitt's protests, France got back Goree – a base for privateers on the flank of the East Indian trade routes. Moreover, the treaty took no account of the interests of Frederick the Great. This ally was left to shift for himself. He never forgave Britain for what he regarded as a betrayal, which rankled long afterwards in the minds of Prussian leaders.

CHAPTER THIRTY-NINE

THE QUARREL WITH AMERICA

The King's Friends — the reign of Bute — the Junius letters — the North Briton — Wilkes sent to the Tower — the conflict with America — the Stamp Act — Rockingham and Burke — the Liberty affair — the biddable Lord North — the Boston "massacre" — the American Patriots — the Boston Tea Party — the Coercion Acts — the Declaration of Rights — Paul Revere's Ride — Concord and Lexington

G EORGE III was, or thought he was, an Englishman born and bred. At any rate he tried to be. He had received a careful education in England from his mother and from the Earl of Bute, who was a Scotsman and in his opponents' eyes a Tory. At first all promised well. The large Tory-minded section of the "Country Party" was at last reconciled to the monarchy, and they rallied to him and to themselves all those elements in the nation which hated the narrow aristocratic domination of the Whig families. George III was thus supported by many "King's Friends", loyal, hungry for power, and eager to help him "turn out the old gang". This he and Bute proceeded to do. In 1761 elections were held throughout England, in which Newcastle was not allowed to control all the royal patronage and many offices in the gift of the Crown were bestowed on supporters of the new monarch. In March Bute was appointed Secretary of State, and Newcastle was shuffled querulously out of office in the following spring. Within two years of his accession the "King's Friends" predominated in the House of Commons. They were not a political party in the modern sense, but they were generally prepared to support almost any administration appointed by the King. The Crown was once more a factor in politics, and young George had beaten the Whigs at their own game.

The first decade of his reign passed in continual and confused manoeuvring between the different Parliamentary groups, some of them accepting the new situation, some making passive resistance to the new tactics of the Crown. George was angry and puzzled at the wrangling of the political leaders. Pitt sat moodily in Parliament, "unconnected and unconsulted". Many people shared Dr Johnson's opinion of the Scots, and Bute, who was much disliked, fell from power early in 1763. His successor, George Grenville, was a mulish lawyer, backed by the enormous electoral power of the Duke of Bedford, of whom "Junius" wrote in his anonymous letters, "I daresay he has bought and sold more than half the representative integrity of the nation."[1] Grenville refused to play the part of "the Minister behind the curtain"; but for two years he clung to office, and must bear a heavy share of responsibility for the alienation of the American colonies.

There were other conflicts. On April 23, 1763, a newspaper called *The North Briton* attacked Ministers as "tools of despotism and corruption. ... They have sent the spirit of discord through the land, and I will prophesy it will never be extinguished but by the extinction of their power." Grenville's Ministry was denounced as a mere reflection of the unpopular Lord Bute. The writer hinted that the peace treaty with France was not only dishonourably but also dishonestly negotiated, and that the King was a party to it. George was incensed. A week later his Secretary of State issued a warrant commanding that the authors, printers, and publishers of "*The North Briton*, No. 45", none of whom was named, should be found and arrested. Searches were made, houses were entered, papers were seized, and nearly fifty suspects were put in prison. Among them was John Wilkes, a rake and a Member of Parliament. He was sent to the Tower. He refused to answer questions. He protested that the warrant was illegal and claimed Parliamentary privilege against the arrest. There was a storm in the country. The legality of "general" warrants which named no actual offender became a constitutional question of the first importance. Wilkes was charged with seditious libel and outlawed. But his case became a national issue when he returned to fight his Parliamentary seat. The radical-minded Londoners welcomed this rebuff to the Government, and in March 1768 he was elected for Middlesex. The next February he was expelled from the House of Commons and there was a by-election. Wilkes stood again, and obtained 1,143 votes against his Government opponent, who polled 296. There were bonfires in London. The election was declared void by Parliament, and Wilkes, now once more in prison for printing an obscene parody of Pope's "Essay on Man", entitled "Essay on Woman", became the idol of the City. Finally his opponent in Middlesex was declared duly elected. When Wilkes was released from gaol in April 1770 London was illuminated to greet him. After a long struggle he was elected Lord Mayor, and again a Member of Parliament.

The whole machinery of eighteenth-century corruption was thus exposed to the public eye. By refusing to accept Wilkes the Commons had denied the right of electors to choose their Members and held themselves out as a closed corporation of privileged beings. Wilkes's cause now found the most powerful champion in England. Pitt himself, now Earl of Chatham, in blistering tones attacked the legality of general warrants and the corruption of politics. His

---

[1] Junius was a mystery political essayist whose tracts were published in *The Public Advertiser* between 1769 and 1771. The editor, Henry Sampson Woodfall, was accused of libel for having printed a Junius letter attacking the King. The jury's verdict was "guilty of publishing only". The most likely Junius was the civil servant and politician Sir Philip Francis (1740–1818), but no one knows for sure.

speeches were indeed the first demands for Parliamentary reform in the eighteenth century.

Nevertheless the outcry against general warrants led directly to important pronouncements by the judges on the liberty of the individual, the powers of the Government, and freedom of speech. Wilkes and the other victims sued the officials who had executed the warrants. The judges ruled that the warrants were illegal. The officials pleaded that they were immune because they were acting under Government powers. This large and sinister defence was rejected by the Chief justice in words which remain a classic statement on the rule of law. "With respect to the argument of State necessity," declared Lord Camden, "or a distinction which has been aimed at between State offences and others, the Common Law does not understand that kind of reasoning, nor do our books take notice of any such distinction." If a Minister of the Crown ordered something to be done which was unlawful, then both he and his servants must answer for it in the ordinary courts of law in exactly the same way as a private person. The Under-Secretary who entered Wilkes's house and took away his papers and the King's Messengers who arrested the printer were mere trespassers and were liable as such. They were guilty of false imprisonment, and the judges refused to interfere when juries awarded large sums by way of compensation. Wilkes obtained £4,000 damages from the Secretary of State himself.

Here indeed was a potent weapon against overbearing Ministers and zealous officials. *Habeas corpus* might, and did, protect the subject from unlawful arrest, or at any rate ensure his speedy release from gaol, but a civil action for false imprisonment hit the authorities where it hurt most, in their private pockets, and the unfettered right of juries to assess the damages at whatever figure they thought fit was a formidable deterrent to such as might be tempted to offend public opinion by relying on "reasons of State". Not until the world wars of the twentieth century was the mere word of a Minister of the Crown enough to legalise the imprisonment of an Englishman.

Freedom of the Press and freedom of speech developed by much the same unspectacular, technical, but effective steps. Long before George I had mounted the throne Parliament declined to renew the Licensing Act. The last relics of the censorship once exercised by the Court of Star Chamber thereby disappeared. But this is not enough if feelings run high, as they did in eighteenth-century politics, when critics of the Government were apt to be put in the dock for seditious libel, and a better safeguard was finally established in the powers of the jury. Through many years and in many trials it was hotly argued that the jury should decide not only whether or not the defendant had published the matter complained of, but also whether or not it was a libel, and Fox's Libel Act eventually established this opinion as law. The letter of the law was thus subjected in each case to the discretion of a jury, and in the last year of the eighteenth century it could be said that "a man may publish anything which twelve of his countrymen think is not blameable". History will not deny some share in the credit for this achievement to John Wilkes.

The contest with America had meanwhile begun to dominate the British political scene. Vast territories had fallen to the Crown on the conclusion of the Seven Years War. From the Canadian border to the Gulf of Mexico the entire hinterland of the American colonies became British soil, and the parcelling out of these new lands led to further trouble with the colonists. Many of them, like George Washington, had formed companies to buy these frontier tracts from the Indians, but a royal proclamation restrained any purchasing and prohibited their settlement. Washington, among others, ignored the ban and wrote to his land agent ordering him "to secure some of the most valuable lands in the King's part [on the Ohio], which I think may be accomplished after a while, notwithstanding the proclamation that restrains it at present, and prohibits the settling of them at all; *for I can never look upon that proclamation in any other light (but this I say between ourselves) than as a temporary expedient to quiet the winds of the Indians.*"[1] This attempt by the British Government to regulate the new lands caused much discontent among the planters, particularly in the Middle and Southern colonies.

George III was also determined that the colonies should pay their share in the expenses of the Empire and in garrisoning the New World. For this there were strong arguments. England had supplied most of the men and the money in the struggle with France for their protection, and indeed their survival; but the methods used by the British Government were ineffective and imprudent. It was resolved to impose a tax on the colonies' imports, and in 1764 Parliament strengthened the Molasses Act. This measure was originally passed in 1733 to protect the West Indian sugar-growers. It created a West Indian monopoly of the sugar trade within the Empire and imposed a heavy duty on foreign imports. It had long been evaded by the colonists, whose only means of acquiring hard cash to pay their English creditors was by selling their goods for molasses in the French and Spanish West Indies. The new regulations were a serious blow.

The results were unsatisfactory on both sides of the Atlantic. The British Government found that the taxes brought in very little money, and the English merchants, already concerned at the plight of their American debtors, had no desire to make colonial finance any more unstable. Indirect taxation of trade being so unfruitful, Grenville and his lieutenant Charles Townshend consulted the Law Officers about levying a direct tax on the colonies. Their opinion was favourable, and Grenville proposed that all colonial legal documents should be stamped, for a fee. The colonial agents in London were informed, and discussed the plan by post with the Assemblies in America. There were no protests, although the colonists had always objected to direct taxation, and in 1765 Parliament passed the Stamp Act.

With two exceptions it imposed no heavy burden. The stamps on legal documents would not in any case produce a large revenue. The English stamp duty brought in £300,000 a year. Its extension to America was only expected

1   Churchill's italics.

to raise another £50,000. But the Act included a tax on newspapers, many of whose journalists were vehement partisans of the extremist party in America, and the colonial merchants were dismayed because the duty had to be paid in bullion already needed for meeting the adverse trade balance with England. The dispute exposed and fortified the more violent elements in America, and gave them a chance to experiment in organised resistance. The future revolutionary leaders appeared from obscurity – Patrick Henry in Virginia, Samuel Adams in Massachusetts, and Christopher Gadsden in South Carolina – and attacked both the legality of the Government's policy and the meekness of most American merchants. A small but well organised Radical element began to emerge. But although there was an outcry and protesting delegates convened a Stamp Act Congress there was no unity of opinion in America.

The personality of George III was now exercising a preponderant influence upon events. He was one of the most conscientious sovereigns who ever sat upon the English throne. Simple in his tastes and unpretentious in manner, he had the superficial appearance of a typical yeoman. But his mind was Hanoverian, with an infinite capacity for mastering detail, and limited success in dealing with large issues and main principles. He possessed great moral courage and an inveterate obstinacy, and his stubbornness lent weight to the stiffening attitude of his Government. His responsibility for the final breach is a high one. He could not understand those who feared the consequences of a policy of coercion. He expressed himself in blunt terms. "It is with the utmost astonishment that I find any of my subjects capable of encouraging the rebellious disposition which unhappily exists in some of my colonies in America. Having entire confidence in the wisdom of my Parliament, the Great Council of the Nation, I will steadily pursue those measures which they have recommended for the support of the constitutional rights of Great Britain and the protection of the commercial interests of my kingdom."

But now, writhing under the domination of Grenville and his friends, alarmed at the growing disorder and disaffection of the country, aware at last of his folly in alienating the Whig families, the King sought a reconciliation. In July 1765 the Marquis of Rockingham, a shy, well-meaning Whig who was disturbed at George's conduct, undertook to form a Government, and brought with him as private secretary a young Irishman named Edmund Burke, already known in literary circles as a clever writer and a brilliant talker. He was much more. He was a great political thinker. Viewing English politics and the English character with something of the detachment of an alien he was able to diagnose the situation with an imaginative insight beyond the range of those immersed in the business of the day and bound by traditional habits of mind.

The political history of the years following 1714 had led to a degeneration and dissolution of parties. The personal activity of the sovereign after 1760 and the emergence of great issues of principle found the Whigs helpless and divided into rival clans. The King's tactics had paralysed them. Burke's aim was to create out of the Rockingham group, high-principled but small in numbers and with no original ideas of its own, an effective political party.[1] He could supply the ideas, but first he had to convince the Whigs that a party could be formed and held together on a ground of common principles. He had to overcome the notion, widely prevalent, that party was in itself a rather disreputable thing, a notion which had been strengthened by Pitt's haughty disdain for party business and organisation. It was an old tradition that politicians not in power need not bother to attend Parliament, but should retire to their country estates and there await the return to royal favour and a redistribution of the sweets of office. Individualists of different schools, such as Shelburne and Henry Fox, consistently opposed Burke's efforts to organise them into a party. "You think", Henry Fox had written to Rockingham, "you can but serve the country by continuing a fruitless Opposition. I think it impossible to serve it at all except by coming into office."

A consistent programme to be advocated in Opposition and realised in office, was Burke's conception of party policy, and the new issues arising plainly required a programme. On Ireland, on America, on India, Burke's attitude was definite. He stood, and he brought his party to stand, for conciliation of the colonies, relaxation of the restraints on Irish trade, and the government of India on the same moral basis as the government of England. At home he proposed to deliver Parliament from its subservience to the Crown by the abolition of numerous sinecures and the limitation of corruption. What he lacked was, in his own words, "the power and purchase" which a strong and well organised party could supply. For years Burke was a voice crying in the wilderness, and, too often rising to tones of frenzy. An orator to be named with the ancients, an incomparable political reasoner, he lacked both judgment and self-control. He was perhaps the greatest man that Ireland has produced. The same gifts, with a dash of English indolence and irony – he could have borrowed them from Charles James Fox, Henry Fox's famous son, who had plenty of both to spare – might have made him Britain's greatest statesman.

Rockingham's Government, which lasted thirteen months, passed three measures that went far to soothe the animosities raised by Grenville on both sides of the Atlantic. They repealed the Stamp Act, and induced the House of Commons to declare general warrants and the seizure of private papers unlawful. At the same time they reaffirmed the powers of Parliament to tax the colonies in a so-called Declaratory Act. But the King was determined to be rid of them, and Pitt, whose mind was clouded by sickness, was seduced by

1   Edmund Burke (1729–97) is often seen as one of the two political thinkers most followed by modern Conservatives when that Party wishes to return to its basic beliefs. The other is Disraeli, but unlike him, Burke offered solutions, not just answers, to the questions he posed. Burke believed in constitutional monarchy and government, but that within that framework, there should be considerable freedom of choice and expression. His thoughts on ridding government of bureaucratic waste and on "less government" would not be out of place in a modern manifesto. For much of the following century Burke's writings cast what Conor Cruise O'Brien called "a long shadow" over British and European political thought. Perhaps Burke's greatest talent was to set people thinking in unconventional directions.

royal flattery and by his own dislike of party into lending his name to a new administration formed on no political principle whatever. His arrogance remained; his powers were failing; his popularity as the "Great Commoner" had been dimmed by his sudden acceptance of the Earldom of Chatham. The conduct of affairs slipped into other hands: Charles Townshend, the Duke of Grafton, and Lord Shelburne. In 1767 Townshend, against the opposition of Shelburne, introduced a Bill imposing duties on American imports of paper, glass, lead, and tea. There was rage in America. The supply of coin in the colonies would be still more depleted, and any surplus from the new revenue was not, as originally stated, to be used for the upkeep of the British garrisons but to pay British colonial officials. This threatened to make them independent of the colonial assemblies, whose chief weapon against truculent governors had been to withhold their salaries. Even so, revolt was still far from their minds.

Intelligent men, like Governor Hutchinson of Massachusetts, preferred not to at all if they could not be enforced, and declared that another repeal would only "facilitate the designs of those persons who appear to be aiming at independency". The Massachusetts Assembly accordingly proposed a joint petition with the other colonial bodies against the new duties. In May 1768 the sloop *Liberty*, belonging to John Hancock, the most prominent Boston merchant, was stopped and searched near the coast by Royal Customs officers. The colonists rescued it by force. By 1769 British exports to America had fallen by one-half. The Cabinet was not seriously apprehensive, but perturbed. It agreed to drop the duties, except on tea. By a majority of one this was carried.

All the signs of a dissolution of the Empire were there for those who could read them. But George III, after twelve years' intrigue, had at last got a docile, biddable Prime Minister. Lord North became First Lord of the Treasury in 1770. A charming man, of good abilities and faultless temper, he presided over the loss of the American colonies. At first all seemed quiet. The American merchants were delighted at the repeal of the import duties, and by the middle of 1770 reconciliation seemed complete, except in Boston. Here Samuel Adams, fertile organiser of resistance and advocate of separation, saw that the struggle was now reaching a crucial stage. Hitherto the quarrel had been at bottom a commercial dispute, and neither the American merchants nor the English Ministers had any sympathy for his ideas. Adams feared that the resistance of the colonies would crumble and the British would reassert their authority unless more trouble was stirred up. This he and other Radical leaders proceeded to do.

News that the duties were withdrawn had hardly reached America when the first blood was shed. Most of the British garrison was stationed in Boston. The troops were unpopular with the townsfolk, and Adams spread evil rumours of their conduct. The "lobsters" in their scarlet coats were insulted and jeered at wherever they appeared. In March 1770 the persistent snowballing by Boston urchins of English sentries outside the barracks caused a riot. In the confusion and shouting some of the troops opened fire and there were casualties. This "massacre" was just the sort of incident that Adams had hoped for. But moderate men of property were nervous, and opinion in the colonies remained disunited and uncertain. The Radicals persisted. In June 1772 rioters burned a British Revenue cutter, H.M.S. *Gaspee*, off Rhode Island. "Committees of Correspondence" were set up throughout Massachusetts, and by the end of the year had spread to seventy-five towns. The Virginian agitators, led by the young Patrick Henry, created a standing committee of their Assembly to keep in touch with the other colonies, and a chain of such bodies was quickly formed. Thus the machinery of revolt was quietly and efficiently created.

Nevertheless the Radicals were still in a minority and there was much opposition to an abrupt break with England. Benjamin Franklin, one of the leading colonial representatives in London, wrote as late as 1773: "There seem to be among us some violent spirits who are for an immediate rupture; but I trust that the general prudence of our country will see that by our growing strength we advance fast to a situation in which our claims must be allowed, that by a premature struggle we may be crippled and kept down, ... that between governed and governing every mistake in government, every encroachment on right, is not worth a rebellion, ... remembering withal that this Protestant country (our mother, though lately an unkind one) is worth preserving, and that her weight in the scales of Europe and her safety in a great degree may depend on our union with her." In spite of the Boston "massacre", the violence on the high seas, and the commercial squabbles, the agitations of Adams and his friends were beginning to peter out, when Lord North committed a fatal blunder.

The East India Company was nearly bankrupt, and the Government had been forced to come to its rescue. An Act was passed through Parliament, attracting little notice among the Members, authorising the company to ship tea, of which it had an enormous surplus, direct to the colonies, without paying import duties, and to sell it through its own agents in America. Thus in effect the company was granted a monopoly. The outcry across the Atlantic was instantaneous. The extremists denounced it as in invasion of their liberties, and the merchants were threatened with ruin. American shippers who brought tea from the British customs-houses and their middle-men who sold it would all be thrown out of business. The Act succeeded where Adams had failed: it united colonial opinion against the British.

The Radicals, who began to call themselves "Patriots", seized their opportunity to force a crisis. In December 1773 the first cargoes arrived in Boston. Rioters disguised as Red Indians boarded the ships and destroyed the cases. "Last night", wrote John Adams, Samuel's cousin, and later the second President of the United States, "three cargoes of Bohea tea were emptied into the sea. ... This is the most magnificent movement of all. There is a dignity, a majesty and sublimity in this last effort of the Patriots that I greatly admire. This destruction of the tea is so bold, so daring, so firm, intrepid, and inflexible, and it must have so important consequences, and so lasting, that I cannot but consider it as an epoch in history. This, however, is but an attack upon property. Another similar exertion of popular power may produce the destruction of lives. Many persons wish that as many dead carcases were floating in the harbour as there are chests of tea. A much less number of lives, however, would remove the causes of all our calamities."

When the news reached London the cry went up for coercion and the reactionaries in the British Government became supreme. In vain Burke and Chatham pleaded for conciliation. Parliament passed a series of "Coercion Acts" which suspended the Massachusetts Assembly, declared the colony to be in Crown hands, closed the port of Boston, and decreed that all judges in the colony were henceforth to be appointed by the Crown. These measures were confined to Massachusetts; only one of them, the Quartering Act, applied to the rest of the colonies, and this declared that troops were to be quartered throughout all of them to preserve order. Thus it was hoped to isolate the resistance. It had the opposite effect.

In September 1774 the colonial assemblies held a congress at Philadelphia. The extremists were not yet out of hand, and the delegates still concentrated on commercial boycotts. An association was formed to stop all trade with England unless the Coercion Acts were repealed, and the Committees of Correspondence were charged with carrying out the plan. A Declaration of Rights demanded the rescinding of some thirteen commercial Acts passed by the British Parliament since 1763. The tone of this document, which was dispatched to London, was one of respectful moderation. But in London all moderation was cast aside. The "sugar interest" in the House of Commons, jealous of colonial competition in the West Indies; Army officers who despised the colonial troops; the Government, pressed for money and blinded by the doctrine that colonies only existed for the benefit of the Mother Country: all combined to extinguish the last hope of peace. The petition was rejected with contempt.

Events now moved swiftly. The Massachusetts Military Governor, General Thomas Gage, tried to enforce martial law, but the task was beyond him. Gage was an able soldier, but he had only four thousand troops and could hold no place outside Boston. The Patriots had about ten thousand men in the colonial militia. In October they set up a "Committee of Safety", and most of the colonies started drilling and arming. Collection of military equipment and powder began. Cannon were seized from Government establishments. Agents were sent to Europe to buy weapons. Both France and Spain refused the British Government's request to prohibit the sale of gunpowder to the Americans, and Dutch merchants shipped it in large glass bottles labelled "Spirits".

The Patriots began accumulating these warlike stores at Concord, a village twenty miles from Boston, where the Massachusetts Assembly, which Parliament had declared illegal, was now in session. Gage decided to seize their ammunition and arrest Samuel Adams and his colleague John Hancock. But the colonists were on the alert. Every night they patrolled the streets of

Boston watching for any move by the English troops. As Gage gathered his men messengers warned the assembly at Concord. The military supplies were scattered among towns farther north and Adams and Hancock moved to Lexington. On April 18, 1775, eight hundred British troops set off in darkness along the Concord road. But the secret was out. One of the patrols, Paul Revere, from his post in the steeple of the North Church, warned messengers by lantern signals. He himself mounted his horse and rode hard to Lexington, rousing Adams and Hancock from their beds and urging them to fight.

At five o'clock in the morning the local militia of Lexington, seventy strong, formed up on the village green. As the sun rose the head of the British column, with three officers riding in front, came into view. The leading officer, brandishing his sword, shouted, "Disperse, you rebels, immediately!" The militia commander ordered his men to disperse. The colonial committees were very anxious not to fire the first shot, and there were strict orders not to provoke open conflict with the British regulars. But in the confusion someone fired. A volley was returned. The ranks of the militia were thinned and there was a general *mêlée*. Brushing aside the survivors, the British column marched on to Concord. But now the countryside was up in arms and the bulk of the stores had been moved to safety. It was with difficulty that the British straggled back to Boston, with the enemy close at their heels. The town was cut off from the mainland. The news of Lexington and Concord spread to the other colonies, and Governors and British officials were expelled. With strategic insight forts on Lake George, at the head of the Hudson valley, were seized by a Patriot force under Benedict Arnold, a merchant from Connecticut. The British were thus denied any help from Canada, and the War of Independence had begun.[1]

---

1 The main events of the War of American Independence may be summarised as follows:
   1775: war breaks out at Lexington and Concord.
   July 4, 1776: Declaration of Independence.
   1776: General Howe defeats Washington at White Plains.
   1777: British surrender at Saratoga.
   1778: Benjamin Franklin signs agreement with France, which joins war on America's side.
   1778: Pitt's last speech to Parliament attacking government policy in the war (Pitt died shortly after this speech).
   1781: British under Cornwallis surrender at Yorktown, thus ending the military campaign.
   1783: Britain recognises American independence by the Treaty of Versailles.

CHAPTER FORTY

THE INDIAN EMPIRE

Rockingham becomes Prime Minister – the Government and the East
India Company – the English in India – rivalry with the French
Compagnie des Indes – Madras attacked – the emergence of Robert
Clive – the Black Hole of Calcutta – the Battle of Plassey – tales of
corruption – Clive as Governor of Bengal – Clive's fall from favour and
suicide – Warren Hastings – the new aristocracy in India

WHEN THE news of the surrender at Yorktown was brought to
Lord North his amiable composure slid from him. He paced
his room, exclaiming in agonised tones, "Oh, God, it is all
over!" The Opposition gathered strongly in the Commons.
There were riotous meetings in London. The Government majority collapsed
on a motion censuring the administration of the Navy. An address to stop the
American war was rejected by a single vote. In March North informed the
Commons that he would resign. "At last the fatal day has come," wrote the
King. North maintained his dignity to the last. After twelve years of service he
left the House of Commons a beaten man. As the Members stood waiting in
the rain for their carriages on that March evening in 1782 they saw North come
down the steps and get into his own vehicle, which had been forewarned and
was waiting at the head of the line. With a courtly bow to the drenched and
hostile Members crowding round him he said, "That, gentlemen, is the
advantage of being in the secret," and drove quickly away. King George, in
the agony of personal defeat, showed greater passion. He talked of abdication
and retiring to Hanover. The violent feeling in the country denied him all
hope of holding a successful election. He was forced to come to terms with the
Opposition. Through the long years of the American war Rockingham and
Burke had waited in patience for the collapse of North's administration. Now
their chance had come. Rockingham made his terms with the King: independence for the colonies and some lessening of the Crown's influence in politics.
George III was forced to accept, and Rockingham took office in March 1782 –
he had but four months to live. It fell to him and his colleague, Lord
Shelburne, to save what they could from the wreckage of the First British
Empire. The first task for this, and the administration which followed, was to
rearrange the understanding between the Government and the powerful East
India Company.

The eighteenth century saw a revolutionary change in the British position in India. The English East India Company, founded simply as a trading venture, grew with increasing speed into a vast territorial Empire. About the year 1700 probably no more than fifteen hundred English people dwelt in India, including wives, children, and transient seamen. The great Empire of the Moguls was disintegrating. For two centuries these Moslem descendants of Tamburlaine had gripped and pacified a portion of the world half as large as the present United States. Early in the eighteenth century this formidable dynasty was shaken by a disputed succession. Invaders from the North soon poured across the frontiers. Delhi was sacked by the Shah of Persia. The Viceroys of the Moguls revolted and laid claim to the sovereignty of the Imperial provinces. Pretenders rose up to challenge the usurpers. In Central India the fierce fighting tribes of the Mahrattas, bound in a loose confederacy, saw and seized their chance to loot and to raid. The country was swept by anarchy and bloodshed.

Hitherto European traders in India, English, French, Portuguese, and Dutch, had plied their wares in rivalry, but so long as "the Great Mogul" ruled in Delhi they had competed in comparative peace and safety. The English East India Company had grown into a solid affair, with a capital of over a million and a quarter pounds and an annual dividend of 9 per cent. The population of Bombay, which Charles II had leased to the Company for ten pounds a year in 1668, had multiplied more than sixfold and exceeded sixty thousand souls. Madras, founded and fortified by the British in 1640, was the chief trading centre on the eastern coast. Calcutta, uninhabited till the servants of the corporation built a factory on the banks of the Hoogli River in 1686, had become a flourishing and peaceful emporium. The French *Compagnie des Indes*, centred at Pondicherry, had also prospered, though, unlike its British rival, it was in effect a Department of State and not a private concern. Both organisations had the same object, the promotion of commerce and the gaining of financial profit. The acquisition of territory played little part in the thoughts and plans of either nation. About 1740 events forced them to change their tune. The Mahrattas slaughtered the Nawab, or Imperial Governor, of the Carnatic, the five-hundred-mile-long province on the south-eastern coast. They threatened Madras and Bombay, and raided the depths of Bengal. It was becoming impossible for the European traders to stand aside. They must either fight on their own or in alliance with Indian rulers or quit. Most of the Dutch had already withdrawn to the rich archipelago of the East Indies; the Portuguese had long since fallen behind in the race; the French and English resolved to stay.

As has so often happened in the great crises of her history, France produced a man. Joseph Dupleix, Governor of Pondicherry since 1742, had long foreseen the coming struggle with Britain. He perceived that India awaited a new ruler. The Mogul Empire was at an end, and a Mahratta Empire seemed unlikely to replace it. Why then should not France seize this glittering, fertile prize? When the War of the Austrian Succession broke out in Europe Dupleix acted with decision. He appealed to the new Nawab of the Carnatic to forbid hostilities within his jurisdiction, where most of the French stations lay. This granted, he proceeded to attack Madras. Its English Governor asked the Nawab to enforce a similar neutrality on the French, but omitted to accompany his request with a suitable bribe. Dupleix, on the other hand, promised to hand over the city once it was captured. Thus reassured, the Nawab stood aside, and after a five-day bombardment the town surrendered on September 10, 1746. Some of its British defenders escaped to the near-by Fort St David. Among them was a young clerk of twenty-one, named Robert Clive.

Dupleix, victorious, refused to surrender Madras to the Nawab and spent the rest of the year repelling his attacks. He then assaulted Fort St David, but news arrived that the war in Europe had ceased and that the peace treaty of Aix-la-Chapelle prescribed that Madras was to be returned to the British in return for the cession of Louisburg, in Nova Scotia, to France. Thus ended a dismal and inglorious opening to the great struggle in India.

Clive had watched these events with anger and alarm, but hitherto there had been few signs in his career to mark him as the man who would reverse his country's fortunes and found the rule of the British in India. He was the son of a small squire, and his boyhood had been variegated and unpromising. Clive had attended no fewer than four schools, and been unsuccessful at all. In his Shropshire market town he had organised and led a gang of adolescent ruffians who extorted pennies and apples from tradesmen in return for not breaking their windows. At the age of eighteen he was sent abroad as a junior clerk in the East India Company at a salary of five pounds a year and forty pounds expenses. He was a difficult and unpromising subordinate. He detested the routine and the atmosphere of the counting-house. Twice, it is said, he attempted suicide, and twice the pistol misfired. Not until he had obtained a military commission and served some years in the armed forces of the Company did he reveal a military genius unequalled in the British history of India. The siege of Madras and the defence of Fort St David had given him a taste for fighting. In 1748 a new upheaval gave him the chance of leadership.

Indian pretenders seized the Mogul viceroyalty of the Deccan and conquered the Carnatic. With a few French soldiers and a couple of thousand Indian troops Dupleix expelled them and placed his own puppets on the throne. The British candidate, Mahomet Ali, was chased into Trichinopoly and fiercely besieged. At a stroke France had become master of Southern India. The next blow would obviously be against the English. Here was the end of any hope of peaceful trading, or of what would nowadays be called non-intervention in Indian affairs, and it became evident that the East India Company must either fight or die. Clive obtained a commission. He made his way to Trichinopoly, and saw for himself that Mahomet Ali was in desperate peril. If he could be rescued and placed on the throne all might be well. But how to do it? Trichinopoly was beset by a combined French and Indian army of vast numbers. The English had very few soldiers, and were so ill-prepared and so short of officers that Clive, still only twenty-five, was given the chief military command. The direct relief of Trichinopoly was impossible, and Clive at once perceived that his blow must be struck elsewhere. Arcot, capital of the Carnatic, had been stripped of troops; most of them were at Trichinopoly besieging Mahomet Ali. Capture Arcot and they would be forced to come back. With two hundred Europeans, six hundred Indians, and eight officers, of whom half were former clerks like himself, Clive set forth. The town fell easily to his assault, and he and his small handful prepared desperately for the vengeance which was to come. Everything turned out as Clive had foreseen. The Indian potentate, dismayed by the loss of his capital, detached a large portion of his troops from Trichinopoly and attacked Clive in Arcot. The struggle lasted for fifty days. Twenty times outnumbered, and close to starvation, Clive's puny force broke the onslaught in a night attack in which he served a gun himself, and the siege was lifted by the threat of an admiring Mahratta chieftain to come to the aid of the British. This was the end of Dupleix, and of much else besides. By 1752 Clive, in combination with Stringer Lawrence, a regular soldier from England, had defeated the French and the French-sponsored usurpers and placed Mahomet Ali on the throne. The Carnatic was safe. Next year Clive, newly wed, but in bad health, sailed to England. He was much enriched by the "presents", as they were politely called, which he had received from Indian rulers. Dupleix struggled on, but was recalled to France in 1754, and died nine years later in poverty and disgrace.

In England Clive used a part of his fortune in an attempt to enter Parliament for a "rotten borough" in Cornwall. He was unsuccessful, and in 1755 he returned to India. He was only just in time, for a new struggle was about to open in the North-East. Calcutta, at the mouth of the Ganges, was earning good dividends. Peace had been kept by a Moslem adventurer from the North-West who had seized and held power for fourteen years. But he died in 1756, and the throne passed to his grandson, Surajah Dowlah, young, vicious, violent, and greedy. Fearing, with some justice, that what came to be called the Seven Years War between Britain and France, lately broken out, would engulf his dominions and reduce him to a puppet like his fellow-princes in the Deccan, he called on both the European communities to dismantle their fortifications. The French at Chandernagore, up-river from Calcutta, returned a soothing answer. The English, aware that war with France was imminent, had extended their fortifications on the river-bank, where the French attack was expected, and ignored his demands. Other frictions increased his anger. In May Surajah Dowlah struck.

Gathering a large army, including guns and Europeans trained to use them, he marched on Calcutta. The landward approach to the city was unfortified, there was mismanagement and confusion, and the evacuation by ships developed into a panic scramble. The small garrison and most of the English civilians fought bravely, but in three days it was all over. They had lived in peace too long. A terrible fate now overtook them. A hundred and forty-six Europeans surrendered after the enemy had penetrated the defences under a flag of truce. They were thrust for the night into a prison cell twenty feet square. By the morning all except twenty-three were dead. The victors departed, having looted the Company's possessions. "Little though he guessed it," says Lord Elton, "the dealings of Surajah Dowlah with the British had ensured they would become the next rulers of India. For the tragedy of the Black Hole had dispelled their last wishful illusion that it might still be possible for them to remain in India as traders and no more. There was an outrage to avenge, and at last they were more than ready to fight."[1]

The news reached Madras in August. The Directors had not yet learnt that war with France had already broken out in Europe but there were rumours, as in Calcutta, of a French attack, both by sea and from the Deccan. They nevertheless gave Clive all their naval power and nearly all their troops. In January 1757, with nine hundred European and fifteen hundred Indian soldiers, he recaptured Calcutta and repulsed Surajah Dowlah's army of forty thousand men. The war with France now compelled him to retreat, but only long enough for him to attack Chandernagore, which he dared not leave in French hands, before hastening back to Madras. In March Chandernagore fell; its garrison, fighting very bravely, withdrew. Then fortune came to Clive's aid. Surajah Dowlah's cruelty was too much, even for his own people. A group of courtiers resolved to depose him and place a new ruler, Mir Jafar, on the throne. Clive agreed to help. On June 23, his army having grown to three thousand men, of whom less than a third were British, he met Surajah Dowlah at Plassey. He was outnumbered seventeen to one. The Hoogli River, now in flood behind him, forbade retreat; the enemy gathered in a semicircle on the open plain. Clive disposed his force along the edge of a mango grove and awaited the onslaught. Then Surajah Dowlah, sensing treachery in his own camp, and listening to the counsel of those plotting to betray him, ordered a withdrawal. Clive had resolved to let him go and make a night attack later on, but a junior officer advanced against orders. It became impossible to check the pursuit. The enemy dispersed in panic, and a few days later Surajah Dowlah was murdered by Mir Jafar's son. For the loss of thirty-six men Clive had become the master of Bengal and the victor of Plassey.

Mir Jafar, who had taken no part in the so-called battle, was placed on the throne. When Clive sailed once more to England in February 1760 Britain was the only European Power left in India. In little more than four years he had brought about a great change upon the Indian scene. The French were still allowed to keep their trading posts, but their influence was destroyed, and nine years later the *Compagnie des Indes* was abolished. Clive had now accumulated a fortune of a quarter of a million pounds. He bought his way into Parliament, as was the custom of the time, and was created an Irish peer. His services in India were not yet over.

1   Lord Elton, *Imperial Commonwealth* (1945). [Churchill]

Modern generations should not mistake the character of the British expansion in India. The Government was never involved as a principal in the Indian conflict. The East India Company was a trading organisation. Its Directors were men of business. They wanted dividends, not wars, and grudged every penny spent on troops and annexations. But the turmoil in the great sub-continent compelled them against their will and their judgment to take control of more and more territory, till in the end, and almost by accident, they established an empire no less solid and certainly more peaceful than that of their Mogul predecessors. To call this process "Imperialist expansion" is nonsense, if by that is meant the deliberate acquisition of political power. Of India it has been well said that the British Empire was acquired in a fit of absence of mind.

Clive's triumph created as many problems as it solved, and the years which followed his departure contain some of the most squalid pages in the history of the British in India. Tales of corruption and the gaining of vast and illicit private fortunes crept back to England. The Directors of the Company suddenly found that they had lost both their dividends and their good name. They appealed to Clive, again made him Governor of Bengal and Commander-in-Chief, and in June 1764 he sailed to India for the last time. His reforms were drastic, high-handed, and in effect more far-reaching than the victory at Plassey. Their success prompted the Mogul Emperor to invite him to extend a British protectorate to Delhi and all Northern India. Clive refused. He had long doubted the ability of the Company to undertake the larger responsibilities of Empire, and five years earlier he had suggested in a letter to Pitt that the Crown should assume the sovereignty of the Company's possessions in India. This advice was disregarded for nearly a century. In January 1767 he returned to England. The British public were critical and ill-informed. Clive was assailed in the House of Commons. He defended himself in an eloquent speech. He pointed out that by his exertions the Directors of the East India Company "had acquired an Empire more extensive than any kingdom in Europe. They had acquired a revenue of four millions sterling and trade in proportion." About the gains which he himself had made he exclaimed in a celebrated passage, "Am I not rather deserving of praise for the moderation which marked my proceedings? Consider the situation in which the victory at Plassey had placed me. A great prince was dependent on my pleasure; an opulent city lay at my mercy; its richest bankers bid against each other for my smiles; I walked through vaults which were thrown open to me alone, piled on either hand with gold and jewels. Mr Chairman, at this moment I stand astonished at my own moderation." The House of Commons unanimously passed a resolution that "Robert Lord Clive rendered great and meritorious services to this country." The vehement, tormented spirit who was the subject of this motion was not appeased. A few years later he died by his own hand.

Clive was soon followed in India by as great a man as himself, but with a somewhat different background. Warren Hastings was poor, but his ancestors had once owned large estates in Worcestershire. The wars of Oliver

Cromwell had compelled his great-grandfather to sell the family home at Daylesford, and from early boyhood Hastings dreamed of winning it back. He served the East India Company as a subordinate through the great period of Clive's triumphs, and a year after Clive's final departure he became a member of the Council in Calcutta. From this position of limited but definite responsibility he witnessed the squalor and confusion which prevailed. The Company's servants continued to build their fortunes at the expense of their employers and of the inhabitants. The Mahrattas seized Delhi and menaced Oudh. Madras was threatened, and even Bombay, hitherto so peaceful, was involved in the civil wars. Between 1769 and 1770 a third of the population of Bengal died of famine. Throughout these ordeals Warren Hastings held fast to an austere way of life. He desired fame and power, and enough money to buy back Daylesford. The gathering of private fortunes he left to others. In 1772 he became Governor of the stricken, preyed-upon, but still wealthy province of Bengal. He made two resolutions: to keep up the Company's dividends and to make the British collect the taxes. By now, however, the whispers and worse on which Clive had been nearly censured by Parliament had taken hold of public opinion in England. Rich adventurers from the East were making and marring the repute of the new Empire in India. The courage and discipline which had won the day at Arcot and at Plassey and had avenged the Black Hole were overlooked. Within nine years nearly three million pounds had been collected as personal rewards by the Company's servants from the inhabitants of Bengal. The instrument for reform happened to be Lord North.

North did his best within his lights. His motto was "Shackle the great", and the year after Hastings became Governor of Bengal he induced Parliament to pass a Regulating Act.[1] The measure was not totally lacking in merit. The administration of British-held territory in India was unified. Bombay and Madras were subjected to a "Governor-General" established at Calcutta, and Warren Hastings was made the first Governor-General, with a salary of twenty-five thousand pounds a year. But in trying to make sure that power was not abused it was made impotent. On paper it was divided between the Nawab of Bengal, the Board of Directors, the Governor-General, and a Council appointed to veto and control him. For years Hastings fought against his shackles. His principal opponent was his new colleague, Philip Francis, the reputed author of the savage *Letters of Junius* which had attacked the Government at home during the agitations over Wilkes. Francis never ceased to intrigue against him, openly and behind his back. But Hastings knew what needed to be done, and he was determined to do it. Though naturally a man of quick temper, he learned the virtues of patience and cool persistence. At one moment the Government tried to recall him. Then two of the most ignorant and hostile members of his Council died, and soon afterwards France, roused by the revolt in America and seeking to regain her power in

1   1773.

India, once again declared war on Britain. Hastings at last was free to act. His liberation came only just in time.

By 1778 a French fleet was approaching the southern coast, Hyder Ali of Mysore was overrunning the Carnatic, the British Governor of Madras had been imprisoned by his own corrupt officials, and Bombay was at war with the Mahrattas. In the space of six years Hastings retrieved everything. His naval forces were weaker than the French, and although they fought no fewer than five engagements they were unable to prevent the French landing on the Madras coast. The Government of Madras was purged and reanimated. Sir Eyre Coote, who had served at Plassey, and was still the ablest British soldier in India, was sent hurriedly southwards. He defeated Hyder Ali at Porto Novo in 1781, and his son Tipu Sultan a year later. Peace was negotiated with the Mahrattas. By 1783 the only active enemies who remained were the French, and their hopes of progress were stopped by the conclusion of the Treaty of Versailles. England had lost one Empire in America and gained another in India.

All this train of action had cost a lot of money. Hastings could get very little help, financial or material, from England, exhausted and overstrained by the conflict in America, Europe, and on the seas. His only course was to raise it on the spot. The inhabitants of Bengal were wealthy. They were also, thanks to British arms and leadership, comparatively safe. They should pay for their protection, and Hastings had been quite ruthless in making them do so. Thus he gathered the funds to rescue Bombay and the Carnatic and to stop the bloodshed once more engulfing Bengal. His critics, and those of the East India Company, were not slow to point out that only a third of the two million pounds he raised was spent on the war. The rest leaked away in familiar directions. But Hastings himself was careless of money and came home with no great fortune. He left India in 1785, not without the gratitude of the inhabitants.

In the beginning Hastings was welcomed and honoured in England. His achievements and victories were some compensation for the humiliations and disasters in America, and the Company had much to thank him for. Soon after Hastings's return a Parliamentary inquiry into his conduct had been set on foot. No personal charge of corruption could be proved against him, but he was arrogant and tactless in his dealings with the politicians of all parties. Headed by Burke, Fox, and Sheridan, Parliament resolved to have his blood. Philip Francis, whom he had wounded in a duel in Calcutta, malignly urged his enemies on. The ancient weapon of impeachment was resurrected and turned against him. The trial opened in Westminster Hall on February 13, 1788. It lasted over seven years. Every aspect and detail of Hastings's administration was scrutinised, denounced, upheld, misunderstood, or applauded. At the end he was acquitted. Though much of the uproar was unfair and uncomprehending, the proceedings proclaimed to the public and the world the support of the British people for Burke's declaration that India should be governed "by those laws which are to be found in Europe, Africa, and Asia, that are found amongst all those principles of equity and humanity implanted in our hearts, which have their existence in the feelings of mankind that are capable of judging".

Hastings was nearly bankrupt by the cost of defending himself. The Company, however, had given him enough money to buy back Daylesford, and many years later, when testifying in the Commons on Indian affairs, the House uncovered in his honour. He never held office again. But at any rate he was more fortunate than his old opponents from France, several of whom had long before been beheaded or made penniless. Posterity has redeemed his name from the slurs of the Whigs.

The impeachment of Warren Hastings was a turning-point in the history of the British in India. The chief power was no longer to be grasped by obscure, brilliant servants of the Company who could seize and merit it, and the post of Governor-General was henceforward occupied by personages distinguished on their own account and drawn from the leading families in England: the Marquess Cornwallis, uncowed by the surrender at Yorktown, the Marquess Wellesley, Lord Minto, the Marquess of Hastings, Lord William Bentinck, and Lord Dalhousie. In effect, though not in name, these men were Viceroys, untempted by the hope of financial gain, impatient of restraint by ill-informed Governments in London, and sufficiently intimate with the ruling circles in Britain to do what they thought right and without fear of the consequences.

CHAPTER FORTY-ONE

PITT THE YOUNGER

Shelburne, North, Fox and Pitt and the aftermath of defeat – agreement with America – towards Parliamentary reform – Tom Paine and The Rights of Man – the industrial revolutions – Pitt the Younger – Dundas and Wilberforce – Free Trade and Adam Smith – the Budget – Pitt's Sinking Fund – the French Revolution – France declares war – the Nore and Spithead mutinies – the Battle of Camperdown – the Battle of the Nile – Napoleon at Marengo – the Act of Union with Ireland – the Irish rebellion – Wolfe Tone – Orangemen – Pitt resigns – the Treaty of Amiens – Napoleon plans invasion of England

W HEN ROCKINGHAM died in July 1782 a formal peace agreement with America had yet to be made and this was left to Lord Shelburne, now entrusted with the new administration. The entire structure of British politics was ruptured in its personal loyalties by the years of defeat to which King George III had led them. Politics were now implacably bitter between three main groups, and none of them was strong enough alone to sustain a Government. Shelburne himself had the support of those who had followed Chatham, including his son, the young William Pitt, who was appointed Chancellor of the Exchequer. But North still commanded a considerable faction, and, smarting at his sovereign's cold treatment after twelve years of faithful service, coveted a renewal of office. The third group was headed by Charles James Fox, vehement critic of North's régime, brilliant, generous-hearted, and inconsistent. Burke, for his part, lacked family connections; he had no great gift for practical politics, and since the death of his patron, Rockingham, was without influence.

Hostility to Shelburne grew and spread. Nevertheless, by negotiations in which he displayed great skill, the Prime Minister succeeded in bringing the world war to an end on the basis of American independence. The French Government were now close to bankrupt. They had only aided the American Patriots in the hope of dismembering the British Empire, and, apart from a few romantic enthusiasts like Lafayette, had no wish to help to create a republic in the New World. His own Ministers had long warned Louis XVI that this might shake his absolute monarchy. Spain was directly hostile to

American independence. She had entered the war mainly because France had promised to help her to recapture Gibraltar in return for the use of her Fleet against England. But the revolt of the Thirteen Colonies had bred trouble among her own overseas possessions, Gibraltar had not fallen, and she now demanded extensive compensation in North America. Although Congress had promised to let France take the lead in peace negotiations, the American Commissioners in Europe realised their danger, and without French knowledge and in direct violation of the Congressional undertaking they signed secret peace preliminaries with England.

The most important issue was the future of the Western lands lying between the Alleghany Mountains and the Mississippi. Shelburne was by no means hostile to the American desire for the West. The difficulty was the Canadian frontier. Franklin and others went so far as to demand the whole province of Canada, but Shelburne knew that to yield to this would bring down his Government. After months of negotiation a frontier was agreed upon which ran from the borders of Maine to the St Lawrence, up the river, and through the Great Lakes to their head. Everything south of this line, east of the Mississippi and north of the borders of Florida, became American territory. This was by far the most important result of the treaty. Shelburne had shown great statesmanship, and frontier wars between Britain and America were, with one exception, prevented by his concessions.

France now made her terms with England. An armistice was declared in January 1783, and the final peace treaty was signed at Versailles later in the year. The French kept their possessions in India and the West Indies. They were guaranteed the right to fish off Newfoundland, and they reoccupied the slave-trade settlements of Senegal on the African coast. The important cotton island of Tobago was ceded to them, but apart from this they gained little that was material. Their main object, however, was achieved. The Thirteen Colonies had been wrested from the United Kingdom, and England's position in the world seemed to have been gravely weakened. Thus ended what some then called the World War. A new state had come into being across the Atlantic, a great future force in the councils of the nations.

England had been heavily battered, but remained undaunted. Her emergence from her ordeal was the work of Shelburne. In less than a year he had brought peace to the world and had negotiated the terms on which it stood. That he received small thanks for his services is a remarkable fact. He resigned after eight months, in February 1783. Later he was created Marquis of Lansdowne, and descendants of his under that name have since played a notable part in British politics. Shelburne's Government was followed by a machine-made coalition between North and Fox. It was said that this combination was too much even for the agile consciences of the age. Fox had made his name by savage personal assaults on North's administration. Only five years before he had publicly declared that any alliance with North was too monstrous to be admitted for a moment. Yet this was what was now presented to an astonished public. Shelburne had lived upon his task. The Fox–North Government had nothing on which to rest their feet. Within nine months this Ministry also collapsed.

The revolt of the American colonies had shattered the complacency of eighteenth-century England. The defects of the political system had plainly contributed to the secession, and the arguments used by the American colonists against the Mother Country lingered in the minds of all Englishmen who questioned the perfection of the Constitution. Demand for some reform of the representation in Parliament begin to stir; but the agitation was now mild and respectable. The main aim of the reformers was to increase the number of boroughs which elected Members of Parliament, and thus reduce the possibilities of Government corruption. There was even talk of universal suffrage and other novel theories of democratic representation. But the chief advocates of reform were substantial landowners or country clergymen like Christopher Wyvill, from Yorkshire, or mature, well-established politicians like Edmund Burke. They would all have agreed that Parliament did not and need not precisely represent the English people. To them Parliament represented, not individuals, but "interests" – the landed interest, the mercantile interest, even the labouring interest, but with a strong leaning to the land as the solid and indispensable basis of the national life. Thus the movement in governing circles was neither radical nor comprehensive. It found expression in Burke's Economic Reform Act of 1782, disfranchising certain classes of Government officials who had hitherto played some part in managing elections. This was a tepid version of the scheme Burke had meant to introduce. No general reform of the franchise was attempted, and when people talked about the rights of Englishmen they meant the sturdy class of yeomen vaunted as the backbone of the country, whose weight in the counties it was desired to increase. Tom Paine's inflammatory pamphlets had a considerable circulation among certain classes, but in Parliament little was heard about the abstract rights of man.[1] In England the revolutionary current ran underground and was caught up in provincial eddies.

Nevertheless the dream of founding a balanced political system on a landed society was becoming more and more unreal. In the last forty years of the eighteenth century exports and imports more than doubled in value and the population increased by over two millions. England was silently undergoing a revolution in industry and agriculture, which was to have more far-reaching effects than the political tumults of the times. Steam-engines provided a new source of power in factories and foundries, which rapidly multiplied. A network of canals was constructed which carried coal cheaply to new industry. New methods of smelting brought a tenfold increase in the output of iron.

[1] Tom Paine (1737–1809), the radical son of a Norfolk Quaker. On the advice of Benjamin Franklin, Paine went to America. His pamphlet, *Common Sense* (1776), made the case for American independence. Back in London, he published (1791) the first part of the widely read *The Rights of Man*. The second part appeared the following year, and Paine, who by then was in Paris, was tried in England for seditious libel. He was later jailed by the French for his opposition to the beheading of Louis XVI; it was then that he wrote *The Age of Reason*. He died in New York.

New roads, with a hard and durable surface, reached out over the country and bound it more closely together. An ever-expanding and assertive industrial community was coming into being. The rapid growth of an urban working class, the gradual extinction of small freeholders by enclosures and improved farming methods, the sudden development of manufactures, the appearance of a prosperous middle class for whom a place must be found in the political structure of the realm, made the demands of reformers seem inadequate. A great upheaval was taking place in society, and the monopoly which the landowners had gained in 1688 could not remain.

Such, in brief were the turmoils and problems which confronted William Pitt when he became Prime Minister of Britain at the age of twenty-four. The elections which carried Pitt into power were the most carefully planned of the century. There has been a legend that a great wave of popular reaction against the personal government of George III brought him into office. In fact it was George himself who turned to Pitt, and the whole electoral machinery built up by the King's agents, headed by the backstairs figure of John Robinson, the Secretary of the Treasury, was put at the disposal of the young politician.[1] In December 1783 Robinson and Pitt met to discuss their plan at a house in Leicester Square belonging to one of Pitt's close associates, Henry Dundas. Robinson drew up a detailed report on the constituencies, and convinced Pitt that a majority in the Commons could be obtained. Three days later Fox and North were dismissed by the King, and the ensuing elections created a majority which William Pitt preserved into the next century. The plan had been justified, and the nation at large accepted the result as the true verdict of the country.

This majority rested on a number of elements – Pitt's personal following; the "Party of the Crown", put at his disposal by George III; the independent country gentlemen; the East India interest, alienated by Fox's attempt to curb their political power; and the Scottish Members, marshalled by Dundas. Here was a rank and file which represented a broad basis of popular favour. With all the renown of his father's name behind him, this grave, precocious young man, eloquent, incorruptible, and hard-working, stood upon the uplands of power. Even at this age he had few close acquaintances. But two men were to play a decisive part in his life, Henry Dundas and William Wilberforce. Dundas, a good-humoured, easy-going materialist, embodied the spirit of eighteenth-century politics, with its buying up of seats, its full-blooded enjoyment of office, its secret influences, and its polished scepticism. He was an indispensable ally, for he commanded both the electoral power of Scotland and the political allegiance of the East India Company, and it was he who kept the new majority together. For Pitt, although personally incorruptible, leant heavily upon the eighteenth-century machinery of government for support.

1   Equally it might be argued that Pitt the Younger was presented to the King as the candidate for Prime Minister and that indeed there was a deep-felt reaction to the old order that had "lost" the Thirteen Colonies.

William Wilberforce, on the other hand, was the friend of Pitt's Cambridge days, and the only person who enjoyed his confidence. Deeply religious and sustained by a high idealism, Wilberforce became the keeper of the young Minister's conscience. He belonged to the new generation which questioned the cheerful complacency of the eighteenth century. The group who gathered round him were known not unkindly as "the Saints". They formed a compact body in the House of Commons, and their prime political aim was the abolition of the slave trade. They drew towards them the religious fervour of the new Evangelical, or "Low Church", movement.[1] Between these contrary characters stood Chatham's son.

The variety of his following, however, limited the scope of his work. From the outset Pitt was overcome by the dead hand of eighteenth-century politics. He failed to abolish the slave trade. He failed to make a settlement in Ireland. He failed to make Parliament more representative of the nation, and the one achievement in these early months was his India Act, which increased rather than limited the opportunities for political corruption. He saw quite clearly the need and justification for reform, but preferred always to compromise with the forces of resistance.

It was in the most practical and most urgent problem, the ordering and reconstruction of the finances of the nation, that Pitt achieved his best work, and created that Treasury tradition of wise, incorruptible management which still prevails. His Ministry coincided with a revolution in economic and commercial thought. In 1776 Adam Smith had published *The Wealth of Nations*, which quickly became famous throughout educated circles. The times were ripe for an exposition of the principles of Free Trade. In steady, caustic prose Adam Smith destroyed the case for Mercantilism. Pitt was convinced. He was the first English statesman to believe in Free Trade, and for a while his Tory followers accepted it. The antiquated and involved system of customs barriers was now for the first time systematically revised. There were sixty-eight different kinds of customs duties, and some articles were subject to many separate and cumulative imposts. A pound of nutmegs paid, or ought to have paid, nine different duties. In 1784 and 1785 Pitt was able to bring a degree of order into this chaos, and the first visible effect of his wide-ranging revision of tariffs was a considerable drop in smuggling. Further reform consolidated the revenue. It is to Pitt that we owe the modern machinery of the "Budget". By gathering around him able officials he reorganised the collection and disbursement of the revenue. The Audit Office was established, and numerous sinecures at the Treasury were abolished. The state of the national finances was lamentable. At the end of 1783 over forty million pounds which had been voted by Parliament for war purposes had not been accounted for. Government credit was low, the Ministry was distrusted. The National Debt stood at two hundred and fifty million pounds, more than two and a half times

---

1 The Saints were Wilberforce's friends in Parliament; they should not be confused with his religious friends beyond Westminster, who were known as the Clapham Sect.

as great as in the days of Walpole. Pitt resolved to acquire a surplus in the revenue and apply it to the reduction of this swollen burden.

In 1786 he brought in a Bill for this purpose. Each year a million pounds would be set aside to buy stock, and the interest would be used to reduce the National Debt. Here was the famous oft-criticised Sinking Fund. The scheme depended on having an annual Budget surplus of revenue over expenditure, and Pitt was often forced in later years, when there was no such surplus, to feed the Sinking Fund with money borrowed at a high rate of interest. His reasons for so costly a procedure were psychological. The soundness of the national finances was judged by the amount in the Sinking Fund, which gave an impression of stability to the moneyed classes of the City. Trade revived, prosperity increased, and what then seemed the handsome sum of ten millions was paid off in ten years.

In this same year, 1786, the Customs and Excise were amalgamated, and a reconstituted Board of Trade established in its modern form. But perhaps the most striking achievement of Pitt's management was the negotiation of the Eden treaty with France – the first Free Trade treaty according to the new economic principles. William Eden, one of Pitt's able young officials, was sent to Paris to get French tariffs against English cotton goods lowered in return for a reduction of English duties on French wines and silks. These did not of course compete with any English product, but the export of Lancashire cotton goods damaged the textile manufacturers in North-Eastern France and increased the discontent among the French industrial classes affected by this enlightened measure.

The hope of further reconstruction and improvement was shattered by war and revolution upon the European scene. For Pitt it was a personal tragedy. His genius lay essentially in business management; his greatest memorials are his financial statements. He knew nothing of the lives of his countrymen outside the limited area of the Metropolis. Even amid the fellowship of the House of Commons and the political clubs he stood aloof. Fully aware of the economic changes in eighteenth-century England, Pitt was less sensitive to signs of political disturbance abroad. He believed firmly in non-intervention, and the break-up of the Old Régime in France left him unimpressed. He watched with quiet malice the quarrel on this issue of his leading Parliamentary opponents, Fox and Burke. His interests lay elsewhere. If the French chose to revolt against their rulers that was their own affair. It might be flattering that they should want a constitutional monarchy like the British, but it was no concern of his. The First Minister was deaf to the zealous campaign of the Whig Opposition in favour of the French revolutionaries, and ignored the warnings of Burke and others who believed that the principles of monarchy, and indeed of civilised society, were endangered by the roar of events across the Channel.

The convulsion which shook France in 1789 was totally different from the revolutions that the world had seen before. The English Revolution had been entirely a domestic affair. So in the main had the American. But the French

Revolution was to spread out from Paris across the whole Continent. It gave rise to a generation of warfare, and its echoes reverberated long into the nineteenth century and afterwards. Every great popular and national movement, until the Bolsheviks gave a fresh turn to events in 1917, was to invoke the principles set forth at Versailles in 1789.

In England the Whigs, and especially the reformers and Radicals, had at first welcomed the French Revolution. They were soon repelled by its excesses. Eighteenth-century London was not without experience of popular upheavals. But in the Wilkes agitations and the riots of 1780 led by Lord George Gordon[1] the law had always gained the upper hand over the mob. Now France gave a frightful demonstration of what happens when the social forces unleashed by reformers break free from all control. Most Englishmen recoiled in horror. In the House of Commons Fox alone, in the broad optimism of his mind, spoke out for the Revolution as long as he conscientiously could. For this he was vehemently attacked by his former friend and ally, Burke, and the number of his faithful followers among the Opposition diminished. In the country similar feelings prevailed. Liberty-loving young men had enthusiastically applauded the events of 1789. "Bliss was it in that dawn to be alive", Wordsworth wrote. Other poets and writers of the fertile new Romantic Movement shared his views. A few years later most of them were disillusioned. Some groups of scientists and political thinkers with progressive opinions also gave their allegiance, as they have done in our own day, to foreign revolutionary ideas. At the meetings of their societies they toasted the Fourteenth of July and the French Constitution. But they were only a small leaven amid the solid English Conservative mass. More dangerous were the Radical working men's clubs which were springing up in the principal towns, generally under middle-class leadership. They kept up a close correspondence with the Jacobins in Paris, and fraternal delegates were sent to the National Assembly and its successor, the Convention. These agitators formed a small but vociferous minority of the British public, and eventually the Government took drastic action against them.

Such was the scene in Britain as the idea of world revolution gathered force in Paris. The unprovoked massacre of political prisoners by the new rulers of France in 1792 was a further shock to the faith of many would-be revolutionaries in the United Kingdom. The execution of the French King in January 1793 was a supreme act of defiance. In his celebrated speech Danton summarised the French Revolutionary attitude: "Allied kings threaten us, and we hurl at their feet as a gage of battle the head of a king." Marat cried, "We must establish the despotism of liberty to crush the despotism of kings." The French Republican armies were a threat not only to the Austrian and Prussian

1 Gordon presented a Parliamentary Petition against the Roman Catholic relief Act of 1778. Parliament rejected the petition and on June 2 there began in London, ten days of anti-Catholic riots (since known as the Gordon Riots) inspired by the Protestant Association. Twelve thousand troops were called out. Between 300 and 700 people died. (Sources produce differing death rates.) Gordon was cleared of High Treason.

enemy, but also to their own Government. It was essential that they should be kept in the field. As a Girondin Minister put it frankly, "Peace is out of the question. We have three hundred thousand men in arms. We must make them march as far as their legs will carry them, or they will return and cut our throats."

In his Budget speech of 1792 Pitt had announced that he believed in fifteen years of peace for Europe. Non-intervention was his policy. Something more vital to Britain than a massacre of aristocrats or a speech in the Convention, something more concrete than a threat of world revolution, had to happen before he would face the issue of war. The spark, as so often in England's history, came from the Netherlands. By November the French decree instructing their generals to pursue the retreating Austrians into any country in which they might take refuge was a clear threat to the neutrality of Holland. A second pronouncement declared the navigation of the Scheldt open between Antwerp and the sea. A week later French men-of-war were bombarding the citadel of Antwerp, and on November 28 the city fell into French hands. The whole delicate balance of eighteenth-century international politics was deranged.

On the last day of January 1793 the French Convention, decreed the annexation of the Austrian Netherlands to the French Republic. The next day France declared war on Great Britain and Holland, firm in the belief that an internal revolution in England was imminent. Pitt now had no choice. English security was imperilled by French occupation of the Flemish coast, and particularly the Scheldt estuary. Trade with the Continent would be endangered, and the English Channel was no longer safe. But for this deliberate provocation from Paris, Pitt might have avoided the issue a little longer. But now, with the Southern Netherlands in French hands and with world revolution in view, the threat was direct and inescapable.

Britain was to be at war for over twenty years, and was now confronted with the task of making a major war effort, with her armed forces more crippled, perhaps, than at any time before by lack of equipment, leaders, and men. The conditions of service and the administration of the Army and Navy were so appalling that it is wonderful that anything was achieved at all. Pitt himself knew nothing of war or strategy, and the conduct of military affairs fell largely upon Henry Dundas, who was first and foremost a business man. In the old tradition of the eighteenth century he advocated a colonial and trade war, which would be popular among the mercantile classes and produce some commercial returns. For several years British resources were dissipated in ill-manned and ill-planned expeditions to the West Indies. It was with the greatest difficulty that any men could be raised for these mistaken enterprises.

If Britain had possessed even a small effective army it would not have been difficult, in concert with allies moving from the Rhine, to strike from the French coast at Paris and overthrow the Government responsible for provoking the conflict. But Pitt was barely able to send five thousand men to help his

Dutch allies protect their frontiers from invasion. The campaigning which followed was no credit to British arms. An attempt to take Dunkirk ended lamentably. By 1795 the British forces on the Continent were driven back upon the mouth of the Ems on the German border, whence they were evacuated home.

Meanwhile the Terror [the Revolution] rose to its height, and in the political frenzy of Paris no one knew when his hour would come. Men and women went by forties and fifties every day to the guillotine. In self-preservation politicians and people combined against Robespierre. It was July 27, 1794, or by the new French reckoning the 9th Thermidor of the year II, for the Revolutionaries had decided to tear up the calendar of Julius Caesar and Pope Gregory and start afresh. On that day, in a furious convulsion, Robespierre was dragged down and sent where he would have sent the rest.

In England the Government had been forced to take repressive measures of a sternness unknown for generations. Republican lecturers were swept into prison. The Habeas Corpus Act was suspended. Distinguished writers were put on trial for treason; but juries could not be prevailed on to convict. The mildest criticism of the Constitution brought the speaker under danger from a new Treason Act. Ireland, governed since 1782 by a Protestant Parliament independent of Westminster, was now on the verge of open rebellion, which, as Pitt saw, could only be averted by liberal concessions to the Irish Catholics. Henry Grattan, the eloquent Irish leader, who had done so much to win more freedom for his country, urged that Catholics should be given both the vote and the right to sit in Parliament and hold office. They got the vote, but seats in Parliament were still denied them.

Few victories came to brighten these dark years. In 1794 the French Channel Fleet, ill-equipped and under-officered, was half-heartedly engaged by Admiral Howe. Three years later, off Cape St Vincent, the Spanish Fleet – Spain being now in alliance with France – was soundly beaten by Jervis and Nelson. But such had been the neglect of conditions of service in the Navy that the ships at Spithead refused to put to sea. The movement spread to the Nore, and for some weeks London was in effect blockaded by the British Fleet, while a French squadron was on the high seas making for Ireland on a vain quest. The men were entirely loyal; indeed, on the King's birthday the salute which they fired was so hearty and the guns so well charged that the fortifications of Sheerness tumbled down. Some slight concessions satisfied the mutineers, and they retrieved their honour in a handsome victory off Camperdown over the Dutch, who were now satellites of France. Meanwhile the Bank of England had suspended cash payments.

On the Continent the French were everywhere triumphant. Bonaparte,[1] having reduced Northern Italy, was preparing to strike at Austria through the Alpine passes. In April 1797 he signed with her the preliminaries of Leoben,

---

1   Napoleon Bonaparte (1769–1821) first came to notice when, as a young officer, he organised and led the successful assault on Fort l'Aiguillette, the key point of the naval base of Toulon, which had been seized by French Royalists in 1793.

converted some months later into the Treaty of Campo Formio. Belgium was annexed to France; the Republic of Venice, with a glorious history reaching into the Dark Ages, became an Austrian province. Milan, Piedmont, and the little principalities of Northern Italy were welded into a new Cisalpine Republic. France, dominant in Western Europe, firmly planted in the Mediterranean, safeguarded against attack from Germany by a secret understanding with Austria, had only to consider what she would conquer next. A sober judgment might have said England, by way of Ireland. Bonaparte thought he saw his destiny in a larger field. In the spring of 1798 he sailed for Egypt. Nelson sailed after him.

During the afternoon of August 1 a scouting vessel from Nelson's fleet signalled that a number of French battleships were anchored in Aboukir Bay, to the east of Alexandria. In a line nearly two miles long the thirteen French "seventy-fours" lay close in to the shallow water, headed west, with dangerous shoals to port. The French Admiral Brueys was convinced that not even an English admiral would risk sailing his ship between the shoals and the French line. But Nelson knew his captains. As evening drew near, the Goliath, followed by the Zealous, cautiously crept to landward of the French van and came into action a few minutes before sundown. Five British ships passed in succession on the land side of the enemy, while Nelson, in the *Vanguard*, led the rest of his fleet to lie to on the starboard of the French line.

The French sailors were many of them on shore and the decks of their vessels were encumbered with gear. They had not thought it necessary to clear the gun ports on their landward side. In the rapidly falling darkness confusion seized their fleet. Relentlessly the English ships, distinguished by four lanterns hoisted in a horizontal pattern, battered the enemy van, passing from one disabled foe to the next down the line. At ten o'clock Brueys's flagship, the *Orient*, blew up. The five ships ahead of her had already surrendered; the rest, their cables cut by shot, or frantically attempting to avoid the inferno of the burning *Orient*, drifted helplessly. In the morning hours three ran ashore and surrendered, and a fourth was burned by her officers. Of the great fleet that had convoyed Napoleon's army to the adventure in Egypt only two ships of the line and two frigates escaped.

Nelson's victory of the Nile cut Napoleon's communications with France and ended his hopes of vast Eastern conquests. He campaigned against the Turks in Syria, but was checked at Acre, where the defence was conducted by Sir Sydney Smith and a force of English seamen. In 1799 he escaped back to France, leaving his army behind him. The British Fleet was once again supreme in the Mediterranean Sea. This was a turning-point. With the capture of Malta in 1800 after a prolonged siege Britain had secured a strong naval base in the Mediterranean, and there was no further need to bring the squadrons home for the winter as in the early part of the war.

But still the British Government could conceive no co-ordinated military plan upon the scale demanded by European strategy. Their own resources were few and their allies seldom dependable. Meanwhile Napoleon again took charge of the French armies in Italy. In June 1800 he beat the Austrians at Marengo, in Piedmont, and France was once more mistress of Europe.

In 1800 the political situation in Britain was dominated by the passing of the Act of Union with Ireland. The shocks and alarums of the previous years determined Pitt to attempt some final settlement in that troubled island. The concessions already won by the Irish from British Governments in difficulty had whetted their appetite for more. At the same time Irish Catholics and Protestants were at each other's throats. In Ulster the Protestants founded the Orange Society for the defence of their religion. In the South the party of United Irishmen under Wolfe Tone had come more and more in their desperation to look to France. Rebellion, French attempts at invasion, and brutal civil war darkened the scene. The hopes that had once been pinned in the independent Parliament at Dublin faded away. Even by eighteenth-century standards this body was shockingly corrupt. Pitt decided that the complete union of the two kingdoms was the only solution. Union with Scotland had been a success. Why not with Ireland too? But the prime requisite for any agreement must be the emancipation of Irish Catholics from the disabilities of the penal laws. Here Pitt was to stumble upon the rock of the conscience of a monarch now half-crazy. Unscrupulous backstairs influences, false colleagues within the Cabinet Council, pressed George III to stand by his coronation oath, which he was assured was involved. Pitt had committed himself to the cause of Catholic freedom without extracting a written agreement from the King. When George refused his assent, on March 14, 1801, Pitt felt bound to resign. Catholic emancipation was delayed for nearly thirty years. The Act of Union had meanwhile been carried through the Irish Parliament by wholesale patronage and bribery against vehement opposition. Grattan made the greatest speech of his career against the Union, but in vain. Westminster absorbed the Irish Members. Bitter fruits were to follow from this in the later nineteenth century.

Pitt was worn and weary, and perplexed by the uncongenial task of organising England for war. He has been blamed by later historians for his incapacity in directing an extensive war, and for his methods of finance, in which he preferred loans to increased taxation, thereby burdening posterity, as others have done since. He chose to incur gigantic debts, and to struggle haphazardly through each year until the dismal close of the campaigning season, living from day to day and hoping for the best. But if Pitt was an indifferent War Minister his successors were no improvement.

Pitt was succeeded by a pinchbeck coalition of King's Friends and rebels from his own party. Masquerading as a Government of National Union, they blundered on for over three years. Their leader was Henry Addington, an able former Speaker of the House of Commons whom no one regarded as a states-man. War-time conditions demanded some form of Coalition Government. The Whig Opposition, if only for their lack of administrative experience, were deemed unfit. In 1800 they had been reduced to impotence by the transformation of the war from one against world revolution to one against world Caesarism. Until the rise of Bonaparte they had steadfastly pleaded for peace and understanding with the revolutionaries. Now they were reduced to points of strategy and military detail upon which they carried no authority. The sense of being the only possible national leader seems to have affected Pitt's actions remarkably little. Young men like Canning and Lord Castlereagh were trained in office under him. And they remained loyal to their chief. As Canning wrote, "Whether Pitt will save us I do not know, but surely he is the only man that can."

In March 1802 Addington's Government made terms with Napoleon by the Treaty of Amiens, and for a time there was a pause in the fighting. Pitt supported the Government over the peace in spite of the arguments of some of his own followers. English tourists flocked to France, Fox among them, all eager to gaze upon the scenes of Revolution and to see at first hand the formidable First Consul, as he now was. But the tourist season was short. In May of the following year war was renewed, and once more mismanaged. Napoleon was now assembling his forces at Boulogne, intent upon the invasion of England.

CHAPTER FORTY-TWO

THE NAPOLEONIC WARS

Pitt returns to power – Nelson returns to the Mediterranean – the Battle of Trafalgar – the Battle of Austerlitz – impeachment of Dundas – the death of Pitt the Younger – the Ministry of All the Talents – the death of Fox – the new men: Castlereagh, Perceval, and Canning – Napoleon rules Europe – the Peninsular War – the Convention of Cintra – Wellington in command – the retreat from Moscow – Napoleon retires to Elba – Talleyrand and the restoration of the French monarchy – Napoleon's return – the Battle of Waterloo – Napoleon exiled to St Helena

I N 1804 Pitt was recalled to power. Feverishly he flung himself into the work of reorganising England's war effort. The French had for the moment cowed the Continent into a passive acceptance of their mastery. The opportunity was now at hand to concentrate the whole weight of the armed forces of France against the stubborn Islanders. Elaborate plans went forward to bring about their subjugation. An enormous army was organised and concentrated at the Channel ports for the invasion of England. A fleet of flat-bottomed boats was built to bring two hundred thousand men across the Channel to what seemed inevitable success. At the crest of his hopes Napoleon had himself crowned by the Pope as Emperor of the French. One thing alone was lacking to his designs – command of the sea. It was essential to obtain naval control of the Channel before embarking upon such an enterprise. Day in, day out, winter and summer, British fleets kept blockade of the French naval bases of Brest and Rochefort on the Atlantic coast and Toulon in the Mediterranean. At all costs a junction of the main French fleets must be prevented. As the American historian Admiral Mahan has said, "It was these distant storm-beaten ships upon which the Grand Army never looked which stood between it and the dominion of the world."

In May 1803 Nelson had returned to the Mediterranean to resume command of his fleet. Here the fate of his country might be decided. It was his task to contain the French fleet in Toulon and stop it from raiding Sicily and the Eastern Mediterranean, or sailing into the Atlantic, whence it might lift the blockade of Rochefort and Brest, force the Channel, and co-operate with the armada from Boulogne. Nelson was well aware of the grim significance of the moment, and all his brilliance as a commander was employed on creating a first-class machine. The crews were reorganised, the ships refitted under dangerous and difficult circumstances. He had no secure base from which to watch Toulon. Gibraltar and Malta were both too far away, and Minorca had been given back to Spain at the Treaty of Amiens. Under such circumstances a literal hemming in of the French was impossible. Nelson's burning desire was to lure them out and fight them. Annihilation was his policy. He kept a screen of frigates watching Toulon, and himself with his battleships lay off Sardinia, alert for interception. Twice in the course of two years the French attempted a sortie, but retired. Throughout this time Nelson never set foot on shore. The constant nightmare in his mind revolved round the direction in which the French would make. For Sicily and Egypt? Or Spain and the Atlantic? He had to cover all escape routes.

In the centre of the web sat Napoleon, and the elaborate scheme for the final blow against England was slowly woven. But the vital instrument in his hand was brittle. The French Navy had suffered a crushing blow in the days of the Revolution. The officer class had been almost wiped out on the guillotine. Discipline was bad and the French Navy in no state to play a decisive rôle. In May 1804 the Emperor had confided the Toulon fleet to Admiral Villeneuve, an excellent seaman, who realised that his ships, except for the luck of circumstance, could only play a defensive part. Napoleon would brook no obstacles, and a complicated series of feints was worked out to deceive the British agents who swarmed into France to gather such information as they could. Spain was dragged into his schemes, her Fleet being a necessary adjunct to the main plan. In the early months of 1805 Napoleon made his final arrangements. Over ninety thousand assault troops, picked and trained, lay in the camps round Boulogne. The French Channel ports were not constructed to take battleships, and the French fleets in the Atlantic and Mediterranean harbours must be concentrated elsewhere to gain command of the Channel. The Emperor fixed upon the West Indies. Here, after breaking the Mediterranean and Atlantic blockades, and drawing off the British Fleet, as he thought, into the waters of the Western Atlantic, his ships were ordered to gather. The combined French and Spanish fleets would then unite with Ganteaume, the admiral of the Brest squadron, double back to Europe, sail up the Channel, and assure the crossing from Boulogne.

Nelson was lying in wait off the Sardinian coastline in April 1805 when news reached him that Villeneuve was at sea, having slipped out of Toulon on the dark night of March 30, sailing, as Nelson did not yet know, in a westerly direction with eleven ships of the line and eight frigates. The fox was out and the chase began. Fortune seemed against Nelson. His frigates lost touch with Villeneuve, and he had first to make sure that the French were not running for Sicily and the Near East. This done, he headed for Gibraltar. Fierce westerly gales prevented him reaching the Straits until May 4, when he learnt that Villeneuve had passed through to Cadiz more than three weeks before. Six Spanish battleships had come out to join him, and the long voyage across the Atlantic began. Nelson, picking up scattered reports from frigates and merchantmen, pieced together the French design. All his qualities were now displayed to the full. Out of perplexing, obscure, and conflicting reports he had fathomed the French plan. There was no evidence to show that Villeneuve had gone to the north, and there could hardly be any reason for his sailing south along the West African coast. Therefore on May 11 Nelson made the momentous decision to sail westwards himself. He had ten ships of the line to follow seventeen of the enemy. The passage was uneventful. In stately procession at an average rate of five and a half knots the English pursued their quarry, and a game of hide-and-seek followed among the West Indian islands. Villeneuve and his Spanish allies reached Martinique on May 14. Nelson made landfall at Barbados on June 4. False intelligence led him to miss Villeneuve in the Caribbean seas. Meanwhile news of his arrival alarmed the French admiral, who was promptly out again in the Atlantic by June 8, heading east. On the 12th Nelson lay off Antigua, where Villeneuve had lain only four days earlier. He again had to make a crucial decision. Was he right in believing that the French were making for Europe? As he wrote in a dispatch, "So far from being infallible, like the Pope, I believe my opinions to be very fallible, and therefore I may be mistaken that the enemy's fleet has gone to Europe; but I cannot think myself otherwise, not withstanding the variety of opinions which a number of good people have formed."

Before leaving the islands Nelson sent a fast sloop back to England with dispatches, and on June 19 it passed Villeneuve's fleet, noting his course and position. The commander of the sloop saw that Villeneuve was heading north-eastwards for the Bay of Biscay, and raced home, reaching Plymouth on July 8. Lord Barham, the new First Lord of the Admiralty, aged seventy-eight and with a lifetime's naval experience, at once realised what was happening. Nelson was sailing rapidly eastwards after Villeneuve, believing he would catch him at Cadiz and head him off the Straits, while the French fleet was making steadily on a more northerly course in the direction of Cape Finisterre. Villeneuve intended to release the Franco-Spanish squadron blockaded at Ferrol, and, thus reinforced, join with Ganteaume from Brest. But Ganteaume, in spite of peremptory orders from Napoleon, failed to break out. Admiral Cornwallis's fleet in the Western Approaches kept him in port. Meanwhile, on orders from Barham at the Admiralty, Admiral Calder intercepted Villeneuve off Finisterre, and here in late July the campaign of Trafalgar opened. Calder's action was indecisive, and the French took refuge in Ferrol.

Nelson meanwhile had reached Cadiz on July 18. There he found Collingwood on guard, but no sign of the enemy. Realising that Villeneuve must have gone north, Nelson replenished his fleet in Morocco and sailed for home waters on the 23rd. On the same day Napoleon arrived at Boulogne. The crisis was at hand and the outlying squadrons of the Royal Navy instinctively gathered at the mouth of the Channel for the defence of the Island. Calder joined Cornwallis off Brest on August 14, and on the next day Nelson arrived with twelve more ships, bringing the main fleet up to a total of nearly forty ships of the line. Thus was the sea-barrier concentrated against the French. Nelson went on alone with his flagship, the *Victory*, to Portsmouth. In the following days the campaign reached its climax. Villeneuve sailed again from Ferrol on August 13 in an attempt to join Ganteaume and enter the English Channel, for Napoleon still believed that the British fleets were dispersed and that the moment had come for invasion. On August 21 Ganteaume was observed to be leaving harbour, but Cornwallis closed in with his whole force and the French turned back. Meanwhile Villeneuve, having edged out into the Atlantic, had changed his mind. Well aware of the shortcomings of his ill-trained fleet, desperately short of supplies, and with many sick on board, he had abandoned the great adventure on August 15 and was already speeding south to Cadiz. The threat of invasion was over.

Early in September dispatches reached London telling that Villeneuve had gone south. Nelson, summoned from his home at Merton, was at once ordered to resume his command. "I hold myself ready to go forth whenever I am desired," he wrote "Although God knows I want rest." Amid scenes of enthusiasm he rejoined the *Victory* at Portsmouth and sailed on September 15. All England realised that her fate now lay in the hands of this frail man. A fortnight later he joined the fleet off Cadiz, now numbering twenty-seven ships of the line. "We have only one great object in view," he wrote to Collingwood, "that of annihilating our enemies." His object was to starve the enemy fleet, now concentrated in Cadiz harbour, and force it out into the open sea and to battle. This involved patrolling the whole adjacent coast. He organised his own ships into blockading squadrons. His energy and inspiration roused the spirit of his captains to the highest pitch. To them he outlined a new and daring plan of battle. He intended to ignore the Admiralty's "Fighting Instructions". To gain a decisive victory, he was resolved to abandon the old formal line of battle, running parallel to the enemy's fleet. He would break Villeneuve's line, when it came out of port, by sailing at right angles boldly into it with two main divisions. While the enemy van was thus cut off and out of touch his centre and rear would be destroyed. After his conference with his captains Nelson wrote, "All approved. It was new, it was singular, it was simple. It must succeed." In a mood of intense exhilaration the fleet prepared for the ordeal ahead. Meanwhile Villeneuve had received orders to sail for Naples in support of Napoleon's new military plans. After learning that he was about to be superseded, he resolved to obey before his successor could arrive. On the morning of October 19 a frigate signalled to Nelson's flagship, "Enemy has their topsail yards hoisted," and some time later, "Enemy ships are coming out of port." On receiving these messages Nelson led his fleet to the south-east to cut off the enemy from the Straits and force them to fight in the open sea. At daybreak on the 21st he saw from the quarterdeck of the *Victory* the battle line of the enemy, consisting of an advance squadron of twelve Spanish ships under Admiral Gravina and twenty-one French ships of the line under Villeneuve. It was seven months since the escape from Toulon, and the first time that Nelson had seen his foes since war had begun again in 1803.

The British fleet lay about ten miles west of the enemy, to the windward, and at six in the morning Nelson signalled his ships to steer east-north-east for the attack in the two columns he had planned. The enemy turned northwards on seeing the advancing squadrons, and Nelson pressed on with every sail set. The clumsy seamanship of his men convinced Villeneuve that flight was impossible, and he hove to in a long sagging line to await Nelson's attack. The English admiral turned to one of his officers. "They have put a good face on it, but I will give them such a dressing as they have never had before." Nelson signalled to Collingwood, who was at the head of the southern column in the *Royal Sovereign*, "I intend to pass through the van of the enemy's line, to prevent him getting into Cadiz." Nelson went down to his cabin to compose a prayer. "May the Great God whom I worship grant to my country, and for the benefit of Europe in general, a great and glorious Victory. ... For myself, I commit my life to Him who made me, and may His blessing light upon my endeavours for serving my country faithfully." The fleets were drawing nearer and nearer. Another signal was run up upon the *Victory*, "England expects every man will do his duty." When Collingwood saw the flutter he remarked testily, "I wish Nelson would stop signalling, as we all know well enough what we have to do," but when the message was reported to him cheers broke out from the ships in his line. A deathly silence fell upon the fleet as the ships drew nearer. Each captain marked down his adversary, and within a few minutes the two English columns thundered into action. The roar of broadsides, the crashing of masts, the rattle of musketry at point-blank range rent the air. The *Victory* smashed through between Villeneuve's flagship, the *Bucentaure*, and the *Redoutable*. The three ships remained locked together, raking each other with broadsides. Nelson was pacing as if on parade on his quarterdeck when at 1.15 p.m. he was shot from the mast-head of the *Redoutable* by a bullet in the shoulder. His backbone was broken, and he was carried below amid the thunder of the *Victory*'s guns. The battle was still raging. By the afternoon of October 21, 1805, eighteen of the enemy ships had surrendered and the remainder were in full retreat. Eleven entered Cadiz, but four more were captured off the coast of Spain. In the log of the *Victory* occurs the passage, "Partial firing continued until 4.30, when a victory having been reported to the Right Hon. Lord Viscount Nelson, K.B. and Commander-in-Chief, he then died of his wound."

The victory was complete and final. The British Fleet, under her most superb commander, like him had done its duty.

In August 1805 the camp at Boulogne broke up, and the French troops set out on their long march to the Danube. The campaign that followed wrecked Pitt's hopes and schemes. In the month of Trafalgar the Austrian General Mack surrendered at Ulm. Austria and Russia were broken at the Battle of Austerlitz. Napoleon's star had once more triumphed, and for England all was to do again. About this time the Prime Minister gave audience to a young general home from India. In forthright terms this officer noted his opinion of Pitt. "The fault of his character," he wrote, "is being too sanguine. ... He conceives a project and then imagines it is done." This severe but not inaccurate judgment was formed by one who was to have many dealings with the armies of the French Emperor. His name was Arthur Wellesley, later Duke of Wellington.

A personal sorrow now darkened Pitt's life. The House of Commons by the casting vote of the Speaker resolved to impeach his close colleague and lifelong companion, Henry Dundas, now Lord Melville, for mal-administration in the Admiralty and for the peculations of certain of his subordinates. The decisive speech against Dundas was made by none other than Wilberforce.[1] The scene in the House of Commons was poignant. Pitt's eyes filled with tears as he listened to Wilberforce attacking his other greatest friend. After the adverse decision the Opposition crowded round him "to see how Pitt took it"; but, encircled by his supporters, he was led from the House. It was this disgrace, rather than the news of Austerlitz, which finally broke the spirit and energy of the Prime Minister. In January 1806 he died. Pitt's successors were staunch in the prosecution of war, but even less adept at it than he. The three years between his death and the rise of Wellington in 1809 were uncheered by fortune.

In 1806 and 1807 there was a brief Ministry of "All the Talents" under Lord Grenville. The talent was largely provided by the Whigs, now in office for the first time since 1783 and the last until 1830. Over twenty years of divorce from power had had an insidious and lowering effect upon the party. Their organisation and their programme dissolved in the perplexed bickering of their leaders. The renewal of the European conflict quenched the hopes of Parliamentary Reform, upon which they had taken their stand in the early 1790s. The rise of Napoleon destroyed their chance of effective opposition to the war. They had maintained a straggling and futile fire against the strategic proposals of the Government. They hoped now to lift some of the restrictions upon Roman Catholics, for they were much oppressed by the problem of Ireland. But in this they failed. The Secretary of State for War, William Windham, produced admirable Paper reforms of the Army. He recommended short-time service, with increased pay. Abolishing the local militia, he passed a Training Act, which made universal military service compulsory. The manhood of England would be called to the colours in batches of two hundred thousand at a time. This was a striking piece of legislation. The Government's tenure of office was redeemed by Fox's abolition of the slave trade, a measure which ranks among the greatest of British achievements, and from which Pitt had always shrunk. It was Fox's last effort. For forty years his warm-hearted eloquence had inspired the Whigs. Almost his whole Parliamentary life was

---

1   Dundas was not a swindler. His post as Treasurer of the Navy made him formally responsible, and he was acquitted in the House of Lords. Dundas, 1st Viscount Melville and Baron Dunira, was the last British minister to be impeached.

spent in Opposition. He died as Secretary of State, nine months after his great rival, Pitt, had gone to the grave.

In 1807 the Whigs fell. They were succeeded by a mixed Government of Tory complexion under the nominal leadership of the Duke of Portland. Its object was to hold together the loyalties of as much of the nation as it could command. In this it was remarkably successful. New figures were appearing in the Tory ranks, trained by Pitt in the daily business of government. George Canning, Spencer Perceval, Viscount Castlereagh, were reaching out for power. Politics centred on the conduct of the War Office and on the personal enmity and rivalry of Canning and Castlereagh. These restless spirits soon impelled the Government to discard the strategies of William Pitt. Active participation in the military and naval struggle for Europe became the order of the day.

Speed was essential, for Napoleon was reaching the height of his career. At Austerlitz he had struck down Russia and Austria. He was already master of the Netherlands, Italy, and the states of the Rhine. At Jena, a year later, he had broken Prussia. The Czar was still in the field, but in June 1807 the Russian Army was defeated at Friedland. There followed the reconciliation of Napoleon and Alexander. The Franco-Russian Alliance, signed at Tilsit on July 7, was the culmination of Napoleon's power. The Emperor of Austria was a cowed and obsequious satellite. The King of Prussia and his handsome Queen were beggars, and almost captives in his train. Napoleon's brothers reigned as kings at The Hague, at Naples, and in Westphalia. His step-son ruled Northern Italy in his name. Spain lent itself to his system, trusting that worse might not befall. Denmark and Scandinavia made haste to obey. Only Britannia remained, unreconciled, unconquered, implacable. There she lay in her Island, mistress of the seas and oceans, ruled by her proud, stubborn aristocracy, facing this immense combination alone, sullen, fierce, and almost unperturbed. Some anxious merchants and manufacturers complained of the British blockade, which materially affected their interests. They stirred up Whig politicians to denounce it. But the Government was founded on land, not trade, and turned a deaf ear. Nevertheless Britain owed much of the power that was to bring her victory to her growing industrial supremacy. Industry knew this. The seeds were now sown for a crop of post-war troubles in which industry was to demand a greater share in the councils of the nation. But for the time being patriotism healed all, or nearly all. It was against this contumacious land, which marred and derided the unity of Europe and challenged the French peace, that Napoleon now directed his whole strength. To venture upon salt water, except for cruiser raids on commerce, was to be sunk or captured. The British blockade wrapped the French Empire and Napoleon's Europe in a clammy shroud. No trade, no coffee, no sugar, no contact with the East, or with the Americans! And no means of ending the deadlock! Napoleon had believed that the marshalling of all Europe under his hands would force England to make terms. But no response came from the Island, which throve upon seaborne trade and whose ruling classes seemed to take as much interest in prize-fighting and fox-hunting as in the world crisis.

Napoleon turned his attention to the Spanish Peninsula. Powerless at sea, he realised that to destroy his one outstanding rival he must turn the weapon of blockade against the Island. English goods must be kept out of the markets of Europe by an iron ring of customs guards stretching from the borders of Russia round the coasts of Northern Europe and Western France and sealing the whole Mediterranean coastline as far as the Dardanelles. Napoleon proclaimed his policy from Berlin. It was a land blockade of sea-power. The weakest link in the immense barrier of French troops and customs officers was the Peninsula of Spain. To complete this amazing plan it was essential to control not only Spain, but also Portugal, the traditional ally of Britain, whose capital, Lisbon, was an important potential base for the British Fleet. Slowly the minds of English Ministers turned to this theatre of coming war. Napoleon was determined to strike through Spain at Lisbon before the British Fleet could sail southwards.

Canning in charge at the Foreign Office, displayed the energy of youth. An English squadron sailed to the Tagus, collected the Portuguese ships, and packed off the Portuguese royal family, Government, and society to the safety of Brazil. A few days later Marshal Junot entered the Portuguese capital, and the following day Napoleon declared war on the country he had just occupied. France and Britain were now locked in their deadliest grip. In reply to Napoleon's Continental System the British Government issued an Order in Council declaring a sea blockade of all French and French-allied ports – in other words, of almost the whole of Europe. Napoleon's decrees and the English Orders wounded the merchant shipping of the neutral countries. The results of this trade war were far-reaching for both sides. The commerce of Europe was paralysed and the nations stirred beneath the French yoke. Interference by British ships with neutral vessels raised with the United States the question of the freedom of the seas. It was a grievous dispute, not to be settled without recourse to war.

Napoleon, insatiable of power, and seeking always to break England and her intangible blockade, resolved to seize the Spanish crown. He enticed King Charles IV of Spain and his son Ferdinand into a trap at Bayonne, and under the threat of a firing squad compelled them to sign documents of abdication. He placed his own brother Joseph on the throne of Spain as a vassal of the French Empire. He was overjoyed with the success of this violence. "Spanish opinion bends to my will. Tranquillity is everywhere re-established," he wrote to Cambacérès;[1] and to his Foreign Secretary Talleyrand on May 16, 1807, "The Spanish business goes well and will soon be entirely settled." But, happily for human freedom, things are not so easy as that. As soon as the Spaniards realised what had happened and that their country was practically

---

1   Duke of Palma, Jean Jacques Régis de Cambacérès (1753–1824). Chancellor from 1804 who is supposed to have been the author of *Code Civil* (more likely the work of his staff) which was the matrix of the *Code Napoléon*.

annexed to France they rose everywhere in spontaneous revolt. Between May 24 and 30 in every hamlet and village throughout the Peninsula they took up what arms they could find and set out for the capital of the province or their local centre, where the same process was already working on a larger scale. Nothing like this universal uprising of a numerous, ancient race and nation, all animated by one thought, had been seen before. The tiny province of Asturias, on the Biscayan shore, separated by the mountains from the rest of Spain, knowing nothing of what the rest were doing, drove out the French governor, seized the arsenal with booty of a hundred thousand muskets, constituted itself an independent Government, declared war upon Napoleon, at the height of his greatness, and sent their envoys to England to appeal for alliance and aid. The envoys landed at Falmouth on the night of June 6, were conveyed by the Admiralty to Canning. Canning understood. From that moment the Peninsular War begin. For the first time the forces unchained by the French Revolution, which Napoleon had disciplined and directed, met, not kings or Old World hierarchies, but a whole population inspired by the religion and patriotism which Joan of Arc had tried in vain to teach to France, and now Spain was to teach to Europe.

The Emperor was very slow to measure the force of the Spanish revolt. He could not understand a people who preferred misgovernment of their own making to rational rule imposed from without. This country, which he had expected to incorporate in his Empire by a personal arrangement with a feeble Government, by a trick, by a trap, without bloodshed or expense, suddenly became his main military problem. He resolved to conquer.

But meanwhile the English had struck a shrewd blow. Canning and his colleagues decided to send an army to the Peninsula to aid the Spanish insurgents. But as the Juntas of Galicia and Andalusia were not as yet willing to accept foreign troops the expedition was sent to Portugal, and in July 1808 disembarked north of Lisbon in the Mondego River. This small British army consisted of thirty thousand well-equipped men. At the head of the first troops to land appeared Sir Arthur Wellesley, whose conduct of the Mahratta war in India had been distinguished. He had gained the Battle of Assaye. He was the younger brother of the Governor-General of India. He was a Member of Parliament and of the Tory administration, and actually held office at this time as Chief Secretary to the Lord-Lieutenant of Ireland. He did not wait for the rest of the army, but immediately took the field. At the combat at Roliça Junot[1] received a sharp repulse. At Vimiero this was repeated on a larger scale. The French columns of assault were broken by the reserved fire of the "thin red line", which now began to attract attention. Junot retreated upon Lisbon.

Sir Arthur Wellesley was superseded in the moment of victory by the arrival of Sir Harry Burrard, who later in the same day made over his

---

1 Marshal Junot (1771–1813), the French commander was a powerful, yet sad figure. He was Napoleon's adjutant, sometime governor of Paris and after Portugal went to Germany and then Russia. He became mentally ill and committed suicide by jumping from a window in the home of his father.

command to Sir Hew Dalrymple. Wellesley's wish to seize the pass of Torres Vedras and thus cut Junot's line of retreat was frustrated by his seniors. But the French commander now sent Kellerman to the British camp to negotiate. He offered to evacuate Portugal if the British would carry him back to France. The Convention of Cintra was signed, and punctiliously executed by the British. Junot and twenty-six thousand Frenchmen were landed from British transports at Rochefort. Wellesley in dudgeon remarked to his officers, "We can now go and shoot red-legged partridges." There was a loud and not unnatural outcry in England at Junot being freed. A military court of inquiry in London exonerated the three commanders, but only one of them was ever employed again.

Napoleon now moved a quarter of a million of his best troops into Spain. The Emperor advanced upon Madrid, driving the Spanish army before him in a series of routs, in which the French cavalry took pitiless vengeance. He astonished his personal staff by his violent energy. Always with the leading troops, he forced the fighting, even at Somo Sierra making his own bodyguard charge the batteries, regardless of loss. In December he entered Madrid, and replaced Joseph, who had hitherto followed with the baggage-train, upon the stolen throne. But the Spanish people were undaunted, and all around the camps of the victorious invaders flickered a horrible guerrilla.

A new English general of high quality had succeeded the commanders involved in the Convention of Cintra. Sir John Moore advanced from Lisbon through Salamanca to Valladolid. He had been lured by promises of powerful Spanish assistance, and he tried by running great risks to turn Spanish hopes into reality. His daring thrust cut or threatened the communications of all the French armies, and immediately prevented any French action in the South of Spain or against Portugal. But Napoleon, watching from Madrid, saw him a prey. At Christmas 1808, with fifty thousand men, with Ney, Soult, and the Old Guard, he marched to intercept and destroy him. On foot with his soldiers Napoleon tramped through the snows of the Guadarrama. He moved with amazing speed. Moore, warned in time, and invoking amphibious power, dropped his communications with Portugal and ordered his transports to meet him at Corunna, on the north-west tip of Spain. It was a race; but when the French horse crossed the Rio Seco they were hurled back, and their general captured, by the cavalry of the English rearguard. Moore had already passed Astorga and was half-way to his haven.

At Astorga the Emperor sat down on the parapet of a bridge to read dispatches brought apace from the capital. After a few moments he rose, and stood absorbed in thought. Then, ordering up his travelling coach, he handed over the pursuit of the British to Soult, and, without offering any explanation to his officers, set off for Valladolid and Paris. He had known for some months that the Austrian armies were assembling and he must expect an Austrian declaration of war, but his summons home was more intimate. His brother, Lucien, and his step-son, Eugène de Beauharnais, warned him of an intrigue, or even plot, against him by Talleyrand and Fouché, his Minister of Police.

Besides, there was now no chance of cutting off the British. The pursuit had become a stern chase. Soult and Ney could have it.

The retreat of the British through the rugged, snow-bound hill country was arduous. The French pressed heavily. Scenes of mass drunkenness where wine stores were found, pillage, stragglers dying of cold and hunger, and the Army chest of gold flung down a precipice to baffle capture darkened the British track. But when, at Lugo, Moore turned and offered battle his army showed so firm a posture that for two days Soult, although already superior, awaited reinforcements. It was now resolved to slip away in the night to Corunna, where the army arrived on January 14, 1809. But the harbour was empty. Contrary winds had delayed the Fleet and transports. There would be a battle after all. On the 16th Soult assaulted Moore with 20,000 against 14,000. He was everywhere repulsed, and indeed counter-attacked. When darkness fell the pursuers had had enough. But both Sir John Moore and his second-in-command, Sir David Baird, had fallen on the field.

Moore's countrymen may well do him justice. By daring, skill, and luck he had ruptured Napoleon's winter campaign and had drawn the Emperor and his finest army into the least important part of Spain, thus affording protection and time for movements to get on foot in all the rest of the Peninsula. He had escaped Napoleon's amazing forward spring and clutch. He died like Wolfe and Nelson, in the hour of victory. His army re-embarked unmolested. His campaign had restored the military reputation of Britain, which had suffered increasing eclipse since the days of Chatham; he had prepared the way for a new figure, destined to lead the armies of Europe upon the decisive field.

When the British sailed away from Corunna no organised forces remained in Spain to hinder Napoleon's Marshals. Everywhere Spanish armies were defeated, and only the implacable guerrilla continued. In the opening months of 1809 the French were again free to move their armies where they pleased in the Peninsula. Soult now entered Portugal and established himself at Oporto. What was left of the original British expedition still occupied Lisbon, and by successive reinforcements was again raised to a strength of thirty thousand men. These, conjoined with an equal number of Portuguese, organised under a British general, Beresford, were sufficient to keep Soult inert for several months, during which he distracted himself with an intrigue to become King. The Government in London were divided in counsel upon what ought to be done. Should they resume a major campaign in the Peninsula or strike at the Netherlands? They decided to split their effort and make an attempt in both quarters. An expedition was mounted to seize the Dutch island of Walcheren, at the mouth of the Scheldt, and occupy Antwerp. It proved a costly diversion, but it seemed a promising plan. Few observers were then convinced that effective success could be won in distant Spain and Portugal. These doubts were not shared by Arthur Wellesley. In April he was reappointed to take command in Lisbon. He was to spend the next five years in the Peninsula, and return to London in triumph by way of the capital of France.

Wellesley resigned his seat in Parliament and his office as Chief Secretary, and reached Lisbon before the end of the month. He could choose between attacking Soult at Oporto or re-entering Spain to engage one or other of the numerous French marshals whose corps were widely spread throughout the Peninsula. He decided first to clear Portugal. By a swift and secret march he reached the Douro, passed a division across it by night in boats and barges, and surprised Soult and his army in the town. With very small loss he compelled the Marshal, whose retreat southwards was also compromised by the operations of Beresford's Portuguese, to withdraw into the mountainous regions of the north. Soult was forced to abandon the whole of his artillery, his wounded, and the bulk of his baggage. He arrived at Orense, in Spanish Galicia, six days later, with an army disordered and exhausted, having lost since he entered Portugal over six thousand men. The passage of the Douro, the surprise of Oporto, and the discomfiture of Soult constituted a brilliant achievement for the new British general and paved the way for further action.

Wellesley now resolved to penetrate into the centre of Spain along the valley of the Tagus, and, joining the Spanish army under Cuesta, to engage Marshal Victor. Soult, his troops reorganised and re-equipped, was moving to join Victor, who would give him a decisive superiority. Wellesley's position at Talavera, a hundred miles south-west of Madrid, became precarious, and his soldiers were near starvation. Marshal Victor conceived himself strong enough to attack without waiting for the arrival of Soult. On the afternoon of July 27, 1809, the armies engaged. The French were fifty thousand strong. Wellesley had twenty thousand British and twenty-four thousand Spaniards, but these latter, though brave, could not be counted upon for serious work in a set battle. Their strength lay in harassing operations. The whole severity of the fighting was borne by sixteen thousand British and thirty thousand Frenchmen. Victor's attacks, which began in earnest on the 28th, were ill-concerted, and were repulsed with heavy loss after fierce mass-fighting with the bayonet. In the afternoon the crisis of the battle was reached. The English Guards, elated by the defeat of the French column in their front, were drawn from their place in the line by the ardour of pursuit. The British centre was open, and a French counter-stroke caused widespread disorder. But Wellesley had brought the 48th Regiment to the scene, who, in perfect array and discipline, advanced through the retreating soldiery, and, striking the French column on the flank, restored the day. A wild cavalry charge by the 23rd Light Dragoons, in which half the regiment fell, cut deeply into the enemy's flanks. By nightfall Marshal Victor accepted defeat and withdrew towards Madrid. The ferocity may be judged from the British losses. Nearly 6,000 men out of Wellesley's total of 20,000 had fallen, killed or wounded; the French had lost 7,500 and twenty guns. The Spaniards claimed to have lost 1,200 men.

Wellesley was in no condition to pursue. The next morning General Robert Craufurd arrived with his Light Brigade, afterwards the famous Light Division, having marched sixty-two miles in twenty-six hours, the most rapid march by foot-soldiers on record. But Wellesley could no longer place any reliance upon the co-operation of his Spanish allies. They engaged the enemy in their own free way, which was certainly not his. Like Sir John Moore before him, he had run enormous risks, and had been saved only by the narrowest of margins. He withdrew unmolested along the Tagus back to Portugal. Not only had he established the reputation of a highly skilful and determined general, but the fighting quality of the British had made a profound impression upon the French. In England there was unwonted satisfaction. Sir Arthur Wellesley was raised to the peerage as Viscount Wellington, and, in spite of Whig opposition, was granted a pension of £2,000 a year for three years. Nelson was gone; Pitt was gone; but here at last was someone to replace them.

The close connection between political developments at home and the fortunes of the generals at the front is a remarkable feature of the history of these years. Each military reverse led to a crisis in the personal relations of the Cabinet Ministers in London. The disgrace of the Convention at Cintra had sharpened the rivalry and mutual dislike of Canning and Castlereagh. The former had been anxious to dismiss all the generals involved; the latter was interested in the political and military careers of the Wellesley brothers. Fortunately Castlereagh had prevailed. Now the two Ministers were at loggerheads over the disaster that threatened the expedition to Walcheren. Tempers were sharpened by the ill-defined and overlapping functions of the Foreign Secretary and the Secretary for War. The failing health of the Duke of Portland, the titular head of the Government, increased the rivalry of the two younger statesmen for the succession to the Premiership. A duel was fought between them, in which Canning was wounded. Both resigned office, and so did Portland. Spencer Perceval, hitherto Chancellor of the Exchequer, took over the Government. He was an unassuming figure, but an adroit debater, and in the conduct of the war a man of considerable resolution. Wellington's cause in Spain was favoured by the new administration. Perceval appointed as his Foreign Secretary the Marquess Wellesley, who steadfastly stood up for his younger brother in the Cabinet. The new War Minister, Lord Liverpool, was also well disposed. The Government did their best to satisfy Wellington's requirements, but, faced with the Whig Opposition and the Tory rebels in the Commons, they were continually obstructed by petty issues. In 1810 the King's renewed madness provoked a fresh crisis. Perceval skilfully averted a change in the political balance of power. George, Prince of Wales, became Regent, but he did not send for his former friends, the Opposition Whigs, as they had fondly hoped. The Prince Regent decided to trust his father's Ministers. It is to his credit that he did so. By frugal finance Perceval was able to maintain supplies and nourish the armed forces. The three years of his Government were marked by quietly growing efficiency.

These were testing years for Wellington. He commanded Britain's sole remaining army on the continent of Europe. Failure would have been disastrous to Britain, and to the patriots in Spain and Portugal; it would also have liberated large numbers of French troops for the reinforcement of Napoleon's ventures elsewhere. We can only speculate upon what further triumphs the Emperor might have enjoyed, even perhaps in Russia, but for the steady drain on his resources caused by Wellington's presence in the Peninsula. All this was not lost upon the English commander. But for the time being caution must be his policy. "As this is the last army England has," he drily wrote, "we must take care of it." Since the start of the Revolutionary wars many British lodgments had been made on the European continent, but none had long survived. The French had always bent every effort to driving the British into the sea. In 1810 they were massing for a fresh attempt. Wellington was resolved that no hasty evacuation would be forced upon him. All the previous winter he had been perfecting a series of fortified lines around Lisbon on the heights of Torres Vedras. This was to form his final bastion, and on these defences he gradually fell back.

The ablest of Napoleon's Marshals, Masséna, now headed the French Army of Portugal. Having overwhelmed Spanish resistance, Masséna advanced across the frontier with eighty thousand men. The British numbered about twenty-five thousand, and their Portuguese allies the same. In September there was a stiff battle at Busaco. Sixty thousand French met fifty thousand Allies, only half of whom were British. But the Portuguese were by now well seasoned. The French were badly mauled and beaten. Wellington's withdrawal nevertheless continued. Suddenly the forward flow of the French came to a halt. Ahead of them rose the formidable lines of Torres Vedras, manned by the undefeated British, and all around extended a countryside deliberately laid waste. Masséna saw before him a prospect of bleak, hungry months, with no hope of successful assault. This was the hinge of the whole campaign. The French paused and dug into winter quarters. Wellington hovered about them, determined, as he put it, "to force them out of Portugal by the distresses they will suffer". So it turned out. In the following spring Masséna gave up. He retreated into Spain, leaving behind him seventeen thousand dead and eight thousand prisoners.

Portugal was now free, and Wellington's successes strengthened the position of the Government at home. Rejoicing in London and Lisbon, however, was mingled with a certain impatience. The British commander had eager critics, even within his own army, who could not appreciate the wisdom of his steadily developing strategy. Wellington himself was unperturbed by cries for haste. He had gauged precisely the size and scope of the task before him. A war of manoeuvre unfolded in 1811 within the Spanish frontiers, and both the French armies blocking his advance were separately met and defeated at Fuentes d'Oñoro and Albuera.

Amid the snows of January 1812 he was at last able to seize Ciudad Rodrigo. Four months later Badajoz fell to a bloody assault. The cost in life was heavy, but the way was opened for an overpowering thrust into Spain. Wellington and Marmont manoeuvred about one another, each watching for the other to make a mistake. It was Marmont who erred, and at Salamanca Wellington achieved his first victory on the offensive in the Peninsular War. King Joseph Bonaparte fled from Madrid, and the British occupied the capital amid the pealing of bells and popular rejoicing. But there was still Soult to be dealt with. Coming up from the south, the French Marshal wheeled round Wellington's flank. He outnumbered the British commander by nearly two to one, and he was careful to offer no opening for promising attack. Wellington fell back once more on the Portuguese frontier. In the year's campaign he had shattered one French army and enabled the whole of Southern Spain to be freed from the French. But meanwhile heavier shadows from the East were falling upon Napoleon's Empire. It was the winter retreat from Moscow.

All through the spring of 1812 the Emperor had been gathering forces on a scale hitherto unknown in Europe, and as the summer came he drew them eastward from all his dominions. For two years past his relations with Russia had been growing more and more embittered. The Czar had gradually become convinced that no general European settlement could be made so long as the French Emperor dominated the scene. Napoleon determined to get his blow in first, and to make it a shattering one. Although his generals and Ministers were reluctant and apprehensive a kind of delirium swept the martial classes of the Empire. The idea of a campaign larger than any yet conceived, more daring than the deeds of Alexander the Great, which might lead to the conquest of all Asia, took possession of the fighting men. Napoleon marshalled beyond the Vistula a group of armies nearly five hundred thousand strong. His Viceroy and stepson Eugene marched from Italy with fifty thousand Italians. Holland, Denmark, and all the states of the Rhine sent their contingents. Austria and Prussia took the field as Napoleon's dutiful allies, each with thirty thousand men. War-ravaged Europe after all these years of strife had never seen such an array. Among these armies moving eastwards were barely two hundred thousand Frenchmen. They formed the central spearhead of attack under the Emperor's direct command. Thus the great drama reached its culmination.

Many voices had warned Napoleon of the hardships and difficulties of campaigning in Russia. Nor did he disregard their advice. He had assembled what seemed for those days abundant transport and supply. It proved unequal to the event. In June 1812 he crossed the Niemen and headed straight for Moscow, some five hundred miles to the east. He was confronted by two main Russian armies totalling two hundred thousand men. His plan was to overwhelm them separately and snatch at the old Russian capital. Before Napoleon the Russian armies fell back, avoiding the traps he set for them and devastating the countryside through which the French had to pass. At Borodino, some sixty miles west of the capital, the Russians turned at bay. There in the bloodiest battle of the nineteenth century General Kutusov inflicted a terrible mauling on Napoleon. Both the armies engaged, each of about a hundred and twenty thousand men, lost a third of their strength. Kutusov withdrew once more, and Moscow fell to the French. But the Russians declined to sue for peace. As winter drew near it was forced on Napoleon's mind that Moscow, burnt to a shell by accident or by design, was untenable by his starving troops. There was nothing for it but retreat through the gathering snows – the most celebrated and disastrous retreat in history. Winter now took its dreadful toll. Rearguard actions however gallant, sapped the remaining French strength. Out of the huge Grand Army launched upon Russia only twenty thousand straggled back to Warsaw. Marshal Ney was said to have been the last Frenchman to quit Russian soil.

On December 5 Napoleon abandoned the remnant of his armies on the Russian frontier and set out by sleigh for Paris. Whatever salvaging could be done he left to his Marshals. For himself he was insensible of disaster. In the spring of 1813 he once more took the field. Half his men were raw recruits, and France was no longer behind him. Germany rose in the hour of his downfall. The spirit of nationalism, diffused by French armies, sprang up to baffle and betray the master of Europe. Coalitions were formed, backed by the finances of Britain. Napoleon was offered the chance of an honourable peace. Thinking that fate could be reversed by genius in battle, he rejected it. One by one his hesitant allies dropped away. Sweden, ruled by the French Marshal Bernadotte; Prussia, Austria, and even Saxony and Bavaria, his own client states, abandoned him. The Czar was resolved upon a march for the Rhine. Central Europe, so long subservient to France, joined the Russian thrust. A series of gigantic engagements were fought in Saxony and Silesia. At last in the three-day battle of Leipzig in October all Napoleon's foes closed in upon him. Nearly half a million men were involved on each side. In this Battle of the Nations Napoleon was overwhelmed and driven westwards to the frontiers of France. The Allies gathered on the borders of their enemy for the first time since 1793. The great Revolutionary and Imperial adventure was drawing to a close.

The forces of opposition to his rule in France openly rose against him. Fouché and Talleyrand, long conspiring in doubt, now put it to themselves that France could only be saved by deserting her Emperor. At the end of March Marshal Marmont, defending Paris, gave up and surrendered the capital. On April 3 Napoleon abdicated and retired to the island of Elba. The long, remorseless tides of war rolled back, and at the Congress of Vienna the Powers prepared for the diplomatic struggle of the peace.

Britain was represented at Vienna by Castlereagh. In 1812 the Prime Minister, Perceval, had been shot dead by a madman in the lobby of the House of Commons. His colleague, Lord Liverpool, took over the administration, and remained in power for fifteen years. Castlereagh rejoined the Government as Foreign Secretary, an office he was to hold until his death. The war Governments of these years have received graceless treatment at the hands of Whig historians. Yet Perceval and Liverpool, Canning and Castlereagh, bore the burden with courage and increasing skill. Castlereagh was now to take an influential part in the reconstruction of Europe. His voice was foremost in proposing a just and honourable peace. He had already in March 1814 negotiated the Treaty of Chaumont between the principal Allies which laid the foundations for the future settlement. In Castlereagh's day there were five

Great Powers in Europe.[1] His object was to concert their interests. Harmony between them was too much to expect. But at least it might be arranged that the jars of international life should not lead inevitably to war.

Castlereagh's principal colleagues at Vienna were Metternich, the Austrian Chancellor, and Talleyrand, the spokesman of France. Metternich was a confirmed believer in the old régime of the eighteenth century; his desire was to put back the clock to pre-Revolutionary days. The supple Talleyrand had served in turn the Revolution, Napoleon, and now the Bourbons; his aim was to salvage for France all that he could from the ruins of the Imperial adventure. It was Talleyrand who persuaded the Powers to restore the Bourbons in the person of Louis XVIII, brother of the executed king. After the glories of the Revolution and the triumphs of Napoleon not even the royalist pen of Chateaubriand could invest the shadowy monarchy with prestige or popularity. Louis, however, represented at least a tradition, a fragment of the political faith of France; above all, he represented peace.

A politic moderation was displayed in the terms offered to the defeated enemy: no indemnity, no occupation by Allied troops, not even the return of the art treasures which had been looted from the galleries of Europe. The foreign conquests of the Emperor were surrendered, but the essential unity of France remained untroubled and the territory over which Louis XVIII ruled was slightly more extensive than that of Louis XVI. The reason for this moderation is not difficult to comprehend. To disrupt France would add too much weight to one or other of the Continental Powers. Besides, it would kindle a flame of vengeance in the hearts of all Frenchmen.

The British were principally concerned with the colonial settlement. Many conquests were returned, yet the Peace of Paris, which was the outcome of the Congress, marks another stage in the establishment of the new Empire which was replacing the lost American colonies. The captured French colonies were surrendered, with the exception of Mauritius, Tobago, and St Lucia. The Dutch recovered their possessions in the East Indies. Sir Stamford Raffles, who had governed with singular success the rich island of Java, saw this British prize given back to its former owners. It was not until some years later that he founded the trading settlement which is now the city of Singapore. At the price of three millions sterling Britain acquired part of Guiana from the Dutch. The Government, however, was most concerned with those possessions which had a strategic value as ports of call. For that reason it held on to Malta, and the key of the route to India, the Cape of Good Hope. From this acquisition in South Africa a troubled saga was to unfold. Dutch Ceylon was kept, and Danish Heligoland, which had proved a fine base for breaking the Continental System[2] and smuggling goods into Germany. These gains

1   They were Austria, Britain, France, Prussia and Russia.
2   The Continental System: a title given to maritime blockades (the Berlin Decrees of 1806 and the Milan Decrees of 1808) against British goods in continental European ports and the British Order in Council of 1807 to close French and allied ports and arrest neutral shipping trading with the French.

were scattered and piecemeal, but, taken together, they represented a powerful consolidation of the Imperial structure.

On the Continent the main preoccupation of the Powers was to draw a cordon sanitaire around France to protect Central Europe from the infections and dangers of revolution. In the North was established a precarious and uneasy union of Calvinist Holland and Catholic Belgium in the Kingdom of the Netherlands – a union which lasted only until 1830. The Rhineland, mainly at the instance of the British Government, was allotted to Prussia. In the South the King of Sardinia regained Piedmont and Savoy, with the old Republic of Genoa as a further sop. Throughout the rest of Italy the authority of Austria stretched unchallenged. Lombardy and Venetia, Trieste and Dalmatia, were placed under direct Austrian rule. Austrian Archdukes reigned in Florence and Modena. The Empress Marie Louise was allotted the Duchy of Parma, more because she was a Habsburg than because she was Napoleon's wife. It was laid down that her son should not succeed her. Bonaparte blood was to be barred from thrones. At Naples for a while Marshal Murat was left in possession of his stolen kingdom. But not for long. Soon the Bourbons were restored, and over them Austrian influence also reigned supreme.

So much for Western Europe. The root trouble lay in the East. Russia wanted Poland, Prussia wanted Saxony. Left to themselves each might have accepted the demands of the other, but this was far from agreeable to either France or Austria. Castlereagh, as fearful of the expansion of Russia as Metternich was of Prussia, took sides against so sweeping a settlement. An alliance between Britain, France, and Austria was formed to resist these pretensions, if necessary even by war. War did not prove necessary. Russia consented to swallow the greater part of Poland, with many professions from the Czar that Polish rights and liberties would be respected. He did not live up to his promises. Prussia, grumbling, accepted two-fifths of Saxony as well as the Rhineland. This compromise was reached only just in time. For while Congress danced at Vienna and the statesmen of Europe replotted the map Napoleon was brooding and scheming in his new retreat at Elba. Long before the wrangling of the Powers had ended he again burst upon the scene.

In the New Year of 1815 peace reigned in Europe and in America. In Paris a stout elderly, easy-going Bourbon sat on the throne of France, oblivious of the mistakes made by his relations, advisers, and followers. His royalist supporters, more royal than their King, were trying the patience of his new-found subjects. The French people, still dreaming of Imperial glories, were ripe for another adventure. At Vienna the Powers of Europe had solved one of their most vexatious problems. They had decided how to apportion the peoples of Saxony and Poland among the hungry victors, Prussia and Russia. But they were still by no means in accord on many details of the map of Europe which they had met to redraw. After the exertions of twenty years of warfare they felt they had earned leisure enough to indulge in haggling, bargains and festivity. A sharp and sudden shock was needed to recall them to their unity of purpose. It came from a familiar quarter.

Napoleon had for nine months been sovereign of Elba. The former master of the Continent now looked out upon a shrunken island domain. He kept about him the apparatus of Imperial dignity. At Porto Ferrajo, his capital, he furnished a palace in the grand manner. He played cards with his mother and cheated according to his recognised custom. He entertained his favourite sister and his faithful Polish mistress. Only his wife, the Empress Marie Louise, and their son were missing. The Austrian Government took care to keep them both in Vienna. The Empress showed no sign of wishing to break her parole. Family Habsburg loyalty meant more to her than her husband.

A stream of curious foreign visitors came to see the fallen Emperor, many from Britain. One of them reported, perhaps not without prejudice, that he looked more like a crafty priest than a great commander. The resident Allied Commissioner on Elba, Sir Neil Campbell, knew better. As the months went by close observers became sure that Napoleon was biding his time. He was keeping a watch on events in France and Italy. Through spies he was in touch with many currents of opinion. He perceived that the restored Bourbons could not command the loyalty of the French. Besides, they had failed to pay him the annual pension stipulated in the treaty of peace. This act of pettiness persuaded Napoleon that he was absolved from honouring the treaty's terms. In February 1815 he saw, or thought he saw, that the Congress of Vienna was breaking up. The Allies were at odds, and France, discontented, beckoned to him. Campbell, the shrewd Scottish watchdog, was absent in Italy. Of all this conjunction of circumstances Napoleon took lightning advantage. On Sunday night, the 26th of February, he slipped out of harbour in his brig, attended by a small train of lesser vessels. At the head of a thousand men he set sail for France. On March 1st he landed near Antibes. The local band, welcoming him, played the French equivalent of *Home, Sweet Home*.

The drama of the Hundred Days had begun, and a bloodless march to Paris ensued. Royalist armies sent to stop the intruder melted away or went over to him. Marshal Ney, "the Bravest of the Brave", who had taken service under the Bourbons, boasted that he would bring his former master back to Paris in an iron cage. He found he could not resist the Emperor's call; he joined Napoleon. Other Marshals who had turned their coats now turned them again. Within eighteen days of his landing Napoleon was installed in the capital. The Bourbons ran for cover, and found it at Ghent. Meanwhile the Emperor proclaimed his peaceful intentions, and at once started shaping his army. He bid for support by promising liberal institutions to the French people. In fact he dreamed of restoring all the old forms of Empire as soon as he had behind him the consolidation of military victory. But the mood of France had changed since the high noon of Austerlitz, Jena, and Wagram. There was enthusiasm, but no longer at the topmost fighting pitch. The Army and its leaders were not what they had been. The frightful losses of the Russian campaign and of Leipzig could not be made good. Since 1805 a hundred and forty-eight French generals had fallen in battle. Of those that remained only half were now loyal to Napoleon. Yet the Emperor remained a formidable figure and a challenge to Europe. The Powers at Vienna acted with un-accustomed speed and unanimity. They declared Napoleon an outlaw. There was no time to lose. Wellington recommended the immediate transport of an army to the Netherlands, to form bases for a march on Paris and prepare for a clash upon the frontiers. Within a month of the escape from Elba Wellington took up his command at Brussels.

The state of his army did not please the Duke. Many of his best troops from the Peninsula had gone to America, including his Chief of Staff, Sir George Murray. With great difficulty the British Government had collected six regiments of cavalry and twenty-five battalions of infantry, consisting partly of Peninsular veterans and partly of untrained boys. The biggest deficiency was in artillery. On the conclusion of the Peace of Paris in 1814 the British Cabinet had ordered the wholesale discharge of gunners and drivers, and the shortage was now serious. But there were, as in all European wars, the Continental allies and auxiliaries. The King of Great Britain was still King of Hanover. Hanoverian troops, on their way home through the Netherlands, were halted and joined the new army. Wellington, at a loss for numbers, tried to persuade the Portuguese to send a few battalions. He had taught them the arts of war, and he was proud of his "fighting cocks", as he called them. But his efforts were in vain. The Dutch and Belgian troops put under his command by the King of the Netherlands looked unreliable. Their countries had for twenty years been occupied by the French, and the Belgians at least had taken not unkindly to French rule. The sympathies of their rank and file would probably waver towards Napoleon. There were contingents also from Nassau and other German provinces. As the summer drew near Wellington assembled a mixed force of eighty-three thousand men, of whom about a third were British. He bluntly cursed, as was his habit, the quality of his untried troops, while bending all his endeavours to train and transform them. The support for his new adventure must be Marshal Blücher.[1] The Prussians had a force of a hundred and thirteen thousand men, but nearly half of them were untrained militia. They lay in Eastern Belgium. Wellington, with his staff, planned a large-scale advance into France. He meant to take the offensive. He did not propose tamely to await a Napoleonic onslaught.

Napoleon could not afford to waste a day. Nor did he do so. His two main enemies stood on his north-eastern frontier within a few days' march of his capital. He must strike immediately at his gathering foes. The moral value of victory would be overwhelming, and the prestige of the British Government would be shaken. His admirers in London, the pacific Whigs, might replace the Tories and proffer a negotiated peace. Louis XVIII would be driven into permanent exile and the Belgian Netherlands restored to French rule. This achieved, he could face with equanimity the menaces of Austria and Russia.

---

1   Gebbard Leberecht von Blücher (1742–1819) the Prussian cavalry commander who, early, in his career was dismissed from the service for an excessive lifestyle and insubordination. Later, he was back in the hussars and when Prussia fought France in 1813, Blücher commanded in Silesia.

During the early days of June tension was heightening. It was plain, or at least predictable, that Napoleon would attempt to rout Wellington's and Blücher's armies separately and piecemeal. But where would he land his first blow? Wellington waited patiently in Brussels for a sign of the Emperor's intention. He and his great opponent were to cross swords for the first time. They were both in their forty-sixth year. Quietly on June 15 Napoleon crossed the Sambrera at Charleroi and Marchiennes, driving the Prussian forward troops before him to within twenty-five miles of Brussels. He had struck at the hinge of the Allied armies. The capture of Brussels would be a great forward stride. Possession of a capital city was always a lure for him, and a source of strength.

Liaison between the British and Prussians was mysteriously defective and hours passed before the news reached Wellington. It seemed as though there was no detailed plan of co-operation between the Allied commanders. Military intelligence, as so often at the neap of events, was confusing and contradictory. There were no British troops on the Waterloo-Charleroi road, which was held thinly by a Dutch-Belgian division. On the night of the 15th, while the French armies massed to destroy the Prussians, the Duchess of Richmond gave a ball in Brussels in honour of the Allied officers. Wellington graced the occasion with his presence. He knew the value of preserving a bold, unruffled face. Amid the dancing he reflected on the belated news which had reached him. At all costs contact must be maintained with the Prussians and the French advance upon Brussels held. Wellington resolved to concentrate on the strategic point of Quatre-Bras. In the early hours of the morning of the 16th Picton's brigade rumbled down the Brussels road to join the Dutch troops already covering this dangerous ground lying open between the British and Prussian array.

For the French everything depended upon beating the Prussians before forcing Wellington north-westwards to the coast. Napoleon had in mind the vision of a shattered British army grimly awaiting transports for home in the Flemish ports. At Corunna and Walcheren such things had happened before. Leaving Ney with the French left, the Emperor swung with sixty-three thousand men and ninety-two guns to meet the main Prussian army, centred in Ligny. But the tardiness and sureness of Wellington's movement deceived him. Realising that so far only a small force held the position at Quatre-Bras, he ordered Ney to attack, and then meet him that evening in Brussels. At two o'clock in the afternoon of the 16th the French went into action on a two-mile front. Wellington himself arrived to take command with a force of seven thousand men and sixteen guns. The brunt of the battle fell upon Picton's leading brigade. After having marched for twelve hours from Brussels these Peninsular veterans steadily pressed on. In vain the French cavalry swirled round them while the Allied Dutch and Belgian infantry were edged from the field. There was little tactical manoeuvre in the fierce struggle which swayed backwards and forwards on that June afternoon at the cross-roads on the way to Brussels. It was a head-on collision in which generalship played no part, though leadership did. Wellington was always at his coolest in the hottest of moments. In this battle of private soldiers the fire-power of the British infantry prevailed. Out of thirty thousand men engaged by nightfall on their side the Allies lost four thousand six hundred; the French somewhat less. But Ney had not gained his objective. Brussels was not in his grasp.

On the French side the staff work had hardly been creditable. D'Erlon, under Napoleon's orders, had marched aimlessly about, at one time in the direction of Ligny and at another towards Quatre-Bras. Napoleon had gained the advantage at the opening of the campaign, but he had not intended that both wings of his army should be in action at once. He seems to have departed from his original plan. At Ligny, however, he won a striking success. Marshal Blücher was out-generalled, his army split in two, battered by the magnificent French artillery, and driven back on Wavre. Again liaison between the Allied armies broke down. Wellington had no immediate information of the outcome at Ligny, nor of the subsequent movements of the Prussians. He had held the French left at Quatre-Bras, but their victory to the east enabled them to concentrate their strength against him and the Brussels road. Wellington's main body had gathered around the village of Quatre-Bras by the time he learnt of the Prussian defeat. Napoleon decided in the small hours of the 17th to send Marshal Grouchy with thirty-three thousand men to pursue the Prussians while he flung his main weight against Wellington. The crisis of the campaign was at hand.

There seems no doubt that in the opening days Wellington had been surprised. As he confessed at the time, Napoleon's movements had "humbugged" him. Years later, when he read French accounts of Quatre-Bras, he declared with his habitual frankness, "Damn them, I beat them, and if I was surprised, if I did place myself in so foolish a position, they were the greater fools for not knowing how take advantage of my faults." Immediately after the battle his methodical mind was in full command of the situation. His plan was to fall back upon a prepared position at Mont St Jean, which British engineers had examined before the campaign of the previous year. There he would accept battle, and all he asked from the Prussians was the support of one corps.

Wellington himself had inspected this Belgian countryside in the autumn of 1814. He had noted the advantages of the ridge at Waterloo. So had the great Duke of Marlborough a century earlier, when his Dutch allies had prevented him from engaging Marshal Villeroi there. His unfought battle was now to unroll. Throughout the night of the 16th and 17th a carefully screened retreat began, and by morning the Waterloo position, a line of defence such as Wellington had already tested in the Peninsula, was occupied. Upon the French must be forced the onus of a frontal attack. Wellington knew that time was playing against his adversary. Swift results must be achieved by Napoleon if he was to establish himself again in France. A line of fortified farms and rolling slopes made up the Allied front, held by sixty-three thousand men and a hundred and fifty-six guns. The French troops failed to harass the retreat. Their staff work had again gone awry. Napoleon was unaware of what had happened at Quatre-Bras, and there was an imminent danger that the Prussians would fall back and unite with Wellington. That was indeed their intention. Blücher and his Chief of Staff, Gneisenau, who was the brain of the Prussian army, were retiring north-west from Ligny in the direction of Brussels. Grouchy, misinformed or misjudging, thought they were moving north-east towards Liège. He remained out of touch and ineffective. Grouchy's was a costly mistake for the French. Meanwhile Napoleon, furious to hear of Wellington's skilful withdrawal, pounded in his carriage down the Brussels road with his advance-guard in a desperate attempt to entrap the British rear. The mercy of a violent storm slowed up progress. The English cavalry galloped for safety through the thunder and torrential rain. An angry scene took place upon the meeting of Napoleon and Ney, who was greeted with the words from the Emperor, "You have ruined France!" As Napoleon reached the ridge of Waterloo and saw the British already in their positions he realised how complete had been their escape.

Late in the morning of the 18th of June the French attacked both flanks of the Allied position, of which the key points were the fortified château of Hougoumont on the right and the farm of La Haye Sainte in the middle. Napoleon promised his staff they would sleep that night in Brussels. And to Soult, who raised some demur, he said, "You think Wellington a great general because he beat you. I tell you this will be a picnic." Then seventy thousand French troops and two hundred and twenty-four guns were concentrated for the decisive assault. Fierce cannonades were launched upon the Allied posts. The battle swayed backwards and forwards upon the grass slopes, and intense fighting centred in the farm of La Haye Sainte, which eventually fell to the French. At Hougoumont, which held out all day, the fighting was heavier still. In the early afternoon one of the most terrific artillery barrages of the time was launched upon Wellington's infantry as preparation for the major cavalry advance of fifteen thousand troopers under Ney. Under the hail of the French guns Wellington moved his infantry farther back over the ridge of Waterloo to give them a little more shelter. On seeing this Ney launched his squadrons in a series of attacks. Everything now depended upon the British muskets and bayonets. Anxiously Wellington looked eastwards for a sign of the Prussians. They were on their way, for Blücher was keeping faith. But the French cuirassiers were upon the Duke. They never reached the infantry squares. As one eye-witness wrote: "As to the so-called charges, I do not think that on a single occasion actual collision occurred. I many times saw the cuirassiers come on with boldness to within some twenty or thirty yards of a square, when, seeing the steady firmness of our men, they invariably edged away and retired. Sometimes they would halt and gaze at the triple row of bayonets, when two or three brave officers would advance and strive to urge the attack, raising their helmets aloft on their sabres; but all in vain, as no efforts could make the men close with the terrible bayonets and meet certain destruction."

No visible decision was achieved. Napoleon, looking through his glasses at the awful *mêlée*, exclaimed, "Will the English never show their backs?"

"I fear," replied Soult, "they will be cut to pieces first." Wellington too had much to disturb him. Although the Prussians had been distantly sighted upon the roads in the early afternoon, they were slow in making their presence felt upon the French right. But by six o'clock in the evening Ney's onslaughts had failed and the Prussians were beating relentlessly upon the wing. They drew off fourteen thousand men from the forces assailing Wellington. The French made a final effort, and desperate fighting with no quarter raged again round the farms. The Imperial Guard itself, with Ney at its head, rolled up the hill, but again the fury of British infantry fire held them. The long-awaited moment to counter-attack had come. Wellington had been in the forefront of danger all day. On his chestnut, Copenhagen, he had galloped everywhere, issuing brusque orders, gruffly encouraging his men. Now he rode along his much-battered line and ordered the advance. "Go on, go on!" he shouted. "They will not stand!" His cavalry swept from the ridge and sabred the French army into a disorganised mass of stragglers. Ney, beside himself with rage, a broken sword in his hand, staggered shouting in vain from one band to another. It was too late. Wellington handed over the pursuit to the Prussians. In agony of soul Napoleon followed the road back to Paris.

Late that night Blücher and Wellington met and embraced. "*Mein lieber Kamerad*," said the old German Field-Marshal, who knew not a word of English, "*quelle affaire!*", which was about all the French he could command. This brief greeting was greatly to Wellington's laconic taste. It was a story he delighted to repeat in later years when he was Lord Warden of the Cinque Ports, recalling his memories at Walmer. The Duke rode back to Brussels. The day had been almost too much even for a man of iron. The whole weight of responsibility had fallen on him. Only the power and example of his own personality had kept his motley force together. The strain had been barely tolerable. "By God!" as he justly said, "I don't think it would have been done if I had not been there." As he took tea and toast and had the casualty lists read to him he broke down and wept.

Napoleon had reached his capital three days after the battle. He had a momentary surge of hope. He would fight again in France a campaign like that of 1814. But no one shared his optimism. The grand officials of the Empire, who owed him their positions and fortunes, had had enough. On June 22 he abdicated and retired to Malmaison. The treacherous Fouché headed a provisional Government and set about treating with the Allies and with Louis XVIII.

Napoleon left Malmaison at the end of June. He made for Rochefort, on the Biscay coast, narrowly evading capture on the way by Blücher's Prussians. Had they taken him they would have shot him. He had thoughts of sailing for America, and he ordered a set of travel books about the transatlantic continent. Perhaps a new Empire might be forged in Mexico, Peru, or Brazil. The alternative was to throw himself upon the mercy of his most inveterate foe. This is what happened. Captain Maitland in the *Bellerophon* was cruising off Rochefort with orders to prevent any French ships from putting to sea. With him Napoleon entered into negotiation. Maitland offered him asylum on his ship. He could not forecast what the British Government would decide to do with his eminent hostage. Nor did he make any promise. Napoleon hoped he might be kept in pleasant captivity in some English country house or Scottish castle. Marshal Tallard and other French generals a century earlier had enjoyed their forced residence in England. The ex-Emperor wrote a flattering letter to the Prince Regent, whom he addressed as "the strongest, the stubbornest, the most generous of my foes". When the Prince read this missive it must have helped to convince him that he and not his generals or his Ministers had really won the war. On this matter he did not need much convincing. The *Bellerophon* anchored in Torbay, and curious Devonshire crowds gazed upon the "Corsican ogre", while Lord Liverpool and the Cabinet deliberated in London. Newspapers clamoured that Napoleon should be put on trial. The Government, acting for the Allies, decided on exile in St Helena, an island about the same size as Jersey, but very mountainous, and far away. Escape from it was impossible. On July 26 the Emperor sailed to his sunset in the South Atlantic. He never permitted himself to understand what had happened at Waterloo. The event was everybody's fault but his own. Six years of life in exile lay before him. He spent them with his small faithful retinue creating the Napoleonic legend of invincibility which was to have so powerful an effect on the France of the future.

The Congress of Vienna had completed its work in June. It remained for the emissaries of the Powers to assemble in Paris and compose a new peace with France. The task took three months. The Prussians pressed for harsh terms. Castlereagh, representing Britain saw that mildness would create the least grievance and guard best against a renewal of war. In this he had the hearty support of Wellington, who now exerted a unique authority throughout Europe. The second Treaty of Paris, concluded in November, was somewhat stiffer than that of 1814. Together with the loss of certain small territories, France was to pay in indemnity of seven hundred million francs and to submit to an Allied army of occupation for three years. Yet no intolerable humiliations were involved. In the moderation of the settlement with France the treaty had its greatest success. Wellington took command of the occupying army. For the next three years he was practically a Great European Power in himself. Castlereagh, with his sombre cast of mind, thought the treaty would be justified if it kept the peace for seven years. He had built better than he knew. Peace reigned for forty years between the Great Powers, and the main framework of the settlements at Vienna and Paris endured until the twentieth century.

The treaties drawn up in 1815 were the last great European settlements until 1919–20. Castlereagh might dismiss the Holy Alliance which was now formed between the three autocratic Powers, Russia, Prussia, and Austria, as "a piece of sublime mysticism and nonsense". Yet for the sake of stability Castlereagh was prepared to see Romanovs, Hohenzollerns, and Habsburgs re-establish their reactionary authority throughout the greater part of Central and Eastern

Europe in defiance of all popular movements for nationality and freedom. Such was the price that Europe paid for the overthrow of Napoleon. Even the principle of legitimacy was discarded when it clashed with the interests of one of the Great Powers. Poland, still independent in 1792, was no longer accounted legitimate in 1814. Part of the kingdom of Saxony and the prince-bishoprics of the Rhine went to Prussia, the Republic of Venice and its Adriatic seaboard to Austria. Legitimacy presented no obstacle to territorial expansion.

The impetus of the French Revolution had been spread by the genius of Napoleon to the four quarters of Europe. Ideals of liberty and nationalism, born in Paris, had been imparted to all the European peoples. In the nineteenth century ahead they were to clash resoundingly with the ordered world for which the Congress of Vienna had striven. If France was defeated and her Emperor fallen, the principles which had inspired her lived on. They were to play a notable part in changing the shape of government in every European country, Britain not excepted.

CHAPTER FORTY-THREE

THE VICTORY PEACE

*Castlereagh and Wellington – the Holy Alliance of Russia, Austria and
Prussia – the Blanketeers' March – the Peterloo Massacre – the Cato
Street conspiracy – the madness of George III – the Regency – Maria
Fitzherbert – Queen Caroline accused of adultery – the rise of Robert
Peel – Castlereagh's suicide – the Monroe Doctrine – the war of
Greek Independence – Canning as Prime Minister – Daniel O'Connell
and the Test election – the Catholic Emancipation Bill – the death of
George IV – William IV, the sailor king*

AFTER A generation of warfare peace had come to Europe in the
summer of 1815. It was to be a long peace, disturbed by civil
commotions and local campaigns, but flaring into no major blaze
until the era of German expansion succeeded the age of French
predominance.

The principal figures in the Government were Lord Liverpool, Lord
Castlereagh, and, after 1818, the Duke of Wellington. Castlereagh and
Wellington towered above their colleagues.[1] Much of the credit for the broad
peace which Europe enjoyed after the fall of Napoleon was due to the robust
common sense and shrewd judgment of Wellington and to the aloof
disinterestedness of Castlereagh. In spite of many setbacks and some military
blunders these men had led the country to victory. Liverpool was the son of
Charles Jenkinson, organiser of Government patronage under George III and
close colleague of the younger Pitt. He was a man of conciliatory temper, a
mild chief, and an easy colleague. He had held a variety of public offices
almost continuously since the start of the war with France. In 1812 he became
Prime Minister, and for fifteen years presided over the affairs of the realm
with tact, patience, and laxity.

Castlereagh had served his political apprenticeship as Chief Secretary for
Ireland. In the difficult days of the negotiation for Union with Ireland, when

1   Robert Banks Jenkinson, 2nd Earl of Liverpool (1770–1828) should never be underrated in
    English political history. A tactful and modest man, Liverpool was often mocked for being
    unimaginative. It was said that, should Liverpool have witnessed The Creation, he would have
    called out in panic "Mon Dieu, conservons nous le chaos!" Perhaps without great vision, he had
    the talent to hold his Party together. (See Sir Llewellyn Woodward, *The Age of Reform
    1815–1870*, Oxford University Press, 1938.)

the powers of patronage were extensively used, he had seen eighteenth-century jobbery at its worst. He had joined the war-time Cabinet as Secretary for War, but was obliged to resign after a celebrated quarrel with his colleague Canning, which led to a duel between them on Putney Heath. In 1812 Castlereagh had returned to the Government and had been appointed to the Foreign Office. He was the architect of the coalition which gained the final victory and one of the principal authors of the treaties of peace. For home affairs he cared little, and he was unable to expound his far-sighted foreign policy with the eloquence that it deserved. Castlereagh was no orator. His cool, collected temperament was stiffened with disdain; he thought it beneath him to inform the public frankly of the Government's plans and measures. Nevertheless he was Leader of the House of Commons. Seldom has that office been filled by a man with fewer natural qualifications for it.

In Wellington all men acknowledged the illustrious General who had met and beaten Napoleon. His conception of politics was simple. He wished to unite all parties, and imbue them with the duty of preserving the existing order. The rest of the Cabinet were Tories of the deepest dye, such as the Lord Chancellor, Eldon; Addington, now Viscount Sidmouth, once Prime Minister and now at the Home Office; and Earl Bathurst, Colonial Secretary, whom Lord Rosebery has described as "one of those strange children of our political system who fill the most dazzling offices with the most complete obscurity". These men had begun their political life under the threat of world revolution. Their sole aim in politics was an unyielding defence of the system they had always known. Their minds were rigid, and scarcely capable of grasping the changes pending in English society. They were the upholders of the landed interest in government, of the Protestant ascendancy in Ireland, and of Anglicanism at home.

Castlereagh resolved that Britain should not abandon the position of authority she had won during the war. Immune from popular passions, race hatreds, or any desire to trample on a fallen enemy, he foresaw the day when France would be as necessary to the balance of Europe and to the interests of Britain as Prussia, Austria, and Russia. With Wellington he stood between France and her vindictive foes. Unrestrained, Prussia, Austria, and Russia would have divided between them the states of Germany, imposed a harsh peace upon France, and fought each other over the partition of Poland. The moderating influence of Britain was the foundation of the peace of Europe.

In the eighteenth century the European Powers had no regular organisation for consulting each other, and little conception of their common interests. The Revolution in France had united them against the common danger, and they were now determined to remain together to prevent a further outbreak. An alliance of the four Great Powers already existed, sworn to confer as occasion demanded upon the problems of Europe. This was now supplemented by a Holy Alliance between the three autocratic rulers on the Continent, the Emperors of Russia and Austria and the King of Prussia. Its main purpose was to intervene in any part of Europe where revolution appeared and in the name of legitimacy instantly to suppress it.

This made small appeal to Castlereagh. He was opposed to any interference in the affairs of sovereign states, however small and whatever liberal complexions their Governments might assume. Although caricatured as a reactionary at home he was no friend to Continental despotism. To him the Quadruple Alliance and the Congress at Vienna were merely pieces of diplomatic machinery for discussing European problems. On the other hand, the Austrian Chancellor Metternich[1] and his colleagues regarded them as instruments for preserving the existing order. This divergence between the Great Powers was in part due to the fact that Britain had a Parliamentary Government which represented, however imperfectly, a nation. Castlereagh's European colleagues were the servants of absolute monarchs. Britain was a world-Power whose strength lay in her ranging commerce and in her command of the seas. Her trade flourished and multiplied independently of the reigning ideas in Europe. Moreover, her governing classes, long accustomed to public debate, did not share the absolutist dreams that inspired, and deluded, the Courts of the autocrats.

In spite of these differences the Congress of Vienna stands as a monument to the success of classical diplomacy. The intricacies of its negotiations were immense. No fewer than twenty-seven separate agreements were concluded during the first six months of 1815, in addition to the formidable Final Act of the Congress itself, and some twenty other treaties signed elsewhere in the same period. Talleyrand,[2] with his background of double-dealing and treachery to his Emperor, nevertheless displayed an unswerving and ingenious determination to restore his country's position in Europe. But to modern eyes Castlereagh was pre-eminent as the genius of the conference. He reconciled opposing views, and his modest expectation that peace might be ensured for seven years was fulfilled more than fivefold. Within three years of the signing of the peace treaty British troops had evacuated French territory, the war indemnity had been paid, and France was received as a respectable nation into the European Congress. Wellington, released from military duties in France, thereupon entered the Cabinet in the not inappropriate office of Master-General of the Ordnance.

At home the Government were faced with the delicate and perplexing task of economic reconstruction. Earlier than her neighbours, Britain enjoyed the

---

1   Prince Metternich (1773–1859). From 1809, Austrian Foreign Minister and supreme diplomatic and political reactionary. He probably did more than any other European leader to constrict constitutional reforms and saw despotism as the most stable form of government. Perhaps ironically, when the government in Vienna fell through the force of European revolution, Metternich fled to England before spending the final years of his life by the Rhine.

2   Charles de Talleyrand-Périgord (1754–1838). For a long time, the powerful courtier in France. Sometime abbot, cynic, intriguer, excommunicant, foreign minister and early supporter and beneficiary of Napoleon, although he later plotted against the Emperor. Masterminded the 1806 Confederation of the Rhine. Later, Louis XVIII's minister of foreign affairs. Generally feared and disliked, he once remarked that war is too serious a thing to be left to military men.

fruits and endured the rigours of the Industrial Revolution. She gained a new domain of power and prosperity. At the same time the growing masses in her ill-built towns were often plunged into squalor and misery, the source of numerous and well-grounded discontents. Her technical lead was due to the ingenuity and success of British inventors and men of business in the eighteenth century and to the fortunate proximity of her main coal and iron deposits to each other and to the coast. Supremacy at sea, the resources of the colonial empire, and the use of capital accumulated from its trade nourished the industrial movement. Steam engines were gradually harnessed to the whole field of contemporary industry. In engineering accurate tools were perfected which brought a vast increase in output. The spinning of cotton was mechanised, and the factory system grew by degrees. The skilled man, self-employed, who had hitherto worked in his home, was steadily displaced. Machinery, the rise of population, and extensive changes in employment all presented a formidable social problem. The Government were by their background and upbringing largely unaware of the causes of the ills which they had to cure. They concentrated upon the one issue they understood, the defence of property. In a society which was rapidly becoming industrial most of them represented the abiding landed interest. They were incapable of carrying out even moderate reforms because of their obsessive fears of bloody revolution.

In the Radical view it was the Government alone, and not chance or Act of God, that was to blame for the misfortunes of the people. The Tory Cabinet in the face of such charges knew not what to do. It was no part of Tory philosophy to leave everything to be settled by the chaffer of the market-place, to trust to good luck and ignore the bad. The Tories of the time recognised and sometimes gloried in the responsibility of the governing classes for the welfare of the whole nation. The tasks of government were well understood to be as Burke had defined them – "the public peace, the public safety, the public order, the public prosperity". It was the last of these that was now foremost. The trouble was that the Government, in the unprecedented conditions that confronted them, had no idea how to secure the public prosperity. And even if they had hit upon a plan they possessed no experienced body of civil servants to put it into effect. As a result the only remedy for misery was private charity or the Poor Law.

It was a misfortune for Britain in these years that the Parliamentary Opposition was at its weakest. A generation in the wilderness had demoralised the Whig Party, which had not been effectively in office since 1783. Like their rivals, they represented the landed class, and also the City of London. The only issues upon which they seriously quarrelled with the Government were Catholic Emancipation and the enfranchisement of the middle classes in the rising industrial towns. In the 1790s the Whigs had favoured the cause of Parliamentary Reform. It had been a useful stick with which to beat the administration of the younger Pitt. But they had been badly scared by the headlong course of events in France. The Radicals who found their way into

Parliament were too few to form an effective Opposition. One of their veteran leaders, John Cartwright, had for forty years in a litter of pamphlets been advocating annual Parliaments and universal suffrage. He was a landed gentleman, liked by many Members, but he never sat in the House of Commons. Under the unreformed franchise no constituency would adopt him.

English political tradition centred in Parliament, and men still looked to Parliament to cure the evils of the day. If Parliament did nothing, then the structure of Parliament must be changed. Agitation therefore turned from airing social discontents to demanding Parliamentary Reform. But the tactics of the Radicals were too much like those of the French Revolutionaries to gain support from the middle classes. Though still denied much weight in Parliament, the middle classes were bound by their fear of revolution to side in the last resort with the landed interest. The Cabinet was thoroughly perturbed. *Habeas corpus* was suspended, and legislation passed against the holding of seditious meetings. Throughout the country a fresh wave of demonstrations followed. A large body of men set out to march from Manchester to London to present a petition against the Government's measures, each carrying a blanket for his night's shelter. This march of the "Blanketeers" disturbed the authorities profoundly. The leaders were arrested and the rank and file quickly dispersed. Another rising in Derbyshire was easily suppressed.

These alarms and excursions revealed the gravity of conditions. Not only was there grinding poverty among the working population, but also a deep-rooted conflict between the manufacturing and agricultural classes. The economy of the country was dangerously out of balance. The war debt had reached alarming proportions. The fund-holders were worried at the instability of the national finances. The country had gone off the gold standard in 1797, and the paper currency had seriously depreciated. In 1812 a Parliamentary committee advised returning to gold, but the Bank of England was strongly adverse and nothing was done. The income tax, introduced by Pitt to finance the war, was highly unpopular, especially among the industrial middle class. It took 10 per cent of all incomes over £150 a year, and there were lower rates for smaller incomes. The yield in 1815 was fifteen million pounds, which was a large proportion of the Budget. Agriculture as well as industry quaked at the end of the war. Much capital had been sunk in land for the sake of high profits. Peace brought a slump in the prices fetched by crops, and landowners clamoured for protection against the importation of cheap foreign corn. This had been granted by the Corn Law of 1815, which excluded foreign wheat unless the domestic price per quarter rose above eighty shillings. The cost of bread went up, and the manufacturing classes had to raise wages to save their workers from hunger. The manufacturers in their turn got the income tax abolished, which helped them but imperilled the Budget.

In 1819 an incident took place which increased the unpopularity and quickened the fears of the Government. A meeting of protest was held at St Peter's Fields, in mid-Manchester, attended by over fifty thousand people, including women and children. The local magistrates lost their heads, and, after reading the Riot Act, ordered the yeomanry to charge. Eleven people were killed, two of them women, and four hundred were injured. This "massacre of Peterloo", as it was called in ironic reference to the Battle of Waterloo, aroused widespread indignation, which was swelled still further when the Government took drastic steps to prevent the recurrence of disorder. Six Acts were passed regulating public meetings, empowering the magistrates to seize seditious literature, forbidding unauthorised drilling in military formations, imposing a heavy tax upon the Press to restrict the circulation of Radical newspapers, regulating the issue of warrants and the bringing of cases to trial. Soon afterwards a conspiracy was discovered against the whole Cabinet. A small gang of plotters was arrested in Cato Street, a turning off the Edgware Road, where they had met to plan to murder all the Ministers at a dinner party and seize the Bank of England.

The attack by the Government upon the traditional principles of English liberty aroused the conscience of the Whigs. They considered that "Peterloo" was no excuse for invading the rights of the subject. They demanded an inquiry. Liberty was at stake, and this was a struggle they well understood. When they were outvoted, however, they took their defeat with some equanimity; for they were as frightened as the Tories by the social unrest that was gripping all Europe

Once again in English history the personal affairs of the royal family now exploded into public view. Victory over Napoleon had been a triumph for the Divine Right of Kings and the cause of monarchy. But the republican influence of the French Revolution had left its mark on public opinion in most European countries, and the vices or incapacity of many monarchs made them easy targets for criticism and abuse. In England King George III had long been intermittently mad, and English politicians had had to reckon with the virtual demise of the Crown for considerable intervals. In 1788 the first madness of the King had confronted Pitt with a grave political crisis. An acrimonious dispute with Fox and the Whigs over the powers that should be exercised by the Prince of Wales as Regent was brought to a conclusion only by George III's sudden recovery. In 1810 the old King finally sank into incurable imbecility. He lived for another ten years, roaming the corridors of Windsor Castle with long white beard and purple dressing-gown. The Prince became Regent, with unrestricted royal prerogatives. To the consternation of his old Whig friends, he had kept his Tory advisers in power and prosecuted the war with vigour. Whatever the faults of George IV, his determination as Regent to support Wellington and Castlereagh and to stand up to Napoleon should earn him an honourable place in his country's history.

The atmosphere of the Court was like that of a minor German principality. All was stiff, narrow, fusty. The spirited lad who was to be George IV soon rebelled against his decorous mother and parsimonious father. A gift for facile friendship, often with dubious personages, alienated him still further from the home circle. In 1784 the Prince had fallen in love. His choice was unfortunate.

Maria Fitzherbert was not only a commoner of obscure family, but also a Roman Catholic. Her morals were impeccable and she would be content with nothing less than marriage. The Prince's Whig friends were alarmed when the heir to the most Protestant throne in Europe insisted on marrying a Roman Catholic widow who had already survived two husbands. Under the Royal Marriages Act the union was illegal, and George's behaviour was neither creditable to himself nor to his position. The clandestine beginnings of this relationship and the volatile temperament of George did their work. Mrs Fitzherbert, prim and quiet, was not the woman to hold him for long. The relationship slid back into the secrecy from which it had unwillingly emerged. It was finally broken off, but not until some years after George had contracted a second, legal, and dynastic marriage.

At the bidding of his parents in 1795 he was wedded to Caroline of Brunswick, a noisy, flighty, and unattractive German princess. George was so appalled at the sight of his bride that he was drunk for the first twenty-four hours of his married life. A few days after his wedding he wrote his wife a letter absolving her from any further conjugal duties. For some years thereafter he consoled himself with Lady Jersey. He acquired a growing hatred for Caroline. A high-spirited, warm-hearted girl was born of their brief union, Princess Charlotte, who found her mother quite as unsatisfactory as her father. In 1814 George banned his wife from Court, and after an unseemly squabble she left England for a European tour, vowing to return to plague her husband when he should accede to the throne.

The Government were perturbed about the problem of the succession. Princess Charlotte married Prince Leopold of Saxe-Coburg, later King of the Belgians, but in 1817 she died in childbirth. Her infant was stillborn. George's brothers, who were all in different ways eccentric, were thoroughly unpopular. Most of them were already illegally involved in long-standing relationships with woman. In 1818, however, the obliging Dukes of Clarence and Kent did their royal duty – for a sum. Kent made a German marriage, and retired to Gibraltar to exercise his martial talents upon the Rock. The offspring of this alliance was the future Queen Victoria.

The Prince of Wales had long played with the idea of divorcing his itinerant wife. But Liverpool's Government were apprehensive. The Prince's extravagance, his lavish architectural experiments at Brighton and Windsor, were already causing them anxiety and giving rise to hostile speeches in Parliament. The Lord Chancellor, bluest of Tories, was vehemently opposed to any idea of divorce. The bench of bishops adopted a similar and suitable attitude. But George was persistent. He got a commission appointed to inquire into the Princess's conduct. It posted to Italy to collect evidence from the unsavoury entourage of Caroline. In July 1819 the Government received a report producing considerable circumstantial evidence against her. George was delighted, Liverpool and the Cabinet dismayed. Ever since 1714 the quarrels of the royal family had provided ammunition for party political warfare. The Opposition would certainly take up the cause of the injured wife.

The Princess's chief legal adviser was Henry Brougham, the ablest of the younger Whigs.[1] This witty, ambitious, and unscrupulous attorney saw the value of the case to his party, though he was unconvinced of his client's innocence. He entered into confidential relations with the Government, hoping a compromise would bring advancement to himself. But in January 1820 the mad old King died and the position of the new sovereign's consort had to be determined. George IV fell seriously ill, but his hatred of Caroline sustained and promoted his recovery. He insisted upon her name being struck from the Church liturgy. The Cabinet presented him with a nervous note pointing out the difficulties of action. But now he was King. He warned them he would dismiss the lot, and threatened to retire to Hanover. The Whigs were as much alarmed as the Tories by the King's determination. They too feared the effect on public opinion outside Parliamentary and political circles. Whatever happened, there would be a scandal which would bring the monarchy into dangerous disrepute.

Caroline now showed her hand. In April 1820 an open letter appeared in the London Press, signed by her, and recounting her woes. The Radical sympathy of the City of London was easily aroused in her favour. Alderman Wood entered into active correspondence with her and promised her a warm reception. The Radicals saw their chance of discrediting the traditional political parties. The Government made a last effort. Brougham was sent to intercept the Queen on her journey to England. A hurried meeting took place at St Omer. But nothing would stop the infuriated woman, whose obstinacy was inflamed by Radical advice. In June she landed, and she drove amid stormy scenes of enthusiasm from Dover to London. Her carriage was hauled most of the way by exuberant supporters. Her arrival produced a tumult of agitation.

The Government reluctantly decided that they must go through with the business. A Secret Committee of the Lords was set up, and their report persuaded Liverpool to agree to introduce a Bill of Pains and Penalties if the Queen were proved guilty of adultery. Popular feeling against the conditions of England was now diverted into a national inquiry into the condition of the monarchy. The characters of the royal personages concerned came under merciless scrutiny. A well-organised campaign was launched on behalf of Queen Caroline, led by the City Radicals, and, now that there was no turning back, by Brougham. Cheering crowds gathered every day outside her house in London. Her appearance in public places was loudly acclaimed. Politicians known to oppose her case were stoned in their carriages. In July the hearing of the charges was opened in Westminster Hall. In lengthy sessions the Attorney-General put the case for the Government, producing unreliable Italian witnesses from Caroline's vagabond Court. Her Master of Ceremonies, Bergami, had installed his numerous relations with bogus titles around her person, and

1   Henry Peter Brougham, 1st Baron Brougham and Vaux (1778–1868) became Lord Chancellor (1830–34). He founded the *Edinburgh Review* in 1802, but his name is more commonly remembered for the one-horse-drawn carriage, the brougham.

this motley company had for some years been touring the Mediterranean countries, earning derision and insults from several Governments. The conflicting and sordid evidence of lackeys and chambermaids was displayed before the audience in Westminster Hall. Stories of keyholes, of indecorous costumes and gestures, regaled the public ear.

The peers thought the Queen guilty, but doubted the wisdom of divorce, and the Bill passed through their House by only nine votes. The Whigs, when compromise had become impossible, voted against the Government. Their leader, Earl Grey, had declared his belief in the innocence of Caroline. The Cabinet now decided that there was small chance of forcing the Bill through the Commons. They withdrew it and the affair was dropped. The London mob rioted in joy; the whole city was illuminated. The windows of the Ministers' houses were broken. Lord Sidmouth, who had prudently kept the newspapers from his daughters, was the first to suffer. But the bubbling effervescence of the masses quickly subsided. Caroline was granted an annuity of £50,000, which she was not too proud to accept. One political result of the crisis was the resignation of George Canning, who had been on friendly terms with the Queen. This gifted pupil of Pitt had rejoined the administration in 1816 as President of the Board of Control, which supervised the Government of India. He had made his influence felt in other spheres as well, and his departure was a serious loss to the Cabinet.

Two more awkward scenes closed this regrettable story. In July 1821 George IV was crowned in pomp at Westminster Abbey. Caroline attempted to force her way into the Abbey, but was turned away because she had no ticket. A month later she died. An attempt by the authorities to smuggle her coffin out of the country was frustrated and a triumphant and tumultuous funeral procession struggled through the City of London. This was the last victory that the Radicals gained from the affair. The political effects of the episode did not end at Canning's resignation. The Tory administration, which consisted largely of ageing reactionaries, had been gravely weakened. It was isolated from general opinion and badly in need of new recruits. The Whigs too had been forced to recognise their lack of popular backing, and the younger Members saw that the "old and natural alliance between the Whigs and the people" was now in danger. They began henceforth to renew their interest in Parliamentary Reform, which soon became the question of the hour.

Modern scholars, delving deeply into family connections and commercial interests, have sought to show that there was no such thing as a two-party system in eighteenth-century Britain. If caution must be the hallmark of history, all that may be said is that the men in power were vigorously opposed by the men who were out, while in between stood large numbers of neutral-minded gentlemen placidly prepared to support whichever group held office. It is not much of a conclusion to come to about a great age of Parliamentary debate. The ins and outs might as well have names, and why not employ the names of Whig and Tory which their supporters cast at one another? At any rate, in the 1820s a Government of Tory complexion had been in power almost without interruption for thirty years.

This Government had successfully piloted the country through the longest and most dangerous war in which Britain had yet been engaged. It had also survived, though with tarnishing reputation, five years of peace-time unrest. But the Industrial Revolution posed a set of technical administrative problems which no aristocratic and agricultural party, Whig or Tory, was capable of handling. The nineteenth century called for a fresh interpretation of the duties of government. New principles and doctrines were arising which were to break up the old political parties and in the Victorian age reshape and recreate them. These developments took time, but already the party built up by the younger Pitt was feeling their stir and stress. Pitt had enlisted the growing mercantile and commercial interests of his day on the Tory side, and his policy of free trade and efficient administration had won over leaders of industry such as the fathers of Robert Peel and William Gladstone. But Pitt's tradition had faded during the years of war. Faithful disciples among the younger men strove to carry on his ideas, but his successors in office lacked his prestige and broad vision.

The younger Tories, headed by George Canning and supported by William Huskisson, spokesman of the merchants, advocated a return to Pitt's policy of free trade. and intelligent commercial legislation. But even they were disunited. The issue of Catholic Emancipation was soon to confuse and split the Tory Party, and on this they were opposed by one of their own generation. Robert Peel during his six years in Ireland had successfully upheld the English ascendancy against heavy discontent and smouldering rebellion. He believed that "an honest despotic Government would be by far the fittest for Ireland". By a mixture of coercion and adroit patronage he had imposed comparative quiet and orderliness. In the nature of things neither his methods nor their results endeared him to the Irish. He had come home convinced that Catholic Emancipation would imperil not only Protestantism in Ireland but the entire political system at Westminster. Long before the nineteenth century was over events proved him right. Meanwhile Peel became Canning's rival for the future leadership of the Tories. Personalities added their complications. Canning had played a leading part in the conception and launching of the Peninsular War. His chief interest lay in foreign affairs. But this field seemed barred to him by his quarrel with Castlereagh. The older Members distrusted him. Brilliant, witty, effervescent, he had a gift for sarcasm which made him many enemies. In August 1822 Canning was offered the post of Governor-General of India. He reconciled himself to this honourable exile; his political life seemed at an end. But then Fate took a hand. In August Castlereagh, his mind unhinged by overwork, cut his throat in the dressing-room of his home. Canning's presence in the Government was now essential: he was appointed Foreign Secretary, and in this office he dominated English politics until his death five years later.

The Ministry had recently been joined by Peel at the Home Office and now

Huskisson went to the Board of Trade. The Government thus had as many as three leading members in the Commons. In 1815 three-quarters of the Cabinet had been in the Lords. The following years saw a more enlightened period of Tory rule. Canning, Peel, and Huskisson pursued bold policies which in many respects were in advance of those propounded by the Whigs. The penal code was reformed by Peel and the London police force is his creation. Huskisson overhauled the tariff system, and continued Pitt's work in abolishing uneconomic taxes and revising the customs duties. Canning urged a scaling down of the duty on corn as the price rose at home. This was bound to bring conflict in the Tory ranks. He realised the distress and the political danger it would cause in the country, and declared on one occasion, "We are on the brink of a great struggle between property and population. Such a struggle is only to be averted by the mildest and most liberal legislation." This soothing task he set before himself, but it was Peel who had to face the crisis when it came.

A crisis in Spain confronted Canning with his first task as Foreign Secretary. The popular elements which had led the struggle against Napoleon now revolted against the autocratic Bourbon Government, formed a revolutionary Junta, and proclaimed a constitution on the model of that set up in France in 1815. Canning had backed the Spanish national rising in 1808, and was naturally sympathetic, but Metternich and the Holy Alliance saw the revolt, which soon spread to the Bourbon Kingdom of Naples, as a threat to the principle of monarchy and to the entire European system. A Congress at Verona in the autumn of 1822 discussed intervention in Spain on behalf of the Bourbons. Wellington had gone out as British representative with instructions from Castlereagh that Britain was to play no part in such a move. Canning vehemently agreed with this view and gave it wide publicity in England, and indeed the whole tradition of British foreign politics was against intervention in the domestic affairs of other states. But Austria and Russia were determined to act. An instrument lay ready to their hand. The ex-enemy, France, coveted respectability. Her restored Bourbon Government feared the revolutionaries and offered to send a military expedition to Spain to recover for King Ferdinand his absolutist powers. This was accepted at Verona. Canning would have nothing to do with it. There was great excitement in London. English volunteers went to Spain to serve in the defence forces of the Spanish "Liberals", a name which entered English politics from this Spanish revolt, while "Conservative" came to us from France. But Canning was equally against official intervention on the side of "Spanish Liberalism", and it was upon this that the Whigs attacked him. These heart-searchings in Britain made little difference to the outcome in Spain. The French expedition met with no serious resistance, and the Spanish Liberals retired to Cadiz and gave in.

A much larger issue now loomed beyond the European scene. Britain had little direct interest in the constitution of Spain, but for two centuries she had competed for the trade of Spain's colonies in South America. Their liberties were important to her. During the wars with Napoleon these colonies had enjoyed the taste of autonomy. They had no relish, when the Bourbons were restored in Madrid, for the revival of royal Spanish rule. These dangers gave Canning great anxiety. The business elements in England, whose support he was keen to command, were acutely sensitive to the peril. He acted with decision. He urged the United States to join Britain in opposing European interference in the countries across the Atlantic. While the Americans meditated on this proposal Canning also made an approach to the French. France had no desire to start an overseas quarrel with Britain. She disclaimed the use of force in South America and forswore colonial ambitions there. Thus was the Holy Alliance checked. As Canning later declared in a triumphant phrase, he had "called the New World into existence to redress the balance of the Old".

The New World meanwhile had something of its own to say. The United States had no wish to see European quarrels transferred across the ocean. They had already recognised the independence of the principal Latin-American republics. They did not want aspiring princes of the royal houses of Europe to be ferried over and set up as monarchs on the democratic continent. Still less would they contemplate European reconquest and colonisation. Canning's suggestion for a joint Anglo-American declaration, began to grow attractive. Two honoured ex-Presidents, Jefferson and Madison, agreed with President Monroe that it would be a welcome and momentous step. They all had in mind Russian designs in the Pacific Ocean, as well as menaces from Europe; for the Russians occupied Alaska, and the territorial claims of the Czar stretched down the Western coast of America to California, where his agents were active. Monroe, however, had in John Quincy Adams a Secretary of State who was cautious and stubborn by temperament and suspicious of Britain. Adams distrusted Canning, whom he earnestly thought to possess "a little too much wit for a Minister of State". He believed that the United States should act on their own initiative. If at some future time Cuba, or even Canada, desired to enlist in the Great Republic, might not a joint statement with Britain about the inviolability of the continent prejudice such possibilities? It was wiser for America to keep her hands free. As Adams noted in his diary, "It would be more candid, as well as more dignified, to avow our principles explicitly to Russia and France, than to come in as a cock-boat in the wake of the British man-of-war." Hence there was propounded on December 2, 1823, in the President's annual message to Congress a purely American doctrine, the Monroe Doctrine, which has often since been voiced in transatlantic affairs. "The American continents", Monroe said, "by the free and independent condition they have assumed and maintain, are henceforth not to be considered as subjects for future colonisation by any European Powers. ... We should consider any attempt on their part to extend their [political] system to any portion of this hemisphere as dangerous to our peace and safety." These were resounding claims. Their acceptance by the rest of the world depended on the friendly vigilance of the "British man-of-war", but this was a fact seldom openly acknowledged. For the best part of a century the Royal Navy remained the stoutest guarantee of freedom in the Americas.

Thus shielded by the British bulwark, the American continent was able to work out its own unhindered destiny.

Monroe's famous message conveyed a warning to Britain as well as to the authoritarian Powers. Canning understood the risks of competition and dispute with the United States upon the continent in which the Americans now claimed predominance. Britain officially recognised the independence of the South American states. Canning's stroke over South America may probably be judged his greatest triumph in foreign policy.

Crisis had meanwhile erupted in the Eastern Mediterranean. After four centuries of subjection to the Turks the spirit of liberty was stirring among the Greeks. They broke into revolt, and in 1822 declared their independence. In England there was widespread enthusiasm for their cause. It appealed to the educated classes who had been brought up on the glories of Thermopylae and Salamis. Subscriptions were raised, and Byron and other British volunteers went to the aid of the Greeks. Before he met his death at Missolonghi Byron was deeply disillusioned. With the aid of an army supplied by Mahomet Ali, the formidable Pasha of Egypt, the Sultan of Turkey was almost everywhere victorious. Unfortunately for the Greeks, the Powers were themselves divided. The Greek revolt had split the Holy Alliance, Austria and Russia taking opposite sides. Canning, like Castlereagh before him, was all for mediation. On the other hand, he feared that Russia would intervene, set up a client state in Greece, and exact her own price from the Turks. If Russia grew at Turkey's expense British interests in the Middle East and in India would be put in jeopardy. Here lay the origins of the "Eastern Question", as it was called, which increasingly preoccupied and baffled the Powers of Europe down to the First World War. After complicated negotiations Britain, France and Russia agreed in 1827 on terms to be put to the Turks. British and French squadrons were sent to Greek waters to enforce them. This was the last achievement of Canning's diplomacy. The next act in the Greek drama was played after his death.

Canning's colleagues had become increasingly critical of the activities of their Foreign Secretary. Wellington was particularly disturbed by what he regarded as Canning's headlong courses. The two wings of the administration were only held together by the conciliatory character of the Prime Minister, and in February 1827 Liverpool had a stroke. A major political crisis followed. Who was now to lead the Government? The whole future of the Tories was at stake. Were they to go upon the road of Wellington or of Canning? The choice of Prime Minister still lay with the Crown, and George IV hesitated for a month before making his decision. It soon became plain that no Government could be constructed which did not include Canning and his friends, and that Canning would accept all or nothing. In April 1827 Canning became Prime Minister, and for a brief hundred days held supreme political power. Canning's Ministry signalled the coming dissolution of the eighteenth-century political system. He held office by courtesy of a section of the Whigs. The only able Tory leader in the House of Commons whom he had lost was

Robert Peel. Peel resigned partly for personal reasons and partly because he knew that Canning was in favour of Catholic Emancipation. But the Opposition Tories and the die-hard Whigs harassed the new Government. Had Canning been granted a longer spell of life the group he led might have founded a new political allegiance. But on August 8, after a short illness, Canning died. He was killed, like Castlereagh, by overwork.

Canning had played a decisive part in the shaping of the new century. In war and in peace he had proved himself a man of large views and active determination. His quick mind and hasty temper made him an uneasy party colleague. As his friend Sir Walter Scott said of him, he wanted prudence. Through Canning, however, the better side of the Pitt tradition was handed on to the future. In many ways he was in sympathy with the new movements stirring in English life. He was also in close touch with the Press and knew how to use publicity in the conduct of government. As with Chatham, his political power was largely based on public opinion and on a popular foreign policy. Belief in Catholic Emancipation marked him as more advanced in view than most of his Tory colleagues. His opposition to Parliamentary Reform was part of the curse which lay upon all English politicians who had had contact with the French Revolution. On this perhaps he might have changed his mind.

A makeshift administration composed of his followers, his Whig allies, and a group of Tories struggled ineptly with the situation. Its leader was the lachrymose Lord Goderich, formerly Chancellor of the Exchequer. More than half the Tory Party, under Peel and Wellington, was in opposition. Quarrels among Whig and Tory members of the Government ruptured its unity. There had been a hitch in carrying out Canning's policy of non-intervention in Greece. Admiral Codrington, one of Nelson's captains, who had fought at Trafalgar and was now in command of the Allied squadron in Greek waters, had on his own initiative destroyed the entire Turkish fleet in the Bay of Navarino. There was alarm in England in case the Russians should take undue advantage of this victory. The battle, which meant much to the Greeks, was disapprovingly described in the King's Speech as an "untoward incident", and the victor narrowly escaped court-martial. The Government, rent by Whig intrigues, abruptly disappeared. There was no question of a purely Whig Government. That party was weak and indifferently led. Wellington and Peel were instructed to form an administration. This they did. Wellington became Prime Minister, with Peel as Home Secretary and Leader of the House of Commons. The old Tories were to fight one more action. It was a stubborn rearguard.

The political views of the new Government were simple – defence of existing institutions, conviction that they alone stood between order and chaos, determination to retreat only if pressed by overwhelming forces. The Government's first retreat was to carry an Opposition measure repealing the Test and Corporation Acts which nominally excluded the Nonconformists from office. After a long struggle they at last achieved political rights and equality. Not so the Catholics. Their emancipation was not merely a matter of principle, a step in the direction of complete religious equality, but it was also an Imperial concern. The greatest failure of British Government was in Ireland. A main dividing line in politics after 1815 was upon this issue of Catholic Emancipation. It had sundered Canning and his followers, together with the Whigs, from Wellington and Peel. A decision had been postponed from year to year by "gentlemen's agreements" among the English politicians. But the patience of the Irish was coming to its end. They were organising under Daniel O'Connell for vehement agitation against England. O'Connell was a landlord and a lawyer. He believed in what later came to be called Home Rule for Ireland under the British Crown. Though not himself a revolutionary, he was a powerful and excitable orator, and his speeches nourished thoughts of violence.

A minor political incident in England fired the train. The leader of Canningites, William Huskisson, had been forced out of the Government along with his followers, and an Irish Protestant landowner, Vesey Fitzgerald, was promoted to one of the vacant Ministerial posts. Appointment to office in those days involved submitting to the electorate at a by-election, and so a poll was due in County Clare. O'Connell stood as candidate, backed by the whole force of his organisation, the Catholic Association. He was of course debarred by existing legislation from taking a seat in Parliament, but in spite of the efforts of the local Protestant gentry he was triumphantly elected. Here was a test case. If the English Government refused to enfranchise the Catholics there would be revolution in Ireland, and political disaster at home.

Peel, whose political career had been built up in Ireland, had long been the symbol of opposition to any concessions to the Catholics. Wellington's position was happier. He was less committed and more able to take without qualm the line of expediency. The position in Ireland was simple. An independent association of the Irish people had sabotaged the official administration. The choice was either Catholic Emancipation or the systematic reconquest of Ireland. In August 1828 Wellington put the matter to the King. "The influence and powers of government in that country are no longer in the hands of the officers of the Government, but have been usurped by the demagogues of the Roman Catholic Association, who, acting through the influence of the Roman Catholic clergy, direct the country as they think proper. ... We have a rebellion impending over us in Ireland." As a general Wellington knew the hopelessness of attempting to repress a national rising. He had seen civil war at close quarters in Spain. He himself came from an Irish family and was familiar with the turbulent island.

The only opponents of Emancipation were the English bishops, the old-fashioned Tories, and the King. The bishops and the Tories could be outvoted; but the King was a more serious obstacle. Wellington could not carry the measure without Peel, and the Whigs could not carry it without the King. This determined Peel. He resigned his High Tory seat at Oxford and bought himself in for Westbury. His offer to stand by Wellington finally persuaded

George IV, who dreaded a Whig administration. Peel himself introduced the Bill for Catholic Emancipation into the House of Commons, and it was carried through Parliament in 1829 with comfortable majorities. Revolution in Ireland was averted. But the unity of the English Tories had received another blow. The "Old Guard", still powerful under the unreformed franchise, never forgave Peel and Wellington for deserting the principle of the Anglican monopoly of power in Great Britain. Toryism meant many different and even conflicting things to its followers, but the supremacy of Protestantism had long been one of its binding political beliefs.

The Duke's administration showed little sign of continuing its Liberal course. After the resignation of the Canningites two important posts had been given to ex-members of Wellington's staff. This military and aide-de-campish Government was increasingly out of touch with political opinion, and the forces of Opposition were gathering. But upon the surface the atmosphere was calm. In June 1830 King George IV died, with a miniature of Mrs Fitzherbert round his neck. "The first gentleman of Europe" was not long mourned by his people. During his last illness his mistress, Lady Conyngham, was busy collecting her perquisites. This once handsome man had grown so gross and corpulent that he was ashamed to show himself in public. His extravagance had become a mania, and his natural abilities were clouded by years of self-indulgence.

George IV was succeeded on the throne by his brother, William, the Duke of Clarence, the most eccentric and least obnoxious of the sons of George III. He had been brought up in the Navy, and had passed a life of total obscurity, except for a brief and ludicrous interval when Canning had made him Lord High Admiral in 1827.[1] For many years he had lived with an actress at Bushey Park. But in the end he, too, had had to do his duty and marry a German princess, Adelaide of Saxe-Meiningen. She proved to be a generous-hearted and acceptable Queen. Good-nature and simplicity of mind were William IV's in equal measure. The gravest embarrassments he caused his Ministers sprang from his garrulity.

It had been expected that the new King might prefer a Whig administration. As Duke of Clarence he had been dismissed from the Admiralty by the Duke of Wellington. But on his accession William IV welcomed and retained the Duke. His reputation for fairness proved to be of political value. "Sailor William" needed every ounce of fairness. There were heavy seas ahead. Revolution had again broken out in France, and the Bourbon monarchy was at an end. As the news swept across the Channel there were mutterings of a coming storm in England.

---

1   Nelson thought William to be a fine sailor. When Nelson was still a junior captain, the two men served together in the West Indies. On one occasion, William fell in love with the daughter of a Spanish admiral in Havana, and it was Nelson who "rescued" the future king from the consequences that that relationship would have brought on the prince and the nation.

CHAPTER FORTY-FOUR

REFORM AND FREE TRADE

New revolution in France — Wellington falls from power — Earl Grey as
Prime Minister — transportation to Australia — Bentham, Mill, and
Cobbett campaign for change — the Reform Bill fails — peers against the
people — the King asked to create new peers — the Reform Act — Melbourne
and Russell lead the Whigs — the rise of Palmerston — abolition of
slavery — Poor Law reform — the Factory Act — the Tolpuddle Martyrs —
the death of King William IV — Victoria becomes Queen — Chartism —
the rise of Disraeli — Prince Albert marries Victoria — Peel becomes
Prime Minister — Gladstone at the Board of Trade — the Anti-Corn Law
League — Cobden and Bright — the Irish famine — Disraeli denounces
Peel — the collapse of Peel's Government

I N 1830 the Liberal forces in Europe stirred again. The July Revolution
in France set up a constitutional monarchy under the house of Orleans.
The new King, Louis Philippe, was the son of the Revolutionary
Philippe Egalité, who had voted for the death of his cousin, Louis XVI,
and himself been guillotined later. Louis Philippe was a wiser and more
honourable man than his father. He was to keep his uneasy throne for eighteen
years, and he also kept his head. Encouraged by events in Paris, the Belgians
rebelled against the Kingdom of the Netherlands in which they had been
incorporated by the peace treaties of 1815. Britain had played a big part in this
arrangement. In 1815 an enlarged united Netherlands had seemed a promising
experiment. After all, it at last realised the dreams of the first William of
Orange in the days of Queen Elizabeth. But the Dutch and Belgians were
divided by language, religion, and commercial interests, and these barriers
could not easily be overcome. The Belgians demanded autonomy, and then
independence. Much diplomatic activity ensued before a peaceful solution was
eventually found. Meanwhile a wave of revolts spread across Germany into
Poland. The Europe of Metternich and the Holy Alliance was severely shaken,
though not yet overturned.

These agitations on the European continent, largely orderly in character
and democratic in purpose, were much acclaimed in England, and their
progress was closely and excitedly studied. The Tory Government and the

Duke of Wellington[1] alone seemed suspicious and hostile. With some reason the Government feared that France might annex Belgium or establish a French prince in Brussels upon a new throne. Wellington was even suspected of intending to restore the Kingdom of the Netherlands by armed force. This was not true. The preservation of peace was his chief care. But Opposition speakers were pleased to attribute to him an aim he did not profess, and the rumour was enough to inflame the hot tempers of the times. Poverty in the villages and on the farms had already led to rioting in South-East England. In the growing towns and cities industrial discontent was driving men of business and their workers into political action. Turmoil, upheaval, even revolution, seemed imminent. Instead there was a General Election.

At the polls the Whigs made gains, but the result was indecisive. The Whig leader was Earl Grey, a friend and disciple of Fox. It is given to few men to carry out late in life a great measure of reform which they have advocated without success for forty years. Such was to be Grey's achievement. He had held office briefly under Fox in the Ministry of 1806.[2] For the rest, since the early years of the younger Pitt he had been not only continuously out of office, but almost without expectation or desire of ever winning it. Now his hour was at hand. Grey was a landowner who regarded politics as a social duty, and much preferred his country estates to the lobbies of Westminster. He had, however, made careful study of the insurrections on the Continent, and realised that they were not as sinister as Wellington thought. His judgment on home affairs was also well directed. He and his colleagues perceived that the agitation which had shaken England since Waterloo issued from two quite separate sources – the middle classes, unrepresented, prosperous, respectable, influenced by the democratic ideas of the French Revolution, but deeply law-abiding in their hunger for political power; and on the other side a bitter and more revolutionary section of working men, smitten by the economic disloca-tion of war and its aftermath, prepared to talk of violence and perhaps even to use it. An alliance with the middle classes and a moderate extension of the franchise would suffice, at any rate for a time, and for this Grey prepared his plans. He had the support of Lord John Russell, son of the Duke of Bedford, who was a man of impulsive mind, with a high devotion to the cause of liberty in the abstract, whatever the practical consequences might be. With them stood Henry Brougham, expectant of office, an advanced politician who had made his name as the defender of Queen Caroline. Brougham was fertile with modern ideas, and a friend of leading Radicals and newspaper editors.

Parliament met in November. There were some who hoped that the Tories would do again what they had done over Catholic Emancipation and, after a rearguard action, reform the franchise themselves. Wellington hoped that the Whigs were too disorganised to form a Government, but his own party was even more disunited. Those who had followed Canning would have nothing

1   Arthur Wellesley, 1st Duke of Wellington (1769–1852) was Prime Minister in 1828–30.
2   First Lord of the Admiralty in the Ministry of "All the Talents" in 1806, Charles Grey, 2nd Earl Grey (1764–1845) resigned over Catholic Emancipation.

more to do with the Tory "Old Guard", and now made common cause with the Whigs. A fortnight later the Tories were defeated and King William IV asked Grey to form a Government. With one brief interval the Whigs had been out of office for nearly fifty years. Now at a bound they were at the summit of power and influence. They were confronted with an ugly scene. French threats to intervene in Belgium made it imperative but unpopular to increase the military estimates. The Chancellor of the Exchequer failed to provide an effective Budget. Law and order were breaking down in the south-eastern counties, and Lord Melbourne, the new Home Secretary, acted decidedly. Over four hundred farm workers were sentenced to transportation.[1] The Radicals were indignant and disillusioned. Only Parliamentary Reform could save the Government, and to this they now addressed themselves.

A secret Cabinet committee was appointed to draft the scheme, and in March 1831 Lord John Russell rose in the House of Commons to move the first Reform Bill. Amid shouting and scornful laughter he read out to their holders a list of over a hundred and fifty "pocket" borough seats which it was proposed to abolish and replace with new constituencies for the unrepresented areas of the Metropolis, the industrial North, and the Midlands. To the Tories this was a violation of all they stood for, an affront to their deepest political convictions, a gross attack on the rights of property. A seat was a thing to be bought or sold like a house or an estate, and a more uniform franchise savoured of an arithmetical conception of politics dangerously akin to French democracy. Many Whigs, too, who had expected a milder measure were at first dumbfounded by the breadth of Russell's proposals. They soon rallied to the Government when they saw the enthusiasm of the country, for the Whigs believed that Reform would forestall revolution. The Tories, on the other hand, feared that it was the first step on the road to cataclysm. To them, and indeed to many Whigs, English government meant the rule, and the duty to rule, of the landed classes in the interests of the community. A wider franchise would mean the beginning of the end of the old system of administration by influence and patronage. Could the King's Government be carried on in the absence of these twin pillars of authority? It was not altogether a vain question. After 1832 Britain was to see many unstable Ministries before the pattern was changed by the rise of disciplined parties with central organisations and busy Whips.

Radical leaders were disappointed by what they conceived to be the moderation of the Bill, but in their various ways they supported it. There was not much in common between them. Jeremy Bentham and James Mill were philosophical advocates of democracy and middle-class education; William Cobbett was a vigorous, independent-minded journalist; Francis Place, the tailor of Charing Cross, and Thomas Attwood, the banker of Birmingham, were active political organisers. But they were all determined that the Bill should not be whittled away by amendment and compromise. Agitation spread

1   Transportation – to the American colonies – started in the seventeenth century. Following the American War of Independence, convicts were, until 1868, transported to Australia.

through the country. There was no economic crisis to distract public attention from the one burning issue or to shake the popular belief that an extension of the right to vote and a redistribution of seats to accord with the Industrial Revolution would cure all national ills. In the House of Commons the Tories fought every inch of the way. The Government was by no means sure of its majority, and although a small block of Irish votes controlled by O'Connell, leader of the emancipated Catholics, was cast for Grey the Bill was defeated. A roar of hatred and disappointment swept the country. Grey asked the King for a dissolution, and William IV had the sense to realise that a refusal might mean revolution. The news caused uproar in the Lords, where a motion was introduced asking the King to reconsider his decision, but as the shouting rose from the benches and peers shook their fists across the floor of the House the thunder of cannon was heard as the King left St James's to come in person to pronounce the dissolution.

Excited elections were held on the single issue of Reform. It was the first time a mandate of this kind had been asked of the British people. They returned an unmistakable answer. The Tories were annihilated in the county constituencies and the Whigs and their allies gained a majority of 136 in the House of Commons. When Parliament reassembled the battle was shifted to the House of Lords. On the night of October 7, 1831, the critical division took place. The peers were sharply divided, and it was twenty-one of the bishops in the Upper House who decided the issue; they were against Reform. Thus the Tories triumphed. The Bill was defeated and a new constitutional issue was raised – the Peers against the People.

Next morning the newspapers, bordered in black, proclaimed the news. Rioting broke out in the Midlands; houses and property were burned; there was wild disorder in Bristol. The associations of Reformers in the country, called Political Unions, strove to harness enthusiasm for the Bill and to steady the public temper. Meanwhile the Government persevered. In December Russell introduced the Bill for the third time, and the Commons carried it by a majority of two to one. In the following May it came again before the Lords. It was rejected by thirty-five votes. There was now no question of another dissolution and Grey realised that only extreme remedies would serve. He accordingly drove to Windsor and asked the King to create enough new peers to carry the Bill. The King refused and the Cabinet resigned. William IV asked Wellington and Peel to form an administration to carry Reform as they had carried Catholic Emancipation, and thus avoid swamping the Lords. But Peel would not comply; he was not prepared to assume Ministerial responsibility for a measure of which he disapproved. Feeling in the country became menacing. Plans were made for strikes and a general refusal of taxes. Banners and placards appeared in the London streets with the caption "To Stop the Duke Go for Gold", and there was a run on the Bank of England. Radical leaders declared they would paralyse any Tory Government which came to power, and after a week the Duke admitted defeat. On the afternoon of May 18 Grey and Brougham called at St James's Palace. The King authorised them to draw up a list of persons who would be made peers and could be counted on to vote for the Whigs. At the same time his private secretary told the leading Tories of the King's decision and suggested that they could avoid such extremities by abstaining. When the Bill was again introduced the Opposition benches were practically empty. It was carried by an overwhelming majority, and became law on June 7, 1832.

The new electors and the Radicals were not content to stop at extending the franchise, and during the next five years the younger politicians forced through an equally extensive reform of public administration. The Whigs became more and more uncomfortable, and Grey, feeling he had done enough, retired in 1834. The new leaders were Lord Melbourne and Lord John Russell. Russell was a Whig of the old school, sensitive to any invasion of political liberty and rights. He saw the need for further reforms in the sphere of government, but the broadening paths of democracy did not beckon him. Melbourne in his youth had held advanced opinions, but his lack of any guiding aim and motive, his want of conviction, his cautious scepticism, denied him and his party any theme or inspiration. Personal friendships and agreeable conversation mattered more to him than political issues. He accepted the office of Prime Minister with reluctance, genuinely wondering whether the honour was worth while. Once in power his bland qualities helped to keep his divided team together. But his administration wore an eighteenth-century air in the midst of nineteenth-century stress.

One of Melbourne's ablest colleagues was Lord Palmerston, who held the Foreign Office for nearly eleven years. Under the wise guidance of Lord Grey, Palmerston had secured a settlement of the Belgian problem which still endures. The Dutch and French were both persuaded to withdraw, Belgian claims to Dutch territory were abated, and Prince Leopold of Saxe-Coburg was installed at Brussels as an independent sovereign. The neutrality of the country was guaranteed by international treaty. Thus was a pledge given which was to be redeemed with blood in 1914. Under Melbourne Palmerston did much as he pleased in foreign affairs. His leading beliefs were two: that British interests must everywhere be stoutly upheld, if necessary by a show of force, and that Liberal movements in the countries of Europe should be encouraged whenever it was within Britain's power to extend them sympathy or even aid. There was a jaunty forthright self-assurance about everything Palmerston did which often gave offence in the staider chancelleries of Europe and alarmed his more nervous colleagues. But his imperturbable spirit gradually won the admiration of the mass of his fellow countrymen. He was in these years building up the popularity which later made him appear the embodiment of mid-Victorian confidence.

The Whig rank and file were perplexed and uncertain. With the passing of the Reform Bill the Whig Party had done its work. Its leaders neither liked nor understood the middle classes. They looked on Radicalism as a fashionable creed to be held in undergraduate days and dropped on reaching maturity, and they perceived, uneasily and dimly, that they were being pushed from behind by mass agitation and organisation into strange and perilous paths. Moreover, their hold on the country was by no means certain. Some quarter of a million voters had been added by the Reform Bill to the electorate, which now numbered nearly 800,000 persons.[1] This meant that about one adult male in six had the vote. However, they by no means gave their undivided support to the Whigs. The strange habit of English electors of voting against Governments which give them the franchise now made itself felt, and it was with great difficulty that the Whig administrations preserved a majority with the help of O'Connell's Irish votes.

Nevertheless the legislation and the commissions of these years were by no means unfruitful. The slaves in the West Indies were finally emancipated in 1833. For the first time in English history the Government made educational grants to religious societies. The Poor Law was reformed on lines that were considered highly advanced in administrative and intellectual circles, though they did not prove popular among those they were supposed to benefit. The first effective Factory Act was passed, though the long hours of work it permitted would horrify the twentieth century and did not satisfy the humanitarians of the time. The whole system of local government was reconstructed and the old local oligarchies abolished. Politics meanwhile centred on the position of the Established Church and the maintenance of order in Ireland, and it was their failure to deal with these issues and to balance their Budgets that in due course ruined the Whigs. Moreover, great forces were at work outside the House of Commons. A large mass of the country still remained unenfranchised. The relations of capital and labour had scarcely been touched by the hand of Parliament, and the activities of the early trade unions frightened the Government into oppressive measures.

The most celebrated case was that of the Tolpuddle "Martyrs" of 1834, when six labourers from that Dorsetshire village of curious name were sentenced to transportation for the technical offence of "administering unlawful oaths" to members of their union. Public agitation eventually secured their pardon, but not until they had served two years in New South Wales.[2] While unrest for many reasons spread, the position of the monarchy itself showed signs of weakness. The Whigs were not the men to bridge the gulf which seemed to yawn between official political circles and the nation.

Sir Robert Peel,[3] on the other hand, was not slow to adjust the Tories to the new times and a speedy reorganisation of their machinery was set on foot. "I presume", he declared in 1833, "the chief object of that party which is called

1 These figures are estimates. Another estimate suggests that while 217,000 had been added to the electoral role, the total was 652,000. The shires remained in the control of important families. There was no secret ballot, and men – there were no women voters – were influenced in their votes by employers and landlords.

2 In the same year (1834) Parliament burned down – but this was not the work of agitators for Reform. A stoker too enthusiastically fed the building's boilers with Treasury wooden tally sticks. The buildings (and a considerable bundle of historical artefacts) were reduced to ashes.

3 Sir Robert Peel (1788–1850) was Prime Minister in 1834–5. Melbourne was Prime Minister between 1835 and 1841, and Peel became Prime Minister again between 1841 and 1847.

Conservative will be to resist Radicalism, to prevent those further encroachments of democratic influence which will be attempted as the natural consequence of the triumph already achieved." He made it clear that the Tories would support administrative changes which increased efficiency, but oppose any weakening of the traditional institutions of the State. A disciplined, purposeful, but not factious Opposition gradually took shape under his leadership. In the following year the party was heartened by a rousing election address which Peel had issued to his constituency. They took their stand upon an enlightened conservation of the best elements in the existing institutions in the country, and Peel showed considerable cleverness in revealing his desire to modify the whole position of the Established Church. The Nonconformist voters did not forget this in the coming years, for religion still counted in politics. As the great Acts of Reform succeeded each other so further interests were antagonised and the Conservative sentiment in the country gradually rallied to Peel. In the elections of 1835 the Tories won a hundred seats, and for some months he presided over a minority Government. Then the Whigs returned, as divided among themselves as ever. They seemed to be playing with fire. They were arousing hopes that no Government could fulfil.

In 1837 King William IV died. Humorous, tactless, pleasant, and unrespected, he had played his part in lowering esteem for the monarchy, and indeed the vices and eccentricities of the sons of George III had by this time almost destroyed its hold upon the hearts of the people. An assault on the institution which had played so great a part in the history of England appeared imminent, and there seemed few to defend it. The new sovereign was a maiden of eighteen. She had been brought up by a dutiful mother who had secluded her in Kensington Palace from both the Court and the nation. Her education was supervised by a German governess, with occasional examinations by Church dignitaries, and a correspondence course on her future duties with her maternal uncle, King Leopold of Belgium. The country knew nothing of either her character or her virtues. "Few people", wrote Palmerston, "have had opportunities of forming a correct judgment of the Princess; but I incline to think that she will turn out to be a remarkable person, and gifted with a great deal of strength of character."

By the time Queen Victoria came to the throne the Whigs had shot their bolt. The Court and the governing circles were isolated and unpopular; the middle classes were fearful of unrest and beginning to vote for the Tories. Meanwhile Lord Melbourne, who had little faith in law-making, with grace and pleasantness was doing nothing. On top of all this there appeared towards the end of the year the first signs of a great economic depression. Conditions in the industrial North soon became as bad as after Waterloo, and in May 1838 a group of working-class leaders published a "People's Charter". Chartism, as it was called, in which some historians discern the beginnings of socialism, was the last despairing cry of poverty against the Machine Age. The Chartists, believing, like the agitators for Reform before 1832, that an extension of the franchise would cure all their miseries, demanded annual Parliaments, universal male suffrage, equal electoral districts, the removal of the property qualification for Membership of Parliament, the secret ballot, and the payment of Members. Their only hope of success was to secure, as the Radicals had done, the backing of a Parliamentary party and of the progressive middle classes. But they deliberately refused to bid for middle-class support. Their leaders quarrelled among themselves and affronted respectable people by threatening and irresponsible speeches. They had no funds, and no organisation such as the Catholic Association had found in the parishes of the Irish clergy, or the Labour Party was to find later in the trade unions. For a time England was flooded with petitions and pamphlets, but the ferment varied in warmth from one part of the country to another. Whenever conditions improved the popular temper cooled, and no united national movement emerged as a permanent force. The few unions which then existed soon deserted the cause and the more prosperous artisans were lukewarm. Agitation revived from time to time in the years that followed, culminating in the revolutionary year of 1848. But in the end the whole muddled, well-intentioned business came to nothing.

Peel drew the right conclusions. He discerned, much more clearly than the Whigs, the causes of the unrest, and, though steadfast against Radicalism, he believed that the remedy lay in efficient administration and an enlightened commercial policy. The younger Tories supported him and like him were oppressed by the division of the country into "two nations", the rich and the poor, as portrayed in the novels of a young Jewish Member of Parliament called Benjamin Disraeli. A small group of Conservatives were already seeking an alliance with the working men against the middle classes.

In 1839 Melbourne offered to resign, but for another two years Victoria kept him in office. His charm had captured her affections.[1] He imparted to her much of his wisdom on men and affairs, without burdening her with his scepticism, and she refused to be separated from her beloved Prime Minister. In February of the following year a new figure entered upon the British scene. The Queen married her cousin, Prince Albert of Saxe-Coburg. The Prince was an upright, conscientious man with far-ranging interests and high ideals. He and the Queen enjoyed for twenty-one years, until his early death, a happy family life, which held up an example much in accord with the desires of her subjects. After the excesses of George IV and his brothers the dignity and repute of the monarchy stood in need of restoration, and this was Victoria and Albert's achievement. At first the Prince found his presence in England resented by the political magnates of the time. They would not let him take a

[1] There is a little more to it than this. Victoria came to the throne when she was only eighteen years old, and Melbourne became her mentor. Moreover, she mistrusted Tories, especially Peel, and in May 1839, when Peel should have been her Prime Minister, he asked her to dismiss those members of her household, the ladies of the bedchamber, whose husbands were supporters of the Whigs. Victoria refused to do as Peel wished, which is why Melbourne stayed on as Prime Minister.

seat in the House of Lords, they cut down his annual allowance, and he was not granted even the title of Prince Consort until 1857. Nevertheless the patronage which he earnestly extended to science, industry, and the arts, and to good causes of many kinds, gradually won him a wide measure of public respect.

Peel, unlike Melbourne, had given the Queen an impression of awkwardness and coldness of manner; but at last in 1841 a General Election brought him to power. Before long he had won her confidence. His abilities now came into full play. He had absolute control of his Cabinet, himself introduced his Government's more important Budgets, and supervised the work of all departments, including that of William Gladstone at the Board of Trade. Tariffs were once again reformed, customs duties greatly reduced, and income tax was reimposed. These measures soon bore fruit. In 1843 trade began to revive, prosperity returned, and the demand for political reform was stilled. Once again the sky seemed clear at Westminster. But a storm was gathering in Ireland.

The immediate issue was the price of bread. To promote foreign commerce Peel had reduced import duties on everything except corn. Dear bread, however, meant either high wages or misery for the masses, and Peel gradually realised that cheap imported food could alone sustain the continued prosperity of the nation. Free Trade in corn seemed imperative, but the political obstacles were formidable. The Tory Party leaned heavily on the votes of the landowners, who had invested much capital in their properties during the Napoleonic wars. Peace had brought cheaper corn from abroad, and the cry for protection had led in 1815 to a prohibition of the import of foreign grain except when the price in the home market was abnormally high. The repeal or modification of this and later Corn Laws now overclouded all other issues. The landowners were accused of using their power in Parliament to safeguard their interests at the expense of the rest of the community. The enmity of the manufacturers and industrialists sharpened the conflict, for the Corn Laws not only caused great distress to the working classes, but angered many employers. Protection in their view prevented them from building up new markets overseas and from competing on fair terms in old ones.

Hostility to the Corn Laws had grown during the depression of 1838–42. An Anti-Corn Law League was formed at Manchester to press for their abolition. It soon exerted a powerful influence on public opinion, and produced two remarkable leaders and organisers who became the Free Trade prophets of nineteenth-century England, Richard Cobden, a calico printer, and John Bright, a Quaker mill-owner. The movement was strongly supported. There were large subscriptions to its funds. The new penny postage, introduced by Sir Rowland Hill in 1840, carried circulars and pamphlets cheaply all over the country. Meetings were held throughout the land. The propaganda was effective and novel: a few simple ideas hammered into the minds of audiences by picked lecturers and speakers. Never had there been such a shrewdly conducted agitation. Monster petitions were sent to Parliament. Cobden persuaded prosperous townspeople to buy forty-shilling freeholds in the county constituencies and thus secure a double vote. This so increased the number of Anti-Corn Law electors that, instead of only petitioning Parliament from outside, the League started influencing it from within. Cobden and Bright's thundering speeches against the landed classes reverberated through the nation.

By 1843, however, Peel was determined to act. His position was very difficult, for some of his followers felt he had betrayed them once already over Catholic Emancipation. But he was sure of himself. Perhaps he believed that his personal ascendancy would carry the majority with him; but he needed time to convince his party, and time was denied him. In August 1845 the potato crop failed in Ireland. Famine was imminent and Peel could wait no longer, but when he put his proposals to the Cabinet several of his colleagues revolted and in December he had to resign. The Whig leader Russell refused to form an administration, and Peel returned to office to face and conquer the onslaught of the Tory Protectionists. Their spokesman, the hitherto little-known Benjamin Disraeli, denounced him not so much for seeking to abolish the Corn Laws as for betraying his position as head of a great party. If Peel, he declared, believed in the measure he should resign, as a large section of his party was traditionally pledged to oppose it. The wilful destruction of a great party by its leader was a political crime, for the true working of English politics depended on the balance of parties and if a leader could not convince his colleagues he should withdraw. Thus Disraeli. But Peel maintained that his duty to the nation was higher than his duty to his party, and he believed it was his mission to carry the abolition of the Corn Laws.

On June 25, 1846, with the help of Whig and Irish votes, the Corn Laws were repealed. Disraeli immediately had his revenge. Turmoil in Ireland destroyed Peel's Government, and by a vote on the same night the great Ministry, one of the strongest of the century, came to an end.[1] Peel had been the dominating force and personality in English politics since the passing of the great Reform Bill. The age over which he resided was one of formidable industrial advance. It was the Railway Age. By 1848 some five thousand miles of railroads had been built in the United Kingdom. Speed of transport and increasing output were the words of the day. Coal and iron production had doubled. Engineering was making great, though as yet hesitating, strides. All the steps were being taken, not by Government, but by enterprisers throughout the country, which were to make Britain the greatest industrial Power of the nineteenth-century world. The days of the land-owning predominance were doomed. Free trade seemed essential to manufacture, and in manufacture Britain was entering upon her supremacy. All this Peel grasped. His Government set an example of initiative which both the Conservative and

---

1   Disraeli never forgave Peel for not giving him a seat in his 1841 Cabinet. Many in the Tory Party never forgave Disraeli for bringing down Peel.

Liberal Parties honoured by imitation in the future. Of his own methods of government he once said, "The fact is, people like a certain degree of obstinacy and presumption in a Minister. They abuse him for dictation and arrogance, but they like being governed." High words perhaps, but they fitted the time.

Early in 1850, Peel fell from his horse while riding in the Green Park and was fatally injured. So died one of the great shapers of British politics in the Victorian Age.

CHAPTER FORTY-FIVE

THE CRIMEAN WAR

Russell as Prime Minister – revolution throughout Europe – the end of
Metternich – the Great Exhibition – Dickens and Ruskin and social
reform – the Eastern Question – the other Canning – Crimea – the Charge
of the Light Brigade – Florence Nightingale – the Battle of Inkerman –
William Russell, the first war correspondent – Palmerston as Prime
Minister – the fall of Sebastopol – the Treaty of Paris – the Indian
Mutiny – the massacre at Cawnpore – Lucknow – Darwin publishes The
Origin of Species – Garibaldi and Italian unity – Gladstone joins the
Whigs – Disraeli as Prime Minister

Towards the middle of the nineteenth century political life in England was still following its long-accustomed habits, which had so far been only slightly changed by the acceptance of the great Reform Bill. The Whigs were in power under Lord John Russell, whose family had served the State since the days of Henry VII. After three and a half centuries of generally smiling fortune the Russells and their friends and connections had acquired an assurance that they knew best how to govern the country in its true interests. Whatever novel agitations might spread among working men in the industrial towns, who as yet enjoyed few votes, the Whig leaders pursued their reasonable, moderate, and undemocratic courses. Lord John's Government, with a few upsets, survived for six years.[1] It achieved little of lasting note, but it piloted Britain through a restless period when elsewhere in Europe thrones were overturned and revolutions multiplied.

In February 1848 the French monarchy fell. A few days of rioting sufficed to eject Louis Philippe,[2] and a Government of romantic outlook and Socialist complexion briefly took control. This in turn collapsed, and by the end of the year a Bonaparte had been elected President of France by an overwhelming majority. Thus, after half a lifetime spent in plotting, exile, and obscurity, Prince Louis Napoleon, nephew of the great Emperor, came to power. He owed his position to the name he bore, to the ineptitude of his rivals, and to

---

1   John Russell, 1st Earl Russell (1792–1878) was Prime Minister in 1846–52 and again in 1865–66.
2   Louis Philippe had come to power after the 1830 Revolution, first as lieutenant-general and then as so-called citizen king, the 'elected' monarch.

the fondness of the French for constitutional experiment. For more than twenty years this amiable, dreamy figure was to play a striking and not always ineffective part upon the European scene.

The peoples of Italy had also broken into revolt against both their own rulers and the Austrian occupiers of Lombardy and Venetia. High hopes were cherished that a united Italian nation might emerge from this commotion. In the Italian provinces enthusiastic conspirators soon found that they could not hold their own against the organised forces of Austria and her allies, nor could the army of the kingdom of Sardinia, which was the only wholly independent Italian state, make much impression on Austrian might. The Italian revolt ended in failure, but not without arousing a widespread sympathy in Britain, which was benevolently exercised when the next attempt at unity was made.

North of the Alps revolutionary nationalism was also stirring in Germany, Austria, and Poland. The Austrian Chancellor, Metternich, who had dominated Central Europe for forty years, was forced to resign by a revolution in Vienna. This aged pillar of Continental absolutism found refuge in an obscure hotel in the England of the Whigs. The Emperor was obliged to abdicate, leaving the Habsburg throne to a young Archduke, Francis Joseph, destined to live through many tribulations and witness the opening years of the First World War. Czechs, Poles, and Hungarians in turn all took up arms, and their gallant risings were eventually suppressed only with the cordial help of the Czar of Russia. In Germany itself the minor monarchs were thrown into disarray, and some into exile, by rebellions and demonstrations. A Parliament met at Frankfort, and after lengthy debate offered the crown of a united Germany to the King of Prussia. This sovereign and his military advisers preferred repressing revolutionaries to accepting favours from them, and the offer was declined. Little came of the events of 1848–49 in Germany, except a powerful impetus to the idea of German unity, and a growing conviction that it could only be achieved with the backing of Prussian arms.

The turmoil in Europe was viewed in England with sympathetic interest, but it went unmatched by any comparable disturbance. The Chartist movement, for some time languishing, took fresh courage from the Republican example in France. It was also stirred by a new economic crisis at home. There was half-hearted talk of revolution, but in the end it was decided to present a new petition to Parliament, reiterating all the old Chartist demands. A meeting was called in April 1848 on Kennington Common, a mile to the south of Westminster Bridge. From there the Chartist leaders proposed to lead an impressive march upon the Houses of Parliament. More spectators than Chartists assembled on that wet spring day. When the police forbade the proposed march the demonstrators quietly dispersed. Their petition was conveyed to the Commons in three cabs. Such was the measure of revolutionary feeling in London in 1848.[1]

---

1   It might be noted that during this period Karl Marx (1818–83) and Friedrich Engels (1820–95) were living in London (having being expelled from Cologne for their extremist views in 1849) and that in this same year, 1848, *The Communist Manifesto* was first published.

In 1849, after opening the new Albert Dock in Liverpool, Prince Albert had been so much impressed by the surging vigour of British industry, and its maritime cause and consequence, that he adopted with enthusiasm a plan for an exhibition on a far larger scale than had ever been seen before. It would display to the country and the world the progress achieved in every field. It would also be international, proclaiming the benefits of free trade between nations and looking forward to the universal peace which it was then supposed must inevitably result from the unhampered traffic in goods. Few people foresaw the war with Russia that was soon to break out.

For two years, against considerable opposition, the Prince headed a committee to further his project. In 1851 the Great Exhibition was opened in Hyde Park. Nineteen acres were devoted to the principal building, the Crystal Palace, designed by an expert glasshouse gardener, Joseph Paxton. Housing most of the exhibits, and enclosing whole trees within its glass and iron structure, it was to be the marvel of the decade. In spite of prophecies of failure, the Exhibition was a triumphant success. Over a million people a month visited it during the six months of its opening. Nearly fourteen thousand exhibits of industrial skill and craft were shown, of which half were British. The Prince was vindicated, and the large profit made by the organisers was invested and put to learned and educational purposes. Queen Victoria described the opening day as "one of the greatest and most glorious in our lives".[1]

The mid-century marks the summit of Britain's preponderance in industry. In another twenty years other nations, among whom industrial progress had started later, had begun to cut down her lead. Until 1870 Britain had mined more than half the world's coal, and in that year her output of pig-iron was still greater than the rest of the world's put together. Foreign trade stood at a figure of nearly 700 millions sterling, as compared with 300 for the United States, 340 for France, and 300 for Germany. But the proportions were rapidly changing. Railways greatly assisted the growth of industry in Germany and America, where coal and iron resources were separated from each other by considerable distances. A challenge was also presented to British agriculture, now that prairie-grown American wheat could be carried to American ports by railroad and shipped across the ocean to European markets. Nevertheless there was no slowing down of industry in Britain. Textiles, the backbone of British exports, filled an insatiable demand in Asia, and the future of the mighty steel and engineering industries seemed assured for a long time to come. In England the rapidly expanding Midlands and North were blackened by the smoke and dust of the pits and forges.

Critics were not wanting of the age of mass production that was now taking shape. Charles Dickens in his novels revealed the plight of the poor, holding

---

1   It is easy to overlook that the success of the Great Exhibition was in large measure due to Henry Cole (1808–82). A designer and civil servant, Cole was the man of enormous energy who really made Prince Albert's ideas work. It was Cole who established the Public Records Office, worked on the setting up of the penny post with Rowland Hill and might be best remembered for publishing the first Christmas card.

up to pity the conditions in which many of them dwelt and ridiculing the State institutions that crudely encompassed them. John Ruskin was another. In the midst of his long life he turned from the study of painting and architecture to modern social problems. His heart lay in the Middle Ages, which he imagined to be peopled by a fraternity of craftsmen harmoniously creating works of art. Peering out upon the Victorian scene, this prophetic figure looked in vain for similar accomplishment. Bad taste in manufacture, bad relations between employers and men aroused his eloquent wrath. His was a voice that cried the way both to new movements in the arts and to Socialism in politics.

Foreign affairs and the threat of war now began to darken the scene. Turkey had troubled the statesmen of Europe for many years. Preoccupation with the conflicts and intrigues of Court and harem had so distracted the Sultans at Constantinople and their chief advisers from the duties of government, and even of defence, that the military empire, which for three centuries had dominated the Eastern world from the Persian Gulf to Budapest, and from the Caspian to Algiers, seemed now on the edge of disruption and collapse. What then would become of its vast territories? To whom would fall the wide, fertile Turkish provinces in Europe and Asia? The urgency and imminence of such questions were sharpened by the evident determination of Russia to seize the Danubian lands, Constantinople, and the Black Sea.

The need to resist Russia was plain to most British observers, though Radicals like Cobden strongly opposed this view. British diplomacy was confused about the best way of achieving its aims. For it was also necessary to keep an eye on the French, who had ambitions for extending their influence in the Levant. Canning had planned to head Russia off from South-East Europe, not by direct opposition, but by founding on the ruins of the Turkish Empire a bloc of small independent states who would stand firm and if necessary fight for the sake of their own survival. With such a programme of emancipation he had hoped to associate not only France, but Russia herself. The creation of the kingdom of Greece was the first and only result of his efforts. But twenty years had gone by and the ruling politicians of England had forgotten the example of Byron, who had died for Greek freedom. They reversed the policy of Canning, and now attempted to check Russian expansion by the opposite method of propping up the decaying system of Turkish rule in South-East Europe. In the execution of this plan the Government was much assisted by Stratford Canning, later Lord Stratford de Redcliffe, the British Ambassador at Constantinople in the 1840s. He was a cousin of George Canning, with a wider knowledge of Turkey, which he had first visited in 1808, than any other Englishman of his day. Proud, difficult, quick-tempered, he enjoyed immense authority with the Turks.

The immediate source and origin of the conflict which now came to a head between Turkey and Russia lay in Jerusalem, where the Greek Orthodox and Roman Catholic Churches disputed the custody of certain shrines. The quarrel would have been unimportant had not the Czar supported the Greek pretensions, and Louis Napoleon, now the Emperor Napoleon III, been anxious to please French Catholics by championing the Latins. After long negotiation the Czar sent his envoy Menschikoff to Constantinople to revive his claims for a general protectorate over the Christians in the Turkish Empire. This, if granted, would have given Russia authority over the many millions of Rumanians, Serbs, Bulgarians, Greeks, and Armenians within the Ottoman domains. The balance of power, for which British Governments always sought in the Near East, as elsewhere, would have been destroyed.

Menschikoff was tactless and his demands angered the Turks. The electric telegraph, recently invented, only reached to Belgrade. Upon Stratford, who had returned to his Embassy, much depended. He was the man on the spot, with considerable freedom from Cabinet control and with strong views on the Russian danger and the need to support Turkey. At home Lord Derby, after a brief spell in office, had been succeeded by Lord Aberdeen, who presided over a coalition Government of Whigs and Peelites, far from united in their opinions. The Prime Minister himself and his Foreign Secretary, Lord Clarendon, were hesitant and favoured appeasement. But Stratford could count on Palmerston, the most popular man in the Cabinet, and on the general hostility in England towards the Russians. Stratford's dispatches do not support the charge that he exceeded his instructions: he recommended the Turks to continue negotiations and not to take too stiff an attitude. But the Turks knew their man, they knew they had his sympathy, and they knew that in the last resort the British Fleet would protect Constantinople and stop Russia seizing the Straits. They accordingly rejected the Russian demands, and on June 2, 1853, the Russian attitude had become so menacing that the Cabinet ordered the British Fleet to Besika Bay, outside the Dardanelles. Napoleon III, eager for British approval and support, agreed to provide a French squadron.

The Fleet reached Besika Bay on June 13. In early July Russian troops crossed the River Pruth and entered Turkish Moldavia. The British Cabinet was still divided, and neither warned the Russians nor promised help to the Turks. The Turks ended the matter by rejecting an offer of mediation by a council of ambassadors. Stratford disapproved of this proposal, known as the Vienna Note, but there is no evidence that he failed to carry out his instructions to advise the Turks to yield. This they could not do since feeling ran so high at Constantinople that the Sultan had little choice but to refuse.

War was not yet certain. The Czar, alarmed at Turkey's resistance, sought a compromise with the help of Austria, but by September Aberdeen and his Cabinet had become so suspicious that they rejected the offer. On October 4 the Sultan declared war on Russia, and soon afterwards attacked the Russians beyond the Danube. Such efforts as Aberdeen and Stratford could still make for peace were extinguished by a Russian onslaught against the Turkish Fleet off Sinope, in the Black Sea. Indignation flared in England, where the action was denounced as a massacre. Palmerston sent in his resignation in December on a domestic issue, but his action was interpreted as a protest against the Government's Eastern policy and Aberdeen was accused of cowardice. Thus England drifted into war. In February 1854 Nicholas recalled his ambassadors from London and Paris, and at the end of March the Crimean War began, with France and Britain as the allies of Turkey.

The operations were ill-planned and ill-conducted on both sides. With the exception of two minor naval expeditions to the Baltic and the White Sea, fighting was confined to Southern Russia, where the great naval fort of Sebastopol, in the Black Sea, was selected as the main Allied objective. The necessity for this enterprise was questionable: the Turks had already driven the Russians out of the Danube valley, there was little danger of an attack upon Constantinople, and it was folly to suppose that the capture of Sebastopol would make much impression on the vast resources of Russia. However, the British expeditionary force was encamped in Turkish territory and some use had to be made of it. Orders from London dispatched it to the Crimea against the wishes of its commander, Lord Raglan. The Allied fleet sailed close by Sebastopol harbour and ceremonial salutes were exchanged between the belligerents. A landing was made at the small town of Eupatoria, to the north-west. The Russian Governor declared that the armies might land, but according to regulations ought immediately to be placed in quarantine. Nobody took any notice of this precaution.

Sebastopol might have been entered by an immediate attack from the north, yet after an initial victory on the Alma in September 1854 the French commander, St Arnaud, who was a sick man and a political appointment, insisted on marching round to the south and beginning a formal siege. With this step Raglan reluctantly concurred; it was against his better judgment. The Russians were thus permitted to bring up reinforcements, and strengthen the fortifications under the direction of the famous engineer Todleben. Unable to complete their investment of the town, the Allies had to beat off fresh Russian field armies which arrived from the interior. The British Army, holding the exposed eastern wing of the lines, had twice to bear the brunt. At Balaclava in October the British cavalry distinguished themselves by two astonishing charges against overwhelming odds. The second of these was the celebrated charge of the Light Brigade, in which 673 horsemen, led by Lord Cardigan, rode up the valley under heavy fire, imperturbably, as if taking part in a review, to attack the Russian batteries. They captured the guns, but only a third of the brigade answered the first muster after the charge. Lord Cardigan calmly returned to the yacht on which he lived, had a bath, dined, drank a bottle of champagne, and went to bed. His brigade had performed an inspiring feat of gallantry. But it was due, like much else in this war, to the blunders of commanders. Lord Raglan's orders had been badly expressed and were misunderstood by his subordinates. The Light Brigade had charged the wrong guns.

The Battle of Inkerman followed, fought in the mists of a November dawn. It was a desperate infantry action, in which the British soldier proved his courage and endurance. Russian casualties were nearly five times as many as those of the Allies. But Inkerman was not decisive. The Russians outnumbered the Allies by two to one, and it became plain that there was no hope of taking Sebastopol before the spring of 1855. Amid storms and blizzards the British Army lay, without tents, huts, food, warm clothes, or the most elemental medical care. Cholera, dysentery, and malarial fever took their dreadful toll. Raglan's men had neither transport nor ambulances, and thousands were lost through cold and starvation because it did not occur to the Government of the greatest engineering country in the world to ease the movement of supplies from the port of Balaclava to the camp by laying down five miles of light railway.

The French and British between them had only 56,000 troops in the Crimea in the terrible winter of 1854–55. Nearly 14,000 of them went to hospital, and many died for want of medical supplies. Most of these casualties were British. The French were much better provided for, while the Russians, who accepted official mismanagement as a matter of course, perished in uncounted numbers on the long route marches through the snow southwards to the Crimea.

Even the War Office was a little shaken by the incompetence and suffering. *The Times*, under its great editor J.T. Delane, sent out the first of all war correspondents, William Russell, and used his reports to start a national agitation against the Government. Aberdeen was assailed from every quarter, and when Parliament reassembled in January a motion was introduced by a Private Member to appoint a commission of inquiry into the state of the army before Sebastopol. It was carried by a majority so large that when the figures were announced they were greeted, not with the usual cheers, but with surprised silence, followed by derisive laughter. Aberdeen resigned, and was succeeded by Palmerston, who accepted the commission of inquiry. Palmerston did not at first command wide confidence, and it was at this moment that Disraeli wrote privately of him, "he is really an impostor, utterly exhausted, and at the best only ginger-beer and not champagne, and now an old painted pantaloon". Disraeli was wrong. Palmerston soon proved himself the man of the hour. The worst mistakes and muddles were cleared up, and at the War Office Sidney Herbert struggled manfully to reform the military administration.

By the summer of 1855 the Allied armies had been reinforced and were in good heart. An assault on Sebastopol was mounted in June, but it failed. This was too much for Raglan. Worn out by the responsibilities of the campaign, he resigned, and ten days later he died. Raglan had been ill-served by his Government and by his quarrelsome subordinates, and he too readily let his good judgment be overridden. This disciple of Wellington, who had lost an arm at Waterloo, deserves a higher niche in military history than is sometimes accorded him. In September Sebastopol at last fell. The futility of the plan of campaign was now revealed. It was impossible to invade Russia from the Crimea. What should the next move be? France by now had four times as many troops in the field as England, and Napoleon III was threatening to withdraw them. A peace party in Paris was making its views felt. The French Emperor was inclined to negotiate, meanwhile reducing operations against Russia to a mere blockade. If the war were to continue, he felt, other Powers would have to be drawn in, and an appeal made to the national sentiments of Poles, Swedes, and other hereditary enemies of the Czar. This was too grandiose even for Palmerston. He privately denounced the French peace party as "a cabal of stock-jobbing politicians", but he realised the war must stop. Threatened by an Austrian ultimatum, Russia agreed to terms, and in February 1856 a peace conference opened in Paris.

The Treaty of Paris, signed at the end of March, removed the immediate causes of the conflict, but provided no permanent settlement of the Eastern Question. Russia surrendered her grip on the mouths of the Danube by abandoning Southern Bessarabia; her claims to a protectorate over the Turkish Christians were set aside; the Dardanelles were closed to foreign ships of war during peace, as they had been before the war; and Turkey's independence was guaranteed by the Powers, in return for a promise of reforms which was not worth the paper it was written on. Russia accepted the demilitarisation of the Black Sea, but repudiated her undertaking when Europe was absorbed by the Franco-Prussian War of 1870. For the time being her expansion was checked, but she remained unappeased. Within twenty years Europe was nearly at war again over Russian ambitions in the Near East. The fundamental situation was unaltered: so long as Turkey was weak so long would her empire remain a temptation to Russian Imperialists and an embarrassment to Western Europe.

With one exception few of the leading figures emerged from the Crimean War with enhanced reputations. Miss Florence Nightingale had been sent out in an official capacity by the Secretary at War, Sidney Herbert. She arrived at Scutari on the day before the Battle of Inkerman, and there organised the first base hospital of modern times. With few nurses and scanty equipment she reduced the death-rate at Scutari from 42 per hundred to 22 per thousand men. Her influence and example were far-reaching. The Red Cross movement, which started with the Geneva Convention of 1864,[1] was the outcome of her work, as were great administrative reforms in civilian hospitals. In an age of proud and domineering men she gave the women of the nineteenth century a new status, which revolutionised the social life of the country, and even made them want to vote. Miss Nightingale herself felt that "there are evils which press much more hardly on women than the want of the suffrage". Lack of education was one, and she favoured better girls' schools and the founding of women's colleges. To these objects she devoted her attention, and by her efforts half the Queen's subjects were encouraged to enter the realms of higher thought.

Palmerston, though now in his seventies, presided over the English scene. With one short interval of Tory government, he was Prime Minister through-out the decade that began in 1855. Not long after the signing of peace with

---

1   The 1864 Geneva Convention laid the ground rules (effective today) for the protection of then, soldiers and sailors, and the neutral status of doctors, nurses, their hospitals and chaplains in war zones, for which Miss Nightingale had campaigned. Those medical workers had to wear some sign of their neutrality and so the Geneva Convention chose the Geneva Cross – a red square cross on a white background.

Russia he was confronted with another emergency which also arose in the East, but this time in Asia. India had been basking under the administration of the East India Company, with only a moderate degree of supervision from London. The Company had its critics in Parliament and elsewhere, but their words had little effect upon its practices. Suddenly there occurred a disturbing outbreak against British rule.

The Indian Mutiny made, in some respects, a more lasting impact on England than the Crimean War. It paved the way for Empire. After it was over Britain gradually and consciously became a world-wide Imperial Power. The causes of the Mutiny lay deep in the past. About the beginning of the nineteenth century a new generation of British administrators and soldiers appeared in India, austere, upright, Bible-reading men, who dreamed of Christianising and Europeanising the sub-continent, and for a while gained a brief promise of success. Hitherto the English, like the Romans in the provinces of their empire, had a neutral policy on religion and no policy at all on Indian education. Regiments held ceremonial parades in honour of Hindu deities, and Hindu and Muslim holidays were impartially and publicly observed. But in England missionary zeal was stirring, and respect for alien creeds gradually succumbed to the desire for proselytisation. For a time enlightened Hindu opinion seemed not unreceptive to elements of the Christian faith. *Suttee*, the burning of widows, *Thugee*, the strangling of travellers by fanatics who deemed it a religious duty, and female infanticide were suppressed.

A more immediate cause of the rising was a series of defeats and reverses suffered by the British. The Russian threat to India had begun to overhang the minds of Englishmen. It was in fact a gross exaggeration to suppose that Russian armies could have crossed the ranges of the Hindu-Kush in force and arrived in the Indus valley. But the menace seemed real at the time. When it was learnt that a small body of Russians had penetrated into the fringes of Afghanistan a British expedition was dispatched in 1839 to Kabul and a British candidate placed on the Afghan throne. The result was disaster. The country rose up in arms. In December 1841, under a promise of safe-conduct, the British garrison of some four thousand troops, accompanied by nearly three times as many women, children, and Afghan camp-followers, began to withdraw through the snow and the mountain passes. The safe-conduct was violated, and nearly all were murdered or taken prisoner. Only a handful of survivors reached India in the following January. A second expedition avenged the treachery in the following year, but the repute of European arms was deeply smitten and the massacre resounded throughout the peninsula.

Another defeat soon followed in the Punjab, the most northerly of the Indian provinces at that time. Here the warrior Sikhs, a reformed Hindu sect, forbidden to touch tobacco or cut their hair above the waist, had long held sway. Encouraged by the news from Afghanistan, and restless after the death of their great leader, Ranjit Singh, who had hitherto held them in check, they resolved to try their hand at invading the Company's territory. In 1845 they crossed the boundary river of the Sutlej, and were met and repulsed two hundred miles north of Delhi. The British installed a regency. Three years later the Sikhs tried to overthrow it. There was a desperate drawn battle deep within the province at Chilianwala, in which three British regiments lost their colours. Shortly afterwards the British forces redeemed their name and the Sikh army was destroyed. The Punjab was pacified by John and Henry Lawrence. These famous brothers ruled with absolute power, untrammelled by the Company and splendidly resourceful. They sent the Koh-i-noor diamond to Queen Victoria, and gained from the formidable warriors of the province an affection and loyalty for the British Crown which was to endure for nearly a century.

This was a period of confident expansion in India, generally undertaken by men on the spot and not always approved by opinion in Britain. Two other major annexations completed the extension of British rule. Possession of Sind, in the lower Indus valley, had been judged necessary to safeguard the command of the north-west coast. It was conquered by Sir Charles Napier, a veteran who had fought at Corunna and in the American war of 1812. The other annexation was that of Oudh, on the borders of Bengal, where an Indian king had long oppressed his subjects. The Marquess of Dalhousie, appointed Governor-General at the age of thirty-five, had no doubts about the benefits conferred on India by British rule and British skill. During his eight years of office he added principalities to the Company's dominion by applying what was called the "doctrine of lapse". This meant that when an Indian ruler died without an heir of his own blood his territory was forfeited. Adopted heirs were not allowed to inherit, though this had long been Hindu custom. In Oudh Dalhousie was more forthright. He bluntly declared that "the British Government would be guilty in the sight of God and man if it were any longer to aid in sustaining by its countenance an administration fraught with suffering to millions". He deposed the king and seized his province in 1856. Next year came the Mutiny, and much of the blame for provoking it was laid at Dalhousie's door.

The East India Company's Army of Bengal had long been of ill-repute. Recruited mainly in the North, it was largely composed of high-caste Hindus. This was bad for discipline. Brahmin privates would question the orders of officers and N.C.O.s of less exalted caste. Power and influence in the regiments frequently depended on a man's position in the religious rather than the military hierarchy. The Company's British officers were often of poor quality, for the abler and more thrusting among them sought secondment to the more spacious fields of civil administration. Many of those who remained at regimental headquarters were out of touch with their men and showed no desire to improve matters. Troops were needed for a war with Burma, but if they crossed the high seas they lost caste. Dalhousie nevertheless made recruits liable for service anywhere in the world. There were grievances about pay and pensions. Other developments, unconnected with this military unrest, added their weight. By the 1850s railways, roads, posts, telegraphs, and schools were beginning to push and agitate their way across the countryside, and were thought by many Indians to threaten an ancient society whose inmost structure and spirit sprang from a rigid and unalterable caste system. If everyone used the same trains and the same schools, or even the same roads, it was argued, how could caste survive? Indian monarchs were apprehensive and resentful of the recent annexations. Hatred smouldered at the repression of *Suttee*. Unfounded stories spread that the Government intended to convert India forcibly to Christianity. The disasters in Afghanistan and the slaughter of the Sikh wars cast doubt on the invincibility of British arms. Many of the sepoys, or Indian soldiers, considered themselves equal or superior to European troops. Thus a legacy of troubles confronted Dalhousie's successor, Lord Canning. He had been in India little more than a year when the introduction of a new type of ammunition provided a spark and focus for the mass of discontent.

In the year of the centenary of Plassey rumours began to flow that the cartridges for the new Enfield rifle were greased with the fat of pigs and cows, animals which Moslem and Hindu respectively were forbidden to eat. The cartridges had to be bitten before they could be inserted in the muzzle. Thus sepoys of both religions would be defiled. There was some truth in the story, for beef-fat had been used in the London arsenal at Woolwich, though it was never used at the Indian factory at Dum-Dum, and as soon as the complaints began no tainted missiles were issued. Nevertheless the tale ran through the regiments in the spring of 1857 and there was much unrest. In April some cavalry troopers at Meerut were court-martialled and imprisoned for refusing to touch the cartridges, and on May 9 they were publicly stripped of their uniforms. An Indian officer told his superiors that the sepoys were planning to break open the jail and release the prisoners. His warning was disbelieved. Next night three regiments mutinied, captured the prison, killed their British officers, and marched on Delhi.

There was nothing at hand to stop them. South of the Punjab fewer than eleven full-strength battalions and ancillary forces, comprising in all about forty thousand British soldiers, were scattered across the vast peninsula, and even these were not on a war footing. The Indian troops outnumbered them by five to one and had most of the artillery. The hot weather had started, distances were great, transport was scarce, the authorities were unprepared. Nevertheless, when the British power was so weak, and India might have been plunged once again into the anarchy and bloodshed from which she had been gradually and painfully rescued, most of the populace remained aloof and at peace, and none of the leading Indian rulers joined the revolt. Of the three armies maintained by the Company only one, that of Bengal, was affected. Gurkhas from Nepal helped to quell the rising. The Punjab remained loyal, and its Sikhs and Moslems respected the colours and disarmed wavering regiments. The valley of the Ganges was the centre of the turmoil.

But at first all went with a rush. The magazine at Delhi was guarded by two British officers and six soldiers. They fought to the last, and when resistance was hopeless they blew it up. The mutineers killed every European in sight, seized the aged King of Delhi, now living in retirement as the Company's pensioner, and proclaimed him Moghul Emperor. The appeal failed and few Moslems rose to support it. For three weeks there was a pause, and then the mutiny spread. British officers would not believe in the disloyalty of their troops and many were murdered. At Cawnpore, on the borders of Oudh, the garrison left the citadel to guard the road. They trusted to the loyalty of the Nana Sahib, the dispossessed adopted son of an Indian ruler, but still a power-ful figure. They were mistaken, and a terrible fate was soon to befall them. At Lucknow, the capital, Henry Lawrence prepared the Residency for what was to be a long and glorious defence. Meanwhile, rightly, perceiving that the key to the revolt lay in Delhi, the British mustered such forces as they could and seized the ridge overlooking the city. They were too few to make an assault, and for weeks in the height of summer three thousand troops, most of whom were British, held the fifty-foot eminence against an enemy twenty or thirty times their number. Early in August Nicholson[1] arrived with reinforcements from the Punjab, having marched nearly thirty miles a day for three weeks. Thus animated, the British attacked on September 14, and after six days' street-fighting, in which Nicholson was killed, the city fell. The poor King was sent to Burma. His two sons were taken prisoners, and summarily shot after an attempt had been made to rescue them. This created a fresh grievance in Indian eyes.

At Cawnpore there was a horrible massacre. For twenty-one days nine hundred British and loyal Indians, nearly half of them women and children, were besieged and attacked by three thousand sepoys with the Nana Sahib at their head. At length, on June 26, they were granted safe-conduct. As they were leaving by boat they were fired upon, and all the men were killed. Such women and children as survived were cast into prison. On the night of July 15 a relieving force under Sir Henry Havelock, a veteran of Indian warfare, was barely twenty miles away. The Nana Sahib ordered his sepoys to kill the prisoners. They refused. Five assassins then cut the captives to death with knives and threw the bodies into a well. Two days later Havelock arrived. "Had any Christian bishop visited that scene of butchery when I saw it", wrote an eye-witness long afterwards, "I verily believe that he would have buckled on his sword." Here and elsewhere the British troops took horrible vengeance. Mutineers were blown from the mouths of cannon, sometimes alive, or their bodies sewn up in the skins of cows and swine.

The rebels turned on Lucknow. Here also there was a desperate struggle. Seventeen hundred troops, nearly half of them loyal sepoys, held the Residency, under Henry Lawrence, against sixty-thousand rebels, for in Oudh, unlike most of India, the population joined the revolt. Food was short and there was much disease. On September 25 Havelock and Outram fought

---

1 John Nicholson (1822–57), a Protestant Irishman and legendary figure in India, was described as the greatest of Henry Lawrence's "Young Men".

their way in, but were beset in their turn, Havelock dying of exhaustion a few days later. In November the siege was raised by Sir Colin Campbell, the new Commander-in-Chief appointed by Lord Palmerston. Campbell had seen service against Napoleon and had a distinguished record in the Crimean War. A fresh threat to Cawnpore compelled him to move on. Outram, reinforced, continued to hold out, and Lucknow was not finally liberated till the following March. No one knows what happened to the Nana Sahib. He disappeared for ever into the Himalayan jungle.

Elsewhere the rising was more speedily crushed. The recapture of Delhi had destroyed all semblance and pretence that the mutiny was a national revolt. Fighting, sporadic but often fierce, continued in the Central Provinces until the end of 1858, but on November the Governor-General, "Clemency" Canning, derisively so called for his mercifulness, proclaimed with truth that Queen Victoria was now sovereign of all India. The first Viceroy, as Canning became, was a son of the renowned Foreign Secretary and Prime Minister. The rule of the East India Company, which had long ceased to be a trading business in India, was abolished. This was the work of the short Conservative Government of Derby and Disraeli. Thus, after almost exactly a century the advice which Clive had given to Pitt was accepted by the British Government. Henceforward there were to be no more annexations, no subsidiary treaties, no more civil wars. Religious toleration and equality before the law were promised to all. Indians for a generation and more were to look back on the Queen's Proclamation of 1858 as a Magna Carta.

The scale of the Indian Mutiny should not be exaggerated. Three-quarters of the troops remained loyal; barely a third of British territory was affected; there had been risings and revolts among the soldiery before; the brunt of the outbreak was suppressed in the space of a few weeks. It was in no sense a national movement, or, as some later Indian writers have suggested, a patriotic struggle for freedom or a war of independence. But terrible atrocities had been committed by both sides. From now on there was an increasing gulf between the rulers and the ruled. The English no longer looked on India as "home", or themselves as crusaders called to redeem and uplift the great multitudes.

While these events unrolled in India the political scene in England remained confused. Peel's conversion to Free Trade had destroyed the party lines which he had done much to draw, and for twenty years in Britain Governments of mixed complexion followed one another. Disraeli and Derby, having broken Peel, found that it took a long time to muster the remnant of the former Tory Protectionists into an effective political party. Rising men like Gladstone, who remained faithful to the Peel tradition, would have nothing to do with them, though on at least one occasion Disraeli tried hard to enlist Gladstone's co-operation. It is an interesting speculation what might have happened had these two bitter opponents and future Prime Ministers at this stage joined hands. The Whigs, under Russell and Palmerston, felt that their main aims had already been accomplished. Palmerston was willing to make improvements in government, but large-scale changes were not to his mind. Russell hankered after a further measure of electoral reform, but that was the limit of his programme. Both conceived of themselves as guardians of the system that they had the fortune to head. In this attitude the two leaders, and Palmerston especially, were probably in harmony with mid-Victorian opinion. Radicalism in these years made little appeal to the voters. Prosperity was spreading through the land, and with it went a lull in the fiercer forms of political agitation. Dignity and deference were the values of the age. If the gentleman was still the admired ideal, the self-made man was also deeply respected. The doctrine of industrious self-help, preached by Samuel Smiles, was widely popular in the middle classes and among many artisans as well. The lessons of the Chartist failure had been learnt, and educating the manual labourer began to seem more important than rousing him to revolution.

Religion in its numerous varieties cast a soothing and uplifting influence on men's minds. Many millions, more than half the total population, were regular attenders at church or chapel, though churchgoers were fewer among the very poor. Religious debate was earnest, sometimes acrimonious, but the contests it bred were verbal. Civil strife for the sake of religion was a thing of the past. The Church of England, earlier in the century, had been stirred from slumber by Evangelical zeal and the lofty ideals of the Oxford Movement. The Low Church and High Church parties, as they were called, strove eloquently for men's souls. About half the churchgoers of England were members of the Anglican communion. Dissent also flourished, and Methodist, Baptist, Presbyterian, Congregational, and Unitarian preachers, gained a wide allegiance. The Church of Rome in England had revived under the impulse of Catholic Emancipation, and was reinforced by the accession of a number of High Anglican clergy, including John Henry Newman, a profound and subtle thinker, later created a Cardinal.

Religious preoccupations were probably more widespread and deeply felt than at any time since the days of Cromwell. But thinking men were also disturbed by a new theory, long foreshadowed in the work of scientists, the theory of evolution. It was given classic expression in *The Origin of Species*, published by Charles Darwin in 1859. This book provoked doubt and perplexity among those who could no longer take literally the Biblical account of creation. But the theory of evolution, and its emphasis on the survival of the fittest in the history of life upon the globe, was a powerful adjunct to mid-Victorian optimism. It lent fresh force to the belief in the forward march of mankind.

The greatest of the European movements in these years was the cause of Italian unity. This long-cherished dream of the Italian peoples was at last realised, though only partially, in 1859 and 1860. The story is well known of how the Italians secured the military aid of Napoleon III for the price of ceding Nice and Savoy to France, and how, after winning Lombardy from the Austrians, the French Emperor left his allies in the lurch. Venice remained unredeemed; still worse, a French army protected the rump of the Papal State in Rome, and for ten years deprived the Italians of their natural capital. But as one small Italian state after another cast out their alien rulers, and merged under a single monarchy, widespread enthusiasm was aroused in England. Garibaldi and his thousand volunteers, who overturned the detested Bourbon Government in Sicily and Naples with singular dash and speed, were acclaimed as heroes in London. These bold events were welcome to Palmerston and his Foreign Secretary, Russell. At the same time the British leaders were suspicious of Napoleon III's designs and fearful of a wider war. Congratulation but non-intervention was therefore their policy. It is typical of these two old Whigs that they applauded the new Italian Government for putting into practice the principles of the English Revolution of 1688. Russell in the House of Commons compared Garibaldi to King William III. History does not relate what the Italians made of this.

In home politics meanwhile a sublime complacency enveloped the Government. Palmerston, like Melbourne before him, did not believe in too much legislation. Good-humour and common sense distinguished him. As the novelist Trollope well said, he was "a statesman for the moment. Whatever was not wanted now, whatever was not practicable now, he drove quite out of his mind." This practical outlook found no favour among the younger and more thrusting Members of the House of Commons. Disraeli, chafing on the Opposition benches, vented his scorn and irritation on this last of the eighteenth-century politicians. "His external system", he once told the House, "is turbulent and aggressive that his rule at home may be tranquil and unassailed. Hence arise excessive expenditure, heavy taxation, and the stoppage of all social improvement. His scheme of conduct is so devoid of all political principle that when forced to appeal to the people his only claim to their confidence is his name." Peel's disciples and followers were no less despairing and powerless. So long as leadership remained in the hands of Palmerston, Russell, and the Whig nobility there could be little hope of advance towards the Liberalism of which they dreamed.

The Tories were little better off. Their nominal head was Lord Derby, who could be brilliant in debate, but was apt to regard politics as an unpleasant duty imposed upon the members of his class. His real interest lay in horse-racing, and he also produced an excellent, translation of Homer. Disraeli had become the leader of his party in the House of Commons. His struggle for power was hard and uphill. A Jew at the head of a phalanx of country gentlemen was an unusual sight in English politics. After the repeal of the Corn Laws protection was not only dead, but, as Disraeli himself said, damned, and he and Derby had agreed to discard it as a party principle. But the search for a new theme was long, painful, and frustrating. Meanwhile he had to play the part of Derby's lieutenant, and their spells of office in 1852 and 1858 were brief and uneventful. Disraeli more than once sought an alliance with the Radicals, and promised them that he would oppose armaments and an aggressive foreign policy. Colonies, he even declared, were "a millstone round our necks". But their chief spokesman, John Bright, was under no illusions. The shrewd Quaker was not to be caught. "Mr Disraeli," he said, "is a man who does what may be called the conjuring for his party. He is what among a tribe of Red Indians would be called the medicine-man." And that was the end of that. Thus foiled, Disraeli returned to his attack on the Whigs. He was convinced that the only way to destroy them was by extending the franchise yet further so as to embrace the respectable artisans and counter the hostility of the middle classes. Patiently he worked on Derby and his colleagues. In his youth he had dreamed of uniting the two nations, the rich and the poor, as the world of his novel Sybil shows, and the 1850s saw the slow emergence of a practical doctrine of Tory democracy. But Disraeli's ideas took time to find acceptance.

Standing apart both from the Whigs and Derby's Tories were the Peelites, of whom the most notable was William Gladstone. Having started his Parliamentary career in 1832 as a strict Tory, he was to make a long pilgrimage into the Liberal camp. The death of Peel had destroyed his allegiance to Toryism and he too was in search of a new theme. The son of a rich Liverpool merchant with slave-owning interests in the West Indies, Gladstone came from the same class as his old leader, and believed, like him, in the new arguments for Free Trade. Though admired as an administrator and an orator, his contemporaries considered him wanting in judgment and principle, but in fact, as Palmerston perceived, he was awaking to the political potentialities of the English middle class. "He might", he said, "be called one of the people; he wished to identify himself with them; he possessed religious enthusiasm, and made it powerful over others from the force of his own intellect." Despite his preoccupations with theology, he comprehended the minds of the new voters better than his colleagues and understood the workings of party better than Peel. "Oxford on the surface, but Liverpool underneath" – such was a contemporary judgment. But, like Disraeli, his progress was slow. He was Chancellor of the Exchequer at the beginning of the Crimean War; then he faded into Opposition. It was fortunate for him that supreme power did not come too soon. Peel had been frustrated by early experience of high office, which prevented him from putting his ideas to the test. Long years of waiting made Gladstone sure of himself.

In 1859, aged nearly fifty, Gladstone joined the Whigs and the pilgrimage was over. His decision was made on an issue of foreign policy, but he again concentrated on finance. As Chancellor of the Exchequer under Palmerston his golden period began – great Budget speeches in the House of Commons, a superb handling of administrative detail, a commercial treaty with France, which opened a new era in Free Trade, and demands for retrenchment in military affairs, which brought him into conflict with his Prime Minister. His finance was a remarkable success. Three brilliant Budgets reduced taxation. Trade was rapidly expanding, and it was soon apparent who would succeed to the leadership of the party. In 1865, in his eighty-first year, Palmerston died. "Gladstone", he declared in his last days, "will soon have it all his own way, and whenever he gets my place we shall have strange doings." The old Whig was right. The eighteenth century died with him. The later Victorian age demanded a new leader, and at long last he had arrived. When Gladstone next appeared before his electors he opened his speech by saying, "At last, my friends, I am come among you, and I am come among you unmuzzled." But the Whigs still hesitated. Gladstone, like Disraeli, wanted to extend the franchise to large sections of the working classes: he was anxious to capture the votes of the new electorate. He prevailed upon the Government, now headed by Russell, to put forward a Reform Bill, but it was defeated on an amendment and the Cabinet resigned. Minority administrations under Derby and Disraeli followed, which lasted for two and a half years.

Disraeli now seized his chance. He introduced a fresh Reform Bill in 1867, which he skilfully adapted to meet the wishes of the House, of which he was Leader. There was a redistribution of seats in favour of the large industrial towns, and nearly a million new voters were added to an existing electorate of about the same number. The Tories were nervous at this startling advance from their original plan. In many towns the working classes would now be in the majority at elections. Derby called it "a leap in the dark". The recent civil war in America seemed a poor recommendation for democracy, and even the Radicals were anxious about how the uneducated masses would behave. But this immediately became clear. The carrying of the second Reform Bill so soon after the death of Palmerston opened a new era in English politics. New issues and new methods began to emerge as Walter Bagehot, the banker and economist, said, "A political country is like an American forest; you have only to cut down the old trees and immediately new trees come up to replace them." In February 1868 Derby resigned from the leadership of the party and Disraeli was at last Prime Minister – as he put it, "at the top of the greasy pole". He had to hold a General Election. The new voters gave their overwhelming support to his opponents, and Gladstone, who had become leader of the Liberal Party, formed the strongest administration that England had seen since the days of Peel.

CHAPTER FORTY-SIX

THE ERA OF EMIGRATION

The migration of the English-speaking peoples – motives and methods – famine – gold – Canada – Wakefield, Durham and the Act of 1840 – the British North American Act – South Africa – conflict with the Dutch – the Great Trek – the Zulu empire – Australia – Botany Bay – origins of the wool trade – tragedy of the Black Drive – New South Wales and her offspring – the Australian Gold Rush – New Zealand – Marsden and the missionaries – the New Zealand Association – the Treaty of Waitangi – the Maori Wars

OCCUPATION OF the empty lands of the globe was vehemently accelerated by the fall of Napoleon. A generation of men and women had toiled or fought in their factories or on their farms, in the fleets and in the armies, and only a very few had had either the wish or the opportunity to seek a new life and new fortunes overseas. Their energies and their hopes had been concentrated on survival and on victory. Suddenly all this was changed. No enemies threatened in Europe. Ships need no longer sail in convoy, and the main outlines of the continents had been charted. Once more the New World offered an escape from the hardships and frustrations of the Old. Fares were cheap and transport was plentiful. The result was the most spectacular migration of human beings of which history has yet had record and a vast enrichment of the trade and industry of Great Britain.

The increasing population of Great Britain added to the pressure. In 1801 it was about eleven millions. Thirty years later it was sixteen millions, and by 1871 it was ten millions more. The numbers grew, and the flow began: in the 1820s a quarter of a million emigrants, in the 1830s half a million, by the middle of the century a million and a half, until sixty-five years after Waterloo no fewer than eight million people had left the British Isles. The motives, methods, and character of the movement were very different from those which had sustained the Pilgrim Fathers and the Stuart plantations of the seventeenth century. Famine drove at least a million Irishmen to the United States and elsewhere. Gold lured hardy fortune-hunters to Australia, and to the bleak recesses of Canada, where they discovered a more practical if less respectable El Dorado than had dazzled the Elizabethan adventurers. Hunger for land and for the profits of the wool trade beckoned the more sober and well-to-do. All this was largely accomplished in the face of official indifference and sometimes of hostility. The American War of Independence had convinced most of the ruling classes in Britain that colonies were undesirable possessions. They did not even have a departmental Secretary of State of their own until 1854. The Government was interested in strategic bases, but if ordinary people wanted to settle in the new lands then let them do so. It might cure unemployment and provide posts for penniless noblemen, but the sooner these communities became completely independent the better and cheaper for the tax-payer in England. Anyway, Greece was more interesting news than New Zealand, and the educated public were much more concerned about the slave-trade than the squalors of the emigrant ships. Thus, as in India, the Second British Empire was founded almost by accident, and with small encouragement from any of the main political parties.

Of the new territories Canada was the most familiar and the nearest in point of distance to the United Kingdom. Her Maritime Provinces had long sent timber to Britain, and rather than return with empty holds the shipowners were content to transport emigrants for a moderate fare. Once they landed, however, the difficulties and the distances were very great. The Maritime Provinces lived a life very much of their own, and many emigrants chose to push on into Lower Canada, or, as it is now called, the Province of Quebec. Pitt in 1791 had sought to solve the racial problems of Canada by dividing her into two parts. In Lower Canada the French were deeply rooted, a compact, alien community, led by priests and seigneurs, uninterested and untouched by the democratic ideas of liberal or revolutionary Europe, and holding stubbornly like the Boers in South Africa to their own traditions and language. Beyond them, to the north-west, lay Upper Canada, the modern Province of Ontario, settled by some of the sixty thousand Englishmen who had left the United States towards the end of the eighteenth century rather than live under the American republic. These proud folk had out of devotion to the British Throne abandoned most of their possessions, and been rewarded with the unremunerative but honourable title of United Empire Loyalists. The Mohawk tribe, inspired by the same sentiments, had journeyed with them. They had hacked a living space out of the forests, and dwelt lonely and remote, cut off from Lower Canada by the rapids of the St Lawrence, and watchful against incursions from the United States. Then there was a vast emptiness till one reached a few posts on the Pacific which traded their wares to China.

These communities, so different in tradition, character, and race, had been rallied into temporary unity by invasion from the United States. French, English, and Red Indians all fought against the Americans, and repulsed them in the three-year struggle between 1812 and 1814. Then trouble began. The French in Lower Canada feared that the immigrants would outnumber and dominate them. The Loyalists in Upper Canada welcomed new settlers who would increase the price of land but were reluctant to treat them as equals.

Moreover, the two Provinces started to quarrel with each other. Upper Canada's external trade had to pass through Lower Canada, and there pay taxes, and disputes occurred about sharing the proceeds. Differences over religion added to the irritations. From about 1820 the Assembly in Lower Canada began to behave like the Parliaments of the early Stuarts and the legislatures of the American colonies, refusing to vote money for the salaries of royal judges and permanent officials. French politicians made vehement speeches. In Upper Canada the new settlers struggled for political equality with the Loyalists. Liberals wanted to make the executive responsible to the Assembly and talked wildly of leaving the Empire, and in 1836 the Assembly in which they held a majority was dissolved.

In the following year both Provinces rebelled, Lower Canada for a month and Upper Canada for a week. There were mobs, firing by troops, shifty compromises, and very few executions. Everything was on a small scale and in a minor key, and no great harm was done, but it made the British Government realise that Canadian affairs required attention. The Whig leaders in London were wiser than George III. They perceived that a tiny minority of insurgents could lead to great troubles, and in 1838 Lord Durham was sent to investigate, assisted by Edward Gibbon Wakefield. His instructions were vague and simple, "To put things right", and meanwhile the Canadian constitution was suspended by Act of Parliament. Durham was a Radical, brilliant, decisive, and hot-tempered. Wakefield was an active theorist on Imperial affairs whose misconduct with a couple of heiresses had earned him a prison sentence and compelled him to spend the rest of his public life behind the scenes. Durham stayed only a few months. His high-handed conduct in dealing with disaffected Canadians aroused much criticism of him at Westminster. Feeling himself deserted by Lord Melbourne's Government, with which he was personally unpopular, but which should nevertheless have stood by him, Durham resigned and returned to England. He then produced the famous report[1] in which he diagnosed and proclaimed the root causes of the trouble and advocated responsible government, carried on by Ministers commanding the confidence of the popular Assembly, a united Canada, and planned settlement of the unoccupied lands. These recommendations were largely put into effect by the Canada Act of 1840, which was the work of Lord John Russell.

Thereafter Canada's progress was swift and peaceful. Her population had risen from about half a million in 1815 to a million and a quarter in 1838. A regular steamship service with the British Isles and cheap transatlantic postage were established in the same year. There were hesitations and doubts in England at the novel idea of making colonies almost completely free and allowing their democratic Assemblies to choose and eject their own Ministers, but the appointment of Durham's son-in-law, Lord Elgin, as Governor-General in 1847 was decisive. Elgin believed, like Durham, that the Governor should represent the sovereign and remain in the background of politics. He

1   *Report on the Affairs of British North America* (1839).

appointed and dismissed Ministers according to the wishes of the Assembly. For this he was blamed or applauded, and even pelted with eggs and stones, according to how it pleased or angered either side. But when he laid down his office seven years later the principle had been firmly accepted by Canadians of all persuasions that popular power must march with popular responsibility, that Ministers must govern and be obeyed so long as they enjoyed the confidence of the majority and should resign when they had lost it. There was hardly any talk now of leaving the Empire or dividing Canada into separate and sovereign units or joining the American Republic. On the contrary, the Oregon Treaty with the United States in 1846 extended the 49th parallel right across the continent as a boundary between the two countries and gave the whole of Vancouver Island to Great Britain.

In the mid-century a movement for the federation of all the Canadian Provinces began to grow and gather support. The Civil War in the United States helped to convince Canadians that all was not perfect in their neighbours' constitution, and the victory of the North also aroused their fears that the exultant Union might be tempted to extend its borders farther still. Canada had already turned her gaze westwards. Between the Province of Ontario and the Rocky Mountains lay a thousand miles of territory, uninhabited save by a few settlers in Manitoba, a roaming-place for Indians, trappers, and wild animals. It was a temptation, so it was argued, to the land-hunger of the United States. Discharged Irish soldiers from the Civil War had already made armed raids across the border which Congress had declared itself powerless to arrest. Might not the Americans press forward, occupy these vacant lands by stealth, and even establish a kind of squatter's right to the prairies? The soil was believed to be fertile and was said to offer a living for white men. In 1867 America purchased the remote and forbidding expanse of Alaska from the Russians for the sum of 7,200,000 dollars, but here, on the doorstep of the Republic, lay a prize which seemed much more desirable and was very easy of access. No one ruled over it except the Hudson's Bay Company, founded in the reign of Charles II, and the Company, believing that agriculture would imperil its fur-trade, was both hostile to settlers and jealous of its own authority. Eleven years before, however, the discovery of gold on the Fraser River had precipitated a rush of fortune-hunters to the Pacific coast. The Company's officials had proved powerless to control the turmoil, and the Government in London had been compelled to extend the royal sovereignty to this distant shore. Thus was born the Crown colony of British Columbia, which soon united with the Island of Vancouver and demanded and obtained self-rule. But between it and Ontario lay a no-man's-land, and something must be done if it was not to fall into the hands of the United States. How indeed could Canada remain separate from America and yet stay alive?

These considerations prompted the British North America Act of 1867, which created the first of the self-governing British Dominions beyond the seas. The Provinces of Ontario, Quebec, New Brunswick, and Nova Scotia were the founding members. They adopted a federal constitution of a very different shape, from that of the United States. All powers not expressly reserved to the Provinces of Canada were assumed by the central Government: the Governor-General, representing the monarch, ruled through Ministers drawn from the majority in her Canadian House of Commons, and Members of the House were elected in numbers proportionate to the population they represented. Thus the way was made easy for the absorption of new territories and Provinces, and on the eve of her Railway Age and westward expansion the political stability of Canada was assured.

When the Parliament of the new Dominion first met, its chief anxiety was about the Western lands. Its members looked to the future, and it is convenient here to chart the results of their foresight. The obvious, immediate step was to buy out the Hudson's Bay Company. This was done two years later for the sum of £300,000. The Company kept its trading rights, and indeed retains them to this day, but it surrendered its territorial sovereignty to the Crown. The process was not accomplished without bloodshed. There was a brief revolt in Manitoba, where wild Indian half-breeds thought that their freedom was endangered, but order was soon restored. Manitoba became a Province of the Dominion in 1870, and in the next year British Columbia was also admitted. By themselves, however, these constitutional steps would not have sufficed to bind the broad stretches of Canada together. The challenging task that faced the Dominion was to settle and develop her empty Western lands before the immigrant tide from America could flood across the 49th parallel. The answer was to build a transcontinental railway.

When the Maritime Provinces joined the federation they had done so on condition they were linked with Ontario by rail, and after nine years of labour a line was completed in 1876. British Columbia made the same demand and received the same promise. It proved much more difficult to fulfil. Capital was scarce, investors were timid, politics were tangled, and much of the country was unknown. At length however a Scotsman, Donald Smith, better known as Lord Strathcona, carried out the plan. His company demanded ten years. Helped by Government funds, they finished their work in half the time, and the Canadian Pacific Railway was opened in 1885. Other lines sprang up, and corn, soon counted in millions of bushels a year, began to flow in from the prairies. Canada had become a nation, and shining prospects lay before her.

South Africa, unlike America, had scanty attractions for the early colonists and explorers. As the half-way house to the Indies many broke their voyage there, but few cared to stay. The Gulf of St Lawrence made it easy to reach the interior of Canada, but the coastline of South Africa, short of natural harbours and navigable rivers, mostly consisted of cliffs and sandhills washed by strong currents and stormy seas. Inland a succession of mountain ranges, running parallel to the coast, barred the way. From the west the ascent was comparatively gradual, but the country was barren and waterless. From the south and east range after range, in many places sheer and precipitous, had to be climbed. Few lands have been more difficult for Europeans to enter than

South Africa, and for them it long remained the "Tavern of the Seas", a port of call on the route to the East.

In the seventeenth century the fleets of the Dutch East India Company, sailing for the Indies or returning home to Amsterdam and Rotterdam, were the most frequent visitors to the Cape, and Table Bay was their halting-place. The establishment of a permanent settlement was discussed, but nothing was done till 1652, when, at the height of their power and in the Golden Age of their civilisation, the Dutch sent Jan van Riebeek, a young ship's surgeon, with three ships to take possession of Table Bay. Colonisation was no part of the plan: they merely wanted to found a port of call for the Company's ships, and almost all the inhabitants were servants of the Company, forbidden to strike out into the new land. After twenty years there were no more than sixty-four free burghers at Table Bay.

The change came at the turn of the seventeenth century , under the Governorship of Simon van der Stel and his son William Adriaan. They encouraged settlers to come out from Holland and take up grants of land, and by 1707 there were over fifteen hundred free burghers. Not all were Dutch; many were Huguenots, Germans, or Swedes, driven into exile by religious persecution; but the Dutch gradually assimilated them. The little community was served and sustained by a local population of negro slaves.

Throughout the eighteenth century the colony prospered and grew. In 1760 the first European crossed the Orange River, and by 1778 the Fish River had been made its eastern boundary. By the end of the century the population numbered about fifteen thousand, and there were three areas of settlement. Cape Town, or "Little Paris" as the settlers called it, was a town and port of five thousand inhabitants, and the Company's headquarters. The agricultural coast-belt near the Cape peninsula offered the farmers a limited prosperity, and life was easy, though primitive. Finally there was the inland plateau and remoter coast-belt, where dwelt the frontiersmen, restless, hard, self-reliant, narrow-minded, isolated from society, and impatient of the restraints of civilised government – the forerunners of the Trekkers and the Transvaal Boers of the nineteenth century.

But Holland had now been slowly overtaken by Britain, and as the century drew to its close it became clear that the Imperial future lay, not with the Dutch, but either with the British or the French. Napoleon's wars ruined the Dutch trade, swept the Dutch ships from the seas, and overthrew the Dutch state. In 1782 the Dutch East India Company had paid its last dividend, and twelve years later declared its bankruptcy, with a deficit of ten million pounds. The consequences were serious. Holland had no longer the power to protect her possessions, and when the Dutch were defeated by the French and the puppet-state of the Batavian Republic was established the British seized Cape Colony as enemy territory. It was finally ceded to them under the peace settlement in of 1814 in return for an indemnity of £6,000,000.

At first they met with no great hostility. The Dutch Company had been unpopular, there was no deliberate policy of Anglicisation, and the Cape kept most of its Dutch customs and traditions. The British dealt forcefully with the eastern frontier, where the settlers were in contact and conflict with a great southward migration of the Bantu peoples from Central Africa. This extended right across the continent, from the Hereros and Damaras in the west to the Nguni coast peoples in the east. There was much cattle-raiding along the line of the Fish River, and fighting between the Dutch and the natives had broken out in 1779. Thus began a long succession of Kaffir wars, lasting for a hundred years. The settlers, scattered in isolated farms over vast stretches of country, found it difficult to defend themselves, and had demanded help from Cape Town. The far-away Dutch authorities had given them no support. It was now the turn of the British.

They decided that the only way to secure the line of the Fish River was to colonise the border with British settlers, and between 1820 and 1821 nearly five thousand of them were brought out from Great Britain. This emigration coincided with a change of policy. Convinced that South Africa was now destined to become a permanent part of the British Empire, the Government resolved to make it as English as they could. English began to replace Dutch as the official language. In 1828 the judicial system was remodelled on the English pattern, Dutch currency was replaced by English, and the English began to dominate the churches and the schools. Thus was born a division which Canada had surmounted. With the same religion, a similar language, a common stock, and kindred political and social traditions, British and Boers nevertheless plunged into racial strife. British methods of government created among the Boers a more bitter antagonism than in any other Imperial country except Ireland.

Anglicisation was not only ill-conceived, it was unsuccessful. The English were to discover, as the Spaniards had learnt in the sixteenth century, that no race has ever clung more tenaciously to its own culture and institutions than the Dutch, and the only result of the new policy in the 1820s and 1830s was to harden those differences of opinion, especially on the native question, which were already beginning to appear. At this time there was much enthusiasm in England for good works, and English missionaries had been active in South Africa since the early years of the century. The missionaries believed and preached that black men were the equals of white men; the settlers regarded the natives primarily as farm-hands and wanted to control them as strictly as possible. When the missionaries got slavery abolished in 1833 the settlers were indignant at such interference, which meant scarcity of labour, a weakening of their authority and prestige, a risk that large numbers of the Bantu would become beggars and vagrants. At first the English settlers agreed with the Dutch, but as soon as the influence of the missionaries, especially Dr John Philip and the London Missionary Society, came to sway the Government and the Colonial Office the Dutch were left alone to nurse their grievances against the English authorities.

The first crisis came in 1834. The settlement of the Fish River area brought no security, and hordes of Bantu swept over the frontier, laying waste the country and destroying the farms. The Governor, Sir Benjamin D'Urban, drove them back, and to prevent another attack he annexed the territory between the Rivers Keis-kamma and Kei, expelled the native raiders, and compensated the settlers by offering them land in this new Province, which was named after Queen Adelaide. This roused the missionaries, and they persuaded the Colonial Secretary, Lord Glenelg, to repudiate D'Urban and abandon the new Province. The settlers lost all compensation, and insult was added to injury when it became known that Glenelg considered that the Kaffirs had an ample justification for the war into which they had rushed. Thus was provoked the Great Trek.

In small parties, accompanied by their women and children and driving their cattle before them, about five thousand Boers set out into the unknown, like the Children of Israel seeking the Promised Land. They were soon followed by many others. Some journeyed over a thousand miles to the banks of the Limpopo, many were attacked by the Matabele and the Zulu, all endured thirst and famine; yet in the unyielding spirit of their Calvinist religion they marched on. The Great Trek was one of the remarkable feats of the nine-teenth century, and its purpose was to shake off British rule for ever. "We quit this colony," wrote Pieter Retief, one of the Boer leaders, "under the full assurance that the English Government has nothing more to require of us, and will allow us to govern ourselves without its interference in future."

For long their fortunes looked dark. It was the time of the Mfecane, the "crushing" of the other native tribes by the military empire of the Zulus under Chaka and his successor Dingaan. The Zulu massacre of thousands of natives gave the Boers room to move, but they moved in great peril. In many lonely places within the laager of their ox-wagons they faced the wild onslaught of the Zulu warriors, and not until December 1838 did they crush Dingaan's forces in a great battle at Blood River. After their victory they established the Republic of Natal around the little town of Pietermaritzburg, with Andries Pretorius as its first President. Their freedom was brief. The British refused to recognise the republic, and after a short struggle in 1845 made it a Province of Cape Colony. There remained the Voortrekkers on the plateau farther west, now reinforced by many refugees from Natal. Here too the British intervened. In 1848 Sir Harry Smith, a brave and energetic soldier who had served under Wellington, annexed the country between the Orange and the Vaal Rivers, defeated Pretorius at Boomplaats, and left only scattered Boer settlements across the Vaal outside the colony.

Soon afterwards there was trouble with the tribes beyond the Orange River, and in particular with the Basuto. In Natal the problem had been met by creating native reserves and re-establishing the old tribal hierarchies under the indirect supervision of the Government. But the Government in London did not care to extend its responsibilities, and in 1852 it recognised the independ-ence of the Transvaal settlers. Two years later, in accordance with the Convention of Bloemfontein, the British withdrew from beyond the Orange River and the Orange Free State was formed. Political dissolution went farther: both Queen Adelaide Province and Natal were made into separate colonies administered directly by the Colonial Office. By 1857 there were five separate republics and three colonies within the territory of the present Union of South Africa. The old colony of the Cape meanwhile prospered, as the production of wool increased by leaps and bounds, and in 1853 an Order in Council established representative institutions in the colony, with a Parliament in Cape Town, though without the grant of full responsible government. Here we may leave South African history for a spell of uneasy peace.

Australia has a long history in the realms of human imagination. The extent of the continent was not accurately known until the middle of the eighteenth century, when Captain James Cook made three voyages between 1768 and 1779, in which he circumnavigated New Zealand, sailed inside the Australian Barrier Reef, sighted the great Antarctic icefields, discovered the Friendly Islands, the New Hebrides, New Caledonia, and Hawaii, and charted the eastern coastline of Australia. Cook was a surveyor trained in the Royal Navy. His reports were official, accurate, and detailed. His news reached Britain at a timely moment. English convicts had long been transported to America, but since the War of Independence the Government had nowhere to send them and many were now dying of disease in the hulks and gaols of London. Why not send the prisoners to the new continent? The younger Pitt's administration shrank from colonial ventures after the disasters in North America, but delay was deemed impossible, and in January 1788 717 convicts were anchored in Botany Bay. A hundred and ninety-eight were women. The Bay had been so named by Sir Joseph Banks, a distinguished amateur of science, who accompanied Cook on one of his voyages. There was not much botany about it now. The convicts were soon moved a few miles north to Port Jackson, within the magnificent expanse of Sydney Harbour. Famine crouched above the settlement, and for long the colony could not supply all its own food. Without training, capital, or the desire to work, the forgers and thieves, poachers and Irish rebels, criminals and political exiles, had neither the will nor the ability to fit themselves to the new land. "The convict barracks of New South Wales", wrote an Australian Governor, "remind me of the monasteries of Spain. They contain a population of consumers who produce nothing." The region had been named by Captain Cook after South Wales. He thought he had detected a resemblance in coastline. But hard-working Wales and its Antipodean namesake had very little else in common at the time.

There were of course a few free settlers from the first, but the full migratory wave did not reach Australia till the 1820s. Even the future Commonwealth's name was not yet determined. "New Holland" and other titles were bestowed upon it in official documents. Driven by the post-war distress in Great Britain and attracted by the discovery of rich pasture in the hinterland of New South Wales, English-speaking emigrants began to trickle into the empty subcontinent and rapidly transformed the character and life of the early communities. The population changed from about fifteen thousand convicts and twenty-one thousand free settlers in 1828 to twenty-seven thousand convicts and over a hundred thousand free settlers in 1841. Free men soon demanded, and got, free government. Transportation to New South Wales was finally abolished in 1840, and two years later a Legislative Council was set up, most of whose members were elected by popular vote.

Wool founded the prosperity of the country, and in time ousted Spanish and German supplies from the world's principal markets. In 1797 a retired Army officer, John MacArthur, had obtained a few merino sheep from the Cape of Good Hope, and his breeding experiments in due course established the famous Australian flocks and changed the whole economy of the continent. The turning point had been the discovery of the Bathurst Plains, beyond the Blue Mountains. Here and to the south of Sydney, and on the Darling Downs to the north, were great sheep-runs, mile after mile of lonely grazing land, open, grassy downs, inhabited only by a few shepherds and thousands upon thousands of silent, soft-footed sheep moving ever farther into the interior. The flocks multiplied swiftly: by 1850 there were more than sixteen million sheep in Australia. This was over sixteen times more sheep than there were men and women. The wool trade for the year was worth nearly two million pounds in sterling.

The British Government, however, distrusted sheep-farming. Not only did it claim that all land under British rule was Crown property, but the Colonial Office was much influenced by Gibbon Wakefield's advocacy of systematic and concentrated colonisation.[1] Wakefield maintained that settlement, wherever it took place, should be controlled and planned, and that to allow individuals to spread haphazard into the interior would hinder administration and reduce the value of the land already settled. His theories had much to commend them, but were quite unsuited to Australia. A series of Land Acts, designed to make land more difficult to obtain by enforcing a minimum price, soon broke down. "Squatters", who needed thousands of acres for their sheep-runs and neither could nor would pay a pound, or even five shillings, for their grazing, struck out into the emptiness and took what they wanted, arguing with force that the land belonged to the people of the colony and that they should be given every facility to occupy it. The Colonial Office surrendered to the pressure of events. The squatters were there to stay, and soon became the most important section of the community. The British Government first compromised by instituting licences which gave them some legal standing, and in 1847 authorised the granting of pastoral leases for a term of years, at the end of which the squatter was to have the first right to purchase the land at its unimproved value.

Long before 1850 the settlement of other parts of Australia had begun. The first to be made from the mother-colony of Port Jackson was in the island of

1 Edward Gibbon Wakefield (1796–1862), an expert in colonisation reform and one of the authors of the Durham Report on Canada. He believed land should be sold at a market price and the profits used to help emigration. In 1853, he emigrated to Wellington, sixteen years after he had been instrumental in forming the New Zealand Association which organised the settlement of that country.

Tasmania, or Van Diemen's Land as it was then called; at Hobart in 1804; and two years later at Launceston. Like New South Wales, Tasmania at first encountered many difficulties. The penal settlements at Macquarie Harbour and Port Arthur had evil reputations; rule was by terror and the labour-gang, and many convicts escaped and lived by bush-ranging, attacking lonely houses at night, and raiding stock-farms when the men were away. Unlike the rest of Australia, where the aboriginal inhabitants, few in number, scattered over vast areas, and, very primitive, scarcely resisted the white settlers, Tasmania had aborigines who were fairly numerous and comparatively advanced. Their defeat was inevitable; their end was tragic. The Black Drive of 1830 was a failure. The entire forces of the colony, organised at a cost of £30,000, attempted in vain to pen the natives in a reserve. But the Tasmanian tribes were extinct by the beginning of the twentieth century.

Tasmania developed in much the same way as New South Wales, and had become a separate colony in 1824. Prosperity came from wool and whaling, and brought a solid upsurge in population. In 1820 there were 6,500 settlers, mostly convicts; twenty years later the population numbered 68,000 and was mostly free. An elected Legislative Council was granted in 1850, and the abolition of transportation three years later placed Tasmania on an equal footing with New South Wales, and enabled her to participate in the general grant of responsible government. From Tasmania a settlement was made at Port Phillip in 1835. At first it was administered by New South Wales, but the settlers quickly demanded independence, and in 1848 they withdrew all other candidates for the Legislative Council and elected Earl Grey, Secretary of State for the Colonies, as "Member for Melbourne". Grey was the son of the Earl Grey of the Reform Bill. The move succeeded: within a few months the Colonial Office agreed to the separation, and in 1851 the new colony of Victoria, complete with representative institutions, was established, with its capital at Melbourne. The young Queen gave her name to this new offshoot of the English-speaking peoples. Its capital commemorates the Whig Prime Minister whom she had found to be the most agreeable of her advisers, and who was now no more.

The third offspring of New South Wales was Queensland. It grew up round the town of Brisbane, but developed more slowly and did not become a separate colony until 1859. By then two other settlements had arisen on the Australian coasts, both independently of New South Wales and the other colonies. In 1834 a body known as "the Colonisation Commissioners for South Australia" had been set up in London, and two years later the first settlers landed near Adelaide. The city was named after William IV's Queen. South Australia was never a convict settlement. It was organised by a group of men under the influence of Gibbon Wakefield, whose elaborate theories were now put into practice. On the whole they succeeded, though a system of dual control by which responsibility was divided between the Government and the Colonisation, or Land Commissioners gave so much trouble that the Commissioners were abolished in 1842. Within seven years the colony numbered

52,000 inhabitants, and had been substantially enriched by the discovery of copper deposits. Along with the eastern colonies, it was presently granted representative institutions.

The other colony, Western Australia, had a very different history. Founded in 1829, it nearly died at birth. With much less fertile soil than the eastern colonies and separated from them by vast and uninhabitable desert, it suffered greatly from lack of labour. Convicts, which the other colonies deemed an obstacle to progress, seemed the only solution, and the British Government, once again encumbered with prisoners, eagerly accepted an invitation to send some out to Perth. In 1849 a penal settlement was established, with much money to finance it. Thus resuscitated, the population trebled within the next ten years but Western Australia did not obtain representative institutions until 1870, after the convict settlement had been abolished, nor full self-government till 1890.

In 1848 gold had been discovered in California, and among the prospectors who crossed the Pacific to try their luck was a certain Edward Hargraves. A few months of digging brought him small success, but he noticed that the gold-beating rocks of California resembled those near Bathurst, in New South Wales. He returned to Australia early in 1851 to test his theory. The first pans of earth proved him right. News of the discovery leaked out, and within a few weeks the Australian Gold Rush had begun. The gold fever swept the eastern colonies. The whole of Australia seemed to be on the move marching out to Bathurst, Ballarat, or Bendigo, with picks and shovels on their shoulders, pots and basins round their waists, an excited, feverish crowd, pouring into mining towns that had sprung up overnight, fully equipped with gambling saloons, bars, and brothels. The Victorian goldfields soon had a population of nearly 100,000. Not all were "diggers", as the miners came to be called, and the hotel-keepers, storekeepers, prostitutes, and other toilers usually fared best. A penniless lollipop-seller made £6,000 a year by opening a public-house on the road to Ballarat. When the miners flocked back to Melbourne or Sydney their money vanished in crazy extravagance and ostentation. Horses were shod with golden shoes, men lit their pipes with banknotes, so the stories ran, and a bridal party attended a wedding in bright pink velvet. When fortunes could be made and lost overnight there seemed no point in steady employment. Squatters lost their shepherds, business houses their clerks, ships their crews. Early in 1852 there were only two policemen left in Melbourne; more than fifty had gone off to the goldfields. Wages doubled and trebled; prices rose fantastically, and the values of land changed with bewildering rapidity. The other colonies, including New Zealand, lost great numbers of men to the goldfields. In a single year 95,000 immigrants entered Victoria; in five months 4,000 men out of a total population, including women and children, of 50,000 left Tasmania for Victoria.

Keeping the peace, setting disputed claims, providing transport, housing, and enough food to stop famine was a grievous burden for the new administration at Melbourne, most of whose staff had also deserted to the goldfields.

For some time there were no more than forty-four soldiers in the whole of Victoria, and in 1853 fifty policemen had to be sent out from London. The diggers probably enjoyed the turbulence they created in the mining towns, but they had a serious grievance against the Government. As with the squatters, the Crown claimed ownership of the land, and demanded a licence fee. The fee was fiercely resented and very difficult to collect, and after many threats the diggers exploded into violence.

On October 6, 1854, a digger was killed in a fight near the Eureka Hotel in Ballarat. The hotel-keeper, Bentley, his wife, and a man named Farrell were accused, but acquitted in spite of the evidence. Ten days later the diggers burned down the hotel, and four of their leaders were arrested. The diggers were now in dangerous mood. They formed the Ballarat Reform League, and issued a political programme which demanded the abolition of licence fees and contained four of the six points of the English Chartists. On November 30 a search for unlicensed miners caused a riot. Led by one Peter Lalor, the diggers began to drill and build a stockade. The local military commander, Captain Thomas, acted with speed and wisdom. He determined to attack before the movement spread. With three hundred men, mainly soldiers, he carried the stockade with a bayonet charge, killing thirty rebels and capturing over a hundred and twenty.

Thus ended what might have become a serious rebellion. Licence fees were soon afterwards abolished and replaced by an export duty on gold. The miners were given the franchise and peace was restored. In the next few years independent diggers were replaced by mining companies, which alone had the resources to carry on underground work. Much the same happened in New South Wales, the only other colony where gold was discovered at this time. Between 1851 and 1861 £124,000,000 worth of it was raised. A more permanent enrichment was the increase in Australian population, which now rose to over a million.

The political repercussions were far-reaching. The increase of population, trade, and revenue made it imperative to reform the makeshift constitutions of 1850, and after long discussion in the colonies a number of schemes were laid before the Colonial Office and approved by the home Government. Between 1855 and 1859 two-chamber Parliaments, elected by popular vote and with Ministers responsible to the Lower House, were introduced in all the Antipodean states except Western Australia, where, as already related, self-government came later.

Great changes were still to unroll, and Australia, as we now know it, was born in 1901 by the association of the colonies in a Commonwealth, with a new capital at Canberra. Federation came late and slowly to the southern continent, for the lively, various, widely separated settlements cherished their own self-rule. Even today most of the Australian population dwells in the settlements founded in the nineteenth century.

Twelve hundred miles to the east of Australia lie the islands of New Zealand. Here, long before they were discovered by Europeans, a Polynesian warrior race, the Maoris, had sailed across the Pacific from the north-east and established a civilisation notable for the brilliance of its art and the strength of its military system. When Captain Cook visited them towards the end of the eighteenth century he judged that they numbered about a hundred thousand. This was probably an overestimate, but here nevertheless was a first formidable obstacle to European colonisation, a cultured people long in possession of the land, independent in spirit and skilled in warfare. Soon after Cook's discovery a small English community gained a footing in the Bay of Islands in the far north, but they were mostly whalers and sealers, shipwrecked mariners, and a few escaped convicts from Australia, enduring a lonely, precarious, and somewhat disreputable existence. They were tolerated by the Maori chiefs, whom they supplied with firearms. They constituted no great threat to Maori life or lands. Resistance to English colonisation was fortified by the arrival of Christian missionaries. In 1814 the Reverend Samuel Marsden set up a mission station in this same Bay of Islands. He was joined by other clerics, and Christianity quickly gained a large ascendancy over the Maoris, many of whom became proselytisers. The missionaries struggled to defeat the power of the traders, and for many years they opposed, in the interests of the Maoris, all schemes for admitting English immigrants. For a time they succeeded, and the Australian colonies had been established for half a century before the first official English settlement was founded. A move to colonise the islands had nevertheless long been afoot in London, impelled by a group of men around Gibbon Wakefield, who had already so markedly influenced the future of Canada and Australia. Wakefield and his friends had founded a New Zealand Association, of which Lord Durham was a member. But the Government was hostile. The missionaries denounced the project as disastrous to the natives, and the Colonial Office refused to sanction its plans.

Wakefield, however, was resolute, and in 1838 his Association formed a private joint-stock company for the colonisation of New Zealand, and a year later dispatched an expedition under his younger brother. Over a thousand settlers went with them, and they founded the site of Wellington in the North Island. News that France was contemplating the annexation of New Zealand compelled the British Government to act. Instead of sanctioning Wakefield's expedition they sent out a man-of-war, under the command of Captain Hobson, to treat with the Maoris for the recognition of British sovereignty. In February 1840 Hobson concluded the Treaty of Waitangi with the Maori chiefs. By this the Maoris ceded to Great Britain all the rights and powers of sovereignty in return for confirmation in "the full and exclusive possession of their lands and estates".

Then, but not till then, the company received official recognition. Two powers were thus established, the Governor at Auckland at the top of the North Island, which Hobson had chosen as the capital, and the company at Wellington. They championed different interests and opposing policies. The company wanted land, as much and as soon as possible. The treaty and the Colonial Office said it belonged to the Maoris. The two authorities struggled and bickered throughout the forties. The treaty was bitterly denounced by the company's settlers, and in 1843 Joseph Somes, Governor of the company, wrote to the Colonial Secretary: "We have always had very serious doubts whether the Treaty of Waitangi, made with naked savages by a consul invested with no plenipotentiary powers, without ratification by the Crown, could be treated by lawyers as anything but a praiseworthy device for amusing and pacifying savages for the moment." The "naked savages", however, were not to be caught. The treaty with Hobson clearly distinguished between the shadow of sovereignty, which they surrendered, and the substance of property, which they retained. The land was their life-blood. "By woman and land are men lost" ran the Maori proverb, and the older chiefs realised that if they lost their land their tribal life would be extinguished. The ingenuity of their laws exasperated settlers who had innocently purchased land for hard cash and found themselves denied possession because the tribe's inalienable rights over the soil were unaffected by private bargains. Nevertheless by 1859 the settlers had occupied seven million acres in the North Island and over thirty-two million acres in the South, where the Maoris were fewer.

The result was the Maori wars, a series of intermittent local conflicts lasting from 1843 to 1872. The scene of the fighting moved from place to place. By the middle of the sixties twenty thousand troops were engaged. The fanatical cult of the Hauhaus and the skill of Te Kooti, a guerrilla leader of genius, taxed all the resources of the colony. The Maoris fought magnificently, and the admiration of the Regular officers for their opponents sharpened their dislike of the settlers. But by 1869 the force of the movement was spent and the risings were defeated. Thereafter the enlightened policy of Sir Donald MacLean, the Minister for Native Affairs, produced a great improvement. The settlers gained some security of tenure. The Maoris realised that the British had come to stay. A series of Native Land Acts, passed in the sixties, protected them against extermination; in 1867 they secured direct representation in the New Zealand legislature, and after declining to 37,000 souls in 1871 by the 1951 census they numbered nearly 100,000.

Despite these years of strife the colony continued to expand. Wakefield, anxious to overcome the opposition of the missionaries, ingeniously persuaded both the Free Church of Scotland and the Church of England to co-operate in establishing two new settlements. These, at Otago and Canterbury, were remarkable applications of his theories. Both were in the South Island, and from 1860 until 1906 it was the South Island, prosperous and comparatively immune from the Maori wars, which contained most of the population. By 1868 the British numbered only about a quarter of a million; twelve years later there were nearly twice as many.

Peace brought prosperity. Great flocks of sheep were reared on the famous Canterbury Plains of the South Island, and a native Corriedale cross-breed was evolved. In the eighteen-sixties gold was found in Otago and Canterbury and there was a temporary boom. The Australian gold discoveries and the swift rise in prices in Melbourne and Sydney gave agriculture a flying start.

Despite a depression in the eighties, the prosperity of New Zealand has continued to grow ever since. The invention of the refrigerator enabled the colony to compete with European and English producers thirteen thousand miles away. The co-operative movement, especially in dairy farming, helped small farmers with little capital to build up an industry of remarkable magnitude, and the Dominion of New Zealand soon possessed the highest external trade in proportion to its numbers of any nation in the world.

New Zealand's political development was no less rapid. Founded in the days of the Durham Report and the first experiments with colonial self-government in Canada, she obtained by the Constitution Act of 1852 a broad measure of independence. Her problems did not, as in the older colonies, centre on the demand for responsible government, but on relations between the central and provincial administrations. Inland travel was so difficult that until late in the nineteenth century the colony remained a number of small, scattered settlements, all differing in the circumstances of their foundation and the character of their interests. This was recognised in the Constitution Act, which set up a number of provincial councils on a democratic basis, each to a considerable extent independent of the General Assembly.

Conflict between the provincial assemblies and the central administration troubled New Zealand politics for twenty years. Some provinces were wealthy, others less so. Otago and Canterbury, stimulated by the discovery of gold, became rich and prosperous, while the settlers in the North Island, harassed by the Maori wars, grew more and more impoverished. At one time Otago and Canterbury wanted to secede. Reform came in 1875, when the constitution was modified, the provinces were abolished, local administration was placed in the hands of county councils, and the powers of the central Government were greatly increased. Thus, on a smaller scale, New Zealand faced and mastered all the problems of federal government thirty years before Australia did. Indeed her political vitality is no less astonishing than her economic vigour. The tradition and prejudices of the past weighed less heavily than in the older countries. Many of the reforms introduced into Great Britain by the Liberal Government of 1906, and then regarded as extreme innovations, had already been accepted by New Zealand. Industrial arbitration, old-age pensions, factory legislation, State insurance and medical service, housing Acts, all achieved between 1890 and the outbreak of the First World War, and State support for co-operative production, testified to the survival and fertility, even in the remote and unfamiliar islands of the Pacific, of the British political genius.

CHAPTER FORTY-SEVEN

THE RISE OF GERMANY

Bismarck – Palmerston restrained – Victoria supports Prussia – war in Europe – the siege of Paris – Napoleon flees to Britain – the Concert of Europe – Gladstone and Disraeli as Prime Ministers – laissez-faire policy – Gladstone and Ireland – the Electoral Reform Act – the Education Act – opening of the universities and Civil Service – Cardwell's Army reforms – the Alabama dispute – Suez Canal shares – another Eastern Question – who controls the Balkans – the Congress of Berlin – Zulu Wars – massacre at Kabul – Gladstone's Midlothian campaign – Joseph Chamberlain and Municipal Socialism – the birth of the National Liberal federation – the death of Disraeli

WHILE THE American Republic was entering upon her ordeal[1] and the restless Napoleon III was consolidating his rule in France an event of great moment took place beyond the Rhine. In 1861 William I of Prussia ascended the throne of Frederick the Great, and marked the first years of his reign with three public appointments whose impact on European history and modern events is incalculable. Count von Moltke became Chief of the General Staff, Count von Roon Minister of War, and – most important of all – Count Otto von Bismarck was recalled from the Embassy in Paris to become Minister-President of Prussia. First as Chancellor of the North German Federation, and finally of the German Empire, this singular genius presided with a cold passion over the unification and Prussianisation of Germany, the elimination of Prussia's nearest European rivals, and the elevation of William to the German Emperor's throne in 1871. He was to serve, or dominate, William I and his two successors uninterruptedly until his clashes with the young Emperor William II finally and acrimoniously ended his tenure in 1890.

Bismarck was well equipped physically, temperamentally, and by training for the gigantic rôle he played. He had served in the Prussian Civil Service and the Pomeranian Provincial Parliament before being appointed Prussian representative at the Federal Diet at Frankfort. He had travelled widely, and

---

1 The American Civil War.

had also gained practical experience by managing the spacious family estates in Pomerania. His last two appointments before becoming Minister-President were at the Prussian Embassies at Petersburg and Paris. He retained from his early career rooted convictions on both ends and means, which he expressed freely and sometimes with brutal frankness. Absolute monarchy was his ideal and aim. Liberalism and Parliamentarianism were anathema. Prussia must be purged of weak and liberal elements so that she could fulfil her destiny of leading and controlling the German-speaking peoples. A decisive struggle with Austria was inevitable.

Before a background of intense, brilliant, and unscrupulous diplomatic activity the three hammer-blows that forged Germany were deliberately prepared and struck. These were the war with Denmark in 1864, by which the Duchies of Schleswig and Holstein were attached to Prussia, the Seven Weeks War of 1866, in which Austria was crushed and her associates in Germany overrun, and as culmination the war against France in 1870.

To ensure freedom of action in other directions Bismarck had always been convinced that Prussia's eastern frontiers must be secure. "Prussia must never let Russian friendship grow cold. Her alliance is the cheapest among all Continental alliances," he had said in Frankfort. Prussia had stood aside from the Crimean War, and before long she had a further opportunity of demonstrating her calculated friendship for the Czar. In 1863 the Poles rose against Russia in a spasm of the hopeless gallantry that has so often characterised the history of that unhappy people. Bismarck gave the Russians his support and encouragement, and even allowed Russian troops to pursue the rebels over the Prussian frontiers. Polish independence, which he had always disliked and feared, was once more extinguished, and Russia was given a proof of Prussian goodwill and a hint of further favours to come.

In the same year Bismarck seized his chance to expand Prussia north-westwards and gain control of the port of Kiel and the neck of the Danish peninsula. With the death of the King of Denmark, without a direct heir, an old dispute about the succession to the Duchies of Schleswig and Holstein came to a head. For centuries the Danish kings had ruled these Duchies as fiefs of the Holy Roman Empire. The Empire had vanished, but the Duchies remained an ill-defined part of the loose German Confederation created at the Congress of Vienna. Schleswig was half Danish in population and the Danes wished to incorporate it in their kingdom. Holstein was wholly German. The conflict of national feeling was inflamed by dynastic issues. Was the Danish King of the new line entitled to succeed to the Duchies? There was a rival claimant in the field. Mounting German patriotism was determined to prevent the parting of the Duchies from the German fatherland.

Bismarck knew well how to cast his line in these troubled waters. The German Confederation had already clashed with the Danes on the issue, and when the new Danish King assumed sovereignty over the Duchies Hanoverians and Saxons united in a Federal Army and occupied Holstein. At this point Bismarck intervened, dragging with him Austria. Austria was still a member of the German Confederation, and with her remaining Italian possessions in mind was hostile to the triumph of nationalism in outlying provinces. In January 1864 an Austro-Prussian ultimatum was dispatched to Copenhagen, and by July Denmark was defeated and overrun and Schleswig was occupied. That superb weapon, the new Prussian Army, had hardly been extended, and its future victims were scarcely made aware of its power.

Palmerston would have liked to intervene, for Britain had guaranteed the integrity of Denmark by the Treaty of Berlin in 1852, which he himself had helped to negotiate. Before the blow fell he had said in the House of Commons: "We are convinced – I am convinced at least – that if any violent attempt were made to overthrow [Danish] rights and interfere with that independence those who made the attempt would find in the result that it would not be Denmark alone with which they would have to contend." But the Cabinet was hesitant and divided and was not prepared to back these imprecise assurances. Queen Victoria held fast to the views of the late Prince Consort and favoured the rise of Prussia. Moreover, Palmerston himself, who had started his Ministerial career during the wars against Napoleon I, was suspicious of France. If a general war were unleashed he feared that Napoleon III might seize the Rhineland and dangerously augment his power in Europe. In fact France turned down tentative British proposals for joint action, conscious that Britain could only put an army of 20,000 on the Continent and that her contribution to a war with Prussia and Austria might well be limited to the easy but indecisive task of naval control of the Baltic. Napoleon III was hoping instead to exact compensations from Prussia, without recourse to war. He was unsuccessful in his double diplomacy. Russia, for her part, was in debt to Bismarck, and with an eye to the future refused to be involved. In these circumstances Palmerston felt he could do no more than press for conferences and mediation. It is not the only time in British history when strength has been lacking to reinforce bold words. Palmerston's words had given the Danes a false sense of security and tempted them to obduracy in an argument where legality did not entirely lie on their side, though some justice did. An ominous precedent was thus set for what the Germans politely called *Realpolitik*, while Britain and France looked on. *Realpolitik* meant that standards of morality in international affairs could be ignored whenever material advantage might be gained. In this instance Denmark, the small victim, was not extinguished, nor were the peace terms unduly onerous. Then and later Bismarck knew the value of a certain hard magnanimity to the vanquished.

The outcome of the war with Denmark was soon to furnish the pretext and occasion for the next and far more important step of eliminating Austria from the German Confederation and vesting its leadership in Prussia. Schleswig and Holstein had become a condominium of Prussia and Austria. Bismarck played upon the awkwardness of this arrangement, maintaining a screen of protests against the indignant but long-suffering Austrians. At the same time he sought support in other quarters. In 1865 he visited Napoleon III at Biarritz. No accurate record of what was said was kept, but Bismarck presumably reiterated the theme he had for some time been impressing on the French Embassy in Prussia: if Prussia was given a free hand against Austria, France might expect Prussian sympathy in extending herself "wherever the French language was spoken". Belgium was clearly meant. Moreover, France could mediate in the final stages, and might even expect a territorial reward in South Germany. Napoleon promised nothing, but was not unreceptive, and Bismarck went home content. He had not committed himself to paper.

Of equal importance was the friendship of Italy, for she too was moving towards unity. Cavour[1] and Garibaldi had brought almost the whole of the peninsula under the rule of the house of Savoy. But Venice, Trieste, and the Southern Tyrol remained in Austrian hands. For these territories the Italians yearned. In April 1866 King Victor Emmanuel signed a secret treaty with Prussia agreeing to attack Austria if war broke out within three months.

The stage was set. France was neutralised. Russia was benevolent. Italy was an ally. Britain counted little in the matter, but in any case her sympathies lay with the Italian Liberation movement, and her relations with Austria had not been good for some years. The provocation to war of Austria and her associates in the German Confederation followed with precision.

Within ten days of the outbreak of war Hanover, Hesse, and Saxony were occupied. The King of Hanover, grandson of George III, fled to England and his country was incorporated in Prussia. Thus disappeared the ancient Electorate which had given Britain her Protestant dynasty in 1714. The Hanoverian State funds were later judiciously used among the ruling circles of other German states to mitigate their resentment against Prussia. The main Prussian armies then marched south into Bohemia, while Bismarck's agents stirred up the Hungarians in the Austrian rear. After a week of manoeuvring, in which the Prussian staff made a remarkable use of railways as an aid to the strategic concentration of their forces, the decisive battle was joined at Sadowa. Over 200,000 men were engaged on either side. The Prussians used a new breech-loading rifle, and its rapidity of fire was conclusive. The Austrians sought to overcome their disadvantage by coming to close quarters, but their belief in their superiority in the use of the bayonet, a vanity common to many nations, proved unfounded. The years of endeavour of Moltke and his Generals bore fruit. The Austrian army was shattered.

Three weeks later the Prussians were within reach of Vienna. At Bismarck's vehement insistence the capital was spared the humiliation of occupation and the peace terms were once again lenient. Bismarck's mind was already turned to his next move, and he set store by future Austrian friendship. "So to limit a victory," he said, "is not only a generous but a most wise policy. But for the victor to benefit from it the recipient must be worthy." Austria's only territorial loss was Venetia, granted to Italy, but she was finally excluded from Germany and her future ambitions had inevitably to lie south-eastwards

---

1   Count Camillo Benso di Cavour (1810–61), after many disappointments, happily saw Victor Emanuel II proclaimed King and died the following year.

among the Slavs. So ended the Seven Weeks War. Prussia had gained five million inhabitants and 25,000 square miles of territory in Germany. The balance of Continental power had changed radically. A premonitory shudder went through France.

Napoleon III tried vainly to extract from Prussia some reward for his neutrality – a policy of asking for tips, as it was contemptuously called. But to a French demand for territories in South Germany Bismarck returned a blank refusal, and published both his and Napoleon's Notes, thus raising suspicions of France and consolidating his own position in non-Prussian Germany. Belatedly France came to realise her full danger. In the logic of Bismarck's methodical planning a Franco-Prussian war lay on the close horizon. In desperate haste Marshal Niel, Minister of War, set in train the reform of the French Army, and Napoleon cast about for allies in the forthcoming struggle. All was vain. Distraught by Napoleon's increasing ill-health and diminished powers of decision and driven by the petulant arrogance of her Parliament and Press, France ran headlong on her fate.

The next four years were marked by growing tension, the steady increase of armaments on both sides, and incidents that lipped the brink of war. The position was perfectly plain to British statesmen and they did their best to mediate. Without a firm commitment to France or Prussia such attempts were necessarily doomed. Neither obvious national interest nor a liking for either side was strong enough to sway Britain. Napoleon's unstable ambitions were suspect in London, and Bismarck, in the words of the British Ambassador in Berlin, seemed to have opted for a *politique de brigandage*.

Once again the German Chancellor succeeded in depriving his adversary of allies. In spite of French blandishments Austria stood aloof. Italy had no reason to turn against her Prussian ally of 1866. French troops still held Rome for the Pope, and a French defeat would compel them to withdraw. Russia, at Bismarck's prompting, seized her advantage to break the treaty bonds placed on her movements in and out of the Black Sea. Bismarck was not greatly concerned with Britain. As he had put it some time before, "What is England to me? The importance of a state is measured by the number of soldiers it can put in the field." Nevertheless in 1870 he sent to *The Times* newspaper the text of a draft treaty apparently proposed by the French four years earlier in which they sought to acquire Belgium in return for supporting Prussia. To Britain, a guarantor of Belgian inviolability, this made intervention on the French side even less attractive.

In that summer Bismarck delivered his stroke. A revolution in Spain had driven out the Bourbon dynasty and the Spanish throne had been vacant for nearly two years. The interim Spanish Government cast about for a suitable royal candidate from the great families of Europe, and the choice finally fell on Prince Leopold of Hohenzollern-Sigmaringen, a member of the elder branch of King William of Prussia's family. The Prince declined the offer. Nevertheless, at Bismarck's suggestion the Spaniards renewed their invitation, and this time it was accepted. The French reaction was violent. To the accompaniment of inflammatory speeches in Parliament the French Ambassador in Prussia was instructed to demand a revocation of Prince Leopold's acceptance, which the French Foreign Minister described as "the disturbance to French detriment of the existing equilibrium of the forces of Europe and the endangering of the interests and honour of France". Nowadays he would no doubt have spoken of encirclement. King William received these remonstrances patiently enough. He privately advised Prince Leopold to withdraw, and within forty-eight hours the Prince complied. The French Press exulted. With fatal importunity the French Ambassador was instructed to demand guarantees that the candidature would never again be renewed. This was too much even for King William. He put off the Ambassador courteously but firmly, and as soon as he was officially informed of Prince Leopold's renunciation he sent the Ambassador a message to say that he regarded the matter as closed.

To Bismarck his sovereign's diplomacy was gall. He believed the fruits of his work to be slipping away and his country to be set on a course of humiliation. Dining in dejection with Moltke and Roon in Berlin, he received from the King at Ems a telegram describing the latest events. The King's telegram gave Bismarck discretion to publish the story if he thought it desirable. Bismarck seized the opportunity, and without literal falsehood so abbreviated the account as to give the impression that the French demands had been rejected in the curtest manner and that their Ambassador had been rebuffed. Well aware that the communiqué – now in Bismarck's words "a red rag to the Gallic bull" – made conflict inevitable, the dinner party broke up content. Roon exclaimed exultantly, "Our God of old lives still, and will not let us perish in disgrace." The French declaration of war followed within a week. The picturesque quality of the incident is somewhat marred by subsequent knowledge that the French Cabinet had decided on war in any case, if King William's attitude was anything less than capitulation. Their deficient military intelligence had led some French leaders to the belief that their military preparations surpassed Prussia's. The next forty days were to give a terrible answer to the contrary.

Prussia placed half a million men in the field, with the same number in reserve. Bavaria, which for two hundred years had supported France upon the European scene, now threw 150,000 men against her. The course of the struggle was brief and fierce. The French fought with all their native dash and gallantry and their infantry weapons were fully up to their enemy's standard. But they were outdated and outclassed in the new dialectic of war, in transport, in the supply system, above all in staff work and training.

From the start things went ill for France. The mobilisation scheme, revised by the Emperor himself, was slow and fearfully confused. Officers searched for non-existent units; reservists in Alsace were sent to camps in the Pyrenees to be equipped before they joined formations within a few miles of their point of departure, many were only able, weeks later, to reach their regiments when these were already dispersed or in retreat. The Germans advanced in three main armies, two, totalling 350,000 men, moving by converging routes on the French fortress of Metz, and the Crown Prince of Prussia, at the head of a force of 220,000, making for Strasbourg. Far in front of the armies drove a cloud of cavalry, blinding and confusing the French and providing their own staffs with accurate information. The greater number of the battles in the open field were joined almost inadvertently by the impetuous advance of the Prussian vanguard, which the excellent organisation of their main forces enabled them to exploit rapidly. On August 4 the Crown Prince defeated part of the French Army of Alsace under Marshal MacMahon at Wissembourg, and two days later, after a major engagement at Wörth, drove the main French force south towards Châlons. Simultaneously the Army of the Rhine, commanded by the Emperor, was compelled to fall back on Metz. At this fortress Napoleon handed over his command to Marshal Bazaine and joined MacMahon at Châlons.

By mid-August the first and second German armies had contrived to get between Metz and Paris. Bazaine fought three bloody battles, which reached their climax at Gravelotte on August 18, where the German cavalry, at great cost, turned the scales. He then retreated into Metz, where he remained with 180,000 of the best of the French Army, a passive and inglorious spectator of the swift development of Moltke's plans. MacMahon and the Emperor advanced to the relief of Metz. The Crown Prince, who had bypassed Strasbourg, came up with the French near Sedan and forced them to retreat into that ancient fortified town on the Belgian frontier. The Germans, whose artillery had early showed a marked superiority, methodically surrounded the French positions and girded them with a circle of fire. Sedan was ill adapted for defence in modern warfare. As the Germans took possession of the heights above the town the position became untenable. After a desperate struggle Napoleon was forced to capitulate with 130,000 men. Only six weeks after the outbreak of war he surrendered his sword to the King of Prussia. Bismarck was present. Their last meeting had been as fellow diplomatists five years before at Biarritz.

Three weeks later the Germans had surrounded Paris, and within a few days Bazaine, through folly, weariness, or worse, as many Frenchmen believed, unnecessarily surrendered the great fortress of Metz. In 1876 a French court, unable to believe that he had acted on grounds other than of cowardice or treason, condemned him to death, though the sentence was not carried out.

The war seemed over. The French Emperor was a prisoner. The Empress had fled to England. Paris was firmly gripped by the besieging armies. A "Government of National Defence" held on in the capital, but in spite of the spirited efforts of one of its members, Gambetta, who escaped from the city in a balloon to stimulate resistance in the provinces, the last French armies on the Loire and the Swiss frontier were not able to achieve anything effective. In January 1871 the siege of Paris was ended.

Negotiations for an armistice opened in Versailles. This time Bismarck drove a relatively hard bargain and exacted a heavy return for every concession he made. The peace treaty with France was considered in its day to be severe. An indemnity of 5,000 million francs in gold was demanded, which was believed to be sufficient to engage the French economy for a long time. It was paid off in three years. The victorious army paraded through the streets of Paris. Alsace and Eastern Lorraine were ceded to Germany. Bitter indeed were the seeds sown thereby.

The final text of the treaty was not signed for several months. Meanwhile France suffered one of the terrible consequences of a major and disintegrating military defeat. In March revolutionaries seized control of Paris, where the French garrison had been greatly depleted by the terms of the armistice. At first the movement, styled the Commune, was inspired by patriotic motives and called on the people of Paris, humiliated by the sight of the triumphant Prussian Army, to rise and continue the struggle. A half-hearted attempt to quell the insurrection failed, and the Provisional French Government withdrew to Versailles leaving Paris under the red flag. Bismarck released French prisoners of war to assist in the subduing of the capital, which now became a full-scale military operation.

As the Government forces under Marshal MacMahon advanced the character of the Commune changed. Its supporters lost interest in repelling the Prussian invaders and became increasingly vicious and bloodthirsty social revolutionaries. Hostages, including the Archbishop of Paris and many priests, were shot, and great national buildings were burned to the ground. MacMahon's troops had to fight their way through barricade after barricade as they closed on the centre of Paris amid all the horrors of civil war. Merciless reprisals were taken on the Communards. By the time order was restored, after some six weeks' fighting, the dead were numbered in tens of thousands. Twenty-five thousand alone are estimated to have been executed as the struggle proceeded. The movement did not spread to any extent to other cities in France. It had been hailed by Communists abroad, and Karl Marx, living in England, saw in it a vindication of the theories of class-warfare which he had been preaching for half a lifetime. In lineal descent from the revolutions of 1789 and 1848, the Commune left scars on the French body politic that are visible to this day.

In the month of the armistice the final touches were put to the tremendous edifice of German unity. Since the autumn the German diplomatic staffs had been at work at Versailles, and on January 18, 1871, in the Hall of Mirrors William I of Prussia received from his fellow sovereigns the title of German Emperor. There had been some dispute over the exact wording of the title. Bismarck, always ready to concede the form for the substance, had decided for the version most likely to spare the susceptibilities of the smaller states. As William left the Hall he pointedly ignored the titanic architect of his fortunes. He had wished to be styled Emperor of Germany.

At Versailles Bismarck's life-work reached its climax. In the face of every obstacle at home and at the cost of the deliberate provocation of three wars

Prussia presided over Germany, and Germany had become one of the two most powerful nations on the Continent. The cost was great. France was embittered, determined on revenge and anxious to gain allies to help her. The Concert of Europe, founded at Vienna,[1] was now fatally cracked and flawed. In the years that followed various efforts were made to revive it, sometimes with temporary success. But gradually the Powers of Europe drifted into two separate camps, with Britain as an uneasy and uncommitted spectator. From this division, growing into an unbridgeable chasm, the eruptions of the twentieth century arose. Britain was slow to recognise the transformation of the scene, and Disraeli – though he exaggerated – was in advance of his time when he declared that the victories of Prussian arms meant a German Revolution, "a greater political event", he forecast, "than the French Revolution of the last century". The era of armed peace had opened. Britain in the age of Gladstone and Disraeli was absorbed in home affairs and in the problems of Ireland and Empire. But the days of an apparent disconnection between European and Colonial affairs were drawing rapidly to a close. Nevertheless so long as Bismarck led Germany, he was careful to do nothing to arouse British hostility. Meanwhile colonial quarrels increasingly darkened the Island's relations with France. Not until Kaiser William III had dismissed the great Chancellor and plunged into provocative policies did Britain fully awake to the Teutonic menace.

We now enter upon a long, connected, and progressive period in British history – the Prime Ministerships of Gladstone and Disraeli. These two great Parliamentarians in alternation ruled the land from 1868 to 1885. For nearly twenty years no one effectively disputed their leadership, and until Disraeli died in 1881 the political scene was dominated by a personal duel on a grand scale. Both men were at the height of their powers, and their skill and oratory in debate gripped and focused public attention on the proceedings of the House of Commons. Every thrust and parry was discussed throughout the country. The political differences between them were no wider than is usual in a two-party system, but what gave the conflict its edge and produced a deep-rooted antagonism was their utter dissimilarity in character and temperament. "Posterity will do justice to that unprincipled maniac, Gladstone," wrote Disraeli, in private, "– extraordinary mixture of envy, vindictiveness, hypocrisy, and superstition; and with one commanding characteristic – whether preaching, praying, speechifying, or scribbling – never a gentleman!" Gladstone's judgment on his rival was no less sharp. His doctrine was "false, but the man more false than his doctrine. ... He demoralised public opinion, bargained with diseased appetites, stimulated passions, prejudices, and selfish desires, that they might maintain his influence ... he weakened the Crown by approving its unconstitutional leanings, and the Constitution by offering any

---

1   The Concert of Europe grew from the Congress of Vienna in 1815, when Austria, Britain, Prussia and Russia formed the Quadruple Alliance. This Concert of four nations met regularly to discuss international politics and the ways to preserve peace – a sort of nineteenth-century mini-United Nations.

price for democratic popularity." Thus they faced each other across the dispatch-boxes of the House of Commons: Gladstone's commanding voice, his hawk-like eyes, his great power to move the emotions, against Disraeli's romantic air and polished, flexible eloquence.

When Gladstone became Prime Minister in 1868 he was deemed a careful and parsimonious administrator who had become a sound Liberal reformer. But this was only one side of his genius. What gradually made him the most controversial figure of the century was his gift of rousing moral indignation both in himself and in the electorate. In two great crusades on the Balkans and on Ireland his dominant theme was that conscience and the moral law must govern political decisions. Such a demand, strenuously voiced, was open to the charge of hypocrisy when, as so often happened, Gladstone's policy obviously coincided with the wellbeing of the Liberal Party. But the charge was false; the spirit of the preacher breathed in Gladstone's speeches. He was willing to break his party rather than deny his conscience. Soon after his conversion to Home Rule for Ireland he said to his lieutenant, Sir William Harcourt, "I am prepared to go forward without anybody." It was a spirit which was to mismanage men and split the Liberals, but it won him a place in the hearts of his followers of which Britain has never seen the like.

To face Gladstone Disraeli needed all the courage and quickness of wit with which he had been so generously endowed. Many Tories disliked and distrusted his reforming views, but he handled his colleagues with a rare skill. He has never been surpassed in the art of party management. In all his attitudes there was a degree of cynicism; in his make-up there was not a trace of moral fervour. Large sections of the working classes were held to Church, Crown, Empire, and aristocracy by practical interests which could be turned to party advantage. Or so he saw it. He never became wholly assimilated to English ways of life, and preserved to his death the detachment which had led him as a young man to make his own analysis of English society. It was this which probably enabled him to diagnose and assess the deeper political currents of his age. Long handicapped by his own party, he led it in the end to an electoral triumph, and achieved for a period the power he had always desired.

Nothing created more bitterness between them than Gladstone's conviction that Disraeli had captured the Queen for the Conservative Party and endangered the Constitution by an unscrupulous use of his personal charm. When Gladstone became Prime Minister Victoria was still in mourning and semi-retirement for Prince Albert, who had died in 1861. She deeply resented his attempts to bring the monarchy back into public life, attempts which culminated in a well-intentioned scheme to make her eldest son the Viceroy of Ireland. Gladstone, though always respectful, was incapable of infusing any kind of warmth into his relationship with her. She once said, according to report, that he addressed her like a public meeting. Disraeli did not make the same mistake. "The principles of the English Constitution," he declared, "do not contemplate the absence of personal influence on the part of the

Sovereign; and, if they did, the principles of human nature would prevent the fulfilment of such a theory." He wrote to the Queen constantly. He wooed her from the loneliness and apathy which engulfed her after Albert's death, and flattered her desire to share in the formulation of policy. At the height of the Eastern crisis in November 1877 he ended a report on the various views of the Cabinet with the following words: "The seventh policy is that of Your Majesty, and which will be introduced and enforced to his utmost by the Prime Minister." Victoria found this irresistible. She complained that Gladstone, when in office, never told her anything. Had he done so after 1880 it might have transmitted to the Conservative Opposition. From then on she was not friendly to her Liberal Governments; she disliked Gladstone and detested the growing Radicalism of his party. But in fact little harm was done; Gladstone was careful to keep the person of the Queen out of political discussion and none of their disagreements was known to the public. He grumbled that "the Queen is enough to kill any man", but he served her patiently, if not with understanding. In any case the development of popular Government based on popular elections was bound to diminish the personal power of the Crown. In spite of her occasional leanings, Victoria remained a constitutional monarch.

Gladstone always said that his Cabinet of 1868 to 1874 was "one of the best instruments of government that ever was constructed". Driven by his boundless energy, it put into effect a long-delayed avalanche of reforms. This was the Golden Age when Liberalism was still an aggressive, unshackling force, and the doctrine of individualism and the philosophy of *laissez-faire*[1] were seeking out and destroying the last relics of eighteenth-century government. The Civil Service, the Army, the universities, and the law were all attacked and the grip of the old landed interest began to crumble. The power of what James Mill had called the "sinister interests" shrivelled bit by bit as the public service was gradually but remorselessly thrown open to talent and industry. Freedom was the keynote, *laissez-faire* the method; no undue extension of Government authority was needed; and the middle class at last acquired a share in the political sphere equal to their economic power. Gladstone came in on the flood; a decisive electoral victory and a country ready for reform gave him his opportunity. The Liberal Party, for a rare moment in equilibrium, was united behind him. The scale and scope of his policy, directed at a series of obvious abuses, was such that Radicals, moderate Liberals, and even Whigs were brought together in agreement. He began with Ireland. "My mission", he had said when the summons from the Queen reached him at his country home in Hawarden, "is to pacify Ireland", and, in spite of bitter opposition and in defiance of his own early principles, which had been to defend property and the Anglican faith, he carried, in 1869, the disestablishment of the Protestant Church of Ireland. This was followed next

---

1   An eighteenth-century concept advocating free trade. By the nineteenth century it meant non-intervention by government – something that appealed to politicians as well as to the leaders of Britain's booming manufacturing classes.

year by a Land Act which attempted to protect tenants from unfair eviction. But Ireland was not so easily to be pacified.

In England the Government found no lack of work to do. After the Electoral Reform of 1867 Robert Lowe, now Chancellor of the Exchequer, had said that "We must educate our masters." Voters ought to know at least how to read and write, and have opened to them the paths to higher knowledge. Thus the extension of the franchise and the general Liberal belief in the value of education led to the launching of a national system of primary schools. This was achieved by W.E. Forster's Education Act of 1870, blurred though it was, like all education measures for some decades to come, by sectarian passion and controversy. At the same time patronage was finally destroyed in the home Civil Service. Entrance to the new administrative class was henceforth possible only through a competitive examination which placed great emphasis on intellectual attainment. Ability, not wealth or family connection, was now the means to advance. In the following year all religious tests at Oxford and Cambridge were abolished. The universities were thrown open to Roman Catholics, Jews, Dissenters, and young men of no belief. The ancient intricacies of the judicial system, so long a nightmare to litigants and a feeding ground for lawyers, were simplified and modernised by the fusion of courts of law and equity. The Judicature Act marked the culmination of a lengthy process of much-needed reform. For centuries litigants had often had to sue in two courts at once about the same matter. Now a single Supreme Court was set up, with appropriate divisions, and procedure and methods of appeal were made uniform. Offices that had survived from the reign of Edward I were swept away in a complete remodelling. All this was accomplished by a generally sound administration, and, what was perhaps closest to Gladstone's own heart, a policy of economy and low taxation.

The sufferings and disgraces of the Crimea had made it evident that the great Duke of Wellington's practices, in the hands of lesser men, had broken down. The Prussian victories in France administered a shock to military and civilian opinion. Reforms were long overdue at the War Office. They were carried out by Gladstone's Secretary of State, Edward Cardwell, one of the greatest of Army reformers. The Commander-in-Chief, the Duke of Cambridge, was opposed to any reform whatever, and the first step was taken when the Queen, with considerable reluctance, signed an Order in Council subordinating him to the Secretary of State. Flogging was abolished. An Enlistment Act introduced short service, which would create an efficient reserve. In 1871 Cardwell went further, and after a hard fight with Service opinion the purchase of commissions was prohibited. The infantry were rearmed with the Martini-Henry rifle, and the regimental system was completely reorganised on a county basis. The War Office was overhauled, though a General Staff was not yet established.

All this was achieved in the space of six brilliant, crowded years, and then, as so often happens in English history, the pendulum swung back. Great reform offends great interests. The Anglicans were hit by several measures;

the Nonconformists found little to please them in the Education Act. The Army and the Court resented Cardwell's onslaught. The working classes were offered little to attract them apart from a Ballot Act which allowed them to exercise the newly won franchise in secret and without intimidation. The settlement for fifteen million dollars of the *Alabama* dispute[1] with the United States, though sensible, was disagreeable to a people long fed on a Palmerstonian diet. They began to suspect that Gladstone was half-hearted in defending British interests. An unsuccessful Licensing Bill, prompted by the Temperance wing of the Liberal Party, estranged the drink interest and founded an alliance between the brewer and the Conservative Party. Gladstone was soon to complain that he had been borne down from power "in a torrent of gin and beer". Disraeli, now at the height of his oratorical powers, painted this portrait of the Ministry: "Her Majesty's new Ministers proceeded in their career like a body of men under the influence of some deleterious drug. Not satiated with the spoliation and anarchy of Ireland, they began to attack every institution and every interest, every class and calling in the country. ... As time advanced it was not difficult to perceive that extravagance was being substituted for energy by the Government. The unnatural stimulus was subsiding. Their paroxysms ended in prostration. Some took refuge in melancholy, and their eminent chief alternated between a menace and a sigh. As I sat opposite the Treasury Bench the Ministers reminded me of one of those marine landscapes not very unusual on the coasts of South America. You behold a range of exhausted volcanoes. Not a flame flickers on a single pallid crest. But the situation is still dangerous. There are occasional earthquakes, and ever and anon the dark rumbling of the sea."

Nevertheless Gladstone's first Government stands high in British history; but there were few fresh Liberal ideals to expound when Parliament was dissolved in 1874. He fought the election on a proposal to abolish the income-tax, which then stood at threepence in the pound, and to the end of his life he always regretted his failure to achieve this object. But the country was now against him and he lost. He went into semi-retirement, believing that the great reforming work of Liberalism had been completed. Most of his Whig friends agreed. The Radicals thought otherwise. All of them were wrong. The "Grand Old Man" was soon to return to politics, and return in a setting and amid a storm which would rend and disrupt the loyalties and traditions of English public life in a manner far more drastic than any of them yet conceived.

While his great adversary devoted his leisure to felling trees at Hawarden and writing articles about Homer Disraeli seized his chance. He had long waited for supreme power. For twenty-five years he had been the leader of the Conservative Party in the House of Commons, and now he was over seventy.

1   During the American Civil War, Britain built a warship named the *Alabama* for the Confederate Navy. The ship had a "good war". After the conflict, the US government demanded compensation on the grounds that Britain had, by building the ship, broken the rules of neutrality.

His physique had never been robust, and his last years, made lonely by the death of his wife, were plagued by gout and other ailments. "Power – it has come to me too late. ... There were days when, on waking, I felt I could move dynasties and Governments; but that has passed away." But at no time had his problems been simple. Apart from the interlude of the Peel Ministry of 1841–46, an interlude which had ended in party disaster, the Tories had been more or less in opposition for close on half a century. Labelled the party of reaction, its members mocked as the heirs of Eldon, Sidmouth, and other hard-shelled old Tories, it now had to face a democratic electorate. The fact that the extension of the franchise had been sponsored by the Tory leader made it no less "a leap in the dark" for them. But Disraeli had no doubts. He remained true to the spirit of the Young England movement, which he had founded a generation before, and he never believed that the working men of England were Radicals or would-be destroyers of the established order. He saw clearly that although many of the new electors were attracted by the ideas of tradition, continuity, and ordered social progress such feelings would never ripen into electoral advantage under the inert conservatism of his own back-benchers. He had not only to win over the electorate, but also to convert his own party.

Disraeli's campaign began long before Gladstone fell. He concentrated on social reform and on a new conception of the Empire, and both prongs of attack struck Gladstone at his weakest points. The Empire had never aroused his interest, and though passionate in defence of the political rights of the working class he cared little for their material claims. Disraeli, on the other hand, proclaimed that "the first consideration of a Minister should be the health of the people". Liberals tried to laugh this off as a "policy of sewage". In his first full session after reaching office Disraeli proceeded to redeem his pledge. He was fortunate in his colleagues, among whom the Home Secretary, Richard Cross, was outstanding in ability. A Trade Union Act gave the unions almost complete freedom of action, an Artisan's Dwelling Act was the first measure to tackle the housing problem, a Sale of Food and Drugs Act and a Public Health Act at last established sanitary law on a sound footing. Disraeli succeeded in persuading much of the Conservative Party not only that the real needs of the electorate included healthier conditions of life, better homes, and freedom to organise in the world of industry, but also that the Conservative Party was perfectly well fitted to provide them. Well might Alexander Macdonald, the miners' leader, declare that "The Conservative Party have done more for the working classes in five years than the Liberals have in fifty." Gladstone had provided the administrative basis for these great developments, but Disraeli took the first considerable steps in promoting social welfare.

The second part of the new Conservative programme, Imperialism, had also been launched before Disraeli came to power. Gladstone's passion for economy in all things military, his caution in Europe, and his indifference to the Empire jarred on a public which was growing ever more conscious of British Imperial glory. Disraeli's appeal was perfectly tuned to the new mood.

"Self-government, in my opinion", he said of the colonies, "when it was conceded, ought to have been conceded as part of a great policy of Imperial consolidation. It ought to have been accompanied by an Imperial tariff, by securities for the people of England for the enjoyment of the unappropriated lands which belonged to the Sovereign as their trustee, and by a military code which should have precisely defined the means and the responsibilities by which the colonies should be defended, and by which, if necessary, this country should call for aid from the colonies themselves. It ought, further, to have been accompanied by the institution of some representative council in the Metropolis which would have brought the colonies into constant and continuous relations with the home Government. All this, however, was omitted because those who advised that policy – and I believe their convictions were sincere – looked upon the colonies of England, looked upon even our connection with India, as a burden upon this country; viewing everything in its financial aspect, and totally passing by those moral and political considerations which make nations great, and by the influence of which men alone are distinguished from the animals.

"Well, what has been the result of this attempt during the reign of Liberalism for the disintegration of the Empire? It has entirely failed. But how has it failed? Through the sympathy of the colonies for the Mother Country. They have decided that the Empire shall not be destroyed; and in my opinion no Minister in this country will do his duty who neglects any opportunity of reconstructing as much as possible our Colonial Empire, and of responding to those distant sympathies which may become the source of incalculable strength and happiness to this land."

At first Disraeli was brilliantly successful. The Suez Canal had been open for six years, and had transformed the strategic position of Great Britain. No longer was the Cape of Good Hope the key to the route to India and the Far East. The Foreign Office had been curiously slow to appreciate this obvious fact and had missed more than one opportunity to control the waterway. In 1875 Disraeli, on behalf of the British Government, bought, for four million pounds, the shares of the Egyptian Khedive Ismail in the Canal. This Turkish satrap was bankrupt and glad to sell; his holding amounted to nearly half the total issue. The route to India was safeguarded, a possible threat to British naval supremacy was removed, and – of fateful importance for the future – Britain was inexorably drawn into Egyptian politics. In the following year Queen Victoria, to her great pleasure, was proclaimed Empress of India. Such a stroke would never have occurred to Gladstone, or, indeed to the next generation of Imperialists. But Disraeli's Oriental, almost mystical, approach to Empire, his emphasis on Imperial symbols, his belief in the importance of outward display, gave his policy an imaginative colour never achieved by his successors. His purpose was to make those colonies which he had once condemned as "millstones round our necks" sparkle like diamonds. New storms in Europe distracted attention from this glittering prospect.

In 1876 the Eastern Question erupted anew. The Crimean War had been mismanaged by the soldiers, and at the peace the diplomats had done no better. Most of the Balkans still remained under Turkish rule, and all attempts to improve the Ottoman administration of Christian provinces had foundered on the obstinacy of the Sultan and the magnitude of the task. Slavs, Rumanians, and Greeks were united in their detestation of the Turk. Revolt offered little hope of permanent success, and they had long looked to the Czar of Russia as their potential liberator. Here was a fine dilemma for the British Government. The possibility of creating independent Balkan states, in spite of Canning's example in the small Greek kingdom, was not yet seriously contemplated. The nice choice appeared to lie between bolstering Turkish power and allowing Russian influence to move through the Balkans and into the Mediterranean by way of Constantinople. The threat had long been present, and the insurrection which now occurred confronted Disraeli with the most difficult and dangerous situation for Great Britain since the Napoleonic wars.

Rebellion broke out in Bosnia and Herzegovina, where forty years later an assassin's bullet was to start the First World War. Germany, Austria, and Russia, united in the League of Three Emperors, proposed that Turkey should be coerced into making serious reforms. Disraeli and his Foreign Secretary, Lord Derby, resisted these plans, arguing that they "must end very soon in the disintegration of Turkey", and to emphasise British support of Turkey a fleet was dispatched to the Dardanelles. But these diplomatic manoeuvres were soon overtaken by the news of terrible Turkish atrocities in Bulgaria. Disraeli, handicapped by faulty reports from his ambassador at Constantinople, who was an admirer of the Turks, failed to measure the deep stir in public opinion. In reply to a Parliamentary question in July he took leave to doubt whether "torture has been practised on a great scale among an Oriental people who seldom, I believe, resort to torture, but generally terminate their connection with culprits in a more expeditious manner". This tone of persiflage fanned into fierce and furious activity the profound moral feeling which was always simmering just below the surface of Gladstone's mind.

In a famous pamphlet, *The Bulgarian Horrors and the Question of the East*, Gladstone delivered his onslaught on the Turks and Disraeli's Government. "Let the Turks now carry away their abuses in the only possible manner, namely, by carrying off themselves. Their Zaptiehs and their Mudirs, their Bimbashis and their Yuzbachis, their Kaimakams and their Pashas, one and all, bag and baggage, shall, I hope, clear out from the provinces they have desolated and profaned. This thorough riddance, this most blessed deliverance, is the only reparation we can make to the memory of those heaps on heaps of dead; to the violated purity alike of matron, of maiden and of child. ... There is not a criminal in a European gaol, there is not a cannibal in the South Sea Islands, whose indignation would not arise and overboil at the recital of that which has been done, which has too late been examined, but which remains unavenged; which has left behind all the foul and all the fierce passions that produced it, and which may again spring up in another more murderous harvest, from the soil soaked and reeking with blood, and in the air tainted with every imaginable deed of crime and shame. ... No Government ever has so sinned; none has proved itself so incorrigible in sin or – which is the same – so impotent for reformation." After this broadside relations between the two great men became so strained that Lord Beaconsfield (as Disraeli now was) publicly described Gladstone as worse than any Bulgarian horror.

At the end of the year a conference of the Great Powers was held in Constantinople at which Lord Salisbury, as the British representative, displayed for the first time his diplomatic talents. Salisbury was the direct descendant of Queen Elizabeth's great servant, William Cecil, and of James I's Minister, Robert Cecil, whose namesake he was. Over a period of twenty years, in both Houses of Parliament, he had been highly critical of his chief. He had joined Disraeli's Government only after much heart-searching. But in office gradually the two men grew together. Salisbury's caustic, far-ranging common sense supplemented Disraeli's darting vision. As Secretary of State for India, and later at the Foreign Office, Salisbury established himself as the next predestined Tory leader. At Constantinople a programme of reform for Turkey was drawn up, but the Turks, sustained in part by a belief that Salisbury's zeal for reform did not entirely reflect the views of his Prime Minister and the British Cabinet, rejected it. The delegates returned to their capitals and Europe waited for war to break out between Russia and Turkey. When it came in the summer of 1877 the mood of the country quickly changed. Gladstone, whose onslaught on the Turks had at first carried all before it, was now castigated as a pro-Russian. Feeling rose as, month after month, in spite of heroic Turkish resistance, especially at Plevna in Bulgaria, the mass of Russian troops moved ponderously towards the Dardanelles. At last, in January 1878, they stood before the walls of Constantinople. Public opinion reached fever-point. The music-hall song of the hour was:

We don't want to fight, but by jingo if we do
We've got the ships, we've got the men, we've got the money too!
We've fought the Bear before, and while we're Britons true
The Russians shall not have Constantinople.

In February, after considerable prevarication, a fleet of British ironclads steamed into the Golden Horn. They lay in the Sea of Marmora, opposite the Russian army, for six uneasy months of truce; the whale, as Bismarck said, facing the elephant.

In March Turkey and Russia signed the Treaty of San Stefano. Andrassy, the Austrian Foreign Minister, in anger called it "an Orthodox Slavic sermon". It gave Russia effective control of the Balkans, and was obviously un-acceptable to the other Great Powers. War again seemed likely, and Lord Derby, who objected to any kind of military preparations, resigned. He was replaced at the Foreign Office by Lord Salisbury, who immediately set about summoning a conference of the Great Powers. They met at the Congress of

Berlin in June and July. Business was dominated by Andrassy, Beaconsfield, Bismarck, and the Russian Minister Gortchakov, a quartet whose combined diplomatic talents would have been difficult to match. The result was that Russia gave up much of what she had momentarily gained at San Stefano. She kept Rumanian Bessarabia, which extended her territories to the mouths of the Danube, but the big Bulgaria which she had planned to dominate was split into three parts, only one of which was granted practical independence. The rest was returned to the Sultan. Austria-Hungary, as we must now call the Habsburg Empire, secured in compensation the right to occupy and administer Bosnia-Herzegovina. By a separate Anglo-Turkish convention Great Britain received Cyprus and guaranteed the territorial integrity of Turkey-in-Asia in return for yet another pledge by the Sultan to introduce proper reforms. Beaconsfield returned from Berlin claiming that he had brought "peace with honour". He had indeed averted war; and for the moment, Russia, blocked in the Balkans, turned her gaze away from Europe to the Far East. The arrangements at Berlin have been much criticised for laying the trail to the war of 1914, but the Eastern Question, as it was then posed before the nations, was virtually insoluble. No settlement could have been more than a temporary one, and the Congress of Berlin in fact ensured the peace of Europe for thirty-six years.

The following weeks saw the zenith of Beaconsfield's career. But fortune soon ceased to smile upon him. Thrusting policies in South Africa and Afghanistan led, in 1879, to the destruction of a British battalion by the Zulus at Isandhlwana and the massacre of the Legation staff at Kabul. These minor disasters, though promptly avenged, lent fresh point to Gladstone's vehement assault upon the Government, an assault which reached its climax in the autumn of 1879 with the Midlothian Campaign. Gladstone denounced a "vigorous, that is to say a narrow, restless, blustering, and self-assertive foreign policy, appealing to the self-love and pride of the community". He argued that Britain should pursue the path of morality and justice, free from the taint of self-interest. Her aims should be self-government for subject peoples and the promotion of a true Concert of Europe. His constant theme was the need for the nation's policy to conform with the moral law. "Remember", he said at Dalkeith, "that the sanctity of life in the hill villages of Afghanistan among the winter snows is as inviolable in the eyes of Almighty God as can be your own." This appeal to morality infuriated the Conservatives, who based their case on the importance of defending and forwarding British interests and responsibilities wherever they might lie. They maintained that Beaconsfield's policy had raised national power and prestige to new heights.

But the force of Gladstone's oratory was too much for the exhausted Ministry. Moreover, their last years in office coincided with the onset of an economic depression, serious enough for industry but ruinous for agriculture. When Beaconsfield dissolved in March 1880 the electoral result was decisive; the Queen was forced to accept as Prime Minister for a second time the man whom she described in a letter to her private secretary, Sir Henry Ponsonby, as "that *half-mad firebrand* who would soon ruin everything".

While the duel between Disraeli and Gladstone held the centre of the stage far-reaching movements were taking shape below the surface of Parliamentary politics. The Reform Act of 1867, in granting the vote to virtually every adult male resident in a borough, killed the modified eighteenth-century régime which had persisted since 1832. The emergence of a mass electorate called for a new kind of politics. Sheer numbers rendered the old techniques ineffective in the large cities. Two things were required: a party policy which would persuade the electors to vote, and an efficient organisation to make sure that they did so. Of the two leaders Gladstone was slow to see the implications of the new age. The great demagogue was bored by the ordinary everyday business of party. Disraeli, on the other hand, produced both a policy and an organisation. Twelve years earlier he had appointed John Gorst as party manager, under whose guidance the Conservative Party was completely overhauled. The Central Office was established and a network of local associations was set up, combined in a National Union. The transition was remarkably smooth, and although there were to be storms in the early 1880s the system created by Disraeli still largely remains at the present time.

In the Liberal camp the situation was very different. Gladstone's coolness and Whig hostility prevented the building of a centralised party organisation. The impulse and impetus came not from the centre, but through the provinces. In 1873 Joseph Chamberlain[1] had become Mayor of Birmingham. Aided by a most able political adviser, Schnadhorst, he built up a party machine which, although based on popular participation, his enemies quickly condemned as a "caucus". A policy of "Municipal Socialism" brought great benefits to Birmingham in the shape of public utilities, slum clearance, and other civic amenities. The movement spread to other towns and cities, and a National Liberal Federation was born. The aim of its promoters was to make the Federation the Parliament of the Liberal movement, which would work out a Radical programme and eventually replace the Whigs by a new set of leaders drawn from its own ranks. This was a novel phenomenon. Unlike Chartism and the Anti-Corn Law League, movements for reform need no longer operate on the fringe of party. Radicalism was now powerful enough to make a bid for control. This change was greatly aided by the clustering of the parties round opposite social poles, a process well under way by 1880, and which Gladstone recognised in the course of his election campaign. "I am sorry," he declared, "to say we cannot reckon upon the aristocracy. We cannot reckon upon what is called the landed interest. We cannot reckon upon the clergy of the Established Church either in England or in Scotland. ... We cannot reckon upon the wealth of the country nor upon the rank of the country. ... In the

---

1   Chamberlain wanted a series of radical "regeneration" programmes for the majority of people. In the 1886 election, he took this a stage further with an independent manifesto, the Unauthorised Programme, which promised, among other things, tax and education reform and allotments for everyone who wanted them.

main these powers are against us. ... We must set them down among our most determined foes." At the election Chamberlain and his followers put forward a programme of reform which was unacceptable to the Whigs, and indeed to Gladstone. Their success exposed and proclaimed the wide changes which the new franchise had wrought in the structure of the party system.

Gladstone and Disraeli had done much to bridge the gap between aristocratic rule and democracy. They both believed that Governments should be active, and the Statute Books for the years between 1868 and 1876 bulge with reforming measures. Elections gradually became a judgment on what the Government of the day had accomplished and an assessment of the promises for the future made by the two parties. By 1880 they were being fought with techniques which differ very little from those used today. Gladstone's Midlothian Campaign, the first broad appeal to the people by a potential Prime Minister underlined the change. It shocked the Queen that he should make a speech about foreign policy from a railway carriage window, but her protest echoed an age that had already passed. This was the way to become "the People's William".

Beaconsfield died a year later. His great task, taken on almost single-handedly, had been to lead the Conservative Party out of the despair of the period after 1846, to persuade it to face the inevitability of democracy, and to endow it with the policies which would meet the new conditions. That he was successful is a remarkable indication of his skill in all matters related to party. He made the Conservatives a great force in democratic politics. The large-scale two-party system with its "swing of the pendulum" begins with him. Tory democracy – working men by hundreds of thousands who voted Conservative – became the dominant factor. The extension of the franchise which had hitherto threatened to engulf the past bore it proudly forward. Whereas the Whigs vanished from the scene, the Tories, though they were slow to realise it, sprang into renewed life and power with a fair future before them. Such was the work of Disraeli, for which his name will be duly honoured.

CHAPTER FORTY-EIGHT

THE FIN DE SIÈCLE

The Venezuelan Dispute – German naval expansion – the origins of America as a world-Power – Gladstone's second term – the Fourth Party of Tories – battle for Home Rule for Ireland – the Boers in revolt – the Pretoria Convention – Cecil Rhodes – Egypt and Sudan – Gordon killed at Khartoum – Reform Bill – the Coercion Acts – Gladstone's Irish Crusade – Charles Stewart Parnell – the Phoenix Park murders – Lord Salisbury as Prime Minister – the 1886 Home Rule Bill falls – the creation of county councils – Salisbury's African policy – the rise of Rosebery, Campbell-Bannerman and Asquith – the Fabians, the Webbs and George Bernard Shaw – Keir Hardie elected to Parliament – the Ashanti Wars – the death of Gladstone – the Battle of Omdurman

B Y THE 1890s the idea of Empire had taken hold of all the great industrial Powers. Britain, France, and Germany were especially active in acquiring new colonies and new markets. This European example was not lost upon America. For these and other reasons a vigorous spirit of self-assertion developed, which first became manifest in the Venezuelan boundary dispute with Britain in 1895.

Ever since the end of the Civil War Anglo-American relations had been distinctly cool. In spite of the settlement of the *Alabama* claims by Gladstone's Government, Britain's sympathy for the South during the great conflict had left its mark upon the Union. Constant bickering agitated the two countries over such matters as seal-fishing in the Behring Sea, the rights of American fishermen in Canadian waters, and interpretations of the Clayton-Bulwer Treaty of 1850 about the proposed Panama Canal. But all these disputes paled before the question of the Venezuelan boundary. The frontier between this South American republic and British Guiana had long been unsettled, and although the United States had frequently offered mediation her advances had always been declined by Britain. In the summer of 1895 the American State Department made yet another move in a communication which President Cleveland described as "a twenty-inch gun note". Britain was accused of violating the Monroe Doctrine, and was required to give a definite answer as to whether she would accept arbitration. Lord Salisbury bided his time, waiting for passions to cool. He replied in November, rejecting arbitration and telling the American Government that its interpretation of the Monroe Doctrine was at fault. Meanwhile Cleveland sent Congress a message announcing that America would fix the boundary line independently and oblige the disputants to accept her decision. For a few days war with Britain seemed possible, and even imminent.[1] But the first patriotic outburst in America soon gave way to more sober feelings. In Britain opinion had reacted less violently. At the height of the crisis news arrived of the Kaiser's telegram to President Kruger in South Africa, congratulating him on the repulse of the Jameson raid. These Imperial perplexities distracted attention in London. British wrath turned against Germany rather than the United States. Too involved in Europe and South Africa to think of quarrelling with America, the British Government agreed to arbitration. Their claims in Guiana were largely conceded by the tribunal. There followed a steady improvement in Anglo-American relations, chiefly because Britain was awakening to the dangers of her isolation. Her growing alarm at German naval expansion led her to make friendly overtures to which the united States were fully ready to respond.

The exuberant pride of Americans could not long be held in check. In the Cuban revolt against Spanish rule it found an outlet. Ever since this revolt began in 1895 American popular sentiment had sympathised with the rebel fight for independence. Tempers rose at tales of Spanish atrocities. General Weyler's policy of herding civilians into concentration camps, where thousands died of disease, was vehemently denounced. These atrocities, sensationally reported and embellished by two rival New York newspapers, led to demands for American intervention. In 1898 popular clamour for war with Spain reached its height. In February the American battleship *Maine*, sent to Cuba to protect American lives and property, was blown up by a mine in Havana harbour, with the loss of most of her crew. At this the Spanish Government hastily made concessions to the United States, which President McKinley was at first disposed to accept. But public indignation was too strong for him, and on April 11 war was declared.

The conflict lasted sixteen weeks, and was marked by a succession of overwhelming American victories. In Cuba an American expeditionary force, despite complaints about the mismanagement of the War Department and incompetent leadership in the field, won a series of rapid battles which brought about the surrender of all the Spanish forces in the island. At sea Commodore Dewey immobilised the main Spanish fleet in an engagement in Manila Bay on May 1. The Caribbean squadron of the Spanish Navy was sunk outside the Cuban port of Santiago. In August Spain sued for peace, and in December a treaty was signed at Paris whereby Cuba became independent. The United States acquired Puerto Rico, Guam, and the Philippines.

---

1   I was returning from a visit to Cuba via America at this time and remember vividly looking at ships off the English coast and wondering which one would be our transport to Canada. [Churchill]

All this did much to heal the wounds remaining from the Civil War. In the wave of patriotism that swept the country Northerner and Southerner alike took pride in the achievements of their common country. Young men from both regions rushed to join the expeditionary force and fought side by side for San Juan Hill. The famous Confederate cavalry leader Joe Wheeler exclaimed that a single battle for the Union flag was worth fifteen years of life. The venture also showed that the American people were now fully aware of their own strength as a world-Power. They began to play an important rôle in the international scene. The Spanish War helped to promote a new and warmer friendship with Britain, for Britain, alone of the European nations, sympathised with the United States in the conflict. This the Americans appreciated, and as the nineteenth century drew to its end the foundations were laid for a closer concert between the two peoples in facing problems of the world.[1] We must now return across the Atlantic from the dazzling prospects that lay before the United States to the English party scene at Westminster.

When Gladstone in 1880 became Prime Minister for the second time his position was not the comfortable one he had held twelve years before. Then, with a determined Cabinet and a united party, he had presided over the enactment of a great series of reforms. Expectation now stood just as high, for a triumphant election campaign had given him a majority of 137 over his Conservative opponents. But almost as soon as the House assembled the Speaker remarked that Gladstone had "a difficult team to drive". So it was to prove. Few periods of office have begun with higher hopes; none has been more disappointing in its outcome.

The main fault lay in the composition of the Liberal Party. For long it had prided itself upon the strength afforded by diversity, but it soon began to find that the divisions between Whig and Radical, Right and Left, were unbridgeable. In the first Gladstone Government there had been little discord. But the old Whig faction thought that reform had gone far enough, and Gladstone himself had some sympathy with them. He disliked intensely the methods of the Radical caucus and scorned their policies of social and economic reform. "Their pet idea", he wrote, "is what they call construction – that is to say, taking into the hands of the State the business of the individual man." Moreover he found the Whigs much better company than Radical newcomers like Joseph Chamberlain. Men such as the Foreign Secretary, Lord Granville, had been his friends and colleagues for many years, and Gladstone never lost his conviction that the natural leaders of the Liberal cause were a small, leisured, cultured aristocracy.

When it came to forming his Cabinet he had to conciliate these same Whigs. The Marquess of Hartington, who had led the party in the Commons

---

1   Churchill's original manuscript gives greater space to this section. But that which has survived
    in this edition begins to illustrate the context of twentieth-century Anglo-American relations and
    some indication of some perspectives of American political thinking that kept her from the
    opening years of the First World War.

during his chief's retirement, had never been happy about Gladstone's onslaught on Disraeli's Eastern policy.[1] He and his friends were fearful of the direction that the Prime Minister's mind and energy were next likely to take. In the upshot only one Radical, Chamberlain, was admitted to the Cabinet, and to him was assigned what was then a lowly office, the Presidency of the Board of Trade. This was Gladstone's first great error. Not only was a Whig Cabinet profoundly unsuited to a time when the Liberal Party was becoming more and more Radical, but its leader was to find himself in direct clash and conflict with his own colleagues on the main political, Imperial and foreign issues of the day, and above all on Ireland. A Cabinet with such deep cleavages was unlikely to prove an effective instrument of government. John Morley, Gladstone's biographer, wrote that it was not only a coalition, but "a coalition of that vexatious kind where those who happened not to agree sometimes seemed to be almost as well pleased with contention as with harmony". Over this ruled the Grand Old Man, as he was already considered in his seventy-first year, his force and energy undimmed, his passions and enthusiasms growing more intense with every year that passed. He towered above his colleagues. When he was away from Cabinet, wrote one of them, it was as though he had "left us mice without the cat".

But the Liberals, or rather the Whigs, were not alone in their troubles and anxieties. Shocked by the onset of democracy and its threat to old, established interests, the Tory leaders proceeded to forget the lessons which Disraeli had tried so long to teach them. Their leader in the Commons was Sir Stafford Northcote, who had once been Gladstone's private secretary and still stood in awe of the great man. His companions on the Front Bench, frightened by the prospect of universal suffrage, clung desperately to the faith, practice, and timidity of their youth. Into the breach stepped a small but extremely able group whose prowess at Parliamentary guerrilla fighting has rarely been equalled, the "Fourth Party" – Lord Randolph Churchill, A.J. Balfour, Sir Henry Drummond Wolff, and John Gorst. They teased and taunted Gladstone without mercy or respect. But Lord Randolph, who quickly rose to special prominence, reserved his fiercest criticism for the leaders of his own side. In a letter to *The Times* he charged them with "a series of neglected opportunities, pusillanimity, combativeness at wrong moments, vacillation, dread of responsibility, repression and discouragement of hard-working followers, collusions with the Government, hankerings after coalitions, jealousies, commonplaces, want of perception". His denunciations were not confined to Parliament. With the motto "Trust the People" and the slogan "Tory Democracy" he appealed to the rank and file over the heads of their

---

1   In Opposition (between 1874 and 1884) Gladstone delivered the most venomous attacks on what he saw as Disraeli's Imperialist policies. In the first of his Midlothian speeches (November 25, 1879) Gladstone said: "We have undertaken to settle the affairs of about a fourth of the entire human race. ... Is not that enough for the ambition of Lord Beaconsfield [Disraeli]? ... all manners of gratuitous, dangerous, ambiguous, impracticable, and impossible engagements are contracted for us in all parts of the world."

nominal leaders. So dramatic was his success that his power soon became almost as strong as Salisbury's.

These were strange years for party warfare. The upsurge of the new forces, Radicalism and Tory Democracy, was playing havoc with the old Parliamentary system. Issues were confused and cut across party lines. Conflict was fierce, but often internecine. Chamberlain and Lord Randolph, though sometimes in bitter disagreement, had far more in common than they had with their own leaders. The confusion was not to be resolved until Gladstone, using Home Rule for Ireland like an axe, divided the political world by forcing men to make a clear and sharp decision about a single great proposal.

It was a constant complaint among Liberals that whenever they succeeded the Tories in office they fell heirs to a set of Imperial complications which involved them in enterprises hateful to their anti-Imperialist sentiments. So it was in 1880. One of their first troubles sprang from South Africa. There the Boer Republic of the Transvaal had long been in difficulties, threatened by bankruptcy and disorders within and by the Zulu warrior kingdom upon its eastern border. To save it from ruin and possible extinction Disraeli's Government had annexed it, an action which at first met with little protest. Disraeli looked forward to a union of all the white communities of South Africa in a self-governing Confederation on the Canadian model, but the times were not yet ripe. A fierce desire for renewed independence began to stir among the Transvaal Boers, and they looked for an opportunity to throw off British rule. As soon as British arms had finally quelled the Zulus in 1879 they felt safe enough to seize their chance. It was perhaps natural that they should expect their freedom from a Liberal Government. Gladstone had denounced the annexation of the Transvaal, but a powerful section of his party favoured the African natives more than the Boers. He himself was convinced that federation was the only solution for the South African puzzle, and he refused to make any immediate change. At the end of 1880 the Boers revolted and a small British force was cut to pieces at Majuba Hill. There was available in South Africa a force large enough to crush the Boers, but Gladstone declined to bow to the outcry for retaliation and continued with the negotiations that had already been under way at the time of Majuba. The outcome was the Pretoria Convention of 1881, which, modified in 1884, gave virtual independence to the Transvaal. This application of Liberal principles provided the foundation of Boer power in South Africa. All might have gone more smoothly in the future but for two developments. Immensely rich goldfields were discovered on the Rand and a large, bustling cosmopolitan mining community was suddenly planted in the midst of the Boer farmers' Republic. Meanwhile at Cape Town Cecil Rhodes had entered politics, resolved to create a vast, all-embracing South African dominion, and endowed by nature with the energy that often makes dreams come true. From these events sprang consequences which have yet to run their course.

As Gladstone had foreseen at the time, Disraeli's purchase of shares in the Suez Canal, brilliant stroke though it was, soon brought all the problems of

Egypt in its wake. When he took office, Egypt, nominally ruled by the Khedive, was in effect under Anglo-French control. The Khedive had only temporarily been saved from bankruptcy by selling his Canal shares. Soon French and British Debt Commissioners were appointed to take charge of his finances, and of much else too. The British Commissioner was Evelyn Baring, later Lord Cromer, and one of the greatest of Imperial proconsuls. With a single break he was to preside over the destinies of Egypt for thirty years. At the end of 1881, however, Anglo-French control was shattered by a nationalist revolt led by Colonel Arabi Pasha. It was backed by the Army and rapidly swept through the whole country. Gladstone tried in vain to apply the principles of the Concert of Europe. A sudden twist in the domestic politics of France forced her to stand aside, and the other European Powers remained aloof. On June 11, 1881, fifty Europeans were killed in riots in Alexandria. Arabi began to fortify the city in such a way as to threaten British ships in the harbour. Hence, exactly a month later, and after warning had been given, the forts were bombarded and the guns silenced. A few days later the Cabinet decided to dispatch an army under Sir Garnet Wolseley to Egypt. The decision was crowned by military success, and Arabi's army was decisively defeated at Tel-el-Kebir on September 13. Gladstone delighted in the victory, but was troubled in his conscience. The Liberal instinct was now to withdraw, but Egypt could not be left a vacuum. To annex her, though logical and expected by the other Powers of Europe, was too repugnant to the Liberal conscience. Gladstone therefore chose the worst of both worlds. The odium of occupation remained on the British, but much authority continued to be exercised by the Commissioners of the Debt, a state of affairs which allowed all the major European Powers to interfere. Nevertheless, after Baring became Consul-General in 1883, and in effect ruler of the country, a new era opened of much-needed reform.

Intervention in Egypt led to an even more perplexing entanglement in the Sudan. This huge territory, more than a thousand miles deep, stretched along the torrid banks of the Nile from the borders of Egypt down almost to the Equator. It formed a part of the Khedive's realm, and in spite of the efforts of British advisers it was woefully misgoverned by Pashas from Cairo. During the same year that the Egyptians revolted against France and Britain the Sudanese rebelled against the Egyptians. They were led by the Mahdi, a Moslem fanatic who quickly destroyed an Egyptian army, and was soon in control of most of the Sudan. Gladstone spoke of the Sudanese as "a people rightly struggling to be free". This was a highly flattering way of describing the Mahdi's forces, whose blood-lust spread terror everywhere in their advance. Either the Sudan must be reconquered or it must be evacuated, and the Government in London chose evacuation. With this the Egyptians had to concur. At the end of 1883 the decision was made to withdraw their outlying garrisons scattered far to the South, for which Britain, as tutor to the Egyptian Army, had a general responsibility. To make the decision was easy; to carry it out more difficult. But on January 14, 1884, General Charles Gordon, who had achieved fame in Chinese wars, left London charged by the Cabinet with the task of evacuation.

Gordon had himself served in the Sudan, and had played a notable part in attempts to suppress the slave trade. He also had a conscience. It was to cost him his life. He arrived in Khartoum in February, and once there he judged that it would be wrong to withdraw the garrisons and abandon the country to the mercy of the Mahdi's Dervishes. He accordingly asked for reinforcements and put forward plans for counter-attack. In London the Government were taken aback by this change of front. They might have foreseen that a commander cast in heroic mould would not readily lend himself to withdrawal. Retreat was never to Gordon's liking. He was resolved to remain in Khartoum until his self-imposed mission was accomplished. His strength of will, often capricious in its expression, was pitted against Gladstone's determination not to be involved in fresh colonial adventures. Lord Randolph Churchill was the first to raise in the House of Commons the problem of Gordon's personal safety. In March he put a blunt question to the Government. "Are they going to remain indifferent", he asked, "to the fate of the one man on whom they have counted to extricate them from their dilemmas, to leave him to shift for himself, and not to make a single effort on his behalf?" Lord Randolph was met with evasive replies. Help for Gordon was to be long in coming, in spite of his urgent appeals, which he backed by dispatches from Baring in Cairo and by the advice of the foremost Imperial soldier of the age, Lord Wolseley. By May Gordon was cut off in Khartoum. Meanwhile the Cabinet, still insistent on the policy of "scuttling out", as Lord Salisbury called it, refused to dispatch a relieving army.

Throughout the spring and summer public opinion in England mounted, and large meetings were held demanding that Gordon must be saved. His stern religious faith, his Bible-reading, his assaults on slavery, his charitable work for the children of the poor, as well as his military prowess, had made him a popular figure, as gallant and noble as one of King Arthur's Knights. But Gladstone's mind was on other things. Reform of the franchise was one, and another was the case of the vehement atheist, Charles Bradlaugh, who had been elected to Parliament but refused his seat, and whose affairs perturbed the House of Commons and the Prime Minister's conscience for over six years.[1] In May Lord Randolph said of Gladstone in the House of Commons: "I have compared his efforts in the cause of General Gordon with his efforts in the cause of Mr Bradlaugh. If a hundredth part of those invaluable moral qualities bestowed upon the cause of a seditious blasphemer had been given to the support of a Christian hero the success of Gordon's mission would have been assured."

Eventually, upon the insistence of Lord Hartington, then Secretary of State

---

1   Charles Bradlaugh (1833–91) iconoclastic editor of the National Reformer who refused to take the oath when elected to Parliament in 1880, but did after the 1886 election and in that same year was prosecuted for carrying an article promoting birth control.

for War, who made it a matter of confidence in the Cabinet, the Government were induced to rescue Gordon. In September Wolseley hastened to Cairo, and in less than a month he had assembled a striking force of ten thousand men. He knew that a rapid foray against the massed spearmen of the Mahdi would accomplish nothing. Speed was essential, but disaster could not be risked. A campaign of six months, soundly based, was the fastest he could hope for. In October he set out from the borders of Egypt upon the eight-hundred-mile advance to Khartoum. Much of his way lay through uncharted reaches of the Nile; rapids and cataracts abounded, and the heat was heavy and wearisome. In the Northern Sudan the River Nile describes an immense bend to the east. Wolseley was aware that time was fatally short. He felt the eyes and anxieties of England focused upon Gordon and himself, and on the distance that lay between them. His main strength must proceed steadily up-river until, all cataracts surmounted, they would be poised for a swoop upon Khartoum. In the meantime he detached the Camel Corps under Sir Herbert Stewart to cut across a hundred and fifty miles of desert and rejoin the Nile to the north of Gordon's capital. Starting on December 30, Stewart acted with resolution. At Abu Klea, on January 17, a hundred and twenty miles short of his goal, Stewart was attacked by a Dervish host. His column of fewer than two thousand men confronted an enemy at least five times as numerous. Under a desperate onset the British square was broken by the Mahdi's fanatical hordes, but the battle was won. Two days later, amid constant harassments, Stewart's advanced troops reached the Nile, but he had been mortally wounded. His successor in command inherited a perilous situation. On January 21 steamers arrived from Khartoum, sent down-river by Gordon. There was a tragic but unavoidable delay while reconnaissances were made and the wounded tended. On the 24th a force of 26 British and 240 Sudanese sailed south on two of the steamers, assailed by Dervish musketry fire from the banks. On the 28th they reached Khartoum. It was too late. Gordon's flag no longer flew over the Residency. He was dead; the city had fallen two days before, after a prodigious display of valour by its defender. He had fallen alone, unsuccoured and unsupported by any of his own countrymen. In the eyes of perhaps half the nation Gladstone was a murderer. The Queen was so distressed that she made her own feelings clear to him in open telegram. Gordon became a national martyr. It was true that he had disobeyed his orders, as indeed he admitted in his journal, but the fact remained that the Cabinet which had sent him out had then virtually abandoned him. The rescuing force, whose efforts had been so nearly crowned with success, retired to Egypt. Thirteen years went by before Gordon was avenged. As Gladstone later confessed, the Government had sent a "hero of heroes" to Khartoum with all the defects and virtues of his type and they had paid the penalty.

The position of the Liberal Party had been equally shaken by its activities at home. While the nation thought only of Gordon the Government was pressing ahead with its one considerable piece of legislation, a Reform Bill which completed the work of democratising the franchise in the counties.[1] Almost every adult male was given a vote. Another Act abolished the remaining small boroughs and, with a few exceptions, divided the country into single-Member constituencies. All this was a logical extension of the Act of 1867, but it exasperated an already difficult situation. Single-Member constituencies stopped the old practice of running a Whig and a Radical in harness. The Liberals and Radicals were quick to press their advantage. Chamberlain had made onslaught after onslaught on the class who "toil not, neither do they spin", and with what is called his Unauthorised Programme,[2] and its famous promise of "three acres and a cow", he now switched his main attack from town to country. The Whigs could not ignore the challenge; the division between them and the Radicals was too deep and fundamental for them ever to work together again, and by the autumn of 1885 Salisbury, the Tory leader in the House of Lords, and now Prime Minister, could assert, and with some truth, that Gladstone's "exhortation to unity was an exhortation to hypocrisy".

Further speculation about the future of English politics was abruptly cut short by the announcement of Gladstone's conversion to the policy of Home Rule. To comprehend the significance and impact of this event we must look back upon the melancholy story of Ireland. In the years since the Great Famine of the 1840s Ireland had continued in her misery. Her peasants, especially in the West, lived in a state of extreme poverty and degradation. General Gordon had thus described them some time before in a letter to *The Times*: "I must say, from all accounts and from my own observation, that the state of our fellow countrymen in the parts I have named is worse than that of any people in the world, let alone Europe." They were "living on the verge of starvation in places in which we would not keep our cattle". Ireland was, and is, a poor country, and in spite of famine and emigration she was still overpopulated. But these misfortunes were greatly aggravated by the policies of the English Government. The Irish peasant was crushed by a land system which he hated not only because it put almost absolute power into the hands of the landlord, but also because it rested on the expropriation of land which he considered, by right, to belong to him. His was a fierce, deep-rooted enmity. It was not just a matter of material poverty, of life passed in a one-roomed hut on a diet of potatoes. He felt he had been robbed of his heritage. For most of the nineteenth century the English answer was to ignore the hate and crush the crime which it produced. In the forty years before 1870 forty-two Coercion Acts were passed. During the same period there was not a single statute to protect the Irish peasant from eviction and rack-renting. This was deliberate; the aim was to make the Irish peasant a day-labourer after the English pattern. But Ireland was not England; the Irish

---

1   In fact, what was called the third Reform Act was introduced in 1884. Gordon was killed in January 1885. An additional measure, the Redistribution Bill, went through Parliament in June 1885.

2   See note on page 580.

peasant clung to his land; he used every means in his power to defeat the alien landlords.

It must not be supposed that the Irish picture can be seen from Britain entirely in black and white. The landlords were mostly colonists from England and of long standing; they believed themselves to be, and in many ways were, a civilising influence in a primitive country. They had often had to fight for their lives and their property. The deep hold of the Roman Catholic Church on a superstitious peasantry had tended on political as well as religious grounds to be hostile to England. Ireland more than once since the days of Queen Elizabeth had threatened to become a stepping-stone to the invasion of Britain from the Continent. Rick-burning, the assassination of landlords, and other acts of terrorism had contributed to a general acceptance in England of the landlord's case. It was hard to grasp that the vicious circle of unrest, heavy-handed repression, and rebellion could only be broken by remedying fundamental grievances.

From the moment when he first took office as Prime Minister Gladstone made Irish Affairs his special concern, until at last they came to dominate his mind to the exclusion of almost everything else. His crusade for Ireland, for such it was, faced formidable opposition. English political society had little sympathy for Irish problems, and indeed many of its leading figures were members of the Irish aristocracy. In his first Ministry Gladstone had dealt successfully with the Irish dislike of an alien Church by disestablishing the Protestant Church of Ireland. His second measure, a Land Act to prevent uncompensated eviction, had been passed in 1870, but proved a failure. Ten more years went by before he became convinced that the Irish peasant had to be given real security in the tenure of his land.

In 1870 Isaac Butt had founded the Home Rule League. It aimed to achieve Home Rule by peaceful, constitutional methods, and its leader, able, courteous, an admirable House of Commons man, put his faith in the persuasive processes of debate. But there was no response to his cause in England and no confidence in his method in Ireland. Effective leadership of the movement soon passed into the hands of Charles Stewart Parnell. Parnell was a landlord, a Protestant, and a newcomer to Parliament. From his mother, the daughter of an American admiral who had won distinction fighting the British, he had acquired a hatred and contempt for English ways and institutions. A patrician in the Irish party, he was a born leader, with a power of discipline and a tactical skill that soon converted Home Rule from a debating topic into the supreme question of the hour. Ruthless in pressing his cause, and defiant of the traditions of the House of Commons, he swiftly gained such a position that an English politician said that "dealing with him was like dealing with a foreign Power".

The root of Parnell's success was the junction of the Home Rule cause with a fresh outburst of peasant agitation. A grave fall in world crop prices in the late seventies and a series of bad harvests accelerated the number of evictions as the impoverished peasants failed to pay their rents. This process was just beginning when, in 1877, Michael Davitt came out of prison after serving a seven-year sentence for treason. Davitt was a remarkable man who, in his love for Ireland and warm human sympathies, made a sharp contrast with Parnell. It was Davitt's belief that Home Rule and the land question could not be separated, and, in spite of opposition from the extreme Irish Nationalists, he successfully founded the Land League in 1879. Its objects were the reduction of rack-rents and the promotion of peasant ownership of the land. Davitt had previously assured himself of the material backing of the Irish in America. When Parnell declared his support for the League the land hunger of the peasant, the political demand for Home Rule, and the hatred of American emigrants for their unforgotten oppressors were at last brought together in a formidable alliance.

At the time none of this was immediately clear to Gladstone; his mind was occupied by the great foreign and Imperial issues that had provoked his return to power. His Government's first answer was to promote an interim Compensation for Disturbance Bill. When this was rejected by the House of Lords in July 1880 Ireland was quick to reply with Terror. In the last quarter of the year nearly two thousand outrages were committed. A new weapon appeared when Parnell advised his followers to make life unbearable for anyone who violated peasant law and custom "by isolating him from his kind as if he were a leper of old". One of the first victims was a land agent, Captain Boycott, whose name has passed into the English language. This was the period of the Land League's greatest success. Funds were pouring in from America and Australia, and, since the League effectively controlled more of Ireland than did the authorities in Dublin Castle, evictions almost ceased.

The Government then decided both to strike at terrorism and to reform the land laws. In March 1881 a sweeping Coercion Act gave to the Irish Viceroy the power, in Morley's phrase, "to lock up anybody he pleased and to detain him for as long as he pleased". It was during the debate on the Coercion Bill that the climax came in Parnell's policy of obstruction. His aim in the House of Commons had been to bring government to a standstill by exploiting the fact that Parliamentary procedure rested on custom rather than rules. From January 31 until February 2 the House sat continuously for forty-one hours, and the end came only when the Speaker took the arbitrary step of "putting the Question that the House should now adjourn". Subsequently a resolution introducing the Closure was passed, thus making the first great breach in the traditional methods of carrying through Parliamentary business.

The Coercion Act was followed immediately by a Land Act which conceded almost everything that the Irish had demanded. The Act was based on the "three Fs" – Fair Rents to be decided by a tribunal, Fixity of Tenure for all who paid their rents, and Free Sale by the tenant. This was far more generous than anything the Irish had expected, but Parnell, driven by Irish-American extremists and by his belief that even greater concessions could be extracted from Gladstone, set out to obstruct the working of the new land courts. The Government had no alternative, under the Coercion Act, but to arrest him. This it did in October. He was asked who would take his place. His reply was "Captain Moonlight". His prophecy was justified. Crime and murder multiplied, and by the spring of 1882 Gladstone was convinced that the policy of coercion had failed.

At the same time Parnell was anxious for release. As the extremists in Ireland were gaining ground it was vital for him to reassert his authority as leader. In April therefore what was called the "Kilmainham Treaty" was concluded, based on the understanding that Parnell would use his influence to end crime and terror in return for an Arrears Bill which would aid those tenants who, because they owed rent, had been unable to take advantage of the Land Act. W.E. Forster, Chief Secretary for Ireland and advocate of coercion, and the Viceroy, Lord Cowper, resigned. They were replaced by Lord Frederick Cavendish and Lord Spencer. Parnell and two of his henchmen were released on May 2, 1882, and it seemed that at last there was some likelihood of peace. But these bright prospects were destroyed by a terrible event. On May 6 Lord Frederick Cavendish landed in Dublin. A few hours after his arrival he was walking in Phoenix Park with his under-secretary, Burke, when both men were stabbed to death. The murderers were a group called the Invincibles. The object of their attack had been Burke. Lord Frederick, whom they did not know, was only killed because he had attempted to defend his companion. The English nation was shocked, the hand of the coercion party was strengthened, and all hope of any immediate conciliation was quenched. Gladstone did what he could to salvage a little from the wreck of his policy. He was now convinced that Parnell was a restraining influence in Ireland and that the only hope of any lasting success was to co-operate with him. This was not a view which commended itself to more than one or two members of his Cabinet. Parnell, for his part, was content to bide his time, and for three years Ireland was relatively quiet and peaceful.

Thus we return to the year 1885. On June 8 the Government was defeated on an amendment to the Budget, and Gladstone promptly resigned. Dissension and division in the Liberal Party had done their work, but a more direct cause was that the Irish Members voted with the Conservative Opposition. Lord Randolph Churchill had given Parnell to understand that a Conservative Government would discontinue coercion, and this was enough to swing Irish support. After some hesitation and difficulty Lord Salisbury formed a Government which was in a minority in the House of Commons. Lord Randolph took office as Secretary for India and his old enemy Northcote was elevated to the House of Lords, Sir Michael Hicks Beach becoming Chancellor of the Exchequer and Leader of the Commons. A most significant appointment was that of the Earl of Carnarvon as Viceroy of Ireland. It was well known that Carnarvon favoured a policy of Home Rule, and on August 1 he met Parnell in a house in Grosvenor Square. He left Parnell with the impression that the Government was contemplating a Home Rule measure. With an election approaching, Parnell had to make his choice. Through his mistress, Mrs O'Shea, who acted as intermediary, he made known to Gladstone the nature of the Conservative approach. Gladstone replied, "It is right I should say that into any counter-bidding of any sort against Lord R. Churchill I for one cannot enter." The truth was that at this time Gladstone had already been converted to Home Rule, but was not prepared to bargain with Parnell, preferring to hold his hand and leave the next move to Salisbury.

When the election came in November Parnell, unable to extract a clear promise of support from Gladstone, ordered the Irish in Britain to vote Conservative. Ireland was not an important issue at these hustings. The election was mainly fought on the unhappy record of the late Government. Chamberlain's Unauthorised Radical Programme provided the only major diversion. The result could not have been more unfortunate. The Liberals lost a number of seats in the boroughs, but made some gains in the counties, where they attracted support from the recently enfranchised workers. In the new House of Commons the Liberal majority over the Conservatives was eighty-six. But Parnell had realised his dream. His followers, their ranks swollen by the operation of the Reform Act in the Irish counties, also numbered eighty-six. The position was exactly what Salisbury had described as "low-water mark – i.e. Tories + Parnellites = Liberals".

In these circumstances Gladstone continued to hope that the Parnellite-Conservative alliance would hold fast and that Home Rule would pass as an agreed measure without undue opposition from the House of Lords. Precedents like Catholic Emancipation, the Repeal of the Corn Laws, and the second Reform Act were much in his mind. To all Parnell's inquiries, put through Mrs O'Shea, he replied that it would be wrong for the Liberals to make any move until the Government had declared its policy. In December he saw A.J. Balfour, Salisbury's nephew, and on the 20th wrote to him, "I feel sure the question can only be dealt with by a Government, and I desire specially on grounds of public policy that it should be dealt with by the present Government." The Conservatives treated this letter with contempt. A few days earlier the political situation had been transformed by the public disclosure of Gladstone's views on Home Rule by his son, Herbert.[1] The "Hawarden Kite", as it came to be called, immediately brought to the surface all those forces which had been struggling, hidden from public view, in the political depths. The split in the Liberal Party which Gladstone had been so anxious to avoid became a reality. The Whigs, already alienated by the growing power of Radicalism, were solid against Home Rule. The attitude of the Conservatives hardened as they sensed the advantages they would gain from Gladstone's dramatic conversion. A possible alliance between them and the Whigs was already in the air. For Parnell the outcome was a disaster. His

---

1   Herbert Gladstone was committed to Home Rule. He was also Liberal MP for Leeds. The *Leeds Mercury* editor, Wemyss Reid (also a Liberal) persuaded Herbert that he should 'leak' his father's thoughts on Home Rule, otherwise the Gladstones' position would be undermined (particularly by Chamberlain). But although Reid got his 'leak', it was an interview Herbert gave to the National Press Agency that started the kite flying.

support had made the Conservatives a present of thirty seats. It proved to be a gift to the enemy.

It is doubtful whether there had ever been substance in Gladstone's hopes. Carnarvon represented himself and not his party or the Cabinet. His approach to Parnell had been tentative and the Government was uncommitted. Salisbury, for his part, was naturally content to have the Irish vote in a critical election, but his Protestantism, his belief in the Union, his loyalty to the landowners and to the Irish minority who had put their faith in the Conservative Party, were all far too strong for him ever to have seriously considered Home Rule. No leader has ever had less of the temperament of a Peel or a Gladstone. Enthusiasm of the kind that splits parties was quite outside Salisbury's nature.

By Christmas 1885 the die was cast. Carnarvon resigned in the New Year, and on January 26 Salisbury's Government announced that it would introduce a Coercion Bill of the most stringent kind. Without hesitation, almost without consultation with his colleagues, Gladstone brought about its defeat on an amendment to the Queen's Speech. There was no doubt that the new Government would be a Home Rule Government, and Harrington and the other leading Whigs refused to join. This was probably inevitable, but Gladstone destroyed any remaining hope of success by his treatment of Chamberlain. In the eyes of the country Chamberlain now stood next to his leader in the Liberal Party. But Gladstone gravely underrated his importance, had refused him the Colonial Office, and sent him to the Local Government Board. Chamberlain's views on Ireland had been changing rapidly during the previous year. His trust in Parnell had been shattered by what he considered the treacherous Irish switch to the Conservative side. The personal relations between the two men had also been poisoned by their intermediary, Captain O'Shea, the husband of Parnell's mistress. Chamberlain was opposed to any large scheme of self-government, and it would have needed all Gladstone's tact and persuasion to win him over. Gladstone made no attempt to do so. Chamberlain was not consulted in the preparation of the Home Rule Bill, and his own scheme for local government reform was ignored. He resigned on March 26, to become Gladstone's most formidable foe.

The Home Rule Bill was introduced into the Commons on April 8, 1886, by Gladstone in a speech which lasted for three and a half hours. He put the case for Home Rule as one of justice for Ireland and freedom for her people. It was an impressive performance, outstanding even in Gladstone's dazzling Parliamentary career. But his appeal to the Liberal principles of liberty and self-government struck against deep emotions. His sudden conversion to the new policy, his dependence upon the Irish vote for continuance in office, and the bitter memories of Irish crimes combined to deepen the fears and prejudices of his opponents. The emotions of race, religion, class, and economic interest all obscured the Liberal arguments which Gladstone used. Fire evoked fire. Gladstone's deep moral feeling found its answer on the other side, which believed him to be a hypocrite or worse. He had embarked on a sudden, destructive crusade. "And why?" asked Lord Randolph Churchill. "For this reason and no other: to gratify the ambition of an old man in a hurry."

The Bill was defeated on the second reading two months after its introduction. Ninety-three Liberals voted against the Government. Gladstone had a difficult decision to make. He could resign or dissolve. He chose the latter course and fought the election on the single issue of Home Rule. His zeal, enthusiasm, and energy were not enough to overcome the mighty forces arrayed against him. The new House contained 316 Conservatives and 78 Liberal Unionists, against 191 Gladstonians and 85 Parnellites. Gladstone resigned immediately, and Salisbury again took office.

Apart from one short spell the Conservatives were to remain in power for twenty years. The long period of Liberal-Whig predominance which had begun in 1830 was over. It had been brought to an end by Whig distaste for social reform and by Gladstone's precipitate conversion to Home Rule. The outlook for the Liberal Party was dark. In committing itself to a policy which was electorally unpopular in England it had not only shed its Right Wing, but also the man who had been by far the most outstanding of its young, reforming leaders. The turn of the wheel had brought fortune to the Conservatives, whose prospects had seemed so gloomy in 1880. The opponents whom they had feared as the irresistible instruments of democracy had delivered themselves into their hands.

It was not immediately perceived in the summer of 1886 that the controversy over Home Rule for Ireland had wrought a deep change in the allegiance of English political parties. Salisbury's Government depended upon the support of the Liberal Unionists, led by Hartington, though their most formidable figure, both in Parliament and in the country, was Joseph Chamberlain. They protested that they were still Liberals, and for ten years they continued to sit on the Liberal side of the House of Commons. This infuriated the followers of Gladstone, many of whom bitterly and publicly likened Chamberlain to Judas Iscariot. It was tacitly accepted, after the failure of a Round Table Conference between the leaders of the two sides, held at the beginning of 1887, that the gulf was too wide to be bridged. This decisive split produced strange bedfellows. Salisbury had to work with the man whom he had denounced as a mob-leader and a "Jack Cade" only a few months before. He had to accept part of Chamberlain's programme as the price of his support. Chamberlain, now tied to the Conservative chariot, was impelled for his part to retract many of his former policies and opinions. On the Liberal side Gladstone, deprived of his Whig supporters, was forced to make concessions to the Radical sections of his party, whose views were far in advance of his own.

Salisbury's Government was not much different from that of the previous year, except that Hicks Beach insisted on standing down from the Leadership of the House of Commons. He argued that "the leader in fact should be leader in name". At the age of thirty-seven therefore Lord Randolph Churchill became Leader of the House and Chancellor of the Exchequer. His career had reached its pinnacle. In the course of six years his skill in debate and political tactics had carried him beyond all his rivals. His position in the Commons was unchallenged by any other member of his party, although many distrusted his methods and disliked his policies. Inside the Cabinet there was little harmony. Lord Randolph's ideas on Tory Democracy struck no spark in Salisbury's traditional Conservatism. The Prime Minister had no great faith in betterment by legislation. He believed that the primary business of government was to administer the existing order, and that the Conservatives owed their first duty to the classes who relied upon them to defend their interests. Lord Randolph wrote to him in November 1886, "I am afraid it is an idle schoolboy's dream to suppose that Tories can legislate – as I did – stupidly. They can govern and make wars and increase taxation and expenditure *à merveille*, but legislation is not their province in a democratic constitution." Salisbury replied, "We must work at less speed and at a lower temperature than our opponents. Our Bills must be tentative and cautious, not sweeping and dramatic." This clash was intensified by Lord Randolph's excursions into the field of foreign affairs. In October he had publicly attacked the reigning policy of friendship for Turkey and declared himself in favour of independence for the Balkan peoples. The differences between the two men, both in character and policy, were fundamental. The final collision occurred over a comparatively trivial point, Lord Randolph's demand for a reduction in the Army and Navy Estimates. He resigned on the eve of Christmas 1886 at the wrong time, on the wrong issue, and he made no attempt to rally support. He lived for another nine years, enduring much ill-health, but already his career lay in ruins.

This dramatic fall came as the finale to a year of political sensations. It was the equivalent on the Conservative side to the Whig defection from Gladstone. Salisbury made George Goschen, a Liberal Unionist of impeccable Whig views, his Chancellor of the Exchequer, thus proclaiming that Tory Democracy was now deemed an unnecessary encumbrance. Thereafter his Government's record in law-making was meagre in the extreme. The main measure was the Local Government Act of 1888, which created county councils and laid the basis for further advance. Three years later school fees were abolished in elementary schools, and a Factory Act made some further attempt to regulate evils in the employment of women and children. It was not an impressive achievement. Even these minor measures were largely carried out as concessions to Chamberlain. From outside the Government he constantly preached the doctrine that the Unionist cause would be best served by a policy of active reform.

Salisbury's interest and that of a large section of public opinion lay in the world overseas, where the Imperialist movement was reaching its climax of exploration, conquest, and settlement. Livingstone, Stanley, Speke, and other travellers had opened up the interior of darkest Africa. Their feats of exploration paved the way for the acquisition of colonies by the European Powers. It was the most important achievement of the period that this partition of Africa was carried out peacefully. The credit is largely due to

Salisbury, who in 1887 became Foreign Secretary as well as Prime Minister, and who never lost sight of the need to preserve peace while the colonial map of Africa was being drawn. The French, seeking consolation for their defeat at the hands of the Prussians in 1870, had been first in the field, with the Germans, in the early eighties, not far behind. Gladstone and Disraeli, had they wished, with the naval and economic power at their disposal, could have annexed much of the continent which their countrymen had mapped and explored. But neither showed any enthusiasm for adventures in tropical Africa. The task of forwarding British interests was largely carried out by men like Cecil Rhodes, Sir William Mackinnon, and Sir George Goldie, who, in spite of the indifference of the Government at home, carved out a great new Empire.

When Salisbury took office he himself promoted no great schemes of Imperial expansion, but he was prepared to back up the men on the spot. The work of consolidation and political control was entrusted after the Elizabethan model, to three chartered companies. The Royal Niger Company operated in Nigeria, the British East Africa Company controlled what is now Kenya and Uganda, and the British South Africa Company acquired the territory of the Rhodesias. All were launched between 1886 and 1889. Rhodesia[1] is the only self-governing member of the British Commonwealth which bears the name of the man who founded it, and foresaw its future. Its capital, Salisbury,[2] commemorates the Prime Minister. Many border disputes with the other colonising Powers arose, but Salisbury pursued a steady policy of settlement by negotiation. It culminated in the signing of agreements with Germany, France, and Portugal in 1890. The German agreement, which was the most important of the three, defined the boundaries of the two countries' possessions in Central and South Africa. As part of the bargain Heligoland was ceded to Germany in compensation for the recognition of the British protectorate of Zanzibar. A future German naval base was traded for a spice island. By 1892 Salisbury had largely succeeded in his aims. The assertion of British control over the Nile Valley and the settlement of the boundaries of the West African colonies were the only outstanding problems.

Salisbury's foreign policy was largely swayed by these colonial affairs. Attached in principle to the idea of the Concert of Europe, he was inevitably drawn closer to Bismarck's Triple Alliance of Germany, Austria-Hungary, and Italy. Britain was in more or less constant conflict with France in West Africa and with Russia in the Near and Far East. The key to Salisbury's success lay in his skilful handling of the innumerable complications that arose between the Powers in an age of intense national rivalries. He once said that "British policy is to drift lazily downstream, occasionally putting out a boat-hook to avoid a collision." No British Foreign Secretary has wielded his diplomatic boat-hook with greater dexterity.

The relentless question of a sullen and embittered Ireland overshadowed domestic politics. "What Ireland wants", Salisbury had asserted before the

1 Now Zimbabwe.
2 Now Harare.

election campaign, "is government – government that does not flinch, that does not vary", and in his nephew, A.J. Balfour, who became Irish Secretary in 1887, he found a man capable of putting into practice the notion that all could be solved by "twenty years of resolute government". The situation that Balfour faced was very difficult. Agricultural prices were steadily falling, but the Government had rejected Parnell's argument that the only way to prevent mass evictions was to reassess rents. The Irish peasants, organised by William O'Brien and John Dillon, had taken matters into their own hands by launching the "Plan of Campaign". The basis of the Plan was that tenants in a body should ask for a reduction of rent. If the landlord refused rents were to be withheld and the money paid into a campaign fund. The Plan was enforced with the terrorist methods which had now become an implacable feature of Irish land disputes. The Government's answer was to make a few concessions, and pass a Crimes Act which gave to the executive arbitrary powers of the most sweeping kind. Balfour stretched his authority to the limit and acted with a determination that fully matched the ruthlessness of his Irish opponents. In defending his actions in the House of Commons he displayed such skill and resource that he rose rapidly to the front rank of Parliamentarians.

Parnell stood aloof from these tumults. He now perceived that Home Rule could only be won by conciliating a broad section of English opinion. But his adherence to cautious and constitutional action was stricken by the publication in *The Times* on April 18, 1887, of a facsimile letter, purporting to bear his signature, in which he was made to condone the Phoenix Park murders. Parnell, while denouncing the letter as a forgery, refused to bring an action in an English court. Such forbearance, and the public acceptance by men as eminent as Salisbury that this and other letters were authentic, convinced most Englishmen of his guilt. But in the following year the Government set up a commission of three judges to investigate the whole field of Irish crime. They had been sitting for six months when, in February 1889, they at last began to probe the letters. They discovered that they had been forged by a decrepit Irish journalist named Richard Piggott. Piggott was betrayed by a fatal inability to spell correctly and crushed by the brilliant cross-examination of Sir Charles Russell. He broke down in the witnessbox, and later confessed. A few days afterwards he blew out his brains in a hotel in Madrid. The effect on the public was most dramatic. For a few months Parnell rode the crest of the wave. Long execration turned into sudden, strange, and short-lived popularity. A General Election was approaching, the Government was out of favour, and nothing, it seemed, could prevent a victory for Gladstone and Home Rule.

But the case was altered. On November 13, 1890, the suit of O'Shea v. O'Shea and Parnell opened in the Divorce Court. A decree *nisi* was granted to Captain O'Shea. Parnell, as co-respondent, offered no defence. He had been living with Mrs O'Shea for ten years. Posterity was to learn that the circumstances were not so dishonourable to Parnell as they then appeared, but public opinion at the time was severe in condemnation. The Nonconformist conscience, powerful in the Liberal Party, reared its head. Gladstone, single-minded for Home Rule, refused to join in the moral censure, but he was convinced that the only way to stop the Conservatives from exploiting Parnell's adultery was for the Irish leader to retire, at any rate for a while. "It'll no' dae", was his constant reply to the suggestion that Parnell should remain. Tremendous pressure was put on the Irish leader. His friend and admirer Cecil Rhodes telegraphed, "Resign – marry – return." It was wise advice. But Parnell was not to be moved; the passion which had burned for so long beneath his cold exterior burst into flame. His pride revolted. He refused to bow to "English hypocrisy", whatever the cost to his country or his cause.

As a last measure Gladstone wrote to Parnell that he would cease to lead the Liberal Party unless the Irishman retired. Before the letter could be delivered the Irish Party confirmed Parnell in his leadership. Gladstone, in despair, sent his letter to the Press. It was an irretrievable step, a public ultimatum. Next morning Gladstone wrote, "For every day, I may say, of those five years we have been engaged in laboriously rolling uphill the stone of Sisyphus. Mr Parnell's decision ... means that the stone is to break away from us and roll down again to the bottom of the hill. I cannot recall the years that have elapsed." The rest of the story is anti-climax. After Parnell had made a bitter attack upon Gladstone the Catholic Church declared against him, and he was disavowed by most of his party. In vain he made a series of wild and desperate efforts to regain power. Within a year he died.

Liberal prospects, which had been so bright in 1889, were now badly clouded. They were not improved by the adoption of the comprehensive "Newcastle Programme" of 1891. In trying to meet the demands of every section of the party this programme gave far more offence than satisfaction. When the election came in the summer of the following year the result was a Home Rule majority of only forty, dependent on the Irish Members. In the House there were 275 Liberals and 82 Irish Nationalists, as against 269 Conservatives and 46 Liberal Unionists. The majority was too thin for Gladstone's purposes, but he formed a Cabinet which included men as gifted as Harcourt, Rosebery, Morley, and Campbell-Bannerman. The brightest star of them all was H.H. Asquith, the most able Home Secretary of the century.

Gladstone was resolute. Work began immediately on a second Home Rule Bill, and in February 1893, he introduced it himself. At the age of eighty-three he piloted the Bill through eighty-two sittings against an Opposition led by debaters as formidable as Chamberlain and Balfour. There have been few more remarkable achievements in the whole history of Parliament. It was all in vain. Passing through the Commons by small majorities, the Bill was rejected on the second reading in the Lords by 419 votes to 41. Thus perished all hope of a united, self-governing Ireland, loyal to the British Crown. A generation later civil war, partition, and the separation of the South from the main stream of world events were to be Ireland's lot. The immediate reaction in England was one of indifference. Encouraged by their victory, the Lords hampered the Government incessantly. Only one major issue was successful, a new Local Government Act, which established urban, rural district, and parish councils. After the defeat of the Home Rule Bill Gladstone fell increasingly out of sympathy with his colleagues. They refused to support his scheme for a dissolution and an attack on the Lords. He, for his part, hated their plans for heavier taxation and increased expenditure on armaments. "The plan is mad," he said of one proposal. "And who are they who propose it? Men who were not born when I had been in public life for years." He resigned on March 3, 1894, fifty-two and a half years after his swearing in as a Privy Counsellor. His parting with his Ministers was affecting. Harcourt made a tearful speech of farewell, and there was much emotion. Gladstone, who remained unmoved, afterwards referred to this meeting as "that blubbering Cabinet". He died in 1898. His career had been the most noteworthy of the century, leaving behind innumerable marks on the pages of history. He was the greatest popular leader of his age, and he has hardly been equalled in his power to move the people on great moral issues. He stands, too, in the very front rank of House of Commons figures. Few of his conceptions were unworthy. Gladstone's achievements, like his failures, were on the grand scale.

In January 1893 the Independent Labour Party had been founded at a conference at Bradford, with J. Keir Hardie, the Scottish miners' leader, as its chairman. The aims of the I.L.P., as it was called, were the popularisation of Socialist doctrine and the promotion of independent working-class candidates at Parliamentary elections. Here was a sign, not much noticed in the great world of politics, of new forces which were coming to the surface in the industrial areas of Britain. The lull which followed the collapse of the Chartist movement had already been broken some years before by an outburst of Socialist propaganda and a wave of Trade Union activity. The first manifestation was the founding in 1881 of the Democratic Federation, which was converted to Marxism by the energy and money of a wealthy exponent of the principles of class-warfare and revolution, H.M. Hyndman. But the working class found Marxism unattractive even when expounded by a rich man, and the movement had little success.

Of far greater importance in England was the emergence about the same time of the Fabian Society, run by a group of young and obscure but highly gifted men, Sidney Webb and George Bernard Shaw among them. They damned all revolutionary theory and set about the propagation of a practical Socialist doctrine. They were not interested in the organisation of a new political party. Socialist aims could be achieved by "permeating" the existing political parties, and, largely through the agency of Sidney and Beatrice Webb, they attained some measure of success. The stream of publications which flowed from the Fabian pens, especially the Fabian Essays of 1889, did much to shape the course of Labour politics. The outlook, in the main, was practical and empirical, owing little to dogmatic theory and nothing to Marx. Great stress was placed on the slow and intricate nature of the change to Socialism – the "inevitability of gradualness".

Most working men knew little of these higher intellectual activities. They were absorbed in efforts to raise their standards of living. During the mid-Victorian years Trade Union Organisation had been largely confined to the skilled and relatively prosperous members of the working class. But in 1889 the dockers of London, a miserably underpaid group, struck for a wage of sixpence an hour. John Burns, one of the organisers of the strike, reminded the dockers of the relief of Lucknow. "This, lads," he said, "is the Lucknow of Labour, and I myself, looking to the horizon, can see a silver gleam – not of bayonets to be imbrued in a brother's blood, but the gleam of the full round orb of the dockers' tanner." It was indeed the Lucknow of Labour. The dockers' victory, made possible by much public sympathy and support, was followed by a rapid expansion of Trade Union Organisation among the unskilled workers.

Throughout the country small groups of Socialists began to form, but they were politically very weak. Their sole electoral success had been the return for West Ham in 1892 of Keir Hardie, who created a sensation by going to the House for his first time accompanied by a brass band and wearing a cloth cap. The greatest difficulty for these Socialist groups was that their fervent beliefs evoked no response either among the mass of working men or among Trade Union leaders, most of whom continued to put their trust in the Liberals and Radicals. But Keir Hardie patiently toiled to woo the Unions away from the Liberal connection. He had some success with the new Unions which had expanded after the dock strike and were willing to support political action. He was greatly aided in his task by the reluctance of the Liberal Party to sponsor working-class candidates for Parliament, apart from a handful, known as "Lib-Labs", most of whom were miners.

The outcome was a meeting sponsored by the Socialist societies and a number of Trade Unions which was held in the Memorial Hall, Farringdon Street, London, on February 27, 1900. It was there decided to set up a Labour Representation Committee, with Ramsay MacDonald as its secretary. The aim of the committee was defined as the establishment of "a distinct Labour group in Parliament who shall have their own Whips and agree upon policy". The Labour Party had been founded. MacDonald in the twentieth century was to become the first Labour Prime Minister. He was to split his party at a moment of national crisis, and die amid the execrations of the Socialists whose political fortunes he had done so much to build.

Gladstone had been succeeded as Prime Minister by Lord Rosebery. Rosebery had the good luck to win the Derby twice during his sixteen months of office. Not much other fortune befell him. Rosebery had a far-ranging mind, above the shifts and compromises indispensable in political life. He had been most at ease as Foreign Secretary, contemplating the larger issues of the world and delicately considering British action. He was the Queen's own choice as Prime Minister, and his Imperialist views made him unpopular with his own party. The Lords continued to obstruct him. At this moment the Chancellor of the Exchequer, Sir William Harcourt, included in his Budget proposals a scheme for the payment of substantial death duties. This caused violent feeling throughout the capitalist class affected. The Cabinet was rent by clashes of personality and the quarrels of Imperialists and "Little Englanders". As Rosebery later said, "I never did have power." His was a bleak, precarious, wasting inheritance. When the Government was defeated on a snap vote in June 1895 it took the opportunity to resign. The quarrels of the Liberal leaders were now no longer confined by the secrecy of the Cabinet, and the years that followed were dark ones for the Liberal Party. At the General Election the Conservative-Liberal Unionist alliance won a decisive victory. Its majority over the Opposition, including the Irish Nationalists, was 152.

Lord Salisbury thereupon formed a powerful administration. He once again combined the offices of Prime Minister and Foreign Secretary, and his position in his own party and in the country was unrivalled. His methods of dispatching business were by now unorthodox. It is said that he sometimes failed to recognise members of his Cabinet when he met them on rare social occasions. He loved to retire to the great Cecil house at Hatfield, whence he discharged his vast responsibilities by a stream of letters written in his own hand. His leisure was spent in making scientific experiments in his private laboratory; he also enjoyed riding a stately tricycle round his park. His authority and prestige derived in part from the air of patrician assurance which marked his public speech and action. In character he presented the aristocratic tradition in politics at its best. He cared little for popular acclaim, and such disinterestedness in a democratic age was accepted and even approved. His deputy and closest adviser was his nephew, Arthur Balfour, who became First Lord of the Treasury. But the man who in the public eye dominated the Government was the Liberal Unionist leader, Joseph Chamberlain, now at the height of his powers and anxious for the office which had been denied to him for so long by the events of 1886. By his own choice Chamberlain became Colonial Secretary. His instinct was a sure one. Interest in home affairs had languished. In its five years of office the Government passed only one substantial reforming measure, the Workmen's Compensation Act of 1897. The excitement of politics lay in the clash of Imperial forces in the continents of Africa and Asia, and it was there that Chamberlain resolved to make his mark.

Chamberlain approached his task with the reforming enthusiasm of his Radical days. A great change had taken place in him. The Municipal Socialist and Republican of his Birmingham years was now the architect of Empire. "It is not enough," he declared, "to occupy certain great spaces of the world's surface unless you can make the best of them – unless you are willing to develop them. We are landlords of a great estate; it is the duty of a landlord to develop his estate." Chamberlain could not fulfil this promise in the way he would have wished, although some advances were made, especially in West Africa. From the moment he took office projects of reform were pushed into the background by the constant eruption of questions inseparable from a policy of expansion.

The first was a small one, that of the Ashanti, who continued to terrorise much of the Gold Coast by their slave-raiding. An expedition was sent against them under Sir Francis Scott, and by January 1896 the Ashanti kingdom had been crushed. The situation in Nigeria was much more difficult, since another Great Power was involved. The French, by moving overland to the south of the Sahara Desert, were attempting to confine the British to the coastal areas by using their superior military strength. Chamberlain, who, as Salisbury said, hated to give anything away, retaliated by organising the West African Frontier Force, under Sir Frederick Lugard. His measures were completely successful; skilful diplomacy backed resolute action, and the Anglo-French Convention of June 1898 drew boundary lines in West Africa which were entirely satisfactory to the British.

A few months later a far more dangerous dispute broke out between Britain and France over the control of the Upper Nile. Since the death of Gordon the Dervishes had held unquestioned sway in the Sudan. Their prophet, the Mahdi, was dead, but his successor, the Khalifa as he was called, kept their loose military empire in his grip. He also cherished ambitions for enlarging his domains at the expense of Egypt and Abyssinia. Meanwhile the Egyptian Army, reorganised and reformed by British officers, successfully defended the Lower Nile and the Red Sea coast from Dervish incursions. In 1896 the time had come for the British Command in Egypt to strike back at the restless fanatics to their south. French moves towards the sources of the Nile were already taking place, and must be forestalled; the Italian settlements on the Red Sea needed support; the slave-trade, which the Dervishes had revived, called for suppression; and at home Lord Salisbury's Government was not averse to an Imperial advance. In March Sir Herbert Kitchener, Sirdar of the Egyptian Army, launched his campaign for the avenging of Gordon and the reconquest of the Sudan. This vast tract of African territory could no longer be left a prey to barbarous rule, or remain a magnet for European rivalries.

The desert and the harsh tropical climate presented a formidable challenge to Kitchener's expedition, and he left nothing to chance. His great capacity, now to be displayed, was his foresight in organisation. The River War on the banks of the Nile was a painstaking operation, well planned and well directed. A single reverse would have aroused an outcry of criticism in Britain, and only carefully calculated risks could be taken. Supply was the chief problem, and to meet the needs of Kitchener's columns far in the interior of the African continent over five hundred miles of railway were built through arid and unsurveyed regions. It was largely an engineers war, enlivened by many short, fierce, gallant actions. Kitchener started the campaign with 15,000 men, and at the end commanded 25,000, of whom 8,000 were British. The Khalifa's forces were at least three times as numerous, devoted to their cause, ferociously brave, and wily in the ways of the desert. After two and a half years the Dervish Army was finally confronted and destroyed outside Khartoum at the Battle of Omdurman on September 2, 1898. This, as described at the time by a young Hussar who took part in the battle, was "the most signal triumph ever gained by the arms of science over barbarians". The Khalifa and his surviving lieutenants were gradually hunted down, and the Sudan then entered upon a period of constructive rule.

Five days after the Battle of Omdurman news reached Khartoum that there were Europeans at Fashoda, a post high up on the White Nile. They were Major Marchand and his officers, with a platoon of West African soldiers, who had marched for two years from the Atlantic coast across 2,500 miles of jungle in the hope of establishing France astride the sources of the Nile between the Congo and Abyssinia. Kitchener himself sailed up-river to meet Marchand in person. Courtesies were exchanged between the two soldiers, but it was evident who held the ground in greater force. For a time the French flag flew alongside the British and the Egyptian at Fashoda fort while matters were referred to London and Paris. In both capitals there was a flurry of talk about war. But French claims to the provinces of the Southern Sudan could not be sustained in the light of the British victory in the River War. The French gave way, and by the Convention of March 1899 the watershed of the Congo and the Nile was fixed as the boundary separating British and French interests. This was virtually the last of the colonial disputes which for some decades had poisoned relations between Britain and France. Henceforward, under the growing menace of Germany, the two countries found themselves in constantly increasing harmony.

These were not the only external preoccupations of the Government. At the end of 1895 a crisis occurred with the United States, when, as has been related, President Cleveland claimed the American right to make an arbitrary settlement of the boundary between British Guiana and Venezuela. Throughout these years Germany was hard at work promoting her plans for the penetration of Asia Minor, and there was much talk of a Berlin-Baghdad railway. To this Salisbury raised no objection. He preferred to see the Germans rather than the Russians busy in Turkey. In the Far East the Russian threat to China, made possible by the building of the trans-Siberian railway, perpetually agitated the Foreign Office. The province of Manchuria, with the naval base of Port Arthur, was falling into the grasp of the Russians. Few foresaw at that time the startling defeats which Japanese arms would shortly inflict upon the Czar. Chamberlain, who had a large say in foreign affairs, was provoked into making an ill-considered bid for an alliance with Germany. Salisbury held aloof, and restrained his ardent colleague, perceiving more perils in a European alliance than in a policy of isolation. His confidence in Britain's power to stand alone was now to be tested. For the great events on the world stage, and the diplomatic manoeuvres that attended them, were for the Island eclipsed by the struggle in South Africa.

CHAPTER FORTY-NINE

THE SOUTH AFRICAN WAR

*The twentieth century reached – the second Boer War – the coming of
Lloyd George – the death of Queen Victoria – the concentration camp
scandal – end of the war in Africa – the death of Cecil Rhodes – the road
to the Great War*

B RITAIN ENTERED the twentieth century in the grip of war. She
placed nearly half a million men in the field, the biggest force she
had hitherto sent overseas throughout her history. The conflict in
South Africa, which began as a small colonial campaign, soon called
for a large-scale national effort. Its course was followed in Britain with intense
interest and lively emotion. Scarcely a generation had gone by since the
Franchise Acts had granted a say in the affairs of State to nearly all adult
males. The power to follow events and to pass judgment upon them had
recently come within the reach of all through free education. Popular journals
had started to circulate among the masses, swiftly bringing news, good, bad,
and sometimes misleading, into millions of homes. Yet the result of this rapid
diffusion of knowledge and responsibility was not, as some had prophesied,
social unrest and revolutionary agitation. On the contrary, the years of the
Boer War[1] saw a surge of patriotism among the vast majority of the British
people, and a widespread enthusiasm for the cause of Empire.

Of course there were vehement critics and dissentients, the pro-Boers, as
they were derisively called. They included some influential Liberal leaders,
and in their train a rising young Welsh lawyer named Lloyd George, who now
first made himself known to the nation by the vigour of his attacks upon the
war and the Government. Nevertheless the general feeling in the country was
staunchly Imperialist. There was pride in the broad crimson stretches on the
map of the globe which marked the span of the British Empire, and confidence
in the Royal Navy's command of the Seven Seas. Europe was envious. Most
of the Powers made plain their sympathy for the Boers, and there were hints
of an allied combination against the Island kingdom. She might not have been
allowed to escape from her colonial war with an easy victory, but her

---

1 There were two Boer Wars. In the first (1880–81) the Transvaal under Paul Kruger (1825–1904)
won its independence by the Pretoria Convention (see above). The second war (1899–1902) is
the more famous, perhaps because it included the sieges of Mafeking and Ladysmith and the
exploits of Robert Baden-Powell.

dominion of the seas caused second thoughts. On the outbreak of war a flying squadron of the Royal Navy was mobilised at Portsmouth, and this upon consideration from many angles proved effective in overawing Europe. The lesson was not lost upon the German Kaiser. The spectacle of British sea-power exercising unchallengeable authority made him redouble his efforts to create a mighty ocean-going German battle fleet. Dire consequences were to flow from his spirit of emulation.

The South African War had its roots deep in the past. Two landlocked Boer Republics, owing a vague suzerainty to Britain, were surrounded on all sides, except for a short frontier with Portuguese Mozambique, by British colonies, protectorates, and territories. Yet conflict was not at first inevitable. The large Dutch population in Cape Colony appeared reconciled to British rule and supported Cecil Rhodes as their Premier. The Orange Free State was friendly, and even in the Transvaal, home of the dourest frontier farmers, a con-siderable Boer party favoured co-operation with Britain. Hopes of an Anglo-Boer federation in South Africa were by no means dead. But all this abruptly changed during the last five years of the nineteenth century.

When Joseph Chamberlain became Colonial Secretary in 1895 he was confronted by a situation of great complexity. The Transvaal had been transformed by the exploitation of the extremely rich goldfields on the Witwatersrand. This was the work of foreign capital and labour, most of it British. Within a few years Johannesburg had developed into a great city. The Uitlanders – or Outlanders, as foreigners were called – equalled the native Boers in number, but the Transvaal Government refused to grant them political rights, even though they contributed all but one-twentieth of the country's taxation. Paul Kruger, the President of the Republic, who had taken part in the Great Trek and was now past his seventieth year, determined to preserve the character and independence of his country. He headed the recalcitrant Dutch, unwilling to make common cause with the British, and opposed to the advance of industry, though ready to feed on its profits. The threat of a cosmopolitan goldfield to a close community of Bible-reading farmers was obvious to him. But his fears were intensified by the encircling motions of Rhodes's British South Africa Company, which already controlled the territories to the north that were to become the Rhodesias, and was now trying to acquire Bechuanaland to the west. Rhodes, who had large financial interests on the Rand, dreamt of a United South Africa and a Cape-to-Cairo railway running through British territory all the way.

The political and economic grievances of the Uitlanders made an explosion inevitable, and Chamberlain by the end of 1895 was ready to meet it. Unknown to him, however, Rhodes had worked out a scheme for an uprising of the British in Johannesburg to be reinforced by the invasion of the Transvaal by a Company force. This was to be led by the Administrator of Rhodesia, Dr Leander Starr Jameson. At the last moment the rising in Johannesburg failed to take place, but Jameson, not having counter-instructions from Rhodes, invaded the Transvaal with five hundred men on

December 29. It was, in Chamberlain's words, "a disgraceful exhibition of filibustering", and it ended in the failure which it deserved. On January 2 Jameson and his force surrendered to the Boers at Doornkop. The raid was a turning-point; the entire course of South African history was henceforth violently diverted from peaceful channels. The atmosphere of the country was poisoned by national and racial prejudice; the Dutch at the Cape, in natural sympathy with the Transvaal Boers, began to growl at the British. Rhodes was forced to resign his Premiership; but his great popularity in England served only to sharpen Boer suspicion of a deep-laid plot against the life of their republics. The Orange Free State threw in its lot with Kruger. In the Transvaal his purpose was strengthened; the party of reaction gained the upper hand and armaments were purchased on a large scale for the conflict that loomed ahead.

The next three years were occupied by long-drawn-out and arduous negotiations, Chamberlain's determination being more than matched by Kruger's tortuous obstinacy. In March 1897 Sir Alfred Milner, an outstanding public servant, became High Commissioner in South Africa. He was an administrator of great talents, but he lacked the gift of diplomacy. Within a few months he had made up his mind; he wrote to Chamberlain, "There is no ultimate way out of the political troubles of South Africa except reform in the Transvaal or war. And at present the chances of reform in the Transvaal are worse than ever." But Chamberlain was anxious to avoid war, except as a last resort, and even then he hoped that the responsibility for its outbreak could be fixed on the Boers. He believed, as did Rhodes, that Kruger, under pressure, would yield. They underestimated the pioneers of the veldt.

The climax was reached in April 1899, when a petition, signed by more than 20,000 Uitlanders, arrived in Downing Street. It was followed in May by a dispatch from Milner which stated that "The spectacle of thousands of British subjects kept permanently in the position of helots ... does steadily undermine the influence and reputation of Great Britain and the respect for the British Government within the Queen's Dominions." A period of negotiation followed, with the British Government demanding a vote for every citizen after five years' residence in the Transvaal and putting forward the old claim to "suzerainty". A conference at Bloemfontein in June between Kruger and Milner settled nothing. Milner was convinced that the Boers, now armed to the teeth, were aiming at the establishment of a Dutch United States of South Africa. Kruger was equally convinced that the British intended to rob the Boers of their freedom and independence. "It is our country you want," he said, as tears ran down his face. Chamberlain made several more attempts to come to an agreement, but by this time both sides were pressing ahead with military preparations. On October 9 the Boers delivered an ultimatum while the British forces in South Africa were still weak. Three days later their troops moved over the border.

At the outbreak of the war the Boers put 35,000 men, or twice the British number, in the field, and a much superior artillery derived from German sources. They crossed the frontiers in several directions. Their army was almost entirely mounted. They were armed with Männlicher and Mauser rifles, with which they were expert shots. Within a few weeks they had invested Ladysmith to the east, and Mafeking and Kimberley to the west. At Ladysmith, on the Natal border, 10,000 men, under Sir George White, were surrounded and besieged after two British battalions had been trapped and forced to surrender with their guns at Nicholson's Nek. At Mafeking a small force commanded by Colonel Baden-Powell was encircled by many times its number under Piet Cronje. At Kimberley Cecil Rhodes himself and a large civilian population were beset. After the seasonal rains there was fresh grazing on the veldt, which had been deliberately stimulated by Boer burnings at the end of the summer. The countryside was friendly to the Boer cause. World opinion was uniformly hostile to the British. Meanwhile a British army corps of three divisions was on the way as reinforcement, under the command of Sir Redvers Buller, and volunteer contingents from the Dominions were offered or forthcoming. The phrase "unmounted men preferred" used in official correspondence was typical of the want of knowledge prevailing at the War Office. The troops were good, but the enemy weapons and conditions were entirely misunderstood.

Kruger had long wanted a salt-water port under his independent control. Beyond the mountain passes of Natal lay Durban harbour, which could be captured if only he could reach it. Durban was linked with the Transvaal by a railway which, by comparison with the long line to Cape Town, was short, manageable, and on his doorstep. Here would be the end of many disputes about customs dues, freight charges, and much else besides, and it was in this region that the main effort of both sides was at first concentrated.

The British army corps, as it arrived, was distributed by Buller in order to show a front everywhere. One division was sent to defend Natal, another to the relief of Kimberley, and a third to the north-eastern district of Cape Colony. Within a single December week each of them advanced against the rifle and artillery fire of the Boers, and was decisively defeated with, for those days, severe losses in men and guns. At Colenso, in Natal, where Buller himself commanded, at the Modder River on the road to Kimberley, and at Stormberg in the east of Cape Colony the Boers held their front and invaded the country before them. Although the losses of under a thousand men in each case may seem small nowadays, they came as a startling and heavy shock to the public in Britain and throughout the Empire, and indeed to the troops on the spot. But Queen Victoria braced the nation in words which have become justly famous. "Please understand," she replied to Balfour when he tried to discuss "Black Week", as it was called, "that there is no one depressed in *this* house. We are not interested in the possibilities of defeat. They do not exist." Lord Roberts of Kindahar, who had won fame in the Afghan Wars, was made the new Commander-in-Chief, Lord Kitchener of Khartoum was appointed his Chief of Staff, and in a few months the two already illustrious generals with an ever-increasing army transformed the scene. Buller meanwhile persevered in Natal.

The new British command saw clearly that forces must be used on a large scale and in combination, and the Boer capitals, Bloemfontein and then Pretoria, became their sure objective. Cronje at Mafeking was deceived into thinking that the main blow would fall on Kimberley, and he shifted the larger portion of his troops to Magersfontein, a few miles south of the diamond centre. Here he entrenched himself and awaited the attack. Kimberley indeed was one of Roberts's objectives, but he gained it by sending General French on a long encirclement, and French's cavalry relieved it on February 15. The threat from the rear now compelled Cronje to quit his earthworks and fall back to the north-east. Twelve days later, after fierce frontal assaults by Kitchener, he surrendered with four thousand men. There after all went with a rush. On the following day Buller relieved Ladysmith; on March 13 Roberts reached Bloemfontein, on May 31 Johannesburg, and on June 5 Pretoria fell. Mafeking was liberated after a siege which had lasted for two hundred and seventeen days, and its relief provoked unseemly celebrations in London. Kruger fled. The Orange Free State and the Transvaal were annexed, and in the autumn of 1900 Roberts went home to England. After almost exactly a year of lively fighting, and with both the rebel capitals occupied, it seemed to the British people that the Boer War was finished, and won. At this Lord Salisbury, on Chamberlain's advice, fought a General Election and gained another spell of power with a large majority.

On January 27, 1901, Queen Victoria died. She lay at Osborne, the country home in the Isle of Wight which she and Prince Albert had designed and furnished fifty-five years before. Nothing in its household arrangements had been changed during the Queen's long widowhood. She had determined to conduct her life according to the pattern set by the Prince; nor did she waver from her resolution. Nevertheless a great change had gradually overtaken the monarchy. The Sovereign had become the symbol of Empire. At the Queen's jubilees in 1887 and 1897 India and the colonies had been vividly represented in the State celebrations. The Crown was providing the link between the growing family of nations and races which the former Prime Minister, Lord Rosebery, had with foresight christened the Commonwealth. Disraeli's vision and Chamberlain's enthusiasm had both contributed to this broadening Imperial theme. The Queen herself was seized with the greatness of her rôle. She sent her sons and grandsons on official tours of her ever-increasing dominions, where they were heartily welcomed. Homage from a stream of colonial dignitaries was received by her in England. She appointed Indian servants to her household, and from them learnt Hindustani. Thus she sought by every means within her power to bind her diverse peoples together in loyalty to the British Crown, and her endeavours chimed with the Imperial spirit of the age. One of her last public acts, when she was over eighty years of age, was to visit Ireland. She had never believed in Irish Home Rule, which seemed to her a danger to the unity of the Empire. Prompted by a desire to recognise the gallantry of her Irish soldiers in South Africa, she travelled to Dublin April 1900, wearing the Shamrock on her bonnet and jacket. Her Irish subjects, even the Nationalists among them, gave her a rousing reception. In Ireland a fund of goodwill still flowed for the Throne, on which English Governments sadly failed to draw.

In England during the Queen's years of withdrawal from the outward shows of public life there had once been restiveness against the Crown, and professed republicans had raised their voices. By the end of the century all this had died away. High devotion to her royal task, domestic virtues, evident sincerity of nature, a piercing and sometimes disconcerting truthfulness – all these qualities of the Queen's had long impressed themselves upon the minds of her subjects. In the mass they could have no knowledge of how shrewd she was in political matters, nor of the wisdom she had accumulated in the course of her dealings with many Ministers and innumerable crises. But they justly caught a sense of a great presiding personage. Even Ministers who in private often found her views impulsive and partisan came to respect the watchful sense of duty that always moved her. She represented staunchness and continuity in British traditions, and as she grew in years veneration clustered round her. When she died she had reigned for nearly sixty-four years. Few of her subjects could remember a time when she had not been their Sovereign. But all reflecting men and women could appreciate the advance of British power and the progress of the British peoples that had taken place during the age to which she gave her name. The Victorian Age closed in 1901, but the sense of purpose and confidence which had inspired it lived on through the ordeals to come.

The war in South Africa meanwhile continued. In the past the Boers had never shown themselves docile or obedient to political authority, even when exercised by their own leaders, and British occupation of their principal townships and British seizure of the railways seemed an insufficient reason for abandoning the struggle. The veldt was wide, and from its scattered farm-houses a man could get news, food, shelter, forage, a fresh horse, and even ammunition. Roberts and Buller had hardly left the shores of South Africa when the war flamed into swift-moving, hard-hitting guerrilla. Botha, Kritzinger, Hertzog, De Wet, De la Rey, to name only five of the more famous commando leaders, soon faced Kitchener with innumerable local battles and reverses which were not to end for another seventeen months. The Boers were only to be subdued by extraordinary British exertions. In February 1901 Botha struck at Natal, and was thrown back by General French after laying waste large areas of the country. The other leaders invaded Cape Colony, hoping to rally its Dutch inhabitants. Very few responded, but they were enough to destroy all hopes of a speedy peace. After the raiders were expelled Kitchener and Botha met at the end of the month to arrange terms. Each of these leaders wanted an amnesty for the Cape rebels; but Milner, the high Commissioner, was adverse, and the Cabinet in London supported him. Thus frustrated, and much against his judgment and personal inclination, Kitchener was driven to what would nowadays be called a "scorched earth" policy. Blockhouses were built along the railway lines; fences were driven across the countryside; then more blockhouses were built along the fences. Movement within the enclosures thus created became impossible for even the most heroic commandos. Then, area by area, every man, woman, and child was swept into concentration camps. Such methods could only be justified by the fact that most of the commandos fought in plain clothes, and could only be subdued by wholesale imprisonment, together with the families who gave them succour. Nothing, not even the incapacity of the military authorities when charged with the novel and distasteful task of herding large bodies of civilians into captivity, could justify the conditions in the camps themselves. By February 1902 more than twenty thousand of the prisoners, or nearly one in every six, had died, mostly of disease. At first the authorities denied that anything was wrong, or that any alleviation was possible, but at length an Englishwoman, Miss Emily Hobhouse, exposed and proclaimed the terrible facts. Campbell-Bannerman, soon to be Prime Minister, but at this time in Opposition, denounced the camps as "methods of barbarism". Chamberlain removed them from military control; conditions thereupon speedily improved, and at last, on March 23, 1902, the Boers sued for peace.

Three days later Cecil Rhodes died of heart disease. In one of his final speeches he thus addressed the Loyalists of Cape Town: "You think you have beaten the Dutch. It is not so. The Dutch are not beaten. What is beaten is Krugerism, a corrupt and evil Government, no more Dutch in essence than English. No! The Dutch are as vigorous and unconquered today as they have ever been; the country is still as much theirs as yours, and you will have to live and work with them hereafter as in the past." Certainly the peace which was signed at Vereeniging on May 31 tried to embody this spirit, and its provisions may be judged magnanimous in the extreme. Thirty-two commandos remained unbeaten in the field. Two delegates from each met the British envoys, and after much discussion they agreed to lay down their arms and ammunition. None should be punished except for certain specified breaches of the usages of war; self-government would be accorded as soon as possible, and Britain would pay three million pounds in compensation. Such, in brief, were the principal terms, of which the last may be reckoned as generous, and was at any rate unprecedented in the history of modern war. Upon the conclusion of peace Lord Salisbury resigned. The last Prime Minister to sit in the House of Lords, he had presided over an unparalleled expansion of the British Empire. He died in the following year, and with him a certain aloofness of spirit, now considered old-fashioned, passed from British politics. All the peace terms were kept, and Milner did much to reconstruct South Africa. Nearly half a million British and Dominion troops had been employed, of whom one in ten became casualties. The total cost in money to the United Kingdom has been reckoned at over two hundred and twenty million pounds.

We have now reached in this account the end of the nineteenth century, and the modern world might reasonably have looked forward to a long period of peace and prosperity. The prospects seemed bright, and no one dreamed that we had entered a period of strife in which command and ascendancy by a single world-Power would be the supreme incentive. Two fearful wars, each of about five years' duration, were to illustrate the magnitude which developments had reached during the climax of the Victorian era. The rise of Germany to world-Power had long been accompanied by national assertiveness and the continuous building up of armaments. No one could attempt to measure the character and consequences of the impending struggles. To fight on till victory was won became the sole objective, and in this the power of the nations engaged was to prove astounding. It seemed so easy in the course of the closing years of the passing century to take as a matter of course the almost universal system of national armies created by general conscription and fed by the measureless resources of industrial progress. Order and organisation were the salient features of modern life, and when Germany threw all her qualities into the task the steps became obvious, and even inevitable. Nay, it could be argued, and perhaps even proved, that the wise and normal method of modern progress, which all the Continent of Europe adopted in one form or another, was the principle of rearmament on the highest scale. Such was the vitality of the human race that it nevertheless flourished undeterred.

Alone of the Great Powers of Europe, which ordained that every man should be trained as a soldier and serve for two or even three years, Great Britain availed herself of her island position and naval mastery to stand outside the universal habit – for such it had become. And yet this abstention was by no means to allay the growth of the danger. On the contrary, in South Africa Britain took, unconsciously no doubt, a leading part in bringing about the crisis. She exhibited herself to all the nations as supreme. For three long years the process of conquering the Boers continued, leaving the rest of Europe and America the facts of Empire and much else to meditate upon. All the Powers began to think of navies in a different mood. Germany saw that her world preponderance would not be achieved without warships of the greatest strength and quality, and France and other nations followed her example. It was indeed a new outlet for national pride and energy, of which Japan, at the opposite side of the globe, took eager advantage. To the vast military staffs were added naval formations which pointed out the logic and importance of all their doings. The conquest of the air was also on the way. Britain would have been content to rule alone in moderation.

Nearly a hundred years of peace and progress had carried Britain to the leadership of the world. She had striven repeatedly for the maintenance of peace, at any rate for herself, and progress and prosperity had been continuous in all classes. The franchise had been extended almost to the actuarial limit, and yet quiet and order reigned. Conservative forces had shown that they could ride the storm, and indeed that there was no great storm between the domestic parties. The great mass of the country could get on with the daily tasks and leave politics to those who were interested as partisans without fear. The national horse had shown that the reins could be thrown on his neck without leading to a furious gallop in this direction or that. No one felt himself left out of the Constitution. An excess of self-assertion would be injurious. Certainly the dawn of the twentieth century seemed bright and calm for those who lived within the unequalled bounds of the British Empire, or sought shelter within its folds. There was endless work to be done. It did not matter which party ruled: they found fault with one another, as they had a perfect right to do. None of the ancient inhibitions obstructed the adventurous. If mistakes were made they had been made before, and Britons could repair them without serious consequences. Active and vigorous politics should be sustained. To go forward gradually but boldly seemed to be fully justified.

The United States remained, save in naval matters, largely aloof from these manifestations. Her thoughts were turned inwards on her unlimited natural resources, as yet barely explored and still less exploited. Her population still owed much of its amazing increase to immigrants from Europe, and these, out of temper with the continent of their origins and perhaps misfortunes, had no wish to see their new home entangled in the struggles of the old. The vast potentialities of America lay as a portent across the globe, as yet dimly recognised, save by the imaginative. But in the contracting world of better communications to remain detached from the pre-occupations of others was rapidly becoming impossible. The status of world-Power is inseparable from its responsibilities. The convulsive climax of the first Great War was finally and inseparably to link America with the fortunes of the Old World and of Britain.

* * * * *

Here is set out a long story of the English-Speaking Peoples. They are now to become Allies in terrible but victorious wars. And that is not the end. Another phase looms before us, in which alliance will once more be tested and in which its formidable virtues may be to preserve Peace and Freedom. The future is unknowable but the past should give us hope.

⋅← INDEX →⋅